ISBN 978-1-333-71369-0
PIBN 10538342

FB &c Ltd, Dalton House, 60 Windsor Avenue, London, SW19 2RR.
Company number 08720141. Registered in England and Wales.

For support please visit www.forgottenbooks.com

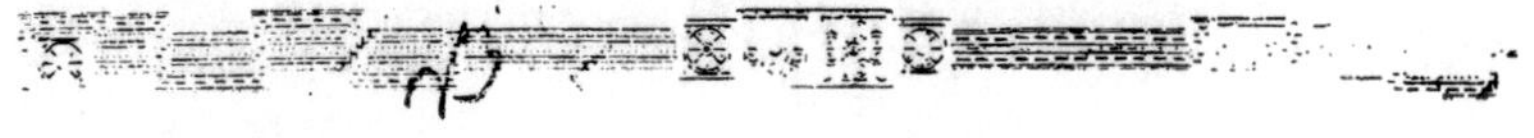

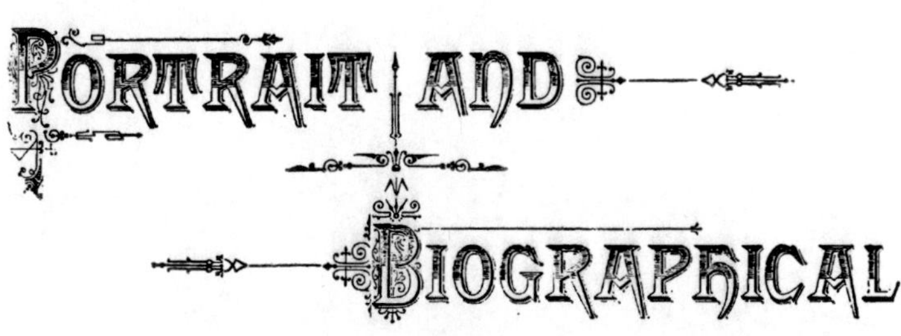

—OF—

WAPELLO COUNTY, IOWA,

CONTAINING

Full Page Portraits and Biographical Sketches of Prominent and Representative Citizens of the County,

TOGETHER WITH

PORTRAITS AND BIOGRAPHIES OF ALL THE GOVERNORS OF IOWA, AND OF THE PRESIDENTS OF THE UNITED STATES.

CHICAGO:
CHAPMAN BROTHERS,
1887.

WE HAVE completed our labors in writing and compiling the PORTRAIT AND BIOGRAPHICAL ALBUM of this county, and wish, in presenting it to our patrons, to speak briefly of the importance of local works of this nature. It is certainly the duty of the present to commemorate the past, to perpetuate the names of the pioneers, to furnish a record of their early settlement, and to relate the story of their progress. The civilization of our day, the enlightenment of the age, and this solemn duty which men of the present time owe to their ancestors, to themselves and to their posterity. demand that a record of their lives and deeds should be made. In local history is found a power to instruct man by precedent, to enliven the mental faculties, and to waft down the river of time a safe vessel in which the names and actions of the people who contributed to raise this region from its primitive state may be preserved. Surely and rapidly the noble men, who in their vigor and prime came early to the county and claimed the virgin soil as their heritage, are passing to their graves. The number remaining who can relate the history of the first days of settlement is becoming small indeed, so that an actual necessity exists for the collection and preservation of historical matter without delay, before the settlers of the wilderness are cut down by time. Not only is it of the greatest importance to render history of pioneer times full and accurate, but it is also essential that the history of the county, from its settlement to the present day, should be treated through its various phases, so that a record, complete and impartial, may be handed down to the future. The present the age of progress, is reviewed, standing out in bold relief over the quiet, unostentatious olden times; it is a brilliant record, which is destined to live in the future; the good works of men, their magnificent enterprises, their lives, whether commercial or military, do not sink into oblivion, but, on the contrary, grow brighter with age, and contribute to build up a record which carries with it precedents and principles that will be advanced and observed when the acts of soulless men will be forgotten and their very names hidden in obscurity.

In the preparation of the personal sketches contained in this volume, unusual care and pains were taken to have them accurate, even in the smallest detail. Indeed, nothing was passed lightly over or treated indifferently; and we flatter ourselves that it is one of the most accurate works of its nature ever published.

As one of the most interesting features of this work, we present the portraits of numerous representative citizens. It has been our aim to have the prominent men of to-day, as well as the pioneers, represented in this department; and we congratulate ourselves on the uniformly high character of the gentlemen whose portraits we present. They are in the strictest sense representative men, and are selected from all the callings and professions worthy to be given. There are others, it is true, who claim equal prominence with those given; but of course it was impossible for us to give portraits of all the leading men and pioneers of the county. We are under great obligation to many of the noble and generous people of this county for kindly and material assistance in the preparation of this ALBUM.

CHICAGO, March, 1887. CHAPMAN BROTHERS.

OF THE

GOVERNORS OF IOWA,

AND OF THE

PRESIDENTS

OF THE

PRESIDENTS.

G. Washington

GEORGE WASHINGTON.

THE Father of our Country was born in Westmorland Co., Va., Feb. 22, 1732. His parents were Augustine and Mary (Ball) Washington. The family to which he belonged has not been satisfactorily traced in England. His great-grandfather, John Washington, emigrated to Virginia about 1657, and became a prosperous planter. He had two sons, Lawrence and John. The former married Mildred Warner and had three children, John, Augustine and Mildred. Augustine, the father of George, first married Jane Butler, who bore him four children, two of whom, Lawrence and Augustine, reached maturity. Of six children by his second marriage, George was the eldest, the others being Betty, Samuel, John Augustine, Charles and Mildred.

Augustine Washington, the father of George, died in 1743, leaving a large landed property. To his eldest son, Lawrence, he bequeathed an estate on the Patomac, afterwards known as Mount Vernon, and to George he left the parental residence. George received only such education as the neighborhood schools afforded, save for a short time after he left school, when he received private instruction in mathematics. His spelling was rather defective. Remarkable stories are told of his great physical strength and development at an early age. He was an acknowledged leader among his companions, and was early noted for that nobleness of character, fairness and veracity which characterized his whole life.

When George was 14 years old he had a desire to go to sea, and a midshipman's warrant was secured for him, but through the opposition of his mother the idea was abandoned. Two years later he was appointed surveyor to the immense estate of Lord Fairfax. In this business he spent three years in a rough frontier life, gaining experience which afterwards proved very essential to him. In 1751, though only 19 years of age, he was appointed adjutant with the rank of major in the Virginia militia, then being trained for active service against the French and Indians. Soon after this he sailed to the West Indies with his brother Lawrence, who went there to restore his health. They soon returned, and in the summer of 1752 Lawrence died, leaving a large fortune to an infant daughter who did not long survive him. On her demise the estate of Mount Vernon was given to George.

Upon the arrival of Robert Dinwiddie, as Lieutenant-Governor of Virginia, in 1752, the militia was reorganized, and the province divided into four military districts, of which the northern was assigned to Washington as adjutant general. Shortly after this a very perilous mission was assigned him and accepted, which others had refused. This was to proceed to the French post near Lake Erie in Northwestern Pennsylvania. The distance to be traversed was between 500 and 600 miles. Winter was at hand, and the journey was to be made without military escort, through a territory occupied by Indians. The trip was a perilous one, and several times he came near losing his life, yet he returned in safety and furnished a full and useful report of his expedition. A regiment of 300 men was raised in Virginia and put in command of Col. Joshua Fry, and Major Washington was commissioned lieutenant-colonel. Active war was then begun against the French and Indians, in which Washington took a most important part. In the memorable event of July 9, 1755, known as Braddock's defeat, Washington was almost the only officer of distinction who escaped from the calamities of the day with life and honor. The other aids of Braddock were disabled early in the action, and Washington alone was left in that capacity on the field. In a letter to his brother he says: "I had four bullets through my coat, and two horses shot under me, yet I escaped unhurt, though death was leveling my companions on every side." An Indian sharpshooter said he was not born to be killed by a bullet, for he had taken direct aim at him seventeen times, and failed to hit him.

After having been five years in the military service, and vainly sought promotion in the royal army, he took advantage of the fall of Fort Duquesne and the expulsion of the French from the valley of the Ohio, to resign his commission. Soon after he entered the Legislature, where, although not a leader, he took an active and important part. January 17, 1759, he married Mrs. Martha (Dandridge) Custis, the wealthy widow of John Parke Custis.

When the British Parliament had closed the port of Boston, the cry went up throughout the provinces that "The cause of Boston is the cause of us all." It was then, at the suggestion of Virginia, that a Congress of all the colonies was called to meet at Philadelphia, Sept. 5, 1774, to secure their common liberties, peaceably if possible. To this Congress Col. Washington was sent as a delegate. On May 10, 1775, the Congress re-assembled, when the hostile intentions of England were plainly apparent. The battles of Concord and Lexington had been fought. Among the first acts of this Congress was the election of a commander-in-chief of the colonial forces. This high and responsible office was conferred upon Washington, who was still a member of the Congress. He accepted it on June 19, but upon the express condition that he receive no salary. He would keep an exact account of expenses and expect Congress to pay them and nothing more. It is not the object of this sketch to trace the military acts of Washington, to whom the fortunes and liberties of the people of this country were so long confided. The war was conducted by him under every possible disadvantage, and while his forces often met with reverses, yet he overcame every obstacle, and after seven years of heroic devotion and matchless skill he gained liberty for the greatest nation of earth. On Dec. 23, 1783, Washington, in a parting address of surpassing beauty, resigned his commission as commander-in-chief of the army to to the Continental Congress sitting at Annapolis. He retired immediately to Mount Vernon and resumed his occupation as a farmer and planter, shunning all connection with public life.

In February, 1789, Washington was unanimously elected President. In his presidential career he was subject to the peculiar trials incidental to a new government; trials from lack of confidence on the part of other governments; trials from want of harmony between the different sections of our own country; trials from the impoverished condition of the country, owing to the war and want of credit; trials from the beginnings of party strife. He was no partisan. His clear judgment could discern the golden mean; and while perhaps this alone kept our government from sinking at the very outset, it left him exposed to attacks from both sides, which were often bitter and very annoying.

At the expiration of his first term he was unanimously re-elected. At the end of this term many were anxious that he be re-elected, but he absolutely refused a third nomination. On the fourth of March, 1797, at the expiraton of his second term as President, he returned to his home, hoping to pass there his few remaining years free from the annoyances of public life. Later in the year, however, his repose seemed likely to be interrupted by war with France. At the prospect of such a war he was again urged to take command of the armies. He chose his subordinate officers and left to them the charge of matters in the field, which he superintended from his home. In accepting the command he made the reservation that he was not to be in the field until it was necessary. In the midst of these preparations his life was suddenly cut off. December 12, he took a severe cold from a ride in the rain, which, settling in his throat, produced inflammation, and terminated fatally on the night of the fourteenth. On the eighteenth his body was borne with military honors to its final resting place, and interred in the family vault at Mount Vernon.

Of the character of Washington it is impossible to speak but in terms of the highest respect and admiration. The more we see of the operations of our government, and the more deeply we feel the difficulty of uniting all opinions in a common interest, the more highly we must estimate the force of his talent and character, which have been able to challenge the reverence of all parties, and principles, and nations, and to win a fame as extended as the limits of the globe, and which we cannot but believe will be as lasting as the existence of man.

The person of Washington was unusally tall; erect and well proportioned. His muscular strength was great. His features were of a beautiful symmetry. He commanded respect without any appearance of haughtiness, and ever serious without being dull.

John Adams

JOHN ADAMS.

JOHN ADAMS, the second President and the first Vice-President of the United States, was born in Braintree (now Quincy), Mass., and about ten miles from Boston, Oct. 19, 1735. His great-grandfather, Henry Adams, emigrated from England about 1640, with a family of eight sons, and settled at Braintree. The parents of John were John and Susannah (Boylston) Adams. His father was a farmer of limited means, to which he added the business of shoemaking. He gave his eldest son, John, a classical education at Harvard College. John graduated in 1755, and at once took charge of the school in Worcester, Mass. This he found but a "school of affliction," from which he endeavored to gain relief by devoting himself, in addition, to the study of law. For this purpose he placed himself under the tuition of the only lawyer in the town. He had thought seriously of the clerical profession but seems to have been turned from this by what he termed "the frightful engines of ecclesiastical councils, of diabolical malice, and Calvanistic good nature," of the operations of which he had been a witness in his native town. He was well fitted for the legal profession, possessing a clear, sonorous voice, being ready and fluent of speech, and having quick perceptive powers. He gradually gained practice, and in 1764 married Abigail Smith, a daughter of a minister, and a lady of superior intelligence. Shortly after his marriage, (1765), the attempt of Parliamentary taxation turned him from law to politics. He took initial steps toward holding a town meeting, and the resolutions he offered on the subject became very popular throughout the Province, and were adopted word for word by over forty different towns. He moved to Boston in 1768, and became one of the most courageous and prominent advocates of the popular cause, and was chosen a member of the General Court (the Legislature) in 1770.

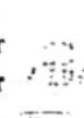

Mr. Adams was chosen one of the first delegates from Massachusetts to the first Continental Congress, which met in 1774. Here he distinguished himself by his capacity for business and for debate, and advocated the movement for independence against the majority of the members. In May, 1776, he moved and carried a resolution in Congress that the Colonies should assume the duties of self-government. He was a prominent member of the committee of five appointed June 11, to prepare a declaration of independence. This article was drawn by Jefferson, but on Adams devolved the task of battling it through Congress in a three days debate.

On the day after the Declaration of Independence was passed, while his soul was yet warm with the glow of excited feeling, he wrote a letter to his wife, which, as we read it now, seems to have been dictated by the spirit of prophecy. "Yesterday," he says, "the greatest question was decided that ever was debated in America; and greater, perhaps, never was or will be decided among men. A resolution was passed without one dissenting colony, 'that these United States are, and of right ought to be, free and independent states.' The day is passed. The fourth of July, 1776, will be a memorable epoch in the history of America. I am apt to believe it will be celebrated by succeeding generations, as the great anniversary festival. It ought to be commemorated as the day of deliverance by solemn acts of devotion to Almighty God. It ought to be solemnized with pomp, shows,

John Adams

JOHN ADAMS.

JOHN ADAMS, the second President and the first Vice-President of the United States, was born in Braintree (now Quincy), Mass., and about ten miles from Boston, Oct. 19, 1735. His great-grandfather, Henry Adams, emigrated from England about 1640, with a family of eight sons, and settled at Braintree. The parents of John were John and Susannah (Boylston) Adams. His father was a farmer of limited means, to which he added the business of shoemaking. He gave his eldest son, John, a classical education at Harvard College. John graduated in 1755, and at once took charge of the school in Worcester, Mass. This he found but a "school of affliction," from which he endeavored to gain relief by devoting himself, in addition, to the study of law. For this purpose he placed himself under the tuition of the only lawyer in the town. He had thought seriously of the clerical profession but seems to have been turned from this by what he termed "the frightful engines of ecclesiastical councils, of diabolical malice, and Calvanistic good nature," of the operations of which he had been a witness in his native town. He was well fitted for the legal profession, possessing a clear, sonorous voice, being ready and fluent of speech, and having quick perceptive powers. He gradually gained practice, and in 1764 married Abigail Smith, a daughter of a minister, and a lady of superior intelligence. Shortly after his marriage, (1765), the attempt of Parliamentary taxation turned him from law to politics. He took initial steps toward holding a town meeting, and the resolutions he offered on the subject became very popular throughout the Province, and were adopted word for word by over forty different towns. He moved to Boston in 1768, and became one of the most courageous and prominent advocates of the popular cause, and was chosen a member of the General Court (the Legislature) in 1770.

Mr. Adams was chosen one of the first delegates from Massachusetts to the first Continental Congress, which met in 1774. Here he distinguished himself by his capacity for business and for debate, and advocated the movement for independence against the majority of the members. In May, 1776, he moved and carried a resolution in Congress that the Colonies should assume the duties of self-government. He was a prominent member of the committee of five appointed June 11, to prepare a declaration of independence. This article was drawn by Jefferson, but on Adams devolved the task of battling it through Congress in a three days debate.

On the day after the Declaration of Independence was passed, while his soul was yet warm with the glow of excited feeling, he wrote a letter to his wife, which, as we read it now, seems to have been dictated by the spirit of prophecy. "Yesterday," he says, "the greatest question was decided that ever was debated in America; and greater, perhaps, never was or will be decided among men. A resolution was passed without one dissenting colony, 'that these United States are, and of right ought to be, free and independent states.' The day is passed. The fourth of July, 1776, will be a memorable epoch in the history of America. I am apt to believe it will be celebrated by succeeding generations, as the great anniversary festival. It ought to be commemorated as the day of deliverance by solemn acts of devotion to Almighty God. It ought to be solemnized with pomp, shows, games, sports, guns, bells, bonfires, and illuminations from one end of the continent to the other, from this time forward for ever. You will think me transported with enthusiasm, but I am not. I am well aware of the toil, and blood and treasure, that it will cost to maintain this declaration, and support and defend these States; yet, through all the gloom, I can see the rays of light and glory. I can see that the end is worth more than all the means; and that posterity will triumph, although you and I may rue, which I hope we shall not."

In November, 1777, Mr. Adams was appointed a delegate to France, and to co-operate with Bemjamin Franklin and Arthur Lee, who were then in Paris, in the endeavor to obtain assistance in arms and money from the French Government. This was a severe trial to his patriotism, as it separated him from his home, compelled him to cross the ocean in winter, and exposed him to great peril of capture by the British cruisers, who were seeking him. He left France June 17, 1779. In September of the same year he was again chosen to go to Paris, and there hold himself in readiness to negotiate a treaty of peace and of commerce with Great Britian, as soon as the British Cabinet might be found willing to listen to such proposels. He sailed for France in November, from there he went to Holland, where he negotiated important loans and formed important commercial treaties.

Finally a treaty of peace with England was signed Jan. 21, 1783. The re-action from the excitement, toil and anxiety through which Mr. Adams had passed threw him into a fever. After suffering from a continued fever and becoming feeble and emaciated he was advised to go to England to drink the waters of Bath. While in England, still drooping and desponding, he received dispatches from his own government urging the necessity of his going to Amsterdam to negotiate another loan. It was winter, his health was delicate, yet he immediately set out, and through storm, on sea, on horseback and foot, he made the trip.

February 24, 1785, Congress appointed Mr. Adams envoy to the Court of St. James. Here he met face to face the King of England, who had so long regarded him as a traitor. As England did not condescend to appoint a minister to the United States, and as Mr. Adams felt that he was accomplishing but little, he sought permission to return to his own country, where he arrived in June, 1788.

When Washington was first chosen President, John Adams, rendered illustiious by his signal services at home and abroad, was chosen Vice President. Again at the second election of Washington as President, Adams was chosen Vice President. In 1796, Washington retired from public life, and Mr. Adams was elected President, though not without much opposition. Serving in this office four years, he was succeeded by Mr. Jefferson, his opponent in politics.

While Mr. Adams was Vice President the great French Revolution shook the continent of Europe, and it was upon this point which he was at issue with the majority of his countrymen led by Mr. Jefferson. Mr. Adams felt no sympathy with the French people in their struggle, for he had no confidence in their power of self-government, and he utterly abhored the class of atheist philosophers who he claimed caused it. On the other hand Jefferson's sympathies were strongly enlisted in behalf of the French people. Hence originated the alienation between these distinguished men, and two powerful parties were thus soon organized, Adams at the head of the one whose sympathies were with England and Jefferson led the other in sympathy with France.

The world has seldom seen a spectacle of more moral beauty and grandeur, than was presented by the old age of Mr. Adams. The violence of party feeling had died away, and he had begun to receive that just appreciation which, to most men, is not accorded till after death. No one could look upon his venerable form, and think of what he had done and suffered, and how he had given up all the prime and strength of his life to the public good, without the deepest emotion of gratitude and respect. It was his peculiar good fortune to witness the complete success of the institution which he had been so active in creating and supporting. In 1824, his cup of happiness was filled to the brim, by seeing his son elevated to the highest station in the gift of the people.

The fourth of July, 1826, which completed the half century since the signing of the Declaration of Independence, arrived, and there were but three of the signers of that immortal instrument left upon the earth to hail its morning light. And, as it is well known, on that day two of these finished their earthly pilgrimage, a coincidence so remarkable as to seem miraculous. For a few days before Mr. Adams had been rapidly failing, and on the morning of the fourth he found himself too weak to rise from his bed. On being requested to name a toast for the customary celebration of the day, he exclaimed "INDEPENDENCE FOREVER." When the day was ushered in, by the ringing of bells and the firing of cannons, he was asked by one of his attendants if he knew what day it was? He replied, "O yes; it is the glorious fourth of July—God bless it—God bless you all." In the course of the day he said, "It is a great and glorious day." The last words he uttered were, "Jefferson survives." But he had, at one o'clock, resigned his spirit into the hands of his God.

The personal appearance and manners of Mr. Adams were not particularly prepossessing. His face, as his portrait manifests, was intellectual and expressive, but his figure was low and ungraceful, and his manners were frequently abrupt and uncourteous. He had neither the lofty dignity of Washington, nor the engaging elegance and gracefulness which marked the manners and address of Jefferson.

Th: Jefferson

THOMAS JEFFERSON.

THOMAS JEFFERSON was born April 2, 1743, at Shadwell, Albermarle county, Va. His parents were Peter and Jane (Randolph) Jefferson, the former a native of Wales, and the latter born in London. To them were born six daughters and two sons, of whom Thomas was the elder. When 14 years of age his father died. He received a most liberal education, having been kept diligently at school from the time he was five years of age. In 1760 he entered William and Mary College. Williamsburg was then the seat of the Colonial Court, and it was the obode of fashion and splendor. Young Jefferson, who was then 17 years old, lived somewhat expensively, keeping fine horses, and much caressed by gay society, yet he was earnestly devoted to his studies, and irreproachable in his morals. It is strange, however, under such influences,that he was not ruined. In the second year of his college course, moved by some unexplained inward impulse, he discarded his horses, society, and even his favorite violin, to which he had previously given much time. He often devoted fifteen hours a day to hard study, allowing himself for exercise only a run in the evening twilight of a mile out of the city and back again. He thus attained very high intellectual culture, alike excellence in philosophy and the languages. The most difficult Latin and Greek authors he read with facility. A more finished scholar has seldom gone forth from college halls; and there was not to be found, perhaps, in all Virginia, a more pureminded, upright, gentlemanly young man.

Immediately upon leaving college he began the study of law. For the short time he continued in the practice of his profession he rose rapidly and distinguished himself by his energy and accuteness as a lawyer. But the times called for greater action. The policy of England had awakened the spirit of resistance of the American Colonies, and the enlarged views which Jefferson had ever entertained, soon led him into active political life. In 1769 he was chosen a member of the Virginia House of Burgesses. In 1772 he married Mrs. Martha Skelton, a very beautiful, wealthy and highly accomplished young widow.

Upon Mr. Jefferson's large estate at Shadwell, there was a majestic swell of land, called Monticello, which commanded a prospect of wonderful extent and beauty. This spot Mr. Jefferson selected for his new home; and here he reared a mansion of modest yet elegant architecture, which, next to Mount Vernon, became the most distinguished resort in our land.

In 1775 he was sent to the Colonial Congress, where, though a silent member, his abilities as a writer and a reasoner soon become known, and he was placed upon a number of important committees, and was chairman of the one appointed for the drawing up of a declaration of independence. This committee consisted of Thomas Jefferson, John Adams, Benjamin Franklin, Roger Sherman and Robert R. Livingston. Jefferson, as chairman, was appointed to draw up the paper. Franklin and Adams suggested a few verbal changes before it was submitted to Congress. On June 28, a few slight changes were made in it by Congress, and it was passed and signed July 4, 1776. What must have been the feelings of that man—what the emotions that swelled his breast—who was charged with the preparation of that Declaration, which, while it made known the wrongs of America, was also to publish her to the world, free, soverign and independent. It is one of the most remarkable papers ever written; and did no other effort of the mind of its author exist, that alone would be sufficient to stamp his name with immortality.

In 1779 Mr. Jefferson was elected successor to Patrick Henry, as Governor of Virginia. At one time the British officer, Tarleton, sent a secret expedition to Monticello, to capture the Governor. Scarcely five minutes elapsed after the hurried escape of Mr. Jefferson and his family, ere his mansion was in possession of the British troops. His wife's health, never very good, was much injured by this excitement, and in the summer of 1782 she died.

Mr. Jefferson was elected to Congress in 1783. Two years later he was appointed Minister Plenipotentiary to France. Returning to the United States in September, 1789, he became Secretary of State in Washington's cabinet. This position he resigned Jan. 1, 1794. In 1797, he was chosen Vice President, and four years later was elected President over Mr. Adams, with Aaron Burr as Vice President. In 1804 he was re-elected with wonderful unanimity, and George Clinton, Vice President.

The early part of Mr. Jefferson's second adminstration was disturbed by an event which threatened the tranquility and peace of the Union; this was the conspiracy of Aaron Burr. Defeated in the late election to the Vice Presidency, and led on by an unprincipled ambition, this extraordinary man formed the plan of a military expedition into the Spanish territories on our southwestern frontier, for the purpose of forming there a new republic. This has been generally supposed was a mere pretext; and although it has not been generally known what his real plans were, there is no doubt that they were of a far more dangerous character.

In 1809, at the expiration of the second term for which Mr. Jefferson had been elected, he determined to retire from political life. For a period of nearly forty years, he had been continually before the public, and all that time had been employed in offices of the greatest trust and responsibility. Having thus devoted the best part of his life to the service of his country, he now felt desirous of that rest which his declining years required, and upon the organization of the new administration, in March, 1809, he bid farewell forever to public life, and retired to Monticello.

Mr. Jefferson was profuse in his hospitality. Whole families came in their coaches with their horses,—fathers and mothers, boys and girls, babies and nurses,—and remained three and even six months. Life at Monticello, for years, resembled that at a fashionable watering-place.

The fourth of July, 1826, being the fiftieth anniversary of the Declaration of American Independence, great preparations were made in every part of the Union for its celebration, as the nation's jubilee, and the citizens of Washington, to add to the solemnity of the occasion, invited Mr. Jefferson, as the framer, and one of the few surviving signers of the Declaration, to participate in their festivities. But an illness, which had been of several weeks duration, and had been continually increasing, compelled him to decline the invitation.

On the second of July, the disease under which he was laboring left him, but in such a reduced state that his medical attendants, entertained no hope of his recovery. From this time he was perfectly sensible that his last hour was at hand. On the next day, which was Monday, he asked of those around him, the day of the month, and on being told it was the third of July, he expressed the earnest wish that he might be permitted to breathe the air of the fiftieth anniversary. His prayer was heard—that day, whose dawn was hailed with such rapture through our land, burst upon his eyes, and then they were closed forever. And what a noble consummation of a noble life! To die on that day,—the birthday of a nation,—the day which his own name and his own act had rendered glorious; to die amidst the rejoicings and festivities of a whole nation, who looked up to him, as the author, under God, of their greatest blessings, was all that was waiting to fill up the record his life.

Almost at the same hour of his death, the kindred spirit of the venerable Adams, as if to bear him company, left the scene of his earthly honors. Hand in hand they had stood forth, the champions of freedom; hand in hand, during the dark and desperate struggle of the Revolution, they had cheered and animated their desponding countrymen; for half a century they had labored together for the good of the country; and now hand in hand they depart. In their lives they had been united in the same great cause of liberty, and in their deaths they were not divided.

In person Mr. Jefferson was tall and thin, rather above six feet in height, but well formed; his eyes were light, his hair originally red, in after life became white and silvery; his complexion was fair, his forehead broad, and his whole countenance intelligent and thoughtful. He possessed great fortitude of mind as well as personal courage; and his command of temper was such that his oldest and most intimate friends never recollected to have seen him in a passion. His manners, though dignified, were simple and unaffected, and his hospitality was so unbounded that all found at his house a ready welcome. In conversation he was fluent, eloquent and enthusiastic; and his language was remarkably pure and correct. He was a finished classical scholar, and in his writings is discernable the care with which he formed his style upon the best models of antiquity.

James Madison

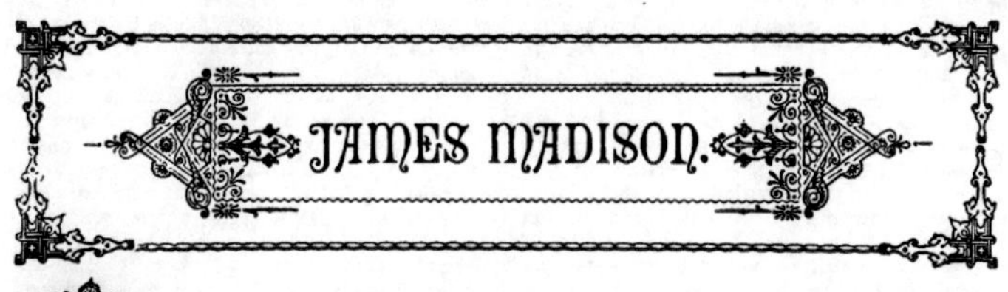

JAMES MADISON, "Father of the Constitution," and fourth President of the United States, was born March 16, 1757, and died at his home in Virginia, June 28, 1836. The name of James Madison is inseparably connected with most of the important events in that heroic period of our country during which the foundations of this great republic were laid. He was the last of the founders of the Constitution of the United States to be called to his eternal reward.

The Madison family were among the early emigrants to the New World, landing upon the shores of the Chesapeake but 15 years after the settlement of Jamestown. The father of James Madison was an opulent planter, residing upon a very fine estate called "Montpelier," Orange Co., Va. The mansion was situated in the midst of scenery highly picturesque and romantic, on the west side of South-west Mountain, at the foot of Blue Ridge. It was but 25 miles from the home of Jefferson at Monticello. The closest personal and political attachment existed between these illustrious men, from their early youth until death.

The early education of Mr. Madison was conducted mostly at home under a private tutor. At the age of 18 he was sent to Princeton College, in New Jersey. Here he applied himself to study with the most imprudent zeal; allowing himself, for months, but three hours' sleep out of the 24. His health thus became so seriously impaired that he never recovered any vigor of constitution. He graduated in 1771, with a feeble body, with a character of utmost purity, and with a mind highly disciplined and richly stored with learning which embellished and gave proficiency to his subsequent career.

Returning to Virginia, he commenced the study of law and a course of extensive and systematic reading. This educational course, the spirit of the times in which he lived, and the society with which he associated, all combined to inspire him with a strong love of liberty, and to train him for his life-work of a statesman. Being naturally of a religious turn of mind, and his frail health leading him to think that his life was not to be long, he directed especial attention to theological studies. Endowed with a mind singularly free from passion and prejudice, and with almost unequalled powers of reasoning, he weighed all the arguments for and against revealed religion, until his faith became so established as never to be shaken.

In the spring of 1776, when 26 years of age, he was elected a member of the Virginia Convention, to frame the constitution of the State. The next year (1777), he was a candidate for the General Assembly. He refused to treat the whisky-loving voters, and consequently lost his election; but those who had witnessed the talent, energy and public spirit of the modest young man, enlisted themselves in his behalf, and he was appointed to the Executive Council.

Both Patrick Henry and Thomas Jefferson were Governors of Virginia while Mr. Madison remained member of the Council; and their appreciation of his intellectual, social and moral worth, contributed not a little to his subsequent eminence. In the year 1780, he was elected a member of the Continental Congress. Here he met the most illustrious men in our land, and he was immediately assigned to one of the most conspicuous positions among them.

For three years Mr. Madison continued in Congress, one of its most active and influential members. In the year 1784, his term having expired, he was elected a member of the Virginia Legislature.

No man felt more deeply than Mr. Madison the utter inefficiency of the old confederacy, with no national government, with no power to form treaties which would be binding, or to enforce law. There was not any State more prominent than Virginia in the declaration, that an efficient national government must be formed. In January, 1786, Mr. Madison carried a resolution through the General Assembly of Virginia, inviting the other States to appoint commissioners to meet in convention at Annapolis to discuss this subject. Five States only were represented. The convention, however, issued another call, drawn up by Mr. Madison, urging all the States to send their delegates to Philadelphia, in May, 1787, to draft a Constitution for the United States, to take the place of that Confederate League. The delegates met at the time appointed. Every State but Rhode Island was represented. George Washington was chosen president of the convention; and the present Constitution of the United States was then and there formed. There was, perhaps, no mind and no pen more active in framing this immortal document than the mind and the pen of James Madison.

The Constitution, adopted by a vote 81 to 79, was to be presented to the several States for acceptance. But grave solicitude was felt. Should it be rejected we should be left but a conglomeration of independent States, with but little power at home and little respect abroad. Mr. Madison was selected by the convention to draw up an address to the people of the United States, expounding the principles of the Constitution, and urging its adoption. There was great opposition to it at first, but it at length triumphed over all, and went into effect in 1789.

Mr. Madison was elected to the House of Representatives in the first Congress, and soon became the avowed leader of the Republican party. While in New York attending Congress, he met Mrs. Todd, a young widow of remarkable power of fascination, whom he married. She was in person and character queenly, and probably no lady has thus far occupied so prominent a position in the very peculiar society which has constituted our republican court as Mrs. Madison.

Mr. Madison served as Secretary of State under Jefferson, and at the close of his administration was chosen President. At this time the encroachments of England had brought us to the verge of war. British orders in council destroyed our commerce, and our flag was exposed to constant insult. Mr. Madison was a man of peace. Scholarly in his taste, retiring in his disposition, war had no charms for him. But the meekest spirit can be roused. It makes one's blood boil, even now, to think of an American ship brought to, upon the ocean, by the guns of an English cruiser. A young lieutenant steps on board and orders the crew to be paraded before him. With great nonchalance he selects any number whom he may please to designate as British subjects; orders them down the ship's side into his boat; and places them on the gun-deck of his man-of-war, to fight, by compulsion, the battles of England. This right of search and impressment, no efforts of our Government could induce the British cabinet to relinquish.

On the 18th of June, 1812, President Madison gave his approval to an act of Congress declaring war against Great Britain. Notwithstanding the bitter hostility of the Federal party to the war, the country in general approved; and Mr. Madison, on the 4th of March, 1813, was re-elected by a large majority, and entered upon his second term of office. This is not the place to describe the various adventures of this war on the land and on the water. Our infant navy then laid the foundations of its renown in grappling with the most formidable power which ever swept the seas. The contest commenced in earnest by the appearance of a British fleet, early in February, 1813, in Chesapeake Bay, declaring nearly the whole coast of the United States under blockade.

The Emperor of Russia offered his services as me ditator. America accepted; England refused. A British force of five thousand men landed on the banks of the Patuxet River, near its entrance into Chesapeake Bay, and marched rapidly, by way of Bladensburg, upon Washington.

The straggling little city of Washington was thrown into consternation. The cannon of the brief conflict at Bladensburg echoed through the streets of the metropolis. The whole population fled from the city. The President, leaving Mrs. Madison in the White House, with her carriage drawn up at the door to await his speedy return, hurried to meet the officers in a council of war. He met our troops utterly routed, and he could not go back without danger of being captured. But few hours elapsed ere the Presidential Mansion, the Capitol, and all the public buildings in Washington were in flames.

The war closed after two years of fighting, and on Feb. 13, 1815, the treaty of peace was signed at Ghent.

On the 4th of March, 1817, his second term of office expired, and he resigned the Presidential chair to his friend, James Monroe. He retired to his beautiful home at Montpelier, and there passed the remainder of his days. On June 28, 1836, then at the age of 85 years, he fell asleep in death. Mrs. Madison died July 12, 1849.

John Tyler

JAMES MONROE.

JAMES MONROE, the fifth President of The United States, was born in Westmoreland Co., Va., April 28, 1758. His early life was passed at the place of nativity. His ancestors had for many years resided in the province in which he was born. When, at 17 years of age, in the process of completing his education at William and Mary College, the Colonial Congress assembled at Philadelphia to deliberate upon the unjust and manifold oppressions of Great Britian, declared the separation of the Colonies, and promulgated the Declaration of Independence. Had he been born ten years before it is highly probable that he would have been one of the signers of that celebrated instrument. At this time he left school and enlisted among the patriots.

He joined the army when everything looked hopeless and gloomy. The number of deserters increased from day to day. The invading armies came pouring in; and the tories not only favored the cause of the mother country, but disheartened the new recruits, who were sufficiently terrified at the prospect of contending with an enemy whom they had been taught to deem invincible. To such brave spirits as James Monroe, who went right onward, undismayed through difficulty and danger, the United States owe their political emancipation. The young cadet joined the ranks, and espoused the cause of his injured country, with a firm determination to live or die with her strife for liberty. Firmly yet sadly he shared in the melancholy retreat from Harleam Heights and White Plains, and accompanied the dispirited army as it fled before its foes through New Jersey. In four months after the Declaration of Independence, the patriots had been beaten in seven battles. At the battle of Trenton he led the vanguard, and, in the act of charging upon the enemy he received a wound in the left shoulder.

As a reward for his bravery, Mr. Monroe was promoted a captain of infantry; and, having recovered from his wound, he rejoined the army. He, however, receded from the line of promotion, by becoming an officer in the staff of Lord Sterling. During the campaigns of 1777 and 1778, in the actions of Brandywine, Germantown and Monmouth, he continued aid-de-camp; but becoming desirous to regain his position in the army, he exerted himself to collect a regiment for the Virginia line. This scheme failed owing to the exhausted condition of the State. Upon this failure he entered the office of Mr. Jefferson, at that period Governor, and pursued, with considerable ardor, the study of common law. He did not, however, entirely lay aside the knapsack for the green bag; but on the invasions of the enemy, served as a volunteer, during the two years of his legal pursuits.

In 1782, he was elected from King George county, a member of the Leglislature of Virginia, and by that body he was elevated to a seat in the Executive Council. He was thus honored with the confidence of his fellow citizens at 23 years of age; and having at this early period displayed some of that ability and aptitude for legislation, which were afterwards employed with unremitting energy for the public good, he was in the succeeding year chosen a member of the Congress of the United States.

Deeply as Mr. Monroe felt the imperfections of the old Confederacy, he was opposed to the new Constitution, thinking, with many others of the Republican party, that it gave too much power to the Central Government, and not enough to the individual States. Still he retained the esteem of his friends who were its warm supporters, and who, notwithstanding his opposition secured its adoption. In 1789, he became a member of the United States Senate; which office he held for four years. Every month the line of distinction between the two great parties which divided the nation, the Federal and the Republican, was growing more distinct. The two prominent ideas which now separated them were, that the Republican party was in sympathy with France, and also in favor of such a strict construction of the Constitution as to give the Central Government as little power, and the State Governments as much power, as the Constitution would warrant. The Federalists sympathized with England, and were in favor of a liberal construction of the Constitution, which would give as much power to the Central Government as that document could possibly authorize.

The leading Federalists and Republicans were alike noble men, consecrating all their energies to the good of the nation. Two more honest men or more pure patriots than John Adams the Federalist, and James Monroe the Republican, never breathed. In building up this majestic nation, which is destined to eclipse all Grecian and Assyrian greatness, the combination of their antagonism was needed to create the right equilibrium. And yet each in his day was denounced as almost a demon.

Washington was then President. England had espoused the cause of the Bourbons against the principles of the French Revolution. All Europe was drawn into the conflict. We were feeble and far away. Washington issued a proclamation of neutrality between these contending powers. France had helped us in the struggle for our liberties. All the despotisms of Europe were now combined to prevent the French from escaping from a tyranny a thousand-fold worse than that which we had endured. Col. Monroe, more magnanimous than prudent, was anxious that, at whatever hazard, we should help our old allies in their extremity. It was the impulse of a generous and noble nature. He violently opposed the President's proclamation as ungrateful and wanting in magnanimity.

Washington, who could appreciate such a character, developed his calm, serene, almost divine greatness, by appointing that very James Monroe, who was denouncing the policy of the Government, as the minister of that Government to the Republic of France. Mr. Monroe was welcomed by the National Convention in France with the most enthusiastic demonstrations.

Shortly after his return to this country, Mr. Monroe was elected Governor of Virginia, and held the office for three years. He was again sent to France to co-operate with Chancellor Livingston in obtaining the vast territory then known as the Province of Louisiana, which France had but shortly before obtained from Spain. Their united efforts were successful. For the comparatively small sum of fifteen millions of dollars, the entire territory of Orleans and district of Louisiana were added to the United States. This was probably the largest transfer of real estate which was ever made in all the history of the world.

From France Mr. Monroe went to England to obtain from that country some recognition of our rights as neutrals, and to remonstrate against those odious impressments of our seamen. But England was unrelenting. He again returned to England on the same mission, but could receive no redress. He returned to his home and was again chosen Governor of Virginia. This he soon resigned to accept the position of Secretary of State under Madison. While in this office war with England was declared, the Secretary of War resigned, and during these trying times, the duties of the War Department were also put upon him. He was truly the armor-bearer of President Madison, and the most efficient business man in his cabinet. Upon the return of peace he resigned the Department of War, but continued in the office of Secretary of State until the expiration of Mr. Madison's administration. At the election held the previous autumn Mr. Monroe himself had been chosen President with but little opposition, and upon March 4, 1817, was inaugurated. Four years later he was elected for a second term.

Among the important measures of his Presidency were the cession of Florida to the United States; the Missouri Compromise, and the "Monroe doctrine."

This famous doctrine, since known as the "Monroe doctrine," was enunciated by him in 1823. At that time the United States had recognized the independence of the South American states, and did not wish to have European powers longer attempting to subdue portions of the American Continent. The doctrine is as follows: "That we should consider any attempt on the part of European powers to extend their system to any portion of this hemisphere as dangerous to our peace and safety," and "that we could not view any interposition for the purpose of oppressing or controlling American governments or provinces in any other light than as a manifestation by European powers of an unfriendly disposition toward the United States." This doctrine immediately affected the course of foreign governments, and has become the approved sentiment of the United States.

At the end of his second term Mr. Monroe retired to his home in Virginia, where he lived until 1830, when he went to New York to live with his son-in-law. In that city he died, on the 4th of July, 1831.

J. Q. Adams

JOHN QUINCY ADAMS.

JOHN QUINCY ADAMS, the sixth President of the United States, was born in the rural home of his honored father, John Adams, in Quincy, Mass., on the 11th cf July, 1767. His mother, a woman of exalted worth, watched over his childhood during the almost constant absence of his father. When but eight years of age, he stood with his mother on an eminence, listening to the booming of the great battle on Bunker's Hill, and gazing on upon the smoke and flames billowing up from the conflagration of Charlestown.

When but eleven years old he took a tearful adieu of his mother, to sail with his father for Europe, through a fleet of hostile British cruisers. The bright, animated boy spent a year and a half in Paris, where his father was associated with Franklin and Lee as minister plenipotentiary. His intelligence attracted the notice of these distinguished men, and he received from them flattering marks of attention.

Mr. John Adams had scarcely returned to this country, in 1779, ere he was again sent abroad. Again John Quincy accompanied his father. At Paris he applied himself with great diligence, for six months, to study; then accompained his father to Holland, where he entered, first a school in Amsterdam, then the University at Leyden. About a year from this time, in 1781, when the manly boy was but fourteen years of age, he was selected by Mr. Dana, our minister to the Russian court, as his private secretary.

In this school of incessant labor and of enobling culture he spent fourteen months, and then returned to Holland through Sweden, Denmark, Hamburg and Bremen. This long journey he took alone, in the winter, when in his sixteenth year. Again he resumed his studies, under a private tutor, at Hague. Thence, in the spring of 1782, he accompanied his father to Paris, traveling leisurely, and forming acquaintance with the most distinguished men on the Continent; examining architectural remains, galleries of paintings, and all renowned works of art. At Paris he again became associated with the most illustrious men of all lands in the contemplations of the loftiest temporal themes which can engross the human mind. After a short visit to England he returned to Paris, and consecrated all his energies to study until May, 1785, when he returned to America. To a brilliant young man of eighteen, who had seen much of the world, and who was familiar with the etiquette of courts, a residence with his father in London, under such circumstances, must have been extremely attractive; but with judgment very rare in one of his age, he preferred to return to America to complete his education in an American college. He wished then to study law, that with an honorable profession, he might be able to obtain an independent support.

Upon leaving Harvard College, at the age of twenty, he studied law for three years. In June, 1794, being then but twenty-seven years of age, he was appointed by Washington, resident minister at the Netherlands. Sailing from Boston in July, he reached London in October, where he was immediately admitted to the deliberations of Messrs. Jay and Pinckney, assisting them in negotiating a commercial treaty with Great Britian. After thus spending a fortnight in London, he proceeded to the Hague.

In July, 1797, he left the Hague to go to Portugal as minister plenipotentiary. On his way to Portugal, upon arriving in London, he met with despatches directing him to the court of Berlin, but requesting him to remain in London until he should receive his instructions. While waiting he was married to an American lady to whom he had been previously engaged,—Miss Louisa Catherine Johnson, daughter of Mr. Joshua Johnson, American consul in London; a lady endownd with that beauty and those accomplishment which eminently fitted her to move in the elevated sphere for which she was destined.

He reached Berlin with his wife in November, 1797; where he remained until July, 1799, when, having fulfilled all the purposes of his mission, he solicited his recall.

Soon after his return, in 1802, he was chosen to the Senate of Massachusetts, from Boston, and then was elected Senator of the United States for six years, from the 4th of March, 1804. His reputation, his ability and his experience, placed him immediately among the most prominent and influential members of that body. Especially did he sustain the Government in its measures of resistance to the encroachments of England, destroying our commerce and insulting our flag. There was no man in America more familiar with the arrogance of the British court upon these points, and no one more resolved to present a firm resistance.

In 1809, Madison succeeded Jefferson in the Presidential chair, and he immediately nominated John Quincy Adams minister to St. Petersburg. Resigning his professorship in Harvard College, he embarked at Boston, in August, 1809.

While in Russia, Mr. Adams was an intense student. He devoted his attention to the language and history of Russia; to the Chinese trade; to the European system of weights, measures, and coins; to the climate and astronomical observations; while he kept up a familiar acquaintance with the Greek and Latin classics. In all the universities of Europe, a more accomplished scholar could scarcely be found. All through life the Bible constituted an important part of his studies. It was his rule to read five chapters every day.

On the 4th of March, 1817, Mr. Monroe took the Presidential chair, and immediately appointed Mr. Adams Secretary of State. Taking leave of his numerous friends in public and private life in Europe, he sailed in June, 1819, for the United States. On the 18th of August, he again crossed the threshold of his home in Quincy. During the eight years of Mr. Monroe's administration, Mr. Adams continued Secretary of State.

Some time before the close of Mr. Monroe's second term of office, new candidates began to be presented for the Presidency. The friends of Mr. Adams brought forward his name. It was an exciting campaign. Party spirit was never more bitter. Two hundred and sixty electoral votes were cast. Andrew Jackson received ninety-nine; John Quincy Adams, eighty-four; William H. Crawford, forty-one; Henry Clay, thirty-seven. As there was no choice by the people, the question went to the House of Representatives. Mr. Clay gave the vote of Kentucky to Mr. Adams, and he was elected.

The friends of all the disappointed candidates now combined in a venomous and persistent assault upon Mr. Adams. There is nothing more disgraceful in the past history of our country than the abuse which was poured in one uninterrupted stream, upon this high-minded, upright, patriotic man. There never was an administration more pure in principles, more conscientiously devoted to the best interests of the country, than that of John Quincy Adams; and never, perhaps, was there an administration more unscrupulously and outrageously assailed.

Mr. Adams was, to a very remarkable degree, abstemious and temperate in his habits; always rising early, and taking much exercise. When at his home in Quincy, he has been known to walk, before breakfast. seven miles to Boston. In Washington, it was said that he was the first man up in the city, lighting his own fire and applying himself to work in his library often long before dawn.

On the 4th of March, 1829, Mr. Adams retired from the Presidency, and was succeeded by Andrew Jackson. John C. Calhoun was elected Vice President. The slavery question now began to assume portentous magnitude. Mr. Adams returned to Quincy and to his studies, which he pursued with unabated zeal. But he was not long permitted to remain in retirement. In November, 1830, he was elected representative to Congress. For seventeen years, until his death, he occupied the post as representative, towering above all his peers, ever ready to do brave battle for freedom, and winning the title of "the old man eloquent." Upon taking his seat in the House, he announced that he should hold himself bound to no party. Probably there never was a member more devoted to his duties. He was usually the first in his place in the morning, and the last to leave his seat in the evening. Not a measure could be brought forward and escape his scrutiny. The battle which Mr. Adams fought, almost singly, against the proslavery party in the Government, was sublime in its moral daring and heroism. For persisting in presenting petitions for the abolition of slavery, he was threatened with indictment by the grand jury, with expulsion from the House, with assassination: but no threats could intimidate him, and his final triumph was complete.

It has been said of President Adams, that when his body was bent and his hair silvered by the lapse of fourscore years, yielding to the simple faith of a little child, he was accustomed to repeat every night, before he slept, the prayer which his mother taught him in his infant years.

On the 21st of February, 1848, he rose on the floor of Congress, with a paper in his hand, to address the speaker. Suddenly he fell, again stricken by paralysis, and was caught in the arms of those around him. For a time he was senseless, as he was conveyed to the sofa in the rotunda. With reviving consciousness, he opened his eyes, looked calmly around and said "*This is the end of earth;*" then after a moment's pause he added, "*I am content.*" These were the last words of the grand "Old Man Eloquent."

Andrew Jackson

ANDREW JACKSON.

ANDREW JACKSON, the seventh President of the United States, was born in Waxhaw settlement, N. C., March 15, 1767, a few days after his father's death. His parents were poor emigrants from Ireland, and took up their abode in Waxhaw settlement, where they lived in deepest poverty.

Andrew, or Andy, as he was universally called, grew up a very rough, rude, turbulent boy. His features were coarse, his form ungainly; and there was but very little in his character, made visible, which was attractive.

When only thirteen years old he joined the volunteers of Carolina against the British invasion. In 1781, he and his brother Robert were captured and imprisoned for a time at Camden. A British officer ordered him to brush his mud-spattered boots. "I am a prisoner of war, not your servant," was the reply of the dauntless boy.

The brute drew his sword, and aimed a desperate blow at the head of the helpless young prisoner. Andrew raised his hand, and thus received two fearful gashes,—one on the hand and the other upon the head. The officer then turned to his brother Robert with the same demand. He also refused, and received a blow from the keen-edged sabre, which quite disabled him, and which probably soon after caused his death. They suffered much other ill-treatment, and were finally stricken with the small-pox. Their mother was successful in obtaining their exchange, and took her sick boys home. After a long illness Andrew recovered, and the death of his mother soon left him entirely friendless.

Andrew supported himself in various ways, such as working at the saddler's trade, teaching school and clerking in a general store, until 1784, when he entered a law office at Salisbury, N. C. He, however, gave more attention to the wild amusements of the times than to his studies. In 1788, he was appointed solicitor for the western district of North Carolina, of which Tennessee was then a part. This involved many long and tedious journeys amid dangers of every kind, but Andrew Jackson never knew fear, and the Indians had no desire to repeat a skirmish with the Sharp Knife.

In 1791, Mr. Jackson was married to a woman who supposed herself divorced from her former husband. Great was the surprise of both parties, two years later, to find that the conditions of the divorce had just been definitely settled by the first husband. The marriage ceremony was performed a second time, but the occurrence was often used by his enemies to bring Mr. Jackson into disfavor.

During these years he worked hard at his profession, and frequently had one or more duels on hand, one of which, when he killed Dickenson, was especially disgraceful.

In January, 1796, the Territory of Tennessee then containing nearly eighty thousand inhabitants, the people met in convention at Knoxville to frame a constitution. Five were sent from each of the eleven counties. Andrew Jackson was one of the delegates. The new State was entitled to but one member in the National House of Representatives. Andrew Jackson was chosen that member. Mounting his horse he rode to Philadelphia, where Congress then held its sessions,—a distance of about eight hundred miles.

Jackson was an earnest advocate of the Democratic party. Jefferson was his idol. He admired Bonaparte, loved France and hated England. As Mr. Jackson took his seat, Gen. Washington, whose second term of office was then expiring, delivered his last speech to Congress. A committee drew up a complimentary address in reply. Andrew Jackson did not approve of the address, and was one of the twelve who voted against it. He was not willing to say that Gen. Washington's administration had been "wise, firm and patriotic."

Mr. Jackson was elected to the United States Senate in 1797, but soon resigned and returned home. Soon after he was chosen Judge of the Supreme Court of his State, which position he held for six years.

When the war of 1812 with Great Britian commenced, Madison occupied the Presidential chair. Aaron Burr sent word to the President that there was an unknown man in the West, Andrew Jackson, who would do credit to a commission if one were conferred upon him. Just at that time Gen. Jackson offered his services and those of twenty-five hundred volunteers. His offer was accepted, and the troops were assembled at Nashville.

As the British were hourly expected to make an attack upon New Orleans, where Gen. Wilkinson was in command, he was ordered to descend the river with fifteen hundred troops to aid Wilkinson. The expedition reached Natchez; and after a delay of several weeks there, without accomplishing anything, the men were ordered back to their homes. But the energy Gen. Jackson had displayed, and his entire devotion to the comrfort of his soldiers, won him golden opinions; and he became the most popular man in the State. It was in this expedition that his toughness gave him the nickname of "Old Hickory."

Soon after this, while attempting to horsewhip Col. Thomas H. Benton, for a remark that gentleman made about his taking a part as second in a duel, in which a younger brother of Benton's was engaged, he received two severe pistol wounds. While he was lingering upon a bed of suffering news came that the Indians, who had combined under Tecumseh from Florida to the Lakes, to exterminate the white settlers, were committing the most awful ravages. Decisive action became necessary. Gen. Jackson, with his fractured bone just beginning to heal, his arm in a sling, and unable to mount his horse without assistance, gave his amazing energies to the raising of an army to rendezvous at Fayettesville, Alabama.

The Creek Indians had established a strong fort on one of the bends of the Tallapoosa River, near the center of Alabama, about fifty miles below Fort Strother. With an army of two thousand men, Gen. Jackson traversed the pathless wilderness in a march of eleven days. He reached their fort, called Tohopeka or Horse-shoe, on the 27th of March. 1814. The bend of the river enclosed nearly one hundred acres of tangled forest and wild ravine. Across the narrow neck the Indians had constructed a formidable breast-work of logs and brush. Here nine hundred warriors, with an ample suply of arms were assembled.

The fort was stormed. The fight was utterly desperate. Not an Indian would accept of quarter. When bleeding and dying, they would fight those who endeavored to spare their lives. From ten in the morning until dark, the battle raged. The carnage was awful and revolting. Some threw themselves into the river; but the unerring bullet struck their heads as they swam. Nearly every one of the nine hundred warrios were killed A few probably, in the night, swam the river and escaped. This ended the war. The power of the Creeks was broken forever. This bold plunge into the wilderness, with its terriffic slaughter, so appalled the savages, that the haggard remnants of the bands came to the camp, begging for peace.

This closing of the Creek war enabled us to concentrate all our militia upon the British, who were the allies of the Indians No man of less resolute will than Gen. Jackson could have conducted this Indian campaign to so successful an issue Immediately he was appointed major-general.

Late in August, with an army of two thousand men, on a rushing march, Gen. Jackson came to Mobile. A British fleet came from Pensacola, landed a force upon the beach, anchored near the little fort, and from both ship and shore commenced a furious assault. The battle was long and doubtful. At length one of the ships was blown up and the rest retired.

Garrisoning Mobile, where he had taken his little army, he moved his troops to New Orleans, And the battle of New Orleans which soon ensued, was in reality a very arduous campaign. This won for Gen. Jackson an imperishable name. Here his troops, which numbered about four thousand men, won a signal victory over the British army of about nine thousand. His loss was but thirteen, while the loss of the British was two thousand six hundred.

The name of Gen. Jackson soon began to be mentioned in connection with the Presidency, but, in 1824, he was defeated by Mr. Adams. He was, however, successful in the election of 1828, and was re-elected for a second term in 1832. In 1829, just before he assumed the reins of the government, he met with the most terrible affliction of his life in the death of his wife, whom he had loved with a devotion which has perhaps never been surpassed. From the shock of her death he never recovered.

His administration was one of the most memorable in the annals of our country; applauded by one party, condemned by the other. No man had more bitter enemies or warmer friends. At the expiration of his two terms of office he retired to the Hermitage, where he died June 8, 1845. The last years of Mr. Jackson's life were that of a devoted Christian man.

M. Van Buren.

MARTIN VAN BUREN.

MARTIN VAN BUREN, the eighth President of the United States, was born at Kinderhook, N. Y., Dec. 5, 1782. He died at the same place, July 24, 1862. His body rests in the cemetery at Kinderhook. Above it is a plain granite shaft fifteen feet high, bearing a simple inscription about half way up on one face. The lot is unfenced, unbordered or unbounded by shrub or flower.

There is but little in the life of Martin Van Buren of romantic interest. He fought no battles, engaged in no wild adventures. Though his life was stormy in political and intellectual conflicts, and he gained many signal victories, his days passed uneventful in those incidents which give zest to biography. His ancestors, as his name indicates, were of Dutch origin, and were among the earliest emigrants from Holland to the banks of the Hudson. His father was a farmer, residing in the old town of Kinderhook. His mother, also of Dutch lineage, was a woman of superior intelligence and exemplary piety.

He was decidedly a precocious boy, developing unusual activity, vigor and strength of mind. At the age of fourteen, he had finished his academic studies in his native village, and commenced the study of law. As he had not a collegiate education, seven years of study in a law-office were required of him before he could be admitted to the bar. Inspired with a lofty ambition, and conscious of his powers, he pursued his studies with indefatigable industry. After spending six years in an office in his native village, he went to the city of New York, and prosecuted his studies for the seventh year.

In 1803, Mr. Van Buren, then twenty-one years of age, commenced the practice of law in his native village. The great conflict between the Federal and Republican party was then at its height. Mr. Van Buren was from the beginning a politician. He had, perhaps, imbibed that spirit while listening to the many discussions which had been carried on in his father's hotel. He was in cordial sympathy with Jefferson, and earnestly and eloquently espoused the cause of State Rights; though at that time the Federal party held the supremacy both in his town and State.

His success and increasing ruputation led him, after six years of practice, to remove to Hudson, the county seat of his county. Here he spent seven years, constantly gaining strength by contending in the courts with some of the ablest men who have adorned the bar of his State.

Just before leaving Kinderhook for Hudson, Mr. Van Buren married a lady alike distinguished for beauty and accomplishments. After twelve short years she sank into the grave, the victim of consumption, leaving her husband and four sons to weep over her loss. For twenty-five years, Mr. Van Buren was an earnest, successful, assiduous lawyer. The record of those years is barren in items of public interest. In 1812, when thirty years of age, he was chosen to the State Senate, and gave his strenuous support to Mr. Madison's administration. In 1815, he was appointed Attorney-General, and the next year moved to Albany, the capital of the State.

While he was acknowledged as one of the most prominent leaders of the Democratic party, he had the moral courage to avow that true democracy did not require that "universal suffrage" which admits the vile, the degraded, the ignorant, to the right of governing the State. In true consistency with his democratic principles, he contended that, while the path leading to the privilege of voting should be open to every man without distinction, no one should be invested with that sacred prerogative, unless he were in some degree qualified for it by intelligence, virtue and some property interests in the welfare of the State.

In 1821 he was elected a member of the United States Senate; and in the same year, he took a seat in the convention to revise the constitution of his native State. His course in this convention secured the approval of men of all parties. No one could doubt the singleness of his endeavors to promote the interests of all classes in the community. In the Senate of the United States, he rose at once to a conspicuous position as an active and useful legislator.

In 1827, John Quincy Adams being then in the Presidential chair, Mr. Van Buren was re-elected to the Senate. He had been from the beginning a determined opposer of the Administration, adopting the "State Rights" view in opposition to what was deemed the Federal proclivities of Mr. Adams.

Soon after this, in 1828, he was chosen Governor of the State of New York, and accordingly resigned his seat in the Senate. Probably no one in the United States contributed so much towards ejecting John Q. Adams from the Presidential chair, and placing in it Andrew Jackson, as did Martin Van Buren. Whether entitled to the reputation or not, he certainly was regarded throughout the United States as one of the most skillful, sagacious and cunning of politicians. It was supposed that no one knew so well as he how to touch the secret springs of action; how to pull all the wires to put his machinery in motion; and how to organize a political army which would, secretly and stealthily accomplish the most gigantic results. By these powers it is said that he outwitted Mr. Adams, Mr. Clay, Mr. Webster, and secured results which few thought then could be accomplished.

When Andrew Jackson was elected President he appointed Mr. Van Buren Secretary of State. This position he resigned in 1831, and was immediately appointed Minister to England, where he went the same autumn. The Senate, however, when it met, refused to ratify the nomination, and he returned home, apparently untroubled; was nominated Vice President in the place of Calhoun, at the re-election of President Jackson; and with smiles for all and frowns for none, he took his place at the head of that Senate which had refused to confirm his nomination as ambassador.

His rejection by the Senate roused all the zeal of President Jackson in behalf of his repudiated favorite; and this, probably more than any other cause, secured his elevation to the chair of the Chief Executive. On the 20th of May, 1836, Mr. Van Buren received the Democratic nomination to succeed Gen. Jackson as President of the United States. He was elected by a handsome majority, to the delight of the retiring President. "Leaving New York out of the canvass," says Mr. Parton, "the election of Mr. Van Buren to the Presidency was as much the act of Gen. Jackson as though the Constitution had conferred upon him the power to appoint a successor."

His administration was filled with exciting events. The insurrection in Canada, which threatened to involve this country in war with England, the agitation of the slavery question, and finally the great commercial panic which spread over the country, all were trials to his wisdom. The financial distress was attributed to the management of the Democratic party, and brought the President into such disfavor that he failed of re-election.

With the exception of being nominated for the Presidency by the "Free Soil" Democrats, in 1848, Mr. Van Buren lived quietly upon his estate until his death.

He had ever been a prudent man, of frugal habits, and living within his income, had now fortunately a competence for his declining years. His unblemished character, his commanding abilities, his unquestioned patriotism, and the distinguished positions which he had occupied in the government of our country, secured to him not only the homage of his party, but the respect ot the whole community. It was on the 4th of March, 1841, that Mr. Van Buren retired from the presidency. From his fine estate at Lindenwald, he still exerted a powerful influence upon the politics of the country. From this time until his death, on the 24th of July, 1862, at the age of eighty years, he resided at Lindenwald, a gentleman of leisure, of culture and of wealth; enjoying in a healthy old age, probably far more happiness than he had before experienced amid the stormy scenes of his active life.

W. H. Harrison

WILLIAM HENRY HARRISON.

WILLIAM HENRY HARRISON, the ninth President of the United States, was born at Berkeley, Va., Feb. 9, 1773. His father, Benjamin Harrison, was in comparatively opulent circumstances, and was one of the most distinguished men of his day. He was an intimate friend of George Washington, was early elected a member of the Continental Congress, and was conspicuous among the patriots of Virginia in resisting the encroachments of the British crown. In the celebrated Congress of 1775, Benjamin Harrison and John Hancock were both candidates for the office of speaker.

Mr Harrison was subsequently chosen Governor of Virginia, and was twice re-elected. His son, William Henry, of course enjoyed in childhood all the advantages which wealth and intellectual and cultivated society could give. Having received a thorough common-school education, he entered Hampden Sidney College, where he graduated with honor soon after the death of his father. He then repaired to Philadelphia to study medicine under the instructions of Dr. Rush and the guardianship of Robert Morris, both of whom were, with his father, signers of the Declaration of Independence.

Upon the outbreak of the Indian troubles, and notwithstanding the remonstrances of his friends, he abandoned his medical studies and entered the army, having obtained a commission of Ensign from President Washington. He was then but 19 years old. From that time he passed gradually upward in rank until he became aid to General Wayne, after whose death he resigned his commission. He was then appointed Secretary of the North-western Territory. This Territory was then entitled to but one member in Congress and Capt. Harrison was chosen to fill that position.

In the spring of 1800 the North-western Territory was divided by Congress into two portions. The eastern portion, comprising the region now embraced in the State of Ohio, was called "The Territory north-west of the Ohio." The western portion, which included what is now called Indiana, Illinois and Wisconsin, was called the "Indiana Territory." William Henry Harrison, then 27 years of age, was appointed by John Adams, Governor of the Indiana Territory, and immediately after, also Governor of Upper Louisiana. He was thus ruler over almost as extensive a realm as any sovereign upon the globe. He was Superintendent of Indian Affairs, and was invested with powers nearly dictatorial over the now rapidly increasing white population. The ability and fidelity with which he discharged these responsible duties may be inferred from the fact that he was four times appointed to this office—first by John Adams, twice by Thomas Jefferson and afterwards by President Madison.

When he began his administration there were but three white settlements in that almost boundless region, now crowded with cities and resounding with all the tumult of wealth and traffic. One of these settlements was on the Ohio, nearly opposite Louisville; one at Vincennes, on the Wabash, and the third a French settlement.

The vast wilderness over which Gov. Harrison reigned was filled with many tribes of Indians. About the year 1806, two extraordinary men, twin brothers, of the Shawnese tribe, rose among them. One of these was called Tecumseh, or "The Crouching Panther;" the other, Olliwacheca, or "The Prophet." Tecumseh was not only an Indian warrior, but a man of great sagacity, far-reaching foresight and indomitable perseverance in any enterprise in which he might engage. He was inspired with the highest enthusiasm, and had long regarded with dread and with hatred the encroachment of the whites upon the hunting-grounds of his fathers. His brother, the Prophet, was an orator, who could sway the feelings of the untutored Indian as the gale tossed the tree-tops beneath which they dwelt.

But the Prophet was not merely an orator: he was, in the superstitious minds of the Indians, invested with the superhuman dignity of a medicine-man or a magician. With an enthusiasm unsurpassed by Peter the Hermit rousing Europe to the crusades, he went from tribe to tribe, assuming that he was specially sent by the Great Spirit.

Gov. Harrison made many attempts to conciliate the Indians, but at last the war came, and at Tippecanoe the Indians were routed with great slaughter. October 28, 1812, his army began its march. When near the Prophet's town three Indlans of rank made their appearance and inquired why Gov. Harrison was approaching them in so hostile an attitude. After a short conference, arrangements were made for a meeting the next day, to agree upon terms of peace.

But Gov. Harrison was too well acquainted with the Indian character to be deceived by such protestations. Selecting a favorable spot for his night's encampment, he took every precaution against surprise. His troops were posted in a hollow square, and slept upon their arms.

The troops threw themselves upon the ground for rest; but every man had his accourtrements on, his loaded musket by his side, and his bayonet fixed. The wakeful Governor, between three and four o'clock in the morning, had risen, and was sitting in conversation with his aids by the embers of a waning fire. It was a chill, cloudy morning with a drizzling rain. In the darkness, the Indians had crept as near as possible, and just then, with a savage yell, rushed, with all the desperation which superstition and passion most highly inflamed could give, upon the left flank of the little army. The savages had been amply provided with guns and ammunition by the English. Their war-whoop was accompained by a shower of bullets.

The camp-fires were instantly extinguished, as the light aided the Indians in their aim. With hideous yells, the Indian bands rushed on, not doubting a speedy and an entire victory. But Gen. Harrison's troops stood as immovable as the rocks around them until day dawned: they then made a simultaneous charge with the bayonet, and swept every thing before them, and completely routing the foe.

Gov. Harrison now had all his energies tasked to the utmost. The British descending from the Canadas, were of themselves a very formidable force; but with their savage allies, rushing like wolves from the forest, searching out every remote farm-house, burning, plundering, scalping, torturing, the wide frontier was plunged into a state of consternation which even the most vivid imagination can but faintly conceive. The war-whoop was resounding everywhere in the forest. The horizon was illuminated with the conflagration of the cabins of the settlers. Gen Hull had made the ignominious surrender of his forces at Detroit. Under these despairing circumstances, Gov. Harrison was appointed by President Madison commander-in-chief of the North-western army, with orders to retake Detroit, and to protect the frontiers.

It would be difficult to place a man in a situation demanding more energy, sagacity and courage; but General Harrison was found equal to the position, and nobly and triumphantly did he meet all the responsibilities.

He won the love of his soldiers by always sharing with them their fatigue. His whole baggage, while pursuing the foe up the Thames, was carried in a valise; and his bedding consisted of a single blanket lashed over his saddle. Thirty-five British officers, his prisoners of war, supped with him after the battle. The only fare he could give them was beef roasted before the fire, without bread or salt.

In 1816, Gen. Harrison was chosen a member of the National House of Representatives, to represent the District of Ohio. In Congress he proved an active member; and whenever he spoke, it was with force of reason and power of eloquence, which arrested the attention of all the members.

In 1819, Harrison was elected to the Senate of Ohio; and in 1824, as one of the presidential electors of that State, he gave his vote for Henry Clay. The same year he was chosen to the United States Senate.

In 1836, the friends of Gen. Harrison brought him forward as a candidate for the Presidency against Van Buren, but he was defeated. At the close of Mr. Van Buren's term, he was re-nominated by his party, and Mr. Harrison was unanimously nominated by the Whigs, with John Tyler for the Vice Presidency. The contest was very animated. Gen. Jackson gave all his influence to prevent Harrison's election; but his triumph was signal.

The cabinet which he formed, with Daniel Webster at its head as Secretary of State, was one of the most brilliant with which any President had ever been surrounded. Never were the prospects of an administration more flattering, or the hopes of the country more sanguine. In the midst of these bright and joyous prospects, Gen. Harrison was seized by a pleurisy-fever and after a few days of violent sickness, died on the 4th of April; just one month after his inauguration as President of the United States.

JOHN TYLER.

JOHN TYLER, the tenth President of the United States. He was born in Charles-city Co., Va., March 29, 1790. He was the favored child of affluence and high social position. At the early age of twelve, John entered William and Mary College and graduated with much honor when but seventeen years old. After graduating, he devoted himself with great assiduity to the study of law, partly with his father and partly with Edmund Randolph, one of the most distinguished lawyers of Virginia.

At nineteen years of age, he commenced the practice of law. His success was rapid and astonishing. It is said that three months had not elapsed ere there was scarcely a case on the docket of the court in which he was not retained. When but twenty-one years of age, he was almost unanimously elected to a seat in the State Legislature. He connected himself with the Democratic party, and warmly advocated the measures of Jefferson and Madison. For five successive years he was elected to the Legislature, receiving nearly the unanimous vote or his county.

When but twenty-six years of age, he was elected a member of Congress. Here he acted earnestly and ably with the Democratic party, opposing a national bank, internal improvements by the General Government, a protective tariff, and advocating a strict construction of the Constitution, and the most careful vigilance over State rights. His labors in Congress were so arduous that before the close of his second term he found it necessary to resign and retire to his estate in Charles-city Co., to recruit his health. He, however, soon after consented to take his seat in the State Legislature, where his influence was powerful in promoting public works of great utility. With a reputation thus canstantly increasing, he was chosen by a very large majority of votes, Governor of his native State. His administration was signally a successful one. His popularity secured his re-election.

John Randolph, a brilliant, erratic, half-crazed man, then represented Virginia in the Senate of the United States. A portion of the Democratic party was displeased with Mr. Randolph's wayward course, and brought forward John Tyler as his opponent, considering him the only man in Virginia of sufficient popularity to succeed against the renowned orator of Roanoke. Mr. Tyler was the victor.

In accordance with his professions, upon taking his seat in the Senate, he joined the ranks of the opposition. He opposed the tariff; he spoke against and voted against the bank as unconstitutional; he strenuously opposed all restrictions upon slavery, resisting all projects of internal improvements by the General Government, and avowed his sympathy with Mr. Calhoun's view of nullification; he declared that Gen. Jackson, by his opposition to the nullifiers, had abandoned the principles of the Democratic party. Such was Mr. Tyler's record in Congress,—a record in perfect accordance with the principles which he had always avowed.

Returning to Virginia, he resumed the practice of his profession. There was a split in the Democratic party. His friends still regarded him as a true Jeffersonian, gave him a dinner, and showered compliments upon him. He had now attained the age of forty-six. His career had been very brilliant. In consequence of his devotion to public business, his private affairs had fallen into some disorder; and it was not without satisfaction that he resumed the practice of law, and devoted himself to the culture of his plantation. Soon after this he removed to Williamsburg, for the better education of his children; and he again took his seat in the Legislature of Virginia.

By the Southern Whigs, he was sent to the national convention at Harrisburg to nominate a President in 1839. The majority of votes were given to Gen. Harrison, a genuine Whig, much to the disappointment of the South, who wished for Henry Clay. To conciliate the Southern Whigs and to secure their vote, the convention then nominated John Tyler for Vice President. It was well known that he was not in sympathy with the Whig party in the North: but the Vice President has but very little power in the Government, his main and almost only duty being to preside over the meetings of the Senate. Thus it happened that a Whig President, and, in reality, a Democratic Vice President were chosen.

In 1841, Mr. Tyler was inaugurated Vice President of the United States. In one short month from that time, President Harrison died, and Mr. Tyler thus found himself, to his own surprise and that of the whole Nation, an occupant of the Presidential chair. This was a new test of the stability of our institutions, as it was the first time in the history of our country that such an event had occured. Mr. Tyler was at home in Williamsburg when he received the unexpected tidings of the death of President Harrison. He hastened to Washington, and on the 6th of April was inaugurated to the high and responsible office. He was placed in a position of exceeding delicacy and difficulty. All his long life he had been opposed to the main principles of the party which had brought him into power. He had ever been a consistent, honest man, with an unblemished record. Gen. Harrison had selected a Whig cabinet. Should he retain them, and thus surround himself with counsellors whose views were antagonistic to his own? or, on the other hand, should he turn against the party which had elected him and select a cabinet in harmony with himself, and which would oppose all those views which the Whigs deemed essential to the public welfare? This was his fearful dilemma. He invited the cabinet which President Harrison had selected to retain their seats. He reccommended a day of fasting and prayer, that God would guide and bless us.

The Whigs carried through Congress a bill for the incorporation of a fiscal bank of the United States. The President, after ten days' delay, returned it with his veto. He suggested, however, that he would approve of a bill drawn up upon such a plan as he proposed. Such a bill was accordingly prepared, and privately submitted to him. He gave it his approval. It was passed without alteration, and he sent it back with his veto. Here commenced the open rupture. It is said that Mr. Tyler was provoked to this measure by a published letter from the Hon. John M. Botts, a distinguished Virginia Whig, who severely touched the pride of the President.

The opposition now exultingly received the President into their arms. The party which elected him denounced him bitterly. All the members of his cabinet, excepting Mr. Webster, resigned. The Whigs of Congress, both the Senate and the House, held a meeting and issued an address to the people of the United States, proclaiming that all political alliance between the Whigs and President Tyler were at an end.

Still the President attempted to conciliate. He appointed a new cabinet of distinguished Whigs and Conservatives, carefully leaving out all strong party men. Mr. Webster soon found it necessary to resign, forced out by the pressure of his Whig friends. Thus the four years of Mr. Tyler's unfortunate administration passed sadly away. No one was satisfied. The land was filled with murmurs and vituperation. Whigs and Democrats alike assailed him. More and more, however, he brought himself into sympathy with his old friends, the Democrats, until at the close of his term, he gave his whole influence to the support of Mr. Polk, the Democratie candidate for his successor

On the 4th of March, 1845, he retired from the harassments of office, to the regret of neither party, and probably to his own unspeakable relief. His first wife, Miss Letitia Christian, died in Washington, in 1842; and in June, 1844, President Tyler was again married, at New York, to Miss Julia Gardiner, a young lady of many personal and intellectual accomplishments.

The remainder of his days Mr. Tyler passed mainly in retirement at his beautiful home,—Sherwood Forest, Charles-city Co., Va. A polished gentleman in his manners, richly furnished with information from books and experience in the world, and possessing brilliant powers of conversation, his family circle was the scene of unusual attractions. With sufficient means for the exercise of a generous hospitality, he might have enjoyed a serene old age with the few friends who gathered around him, were it not for the storms of civil war which his own principles and policy had helped to introduce.

When the great Rebellion rose, which the State-rights and nullifying doctrines of Mr. John C. Calhoun had inaugurated, President Tyler renounced his allegiance to the United States, and joined the Confederates. He was chosen a member of their Congress; and while engaged in active measures to destroy, by force of arms, the Government over which he had once presided, he was taken sick and soon died.

JAMES K. POLK, the eleventh President of the United States, was born in Mecklenburg Co., N. C., Nov. 2, 1795. His parents were Samuel and Jane (Knox) Polk, the former a son of Col. Thomas Polk, who located at the above place, as one of the first pioneers, in 1735.

In the year 1806, with his wife and children, and soon after followed by most of the members of the Polk family, Samuel Polk emigrated some two or three hundred miles farther west, to the rich valley of the Duck River. Here in the midst of the wilderness, in a region which was subsequently called Maury Co., they reared their log huts, and established their homes. In the hard toil of a new farm in the wilderness, James K. Polk spent the early years of his childhood and youth. His father, adding the pursuit of a surveyor to that of a farmer, gradually increased in wealth until he became one of the leading men of the region. His mother was a superior woman, of strong common sense and earnest piety.

Very early in life, James developed a taste for reading and expressed the strongest desire to obtain a liberal education. His mother's training had made him methodical in his habits, had taught him punctuality and industry, and had inspired him with lofty principles of morality. His health was frail; and his father, fearing that he might not be able to endure a sedentary life, got a situation for him behind the counter, hoping to fit him for commercial pursuits.

This was to James a bitter disappointment. He had no taste for these duties, and his daily tasks were irksome in the extreme. He remained in this uncongenial occupation but a few weeks, when at his earnest solicitation his father removed him, and made arrangements for him to prosecute his studies. Soon after he sent him to Murfreesboro Academy. With ardor which could scarcely be surpassed, he pressed forward in his studies, and in less than two and a half years, in the autumn of 1815, entered the sophomore class in the University of North Carolina, at Chapel Hill. Here he was one of the most exemplary of scholars, punctual in every exercise, never allowing himself to be absent from a recitation or a religious service.

He graduated in 1818, with the highest honors, being deemed the best scholar of his class, both in mathematics and the classics. He was then twenty-three years of age. Mr. Polk's health was at this time much impaired by the assiduity with which he had prosecuted his studies. After a short season of relaxation he went to Nashville, and entered the office of Felix Grundy, to study law. Here Mr. Polk renewed his acquaintance with Andrew Jackson, who resided on his plantation, the Hermitage, but a few miles from Nashville. They had probably been slightly acquainted before.

Mr. Polk's father was a Jeffersonian Republican, and James K. Polk ever adhered to the same political faith. He was a popular public speaker, and was constantly called upon to address the meetings of his party friends. His skill as a speaker was such that he was popularly called the Napoleon of the stump. He was a man of unblemished morals, genial and courteous in his bearing, and with that sympathetic nature in the joys and griefs of others which ever gave him troops of friends. In 1823, Mr. Polk was elected to the Legislature of Tennessee. Here he gave his strong influence towards the election of his friend, Mr. Jackson, to the Presidency of the United States.

In January, 1824, Mr. Polk married Miss Sarah Childress, of Rutherford Co., Tenn. His bride was altogether worthy of him,—a lady of beauty and culture. In the fall of 1825, Mr. Polk was chosen a member of Congress. The satisfaction which he gave to his constituents may be inferred from the fact, that for fourteen successive years, until 1839, he was continued in that office. He then voluntarily withdrew, only that he might accept the Gubernatorial chair of Tennessee. In Congress he was a laborious member, a frequent and a popular speaker. He was always in his seat, always courteous; and whenever he spoke it was always to the point, and without any ambitious rhetorical display.

During five sessions of Congress, Mr. Polk was Speaker of the House Strong passions were roused, and stormy scenes were witnessed; but Mr. Polk performed his arduous duties to a very general satisfaction, and a unanimous vote of thanks to him was passed by the House as he withdrew on the 4th of March, 1839.

In accordance with Southern usage, Mr. Polk, as a candidate for Governor, canvassed the State. He was elected by a large majority, and on the 14th of October, 1839, took the oath of office at Nashville. In 1841, his term of office expired, and he was again the candidate of the Democratic party, but was defeated.

On the 4th of March, 1845, Mr. Polk was inaugurated President of the United States. The verdict of the country in favor of the annexation of Texas, exerted its influence upon Congress; and the last act of the administration of President Tyler was to affix his signature to a joint resolution of Congress, passed on the 3d of March, approving of the annexation of Texas to the American Union. As Mexico still claimed Texas as one of her provinces, the Mexican minister, Almonte, immediately demanded his passports and left the country, declaring the act of the annexation to be an act hostile to Mexico.

In his first message, President Polk urged that Texas should immediately, by act of Congress, be received into the Union on the same footing with the other States. In the meantime, Gen. Taylor was sent with an army into Texas to hold the country. He was sent first to Nueces, which the Mexicans said was the western boundary of Texas. Then he was sent nearly two hundred miles further west, to the Rio Grande, where he erected batteries which commanded the Mexican city of Matamoras, which was situated on the western banks.

The anticipated collision soon took place, and war was declared against Mexico by President Polk. The war was pushed forward by Mr. Polk's administration with great vigor. Gen. Taylor, whose army was first called one of "observation," then of "occupation," then of "invasion," was sent forward to Monterey. The feeble Mexicans, in every encounter, were hopelessly and awfully slaughtered. The day of judgement alone can reveal the misery which this war caused. It was by the ingenuity of Mr. Polk's administration that the war was brought on.

'To the victors belong the spoils." Mexico was prostrate before us. Her capital was in our hands. We now consented to peace upon the condition that Mexico should surrender to us, in addition to Texas, all of New Mexico, and all of Upper and Lower California. This new demand embraced, exclusive of Texas, eight hundred thousand square miles. This was an extent of territory equal to nine States of the size of New York. Thus slavery was securing eighteen majestic States to be added to the Union. There were some Americans who thought it all right: there were others who thought it all wrong. In the prosecution of this war, we expended twenty thousand lives and more than a hundred million of dollars. Of this money fifteen millions were paid to Mexico.

On the 3d of March, 1849, Mr. Polk retired from office, having served one term. The next day was Sunday. On the 5th, Gen. Taylor was inaugurated as his successor. Mr. Polk rode to the Capitol in the same carriage with Gen. Taylor; and the same evening, with Mrs. Polk, he commenced his return to Tennessee. He was then but fifty-four years of age. He had ever been strictly temperate in all his habits, and his health was good. With an ample fortune, a choice library, a cultivated mind, and domestic ties of the dearest nature, it seemed as though long years of tranquility and happiness were before him. But the cholera—that fearful scourge—was then sweeping up the Valley of the Mississippi. This he contracted, and died on the 15th of June, 1849, in the fifty-fourth year of his age, greatly mourned by his countrymen.

Zachary Taylor

ZACHARY TAYLOR.

ZACHARY TAYLOR, twelfth President of the United States, was born on the 24th of Nov., 1784, in Orange Co., Va. His father, Colonel Taylor, was a Virginian of note, and a distinguished patriot and soldier of the Revolution. When Zachary was an infant, his father with his wife and two children, emigrated to Kentucky, where he settled in the pathless wilderness, a few miles from Louisville. In this frontier home, away from civilization and all its refinements, young Zachary could enjoy but few social and educational advantages. When six years of age he attended a common school, and was then regarded as a bright, active boy, rather remarkable for bluntness and decision of character He was strong, fearless and self-reliant, and manifested a strong desire to enter the army to fight the Indians who were ravaging the frontiers. There is little to be recorded of the uneventful years of his childhood on his father's large but lonely plantation.

In 1808, his father succeeded in obtaining for him the commission of lieutenant in the United States army; and he joined the troops which were stationed at New Orleans under Gen. Wilkinson. Soon after this he married Miss Margaret Smith, a young lady from one of the first families of Maryland.

Immediately after the declaration of war with England, in 1812, Capt. Taylor (for he had then been promoted to that rank) was put in command of Fort Harrison, on the Wabash, about fifty miles above Vincennes. This fort had been built in the wilderness by Gen. Harrison, on his march to Tippecanoe. It was one of the first points of attack by the Indians, led by Tecumseh. Its garrison consisted of a broken company of infantry numbering fifty men, many of whom were sick.

Early in the autumn of 1812, the Indians, stealthily, and in large numbers, moved upon the fort. Their approach was first indicated by the murder of two soldiers just outside of the stockade. Capt. Taylor made every possible preparation to meet the anticipated assault. On the 4th of September, a band of forty painted and plumed savages came to the fort, waving a white flag, and informed Capt. Taylor that in the morning their chief would come to have a talk with him. It was evident that their object was merely to ascertain the state of things at the fort, and Capt. Taylor, well versed in the wiles of the savages, kept them at a distance.

The sun went down; the savages disappeared, the garrison slept upon their arms. One hour before midnight the war whoop burst from a thousand lips in the forest around, followed by the discharge of musketry, and the rush of the foe. Every man, sick and well, sprang to his post. Every man knew that defeat was not merely death, but in the case of capture, death by the most agonizing and prolonged torture. No pen can describe, no immagination can conceive the scenes which ensued. The savages succeeded in setting fire to one of the block-houses. Until six o'clock in the morning, this awful conflict continued. The savages then, baffled at every point, and gnashing their teeth with rage, retired. Capt. Taylor, for this gallant defence, was promoted to the rank of major by brevet.

Until the close of the war, Major Taylor was placed in such situations that he saw but little more of active service. He was sent far away into the depths of the wilderness, to Fort Crawford, on Fox River, which empties into Green Bay. Here there was but little to be done but to wear away the tedious hours as one best could. There were no books, no society, no intellectual stimulus. Thus with him the uneventful years rolled on Gradually he rose to the rank of colonel. In the Black-Hawk war, which resulted in the capture of that renowned chieftain, Col Taylor took a subordinate but a brave and efficient part.

For twenty-four years Col. Taylor was engaged in the defence of the frontiers, in scenes so remote, and in employments so obscure, that his name was unknown beyond the limits of his own immediate acquaintance. In the year 1836, he was sent to Florida to compel the Seminole Indians to vacate that region and retire beyond the Mississippi, as their chiefs by treaty, had promised they should do. The services rendered here secured for Col. Taylor the high appreciation of the Government; and as a reward, he was elevated to the rank of brigadier-general by brevet; and soon after, in May, 1838, was appointed to the chief command of the United States troops in Florida.

After two years of such wearisome employment amidst the everglades of the peninsula, Gen. Taylor obtained, at his own request, a change of command, and was stationed over the Department of the Southwest. This field embraced Louisiana, Mississippi, Alabama and Georgia. Establishing his headquarters at Fort Jessup, in Louisiana, he removed his family to a plantation which he purchased, near Baton Rogue. Here he remained for five years, buried, as it were, from the world, but faithfully discharging every duty imposed upon him.

In 1846, Gen. Taylor was sent to guard the land between the Nueces and Rio Grande, the latter river being the boundary of Texas, which was then claimed by the United States. Soon the war with Mexico was brought on, and at Palo Alto and Resaca de la Palma, Gen. Taylor won brilliant victories over the Mexicans. The rank of major-general by brevet was then conferred upon Gen. Taylor, and his name was received with enthusiasm almost everywhere in the Nation. Then came the battles of Monterey and Buena Vista in which he won signal victories over forces much larger than he commanded.

His careless habits of dress and his unaffected simplicity, secured for Gen. Taylor among his troops, the *sobriquet* of "Old Rough and Ready.'

The tidings of the brilliant victory of Buena Vista spread the wildest enthusiasm over the country. The name of Gen. Taylor was on every one's lips. The Whig party decided to take advantage of this wonderful popularity in bringing forward the unpolished, unlettered, honest soldier as their candidate for the Presidency. Gen. Taylor was astonished at the announcement, and for a time would not listen to it; declaring that he was not at all qualified for such an office. So little interest had he taken in politics that, for forty years, he had not cast a vote. It was not without chagrin that several distinguished statesmen who had been long years in the public service found their claims set aside in behalf of one whose name had never been heard of, save in connection with Palo Alto, Resaca de la Palma, Monterey and Buena Vista. It is said that Daniel Webster, in his haste remarked, "It is a nomination not fit to be made."

Gen. Taylor was not an eloquent speaker nor a fine writer. His friends took possession of him, and prepared such few communications as it was needful should be presented to the public. The popularity of the successful warrior swept the land. He was triumphantly elected over two opposing candidates,—Gen. Cass and Ex-President Martin Van Buren. Though he selected an excellent cabinet, the good old man found himself in a very uncongenial position, and was, at times, sorely perplexed and harassed. His mental sufferings were very severe, and probably tended to hasten his death. The pro-slavery party was pushing its claims with tireless energy; expeditions were fitting out to capture Cuba; California was pleading for admission to the Union, while slavery stood at the door to bar her out. Gen. Taylor found the political conflicts in Washington to be far more trying to the nerves than battles with Mexicans or Indians.

In the midst of all these troubles, Gen. Taylor, after he had occupied the Presidential chair but little over a year, took cold, and after a brief sickness of but little over five days, died on the 9th of July, 1850. His last words were, "I am not afraid to die. I am ready. I have endeavored to do my duty." He died universally respected and beloved. An honest, unpretending man, he had been steadily growing in the affections of the people; and the Nation bitterly lamented his death.

Gen. Scott, who was thoroughly acquainted with Gen. Taylor, gave the following graphic and truthful description of his character:—"With a good store of common sense, Gen. Taylor's mind had not been enlarged and refreshed by reading, or much converse with the world. Rigidity of ideas was the consequence. The frontiers and small military posts had been his home. Hence he was quite ignorant for his rank, and quite bigoted in his ignorance. His simplicity was child-like, and with innumerable prejudices, amusing and incorrigible, well suited to the tender age. Thus, if a man, however respectable, chanced to wear a coat of an unusual color, or his hat a little on one side of his head; or an officer to leave a corner of his handkerchief dangling from an outside pocket,—in any such case, this critic held the offender to be a coxcomb (perhaps something worse), whom he would not, to use his oft repeated phrase, 'touch with a pair of tongs.'

"Any allusion to literature beyond good old Dilworth's spelling-book, on the part of one wearing a sword, was evidence, with the same judge, of utter unfitness for heavy matchings and combats. In short, few men have ever had a more comfortable, labor-saving contempt for learning of every kind."

Millard Fillmore

MILLARD FILLMORE.

MILLARD FILLMORE, thirteenth President of the United States, was born at Summer Hill, Cayuga Co., N. Y., on the 7th of January, 1800. His father was a farmer, and owing to misfortune, in humble circumstances. Of his mother, the daughter of Dr. Abiathar Millard, of Pittsfield, Mass., it has been said that she possessed an intellect of very high order, united with much personal loveliness, sweetness of disposition, graceful manners and exquisite sensibilities. She died in 1831; having lived to see her son a young man of distinguished promise, though she was not permitted to witness the high dignity which he finally attained.

In consequence of the secluded home and limited means of his father, Millard enjoyed but slender advantages for education in his early years. The common schools, which he occasionally attended were very imperfect institutions; and books were scarce and expensive. There was nothing then in his character to indicate the brilliant career upon which he was about to enter. He was a plain farmer's boy; intelligent, good-looking, kind-hearted. The sacred influences of home had taught him to revere the Bible, and had laid the foundations of an upright character. When fourteen years of age, his father sent him some hundred miles from home, to the then wilds of Livingston County, to learn the trade of a clothier. Near the mill there was a small villiage, where some enterprising man had commenced the collection of a village library. This proved an inestimable blessing to young Fillmore. His evenings were spent in reading. Soon every leisure moment was occupied with books. His thirst for knowledge became insatiate; and the selections which he made were continually more elevating and instructive. He read history, biography, oratory; and thus gradually there was enkindled in his heart a desire to be something more than a mere worker with his hands; and he was becoming, almost unknown to himself, a well-informed, educated man.

The young clothier had now attained the age of nineteen years, and was of fine personal appearance and of gentlemanly demeanor. It so happened that there was a gentleman in the neighborhood of ample pecuniary means and of benevolence,—Judge Walter Wood,—who was struck with the prepossessing appearance of young Fillmore. He made his acquaintance, and was so much impressed with his ability and attainments that he advised him to abandon his trade and devote himself to the study of the law. The young man replied, that he had no means of his own, no friends to help him and that his previous education had been very imperfect. But Judge Wood had so much confidence in him that he kindly offered to take him into his own office, and to loan him such money as he needed. Most gratefully the generous offer was accepted.

There is in many minds a strange delusion about a collegiate education. A young man is supposed to be liberally educated if he has graduated at some college. But many a boy loiters through university halls and then enters a law office, who is by no means as well prepared to prosecute his legal studies as was Millard Fillmore when he graduated at the clothing-mill at the end of four years of manual labor, during which every leisure moment had been devoted to intense mental culture.

In 1823, when twenty-three years of age, he was admitted to the Court of Common Pleas. He then went to the village of Aurora, and commenced the practice of law. In this secluded, peaceful region, his practice of course was limited, and there was no opportunity for a sudden rise in fortune or in fame. Here, in the year 1826, he married a lady of great moral worth, and one capable of adorning any station she might be called to fill,—Miss Abigail Powers.

His elevation of character, his untiring industry, his legal acquirements, and his skill as an advocate, gradually attracted attention; and he was invited to enter into partnership under highly advantageous circumstances, with an elder member of the bar in Buffalo. Just before removing to Buffalo, in 1829, he took his seat in the House of Assembly, of the State of New York, as a representative from Erie County. Though he had never taken a very active part in politics, his vote and his sympathies were with the Whig party. The State was then Democratic, and he found himself in a helpless minority in the Legislature, still the testimony comes from all parties, that his courtesy, ability and integrity, won, to a very unusual degree the respect of his associates.

In the autumn of 1832, he was elected to a seat in the United States Congress. He entered that troubled arena in some of the most tumultuous hours of our national history. The great conflict respecting the national bank and the removal of the deposits, was then raging.

His term of two years closed; and he returned to his profession, which he pursued with increasing reputation and success. After a lapse of two years he again became a candidate for Congress; was re-elected, and took his seat in 1837. His past experience as a representative gave him strength and confidence. The first term of service in Congress to any man can be but little more than an introduction. He was now prepared for active duty. All his energies were brought to bear upon the public good. Every measure received his impress.

Mr. Fillmore was now a man of wide repute, and his popularity filled the State, and in the year 1847, he was elected Comptroller of the State.

Mr. Fillmore had attained the age of forty-seven years. His labors at the bar, in the Legislature, in Congress and as Comptroller, had given him very considerable fame. The Whigs were casting about to find suitable candidates for President and Vice-President at the approaching election. Far away, on the waters of the Rio Grande, there was a rough old soldier, who had fought one or two successful battles with the Mexicans, which had caused his name to be proclaimed in trumpet-tones all over the land. But it was necessary to associate with him on the same ticket some man of reputation as a statesman.

Under the influence of these considerations, the names of Zachary Taylor and Millard Fillmore became the rallying-cry of the Whigs, as their candidates for President and Vice-Peesident. The Whig ticket was signally triumphant. On the 4th of March, 1849, Gen. Taylor was inaugurated President, and Millard Fillmore Vice-President, of the United States.

On the 9th of July, 1850, President Taylor, but about one year and four months after his inauguration, was suddenly taken sick and died. By the Constitution, Vice-President Fillmore thus became President. He appointed a very able cabinet, of which the illustrious Daniel Webster was Secretary of State.

Mr. Fillmore had very serious difficulties to contend with, since the opposition had a majority in both Houses. He did everything in his power to conciliate the South; but the pro-slavery party in the South felt the inadequacy of all measures of transient conciliation. The population of the free States was so rapidly increasing over that of the slave States that it was inevitable that the power of the Government should soon pass into the hands of the free States. The famous compromise measures were adopted under Mr. Fillmcre's administration, and the Japan Expedition was sent out. On the 4th of March, 1853, Mr. Fillmore, having served one term, retired.

In 1856, Mr. Fillmore was nominated for the Presidency by the "Know Nothing" party, but was beaten by Mr. Buchanan. After that Mr. Fillmore lived in retirement. During the terrible conflict of civil war, he was mostly silent. It was generally supposed that his sympathies were rather with those who were endeavoring to overthrow our institutions. President Fillmore kept aloof from the conflict, without any cordial words of cheer to the one party or the other. He was thus forgotten by both. He lived to a ripe old age, and died in Buffalo. N. Y., March 8, 1874.

Franklin Pierce

FRANKLIN PIERCE.

FRANKLIN PIERCE, the fourteenth President of the United States, was born in Hillsborough, N. H., Nov. 23, 1804. His father was a Revolutionary soldier, who, with his own strong arm, hewed out a home in the wilderness. He was a man of inflexible integrity; of strong, though uncultivated mind, and an uncompromising Democrat. The mother of Franklin Pierce was all that a son could desire,—an intelligent, prudent, affectionate, Christian woman. Franklin was the sixth of eight children.

Franklin was a very bright and handsome boy, generous, warm-hearted and brave. He won alike the love of old and young. The boys on the play ground loved him. His teachers loved him. The neighbors looked upon him with pride and affection. He was by instinct a gentleman; always speaking kind words, doing kind deeds, with a peculiar unstudied tact which taught him what was agreeable. Without developing any precocity of genius, or any unnatural devotion to books, he was a good scholar; in body, in mind, in affections, a finely-developed boy.

When sixteen years of age, in the year 1820, he entered Bowdoin College, at Brunswick, Me. He was one of the most popular young men in the college. The purity of his moral character, the unvarying courtesy of his demeanor, his rank as a scholar, and genial nature, rendered him a universal favorite. There was something very peculiarly winning in his address, and it was evidently not in the slightest degree studied: it was the simple outgushing of his own magnanimous and loving nature.

Upon graduating, in the year 1824, Franklin Pierce commenced the study of law in the office of Judge Woodbury, one of the most distinguished lawyers of the State, and a man of great private worth. The eminent social qualities of the young lawyer, his father's prominence as a public man, and the brilliant political career into which Judge Woodbury was entering, all tended to entice Mr. Pierce into the facinating yet perilous path of political life. With all the ardor of his nature he espoused the cause of Gen. Jackson for the Presidency. He commenced the practice of law in Hillsborough, and was soon elected to represent the town in the State Legislature. Here he served for four years. The last two years he was chosen speaker of the house by a very large vote.

In 1833, at the age of twenty-nine, he was elected a member of Congress. Without taking an active part in debates, he was faithful and laborious in duty, and ever rising in the estimation of those with whom he was associatad.

In 1837, being then but thirty-three years of age, he was elected to the Senate of the United States; taking his seat just as Mr. Van Buren commenced his administration. He was the youngest member in the Senate. In the year 1834, he married Miss Jane Means Appleton, a lady of rare beauty and accomplishments, and one admirably fitted to adorn every station with which her husband was honored. Of the three sons who were born to them, all now sleep with their parents in the grave.

In the year 1838, Mr. Pierce, with growing fame and increasing business as a lawyer, took up his residence in Concord, the capital of New Hampshire. President Polk, upon his accession to office, appointed Mr. Pierce attorney-general of the United States; but the offer was declined, in consequence of numerous professional engagements at home, and the precariuos state of Mrs. Pierce's health. He also, about the same time declined the nomination for governor by the Democratic party. The war with Mexico called Mr. Pierce in the army. Receiving the appointment of brigadier-general, he embarked, with a portion of his troops, at Newport, R. I., on the 27th of May, 1847. He took an important part in this war, proving himself a brave and true soldier.

When Gen. Pierce reached his home in his native State, he was received enthusiastically by the advocates of the Mexican war, and coldly by his opponents. He resumed the practice of his profession, very frequently taking an active part in political questions, giving his cordial support to the pro-slavery wing of the Democratic party. The compromise measures met cordially with his approval; and he strenuously advocated the enforcement of the infamous fugitive-slave law, which so shocked the religious sensibilities of the North. He thus became distinguished as a "Northern man with Southern principles." The strong partisans of slavery in the South cousequently regarded him as a man whom they could safely trust in office to carry out their plans.

On the 12th of June, 1852, the Democratic convention met in Baltimore to nominate a candidate for the Presidency. For four days they continued in session, and in thirty-five ballotings no one had obtained a two-thirds vote. Not a vote thus far had been thrown for Gen. Pierce. Then the Virginia delegation brought forward his name. There were fourteen more ballotings, during which Gen. Pierce constantly gained strength, until, at the forty-ninth ballot, he received two hundred and eighty-two votes, and all other candidates eleven. Gen. Winfield Scott was the Whig candidate. Gen. Pierce was chosen with great unanimity. Only four States—Vermont, Massachusetts, Kentucky and Tennessee—cast their electoral votes against him. Gen. Franklin Pierce was therefore inaugurated President of the United States on the 4th of March, 1853.

His administration proved one of the most stormy our country had ever experienced. The controversy between slavery and freedom was then approaching its culminating point. It became evident that there was an "irrepressible conflict" between them, and that this Nation could not long exist "half slave and half free." President Pierce, during the whole of his administration, did every thing he could to conciliate the South; but it was all in vain. The conflict every year grew more violent, and threats of the dissolution of the Union were borne to the North on every Southern breeze.

Such was the condition of affairs when President Pierce approached the close of his four-years' term of office. The North had become thoroughly alienated from him. The anti-slavery sentiment, goaded by great outrages, had been rapidly increasing; all the intellectual ability and social worth of President Pierce were forgotten in deep reprehension of his administrative acts. The slaveholders of the South, also, unmindful of the fidelity with which he had advocated those measures of Government which they approved, and perhaps, also, feeling that he had rendered himself so unpopular as no longer to be able acceptably to serve them, ungratefully dropped him, and nominated James Buchanan to succeed him.

On the 4th of March, 1857, President Pierce retired to his home in Concord. Of three children, two had died, and his only surviving child had been killed before his eyes by a railroad accident; and his wife, one of the most estimable and accomplished of ladies, was rapidly sinking in consumption. The hour of dreadful gloom soon came, and he was left alone in the world, without wife or child.

When the terrible Rebellion burst forth, which divided our country into two parties, and two only, Mr. Pierce remained steadfast in the principles which he had always cherished, and gave his sympathies to that pro-slavery party with which he had ever been allied. He declined to do anything, either by voice or pen, to strengthen the hand of the National Government. He continued to reside in Concord until the time of his death, which occurred in October, 1869. He was one of the most genial and social of men, an honored communicant of the Episcopal Church, and one of the kindest of neighbors. Generous to a fault, he contributed liberally for the alleviation of suffering and want, and many of his townspeople were often gladened by his material bounty.

James Buchanan

JAMES BUCHANAN, the fifteenth President of the United States, was born in a small frontier town, at the foot of the eastern ridge of the Alleghanies, in Franklin Co., Penn., on the 23d of April, 1791. The place where the humble cabin of his father stood was called Stony Batter. It was a wild and romantic spot in a gorge of the mountains, with towering summits rising grandly all around. His father was a native of the north of Ireland; a poor man, who had emigrated in 1783, with little property save his own strong arms. Five years afterwards he married Elizabeth Spear, the daughter of a respectable farmer, and, with his young bride, plunged into the wilderness, staked his claim, reared his log-hut, opened a clearing with his axe, and settled down there to perform his obscure part in the drama of life. In this secluded home, where James was born, he remained for eight years, enjoying but few social or intellectual advantages. When James was eight years of age, his father removed to the village of Mercersburg, where his son was placed at school, and commenced a course of study in English, Latin and Greek. His progress was rapid, and at the age of fourteen, he entered Dickinson College, at Carlisle. Here he developed remarkable talent, and took his stand among the first scholars in the institution. His application to study was intense, and yet his native powers enabled him to master the most abstruse subjects with facility.

In the year 1809, he graduated with the highest honors of his class. He was then eighteen years of age; tall and graceful, vigorous in health, fond of athletic sport, an unerring shot, and enlivened with an exuberant flow of animal spirits. He immediately commenced the study of law in the city of Lancaster, and was admitted to the bar in 1812, when he was but twenty-one years of age. Very rapidly he rose in his profession, and at once took undisputed stand with the ablest lawyers of the State. When but twenty-six years of age, unaided by counsel, he successfully defended before the State Senate one of the judges of the State, who was tried upon articles of impeachment. At the age of thirty it was generally admitted that he stood at the head of the bar; and there was no lawyer in the State who had a more lucrative practice.

In 1820, he reluctantly consented to run as a candidate for Congress. He was elected, and for ten years he remained a member of the Lower House. During the vacations of Congress, he occasionally tried some important case. In 1831, he retired altogether from the toils of his profession, having acquired an ample fortune.

Gen. Jackson, upon his elevation to the Presidency, appointed Mr. Buchanan minister to Russia. The duties of his mission he performed with ability, which gave satisfaction to all parties. Upon his return, in 1833, he was elected to a seat in the United States Senate. He there met, as his associates, Webster, Clay, Wright and Calhoun. He advocated the measures proposed by President Jackson, of making reprisals against France, to enforce the payment of our claims against that country; and defended the course of the President in his unprecedented and wholesale removal from office of those who were not the supporters of his administration. Upon this question he was brought into direct collision with Henry Clay. He also, with voice and vote, advocated expunging from the journal of the Senate the vote of censure against Gen. Jackson for removing the deposits. Earnestly he opposed the abolition of slavery in the District of Columbia, and urged the prohibition of the circulation of anti-slavery documents by the United States mails.

As to petitions on the subject of slavery, he advocated that they should be respectfully received; and that the reply should be returned, that Congress had no power to legislate upon the subject. "Congress," said he, "might as well undertake to interfere with slavery under a foreign government as in any of the States where it now exists."

Upon Mr. Polk's accession to the Presidency, Mr. Buchanan became Secretary of State, and as such, took his share of the responsibility in the conduct of the Mexican War. Mr. Polk assumed that crossing the Nueces by the American troops into the disputed territory was not wrong, but for the Mexicans to cross the Rio Grande into that territory was a declaration of war. No candid man can read with pleasure the account of the course our Government pursued in that movement.

Mr. Buchanan identified himself thoroughly with the party devoted to the perpetuation and extension of slavery, and brought all the energies of his mind to bear against the Wilmot Proviso. He gave his cordial approval to the compromise measures of 1850, which included the fugitive-slave law. Mr. Pierce, upon his election to the Presidency, honored Mr. Buchanan with the mission to England.

In the year 1856, a national Democratic convention nominated Mr. Buchanan for the Presidency. The political conflict was one of the most severe in which our country has ever engaged. All the friends of slavery were on one side; all the advocates of its restriction and final abolition, on the other. Mr. Fremont, the candidate of the enemies of slavery, received 114 electoral votes. Mr. Buchanan received 174, and was elected. The popular vote stood 1,340,618, for Fremont, 1,224,750 for Buchanan. On March 4th, 1857, Mr. Buchanan was inaugurated.

Mr. Buchanan was far advanced in life. Only four years were waiting to fill up his threescore years and ten. His own friends, those with whom he had been allied in political principles and action for years, were seeking the destruction of the Government, that they might rear upon the ruins of our free institutions a nation whose corner-stone should be human slavery. In this emergency, Mr. Buchanan was hopelessly bewildered He could not, with his long-avowed principles, consistently oppose the State-rights party in their assumptions. As President of the United States, bound by his oath faithfully to administer the laws, he could not, without perjury of the grossest kind, unite with those endeavoring to overthrow the republic. He therefore did nothing.

The opponents of Mr. Buchanan's administration nominated Abraham Lincoln as their standard bearer in the next Presidential canvass. The pro-slavery party declared, that if he were elected, and the control of the Government were thus taken from their hands, they would secede from the Union, taking with them, as they retired, the National Capitol at Washington, and the lion's share of the territory of the United States.

Mr. Buchanan's sympathy with the pro-slavery party was such, that he had been willing to offer them far more than they had ventured to claim. All the South had professed to ask of the North was non-intervention upon the subject of slavery. Mr. Buchanan had been ready to offer them the active co-operation of the Government to defend and extend the institution.

As the storm increased in violence, the slaveholders claiming the right to secede, and Mr. Buchanan avowing that Congress had no power to prevent it, one of the most pitiable exhibitions of governmental imbecility was exhibited the world has ever seen. He declared that Congress had no power to enforce its laws in any State which had withdrawn, or which was attempting to withdraw from the Union. This was not the doctrine of Andrew Jackson, when, with his hand upon his sword-hilt, he exclaimed, "The Union must and shall be preserved!"

South Carolina seceded in December, 1860; nearly three months before the inauguration of President Lincoln. Mr. Buchanan looked on in listless despair. The rebel flag was raised in Charleston; Fort Sumpter was besieged; our forts, navy-yards and arsenals were seized; our depots of military stores were plundered; and our custom-houses and post-offices were appropriated by the rebels.

The energy of the rebels, and the imbecility of our Executive, were alike marvelous. The Nation looked on in agony, waiting for the slow weeks to glide away, and close the administration, so terrible in its weakness At length the long-looked-for hour of deliverance came, when Abraham Lincoln was to receive the scepter.

The administration of President Buchanan was certainly the most calamitous our country has experienced. His best friends cannot recall it with pleasure. And still more deplorable it is for his fame, that in that dreadful conflict which rolled its billows of flame and blood over our whole land, no word came from his lips to indicate his wish that our country's banner should triumph over the flag of the rebellion. He died at his Wheatland retreat, June 1, 1868.

A. Lincoln

ABRAHAM LINCOLN, the sixteenth President of the United States, was born in Hardin Co., Ky., Feb. 12, 1809. About the year 1780, a man by the name of Abraham Lincoln left Virginia with his family and moved into the then wilds of Kentucky. Only two years after this emigration, still a young man, while working one day in a field, was stealthily approached by an Indian and shot dead. His widow was left in extreme poverty with five little children, three boys and two girls. Thomas, the youngest of the boys, was four years of age at his father's death. This Thomas was the father of Abraham Lincoln, the President of the United States whose name must henceforth forever be enrolled with the most prominent in the annals of our world.

Of course no record has been kept of the life of one so lowly as Thomas Lincoln. He was among the poorest of the poor. His home was a wretched log-cabin; his food the coarsest and the meanest. Education he had none; he could never either read or write. As soon as he was able to do anything for himself, he was compelled to leave the cabin of his starving mother, and push out into the world, a friendless, wandering boy, seeking work. He hired himself out, and thus spent the whole of his youth as a laborer in the fields of others.

When twenty-eight years of age he built a log-cabin of his own, and married Nancy Hanks, the daughter of another family of poor Kentucky emigrants, who had also come from Virginia. Their second child was Abraham Lincoln, the subject of this sketch. The mother of Abraham was a noble woman, gentle, loving, pensive, created to adorn a palace, doomed to toil and pine, and die in a hovel. "All that I am, or hope to be," exclaims the grateful son "I owe to my angel-mother."

When he was eight years of age, his father sold his cabin and small farm, and moved to Indiana. Where two years later his mother died.

Abraham soon became the scribe of the uneducated community around him. He could not have had a better school than this to teach him to put thoughts into words. He also became an eager reader. The books he could obtain were few; but these he read and re-read until they were almost committed to memory.

As the years rolled on, the lot of this lowly family was the usual lot of humanity. There were joys and griefs, weddings and funerals. Abraham's sister Sarah, to whom he was tenderly attached, was married when a child of but fourteen years of age, and soon died. The family was gradually scattered. Mr. Thomas Lincoln sold out his squatter's claim in 1830, and emigrated to Macon Co., Ill.

Abraham Lincoln was then twenty-one years of age. With vigorous hands he aided his father in rearing another log-cabin. Abraham worked diligently at this until he saw the family comfortably settled, and their small lot of enclosed prairie planted with corn, when he announced to his father his intention to leave home, and to go out into the world and seek his fortune. Little did he or his friends imagine how brilliant that fortune was to be. He saw the value of education and was intensely earnest to improve his mind to the utmost of his power. He saw the ruin which ardent spirits were causing, and became strictly temperate; refusing to allow a drop of intoxicating liquor to pass his lips. And he had read in God's word, "Thou shalt not take the name of the Lord thy God in vain;" and a profane expression he was never heard to utter. Religion he revered. His morals were pure, and he was uncontaminated by a single vice.

Young Abraham worked for a time as a hired laborer among the farmers. Then he went to Springfield, where he was employed in building a large flat-boat. In this he took a herd of swine, floated them down the Sangamon to the Illinois, and thence by the Mississippi to New Orleans. Whatever Abraham Lincoln undertook, he performed so faithfully as to give great satisfaction to his employers. In this adventure his employers were so well pleased, that upon his return they placed a store and mill under his care.

In 1832, at the outbreak of the Black Hawk war, he enlisted and was chosen captain of a company. He returned to Sangamon County, and although only 23 years of age, was a candidate for the Legislature, but was defeated. He soon after received from Andrew Jackson the appointment of Postmaster of New Salem, His only post-office was his hat. All the letters he received he carried there ready to deliver to those he chanced to meet. He studied surveying, and soon made this his business. In 1834 he again became a candidate for the Legislature, and was elected Mr. Stuart, of Springfield, advised him to study law. He walked from New Salem to Springfield, borrowed of Mr. Stuart a load of books, carried them back and began his legal studies. When the Legislature assembled he trudged on foot with his pack on his back one hundred miles to Vandalia, then the capital. In 1836 he was re-elected to the Legislature. Here it was he first met Stephen A. Douglas. In 1839 he removed to Springfield and began the practice of law. His success with the jury was so great that he was soon engaged in almost every noted case in the circuit.

In 1854 the great discussion began between Mr. Lincoln and Mr. Douglas, on the slavery question. In the organization of the Republican party in Illinois, in 1856, he took an active part, and at once became one of the leaders in that party. Mr. Lincoln's speeches in opposition to Senator Douglas in the contest in 1858 for a seat in the Senate, form a most notable part of his history. The issue was on the slavery question, and he took the broad ground of the Declaration of Independence, that all men are created equal. Mr. Lincoln was defeated in this contest, but won a far higher prize.

The great Republican Convention met at Chicago on the 16th of June, 1860. The delegates and strangers who crowded the city amounted to twenty-five thousand. An immense building called "The Wigwam," was reared to accommodate the Convention. There were eleven candidates for whom votes were thrown. William H. Seward, a man whose fame as a statesman had long filled the land, was the most prominent. It was generally supposed he would be the nominee. Abraham Lincoln, however, received the nomination on the third ballot. Little did he then dream of the weary years of toil and care, and the bloody death, to which that nomination doomed him: and as little did he dream that he was to render services to his country, which would fix upon him the eyes of the whole civilized world, and which would give him a place in the affections of his countrymen, second only, if second, to that of Washington.

Election day came and Mr. Lincoln received 180 electoral votes out of 203 cast, and was, therefore, constitutionally elected President of the United States. The tirade of abuse that was poured upon this good and merciful man, especially by the slaveholders, was greater than upon any other man ever elected to this high position. In February, 1861, Mr. Lincoln started for Washington, stopping in all the large cities on his way making speeches. The whole journey was frought with much danger. Many of the Southern States had already seceded, and several attempts at assassination were afterwards brought to light. A gang in Baltimore had arranged, upon his arrival to "get up a row," and in the confusion to make sure of his death with revolvers and hand-grenades. A detective unravelled the plot. A secret and special train was provided to take him from Harrisburg, through Baltimore, at an unexpected hour of the night. The train started at half-past ten; and to prevent any possible communication on the part of the Secessionists with their Confederate gang in Baltimore, as soon as the train had started the telegraph-wires were cut. Mr. Lincoln reached Washington in safety and was inaugurated, although great anxiety was felt by all loyal people.

In the selection of his cabinet Mr. Lincoln gave to Mr. Seward the Department of State, and to other prominent opponents before the convention he gave important positions.

During no other administration have the duties devolving upon the President been so manifold, and the responsibilities so great, as those which fell to the lot of President Lincoln. Knowing this, and feeling his own weakness and inability to meet, and in his own strength to cope with, the difficulties, he learned early to seek Divine wisdom and guidance in determining his plans, and Divine comfort in all his trials, both personal and national. Contrary to his own estimate of himself, Mr. Lincoln was one of the most courageous of men. He went directly into the rebel capital just as the retreating foe was leaving, with no guard but a few sailors. From the time he had left Springfield, in 1861, however, plans had been made for his assassination, and he at last fell a victim to one of them. April 14, 1865, he, with Gen. Grant, was urgently invited to attend Fords' Theater. It was announced that they would be present. Gen. Grant, however, left the city. President Lincoln, feeling, with his characteristic kindliness of heart, that it would be a disappointment if he should fail them, very reluctantly consented to go. While listening to the play an actor by the name of John Wilkes Booth entered the box where the President and family were seated, and fired a bullet into his brains. He died the next morning at seven o'clock.

Never before, in the history of the world was a nation plunged into such deep grief by the death of its ruler Strong men met in the streets and wept in speechless anguish. It is not too much to say that a nation was in tears. His was a life which will fitly become a model. His name as the savior of his country will live with that of Washington's, its father; his countrymen being unable to decide which is the greater.

Andrew Johnson

ANDREW JOHNSON, seventeenth President of the United States. The early life of Andrew Johnson contains but the record of poverty, destitution and friendlessness. He was born December 29, 1808, in Raleigh, N. C. His parents, belonging to the class of the "poor whites" of the South, were in such circumstances, that they could not confer even the slightest advantages of education upon their child. When Andrew was five years of age, his father accidentally lost his life while herorically endeavoring to save a friend from drowning. Until ten years of age, Andrew was a ragged boy about the streets, supported by the labor of his mother, who obtained her living with her own hands.

He then, having never attended a school one day, and being unable either to read or write, was apprenticed to a tailor in his native town. A gentleman was in the habit of going to the tailor's shop occasionally, and reading to the boys at work there. He often read from the speeches of distinguished British statesmen. Andrew, who was endowed with a mind of more than ordinary native ability, became much interested in these speeches; his ambition was roused, and he was inspired with a strong desire to learn to read.

He accordingly applied himself to the alphabet, and with the assistance of some of his fellow-workmen, learned his letters. He then called upon the gentleman to borrow the book of speeches. The owner, pleased with his zeal, not only gave him the book, but assisted him in learning to combine the letters into words. Under such difficulties he pressed onward laboriously, spending usually ten or twelve hours at work in the shop, and then robbing himself of rest and recreation to devote such time as he could to reading.

He went to Tennessee in 1826, and located at Greenville, where he married a young lady who possessed some education. Under her instructions he learned to write and cipher. He became prominent in the village debating society, and a favorite with the students of Greenville College. In 1828, he organized a working man's party, which elected him alderman, and in 1830 elected him mayor, which position he held three years.

He now began to take a lively interest in political affairs; identifying himself with the working-classes, to which he belonged. In 1835, he was elected a member of the House of Representatives of Tennessee. He was then just twenty-seven years of age. He became a very active member of the legislature, gave his adhesion to the Democratic party, and in 1840 "stumped the State," advocating Martin Van Buren's claims to the Presidency, in opposition to those of Gen. Harrison. In this campaign he acquired much readiness as a speaker, and extended and increased his reputation.

In 1841, he was elected State Senator; in 1843, he was elected a member of Congress, and by successive elections, held that important post for ten years. In 1853, he was elected Governor of Tennessee, and was re-elected in 1855. In all these responsible positions, he discharged his duties with distinguished ability, and proved himself the warm friend of the working classes. In 1857, Mr. Johnson was elected United States Senator.

Years before, in 1845, he had warmly advocated the annexation of Texas, stating however, as his reason, that he thought this annexation would probably prove "to be the gateway out of which the sable sons of Africa are to pass from bondage to freedom, and become merged in a population congenial to themselves." In 1850, he also supported the compromise measures, the two essential features of which were, that the white people of the Territories should be permitted to decide for themselves whether they would enslave the colored people or not, and that the free States of the North should return to the South persons who attempted to escape from slavery.

Mr. Johnson was never ashamed of his lowly origin: on the contrary, he often took pride in avowing that he owed his distinction to his own exertions. "Sir," said he on the floor of the Senate, "I do not forget that I am a mechanic; neither do I forget that Adam was a tailor and sewed fig-leaves, and that our Savior was the son of a carpenter."

In the Charleston-Baltimore convention of 1860, he was the choice of the Tennessee Democrats for the Presidency. In 1861, when the purpose of the Southern Democracy became apparent, he took a decided stand in favor of the Union, and held that "slavery must be held subordinate to the Union at whatever cost." He returned to Tennessee, and repeatedly imperiled his own life to protect the Unionists of Tennesee. Tennessee having seceded from the Union, President Lincoln, on March 4th, 1862, appointed him Military Governor of the State, and he established the most stringent military rule. His numerous proclamations attracted wide attention. In 1864, he was elected Vice-President of the United States, and upon the death of Mr. Lincoln, April 15, 1865, became President. In a speech two days later he said, "The American people must be taught, if they do not already feel, that treason is a crime and must be punished; that the Government will not always bear with its enemies; that it is strong not only to protect, but to punish * * The people must understand that it (treason) is the blackest of crimes, and will surely be punished." Yet his whole administration, the history of which is so well known, was in utter inconsistency with, and the most violent opposition to, the principles laid down in that speech.

In his loose policy of reconstruction and general amnesty, he was opposed by Congress; and he characterized Congress as a new rebellion, and lawlessly defied it, in everything possible, to the utmost. In the beginning of 1868, on account of "high crimes and misdemeanors," the principal of which was the removal of Secretary Stanton, in violation of the Tenure of Office Act, articles of impeachment were preferred against him, and the trial began March 23.

It was very tedious, continuing for nearly three months. A test article of the impeachment was at length submitted to the court for its action. It was certain that as the court voted upon that article so would it vote upon all. Thirty-four voices pronounced the President guilty. As a two-thirds vote was necessary to his condemnation, he was pronounced acquitted, notwithstanding the great majority against him. The change of one vote from the *not guilty* side would have sustained the impeachment.

The President, for the remainder of his term, was but little regarded. He continued, though impotently, his conflict with Congress. His own party did not think it expedient to renominate him for the Presidency. The Nation rallied, with enthusiasm unparalleled since the days of Washington, around the name of Gen. Grant. Andrew Johnson was forgotten. The bullet of the assassin introduced him to the President's chair. Notwithstanding this, never was there presented to a man a better opportunity to immortalize his name, and to win the gratitude of a nation. He failed utterly. He retired to his home in Greenville, Tenn., taking no very active part in politics until 1875. On Jan. 26, after an exciting struggle, he was chosen by the Legislature of Tennessee, United States Senator in the forty-fourth Congress, and took his seat in that body, at the special session convened by President Grant, on the 5th of March. On the 27th of July, 1875, the ex-President made a visit to his daughter's home, near Carter Station, Tenn. When he started on his journey, he was apparently in his usual vigorous health, but on reaching the residence of his child the following day, was stricken with paralysis, rendering him unconscious. He rallied occasionally, but finally passed away at 2 A.M., July 31, aged sixty-seven years. His funeral was attended at Geenville, on the 3d of August, with every demonstration of respect.

U. S. Grant

ULYSSES S. GRANT, the eighteenth President of the United States, was born on the 29th of April, 1822, of Christian parents, in a humble home, at Point Pleasant, on the banks of the Ohio. Shortly after his father moved to Georgetown, Brown Co., O. In this remote frontier hamlet, Ulysses received a common-school education. At the age of seventeen, in the year 1839, he entered the Military Academy at West Point. Here he was regarded as a solid, sensible young man of fair abilities, and of sturdy, honest character. He took respectable rank as a scholar. In June, 1843, he graduated, about the middle in his class, and was sent as lieutenant of infantry to one of the distant military posts in the Missouri Territory. Two years he past in these dreary solitudes, watching the vagabond and exasperating Indians.

The war with Mexico came. Lieut. Grant was sent with his regiment to Corpus Christi. His first battle was at Palo Alto. There was no chance here for the exhibition of either skill or heroism, nor at Resaca de la Palma, his second battle. At the battle of Monterey, his third engagement, it is said that he performed a signal service of daring and skillful horsemanship. His brigade had exhausted its ammunition. A messenger must be sent for more, along a route exposed to the bullets of the foe. Lieut. Grant, adopting an expedient learned of the Indians, grasped the mane of his horse, and hanging upon one side of the animal, ran the gauntlet in entire safety.

From Monterey he was sent, with the fourth infantry, to aid Gen. Scott, at the siege of Vera Cruz. In preparation for the march to the city of Mexico, he was appointed quartermaster of his regiment. At the battle of Molino del Rey, he was promoted to a first lieutenancy, and was brevetted captain at Chapultepec.

At the close of the Mexican War, Capt. Grant returned with his regiment to New York, and was again sent to one of the military posts on the frontier. The discovery of gold in California causing an immense tide of emigration to flow to the Pacific shores, Capt. Grant was sent with a battalion to Fort Dallas, in Oregon, for the protection of the interests of the immigrants. Life was wearisome in those wilds. Capt. Grant resigned his commission and returned to the States; and having married, entered upon the cultivation of a small farm near St. Louis, Mo. He had but little skill as a farmer. Finding his toil not remunerative, he turned to mercantile life, entering into the leather business, with a younger brother, at Galena, Ill. This was in the year 1860. As the tidings of the rebels firing on Fort Sumpter reached the ears of Capt. Grant in his counting-room, he said,—"Uncle Sam has educated me for the army; though I have served him through one war, I do not feel that I have yet repaid the debt. I am still ready to discharge my obligations. I shall therefore buckle on my sword and see Uncle Sam through this war too."

He went into the streets, raised a company of volunteers, and led them as their captain to Springfield, the capital of the State, where their services were offered to Gov. Yates. The Governor, impressed by the zeal and straightforward executive ability of Capt. Grant, gave him a desk in his office, to assist in the volunteer organization that was being formed in the State in behalf of the Government. On the 15th of

June, 1861, Capt. Grant received a commission as Colonel of the Twenty-first Regiment of Illinois Volunteers. His merits as a West Point graduate, who had served for 15 years in the regular army, were such that he was soon promoted to the rank of Brigadier-General and was placed in command at Cairo. The rebels raised their banner at Paducah, near the mouth of the Tennessee River. Scarcely had its folds appeared in the breeze ere Gen. Grant was there. The rebels fled. Their banner fell, and the star and stripes were unfurled in its stead.

He entered the service with great determination and immediately began active duty. This was the beginning, and until the surrender of Lee at Richmond he was ever pushing the enemy with great vigor and effectiveness. At Belmont, a few days later, he surprised and routed the rebels, then at Fort Henry won another victory. Then came the brilliant fight at Fort Donelson. The nation was electrified by the victory, and the brave leader of the boys in blue was immediately made a Major-General, and the military district of Tennessee was assigned to him.

Like all great captains, Gen. Grant knew well how to secure the results of victory. He immediately pushed on to the enemies' lines. Then came the terrible battles of Pittsburg Landing, Corinth, and the siege of Vicksburg, where Gen. Pemberton made an unconditional surrender of the city with over thirty thousand men and one-hundred and seventy-two cannon. The fall of Vicksburg was by far the most severe blow which the rebels had thus far encountered, and opened up the Mississippi from Cairo to the Gulf.

Gen. Grant was next ordered to co-operate with Gen. Banks in a movement upon Texas, and proceeded to New Orleans, where he was thrown from his horse, and received severe injuries, from which he was laid up for months. He then rushed to the aid of Gens. Rosecrans and Thomas at Chattanooga, and by a wonderful series of strategic and technical measures put the Union Army in fighting condition. Then followed the bloody battles at Chattanooga, Lookout Mountain and Missionary Ridge, in which the rebels were routed with great loss. This won for him unbounded praise in the North. On the 4th of February, 1864, Congress revived the grade of lieutenant-general, and the rank was conferred on Gen. Grant. He repaired to Washington to receive his credentials and enter upon the duties of his new office.

Gen. Grant decided as soon as he took charge of the army to concentrate the widely-dispersed National troops for an attack upon Richmond, the nominal capital of the Rebellion, and endeavor there to destroy the rebel armies which would be promptly assembled from all quarters for its defence. The whole continent seemed to tremble under the tramp of these majestic armies, rushing to the decisive battle field. Steamers were crowded with troops. Railway trains were burdened with closely packed thousands. His plans were comprehensive and involved a series of campaigns, which were executed with remarkable energy and ability, and were consummated at the surrender of Lee, April 9, 1865.

The war was ended. The Union was saved. The almost unanimous voice of the Nation declared Gen. Grant to be the most prominent instrument in its salvation. The eminent services he had thus rendered the country brought him conspicuously forward as the Republican candidate for the Presidential chair.

At the Republican Convention held at Chicago, May 21, 1868, he was unanimously nominated for the Presidency, and at the autumn election received a majority of the popular vote, and 214 out of 294 electoral votes.

The National Convention of the Republican party which met at Philadelphia on the 5th of June, 1872, placed Gen. Grant in nomination for a second term by a unanimous vote. The selection was emphatically indorsed by the people five months later, 292 electoral votes being cast for him.

Soon after the close of his second term, Gen. Grant started upon his famous trip around the world. He visited almost every country of the civilized world, and was everywhere received with such ovations and demonstrations of respect and honor, private as well as public and official, as were never before bestowed upon any citizen of the United States.

He was the most prominent candidate before the Republican National Convention in 1880 for a renomination for President. He went to New York and embarked in the brokerage business under the firm name of Grant & Ward. The latter proved a villain, wrecked Grant's fortune, and for larceny was sent to the penitentiary. The General was attacked with cancer in the throat, but suffered in his stoic-like manner, never complaining. He was re-instated as General of the Army and retired by Congress. The cancer soon finished its deadly work, and July 23, 1885, the nation went in mourning over the death of the illustrious General.

Sincerely
R. B. Hayes

RUTHERFORD B. HAYES, the nineteenth President of the United States, was born in Delaware, O., Oct. 4, 1822, almost three months after the death of his father, Rutherford Hayes. His ancestry on both the paternal and maternal sides, was of the most honorable character. It can be traced, it is said, as far back as 1280, when Hayes and Rutherford were two Scottish chieftains, fighting side by side with Baliol, William Wallace and Robert Bruce. Both families belonged to the nobility, owned extensive estates, and had a large following. Misfortune overtaking the family, George Hayes left Scotland in 1680, and settled in Windsor, Conn. His son George was born in Windsor, and remained there during his life. Daniel Hayes, son of the latter, married Sarah Lee, and lived from the time of his marriage until his death in Simsbury, Conn. Ezekiel, son of Daniel, was born in 1724, and was a manufacturer of scythes at Bradford, Conn. Rutherford Hayes, son of Ezekiel and grandfather of President Hayes, was born in New Haven, in August, 1756. He was a farmer, blacksmith and tavern-keeper. He emigrated to Vermont at an unknown date, settling in Brattleboro, where he established a hotel. Here his son Rutherford Hayes, the father of President Hayes, was born. He was married, in September, 1813, to Sophia Birchard, of Wilmington, Vt., whose ancestors emigrated thither from Connecticut, they having been among the wealthiest and best famlies of Norwich. Her ancestry on the male side are traced back to 1635, to John Birchard, one of the principal founders of Norwich. Both of her grandfathers were soldiers in the Revolutionary War.

The father of President Hayes was an industrious frugal and opened-hearted man. He was of a mechanical turn, and could mend a plow, knit a stocking, or do almost anything else that he choose to undertake. He was a member of the Church, active in all the benevolent enterprises of the town, and conducted his business on Christian principles. After the close of the war of 1812, for reasons inexplicable to his neighbors, he resolved to emigrate to Ohio.

The journey from Vermont to Ohio in that day, when there were no canals, steamers, nor railways, was a very serious affair. A tour of inspection was first made, occupying four months. Mr. Hayes determined to move to Delaware, where the family arrived in 1817. He died July 22, 1822, a victim of malarial fever, less than three months before the birth of the son, of whom we now write. Mrs. Hayes, in her sore bereavement, found the support she so much needed in her brother Sardis, who had been a member of the household from the day of its departure from Vermont, and in an orphan girl whom she had adopted some time before as an act of charity.

Mrs. Hayes at this period was very weak, and the

subject of this sketch was so feeble at birth that he was not expected to live beyond a month or two at most. As the months went by he grew weaker and weaker, so that the neighbors were in the habit of inquiring from time to time "if Mrs. Hayes' baby died last night." On one occasion a neighbor, who was on familiar terms with the family, after alluding to the boy's big head, and the mother's assiduous care of him, said in a bantering way, "That's right! Stick to him. You have got him along so far, and I shouldn't wonder if he would really come to something yet."

"You need not laugh," said Mrs. Hayes. "You wait and see. You can't tell but I shall make him President of the United States yet." The boy lived, in spite of the universal predictions of his speedy death; and when, in 1825, his older brother was drowned, he became, if possible, still dearer to his mother.

The boy was seven years old before he went to school. His education, however, was not neglected. He probably learned as much from his mother and sister as he would have done at school. His sports were almost wholly within doors, his playmates being his sister and her associates. These circumstances tended, no doubt, to foster that gentleness of disposition, and that delicate consideration for the feelings of others, which are marked traits of his character.

His uncle Sardis Birchard took the deepest interest in his education; and as the boy's health had improved, and he was making good progress in his studies, he proposed to send him to college. His preparation commenced with a tutor at home; but he was afterwards sent for one year to a professor in the Wesleyan University, in Middletown, Conn. He entered Kenyon College in 1838, at the age of sixteen, and was graduated at the head of his class in 1842.

Immediately after his graduation he began the study of law in the office of Thomas Sparrow, Esq., in Columbus. Finding his opportunities for study in Columbus somewhat limited, he determined to enter the Law School at Cambridge, Mass., where he remained two years.

In 1845, after graduating at the Law School, he was admitted to the bar at Marietta, Ohio, and shortly afterward went into practice as an attorney-at-law with Ralph P. Buckland, of Fremont. Here he remained three years, acquiring but a limited practice, and apparently unambitious of distinction in his profession.

In 1849 he moved to Cincinnati, where his ambition found a new stimulus. For several years, however, his progress was slow. Two events, occurring at this period, had a powerful influence upon his subsequent life. One of these was his marrage with Miss Lucy Ware Webb, daughter of Dr. James Webb, of Chilicothe; the other was his introduction to the Cincinnati Literary Club, a body embracing among its members such men as Chief Justice Salmon P. Chase, Gen. John Pope, Gov. Edward F. Noyes, and many others hardly less distinguished in after life. The marriage was a fortunate one in every respect, as everybody knows. Not one of all the wives of our Presidents was more universally admired, reverenced and beloved than was Mrs. Hayes, and no one did more than she to reflect honor upon American womanhood. The Literary Club brought Mr. Hayes into constant association with young men of high character and noble aims, and lured him to display the qualities so long hidden by his bashfulness and modesty.

In 1856 he was nominated to the office of Judge of the Court of Common Pleas; but he declined to accept the nomination. Two years later, the office of city solicitor becoming vacant, the City Council elected him for the unexpired term.

In 1861, when the Rebellion broke out, he was at the zenith of his professional life. His rank at the bar was among the the first. But the news of the attack on Fort Sumpter found him eager to take up arms for the defense of his country.

His military record was bright and illustrious. In October, 1861, he was made Lieutenant-Colonel, and in August, 1862, promoted Colonel of the 79th Ohio regiment, but he refused to leave his old comrades and go among strangers. Subsequently, however, he was made Colonel of his old regiment. At the battle of South Mountain he received a wound, and while faint and bleeding displayed courage and fortitude that won admiration from all.

Col. Hayes was detached from his regiment, after his recovery, to act as Brigadier-General, and placed in command of the celebrated Kanawha division, and for gallant and meritorious services in the battles of Winchester, Fisher's Hill and Cedar Creek, he was promoted Brigadier-General. He was also brevetted Major-General, "for gallant and distinguished services during the campaigns of 1864, in West Virginia." In the course of his arduous services, four horses were shot from under him, and he was wounded four times.

In 1864, Gen. Hayes was elected to Congress, from the Second Ohio District, which had long been Democratic. He was not present during the campaign, and after his election was importuned to resign his commission in the army; but he finally declared, "I shall never come to Washington until I can come by the way of Richmond." He was re-elected in 1866.

In 1867, Gen Hayes was elected Governor of Ohio, over Hon. Allen G. Thurman, a popular Democrat. In 1869 was re-elected over George H. Pendleton. He was elected Governor for the third term in 1875.

In 1876 he was the standard bearer of the Republican Party in the Presidential contest, and after a hard long contest was chosen President, and was in augurated Monday, March 5, 1875. He served his full term, not, however, with satisfaction to his party, but his administration was an average one.

J. A. Garfield

JAMES A. GARFIELD, twentieth President of the United States, was born Nov. 19, 1831, in the woods of Orange, Cuyahoga Co., O His parents were Abram and Eliza (Ballou) Garfield, both of New England ancestry and from families well known in the early history of that section of our country, but had moved to the Western Reserve, in Ohio, early in its settlement.

The house in which James A. was born was not unlike the houses of poor Ohio farmers of that day. It was about 20 x 30 feet, built of logs, with the spaces between the logs filled with clay. His father was a hard working farmer, and he soon had his fields cleared, an orchard planted, and a log barn built. The household comprised the father and mother and their four children—Mehetabel, Thomas, Mary and James. In May, 1823, the father, from a cold contracted in helping to put out a forest fire, died. At this time James was about eighteen months old, and Thomas about ten years old. No one, perhaps, can tell how much James was indebted to his brother's toil and self-sacrifice during the twenty years succeeding his father's death, but undoubtedly very much. He now lives in Michigan, and the two sisters live in Solon, O., near their birthplace.

The early educational advantages young Garfield enjoyed were very limited, yet he made the most of them. He labored at farm work for others, did carpenter work, chopped wood, or did anything that would bring in a few dollars to aid his widowed mother in her struggles to keep the little family together. Nor was Gen. Garfield ever ashamed of his origin, and he never forgot the friends of his struggling childhood, youth and manhood, neither did they ever forget him. When in the highest seats of honor, the humblest friend of his boyhood was as kindly greeted as ever. The poorest laborer was sure of the sympathy of one who had known all the bitterness of want and the sweetness of bread earned by the sweat of the brow. He was ever the simple, plain, modest gentleman.

The highest ambition of young Garfield until he was about sixteen years old was to be a captain of a vessel on Lake Erie. He was anxious to go aboard a vessel, which his mother strongly opposed. She finally consented to his going to Cleveland, with the understanding, however, that he should try to obtain some other kind of employment. He walked all the way to Cleveland. This was his first visit to the city. After making many applications for work, and trying to get aboard a lake vessel, and not meeting with success, he engaged as a driver for his cousin, Amos Letcher, on the Ohio & Pennsylvania Canal. He remained at this work but a short time when he went home, and attended the seminary at Chester for about three years, when he entered Hiram and the Eclectic Institute, teaching a few terms of school in the meantime, and doing other work. This school was started by the Disciples of Christ in 1850, of which church he was then a member. He became janitor and bell-ringer in order to help pay his way. He then became both teacher and pupil. He soon "exhausted Hiram" and needed more; hence, in the fall of 1854, he entered Williams College, from which he graduated in 1856, taking one of the highest honors of his class. He afterwards returned to Hiram College as its President. As above stated, he early united with the Christian or Diciples Church at Hiram, and was ever after a devoted, zealous member, often preaching in its pulpit and places where he happened to be. Dr. Noah Porter, President of Yale College, says of him in reference to his religion:

"President Garfield was more than a man of strong moral and religious convictions. His whole history, from boyhood to the last, shows that duty to man and to God, and devotion to Christ and life and faith and spiritual commission were controlling springs of his being, and to a more than usual degree. In my judgment there is no more interesting feature of his character than his loyal allegiance to the body of Christians in which he was trained, and the fervent sympathy which he ever showed in their Christian communion. Not many of the few 'wise and mighty and noble who are called' show a similar loyalty to the less stately and cultured Christian communions in which they have been reared. Too often it is true that as they step upward in social and political significance they step upward from one degree to another in some of the many types of fashionable Christianity. President Garfield adhered to the church of his mother, the church in which he was trained, and in which he served as a pillar and an evangelist, and yet with the largest and most unsectarian charity for all 'who love our Lord in sincerity.'"

Mr. Garfield was united in marriage with Miss Lucretia Rudolph, Nov. 11, 1858, who proved herself worthy as the wife of one whom all the world loved and mourned. To them were born seven children, five of whom are still living, four boys and one girl.

Mr. Garfield made his first political speeches in 1856, in Hiram and the neighboring villages, and three years later he began to speak at county mass-meetings, and became the favorite speaker wherever he was. During this year he was elected to the Ohio Senate. He also began to study law at Cleveland, and in 1861 was admitted to the bar. The great Rebellion broke out in the early part of this year, and Mr. Garfield at once resolved to fight as he had talked, and enlisted to defend the old flag. He received his commission as Lieut.-Colonel of the Forty-second Regiment of Ohio Volunteer Infantry, Aug. 14, 1861. He was immediately put into active service, and before he had ever seen a gun fired in action, was placed in command of four regiments of infantry and eight companies of cavalry, charged with the work of driving out of his native State the officer (Humphrey Marshall) reputed to be the ablest of those, not educated to war whom Kentucky had given to the Rebellion. This work was bravely and speedily accomplished, although against great odds. President Lincoln, on his success commissioned him Brigadier-General, Jan. 10, 1862; and as "he had been the youngest man in the Ohio Senate two years before, so now he was the youngest General in the army." He was with Gen. Buell's army at Shiloh, in its operations around Corinth and its march through Alabama. He was then detailed as a member of the General Court-Martial for the trial of Gen. Fitz-John Porter. He was then ordered to report to Gen. Rosecrans, and was assigned to the "Chief of Staff."

The military history of Gen. Garfield closed with his brilliant services at Chickamauga, where he won the stars of the Major-General.

Without an effort on his part Gen. Garfield was elected to Congress in the fall of 1862 from the Nineteenth District of Ohio. This section of Ohio had been represented in Congress for sixty years mainly by two men—Elisha Whittlesey and Joshua R. Giddings. It was not without a struggle that he resigned his place in the army. At the time he entered Congress he was the youngest member in that body. There he remained by successive re-elections until he was elected President in 1880. Of his labors in Congress Senator Hoar says: "Since the year 1864 you cannot think of a question which has been debated in Congress, or discussed before a tribunel of the American people, in regard to which you will not find, if you wish instruction, the argument on one side stated, in almost every instance better than by anybody else, in some speech made in the House of Representatives or on the hustings by Mr. Garfield."

Upon Jan. 14, 1880, Gen. Garfield was elected to the U. S. Senate, and on the eighth of June, of the same year, was nominated as the candidate of his party for President at the great Chicago Convention. He was elected in the following November, and on March 4, 1881, was inaugurated. Probably no administration ever opened its existence under brighter auspices than that of President Garfield, and every day it grew in favor with the people, and by the first of July he had completed all the initiatory and preliminary work of his administration and was preparing to leave the city to meet his friends at Williams College. While on his way and at the depot, in company with Secretary Blaine, a man stepped behind him, drew a revolver, and fired directly at his back. The President tottered and fell, and as he did so the assassin fired a second shot, the bullet cutting the left coat sleeve of his victim, but inflicting no further injury. It has been very truthfully said that this was "the shot that was heard round the world" Never before in the history of the Nation had anything occurred which so nearly froze the blood of the people for the moment, as this awful deed. He was smitten on the brightest, gladdest day of all his life, and was at the summit of his power and hope. For eighty days, all during the hot months of July and August, he lingered and suffered. He, however, remained master of himself till the last, and by his magnificent bearing was teaching the country and the world the noblest of human lessons—how to live grandly in the very clutch of death. Great in life, he was surpassingly great in death. He passed serenely away Sept. 19, 1883, at Elberon, N. J., on the very bank of the ocean, where he had been taken shortly previous. The world wept at his death, as it never had done on the death of any other man who had ever lived upon it. The murderer was duly tried, found guilty and executed, in one year after he committed the foul deed.

C. A. Arthur.

CHESTER A. ARTHUR, twenty-first President of the United States was born in Franklin County, Vermont, on the fifth of October, 1830, and is the oldest of a family of two sons and five daughters. His father was the Rev. Dr. William Arthur, a Baptist clergyman, who emigrated to this country from the county Antrim, Ireland, in his 18th year, and died in 1875, in Newtonville, near Albany, after a long and successful ministry.

Young Arthur was educated at Union College, Schenectady, where he excelled in all his studies. After his graduation he taught school in Vermont for two years, and at the expiration of that time came to New York, with $500 in his pocket, and entered the office of ex-Judge E. D. Culver as student. After being admitted to the bar he formed a partnership with his intimate friend and room-mate, Henry D. Gardiner, with the intention of practicing in the West, and for three months they roamed about in the Western States in search of an eligible site, but in the end returned to New York, where they hung out their shingle, and entered upon a successful career almost from the start. General Arthur soon afterward married the daughter of Lieutenant Herndon, of the United States Navy, who was lost at sea. Congress voted a gold medal to his widow in recognition of the bravery he displayed on that occasion. Mrs. Arthur died shortly before Mr. Arthur's nomination to the Vice Presidency, leaving two children.

Gen. Arthur obtained considerable legal celebrity in his first great case, the famous Lemmon suit, brought to recover possession of eight slaves who had been declared free by Judge Paine, of the Superior Court of New York City. It was in 1852 that Jonathan Lemmon, of Virginia, went to New York with his slaves, intending to ship them to Texas, when they were discovered and freed. The Judge decided that they could not be held by the owner under the Fugitive Slave Law. A howl of rage went up from the South, and the Virginia Legislature authorized the Attorney General of that State to assist in an appeal. Wm. M. Evarts and Chester A. Arthur were employed to represent the People, and they won their case, which then went to the Supreme Court of the United States. Charles O'Conor here espoused the cause of the slave-holders, but he too was beaten by Messrs. Evarts and Arthur, and a long step was taken toward the emancipation of the black race.

Another great service was rendered by General Arthur in the same cause in 1856. Lizzie Jennings, a respectable colored woman, was put off a Fourth Avenue car with violence after she had paid her fare. General Arthur sued on her behalf, and secured a verdict of $500 damages. The next day the company issued an order to admit colored persons to ride on their cars, and the other car companies quickly followed their example. Before that the Sixth Avenue Company ran a few special cars for colored persons and the other lines refused to let them ride at all.

General Arthur was a delegate to the Convention at Saratoga that founded the Republican party. Previous to the war he was Judge-Advocate of the Second Brigade of the State of New York, and Governor Morgan, of that State, appointed him Engineer-in-Chief of his staff. In 1861, he was made Inspector General, and soon afterward became Quartermaster-General. In each of these offices he rendered great service to the Government during the war. At the end of Governor Morgan's term he resumed the practice of the law, forming a partnership with Mr. Ransom, and then Mr. Phelps, the District Attorney of New York, was added to the firm. The legal practice of this well-known firm was very large and lucrative, each of the gentlemen composing it were able lawyers, and possessed a splendid local reputation, if not indeed one of national extent.

He always took a leading part in State and city politics. He was appointed Collector of the Port of New York by President Grant, Nov. 21 1872, to succeed Thomas Murphy, and held the office until July, 20, 1878, when he was succeeded by Collector Merritt.

Mr. Arthur was nominated on the Presidential ticket, with Gen. James A. Garfield, at the famous National Republican Convention held at Chicago in June, 1880. This was perhaps the greatest political convention that ever assembled on the continent. It was composed of the leading politicians of the Republican party, all able men, and each stood firm and fought vigorously and with signal tenacity for their respective candidates that were before the convention for the nomination. Finally Gen. Garfield received the nomination for President and Gen. Arthur for Vice-President. The campaign which followed was one of the most animated known in the history of our country. Gen. Hancock, the standard-bearer of the Democratic party, was a popular man, and his party made a valiant fight for his election.

Finally the election came and the country's choice was Garfield and Arthur. They were inaugurated March 4, 1881, as President and Vice-President. A few months only had passed ere the newly chosen President was the victim of the assassin's bullet. Then came terrible weeks of suffering,—those moments of anxious suspense, when the hearts of all civilized nations were throbbing in unison, longing for the recovery of the noble, the good President. The remarkable patience that he manifested during those hours and weeks, and even months, of the most terrible suffering man has often been called upon to endure, was seemingly more than human. It was certainly Godlike. During all this period of deepest anxiety Mr. Arthur's every move was watched, and be it said to his credit that his every action displayed only an earnest desire that the suffering Garfield might recover, to serve the remainder of the term he had so auspiciously begun. Not a selfish feeling was manifested in deed or look of this man, even though the most honored position in the world was at any moment likely to fall to him.

At last God in his mercy relieved President Garfield from further suffering, and the world, as never before in its history over the death of any other man, wept at his bier. Then it became the duty of the Vice President to assume the responsibilities of the high office, and he took the oath in New York, Sept. 20, 1881. The position was an embarrassing one to him, made doubly so from the facts that all eyes were on him, anxious to know what he would do, what policy he would pursue, and who he would select as advisers. The duties of the office had been greatly neglected during the President's long illness, and many important measures were to be immediately decided by him; and still farther to embarrass him he did not fail to realize under what circumstances he became President, and knew the feelings of many on this point. Under these trying circumstances President Arthur took the reins of the Government in his own hands; and, as embarrassing as were the condition of affairs, he happily surprised the nation, acting so wisely that but few criticised his administration. He served the nation well and faithfully, until the close of his administration, March 4, 1885, and was a popular candidate before his party for a second term. His name was ably presented before the convention at Chicago, and was received with great favor, and doubtless but for the personal popularity of one of the opposing candidates, he would have been selected as the standard-bearer of his party for another campaign. He retired to private life carrying with him the best wishes of the American people, whom he had served in a manner satisfactory to them and with credit to himself.

Grover Cleveland

S. Grover Cleveland.

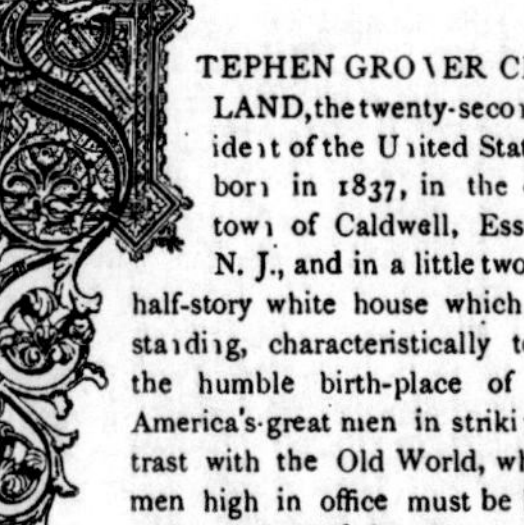

TEPHEN GROVER CLEVELAND, the twenty-second President of the United States, was born in 1837, in the obscure town of Caldwell, Essex Co., N. J., and in a little two-and-a-half-story white house which is still standing, characteristically to mark the humble birth-place of one of America's great men in striking contrast with the Old World, where all men high in office must be high in origin and born in the cradle of wealth. When the subject of this sketch was three years of age, his father, who was a Presbyterian minister, with a large family and a small salary, moved, by way of the Hudson River and Erie Canal, to Fayetteville, in search of an increased income and a larger field of work. Fayetteville was then the most straggling of country villages, about five miles from Pompey Hill, where Governor Seymour was born.

At the last mentioned place young Grover commenced going to school in the "good, old-fashioned way," and presumably distinguished himself after the manner of all village boys, in doing the things he ought not to do. Such is the distinguishing trait of all geniuses and independent thinkers. When he arrived at the age of 14 years, he had outgrown the capacity of the village school and expressed a most emphatic desire to be sent to an academy. To this his father decidedly objected. Academies in those days cost money; besides, his father wanted him to become self-supporting by the quickest possible means, and this at that time in Fayetteville seemed to be a position in a country store, where his father and the large family on his hands had considerable influence. Grover was to be paid $50 for his services the first year, and if he proved trustworthy he was to receive $100 the second year. Here the lad commenced his career as salesman, and in two years he had earned so good a reputation for trustworthiness that his employers desired to retain him for an indefinite length of time. Otherwise he did not exhibit as yet any particular "flashes of genius" or eccentricities of talent. He was simply a good boy.

But instead of remaining with this firm in Fayetteville, he went with the family in their removal to Clinton, where he had an opportunity of attending a high school. Here he industriously pursued his studies until the family removed with him to a point on Black River known as the "Holland Patent," a village of 500 or 600 people, 15 miles north of Utica, N. Y. At this place his father died, after preaching but three Sundays. This event broke up the family, and Grover set out for New York City to accept, at a small salary, the position of "under-teacher" in an asylum for the blind. He taught faithfully for two years, and although he obtained a good reputation in this capacity, he concluded that teaching was not his calling for life, and, reversing the traditional order, he left the city to seek his fortune, instead of going to a city. He first thought of Cleveland, Ohio, as there was some charm in that name for him; but before proceeding to that place he went to Buffalo to ask the advice of his uncle, Lewis F. Allan, a noted stock-breeder of that place. The latter did not speak enthusiastically. "What is it you want to do, my boy?" he asked. "Well, sir, I want to study law," was the reply. "Good gracious!" remarked the old gentleman; "do you, indeed? What ever put that into your head? How much money have you got?" "Well, sir, to tell the truth, I haven't got any."

After a long consultation, his uncle offered him a place temporarily as assistant herd-keeper, at $50 a year, while he could "look around." One day soon afterward he boldly walked into the office of Rogers, Bowen & Rogers, of Buffalo, and told them what he wanted. A number of young men were already engaged in the office, but Grover's persistency won, and he was finally permitted to come as an office boy and have the use of the law library, for the nominal sum of $3 or $4 a week. Out of this he had to pay for his board and washing. The walk to and from his uncle's was a long and rugged one; and, although the first winter was a memorably severe one, his shoes were out of repair and his overcoat—he had none—yet he was nevertheless prompt and regular. On the first day of his service here, his senior employer threw down a copy of Blackstone before him with a bang that made the dust fly, saying "That's where they all begin." A titter ran around the little circle of clerks and students, as they thought that was enough to scare young Grover out of his plans; but in due time he mastered that cumbersome volume. Then, as ever afterward, however, Mr. Cleveland exhibited a talent for executiveness rather than for chasing principles through all their metaphysical possibilities. "Let us quit talking and go and do it," was practically his motto.

The first public office to which Mr. Cleveland was elected was that of Sheriff of Erie Co., N. Y., in which Buffalo is situated; and in such capacity it fell to his duty to inflict capital punishment upon two criminals. In 1881 he was elected Mayor of the City of Buffalo, on the Democratic ticket, with especial reference to the bringing about certain reforms in the administration of the municipal affairs of that city. In this office, as well as that of Sheriff, his performance of duty has generally been considered fair, with possibly a few exceptions which were ferreted out and magnified during the last Presidential campaign. As a specimen of his plain language in a veto message, we quote from one vetoing an iniquitous street-cleaning contract: "This is a time for plain speech, and my objection to your action shall be plainly stated. I regard it as the culmination of a most bare-faced, impudent and shameless scheme to betray the interests of the people and to worse than squander the people's money." The New York *Sun* afterward very highly commended Mr. Cleveland's administration as Mayor of Buffalo, and thereupon recommended him for Governor of the Empire State. To the latter office he was elected in 1882, and his administration of the affairs of State was generally satisfactory. The mistakes he made, if any, were made very public throughout the nation after he was nominated for President of the United States. For this high office he was nominated July 11, 1884, by the National Democratic Convention at Chicago, when other competitors were Thomas F. Bayard, Roswell P. Flower, Thomas A. Hendricks, Benjamin F. Butler, Allen G. Thurman, etc.; and he was elected by the people, by a majority of about a thousand, over the brilliant and long-tried Republican statesman, James G. Blaine. President Cleveland resigned his office as Governor of New York in January, 1885, in order to prepare for his duties as the Chief Executive of the United States, in which capacity his term commenced at noon on the 4th of March, 1885. For his Cabinet officers he selected the following gentlemen: For Secretary of State, Thomas F. Bayard, of Delaware; Secretary of the Treasury, Daniel Manning, of New York; Secretary of War, William C. Endicott, of Massachusetts; Secretary of the Navy, William C. Whitney, of New York; Secretary of the Interior, L. Q. C. Lamar, of Mississippi; Postmaster-General, William F. Vilas, of Wisconsin; Attorney-General, A. H. Garland, of Arkansas.

The silver question precipitated a controversy between those who were in favor of the continuance of silver coinage and those who were opposed, Mr. Cleveland answering for the latter, even before his inauguration.

GOVERNORS.

Ansel Briggs

Ansel Briggs.

ANSEL BRIGGS, the first gentleman chosen to fill the gubernatorial chair of Iowa after its organization as a State, was a native of Vermont, and was born Feb. 3, 1806. His parents, who likewise were New Englanders, were Benjamin and Electa Briggs. The boyhood of our subject was passed in his native State, and in attendance upon the common schools he received a fair education which was subsequently improved by a term at Norwich Academy. When a young man he removed with his parents to Cambridge, Guernsey Co., Ohio, where young Briggs engaged in the work of establishing stage lines. He also here embarked in political affairs and as a Whig ran for the office of County Auditor but was defeated by John Ferguson, a Jackson Democrat.

After remaining in Ohio for six years, the glowing accounts of the fair fields and the fertile prairies of the Territory of Iowa, led him westward across the Father of Waters. He had previously united his fortunes in life with Nancy M. Dunlap, daughter of Major Dunlap, an officer in the War of 1812. Even prior to this marriage he had chosen a wife, a lady who was born on the same day and year as himself, but of whom he was soon bereft. He brought with him to Iowa his little family and located at Andrew, in Jackson County. Seeing the opportunity here for resuming his former business, he began opening up stage lines, frequently driving the old stage coach himself. He made several contracts with the Postoffice Department for carrying the United States mails weekly between Dubuque and Davenport, Dubuque and Iowa City and other routes, thus opening up and carrying on a very important enterprise. Politically, Gov. Briggs was a Democrat, and on coming to Iowa identified himself with that party. In 1842 he was chosen a member of the Territorial House of Representatives from Jackson County, and subsequently was elected Sheriff of the same county. He had taken a leading part in public affairs, and upon the formation of the State Government in 1846, he became a prominent candidate for Governor, and though his competitors in his own party were distinguished and well-known citizens, Mr. Briggs received the nomination. The convention was held in Iowa City, on Thursday, Sept. 24, 1846, and assembled to nominate State officers and two Congressmen. It was called to order by F. D. Mills, of Des Moines County. William Thompson, of Henry County, presided, and J. T. Fales, of Dubuque, was Secretary. The vote for Governor in the convention stood: Briggs, sixty-two; Jesse Williams, thirty-two, and William Thompson, thirty-one. The two latter withdrew, and Briggs was then chosen by acclamation. Elisha Cutler, Jr., of Van Buren County, was nominated for Secretary of State; Joseph T. Fales, of Linn, for Auditor, and Morgan Reno, of Johnson, for Treasurer. S. C. Hastings and Sheperd Leffler were nominated for Congress. The election was held Oct. 28, 1846, the entire Democratic ticket being successful. Briggs received 7,626 votes and his competitor, Thomas McKnight, the Whig candidate, 7,379, giving Briggs a majority of 247.

The principal question between the two leading parties, the Democratic and the Whig, at this period, was that of the banking system. It is related that a short time prior to the meeting of the convention which nominated Mr. Briggs, that in offering a toast at a banquet, he struck the key-note which made him the popular man of the hour. He said, "No banks but earth and they well tilled." This was at once caught up by his party and it did more to secure him the nomination than anything else. His administration was one void of any special interest. He labored in harmonious accord with his party, yet frequently exhibited an independence of principle, characteristic of his nature. The Missouri boundary question which caused a great deal of excited controversy at this period, and even a determination to resort to arms, was handled by him with great ability.

On his election as Executive of the State, Gov. Briggs sold out his mail contract, but after the expiration of his term of service he continued his residence in Jackson County. In 1870 he removed to Council Bluffs. He had visited the western part of the State before the day of railroads in that section, making the trip by carriage. On the occasion he enrolled himself as one of the founders of the town of Florence on the Nebraska side of the river and six miles above Council Bluffs, and which for a time was a vigorous rival of Omaha. During the mining excitement, in 1860, he made a trip to Colorado, and three years later, in company with his son John and a large party, went to Montana, where he remained until the year 1865, when he returned to his home in Iowa.

As above stated, Gov. Briggs was twice married, his first wife being his companion for a brief time only. His second wife bore him eight children, all of whom died in infancy save two, and of these latter, Ansel, Jr., died May 15, 1867, aged twenty-five years. John S. Briggs, the only survivor of the family, is editor of the *Idaho Herald*, published at Blackfoot, Idaho Territory. Mrs. Briggs died Dec. 30, 1847, while her husband was Governor of the State. She was a devoted Christian lady, a strict member of the Presbyterian Church, and a woman of strong domestic tastes. She was highly educated, and endowed by nature with that womanly tact and grace which enabled her to adorn the high position her husband had attained. She dispensed a bounteous hospitality, though her home was in a log house, and was highly esteemed and admired by all who met her.

Gov. Briggs went in and out among his people for many years after his retirement from the executive office, and even after his return from the Montana expedition. He was admired for his able services rendered so unselfishly during the pioneer period of the now great and populous State. His last illness, ulceration of the stomach, was of brief duration, lasting only five weeks, indeed only three days before his death he was able to be out. His demise occurred at the residence of his son, John S. Briggs, in Omaha, Neb., at half-past three of the morning of May 5, 1881. His death was greatly mourned all over the State. Upon the following day, Gov. Gear issued a proclamation reciting his services to the State, ordering half-hour guns to be fired and the national flag on the State capitol to be put at half-mast during the day upon which the funeral was held, which was the following Sunday succeeding his death.

S. Hempstead

Stephen Hempstead.

STEPHEN HEMPSTEAD, second Governor of Iowa, is a native of Connecticut, where, at New London, he was born Oct. 1, 1812. He resided in that State with his parents until 1828, when the family came West, locating upon a farm near Saint Louis. This was the home of young Stephen until 1830, when he went to Galena, Ill., where he served in the capacity of a clerk in a commission house for a time. He was there during the exciting period of the Black Hawk troubles, and was an officer in an artillery company which had been organized for the protection of Galena. After the defeat of Black Hawk and the consequent termination of Indian troubles, he entered the Illinois College at Jacksonville, where he remained for about two years. On account of difficulties which he got into about sectarianism and abolitionism, he left the college and returned to Missouri. He shortly afterward entered the office of Charles S. Hempstead, a prominent lawyer of Galena, and began the study of the profession in which he afterward became quite proficient. In 1836 he was admitted to practice in all the courts of the Territory of Wisconsin, which at the time embraced the Territory of Iowa, and the same year located at Dubuque, being the first lawyer who began the practice of his profession at that place.

As might be expected in a territory but thinly populated, but one which was rapidly settling up, the services of an able attorney would be in demand in order to draft the laws. Upon the organization of the Territorial Government of Iowa in 1838, he was, with Gen. Warner Lewis, elected to represent the northern portion of the Territory in the Legislative Council, which assembled in Burlington that year. He was Chairman of the Committee Judiciary, and at the second session of that body was elected its President. He was again elected a member of the Council, in 1845, over which he also presided. In 1844 he was elected one of the delegates of Dubuque County, for the first convention to frame a constitution for the State. In 1848, in company with Judge Charles Mason and W. G. Woodward, he was appointed by the Legislature Commissioner to revise the laws of the State, which revision, with a few amendments, was adopted as the code of Iowa in 1851.

In 1850 Mr. Hempstead was elected Governor of

the State, and served with ability for four years, that being the full term under the Constitution at the time. He received 13,486 votes against 11,-403 cast for his opponent, James L. Thompson. After the vote had been canvassed a committee was appointed to inform the Governor-elect that the two Houses of the Legislature were ready to receive him in joint convention, in order that he might receive the oath prescribed by the Constitution. Gov. Hempstead, accompanied by the retiring Executive, Gov. Briggs, the Judges of the Supreme Court and the officers of State, entered the hall of the House where the Governor-elect delivered his inaugural message, after which the oath was administered by the Chief Justice of the Supreme Court. This was an important period in the history of the State, being at a time when the public affairs were assuming definite shape, and indeed it was what might be termed the formative period. The session of the Legislature passed many important acts which were approved by the Governor, and during his term there were fifty-two new counties formed. Gov. Hempstead in his message to the Fourth General Assembly in December, 1852, stated that among other things, the population of the State according to the Federal census was 192,-214, and that the State census showed an increase for one year of 37,786. He also stated that the resources of the State for the coming two years would be sufficient to cancel all that part of funded debt which was payable at its option.

Among the numerous counties organized was one named Buncombe, which received its name in the following way: The Legislature was composed of a large majority favoring stringent corporation laws and the liability of individual stockholders for corparate debts. This sentiment, on account of the agitation of railroad enterprises then being inaugurated, brought a large number of prominent men to the capital. To have an effect upon the Legislature, they organized a "lobby Legislature" and elected as Governor, Verplank Van Antwerp, who delivered to the self-constituted body a lengthy message in which he sharply criticized the regular General Assembly. Some of the members of the latter were in the habit of making long and useful speeches much to the hindrance of business. To these he especially referred, charging them with speaking for "Buncombe," and recommended that as a lasting memorial a county should be called by that name. This suggestion was readily seized on by the Legislature, and the county of Buncombe was created with few dissenting voices. However, the General Assembly, in 1862, changed the name to Lyon, in honor of Gen. Nathaniel Lyon who was killed in the early part of the Civil War.

The season of 1851 was one of great disappointment to the pioneers of Iowa, and much suffering was the result of the bad season of that year. By the year 1854, the State had fully recovered from the depression thus produced, and that year as well as the following, the emigration from the East was unprecedented. The prairies of Illinois were lined day after day with a continuous caravan of emigrants pushing on toward Iowa. During a single month 1743 wagons bound for Iowa passed through Peoria. So remarkable had been the influx of people into the State, that in an issue of the Burlington *Telegraph* appeared the following statement: "Twenty thousand emigrants have passed through the city within the last thirty days, and they are still crossing the Mississippi at the rate of 600 a day."

At the expiration of his term of service, which occurred in the latter part of the year 1854, Gov. Hempstead returned to his old home at Dubuque. In 1855 he was elected County Judge of Dubuque County, and so acceptably did he serve the people that for twelve years he was chosen to fill that position. Under his administration the principal county building, including the jail, poorhouse, as well as some valuable bridges, were erected. Owing to ill-health he was compelled to retire from public life, passing the remainder of his days in quietude and repose at Dubuque. There he lived until Feb. 16, 1883, when, at his home, the light of his long and eventful life went out. The record he has made, which was an honorable and distinguished one, was closed, and Iowa was called upon to mourn the loss of one of her most distinguished pioneer citizens. He had been an unusually useful man of the State and his services, which were able and wise, were rendered in that unselfish spirit which distinguished so many of the early residents of this now prosperous State.

JAMES W. GRIMES, the third gentleman to fill the Executive Chair of the State of Iowa, was born in the town of Deering, Hillsborough Co., N. H., Oct. 20, 1816. His parents, John and Elizabeth (Wilson) Grimes, were also natives of the same town. The former was born on the 11th of August, 1772, and the mother March 19, 1773. They became the parents of eight children, of whom James was the youngest and became one of the most distinguished citizens of Iowa. He attended the district schools and in early childhood evinced an unusual taste for learning. Besides attending the district schools, the village pastor instructed him in Greek and Latin. After completing his preparations for college, which he did at Hampton Academy, he entered Dartmouth College, in August, 1832, which was in the sixteenth year of his age. He was a hard student, advanced rapidly, and in February, 1835, bid adieu to the college halls, and with James Walker, of Peterborough, N. H., be began the study of his chosen profession.

Feeling that his native State afforded too limited advantages, and, in fact, being of a rather adventurous disposition, as well as ambitious, he desired broader fields in which to carve for himself a fortune. He accordingly left the home that had sheltered him during his boyhood days, and turning his face Westward proceeded until he had crossed the great Father of Waters. It was in 1836, and young Grimes was indeed young to thus take upon himself such responsibilities; but possessing business tact, determination and tenacity, as well as an excellent professional training, he determined to open an office in the then new town of Burlington, Iowa. Here he hung out his shingle, and ere long had established a reputation which extended far beyond the confines of the little city.

In April, 1837, he was appointed City Solicitor, and entering upon the duties of that office he assisted in drawing up the first police laws of that town. In 1838 he was appointed Justice of the Peace, and became a law partner of William W. Chapman, United States District Attorney for Wisconsin Territory. In the early part of the year 1841 he formed a partnership with Henry W. Starr, Esq., which continued twelve years. This firm stood at the head of the legal profession in Iowa. Mr. Grimes was widely known as a counselor with superior knowledge of the law, and with a clear sense of truth and justice. He was chosen one of the Representatives of Des Moines County in the first Legislative Assembly of the Territory of Iowa, which convened at Burlington, Nov. 12, 1838; in the sixth, at Iowa City, Dec. 4, 1843; and in the fourth General Assembly of the State, at Iowa City, Dec. 6, 1852. He early took front rank among the public men of Iowa. He was Chairman of the Judiciary Committee in the House of Representatives of the first Legislative Assembly of the Territory, and all laws for the new Territory passed through his hands.

Mr. Grimes had become prominently identified with the Whig party, and being distinguished as an able lawyer, as well as a fair-minded, conscientious man, he was a prominent candidate for Governor before the convention which met in February, 1854. It was the largest convention of that party ever held in Iowa and the last. He was chosen as a nominee for Governor, was duly elected, and in December, 1854, assumed the duties of the office. Shortly after his election it was proposed that he should go to the United States Senate, but he gave his admirers to understand that he was determined to fill the term of office for which he had been chosen. This he did, serving the full term to the entire satisfaction of all parties. He was a faithful party leader, and so able were his services that, while at the time of his election as Governor Democracy reigned supreme in the State and its representatives in Congress were allied to the slave power, he turned the State over to the Republican party.

His term of office expired Jan. 14, 1858, when he retired from the Executive Chair, only, however, to assume the responsibilities of a United States Senator. Upon the 4th of March of the following year he took his seat in the Senate and was placed upon the Committee on Naval Affairs, upon which he remained during his Senatorial career, serving as Chairman of that important committee from December, 1864. Jan. 16, 1864, Mr. Grimes was again chosen to represent Iowa in the Senate of the United States, receiving all but six of the votes of the General Assembly in joint convention.

His counsel was often sought in matters of great moment, and in cases of peculiar difficulty. Always ready to promote the welfare of the State, he gave, unsolicited, land worth $6,000 to the Congregational College, at Grinnell. It constitutes the "Grimes foundation," and "is to be applied to the establishment and maintenance in Iowa College, forever, of four scholarships, to be awarded by the Trustees, on the recommendation of the faculty, to the best scholars, and the most promising, in any department, who may need and seek such aid, and without any regard to the religious tenets or opinions entertained by any person seeking either of said scholarships." These terms were imposed by Mr. Grimes, and assumed July 20, 1865, by the Trustees. He received the honorary degree of LL.D. in 1865 from Dartmouth College, and also from Iowa College. He also aided in founding a public library in Burlington, donating $5,000, which was expended in the purchase of costly books, and subsequently sent from Europe 256 volumes in the German language, and also contributed 600 volumes of public documents.

In January, 1869, he made a donation of $5,000 to Dartmouth College, and $1,000 to the "Social Friend," a literary society of which he was a member when in college.

His health failing, Mr. Grimes sailed for Europe, April 14, 1869, remaining abroad two years, reaching home Sept. 22, 1871, apparently in improved health and spirits. In November he celebrated his silver wedding, and spent the closing months of his life with his family. He voted at the city election, Feb. 5, 1872, and was suddenly attacked with severe pains in the region of the heart, and died after a few short hours of intense suffering.

Senator Grimes was united in marriage at Burlington, Ia., Nov. 9, 1846, with Miss Sarah Elizabeth Neally. Mr. Grimes stood in the foremost ranks among the men of his time, not only in the State but of the nation. The young attorney who left the granite hills of New Hampshire for the fertile prairies of the West, distinguished himself both as an attorney and a statesman. His personal history is so inseparably interwoven in that of the history of the State that a sketch of his life is indeed but a record of the history of his adopted State during the years of his manhood and vigor.

R. P. Lowe

RALPH P. LOWE, the fourth Governor of the State of Iowa, was born in Ohio in the year 1808, and like many others of the distinguished men of Iowa, came within her borders in early pioneer times. He was a young man but a little over thirty years of age when he crossed the great Father of Waters, settling upon its western bank at the then small village of Muscatine. He at once identified himself with the interests of the growing city, and ere long became quite prominent in local affairs and of recognized ability in questions of public policy. He was shortly afterward chosen as a representative from Muscatine County to the Constitutional Convention of 1844, which framed the Constitution which was rejected by the people.

After this constitutional convention, Mr. Lowe took no further part in public matters for a number of years. He removed to Lee County about 1849 or '50, where he became District Judge as a successor to George H. Williams, who was afterward famous as President Grant's Attorney General. He was District Judge five years, from 1852 to 1857, being succeeded by Judge Claggett. In the summer of 1857 he was nominated by the Republicans for Governor of Iowa, with Oran Faville for Lieutenant-Governor. The Democracy put in the field Benjamin M. Samuels for Governor and George Gillaspy for Lieutenant-Governor. There was a third ticket in the field, supported by the American or "Know-Nothing" party, and bearing the names of T. F. Henry and Easton Morris. The election was held in October, 1857, and gave Mr. Lowe 38,498 votes, against 36,088 for Mr. Samuels, and 1,006 for Mr. Henry.

Hitherto the term of office had been four years, but by an amendment to the Constitution this was now reduced to two. Gov. Lowe was inaugurated Jan. 14, 1858, and at once sent his first message to the Legislature. Among the measures passed by this Legislature were bills to incorporate the State Bank of Iowa; to provide for an agricultural college; to authorize the business of banking; disposing of the land grant made by Congress to the Des Moines Valley Railroad; to provide for the erection of an institution for the education of the blind, and to provide for taking a State census.

No events of importance occurred during the administration of Gov. Lowe, but it was not a period of uninterrupted prosperity. The Governor said in his biennial message of Jan. 10, 1860, reviewing the preceeding two years: "The period that has elapsed since the last biennial session has been one of great disturbing causes, and of anxious solicitude to all classes of our fellow-citizens. The first year of this period was visited with heavy and continuous rains, which reduced the measure of our field crops below one-half of the usual product, whilst the financial revulsion which commenced upon the Atlantic coast in the autumn of 1857, did not reach its climax for evil in our borders until the year just past."

He referred at length to the claim of the State against the Federal Government, and said that he had appealed in vain to the Secretary of the Interior for the payment of the 5 per cent upon the military land warrants that the State is justly entitled to, which then approximated to a million of dollars. The payment of this fund, he said, "is not a mere favor which is asked of the General Government, but a subsisting right which could be enforced in a court of justice, were there a tribunal of this kind clothed with the requisite jurisdiction."

The subject of the Des Moines River grant received from the Governor special attention, and he gave a history of the operations of the State authorities in reference to obtaining the residue of the lands to which the State was entitled, and other information as to the progress of the work. He also remarked "that under the act authorizing the Governor to raise a company of mounted men for defense and protection of our frontier, approved Feb. 9, 1858, a company of thirty such men, known as the Frontier Guards, armed and equipped as required, were organized and mustered into service under the command of Capt. Henry B. Martin, of Webster City, about the 1st of March then following, and were divided into two companies, one stationed on the Little Sioux River, the other at Spirit Lake. Their presence afforded security and gave quiet to the settlements in that region, and after a service of four months they were disbanded.

"Late in the fall of the year, however, great alarm and consternation was again felt in the region of Spirit Lake and Sioux River settlements, produced by the appearance of large numbers of Indians on the border, whose bearing was insolent and menacing, and who were charged with clandestinely running off the stock of the settlers. The most urgent appeals came from these settlers, invoking again the protection of the State. From representations made of the imminence of their danger and the losses already sustained, the Governor summoned into the field once more the frontier guards. After a service of four or five months they were again discharged, and paid in the manner prescribed in the act under which they were called out."

Gov. Lowe was beaten for the renomination by Hon. S. J. Kirkwood, who was considered much the stronger man. To compensate him for his defeat for the second term, Gov. Lowe was appointed one of the three Judges under the new Constitution. He drew the short term, which expired in 1861, but was returned and served, all told, eight years. He then returned to the practice of law, gradually working into a claim business at Washington, to which city he removed about 1874. In that city he died, on Saturday, Dec. 22, 1883. He had a large family. Carleton, one of his sons, was an officer in the Third Iowa Cavalry during the war.

Gov. Lowe was a man of detail, accurate and industrious. In private and public life he was pure, upright and honest. In religious faith he was inclined to be a Spiritualist.

THE fifth Governor of Iowa was Samuel J. Kirkwood. He was born in Hartford County, Md., on his father's farm, Dec. 20, 1813. His father was twice married, first to a lady named Coulson, who became the mother of two sons. After the death of this companion, the elder Kirkwood was united in marriage with Mary Alexander, who bore him three children, all of whom were sons. Of this little family Samuel was the youngest, and when ten years of age was sent to Washington City to attend a school taught by John McLeod, a relative of the family. Here he remained for four years, giving diligent attention to his studies, at the close of which time he entered a drug store at Washington as clerk. In this capacity he continued with the exception of eighteen months, until he reached his majority. During the interval referred to, young Kirkwood was living the life of a pedagogue in York County, Pa.

In the year 1835, Samuel quit Washington and came westward to Richland County, Ohio. His father and brother had preceded him from Maryland, locating upon a timbered farm in the Buckeye State. Here Samuel lent them valuable assistance in clearing the farm. He was ambitious to enter the legal profession, and in the year 1841, an opportunity was afforded him to enter the office of Thomas W. Bartley, afterward Governor of Ohio. The following two years he gave diligent application to his books, and in 1843, was admitted to practice by the Supreme Court of Ohio. He was then fortunate enough to form an association in the practice of his profession with his former preceptor, which relations continued for eight years.

From 1845 to 1849 he served as Prosecuting Attorney of his county. In 1849 he was elected as a Democrat to represent his county and district in the Constitutional Convention. In 1851 Mr. Bartley, his partner, having been elected to the Supreme Judiciary of the State, Kirkwood formed a partnership with Barnabas Barns, with whom he continued to practice until the spring of 1855, when he removed to the West.

Up to 1854 Mr. Kirkwood had acted with the Democratic party. But the measures proposed and sustained that year by the Democracy in Congress, concentrated in what was known as the Kansas-Nebraska Act, drove him with hosts of anti-slavery Democrats out of the party. He was besought by the opposition in the "Richland District" to become their candidate for Congress, but declined. In 1855 he came to Iowa and settled two miles northwest of Iowa City, entering into a partnership with his brother-in-law, Ezekiel Clark, in the milling business, and kept aloof from public affairs. He could not long conceal his record and abilities from his neighbors, however, and in 1856 he was elected to the State Senate from the district composed of the counties of Iowa and Johnson, and served in the last session of the Legislature held at Iowa City and the first one held at Des Moines.

In 1859 Mr. Kirkwood was made the standard-bearer of the Republicans of Iowa, and though he had as able and popular a competitor as Gen. A. C. Dodge, he was elected Governor of Iowa by a majority of over 3,000. He was inaugurated Jan. 11, 1860. Before the expiration of his first term came the great Civil War. As Governor, during the darkest days of the Rebellion, he performed an exceedingly important duty. He secured a prompt response by volunteers to all requisitions by the Federal Government on the State for troops, so that during his Governorship no "draft" took place in Iowa, and no regiment, except the first, enlisted for less than three years. At the same time he maintained the State's financial credit. The Legislature, at its extra session in 1861, authorized the sale of $800,000 in bonds, to assist in arming and equipping troops. So frugally was this work done, that but $300,000 of the bonds were sold, and the remaining $500,000 not having been required, the bonds representing this amount were destroyed by order of the succeeding Legislature.

In October, 1861, Gov. Kirkwood was, with comparatively little opposition, re-elected—an honor accorded for the first time in the history of the State. His majority was about 18,000. During his second term he was appointed by President Lincoln to be Minister to Denmark, but he declined to enter upon his diplomatic duties until the expiration of his term as Governor. The position was kept open for him until that time, but, when it came, pressing private business compelled a declination of the office altogether.

In January, 1866, he was a prominent candidate before the Legislature for United States Senator. Senator Harlan had resigned the Senatorship upon his appointment to the office of Secretary of the Interior by President Lincoln, just before his death, but had withdrawn from the cabinet soon after the accession of Mr. Johnson to the Presidency. In this way it happened that the Legislature had two terms of United States Senator to fill, a short term of two years, to fill Harlan's unexpired term, and a long term of six years to immediately succeed this; and Harlan had now become a candidate for his own successorship, to which Kirkwood also aspired. Ultimately, Kirkwood was elected for the first and Harlan for the second term. During his brief Senatorial service, Kirkwood did not hesitate to measure swords with Senator Sumner, whose natural egotism had begotten in him an arrogant and dictatorial manner, borne with humbly until then by his colleagues, in deference to his long experience and eminent ability, but unpalatable to an independent Western Senator like Kirkwood.

At the close of his Senatorial term, March 4, 1867, he resumed the practice of law, which a few years later he relinquished to accept the Presidency of the Iowa City Savings Bank. In 1875 he was again elected Governor, and was inaugurated Jan. 13, 1876. He served but little over a year, as early in 1877 he was chosen United States Senator He filled this position four years, resigning to become Secretary of the Interior in President Garfield's Cabinet. In this office he was succeeded, April 17, 1882, by Henry M. Teller, of Colorado.

Gov. Kirkwood returned to Iowa City, his home, where he still resides, being now advanced in years. He was married in 1843, to Miss Jane Clark, a native of Ohio.

In 1886 Mr. Kirkwood was nominated for Congress by the Republicans of his district. Considerable interest was manifested in the contest, as both the Labor and Democratic parties had popular candidates in the field.

J. M. Stone

WILLIAM M. STONE, the sixth Governor of Iowa, was born Oct. 14, 1827. His parents, Truman and Lavina (North) Stone, who were of English ancestry, moved to Lewis County, N. Y., when William was but a year old. William's grandfather, Aaron Stone, was in the second war with England. When our subject was six years of age his parents moved into Ohio, locating in Coshocton County. Like many other self-made men, William M. had few advantages. He never attended a school of any kind more than twelve months. In boyhood he was for two seasons a team-driver on the Ohio Canal. At seventeen he was apprenticed to the chairmaker's trade, and he followed that business until he was twenty-three years of age, reading law meantime during his spare hours, wherever he happened to be. He commenced at Coshocton, with James Mathews, who afterward became his father-in-law; continued his reading with Gen. Lucius V. Pierce, of Akron, and finished with Ezra B. Taylor, of Ravenna. He was admitted to the bar in August, 1851, by Peter Hitchcock and Rufus P. Ranney, Supreme Judges, holding a term of court at Ravenna.

After practicing three years at Coshocton with his old preceptor, James Mathews, he, in November, 1854, settled in Knoxville, which has remained his home since. The year after locating here Mr. Stone purchased the Knoxville *Journal*, and was one of the prime movers in forming the Republican party in Iowa, being the first editor to suggest a State Convention, which met Feb. 22, 1856, and completed the organization. In the autumn of the same year he was a Presidential elector on the Republican ticket.

In April, 1857, Mr. Stone was chosen Judge of the Eleventh Judicial District. He was elected Judge of the Sixth Judicial District when the new Constitution went into operation in 1858, and was serving on the bench when the American flag was stricken down at Fort Sumter. At that time, April, 1861, he was holding court in Fairfield, Jefferson County, and when the news came of the insult to the old flag he immediately adjourned court and prepared for what he believed to be more important duties—duties to his country.

In May he enlisted as a private; was made Captain of Co. B, Third Iowa Inf., and was subsequently promoted to Major. With that regiment he was at the battle of Blue Mill, Mo., in September, 1861, where he was wounded. At Shiloh, the following spring, he commanded the regiment and was taken prisoner. By order of Jefferson Davis he was paroled for the time of forty days, with orders to repair to Washington, and if possible secure an agreement for a cartel for a general exchange of prisoners, and to return as a prisoner if he did not succeed. Failing to secure that result within the period specified, he returned to Richmond and had his parole extended fifteen days; repairing again to Washington, he effected his purpose and was exchanged.

In August, 1862, he was appointed by Gov. Kirkwood Colonel of the Twenty-second Iowa Infantry, which rendezvoused and organized at Camp Pope, Iowa City, the same month. The regiment was occupied for several months in guarding supply stores and the railroad, and escorting supply trains to the Army of the Southeast Missouri until Jan. 27, 1863, when it received orders to join the army under Gen. Davidson, at West Plains, Mo. After a march of five days it reached its destination, and was brigaded with the Twenty-first and Twenty-third Iowa regiments, Col. Stone commanding, and was designated the First Brigade, First Division, Army of Southeast Missouri. April 1 found Col. Stone at Milliken's Bend, La., to assist Grant in the capture of Vicksburg. He was now in immediate command of his regiment, which formed a part of a brigade under Col. C. L. Harris, of the Eleventh Wisconsin. In the advance upon Port Gibson Col. Harris was taken sick, and Col. Stone was again in charge of a brigade. In the battle of Port Gibson the Colonel and his command distinguished themselves, and were successful. The brigade was in the reserve at Champion Hills, and in active skirmish at Black River.

On the evening of May 21 Col. Stone received Gen. Grant's order for a general assault on the enemy's lines at 10 A. M. on the 22d. In this charge, which was unsuccessful, Col. Stone was again wounded, receiving a gunshot in the left forearm. Col. Stone commanded a brigade until the last of August, when, being ordered to the Gulf Department, he resigned. He had become very popular with the people of Iowa.

He was nominated in a Republican convention, held at Des Moines in June, 1863, and was elected by a very large majority. He was breveted Brigadier-General in 1864, during his first year as Governor. He was inaugurated Jan. 14, 1864, and was re-elected in 1865, his four years in office closing Jan. 16, 1868. His majority in 1863 was nearly 30,000, and in 1865 about 16,500. His diminished vote in 1865 was due to the fact that he was very strongly committed in favor of negro suffrage.

Gov. Stone made a very energetic and efficient Executive. Since the expiration of his gubernatorial term he has sought to escape the public notice, and has given his time to his private business interests. He is in partnership with Hon. O. B. Ayres, of Knoxville, in legal practice.

He was elected to the General Assembly in 1877, and served one term.

In May, 1857, he married Miss Carloact Mathews, a native of Ohio, then residing in Knoxville. They have one son—William A.

SAMUEL MERRILL, Governor from 1868 to 1872, was born in Oxford County, Maine, Aug. 7, 1822. He is a descendant on his mother's side of Peter Hill, who came from England and settled in Maine in 1653. From this ancestry have sprung most of the Hills in America. On his father's side he is a decendant of Nathaniel Merrill, who came from England in 1636, and located in Massachusetts. Nathaniel had a son, Daniel, who in turn had a son named John, and he in turn begat a son called Thomas. The latter was born Dec. 18, 1708. On the 4th of August, 1728, was born to him a son, Samuel, who was married and had a family of twelve children, one of whom, Abel, was taken by his father to Boston in 1750. Abel was married to Elizabeth Page, who had five children, one of whom, Abel, Jr., was the father of our subject. He married Abigail Hill June 25, 1809, and to them were born eight children, Samuel being the youngest but one. At the age of sixteen Samuel moved with his parents to Buxton, Maine, the native place of his mother, where his time was employed in turns in teaching and attending school until he attained his majority. Having determined to make teaching a profession, and feeling that the South offered better opportunities, he immediately set out for that section. He remained, however, but a short time, as he says "he was born too far North." Suspicion having been raised as to his abolition principles and finding the element not altogether congenial, he soon abandoned the sunny South and went to the old Granite State, where the next several years were spent in farming. In 1847 he moved to Tamworth, N. H., where he engaged in the mercantile business in company with a brother, in which he was quite successful. Not being satisfied with the limited resources of Northern New England he determined to try his good fortune on the broad prairies of the fertile West.

It was in the year 1856 that Mr. Merrill turned his face toward the setting sun, finding a desirable location near McGregor, Iowa, where he established a branch house of the old firm. The population increased, as also did their trade, and their house became one of the most extensive wholesale establishments on the Upper Mississippi. During all these years of business Mr. Merrill took an active part in politics. In 1854 he was chosen on the abolition ticket to the Legislature of New Hampshire. The following year he was again returned to the Legislature, and doubtless had he remained in that State would have risen still higher. In coming to Iowa his experience and ability were demanded by his neighbors, and he was here called into public service. He was sent to the Legislature, and though assembled with the most distinguished men of his time, took a leading part in the important services demanded of that body. The Legislature was convened in an extra session of 1861, to provide for the exigencies of the Rebellion, and in its deliberations Mr. Merrill took an active part.

In the summer of 1862, Mr. Merrill was commissioned Colonel of the 21st Iowa Infantry, and immediately went to the front. At the time Marmaduke was menacing the Union forces in Missouri, which called for prompt action on the part of the Union Generals. Col. Merrill was placed in command, with detachments of the 21st Iowa and 99th Illinois, a portion of the 3d Iowa Cavalry and two pieces of artillery, with orders to make a forced march to Springfield, he being at the time eighty miles distant. On the morning of Jan. 11, 1863, he came across a body of Confederates who were advancing in heavy force. Immediate preparations for battle were made by Col. Merrill, and after briskly firing for an hour, the enemy fell back. Merrill then moved in the direction of Hartville, where he found the enemy in force under Marmaduke, being about eight thousand strong, while Merrill had but one-tenth of that number. A hot struggle ensued in which the Twenty-first distinguished itself. The Confederate loss was several officers and three hundred men killed and wounded, while the Union loss was but seven killed and sixty-four wounded. The following winter the regiment performed active service, taking part in the campaign of Vicksburg. It fought under McClernand at Port Gibson, and while making the famous charge of Black River Bridge, Col. Merrill was severely wounded through the hip. He was laid up from the 17th of May to January, when he again joined his regiment in Texas, and in June, 1864, on account of suffering from his wound, resigned and returned to McGregor. In 1867 Mr. Merrill was chosen Governor of the State, being elected upon the Republican ticket. He served with such satisfaction, that in 1869 he was re-nominated and accordingly elected.

Under the administration of Gov. Merrill, the movement for the erection of the new State House was inaugurated. The Thirteenth General Assembly provided for the building at a cost of $1,500,000, and made an appropriation with which to begin the work of $150,000. With this sum the work was begun, and Nov. 23, 1871, the corner stone was laid in the presence of citizens from all parts of the State. On this occasion the Governor delivered the address. It was an historical view of the incidents culminating in the labors of the day. It was replete with historical facts, showed patient research, was logical and argumentative, and at times eloquent with the fire and genius of American patriotism. It is a paper worthy of the occasion, and does justice to the head and heart that conceived it.

During the gubernatorial career of Gov. Merrill, extending through two terms, from January, 1868, to January, 1872, he was actively engaged in the discharge of his official duties, and probably no incumbent of that office ever devoted himself more earnestly to the public good, standing by the side of Gov. Fairchild, of Wisconsin. The two were instrumental in placing the slack-water navigation between the Mississippi and the Lakes in the way of ultimate and certain success. The Governor treated this subject to great length and with marked ability in his message to the Thirteenth General Assembly, and so earnest was he in behalf of this improvement, that he again discussed it in his message to the Fourteenth General Assembly. In the instigation of the work the Governors of the different States interested, called conventions, and through the deliberations of these assemblies the aid of the General Government was secured.

Samuel Merrill was first married to Catherine Thomas, who died in 1847, fourteen months after their marriage. In January, 1851, he was united in marriage with a Miss Hill, of Buxton, Maine. She became the mother of four children, three of whom died young, the eldest living to be only two and a half years old.

After the expiration of his public service he returned to McGregor, but shortly afterward removed to Des Moines, where he is now residing, and is President of the Citizens' National Bank.

Thus briefly have been pointed out the leading features in the life of one of Iowa's most prominent citizens, and one who has made an honorable record both in public positions and private enterprises. He is highly esteemed in the city where he resides and is regarded as one of the faithful representatives of the sons of New England. In stature he is fully six feet high and finely proportioned.

C. C. Carpenter

CYRUS CLAY CARPENTER, Governor of Iowa from 1872 to 1875, inclusive, was born in Susquehanna County, Pa., Nov. 24, 1829. He was left an orphan at an early age, his mother dying when he was at the age of ten years, and his father two years later. He was left in destitute circumstances, and went first to learn the trade of a clothier, which, however, he abandoned after a few months, and engaged with a farmer, giving a term in the winter, however, to attendance upon the district school. When eighteen he began teaching school, and the following four years divided his time between teaching and attending the academy at Hartford. At the conclusion of this period he went to Ohio, where he engaged as a teacher for a year and a half, spending the summer at farm work.

In the year 1854 Mr. Carpenter came further westward, visiting many points in Illinois and Iowa, arriving at Des Moines, then a village of some 1,200 inhabitants. This place, however, not offering a favorable location, he proceeded on his journey, arriving in Fort Dodge June 28, 1854. Owing to his being without funds he was compelled to travel on foot, in which way the journey to Fort Dodge was made, with his entire worldly possessions in a carpet-sack which he carried in his hand. He soon found employment at Fort Dodge, as assistant to a Government surveyor. This work being completed, young Carpenter assisted his landlord in cutting hay, but soon secured another position as a surveyor's assistant. In the early part of the following January he engaged in teaching school at Fort Dodge, but in the spring was employed to take charge of a set of surveyors in surveying the counties of Emmet and Kossuth.

On his return to Fort Dodge he found the land-office, which had been established at that place, was about to open for the sale of land. Being familiar with the country and the location of the best land, he opened a private land-office, and found constant and profitable employment for the following three years, in platting and surveying lands for those seeking homes. During this period he became extensively known, and, being an active Republican, he was chosen as a standard-bearer for his section of the State. He was elected to the Legislature in the autumn of 1857. In 1861, on the breaking out of the Rebellion, he volunteered and was assigned to duty as Commissary of Subsistence, much of the time being Chief Commissary of the left wing of the 16th Army Corps. In 1864 he was promoted Lieutenant-Colonel and assigned to duty on the staff of Gen. Logan, as Chief Commissary of the 15th Army Corps. He continued in the service until the close of the war, and in August, 1865, was mustered out.

Upon the close of his service to his country he returned to his home at Fort Dodge, but, owing to so many changes which had taken place, and such an influx of enterprising men into the city, he found his once prosperous business in the hands of others. He turned his attention to the improvement of a piece of land, where he remained until his election, in the autumn of 1866, as Register of the State Land-Office. He was re-elected in 1868, and refused the nomination in 1870. This position took him to Des Moines, but in 1870 he returned to Fort Dodge. During the summer of the following year he was nominated by the Republican party for Governor. He was elected, and inaugurated as Chief Executive of Iowa Jan. 11, 1872. In 1873 he was renominated by his party, and October 14 of that year was re-elected, his inauguration taking place Jan. 27, 1874. Gov. Carpenter was an able, popular and faithful Executive, and was regarded as one of the most honest, prominent and unselfish officials the State ever had. Plain, unassuming, modest, he won his public position more through the enthusiasm of his friends than by any personal effort or desire of his own. Everywhere, at all times and upon all occasions, he demonstrated that the confidence of his friends was justified. He took an active part in the great question of monopolies and transportation evils, which during his administration were so prominent, doing much to secure wise legislation in these respects.

Gov. Carpenter has been regarded as a public speaker of more than ordinary ability, and has upon many occasions been the orator, and always appreciated by the people.

At the expiration of his second term as Governor Mr. Carpenter was appointed Second Comptroller of the United States Treasury, which position he resigned after a service of fifteen months. This step was an evidence of his unselfishness, as it was taken because another Bureau officer was to be dismissed, as it was held that Iowa had more heads of Bureaus than she was entitled to, and his resigning an office of the higher grade saved the position to another. In 1881 he was elected to Congress, and served with ability, and in the Twentieth General Assembly of Iowa he represented Webster County.

Gov. Carpenter was married, in March, 1864, to Miss Susan Burkholder, of Fort Dodge. No children have been born to them, but they have reared a niece of Mrs. Carpenter's.

During his entire life Mr. Carpenter has been devoted to the principles of Reform and the best interests of all classes of citizens who, by adoption or by birth-right, are entitled to a home upon our soil and the protection of our laws, under the great charter of "Life, Liberty and the Pursuit of Happiness." In an address in 1852 he took advanced views upon the leading subjects of public interest. He had already laid the foundation for that love of freedom which afterwards found an ample field of labor with the Republican party. There was nothing chimerical in his views. He looked at every strata of human society, and, from the wants of the masses, wisely devined duty and prophesied destiny. He would have the people of a free Republic educated in the spirit of the civilization of the age. Instead of cultivating a taste for a species of literature tending directly to degrade the mind and deprave the heart, thereby leading back to a state of superstition and consequent barbarism, he would cultivate principles of temperance, industry and economy in every youthful mind, as the indispensable ingredients of good citizens, or subjects upon whose banner will be inscribed Liberty, Equality, Fraternity.

Thus early in life Mr. Carpenter saw the destined tendency of our American institutions, and the advancing civilization of the age. He saw it in the peace congress, whose deliberations have made the Rhine thrice immortal. He saw it in the prospective railway, which he believed would one day unite the shores of the Atlantic with those of the Pacific—a fact realized by the construction of the great continental railway.

It was thus early that he began to study the wants of the world, and with what clearness and directness may be seen by the correctness of his vision and the accomplishment of what he considered an inevitable necessity.

Thus, growing up into manhood, and passing onward in the rugged pathway of time, disciplined in political economy and civil ethics in the stern school of experience, he was prepared to meet every emergency with a steady hand; to bring order out of discord, and insure harmony and prosperity.

Gov. Carpenter is now engaged in the quiet pursuits of farm life, residing at Fort Dodge, where he is highly esteemed as one of her purest minded and most upright citizens.

J. G. Newbold

JOSHUA G. NEWBOLD, the ninth Governor of Iowa, is a native of Pennsylvania. He comes from that excellent stock known as the Friends, who very early settled in New Jersey. Joshua G. is the son of Barzilla and Catherine (House) Newbold, and was born in Fayette County, May 12, 1830. He was born a farmer's boy and was reared in the vigorous employment of farm work. When he was eight years of age the family moved to Westmoreland County, Pa., where, in the common schools and in a select school or academy, young Newbold received his education. When sixteen years of age he accompanied the family on their return to Fayette County. Here for the following eight years he assisted his father in running a flouring-mill as well as devoting much of his time to teaching school. When about nineteen years of age our subject began the study of medicine, devoting much of his time while teaching to his medical books. He, however, abandoned the idea of becoming a physician and turned his attention to different walks in life.

In the month of March, 1854, Mr. Newbold removed to Iowa, locating on a farm, now partly in the corporation of Mount Pleasant, Henry County. At the end of one year he removed to Cedar Township, Van Buren County, there merchandising and farming till about 1860, when he removed to Hillsboro, Henry County, and pursued the same callings.

In 1862, when the call was made for 600,000 men to finish the work of crushing the Rebellion, Mr. Newbold left his farm in the hands of his family and his store in charge of his partner, and went into the army as Captain of Company C, 25th Regiment of Iowa Infantry. He served nearly three years, resigning just before the war closed, on account of disability. During the last two or three months he served at the South he filled the position of Judge Advocate, with headquarters at Woodville, Ala.

His regiment was one of those that made Iowa troops famous. It arrived at Helena, Ark., in November, 1862, and sailed in December following on the expedition against Vicksburg by way of Chickasaw Bayou. At the latter place was its first engagement. Its second was at Arkansas Post, and there it suffered severely, losing in killed and wounded more than sixty.

After Lookout Mountain it joined in the pursuit of Bragg's flying forces to Ringgold, where it engaged the enemy in their strong works, November 27, losing twenty-nine wounded. The following year it joined Sherman in his Atlanta Campaign, then on the famous march to the sea and through the Carolinas.

On returning to Iowa he continued in the mercantile trade at Hillsboro for three or four years, and then sold out, giving thereafter his whole attention to agriculture, stock-raising and stock-dealing, making the stock department an important factor in his business for several years. Mr. Newbold was a member of the 13th, 14th and 15th General Assemblies, representing Henry County, and was Chairman of the School Committee in the 14th, and of the committee on appropriations in the 15th General Assembly. In the 15th (1874) he was temporary Speaker during the deadlock in organizing the House. In 1875 he was elected Lieutenant Governor on the Republican ticket with Samuel J. Kirkwood.

His Democratic competitor was E. D. Woodward, who received 93,060 votes. Mr. Newbold received 134,166, or a majority of 31,106. Governor Kirkwood being elected United States Senator during that session, Mr. Newbold became Governor, taking the chair Feb. 1, 1877, and vacating it for Gov. Gear in January, 1878.

Gov. Newbold's message to the Legislature in 1878, shows painstaking care and a clear, business-like view of the interests of the State. His recommendations were carefully considered and largely adopted. The State's finances were then in a less creditable condition than ever before or since, as there was an increasing floating debt, then amounting to $340,826.56, more than $90,000 in excess of the Constitutional limitation. Said Gov. Newbold in his message: "The commonwealth ought not to set an example of dilatoriness in meeting its obligations. Of all forms of indebtedness, that of a floating character is the most objectionable. The uncertainty as to its amount will invariably enter into any computation made by persons contracting with the State for supplies, material or labor. To remove the present difficulty, and to avert its recurrence, I look upon as the most important work that will demand your attention."

One of the greatest problems before statesmen is that of equal and just taxation. The following recommendation shows that Gov. Newbold was abreast with foremost thinkers, for it proposes a step which yearly finds more favor with the people: "The inequalities of the personal-property valuations of the several counties suggest to my mind the propriety of so adjusting the State's levy as to require the counties to pay into the State treasury only the tax on realty, leaving the corresponding tax on personalty in the county treasury. This would rest with each county the adjustment of its own personal property valuations, without fear that they might be so high as to work injustice to itself in comparison with other counties."

Gov. Newbold has always affiliated with the Republican party, and holds to its great cardinal doctrines, having once embraced them, with the same sincerity and honesty that he cherishes his religious sentiments. He has been a Christian for something like twenty-five years, his connection being with the Free-Will Baptist Church. He found his wife, Rachel Farquhar, in Fayette County, Pa., their union taking place on the 2d of May, 1850. They have had five children and lost two. The names of the living are Mary Allene, Emma Irene and George C.

The Governor is not yet an old man, and may serve his State or county in other capacities in the coming years.

John H. Gear.

JOHN H. GEAR, the tenth gentleman to occupy the Executive Chair of Iowa, is still a resident of Burlington. He is a native of the Empire State, where in the city of Ithica, April 7, 1825, he was born. Rev. E. G. Gear, his father, was born in New London, Conn., in 1792, and became a distinguished clergyman of the Protestant Episcopal Church. His family had removed with him, while he was still young, to Pittsfield, Mass., and in the year 1816, after his ordination as a clergyman of the Episcopal Church, he went to New York and located at Onondaga Hill near the city of Syracuse. Shortly after this settlement, the young minister was united in marriage with Miss Miranda E. Cook. After serving various congregations in Western New York for many years, he determined to become a pioneer in Northern Illinois, which at the time, in the year 1836, was being rapidly settled up. He found a desirable location at Galena where he remained until 1838, when he received the appointment as Chaplain in the United States army while located at Fort Snelling, Minn. He lived a long and active life, doing much good, quitting his labors in the year 1874 at the advanced age of eighty-two years.

The only son born to Mr. and Mrs. E. G. Gear was J. H., afterward the distinguished Governor of Iowa. As above stated the birth occurred in 1825. In 1843, when still a young man, he came West to Burlington, where he has since continued to reside, her most distinguished citizen. Shortly after his arrival in the young city, he embarked in his mercantile career, engaging at the time with the firm of Bridgman & Bros., in the capacity of a clerk. Remaining with this firm for a little over a year, he left them for an engagement with W. F. Coolbaugh, who at one time was President of the Union National Bank, of Chicago, and who at that early period was the leading merchant of Eastern Iowa. He served Mr. Coolbaugh so faithfully, and with such marked ability for the following five years, that, when desirous of a partner in his business, the wealthy merchant could find no one in whom he could place greater confidence and with whom he could trust his extensive business relations that pleased him better than the young clerk. Accordingly he was associated as a partner under the firm name of W. F. Coolbaugh & Co. Under this arrangement the firm did a prosperous business for the following five years, when Mr. Gear purchased the entire business, which he carried on with marked success until he became known as the oldest wholesale grocer in the State. He is at present, besides filling other prominent business relations, President of the Rolling Mill Co., of Galesburg.

Mr. Gear has been honored by his fellow-citizens with many positions of trust. In 1852 he was elected Alderman; in 1863 was elected Mayor over A. W. Carpenter, being the first Republican up to that time who had been elected in Burlington on a party issue. In 1867 the Burlington, Cedar Rapids & Minnesota Railroad Company was organized, and he was chosen as its President. His efforts highly contributed to the success of the enterprise, which did much for Burlington. He was also active in promoting the Burlington & Southwestern Railway, as well as the Burlington & Northwestern narrow-gauge road.

He has always acted with the Republican party, and in 1871 was nominated and elected a member of the House of Representatives of the 14th General Assembly. In 1873 he was elected to the 15th General Assembly. The Republican caucus of the House nominated him for Speaker by acclamation, and after a contest of two weeks he was chosen over his opponent, J. W. Dixon. He filled the position of Speaker very acceptably, and at the close of the session all the members of the House, independent of party affiliations, joined in signing their names to a resolution of thanks, which was engraved and presented to him. In 1875 he was the third time nominated to the Assembly by the Republican party, and while his county gave a large Democratic vote he was again elected. He was also again nominated for Speaker by the Republican caucus, and was elected by a handsome majority over his competitor, Hon. John Y. Stone. He is the only man in the State who ever had the honor of being chosen to this high position a second time. He enjoys the reputation of being an able parliamentarian, his rulings never having been appealed from. At the close of the session he again received the unanimous thanks of the House of Representatives for his courtesy and impartiality, and for the able and satisfactory manner in which he had presided over that body.

In 1877 he was nominated for Governor by the Republican convention which met at Des Moines, June 28, and at the election held the following October he received 121,546 votes, against 79,353 for John P. Irish, 10,639 for Elias Jessup and 38,-228 for D. P. Stubbs. His plurality over Irish was 42,193. He was inaugurated Jan. 17, 1878, and served four years, being re-elected in 1879 by the following handsome vote: Gear, 157,571; Trimble, 85,056; Campbell, 45,439; Dungan, 3,258; Gear's majority over all competitors, 23,828. His second inauguration occurred in January of the year 1880.

Gov. Gear's business habits enabled him to discharge the duties of his office with marked ability. He found the financial condition of the State at a low ebb, but raised Iowa's credit to that of the best of our States. In his last biennial message he was able to report: "The warrants out-standing, but not bearing interest, Sept. 30, 1881, amounted to $22,093.74, and there are now in the treasury ample funds to meet the current expenses of the State. The war and defense debt has been paid, except the warrants for $125,000 negotiated by the Executive, Auditor and Treasurer, under the law of the 18th General Assembly, and $2,500 of the original bonds not yet presented for payment. The only other debt owing by the State amounts to $245,435.19, due to the permanent school fund, a portion of which is made irredeemable by the Constitution. These facts place Iowa practically among the States which have no debt, a consideration which must add much to her reputation. The expenses of the State for the last two years are less than those of any other period since 1869, and this notwithstanding the fact that the State is to-day sustaining several institutions not then in existence; namely, the hospital at Independence, the additional penitentiary, the Normal School and the asylum for the feeble-minded children, besides the girl's department of the reform school. The State also, at present, makes provision for fish culture, for a useful weather service, for sanitary supervision by a Board of Health, for encouraging immigration to the State, for the inspection of coal mines by a State Inspector, and liberally for the military arm of the Government."

Gov. Gear is now in the sixty-first year of his age, and is in the full vigor of both his mental and physical faculties. He was married in 1852 to Harriet S. Foot, formerly of the town of Middlebury, Vermont, by whom he has had four children, two of whom are living.

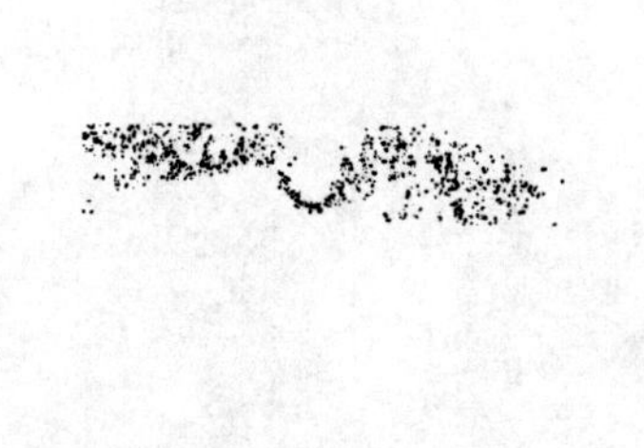

B. R. Sherman

Buren R. Sherman.

ONE of the most distinguished gentlemen who was ever honored with the position of Chief Executive of the State is Buren R. Sherman, the eleventh Governor of Iowa, who is a native of New York. It was in the town of Phelps, in Ontario County, that he was born to his parents, Phineas L. and Eveline (Robinson) Sherman, on the 28th of May, 1836, and was the third son of a distinguished family of children. His parents were likewise natives of the Empire State. Buren R. attended the public schools of his neighborhood, but was subsequently given advantages of the schools at Almira, N. Y., where he acquired a very thorough knowledge of the English branches. His father, who was a mechanic, advised him at the close of his studies to apprentice himself to learn some trade. He accordingly made such arrangements with S. Ayers, of Almira, to learn the trade of a watchmaker. In 1855, however, he left this position and joined his family on their removal to the then new State of Iowa. They settled upon a piece of unbroken prairie land on what is now Geneseo Township, Tama County, his father having previously purchased land from the Government. Here Buren R. labored diligently in developing his father's fields, devoting, however, leisure hours which he was granted, to the study of law. Before leaving his Eastern home he had decided upon that profession and began its study while yet in Almira. He soon secured a position as a book-keeper in a neighboring town, and with the wages earned there, materially assisted his father in the development of their home farm. In the meantime he had applied himself diligently to the study of his books, and so studious had he been that in the summer of 1859, he was enabled to pass a creditable examination and to be admitted to the bar. The following spring the young attorney moved to Vinton, hung out his shingle and began the practice of his profession. He was associated with Hon. William Smyth, formerly District Judge, and J. C. Traer, under the firm name of Smyth, Traer & Sherman. The new firm rapidly grew into prominence, building up a prosperous practice, when Mr. Sherman withdrew to tender his services to the Government in defense of her integrity and honor.

It was early in 1861, directly after the enemy had assaulted the American flag on Sumter, that the young attorney enlisted in Co. C, 13th Iowa Vol.

Inf., and immediately went to the front. He entered the service as Second Sergeant, and in February, 1862, was made Second Lieutenant of Company E. On the 6th of April following he was very severely wounded at the battle of Pittsburgh Landing, and while in the hospital was promoted to the rank of Captain. He returned to his company while yet obliged to use his crutches, and remained on duty till the summer of 1863, when, by reason of his wound, he was compelled to resign and return home. Soon after returning from the army he was elected County Judge of Benton County, and re-elected without opposition in 1865. In the autumn of 1866 he resigned his judgeship and accepted the office of Clerk of the District Court, to which he was re-elected in 1868, 1870 and 1872, and in December, 1874, resigned in order to accept the office of Auditor of State, to which office he had been elected by a majority of 28,425 over J. M. King, the "anti-monopoly" candidate. In 1876 he was renominated and received 50,272 more votes than W. Growneweg (Democrat) and Leonard Browne (Greenback) together. In 1878 he was again chosen to represent the Republican party in that office, and this time received a majority of 7,164 over the combined votes of Col. Eiboeck (Democrat) and G. V. Swearenger (Greenback). In the six years that he held this office, he was untiring in his faithful application to routine work and devotion to his special share of the State's business. He retired with such an enviable record that it was with no surprise the people learned, June 27, 1881, that he was the nominee of the Republican party for Governor.

The campaign was an exciting one. The General Assembly had submitted to the people the prohibitory amendment to the Constitution. This, while not a partisan question, became uppermost in the mind of the public. Mr. Sherman received 133,330 votes, against 83,244 for Kinne and 28,112 for D. M. Clark, or a plurality of 50,086 and a majority of 21,974. In 1883 he was re-nominated by the Republicans, as well as L. G. Kinne by the Democrats. The National party offered J. B. Weaver. During the campaign these candidates held a number of joint discussions at different points in the State. At the election the vote was: Sherman, 164,182; Kinne, 139,093; Weaver, 23,089; Sherman's plurality, 25,089; majority, 2,000. In his second inaugural Gov. Sherman said:

"In assuming, for the second time, the office of Chief Magistrate for the State, I fully realize my grateful obligations to the people of Iowa, through whose generous confidence I am here. I am aware of the duties and grave responsibilities of this exalted position, and as well what is expected of me therein. As in the past I have given my undivided time and serious attention thereto, so in the future I promise the most earnest devotion and untiring effort in the faithful performance of my official requirements. I have seen the State grow from infancy to mature manhood, and each year one of substantial betterment of its previous position.

"With more railroads than any State, save two; with a school interest the grandest and strongest, which commands the support and confidence of all the people, and a population which in its entirety is superior to any other in the sisterhood, it is not strange the pride which attaches to our people. When we remember that the results of our efforts in the direction of good government have been crowned with such magnificent success, and to-day we have a State in most perfect physical and financial condition, no wonder our hearts swell in honest pride as we contemplate the past and so confidently hope for the future. What we may become depends on our own efforts, and to that future I look with earnest and abiding confidence."

Gov. Sherman's term of office continued until Jan. 14, 1886, when he was succeeded by William Larrabee, and he is now, temporarily, perhaps, enjoying a well-earned rest. He has been a Republican since the organization of that party, and his services as a campaign speaker have been for many years in great demand. As an officer he has been able to make an enviable record. Himself honorable and thorough, his management of public business has been of the same character, and such as has commended him to the approval of his fellow-citizens.

He was married, Aug. 20, 1862, to Miss Lena Kendall, of Vinton, Iowa, a young lady of rare accomplishments and strength of character. Their union has been happy in every respect. They have two children—Lena Kendall and Oscar Eugene.

William Larrabee.

WILLIAM LARRABEE, the present able Governor of Iowa, and the twelfth gentleman selected by the people as the Chief Magistrate of the great Commonwealth, is a native of Connecticut. His ancestors were among the French Huguenots who came to America early in the seventeenth century and located in Connecticut. At that time they bore the name of d'Larrabee. Adam Larrabee, the father of William, was born March 14, 1787, and was one of the early graduates of the West Point Military Academy. He served his country during the War of 1812, with distinction, holding the position of Second Lieutenant, to which he was commissioned March 1, 1811. He was promoted to the Captaincy of his company Feb. 1, 1814, and on the 30th of the following March, at the battle of Lacole Mills, during Gen. Wilkinson's campaign on the Saint Lawrence River, he was severely wounded in the lung. He eventually recovered from the injury and was united in marriage to Hannah G. Lester. This much esteemed lady was born June 3, 1798, and died on the 15th of March, 1837. Capt. Larrabee lived to an advanced age, dying in 1869, at the age of eighty-two years.

As above mentioned, William, our subject, was born in Connecticut the town of Ledyard being the place of his birth and Jan. 20, 1832, the date. He was the seventh child in a family of nine children, and passed the early years of his life upon a rugged New England farm, enjoying very meager educational advantages. He attended, during the winter seasons, the neighboring district schools until he reached the age of nineteen years, when, during the following two winters, he filled the position of schoolmaster. He was ambitious to do something in life for himself that would bring fortune and distinction, but in making his plans for the future he was embarrassed by a misfortune which befell him when fourteen years of age. In being trained to the use of firearms under his father's direction, an accidental discharge resulted in the loss of the sight in the right eye. This consequently unfitted him for many employments usually sought by ambitious young men. The family lived near the seashore, only two miles away, and in that neighborhood it was the custom for at least one son in each family to go upon the sea as a sailor. The two eldest brothers of our subject had chosen this occupation while the third remained in charge of the home farm. William was thus left free to chose for himself and, like many of the youths of that day, he wisely turned his face Westward. The year 1853 found him on this journey toward the setting sun, stopping only when he came to the broad and fertile prairies of the new State of Iowa. He first joined his elder sister. Mrs.

E. H. Williams, who was at that time living at Garnavillo, Clayton County. It was this circumstance which led the young boy from Connecticut to select his future home in the northeastern portion of Iowa. He resumed his occupation as a pedagogue, teaching, however, but one winter, which was passed at Hardin. The following three years he was employed in the capacity of foreman on the Grand Meadow farm of his brother-in-law, Judge Williams.

In 1857 he bought a one-third interest in the Clermont Mills, and located at Clermont, Fayette County. He soon was able to buy the other two-thirds, and within a year found himself sole owner. He operated this mill until 1874 when he sold to S. M. Leach. On the breaking out of the war he offered to enlist, but was rejected on account of the loss of his right eye. Being informed he might possibly be admitted as a commissioned officer, he raised a company and received a commission as First Lieutenant, but was again rejected for the same disability.

After selling the mill Mr. Larrabee devoted himself to farming, and started a private bank at Clermont. He also, experimentally, started a large nursery, but this resulted only in confirming the belief that Northern Iowa has too rigorous a climate for fruit-raising.

Mr. Larrabee did not begin his political career until 1867. He was reared as a Whig and became a Republican on the organization of that party. While interested in politics he generally refused local offices, serving only as Treasurer of the School Board prior to 1867. In the autumn of that year, on the Republican ticket, he was elected to represent his county in the State Senate. To this high position he was re-elected from time to time, so that he served as Senator continuously for eighteen years before being promoted to the highest office in the State. He was so popular at home that he was generally re-nominated by acclamation, and for some years the Democrats did not even make nominations. During the whole eighteen years Senator Larrabee was a member of the principal committee, that on Ways and Means, of which he was generally Chairman, and was also a member of other committees. In the pursuit of the duties thus devolving upon him, he was indefatigable. It is said that he never missed a committee meeting. Not alone in this, but in private and public business of all kinds, his uniform habit is that of close application to work. Many of the important measures passed by the Legislature owe their existence or present form to him.

He was a candidate for the gubernatorial nomination in 1881, but entered the contest too late, as Gov. Sherman's following had been successfully organized. In 1885 it was generally conceded before the meeting of the convention that he would be nominated, which he was, and his election followed as a matter of course. He was inaugurated Jan. 14, 1886, and so far has made an excellent Governor. His position in regard to the liquor question, that on which political fortunes are made and lost in Iowa, is that the majority should rule. He was personally in favor of high license, but having been elected Governor, and sworn to uphold the Constitution and execute the laws, he proposes to do so.

A Senator who sat beside him in the Senate declares him to be "a man of the broadest comprehension and information, an extraordinarily clear reasoner, fair and conscientious in his conclusions, and of Spartan firmness in his matured judgment," and says that "he brings the practical facts and philosophy of human nature, the science and history of law, to aid in his decisions, and adheres with the earnestness of Jefferson and Sumner to the fundamental principles of the people's rights."

Gov. Larrabee was married Sept. 12, 1861, at Clermont, to Anna M. Appelman, daughter of Capt. G. A. Appelman. Gov. Larrabee has seven children—Charles, Augusta, Julia, Anna, William, Frederic and Helen.

Wapello County,

Iowa.

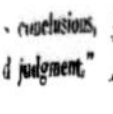

BIOGRAPHICAL.

INTRODUCTORY.

THE time has arrived when it becomes the duty of the people of this county to perpetuate the names of their pioneers, to furnish a record of their early settlement, and relate the story of their progress. The civilization of our day, the enlightenment of the age and the duty that men of the present time owe to their ancestors, to themselves and to their posterity, demand that a record of their lives and deeds should be made. In biographical history is found a power to instruct man by precedent, to enliven the mental faculties, and to waft down the river of time a safe vessel in which the names and actions of the people who contributed to raise this country from its primitive state may be preserved. Surely and rapidly the great and aged men, who in their prime entered the wilderness and claimed the virgin soil as their heritage, are passing to their graves. The number remaining who can relate the incidents of the first days of settlement is becoming small indeed, so that an actual necessity exists for the collection and preservation of events without delay, before all the early settlers are cut down by the scythe of Time.

To be forgotten has been the great dread of mankind from remotest ages. All will be forgotten soon enough, in spite of their best works and the most earnest efforts of their friends to perserve the memory of their lives. The means employed to prevent oblivion and to perpetuate their memory has been in proportion to the amount of intelligence they possessed. The pyramids of Egypt were built to perpetuate the names and deeds of their great rulers. The exhumations made by the archeologists of Egypt from buried Memphis indicate a desire of those people to perpetuate the memory of their achievements. The erection of the great obelisks were for the same purpose. Coming down to a later period, we find the Greeks and Romans erecting mausoleums and monuments, and carving out statues to chronicle their great achievements and carry them down the ages. It is also evident that the Mound-builders, in piling up their great mounds of earth, had but this idea—to leave something to show that they had lived. All these works, though many of them costly in the extreme, give but a faint idea of the lives and characters of those whose memory they were intended to perpetuate, and scarcely anything of the masses of the people that then lived. The great pyramids and some of the obelisks remain objects only of curiosity; the mausoleums, monuments and statues are crumbling into dust.

It was left to modern ages to establish an intelligent, undecaying, immutable method of perpetuating a full history—immutable in that it is almost unlimited in extent and perpetual in its action; and this is through the art of printing.

To the present generation, however, we are indebted for the introduction of the admirable system of local biography. By this system every man, though he has not achieved what the world calls greatness, has the means to perpetuate his life, his history, through the coming ages.

The scythe of Time cuts down all; nothing of the physical man is left. The monument which his children or friends may erect to his memory in the cemetery will crumble into dust and pass away; but his life, his achievements, the work he has accomplished, which otherwise would be forgotten, is perpetuated by a record of this kind.

To preserve the lineaments of our companions we engrave their portraits, for the same reason we collect the attainable facts of their history. Nor do we think it necessary, as we speak only truth of them, to wait until they are dead, or until those who know them are gone: to do this we are ashamed only to publish to the world the history of those whose lives are unworthy of public record.

Chas. L. Blake

CHARLES F. BLAKE, President of the Iowa National Bank, of Ottumwa, is a native of Germany, and was born near Minden, Prussia, Oct. 12, 1823. His parents, Carl F. and Mary (Niemann) Blake, resided on a farm in their native country until 1836, when, accompanied by their seven children, they emigrated to the United States and first made settlement in Hamilton County, Ohio. Six months later the family removed to Clermont County, same State, and located near Milford, and in 1840 made another move, this time taking up their residence on a farm near Indianapolis, Ind. In 1845 they came to Iowa, and settling at Ottumwa, being among the earliest pioneers of this section, they continued to reside there an unbroken family until 1853, when the demise of the father occurred, his age being fifty-eight years. The mother died Oct. 25, 1870. The seven children are: Christina L., who married Martin Gehringer, and removed to Indianapolis, but came to Ottumwa in 1843, afterward removed to Lee County, and about 1848 moved to Louisiana, and have not been heard from since; it is supposed both died from the cholera; the other children are, Charles F., our subject; Mary C., wife of N. C. Hill, of this county; Christian F., a farmer of Oregon; John H., residing in Grant County, Oregon; Sophia married David Gephart, and departed this life in Wapello County, leaving several children; Ellen M. is the wife of John Scheiwe, a resident of Ottumwa.

After emigrating to the United States Mr. Blake of this notice worked for various parties, following no particular trade but working at whatever he could find to do to earn an honest dollar. In the spring of 1850 he crossed the plains to California, and engaged in placer mining in that State for one year. He became interested in a quartz mining company there, one of the first on the Pacific slope, and continued his relationship with the company for about a year, when he sold out. He had become the happy possessor of $1,800 in cash before he started home. On arriving here he at once engaged in clerking for James Hawley in a general store, having invested the means which he brought from the land of gold in purchasing the interest of the heirs to his father's estate and also a little town property. He continued clerking until 1857, and from that time until 1863 he was interested in no particular business except looking after his property.

During the year 1863 two clerks in the employ

of James L. Taylor, at Ottumwa, having enlisted in the war, Mr. Blake entered Mr. Taylor's store in the capacity of book-keeper and custodian of finances, and held that position until the spring of 1865. He then, with W. T. Harper, took an interest in the business, and the firm of Taylor, Blake & Co. sprang into existence, and our subject continued his relations therewith until 1874. It did a wholesale and retail business and met with signal success. In 1873 Mr. Blake entered the Iowa National Bank, of which he was one of the original stockholders, and in the fall of that year became its President. This honorable and responsible position he has since continued to hold, devoting the major portion of his time to its interest. In the spring of 1881 Mr. Blake, in company with E. E. Bruce and W. B. Goodall, organized the present firm of Blake, Bruce & Co., wholesale druggists, Mr. Blake is one of the original organizers of the Ottumwa Starch Works, and one of the re-organizers of the Ottumwa Cutlery Company, and is still interested in both. He was also one of the original stockholders of the D. & M. R. R., and one of the number who assisted in raising $100,000 for the Wabash Railroad Company.

Coming to Ottumwa at an early day and investing in a small portion of her present site, our subject continued to hold to his property, and as the city increased in population and the surrounding country was more thickly settled the city property bgan to increase in value, and in 1859 he laid it off in lots and added Blake's addition to the city. He also added to his acreage outside of the city, and at present is the proprietor of 2,500 acres of land located near Ottumwa, which is growing in value every year.

In the early part of 1886 Mr. Blake became one of the proprietors of valuable mining property in Montana, in connection with J. O. Briscoe. He is also a part owner of the celebrated Frohner Mine which, after careful investigation, was purchased by them and others. For the past year the work has been principally that of development, but sufficient profit has been realized to pay for the mine and insure a surplus of $25,000. This for the first year is a very unusual showing in mining operations. The Frohner is situated in the Red Mountain district on the Lump Gulch Slope, and is regarded by prominent mineralogists as a section of the most valuable property in Montana. The Minah, another mine owned jointly by Mr. Blake and Mr. Briscoe, has also proved of great value, its success being simply marvelous.

With that caution which has characterized all his business transactions, Mr Blake secured an interest in mining property only after the most careful and methodical investigation. The results have proved the accuracy of his judgment and the keenness and penetration which have enabled him, almost without exception, to achieve success. These qualities also have enabled him to become one of the most useful citizens and valued members of the community.

Mr. Blake was married, in 1856, to Miss Polly Kingsley, daughter of Cyrus and Hannah (Sears) Kingsley. She was born in Onondaga County, N. Y., Jan. 1, 1819, and died in 1876, leaving two children: Juliette K., wife of Calvin Manning, and Cyrus K., also married, and connected with the Bank of Ottumwa. In 1877 Mr. Blake married Mrs. Jennie E. Stevens, *nee* Webb, by whom he has one son, Frederick C. In addition to his other business, Mr. Blake holds the office of Treasurer of the Iowa Mutual Aid Society, and Ottumwa City School District, and is one of the foremost citizens of the city and county in which he resides.

In the history of Mr. Blake we find an excellent example for young men who are just embarking in the field of active life, of what may be accomplished by a man beginning poor, but honest, prudent and industrious. In early life he enjoyed but few advantages. His school days were limited, nor had he wealth or position to aid him in starting in life. To win success he relied upon his own efforts and conduct. In monetary and mercantile fields he is known to be a man of undoubted integrity and substantial ability. In his social and public life he is one who is capable of forming his own opinions and resolutely adhering to them. His career as a citizen of the county has been one eminently worthy and useful to the community, and it is with pleasure we present his portrait in this connection as one of the leading men, not only of the county, but of the State.

Looking back over this short record the reader will see that the subject of this notice is a self-made man in every respect that word implies, and that his success in life is attributable, not as the recipient of a legacy, but through his own energy, perseverance and good judgment.

ROBERT FELLOWS, a prominent citizen of Ottumwa, and closely identified with its business and industrial interests, is a native of Monroe County, N. Y., born in the town of Penfield, Oct. 7, 1817. He is the son of Henry and Sophia (Sanburn) Fellows, the former a native of Berkshire, Mass. His father was a General in the Revolutionary War under command of Gen. Washington, and was on his staff. His mother was born in Connecticut, and went to New York with her parents at an early day, settling in Ontario County, where they owned a large tract of land, which her father afterward sold for the sum of eighteen cents per acre.

Henry Fellows entered upon the practice of his profession at Canandaigua, N. Y., and after becoming a resident of that State was prominently identified with its political affairs. He was elected to the State Legislature for two terms, and held the office of Justice of the Peace after he had become designated as an "old man." But he retained his mental faculties to a surprising degree, and performed the duties of his office correctly and acceptably.

Robert Fellows was reared upon a farm, and gained a good insight into the nursery business, conducted at that time by his father. He received careful home training, and completed his education in the High School at Penfield, N. Y. His first vote was cast for Gen. Harrison as President, and he has not missed voting at a presidential election since that time. He was married, in 1837, to Miss Caroline E. Crampton, of Connecticut, and, crossing the Mississippi in 1867, came to the city of Ottumwa, where he engaged in the ferry business, farming and stock-raising, which he prosecuted for a term of five years. He then purchased the residence which he now occupies and where he is passing his later days surrounded by the comforts which his early industry was the means of providing. He is a Republican in politics, and in all respects has been considered among the best citizens of Ottumwa. He has visited the East several times since taking up his residence in Wapello County, and among old friends and associations reviewed with pleasure the scenes of his childhood and youth.

The Fellows family of Penfield is one of the oldest in Monroe County, N. Y. Henry Fellows, Sr., now deceased, was a brother-in-law of Daniel Penfield, who came from Sheffield, Mass., and settled in that town. Mr. Henry Fellows was a soldier in the Revolutionary War, and one of the military advisers of Gen. Washington, being a part of the time on the staff of the great commander, and at other times was at the head of one of the divisions of the army. Wherever placed he was notable for skill, energy and courage, and retained the confidence of the Commander-in-Chief of the army, as well as that of the soldiers and citizens, until the close of the war. His son Henry, the father of our subject, was a gentleman of fine education, a graduate of Williams College, and commenced his professional career at Canandaigua, N. Y., about seventy years ago. There he formed the acquaintance of and married Miss Sophia Sanburn, her mother being Mrs. Hannah Sanburn, the first white woman coming to that section of the country in its earlier history, sixty-one years ago. Henry Fellows, Jr., and Daniel Penfield settled in the town of the same name fifty-seven years ago. Mr. Fellows built his mansion there, and in this were born to him and his wife seven of their ten children, the record of whom is as follows: Henry was the eldest; Mary became the wife of Daniel Lewis; John Charles was the next in order of birth, and then Robert, the subject of our sketch; Jane became the wife of John L. Livingston; Charlotte married George Parmeter, and Sophia, C. M. Hawley, of Chicago; Cornelia is the widow of Nathan Hall, and George was the youngest in order of birth; the deceased are May and George.

Henry Fellows, Sr., for the space of sixty years, was prominently identified with the business interests of his locality, and filled many offices of trust and emolument. He represented his county several terms in the General Assembly of New York State, and was greatly esteemed for his kindly and sympathetic nature and his active benevolence. He was the encourager and supporter of every worthy enterprise, and both in his public and private life lived above reproach. He was also fortunate in securing in his wife a companion fully suited to his qualities of mind and character. It was doubtless due to her ready sympathy and mental capacities that he was enabled to make for himself so noble a record as a man and citizen, and they transmitted to their children in a marked degree those principles of honor and integrity which they made the rule of their own lives and by which they builded so well for the generations to come.

EDWARD L. BURTON. There is scarcely a person in the county to whom the name which stands at the head of this sketch is not familiar; for nearly thirty years he has been prominent professionally in all its courts, and there has scarcely been a case of importance, except when he was upon the bench, during that time, in which he has not taken an active and leading part. He is a native of Waterloo, Seneca Co., N. Y., where he was born on the 18th day of February, 1831; his father, John Burton, Esq., was one of the pioneer settlers of Seneca County, moving there as early as 1812; was a soldier in the last war with England; a careful and accurate surveyor, having surveyed, it is said, nearly every farm in the county; and a lawyer of prominence in that part of the State. His mother, Elizabeth Hooper, was the daughter of Portius Hooper, also an early settler of Seneca County, and a grand-daughter of Gen. Clark of Revolutionary fame. He received a thorough legal education in the office of his father and his brother, William H. Burton, the latter also a prominent lawyer, which he completed at the law school of Prof. Fowler, at Ballston Springs, N. Y.

Mr. Burton turned his steps westward, and settled in Keokuk County, this State, in 1855, where he practiced law until his removal to Ottumwa in January, 1859. Here he formed a partnership with Hon. H. B. Hendershott, then, as now, an able and distinguished attorney and jurist; this partnership continued for twelve years, the firm enjoying a large and lucrative practice, when it was dissolved with mutual good-will, Mr. Burton retiring. In 1872 he formed a partnership with Hon. Edward H. Stiles, of the Ottumwa bar, and now of Kansas City, Mo.

In politics Judge Burton has always been identified with the Democratic party, which has frequently honored him by placing his name upon its ticket for important offices; but the party having generally been in the minority, never succeeded in making the official duties of Mr. Burton interfere with his legal practice until October, 1878, when he was overwhelmingly elected Judge of the District Court of the Second Judicial District; in this contest Judge Burton's majority over his competitor, Capt. Fee, of Centerville, Iowa, was nearly 2,500. The following sketch of Judge Burton was written by a friend immediately after his election to the Judgeship:

"The biographies of men should properly be written after they are dead; yet it may with propriety be said that among the leaders of the bar of Iowa, Mr. Burton deserves, by reason of his preeminent talents, to rank conspicuously; and were he as ambitious of distinction as some of his compeers who are striving to mount the ladder of professional fame, he would before this have been regarded as having attained the topmost round. He has all the real qualifications that go to make up the able and successful lawyer—a sound judgment, nice discrimination, quickness and accuracy of expression. He is universally recognized by the people of this county and district, as well as the Supreme Court of the State, as one of the ablest practitioners of this section. It has been the good fortune of the writer to witness in the State and Federal courts the forensic efforts of nearly all the leading lawyers in the State, and he is frank to say that, while Mr. Burton has some superiors as an advocate, yet, for readiness and legal accuracy, strength and perspicuity of argument, he has yet to see his superior. That he will fill the Judgeship, to which he has been recently elected, with distinguished ability and fairness, can scarcely be doubted. With him we feel assured there will be no pre-judgment, nor will his decisions be influenced by any timorous considerations of policy, or warp from their just bearings by feelings of personal favor or personal enmity. There is in the life of Lord Coke a single instance which is sufficient to justly perpetuate his fame and relieve it from the dark shadows which his intolerance and persecutive disposition has cast upon it: When he and his associates of the bench were summoned before an angry King, because they had ventured to protest against his claimed right to prohibit the hearing of any cause in which his prerogative was concerned, it is said that all save Coke threw themselves upon their knees and prayed for pardon; and when the King imperiously put the question: 'In the case where the King believes his prerogative or interests to be concerned and requires the Judges to attend him for their advice ought they not to stay proceedings until His Majesty has consulted them?' all but Coke responded eagerly in the affirmative. But he replied: 'When that case happens, I shall do that which it shall be fit for a Judge to do.'

"This historic incident, if we may be allowed to use it, illustrates the spirit of independence which, in our opinion, will characterize Mr. Burton's course as a Judge. Had Mr. Burton been identified with the political party that has had control of the State for the past twenty years, he would in all probability, have been placed before this on the Supreme Bench; and we may add, should his party succeed in regaining the lost scepter, it would show its wisdom and sagacity by placing Judge Burton in a position which he would both strengthen and adorn."

Judge Burton began his official duties as Judge of the Second Judicial District on the 1st day of January, 1879; in the discharge of those duties his friends were not disappointed in him. The duties of the bench were pleasant to him, and he seemed to feel perfectly at home. His ability for dispatching business was more than ordinary, and the court dockets, which were from one to two years behind, soon began to assume their proper proportions. On the bench he was ready and prompt to decide, seldom hearing arguments of any considerable length. In one term of four weeks in this county he tried twenty-two jury cases, besides transacting the other business of the term. His relations with the bar and officers of the court were always of the most friendly character. In the estimation of the bar, his main fault was in working them too hard, and insisting upon too much speed in the dispatch of business.

At the close of his first term Judge Burton was re-elected by an increased majority, his competitor being Hon. Henry L. Dashiel, of Albia, Monroe County. Judge Burton's record in the Supreme Court of this State is among the best, a very large per cent of his judgments being affirmed. During the eight years he was upon the bench many new questions were raised, some of them requiring the most careful study in their determination.

Judge Burton retired from the bench Jan. 1, 1887, and resumed again the practice of the law, and there is little doubt that he will take his place again among the prominent lawyers of the State. In private life he is domestic in his tastes, always cheerfully welcoming his friends to his home, and is pleased at their coming, but seldom seeks society outside of his own family.

The wife of Judge Burton, formerly Miss Mary J. Crocker, is a daughter of the late Col. James G. Crocker, formerly of Fairfield, Jefferson County, but more recently of Lancaster, Keokuk County, and sister of that distinguished soldier and civilian, Gen. M. M. Crocker, whom the people of Iowa delighted to honor, and whose memory they hold dear.

JAMES H. JORDAN, an intelligent farmer and stock-grower of Salt Creek Township, Davis Co., Iowa, is located on section 1, and forms one of the useful factors of an excellent community. He is the second of the family of eight children of Gen. Peter and Sarah (Baker) Jordan, both of whom are natives of Kentucky. The other members of the family were, R. V., Thomas J., Garret, John, Peter and Nancy Jane, the four latter deceased. The grandfather of James H. Jordan moved from Virginia to Kentucky at a very early day, while the Indians were yet in possession of that section of country, and there raised the children whose names have been given above. His father enlisted in the War of 1812, under Gen. Harrison, with the rank of Captain. He was subsequently promoted Brigadier General, and participated in the battle of New Orleans. He was a man of more than ordinary ability, and served in both branches of the Legislature of Kentucky. He was also Sheriff of Mercer County, Ky., for a number of years, and for a time was Associate Justice of the County Court of that State. In 1822 the subject of this sketch moved from Kentucky to St. Louis, Mo., whence after a short time he proceeded up the Mississippi River to Rock Island. He then procured a license to trade with the Indians, which business he continued until 1844. In the meantime he made claim to a tract of land which he occupied until it came into market, and then purchased the same of the Government. His present homestead comprises that claim. From time to time he has added to his original purchase, until he now owns over 1,600 acres of good land, and has a farm finely improved, with all modern conveniences.

Mr. Jordan in 1838, was married to Miss Frances Williams, a native of Kentucky, who was born in 1817 and the daughter of John and Fannie (Brent) Williams. Three children have been born to this union: H. C., now living in the village of Eldon, Wapello County; Sarah, the wife of Abraham Hinkle, of Van Buren County, and Victor P., deceased.

James H. Jordan is truly a pioneer, and few men now living have endured as much or witnessed such great changes in a country. For years he lived among the Indians, meeting with but few whites in that time. He assisted Gen. Street to lay out the Government post at the present village of Agency, and in all respects has been a useful and worthy citizen. His life has been full of adventure, and the true story of life among the Indians and the early settlers of this country, would form a tale stranger than fiction.

Mr. Jordan is a well-preserved man, and has lived to enjoy the fruits of a life well spent. At his hospitable fireside have gathered many of the pioneers of Davis and Wapello Counties, and those who are yet living have a kindly and pleasant recollection of the welcome always extended to the wayfarer. His wife yet remains with him in their pleasant home, the two enjoying life as well as they did forty years ago. Mr. Jordan is a member of the I. O. O. F., and in politics still adheres to the principles of Thomas Jefferson and Andrew Jackson.

LAWRENCE GUGGERTY, a self-made man, successful farmer and stock-dealer, is pleasantly situated on his fine farm on section 31, Cass Township, where he is surrounded with all the luxuries of a home life, and is meeting with success in the prosecution of his chosen vocation. Mr. Guggerty was born April 17, 1831, in County Meath, Ireland, and is the son of Owen and Julia (Riley) Guggerty, who became the parents of nine children. The record is as follows: Owen, Jr., is a farmer, and resides in Wisconsin; Patrick and Bartholomew reside with the subject of this notice; Hugh is deceased; Margaret has not been heard from for years, and her residence is consequently unknown; John is a railroad employe, and is engaged in his labors near Jacksonville, Ill., and Lawrence is the subject of this notice.

When Lawrence Guggerty was but three months old his mother was left a widow, the father's death taking place in August, 1831. He was a member of the Catholic Church, and a successful stock-dealer in the old country, highly respected by all who knew him. The mother of our subject departed this life in May, 1863, having attained the age of seventy-four years. She was also a member of the Catholic Church, and both husband and wife are buried side by side in County Meath, Ireland.

In 1849, our subject, in company with his sister Margaret, came to this country, landing in New York May 1 of that year. From the metropolis he went to Utica, the same State, and in the neighborhood of that city engaged in working on the farm of John M. Crane. After laboring there for about eleven months he made up his mind to go further West, and we next hear of him in Jo Daviess County, Ill., where he worked on the Illinois Central Railroad. This vocation he continued until 1857, when he went to Batavia, Iowa, and in company with Luke O'Brien took a contract to grade a part of the railroad bed. Their first contract amounted to $3,500, after which they took another of six miles. The latter one was taken in 1860 and completed in 1861. The partners then engaged in buying horses for the army, and continued in that business until 1863, when they again embarked in contracting. This time they took a contract for the building of sixty miles of railroad bed.

The firm continued in existence, meeting with success, until 1871, when Mr. O'Brien withdrew, and Mr. Guggerty then formed a partnership with Martin Flynn, and the new firm had at one time a contract for the building of about twenty miles of grading for the C., B. & Q. R. R., and forty-five miles on the Northwestern, also forty-one miles of grade south of Des Moines, and a forty-five mile contract between Rutland and Gilmore. All these contracts were fulfilled to the satisfaction of the companies, and thus we see that Mr. Guggerty has had considerable to do with the upbuilding of the great West, giving employment to thousands of men and teams.

In 1859 Mr. Guggerty began to invest his surplus funds in land, buying at that time eighty acres. He has added thereto as the years rolled by until at the present time he is the proprietor of 1,343 acres of land, all within the boundaries of Wapello County and in Cass Township. He also owns 320 acres in Palo Alto County, this State, making his landed possessions in the State 1,663 acres. He is also extensively engaged in stock feeding and raising, and has about 145 head of cattle, and in this department of his vocation is meeting with signal success.

On the 8th of January, 1861, Mr. Guggerty was united in marriage with Miss Bridget Gallespie. She was born March 17, 1840, and is a daughter of William and Bridget (McTye) Gallespie, who emigrated to this country in 1845. The father died in 1862, aged seventy years; the mother died while in her sixtieth year. Both were members of the Catholic Church. To the union of Mr. and Mrs. Guggerty have been given ten children: Maggie A. was born Oct. 12, 1862; Julia, March 15, 1864; John T., Aug. 23, 1866; Mary A., Sept. 28, 1868; Patrick L., Dec. 2, 1870; Bartholomew E., Jan. 7, 1872; William Eugene, Dec. 23, 1874; Bridget E., Jan. 14, 1876; Agnes Amy, June 8, 1878, and the youngest died in infancy. Mr. and Mrs. Guggerty are members of the Catholic Church.

In 1883 Mr. Guggerty held a lien on the Wabash Railroad for $35,000, and being unable to obtain his money was forced to advertise the road for sale. It was placed in a Receiver's hands, and our subject obtained his honest dues. In fact he has never lost any money in all his dealings with railroads. He has now withdrawn from contracting, and has erected himself a beautiful farm residence within a stone's throw of the C., B. & Q. R. R., where he can sit upon his front porch and see the iron horse as it pulls its thousands to some Eastern seashore or metropolis.

RICHARD H. WARDEN, city editor of the Ottumwa *Courier*, has been a resident of this city since the spring of 1848. Besides being an able journalist, he is a practical printer, and is thus well fitted for the duties of his present position, for it is a notable fact that the most eminent journalists of our country began life as printer boys, and thus obtained an insight into the details of newspaper work more correctly than could have been secured in any other manner

The subject of this history is a native of Kentucky, and first opened his eyes to the light in the city of Maysville, on the 8th of March, 1826. He is the son of Richard and Elizabeth (Chunn) Warden, and when but eight years of age removed with his parents from his native State to Clermont County, Ohio, where they located in the town of Bethel, of which they remained residents for about three years, and where his father died in 1839. Mrs. Warden subsequently removed to Decatur County, Ind., and there married Col. John Kane, of Williamsburg, Ohio. She subsequently returned to Ohio, and died in Williamsburg in 1874.

Richard H. Warden learned the printer's trade at Batavia, Ohio, in the office of Andrew M. Guest, and worked as a journeyman until the spring of 1846. He then took charge of the *Clinton Repub-*

lican at Wilmington, Ohio, which was owned by David Fisher, then Member of Congress from the Second Ohio District. In this capacity young Warden was employed until 1848, and then crossing the Mississippi, came to Ottumwa. Soon afterward, in company with J. H. D. Street, he established the *Des Moines Courier*, with which paper he was connected as editor and publisher until Dec. 20, 1856. He then sold out, determined to change his occupation, and engaged in the hotel and mercantile business.

Mr. Warden had been carefully trained in principles of honor and rectitude, and was a young man of more than ordinary ability. After coming to this section his excellent personal traits of character received ready recognition, and he was at once taken into the confidence of his fellow-townsmen. In April, 1849, he was appointed Postmaster of Ottumwa, which office he occupied for a period of four years and two months. During the progress of the late war, in August, 1862, he enlisted as a private in Co. E, 36th Iowa Vol. Inf., was elected First Lieutenant, and mustered in at Keokuk. His regiment subsequently became a part of the 7th Army Corps, under Gen. E. O. C. Ord.

Lieut. Warden participated with his regiment in the Yazoo expedition, battles of Helena and Little Rock, and various other minor engagements. In December, 1863, he was sent home on recruiting service, and was thus engaged until April, 1864, during which time he enlisted 165 men. While in the service he was aide-de-camp to Gens. Asboth and Prentiss, being also Assistant Adjutant-General of the 2d Brigade, 1st Division of Steele's Army Corps. From June 10 to Dec. 4, 1864, he served as Post Adjutant at Little Rock, Ark., and soon afterward, on account of dangerous illness in his family, he resigned his commission and returned home.

After the close of his military services Mr. Warden returned to Ottumwa, being appointed Assistant Assessor of Internal Revenue, and was connected with the revenue service for ten years. Since 1869 he has been continuously with the *Courier*, either as general editor, business manager, or city editor. He has been associated with the press of the State longer than any other editor now engaged upon an Iowa newspaper. His ability as a journalist is unquestioned. He is a terse and forcible writer, fearless in his denunciation of wrong and courageous in maintaining the right.

Richard H. Warden and Miss Virginia C. Adams were united in marriage in Ottumwa on the 26th of February, 1851. Mrs. W. is a native of Louisville, Ky., and the date of her birth was the 20th of October, 1832. By her union with our subject she has become the mother of seven children, three of whom died in infancy. The living are George A., Nettie C., Annie, and Clara C. Mr. W. is a Republican in politics, and active in all worthy public enterprises. He has been a member of the Common Council of Ottumwa and City Treasurer, and his fellow-townsmen in numerous other ways have manifested for him their high esteem.

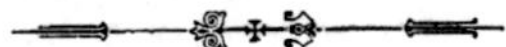

CAPT. TIMOTHY EGAN, of the firm of Moriarty, Egan & Co., transacting an extensive wholesale grocery business in Ottumwa, Iowa, is a native of the Empire State, having been born in Lewis County, near Booneville, on the 1st of January, 1838. He is the son of Timothy and Margaret (Tierney) Egan. Timothy Egan, Sr., was a native of Ireland, possessing all the generous characteristics of the Celtic race, and while a young man emigrated to the United States and became a contractor on the Black River Canal. He possessed fine abilities, and had received a liberal education. The parental family included eight children, four of whom are living, the record being as follows: James, of Syracuse, N. Y., during the progress of the late Civil War, enlisted as a soldier of the Union in the 35th New York Infantry, and served until the close; Edward, of Salt Lake City, is owner of the White House Hotel, and has been an extensive cattle dealer, having now accumulated a competency; Ann became the wife of Lawson Cunningham, of Sterlingville, Jefferson Co., N. Y., and Timothy is our subject. The father died in Jefferson County, N. Y., in 1849; the mother is still living in Ottumwa, at the advanced age of seventy-nine years.

The subject of this biography received his early

education in the district schools, and remained with his parents until after he had attained to years of manhood. In 1861, the late war being then in progress, he enlisted in the 35th New York Infantry, becoming a member of Company F, and was first stationed with his regiment at Elmira, N. Y. A short time afterward they were ordered to Arlington Heights, where the regiment assisted in building the forts, and young Egan engaged, with his comrades, in the various battles and skirmishes which they afterward encountered. They marched to Manassas, where they found a detachment of the enemy under Gen. Patrick, and thence, returning to Alexandria and Fredericksburg, participated in the first engagement, and were the first to open fire. They afterward met the enemy at Rappahannock and Culpeper, Va., where they covered Gen. Banks' division, and wound up with considerable skirmishing. Subsequently they engaged in the battle of Bull Run, and were then sent to Maryland and went into the fight at South Mountain, where Gen. Reno was killed; thence to Antietam, where the regiment lost heavily and where Mr. Egan was wounded with a piece of shell in the groin, and received a bullet in the left foot and calf of the leg. He was confined in the hospital at Georgetown, and after an absence from his regiment of four months, rejoined it at Hatchie River. After various other engagements they proceeded to Fredericksburg, where occurred the last general engagement of the regiment, their term of service having expired. Mr. Egan returned to Jefferson County, N. Y., and raised Company C, of the 186th New York Volunteers, of which he was commissioned Captain, this being in the fall of 1863. He, with his command, was assigned to the 5th Corps under Gen. Warren, with which they remained until the close of the war. Capt. Egan was present at the grand review in Washington, and was mustered out as Captain at Sackett's Harbor, after which he returned to his native county.

In March, 1866, Capt. Egan decided to visit the western country, and accordingly crossed the Father of Waters and came into Iowa, locating in Ottumwa, where he was employed by the marble firm of M. B. Root & Son, with whom he remained until the following year. In 1868 he purchased a stock of hardware, and associated himself in partnership with Mr. Harper, and they engaged in trade under the name and style of Egan & Harper. They were soon afterward burned out, but fortunately were insured to the full extent of loss. The firm then purchased the interest of Mr. William Doggett, and was re-organized, becoming Egan, Harper & Co. In 1881 Mr. Egan sold his interest, and the following year established the present business.

Capt. Egan was married in Jefferson County, N. Y., near Watertown, in 1868, to Miss Mary Benoit, who was a native of Northern New York. They became the parents of three children, of whom one only is living—Alfred T. They occupy a pleasant home in this city, and Mr. Egan, socially as well as in a business point of view, is reckoned among the leading citizens of the county. He is essentially a self-made man, and self-educated, only enjoying the privilege of three months' schooling when a boy of eleven years old. His education was completed while in the army, by studying nights and whenever opportunity occurred. He is Republican in politics, and has filled the various local offices of his township. He is at present Alderman from the Fourth Ward, and socially a member of Cloutman Post No. 69.

SMITH AUGUSTUS SPILMAN, M. D., a successful physician and surgeon, has been a resident of Ottumwa since 1876, and by his straightforward business methods and unquestioned medical skill has secured the approval and esteem of his fellow-citizens. He is a native of Jennings County, Ind., and was born on the 6th of March, 1853, his parents being John D. and Amelia (Percival) Spilman, natives of Kentucky, who came to Indiana before their marriage. After this event John D. Spilman located upon a farm and engaged in agricultural pursuits, which he afterward abandoned and interested himself in trade. In 1860 they removed to Decatur County, Ind., where he became prominent in public affairs, being elected County

Auditor, which position he occupied for eight years. He was strongly Republican in politics, and acted as Chairman of the Republican Central Committee. He was a man of rare intelligence, an extensive reader, and kept himself thoroughly posted upon all matters of general interest. During the progress of the late war, in 1862, he enlisted in the 76th Indiana Infantry, and served as a soldier until the close of his term of enlistment, his duties in the service confining him mostly within the boundaries of Kentucky.

John D. Spilman was a thoroughly religious man, prominently connected with the Methodist Episcopal Church and licensed as a local preacher. After the close of the war he removed across the Mississippi into Iowa, becoming a resident of Wapello County, and died Aug. 19, 1876. He belonged to the I. O. O. F. and Masonic fraternity, being a master of the latter order, and one of its most interesting public speakers. His wife, the mother of our subject, survived her husband until 1881, and then departed to join him in the silent land. She was a most amiable Christian, highly respected by all who knew her; she sympathized thoroughly with her husband in his opinions and projects, and with him was also a devoted member of the Methodist Church.

The subject of our sketch received his primary education in the schools of Greensburg, Ind., and in 1876 entered the office of Dr. C. G. Lewis, of Ottumwa, one of the most eminent physicians of this locality. After pursuing a thorough course of study there Mr. Spilman entered the Chicago Medical College, the medical department of the Northwestern University, graduating in the class of 1879. He then returned to Ottumwa and was admitted to partnership with his preceptor, Dr. Lewis, and they operated together until September, 1882, since which time Dr. Spilman has practiced alone. He is an honored member of the profession in this vicinity, and a member of Wapello and Des Moines Valley Medical Societies, holding in the latter the position of Secretary and Treasurer. He is also connected with the State Medical Society and the American Medical Association.

Dr. Spilman gives his entire attention to the duties of his profession, in which he is ambitious to excel, and is making fine progress in that direction. He is a close student, an extensive reader, and fully deserves the success which he has hitherto enjoyed. Socially he belongs to the Masonic fraternity, and is also a Knight of Pythias. He has passed all the chairs and represented the order in the Grand Lodge, holding at present the office in this district of Deputy Grand Chancellor, and is also connected with the Sons of Veterans, in which he holds the position of Surgeon-General and ranks as Brigadier-General.

The subject of our sketch was married, Sept. 23, 1873, to Miss Mary J. Kiser, a native of Indiana. Mrs. Mary J. Spilman remained the companion of her husband for only a little more than two years, dying in April, 1876, and leaving one child—Mattie A. The Doctor was married the second time on the 4th of December, 1879, to Miss Mary Ball, of Ottumwa, who died on the 2d of March, 1881. Dr. Spilman contracted a third marriage on Dec. 29, 1886, with Miss Alice Sellers, of Oskaloosa, Iowa.

JAMES ADAMS, the first white man who made settlement in what is now Adams Township, and which was named after him, also established the first blacksmith-shop in the township, and operated this in connection with the improvement and cultivation of his farm. He was born in Canada, and when a young man moved to Licking County, Ohio, thence came to Van Buren County, Iowa, in 1842, when the New Purchase was first opened up for settlement, and subsequently moved to this county. As may be supposed he became prominent in the affairs of his township, and was greatly respected for his sterling worth of character. He was twice married before leaving Canada, his second wife having been Miss Sarah Barton, by whom he became the father of five children. He was a straightforward business man, and a member of the Baptist Church.

One of his sisters married Theophilus Blake, Sr., well known as the founder of Blakesburg in Adams Township, and of whom a sketch will be found in another part of this ALBUM.

H. B. Hendershott

JUDGE HENRY B. HENDERSHOTT, a valued citizen of Ottumwa, and whose portrait is given on the opposite page, is a descendant of excellent old Welsh and German families, and possesses in a goodly degree the worthy traits of his ancestors. He was born in Miami County, Ohio, on the 15th of May, 1816; his father was a native of New Jersey and his mother of Ohio. Soon after the birth of their son, our subject, in the autumn of the same year they removed to the Territory of Illinois, and located in Madison County, where the early life of Henry Hendershott was passed, amid the wild scenes of a pioneer's life. His opportunities for securing an education were very limited, only being able to attend school during the winter seasons, and then often obliged to walk three or four miles in order to reach the public institution of learning. At an early period in his life he gave unmistakable indications of great resolution and force of character, which his later years fully established. At the age of nineteen years he started out alone and on foot for Illinois College, at Jacksonville. When he reached the place he had but $2.50 in his pocket, and a very scanty wardrobe. He laid his case before the faculty of the college, of which Rev. Edward Beecher was President, and they, appreciating the worthiness of his undertaking, extended to him all the encouragement in their power. At that time there was a large farm and workshop attached to the college, and during such spare hours as he could obtain from his studies, young Hendershott applied himself to work, receiving twelve and one-half cents per hour. He remained two years in college, alternating work with study and keeping equal pace with his classmates. At length he found it necessary to find something to do which would contribute more liberally to his support.

Mr. Hendershott, in 1837, after leaving college, proceeded westward to Burlington, Iowa. He secured a position as clerk in the post-office, and was afterward employed in the Recorder's office. He still continued the pursuit of his studies during his leisure moments, and took up the study of law under the instruction of Judge David Rorer and M. D. Browning. He had been faithful to his duties in the Recorder's office, and in 1839 was appointed Deputy Clerk of the District Court of Des Moines County, by the Hon. Charles Mason of that court. Here he remained for two years, in the meantime continuing his studies, and was finally admitted to the bar in 1841. The following year he removed to Mt. Pleasant, Henry County, and soon afterward to Fairfield, Jefferson County. Thence he went to Agency City, and on the 16th of May, 1844, came to Ottumwa, where he located permanently, being one of the most honored pioneers and highly respected citizens of the place.

In February, 1844, previous to becoming a resident here, Mr. H. was appointed, by Judge Mason, Clerk of the District Court of Wapello County, which office he held until the following September. While acting as Clerk it became his duty, by an act of the Legislature, to organize the county. On the 17th day of December of the following year he was appointed by Gov. James Clark to the office of District Prosecutor for the Seventh District of Iowa, and not quite a year from that time, on the 17th of September, 1846, Gov. Clark commissioned him Colonel of the 2d Regiment, 1st Brigade, 4th Division, Iowa Militia. On the 10th of April, 1849, he was commissioned by Hon. George W. Jones, Surveyor-General of Wisconsin and Iowa, as surveyor to sectionize townships. At the September term of the United States Court, in 1848, he was appointed by that court to the responsible position of Commissioner of Iowa, to act in conjunction with Joseph C. Brown, Commissioner from Missouri, in determining the vexed question of the boundary line between those States. In the meantime Mr. Brown died, and Hon. Robert W. Wells was appointed his successor. Mr. Wells, finding that the duties of Commissioner interfered with those of a Judge, resigned, and Hon. W. G. Minor was appointed to succeed him. The joint services of Judge Hendershott and Mr. Minor gave entire satisfaction, and their report was accepted as a final settlement of a prolonged and bitter dispute over the line.

In the summer of 1850 Judge H. was elected to represent the counties of Wapello, Monroe and Lucas in the State Senate, where he served four years. In this body he was a member of the Judiciary Committee, and took an active part in forming the code of 1851. In January following he was elected a member of the Iowa Historical and Geological Society. He was Clerk of the City Council in 1852–53, and again in 1855. Four years later he was a member of the City Council. In the meantime, however, in 1856, the subject of our sketch had been elected Judge of the District Court for the Third Judicial District, the duties of which position he performed with great credit to himself and acceptability to the bar and the people. It may be said, without disparagement to others, that the reports of cases decided by the Supreme Court of the State will show a less proportion of Judge Hendershott's rulings reversed than those of any other Judge in the State. Upon retiring from the bench the bar tendered him a complimentary supper, at which resolutions of approval of his services were passed.

On the 8th day of June, 1845, Judge Hendershott was united in marriage with Miss Mary W. Jeffries, daughter of Judge Paul C. Jeffries, of Ottumwa. She was born in Mecklenburg County, Va., in 1820, and by her marriage with our subject became the mother of seven sons and one daughter. The family residence at Ottumwa is one of the most attractive in the city and the abode of comfort and luxury. Within its hospitable doors the cultured citizens of Ottumwa often gather with expressions of good-will and friendship toward their honored fellow-citizen and his amiable and excellent lady.

Since 1850, with the exception of the time he was actually engaged in the duties of State Senator and during the time he acted as Judge of the District Court, Mr. Hendershott has been actively engaged in the practice of his profession. In 1876 he was the Democratic nominee for Congress in the Sixth District of Iowa, which was then Republican by 5,000 majority. Though his defeat was to be expected he yet ran several hundred votes ahead of his ticket.

Judge Hendershott has filled many offices of responsibility and honor, and always with industry, vigor and ability. He is a fluent, forcible and convincing speaker. His personal character is above reproach, and he has always been a staunch friend and supporter of education, morality and sobriety. He is, in all respects, an honored representative of the pioneer element of Wapello County, and has arisen to his present position by the exercise of his own native talent and resolution.

J. M. SPRINGER, trainmaster of the C., B. & Q. R. R. and stationed at Ottumwa, has been a resident of the Hawkeye State since 1852, having come here with his parents when a child of two years old. He was born in Dayton County, Ohio, on the 12th of October, 1850. Two years later his parents crossed the Mississippi and settled in Wapello County. Here their son, our subject, was reared and attended the district schools until the age of fourteen years. He seemed to have a natural inclination for railroading, and at the age mentioned, boarded the trains of the C., B. & Q. R. R., as newsboy. At the age of fifteen his active experience commenced as a brakeman, and three years later he was conductor on a freight train. In 1870 he accompanied Henry Teilson, a Superintendent of the C., B. & Q. R. R., as freight conductor in Oregon, Mr. Teilson being Superintendent of the Oregon & California Railroad, after which young Springer ran a passenger train for two years. In the spring of 1874 he returned to Ottumwa, where he was given a train and occupied a responsible position until 1882. He was then appointed trainmaster, the duties of which he has fulfilled faithfully since that time. He is a gentleman of fine address, courteous and agreeable, and thoroughly posted in railroad matters. He is a great favorite among the fraternity, and a member in good standing of the Brotherhood of Railway Conductors, and the A. O. U. W.

Upon his return from Oregon, J. M. Springer was united in marriage with Miss Emma Fiedler, their union taking place in 1874. Mrs. Springer is a sister of Frank Fiedler, of Ottumwa. Of this union there have been born four children—Harry J., Willie H., Maxon G. and Frank J.

Mr. Springer has literally grown up with the county, and has taken an active interest in its welfare, being the encourager and supporter of every worthy enterprise having for its object the promotion of education, morality and sobriety, and in a residence of over thirty years has secured for himself the respect and esteem of his fellow-citizens.

George Springer, the father of our subject, was born in Pennsylvania, whence he removed when a boy to Maryland. Later, he went to Dayton, Ohio, and after a time proceeding still further westward, located at Brownsville, Ind., where he was united in marriage with Miss Jane Conway. In 1852 they crossed the Father of Waters, and coming into the Hawkeye State, located in Wapello County. The parental household consisted of ten children, five of whom are still living, as follows: John, of Agency City; J. M., of our sketch; Ellen, the wife of Chris Heller, of this county, and Frank and Charlie, twins, of Ottumwa, both being conductors on the C., B. & Q. R. R. The father of the family folded his hands for his final rest in 1873, leaving behind him a record of kindly acts and a blameless life. The mother is still living with her son in Agency City. Both parents were connected with the Baptist Church, and carried out in their daily lives the principles which they religiously professed.

CHARLES E. and LIZZIE R. McKINNEY, subjects of this biography, are natives of Nauvoo, Ill., and the children of R. W. and Mary (Beck) McKinney, natives of Ohio, who removed from their native State to Nauvoo after their marriage at an early period in the history of the Prairie State. From there they removed to Bushnell, Ill., where they still live, the father engaged in the practice of law. The parental household consisted of seven children, two of whom died in infancy. The five surviving received careful home training and a good education, and inherited from their parents a more than ordinary amount of intelligence, with considerable literary ability.

Charles E. and Lizzie R. McKinney are proprietors of the Eldon *Review*, which was established in 1881, by E. H. Thomas, as an independent paper. It was purchased by the brother and sister in April, 1885, and is being conducted with ability and success. It is a seven-column folio, issued weekly, and its present publishers are maintaining its first character as an independent journal.

Charles E. McKinney learned the printer's trade at Nauvoo, Ill., and afterward was employed as a journeyman in Bushnell, Ill. Miss McKinney was formerly a teacher of the graded schools in Bushnell, Macomb and Keokuk, Iowa, and is possessed of fine literary talent, and has been a popular contributor to the journals of St. Louis, Chicago, Kansas City, Burlington, and other leading cities. She seems to have inherited in a large measure the talents of her father, who has also contributed many interesting articles to the various leading magazines of the country, among those which attracted attention being a discussion of the Mormon question in the pages of the *North American Review*. He also assisted in the compilation of Beadle's "History of Mormonism," and other important and interesting works. The remaining children of the parental family are as follows: R. M. is engaged as bookkeeper in a bank at Burlington, Iowa: W. C. is a dentist of Havana, Ill.; E. H. is a teacher at Bushnell, Ill.

The publishers of the Eldon *Review* bid fair to follow in the footsteps of their father, possessing a large share of his mental capacities, and conducting their paper with intelligence and ability. Its circulation is steadily increasing and they are building up a flattering patronage.

EDWARD MORIARTY, senior member of the wholesale grocery firm of Moriarty, Egan & Co., of Ottumwa, is one of the leading and most enterprising citizens of Wapello County. The firm with which he is connected carries on an extensive business and is regarded as one of the most substantial in this section of the State.

Mr. Moriarty is a native of Portsmouth, Ohio, and was born Feb. 17, 1842. His parents were Morris P. and Mary (Pheney) Moriarty, natives of Ireland, who emigrated to America in about 1835. After coming to this country Morris Moriarty became engaged as an employe in the construction of railroads and afterward engaged in mercantile pursuits at Agency City, Iowa, and at Ottumwa. He was stricken down in the prime of life, dying in 1863, leaving his widow and a family of seven children mainly dependent upon the eldest son, our subject, for their support. This duty Mr. M. fulfilled in the most admirable manner, providing generously for the education of his brothers and sisters, who are now highly respected members of society and occupy their rightful position among the cultured people of this vicinity. In the meantime he did not neglect his own education, and after an attendance at the primary schools entered St. Joseph College in Perry County, Ohio, where he pursued a thorough course of study and subsequently attended Sinsinawa Mound College, in Wisconsin, where he graduated in 1862, at the age of twenty years. The year following he came to Ottumwa and established himself in the grocery business, meeting with success from the start, and by his straightforward business methods and courteous demeanor toward his customers, secured a large and profitable patronage. In 1875 he removed to Red Oak, Montgomery County, and, associating with him one of his brothers, commenced dealing in groceries at wholesale and was attended with the same success which marked his first business venture. Seven years later, in 1882, he organized the present firm at Ottumwa and which, conducted by the business methods which Mr. M. had heretofore so successfully pursued, has become one of the leading houses of its line in this section of the State.

The marriage of Edward Moriarty and Miss Helen O'Keefe, of Plattsmouth, Neb., was celebrated Feb. 7, 1877, and of this union there have been born four children, three of whom are living, viz: Edward, Morris and Leo. They occupy a handsome residence in this city and are surrounded by all the comforts and luxuries which a cultivated taste and ample means afford. Their dwelling is equipped with all the modern improvements—gas, hot and cold water pipes, bath, etc.

Politically Mr. M. is Democratic and uniformly casts his vote in support of the principles of his party. He is prominently identified with the business and industrial interests of this community and contributes cheerfully of his time and means for the promotion of every worthy enterprise connected with the welfare of his city and county. He and his wife are both members of the Catholic Church.

CHARLES HARLEN, a highly respected resident of Green Township, is a native of Sweden, born March 1, 1849, and the son of Munson and Carrie (Anderson) Harlen. His father was a farmer by occupation, and he was reared under the parental roof, attending the schools of his native country and assisting in the duties around the homestead. When he became of suitable age he learned the trade of a wagon-maker, at which he worked for three years in his own country, or until 1868. Then, believing that he could improve his fortune by coming to America, he bid farewell to home and the associations of his youth and started for the New World. After a prosperous voyage he landed at New York City, and turning his steps directly westward, journeyed to the Prairie State, making his first location in Princeton, Bureau County. He there engaged as a farm laborer for four months, and then, going to New Boston, Mercer County, he engaged at his former occupation, wagon-making, and remained there two and a half years. He then crossed the Mississippi and came into Iowa, working at his trade, and after four months thus employed came to Ottumwa in the spring of 1871. He there engaged to work for Mr. Hartman, who was carrying on a wagon manufactory, and remained in Ottumwa until the following spring, when he was employed by the C., B. & Q. R. R. Co., as Car Inspector, which position he held for the following seven years. He then went upon the road as a brakeman for two months, and then purchased a grocery store at Dudley, Iowa, which he operated for a short time and then returned to Ottumwa. He next engaged as a teamster for two years, and in 1879, having all this time practiced a strict economy, he purchased ninety acres of land in Green Township, on section 16, which constitutes his present home. He has brought his land to a good state of cultivation, has a comfortable farm dwelling, good barns and outhouses, and everything necessary for the carrying on of agriculture after the most improved methods.

Charles Harlen and Miss Christina Jeppson were married Nov. 21, 1874. She is a native of his own country, and they have become the parents of five children, as follows: Clara Matilda was born Aug. 18, 1875; Juliet Ellen, born Nov. 3, 1877, died April 3, 1878; Ella Juliet, born July 10, 1879; Carl Alben, July 12, 1882, and Harriett Alvira, July 12, 1885. Mr. and Mrs. H. are members in good standing of the Lutheran Church at Ottumwa. Mr. H. is quiet and undemonstrative, attending strictly to his own affairs, and in every respect is an honorable member of his community. Aside from his general farming operations he is giving considerable attention to the breeding of fine stock, of which he has a number of valuable animals. In politics he is Republican. A view of the residence of Mr. Harlen will be found on another page.

SAMUEL RAYL. Among the well-to-do and successful farmers of Agency Township, and a gentleman who has attained success in life through industry and economy, is the gentleman whose biography we now write. He is at present engaged in the calling which he has followed the greater portion of his life on his fine farm in Agency Township, and in addition to the cultivation of the cereals, is devoting considerable time to stock-raising. Mr. Rayl was born in Fayette County, Pa., Sept. 2, 1815, and is the son of Samuel and Nancy (Flick) Rayl, the former a native of Pennsylvania, and the latter of German ancestry.

The subject of this notice learned the carpenter's trade in early years from his father, a man well skilled as a carpenter and builder, who departed this life in Middleburg, Va. His wife, the mother of our subject, died in Pennsylvania.

Samuel Rayl after learning the carpenter's trade worked at the same with his father until he was about twenty-two years of age. He then went to Brooke County, Va., and located at Bethany, a small town, where he worked for Alexander Campbell, the great defender of primitive Christianity, and often falsely referred to as the founder of the Christian Church. Bethany College, the institution of which Mr. Campbell was so long President, was in process of building, and Mr. Rayl was employed in its erection. After the completion of the college Mr. Rayl went to Greene County, Pa. Prior to this, however, in 1842, he was married to Miss Ellen, the daughter of Maj. Garrett Snedeker, who was born in Brooke County, Va., and lived as the faithful wife and companion of our subject until June 3, 1886, when she passed to the land of the hereafter. Their union was blest by the birth of two children: Samuel G., who married a daughter of Maj. S. Cramer, and lives near our subject, and Elizabeth C., wife of George M. Shear, a resident of Pleasant Township.

Mr. Rayl came to Iowa in 1855, from Pennsylvania, and settling in Competine Township, was occupied in farming until March 1, 1865, when he purchased the farm he now occupies in Agency Township, consisting of 240 acres on the home farm and also sixty acres of timber. He has two good houses on his place, together with excellent barns and first-class improvements, and is meeting with that success which energy, perseverance and good judgment will invariably bring. In politics Mr. Rayl votes with the Republican party. He is a gentleman honored and respected for his sterling worth and integrity, and for his straightforward and manly dealings with his fellow-man.

JACOB MILLISACK, a prominent citizen of Wapello County, was born in Washington County, Pa., Jan. 9, 1800, being a son of Philip and Mary Millisack, both of whom were natives of Lancaster County, Pa., and of German parentage. When twelve years old our subject began to learn the trade of a hatter in Washington, Pa., and served the following six years as an apprentice. His father had died when he was under six years, and at twelve his heart was saddened and the world made lonely and desolate by the death of his mother. He bravely went to work, however, making the most of life, and in 1820 he went into Carroll County, Ohio, where he established himself in the hatter's business and carried on quite an extensive trade for ten years. He then sold out and engaged in general merchandising quite profitably for twenty-five years following.

On the 18th of November, 1864, our subject came to Ottumwa, in the vicinity of which he had been buying land for five or six years previously, and retired from active business, and to-day is comfortably settled in a pleasant home at 118 Second Street West.

As might be expected Mr. Millisack had but meager advantages for an education, but by a course of entensive reading he has become well educated and well informed upon general matters. He was one of the prominent men of Carroll County, Ohio, for a period of forty years, always taking an active part in everything tending to advance the general welfare of the people. He was a strong friend of liberty and a colleague in the noble work of anti-slavery with the illustrious William Loyd Garrison. He was the first to ring the town bell when the Emancipation Proclamation was issued, getting up at midnight in mid-winter to do this.

Our subject was married, July 12, 1821, to Miss Sarah, daughter of Isaac and Betsy (McNabb) Holmes, natives respectively of New Jersey and Ohio. To them were born eleven children, of whom the record is as follows: Martha, born Nov. 12, 1822, became the wife of Thomas Cummings, of Leesburg, Ohio, and died April 15, 1849; Thomas is a clerk in Ottumwa; Wesley, a resident of Agency, this county; Jeremiah died in infancy; Isaac is a clerk at Ottumwa; Mary is the wife of W. F. Carroll, of Ottumwa; Jacob C. is farming near Drakesville, Davis County; Phebe is the wife of J. McCoy, of Leesburg, Ohio; William, born March 31, 1839, died in the late war, serving as Quartermaster Sergeant; Edward is a resident of Des Moines.

Mr. Millisack began life a poor boy, but by the exercise of his excellent business talent has made of life quite a success. In his political views at present he is a Greenbacker.

The wife of our subject died Jan. 21, 1884, aged eighty-four years and seven months. They had lived together for sixty-two years, nine months and seven days. She was a devoted Spiritualist, and it was written of her that "Her work of a lifetime, like that of Jacob Millisack, was well done." When he in the darkest and most dangerous hours of the great battle for human rights, stood, as one man to a thousand, she was his strength and his support, and with courage undaunted they mutually pledged their lives, fortunes and honor in support of a principle that has since liberated four millions of people who were then marketed like beasts, but now free as the winds of Heaven. Who could do more? In the life and career of our venerable subject, who has now lived to almost fourscore and ten years, we find a noble specimen and example of the pioneer of the great West. Since the Revolutionary contest, he has witnessed the most important events in the history of our country, and been an active participant therein. The reader will observe that in all the great questions of human liberty and free thought that have agitated the minds of the American people in the last seventy years, Jacob Millisack has always been found on the side of right and progress. Always a keen and active thinker, logical in his conclusions, and eloquent in the expressions of his sentiments.

NELS HALL, a prosperous farmer and stock-raiser of Polk Township, owns and occupies 116 acres of land on section 32, and is a fine specimen of the thrifty and industrious Scandinavian farmer. He was born in Sweden on the 11th of February, 1839, and is the son of Nels and Sisly (Gunison) Hall, who emigrated from their native land in 1855, setting sail from Sweden on the 15th of October, and after a voyage of six weeks landed at Boston Harbor, and from there proceeded directly toward the prairies of Illinois. They located in the city of Moline, where they remained one year, and then, crossing the Mississippi, came into Wapello County, Iowa, and purchasing a small farm in Polk Township began the improvement and cultivation of a farm. They were prospered in their undertaking, and in the course of time the father of our subject added to his landed interests until he became the owner of 106 acres, which he brought to a good state of cultivation. The parental household included six children, five of whom are yet living and of whom the record is as follows: Hannah became the wife of Peter Oakley, and resides in Moline, Ill.; Nels, our subject, was next in order of birth; William died at the age of twenty-nine years in Montana Territory, and there his remains are buried; Augusta married Percy Swanson, a farmer of Red Oak, Iowa; John is a farmer of Nebraska; Emma, the wife of Charles Carlson, resides in Moline.

Nels Hall, Jr., was married to Miss Emma Petersen in 1863. Mrs. H. is a native of the same country as her husband, and was born May 9, 1845. She is the daughter of Nels P. and Mary (Anderson) Petersen, and came to this country with her father, her mother having died in Sweden when Mrs. H. was a young child. Her father is still living in Polk Township. Of the marriage of our subject and his wife there were five children, viz.: John W., born July 13, 1866; Charles E., Dec. 1, 1867; Frank W., Nov. 27, 1870; Guy F., March 30, 1873, and Ellen A., Aug. 19, 1883. The family have been well raised and are prominently connected with the Lutheran Church. Mr. H. is Democratic in politics and uniformly casts his vote in support of the principles of that party.

In the spring of 1860 he went overland to Colorado, and there engaged in teaming and mining for a period of three years, in that time being fully satisfied with his experiences in the Far West, and contented to return to a a more civilized locality.

WILLIAM HOBBS, deceased, was a highly respected farmer of Center Township, who came from his native State of Maryland, to Wapello County, Iowa, in 1850, accompanied by his family. They settled upon a tract of uncultivated land, moved into a rude log cabin, and experienced many of the privations and hardships of pioneer life. Mr. Hobbs had been reared to habits of industry, and after settling upon his land in Center Township he industriously proceeded with its improvement and cultivation and in due time reaped the reward of his labors. He was a good man in every respect, honest and upright in his dealings, and enjoyed to more than a usual degree the confidence and esteem of his neighbors. Although never identified with any church organization, he was peculiarly benevolent and charitable, ready to assist at every call of distress and to contribute of his time and means to the promotion of every worthy enterprise. His name is held in kindly remembrance by a large circle of friends and acquaintances as an example which the rising generation would be wise to follow.

Mr. Hobbs was born near the city of Baltimore in 1794, where he received a common-school education and grew to manhood. He was a soldier in the War of 1812, and with his comrades fought bravely near Washington at the time of the burning of that city. He was also at the battle of Bladensburg, and for his military services received a pension in his later years. At the close of this war Mr. Hobbs left his native State and went to Kentucky. He was subsequently married to Miss Emily Tennant of the latter State, and they became the parents of ten children, eight of whom are still living and recorded as follows: Richard is a resident of Vermilion County, Ill.; Elizabeth became the wife of Erastus Day, of Wapello County, Iowa; Mary E. married Jacob N. Moore, and lives in Burlington, Iowa; Achsah was married to William M. Day, of Putnam County, Ind.; Samuel lives in Palo County, Iowa; John, in Dallas County, Tex.; William, in Centralia, Iowa, and Rachel, the wife of B. J. Boulton, resides in Ottumwa. After his marriage in Kentucky, Mr. Hobbs with his young wife went into Indiana, where they remained until 1850, then crossed the Father of Waters and came to this county, as before stated.

J. JACKSON CRIDER, M. D., founder and proprietor of Crider Medical Institute, of Ottumwa, Iowa, is a native of Virginia, and was born in Abingdon, Washington County, on the 15th of October, 1831. He is the son of William A. and Elizabeth (Hinton) Crider, natives of Washington County, Va., and of English and German descent. After their marriage and the birth of our subject, they removed from Virginia to Indiana, becoming residents of that section in 1838. Here J. Jackson attended the district schools, where he received his primary education, and later attended Asbury University at Greencastle, Ind., from which he graduated in the class of 1850. During this time he entered upon the study of medicine under the tutelage of J. Hall, of Greenfield, Ind. The following year he went to Lancaster, Pa., and entered the office of Dr. Michael Crider, his uncle, one of the most eminent physicians and surgeons in the country at that time. With him he remained for a period of three years, and in 1854 went to New York, and for the following fifteen years practiced as a specialist in throat and lung diseases, diseases of the air passages, and female complaints. In 1870, wishing to avail himself of still higher opportunities of knowledge, he attended a course of lectures at the A. M. University of Pennsylvania, in the meantime pursuing a scientific course of study, and graduated with the highest honors of his class. Ten years later the school suspended operations and never resumed.

Dr. Crider crossed the Mississippi in 1871, and made his location in Ottumwa, Iowa. The following year he completed his preparations for founding the Crider Institute, which has been in successful operation since that time. It receives patients from all the States in the Union and the Canadas. As an illustration of its popularity and success it may be proper to state that the receipts of this institution for one year have aggregated the sum of $27,000. It is pleasantly and healthfully located on the corner of Second and Washington streets, the building being three stories in height, and supplied with all modern conveniences and improvements, and patients are brought from all points on the six railroads leading into the city.

Dr. Crider was married, in Boone County, Ind., his wife's native place, to Miss Mary E. Johns, on the 15th of June, 1854. Mrs. C. is the daughter of Jacob Johns, a prominent stock-raiser of that county. Her birth occurred on the 3d of April, 1838, and by her union with our subject she has become the mother of four children: Wilber E., the assistant of his father; Sarah E., the wife of I. D. Morey, a stock-dealer of Ottumwa; Eva A., who married D. R. Smith, Superintendent of the Homes State Gold Mills of Lead City, Dak., and Ida M., who is unmarried and living at home. The family residence is pleasantly located, and its inmates are apparently enjoying all the comforts and many of the luxuries of life. They are regular attendants of the Presbyterian Church, and socially Dr. Crider belongs to the I. O. O. F.

JAMES M. PECK, Sr., an intelligent farmer and stock-grower, is pleasantly located on section 1, Center Township. Few men are better known in Wapello County, he being first among the pioneers, the first Sheriff of the county, and one of its organizers.

Mr. Peck was born near the Catawba River, Botetourt County, Va., Feb. 15, 1818. He is a son of Jacob F. and Jane (Waggoner) Peck, both of whom were natives of the same State, the father being of German, and the mother of Scotch descent. Jacob F. Peck was a farmer, and made a specialty of raising hemp and tobacco. These products he shipped on Craig's Creek, to the James River, principally on keelboats to various markets. In the War of 1812 he served as a soldier, with the rank of Orderly Sergeant.

When James M. Peck was but seven years of age his parents moved from Virginia to Tillico Plain, Monroe Co., E. Tenn., and settled upon a farm where they remained until their death. His mother died about Feb. 1, 1870, and his father in 1874. As may be inferred, the subject of this sketch was reared upon a farm and his educational advantages were limited indeed. On the 28th of May, 1840, he was united in marriage with Miss Sarah E. Rider, of Monroe County, Tenn., the daughter of Alexander and Rachael A. (Talbot) Rider, also natives of that State. Mr. Rider died Jan. 1, 1872. Eight children have been born to Mr. and Mrs. Peck: Thomas J. is now deceased; James Monroe is engaged in the livery business in Ottumwa; Andrew J. is engaged in the same business at South Ottumwa; Mary, George M., John H. and Charles F. are deceased; Martha J., the wife of Henry P. Mudge, lives at Council Bluffs.

In the fall of 1841, with his wife and one child, Mr. Peck moved overland from Tennessee to Mt. Pleasant, Henry Co., Iowa, by means of two horses and a wagon, being seven weeks on the road. In the fall of 1842 he came to what is now Wapello County, and selected a claim. On this he subsequently erected a cabin in which he moved, and when the land came into market he entered 165 acres at $1.25 per acre. Upon this farm he has since continued to reside. The old log house has since been replaced by one of the neatest farm dwellings in Wapello County, together with a good barn and all necessary out-buildings. He has made a specialty of stock-raising, including graded Short-horn cattle and Hambletonian horses, and is now breeding the Norman stock, of which he has now upon the farm some very fine roadsters.

Upon the organization of the county, Mr. Peck was appointed the first Sheriff, and held the office until the next general election. In politics he has always been a stanch supporter of the principles of the Democratic party, and socially belongs to the I. O. O. F.

HENRY DORNSIFE, a successful farmer and dairyman, residing on section 26, Washington Township, is a native of Lewistown, Pa., where he was born Nov. 20, 1819. He is a son of Romanus and Catherine (Atler) Dornsife, both natives of Germany. They emigrated to the United States in 1817, where the father of our subject followed the trade of a blacksmith until his demise, which event occurred in Lewistown, Pa., in 1827. His good wife died in Maryland about the year 1851.

After the death of his father our subject went to live with his uncle, Henry Dornsife, and made that his home until he attained the age of manhood. It was there that he learned the trade of blacksmith under the instruction of his uncle, and worked at the same until 1841. During that year he went to Ohio, and while there, in 1844, he was united in marriage with Martha A. Trego, born in Ross County, that State, in 1820. By this union six children were born—Jerome, Napoleon, Wellington, Rosa, Alice and Frances. The mother died in 1858, four years after our subject had left Ohio and made settlement in Agency Township, this county, on what is known as Agency Farm.

In 1859 Mr. Dornsife formed a second matrimonial alliance, Mrs. Jane M. Harris, born in Switzerland, Ind., April 24, 1829, being the other contracting party. Of this latter union four children—Clara, Mattie, May and Lewie—have been born. As intimated Mr. Dornsife came to this county in 1854, from Pickaway County, Ohio, and has made this his residence until the present time. He is a blacksmith, also a wagon and carriage maker, and followed the manufacture of wagons and buggies for a number of years, making shipments as far west as Oregon, and has the reputation of being one of the very best horse-shoers in the State of Iowa. This latter trade he certainly ought to be proficient in for he has followed it upward of forty years.

Mr. Dornsife is at present the owner of 100 acres of finely improved land, on which he has a frame residence, a good barn and substantial out-buildings, and all necessary improvements used in the carrying on of a well-improved farm. He and his wife are consistent Christians and hold fellowship with the Methodist Episcopal Church. A lithographic view of his residence is shown on another page.

C H. PROSSER, of Center Township, owns and occupies a snug homestead on section 2, where he has prosecuted farming since locating here in 1886. From a tract of uncultivated land he has opened up a fine farm and ranks among the best residents of this section.

Mr. Prosser is a native of Pittsburgh, Pa., and was born in 1845, being the son of John and Margaret (Gittins) Prosser, natives respectively of Wales and Pennsylvania. His father emigrated to the United States in 1832, and settled in Philadelphia, Pa., whence he removed to Pittsburgh, where he was married, and where the subject of our sketch received his early education. When he was a lad of eleven years the latter came to Iowa with his parents, arriving in Wapello County on the 14th of June, 1856. They located in Ottumwa, where they lived for about fourteen months, and then took possession of a tract of land in Center

Township, where they established a comfortable home and spent the remainder of their days.

In 1869, at the age of twenty-four years, young Prosser was united in marriage with Miss Hester Golden, a native of Mercer County, Pa., and the daughter of James Golden, of England. Of this union there were born seven children, viz., Margaret R., Fannie Esther, Mollie, Warren Henry, Frederick William, Christopher Golden and Grace Elva.

During the progress of the late Civil War, Mr. Prosser enlisted as a soldier of the Union Army on the 12th of January, 1863. On account of disability he was not permitted to serve, but not considering the reason sufficient, he proffered his services in another regiment, the 36th Iowa, Company H, in which he served twenty-two months or until the close of the war. He participated in several minor engagements, and after peace had been declared, returned to his family in Center Township. He engaged in milling twelve miles south of Ottumwa the following year, and after being thus occupied for twelve months, disposed of his interest there and engaged in the same business at Richmond until 1872, when he abandoned milling and was occupied in farm pursuits for the following two and a half years. After this he became a resident of Monroe County for five years, and then returned to the farm in Center Township, where he has since resided and been industriously engaged in the varied duties of an agriculturist. Politically Mr. Prosser endorses the principles of the Republican party, and religiously he is connected with the Methodist Episcopal Church.

GEORGE GRISWOLD, attorney at law of Ottumwa, and a native of Wayne County, N. Y., removed from his native State, in 1851, with his parents, and proceeding westward crossed the Mississippi into the Hawkeye State, of which he has since been a resident. He has distinguished himself as a leading citizen, a man of honor and honesty, and enjoys the respect and esteem of his fellow-townsmen in a marked degree. The birth of our subject occurred on the 10th of January, 1836, his parents being William H. an Sallie (Onderdonk) Griswold, natives of the same State as their son. William Griswold was Democratic in politics and a prominent man in whatever locality he made his home. He had been an officeholder in his native State, and after coming to Iowa was a member of the State Legislature in 1855–56, during the last session held in Iowa City. He was a man of fine abilities, an extensive reader, and well posted in the affairs of his county and the country at large. At the breaking out of the Rebellion he was decidedly on the side of the North, and was known as a War Democrat. After a busy life filled with good deeds he departed this life in May, 1884, at the advanced age of eighty years. His wife, the mother of our subject, is still living, and is seventy-seven years of age.

The household circle of the parents of our subject included nine children, five sons and four daughters, all of whom, with one exception, lived to adult years, and six are still surviving. Henry and James are engaged in agricultural pursuits in Lee County, Iowa; Charles is in Montana; George, our subject, is the next in order of birth; Almira is the wife of C. T. Moon, of Lee County, Iowa, and Mary married D. F. Miller, an attorney at law of Ottumwa.

George Griswold completed his education in the literary and law department of the Iowa State University in 1874, after close application and long-continued study. He was united in marriage with Miss Mary L. Morgan, in 1864. Mrs. G. is the daughter of T. A. and Sylvia Morgan, of Wapello County, and also a graduate of the State University of Iowa. Of this union there were born eight children, two sons and six daughters, as follows: Morgan, Edna, Daisy, George and May (twins), Ann, Alice and Myra. Mr. and Mrs. G. have given their children excellent educational advantages, and they are regular attendants of the Episcopal Church, of which Mr. and Mrs. G. are members in good standing.

After graduating from the State University Mr. Griswold was admitted to the bar in Iowa City, and received his certificate to practice in all the courts of the State. Before completing his studies he had been actively engaged in the cause of education, and for a time occupied the position of Principal of the schools at Ft. Madison. He first read law in the office of Judge Beck, of Ft. Madison, and before he commenced the practice of his profession was Deputy Clerk of Wapello County, Iowa, for four years, and then drifted into the abstract business.

The Griswolds are an old and prominent family, and from the records which have been preserved for several generations we extract the following concerning the ancestry of our subject: Edward Griswold, whose name stands at the head of the record, was born in Wales and descended from Welsh ancestry. He removed to England in early life, where he married and spent the remainder of his days. He became the father of four sons—Mathew, Thomas, John and George. By his request all emigrated to America, landing at Saybrook, at the mouth of the Connecticut River, where Mathew and George located; Thomas settled at Windsor, and John at Weathersfield, Vt. Mathew afterward went to the settlement of Lyme, opposite Saybrook. The Lyme branch of the family became distinguished as having furnished two Governors of Connecticut—Mathew, who married a daughter of Gov. Roger Wolcott, and Roger Griswold, who first was a Member of Congress and afterward Governor. A sketch of these may be seen on page 33 of "Connecticut Historical Collections."

John Griswold, the son of George and grandson of Edward, was born at Saybrook, and married Miss Isabella Price, the daughter of Col. Walter Price, and settled at Killingworth, where they both spent the remainder of their lives. Their son, Daniel Griswold, was also born at Killingworth, where he spent his entire life; he married Miss Jerusha Stevens. Capt. Daniel Griswold, the son of the last mentioned, was born in Killingworth Dec. 1, 1729. He commanded a company of Connecticut militia during the French War, and married Miss Mary Bushnell, in Saybrook, in October, 1750. He removed to Fairfield, Herkimer Co., N. Y., forty years later, and there died on the 10th of May, 1814. His wife died the following year, on the 5th of February, at the same place. Their sons were named Edward, John, Francis, Aaron, Simeon and William, all now deceased, William, the youngest, having departed this life Nov. 15, 1853.

Simeon Griswold, son of Daniel, Jr., was born in Killingworth in 1773. He married Miss Rachel Willard at Fairfield, Herkimer Co., N. Y., in 1797; they became the parents of eleven children: John, Aaron, Horatio, William H. (the father of the subject of this sketch, and who was named after William Hurd who married his father's sister), Alfred, Simeon, Sallie, Maria, Joseph, Lorenzo and James H.

The record of the Willard family, ancestors of the mother of our subject, is as follows: Maj. Simon Willard, the first of the name in America, was a native of the county of Kent, England, from which he emigrated in about 1830, and settled in Concord, near Boston, Mass. He was one of the most distinguished leaders in the settlement of that town. He traded with the Indians and assisted in making the first purchase of land from them. He was for a time Town Clerk, and was subsequently a member of the Colonial Legislature.

In 1660 Simon Willard removed to Lancaster, and was promoted to the rank of Major, having command of the Massachusetts force in the Phillip's War. He superintended the construction of the military defenses in the several towns, and in other ways rendered important services during that period. His first wife was Miss Mary Sharp, and his second, Miss Elizabeth Dunstan, a sister of President Dunstan, of Harvard College. His third marriage was with Miss Mary Dunstan, a sister of his second wife, and of the three marriages he became the father of seventeen children, nine sons and eight daughters. His eldest son, Josiah, was the ancestor of the Connecticut branch of the family whose descendants settled in Hartford, Weathersfield, Killingworth and Saybrook. Josiah, the son of Samuel, settled in Saybrook, and was the father of Col. Samuel Willard and Charles. He was a lawyer by profession and held the office of District Attorney of Middlesex County. The Samuels all died and were buried near each other in the old burial-ground at Saybrook where their monuments are still to be seen. Joseph Willard was born in Saybrook June 16, 1750. He had two brothers, Nathaniel and Samuel, the latter of whom was taken prisoner by the British in the Revolutionary War and died on board the old Jersey prison-ship in New York Harbor. Joseph married Miss Rachel Reeves, and moved to Fairfield, Herkimer Co., N. Y., in 1795, where he died in 1832, and his wife in 1829. Their family consisted of four sons and four daughters, of whom two sons and two daughters are still living.

H. J. DUNCAN, Deputy United States Marshal of the Southern District of Iowa, is one of the most esteemed residents of Ottumwa, respected alike for his business talents and his innate worth of character. Mr. Duncan is a native of Missouri, and was born in the little city of Linnville on the 28th of October, 1847. He is the son of Thomas H. P. and Susan (Browner) Duncan, both natives of Kentucky, who removed across the Mississippi and settled in Missouri at an early period in the history of that State. Mr. Duncan was engaged in mercantile pursuits for many years in Mercer County, Mo., being the first merchant to establish trade in that section. His store was located on the State line, one half in Missouri and the other half in Iowa. He was a gentleman of great energy and enterprise, and became one of the leading business men of Mercer County. He was also a slave-holder, and at the time of the border war, resulting from the attempt to extend slavery into Iowa and Kansas, he was given a certain length of time to get his slaves over into Missouri.

The parental household of our subject included six children—three sons and three daughters—of whom the record is as follows: William D. is deceased; Basil B., at the time of the rebellion in Cuba, went into that locality, was commissioned Captain, and when last heard from was in South America; H. J. is our subject; Mary M. became the wife of J. Wilson, of Des Moines; Nora E. married Hugh Week, of Bonaparte. Thomas H. P. Duncan departed this life in 1866. His wife, the mother of our subject, is still living at the old homestead in Mercer County, Mo.

The subject of this biography received his early education in the schools of Mt. Pleasant, which was limited to an attendance of two terms. His natural love of books, however, inclined him to employ his leisure moments profitably, and his inquiring mind resulted in his possession of a fund of knowledge superior to that of many who had the privilege of obtaining a collegiate education. He is thoroughly posted in regard to matters of public interest, has a retentive memory, and is remarkably interesting to converse with.

The marriage of Mr. Duncan occurred in Ottumwa, in December, 1870, the maiden of his choice being Miss Kate Dunnett, of Ohio, and they became the parents of three children—Hazzie, Eddie and Harry J., Jr. They are pleasantly located in Ottumwa, and are surrounded by all the comforts of life.

Mr. Duncan received the appointment of Deputy United States Marshal in 1880, and after the resignation of the Marshal he was continued in the office under Edward Campbell, Chief Marshal, and has fulfilled the duties of his position in a manner reflecting credit upon himself and the good judgment of those who secured his appointment. In politics he is a staunch supporter of the Democratic party, decided in his views, and fearless in the expression of those principles which he believes to be synonymus with truth and justice.

LEWIS COBLER, an old and respected resident of Highland Township, in former years owned an extensive tract of land and was successfully engaged in farming and stock-raising. He is now retired from active labor, and is spending the sunset of life in the comfort and quiet which he has justly earned by habits of industry and economy.

Our subject was born in Adams County, Ohio, in 1810, and is the son of David and Anna (Freeman) Cobler, natives respectively of Pennsylvania and Maryland. He was reared to farming pursuits, and in 1828 left his native State and went to Indiana, where he located on the Wabash River, near La Fayette, and lived for fifteen years. His marriage took place Nov. 7, 1833, the maiden of his choice being Miss Nancy Travis, a native of Scioto County, Ohio, who became the mother of six children. The record is as follows: Mary Ann became the wife of Jacob Goudy, of Nebraska; David lives in Wapello County; Edie who married Henry Miller, and Sarepta, Mrs. Jackson Harman, live in Pleasant Township; Minerva married Mr. James Work, and they live in the north part of the State; Rhoda Jane, Mrs. Thomas Rhiner, lives in Dahlonega Township. The mother of these children, who was born in January, 1813, died Jan. 6, 1873.

Mr. Cobler commenced life a poor boy, and earned his first money by grubbing stumps at twenty-five cents per day. He climbed up, however, step by step, and in due time became the owner of 483 acres of land. He assisted his children to start in life, and is a hale, hearty and happy old gentleman, enjoying the esteem of his community and taking abundant comfort in the consciousness of a well-spent life.

David Cobler, son of the above-mentioned gentleman, is pleasantly located in Highland Township, and is carrying on agriculture and stock-raising in an intelligent and successful manner. He makes a specialty of raising mules, and usually keeps a stable of twenty fine specimens, ready for the market. His farm consists of 325 acres of valuable land on section 29, which he has brought to a fine state of cultivation.

David Cobler was born in Tippecanoe County, Ind., in 1837, and has been a resident of Wapello County since 1842. He received a limited education as the school facilities in the place of his birth were few. After arriving at years of manhood he was united in marriage in 1861, to Miss Guelma Hoover, a native of Indiana, and by whom he became the father of five children: One died in infancy; Emma became Mrs. Elwood Buckner, and Marion lives in Highland Township; Charlie and Lewis are at home. The mother of these children died in 1872, and the following year Mr. Cobler was married to Miss Sarah Belle Hedrick, of this county. Of this marriage there were also born five children as follows, all at home: Mary, Katie, Frederick, Elizabeth and David J.

Mr. Cobler and his family occupy a handsome farm dwelling (a view of which appears on another page), and are surrounded by all the comforts of life. He is the stanch friend of education, is a member of the School Board, and the supporter and encourager of every measure calculated to promote the welfare of his community.

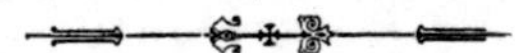

DANIEL ZOLLARS, one of the prosperous and highly respected citizens of Ottumwa, has been a resident of Wapello County for over thirty-three years and has fully established himself in the respect and confidence of his fellow-citizens. In early life he was engaged in farming pursuits, and after coming to this county purchased 330 acres of land near Eddyville, which was mostly unimproved. He there erected a steam sawmill, as it was impossible to get lumber to improve with, and was patronized by people living a great distance from the mill. He also purchased land in the city limits of Ottumwa, which he laid off into town lots and sold, the proceeds yielding him a handsome profit, while at the same time the property furnished comfortable and economical homes to the enterprising members of the rapidly growing community. He has laid off four additions to the city of five acres, and three other additions of twenty acres each, and he still owns a farm of 100 acres in Washington Township besides 200 acres near Centerville and a valuable lot fronting the public square in Albia.

The subject of our sketch was born in Pennsylvania in 1808, and is the son of John and Frances (Hahn) Zollars. When he was four years old his parents moved to Harrison County, Ohio, where our subject was reared on a farm and lived until he came to Iowa in 1854. His parents settled about ten miles west of Ottumwa, and he lived with them there ten years, engaged in farming pursuits. He was a young men of energy and enterprise, as will be seen by the foregoing history, and in a brief time became prominently identified with the business and industrial interests of this section.

The marriage of Mr. Zollars and Miss Mary A. Druckamiller took place on the 7th of June, 1831, in Ohio. Mrs. Z. was a native of Harrison County, that State, and the daughter of Frederick and Margaret (Winings) Druckamiller, both natives of Pennsylvania. Of this union there were born seven children, only three of whom are now living: William died Jan. 27, 1872, at the age of thirty-nine years; Elmira is the wife of Isaac Millisack, of Ottumwa; Sarah J. married James Stevenson, and died in Kirkville in 1860; Thomas J., born July 7, 1839, is an insurance agent of Denver, Col.; he served three years as Captain in the 4th Iowa Cavalry, being at the siege and capture of Vicksburg, and participating with his regiment in the various engagements until the close of the war. He finished his education at Wesleyan University, Mt. Pleasant, Iowa; Malinda died at the age of two years; Margaret became the wife of Joseph Harman, of Ottumwa; Emma died at the age of ten years.

Mr. Zollars commenced life a poor boy, at the foot of the ladder, and has climbed up to his present position solely by the exercise of his own native talents. In early life he was trained to habits of industry, and has never considered it a hardship or a disgrace to engage in honest labor. He has been an important factor in the growth and development of this section, and is one of the valued members of the community. Mr. and Mrs. Z. are members of the Methodist Episcopal Church, and politically Mr. Z. votes with the Republican party.

FRANK DUNGAN, Mayor of the city of Ottumwa, is a gentleman of decided ability, finely educated, well informed, and accredited by all as being admirably adapted to the responsible position which he occupies. He is a native of Beaver County, Pa., the date of his birth being July 30, 1848. His parents were George W. and Nancy (Ferris) Dungan, both natives of Pennsylvania. They removed from their native State to Iowa in 1856, and located in Knoxville, Marion County, where the father of our subject was occupied as a miller for the following six years. His mill then being destroyed by fire, he removed to Chariton, Lucas County, which remained his home until he departed from the scene of his earthly labors. His wife, the mother of our subject, is still living in Ottumwa. The parental household consisted of six children, five of whom are living, viz.: Frank, our subject; Edwin, a grocer of Ottumwa; Mary, the wife of Chancey Smith, a native of Buffalo, N. Y.; Horace, a locating agent for the Lombard Investment Company, and William D., Cashier of the Lombard Investment Company, of Sioux City, and closely resembling his father in point of intellect and ability.

Mayor Dungan was eight years of age when his parents came to the Hawkeye State. His early education was somewhat limited, and at the age of thirteen years he entered the store of O. L. Palmer, as clerk, at Chariton, Iowa, with whom he remained until he was of suitable age to engage in business for himself, when he became a partner of O. L. Palmer, with whom he continued until 1872, and then came to Ottumwa. He then decided to go across the plains to California, with the intention of making his future home in the Golden State. He was not, however, satisfied with his experience on the Pacific coast, and being disappointed in finding a desirable location, returned to Iowa and engaged as a traveling salesman for the firm of Lawrence & Garner. At the expiration of two years he purchased the interest of Mr. G., and the latter retiring, the firm became Lawrence & Dungan, who continued the business as wholesale dealers in dry-goods, boots and shoes. In July, 1883, Mr. D. was identified with the organization of Manning, Cushing & Co., wholesale boot-and-shoe firm, with which he was connected for the following two years, and closely following upon this, in March, 1886, Mr. D. was elected Mayor of Ottumwa, which position he has filled with great discretion and dignity.

The subject of our sketch was united in marriage with Miss Nellie Godfrey, in May, 1872. Mrs. D. is a daughter of George Godfrey, a native of Indiana, and was born in this city in August, 1854. They have become the parents of one child, a daughter, Matie. They occupy a handsome residence and are surrounded by the comforts and refinements of life.

Mr. D. is connected with the Masonic fraternity as a member of Empire Lodge No. 269, and also belongs to Clinton Chapter No. 12. He is a member of the K. of P., Wapello Lodge No. 12, of which he has held the position of Treasurer for two years. He was a charter member of the Modern Woodmen of America in this locality and holds the office of Grand Consul in this order. Mr. Dungan proposes to enter extensively into the manufacture of the miner's coal drill, a new patent, after his term of office as Mayor expires in March next, locating their business in Ottumwa.

HON. GREGG A. MADISON, retired from an active business career, and passing the sunset of life in peace and quiet, in the enjoyment of a splendid competency, at Ottumwa, Iowa, was born in Juniata County, Pa., Feb. 22, 1818. The parents of our subject, Joseph and Agnes (Alzeo) Madison, were born on the Emerald Isle, and both natives of County Tyrone, whence they emigrated to the United States in childhood. They were married in this country, and became the parents of eleven children, of whom the subject of this notice is the youngest.

Gregg Madison received but a limited education, as there were no free schools in the locality in which his parents resided, and the time passed in the school-room hardly exceeded a year. He labored to assist in the maintenance of the family, and when seventeen years of age served an apprenticeship of three years to the wagon-making trade with Samuel Riddle, of Mifflin, Pa. While following his trade in Huntingdon County, Pa., he made the acquaintance of a German scholar, and a teacher in the seminary at Huntingdon. From this gentleman Mr. Madison received instruction in his studies, and made considerable progress. He subsequently studied law, and was admitted to the bar at Huntingdon in 1848. He now had a profession but an empty pocket, and not being able to secure clients, or rather to pay board and wait for them, he secured a job of rafting timber on the rivers for bridges for the Pennsylvania Central Railroad, which was then in process of construction. The company formed such a good opinion of our subject that when he had finished his contract they hired him by the month, paying him $40, which they increased from year to year, and at the expiration of five years he was the recipient of the handsome salary of $3,500, and was presented by the company with $500 in cash besides.

In 1856 Mr. Madison came to Iowa, arriving at Ottumwa on the first day of July. He had at that time about $10,000 in money besides some real estate, and at once erected the first circular steam sawmill in this part of the State, locating it in Davis County, near the Wapello County line, and operated it with signal success for about two years. Upon the breaking out of the late Civil War our subject raised a goodly number of men and accompanied them to Keokuk, where they were divided into two companies, and John M. Hedrick was made Captain of Company K, and Mr. Madison of Company D. The latter was Captain prior to the division of the men, but as he had about 170 men after the division it was necessary to organize a new company. His company was mustered into service with the 15th regiment, and he served as Captain of the same until 1863, when he resigned his commission, because he was not the man to tolerate imposition even from a superior officer. While in the army he participated in the battles of Shiloh, Iuka and Corinth. His men never smelled powder except Capt. Madison was with them and inhaled it at the same time. He was a brave soldier, but, on account of jealousy, other officers were jumped over him in rank, and Capt. Madison resigned. Returning home from the war our subject purchased a steam sawmill, which he operated in connection with his farming for a number of years, and then, in company with J. G. Baker and Tolon Grey, took a contract for the furnishing of ties for the C., B. & Q. R. R., and furnished upward of 300,000 ties for that company.

In 1880 Capt. Madison went to Texas, where he took a contract for the delivery of lumber and ties to the Texas Pacific Railroad. He was occupied in the fulfilling of this contract for about three years, when he returned to Ottumwa, and has since resided here. Mr. Madison is at present the owner of about 1,600 acres of land in Wapello County, about 1,000 acres in Hancock and Cerro Gordo Counties, 100 acres in Davis County, and about 3,000 acres in Texas. He has rented all of his land which is under cultivation.

In politics Capt. Madison is a Democrat. He

represented his district in the General Assembly in 1875–76, and was also a member of the Senate in 1878–80. His term expired in the Senate while he was in Texas, or he no doubt would have been re-elected. He was elected Mayor of Ottumwa in 1884, and re-elected in 1885. He was a candidate for the Senate in 1885, and was defeated by only twenty-one votes.

Capt. Madison was united in marriage with Miss Sarah J. Livingtone in 1863. She was a native of Indiana, and has borne our subject three children, all daughters: Ellen married Anson Headley, telegraph operator for the C., R. I. & P. R. R. at Keokuk; Mary is the wife of Harry Reigg, an engineer on the C., B. & Q. R. R.; Rhoda resides at home. Mr. Madison has never connected himself with any secret society. His success in life is due to his own good judgment and energetic perseverance.

CAPT. GEORGE P. NORRIS, an honored resident of the city of Ottumwa, crossed the Mississippi in 1845, and came into Iowa while it was yet a Territory, thus being entitled to rank among the pioneers of the Hawkeye State. He was born in Compton, Canada, on the 13th of May, 1831, and is the son of Samuel S. Norris (see sketch elsewhere in this book), and when a lad of six years old went with his parents from the Dominion into the State of New Hampshire, thence removing to Bloomington, Ill., where they remained for about seven or eight years, and then proceeded farther westward, locating in Ottumwa.

The early education of our subject was received in the common schools, and after completing his studies there he attended two terms at Knox College, in Galesburg, Ill. Several years later, in 1852, he started across the plains to Sacramento, Cal. He drove an ox-team, and starting out on the 13th of May, arrived at Hangtown, now Placerville, on the 15th of October. At this place he entered the mines, and the first pan of dirt which he washed out contained gold to the value of $2.50. He remained in that vicinity, operating along Spanish Gulch and Coon Hill for a period of six years, then, in 1858, returned to Iowa via the Isthmus of Panama and New York.

In 1861, Mr. Norris having come westward to Iowa, was united in marriage on the 18th of June with Miss Roxey Murray. Mrs. Norris is the daughter of George, Jr., and Wealthy (Landon) Murray, who was born at Clinton, N. Y., Nov. 22, 1799, and died on the 17th of January, 1886. Mr. Murray was born Nov. 5, 1800, and departed this life in 1851, at Youngstown, Ohio, where he had located in 1836. The parental family of Mrs. Norris consisted of eight children, five of whom are living, as follows: Helen became the wife of H. S. Doolittle, of Decatur, Ala.; Eliza married B. A. Darby, of Meadville, Pa., and Gertrude became Mrs. Calvin G. Packard, of Missouri Valley, Iowa; Roxey became the wife of our subject, and George W. lives in Rochester, N. Y.; he served as a soldier in the Union army and was a member of the 47th Iowa Infantry, losing both eyes in the service

Mr. and Mrs. Norris became the parents of six children, as follows: James W., Jr., was born April 6, 1862; Mary F., born July 7, 1865, became the wife of Edward Loomis, of Ottumwa; Frederick L. was born June 17, 1867; Nettie W., May 3, 1870; Helen A., Oct. 7, 1876; Julia R., July 30, 1880.

During the progress of the late war Mr. Norris, in April, 1862, enlisted in Co. E, 7th Iowa Vol. Cav., which company he assisted in raising, and was commissioned First Lieutenant. He served four years, or until the close of the war, and was mustered out on the 17th day of May, 1866, at Ft. Leavenworth, Kan., after having made a good record and receiving decided manifestations of approval from his superior officers. After the close of his military services Mr. Norris returned to Ottumwa and, on account of his son's health, went to Scott County, Minn., and was engaged in milling for the following ten years. His son then having recovered, he returned to Ottumwa.

Mr. Norris has been identified with the interests of Wapello County for a period of forty-two years, and has viewed with pride and pleasure the rapid development of its resources and the onward march of civilization. He has aided in the best manner possible in promoting its educational facilities, and has been a stanch friend of temperance, morality and good order. He is held in the highest respect in this community for his worth and liberality.

L. A. Myers

Mrs L. A. Myers

L. A. MYERS, one of the earliest and most highly respected pioneers of Wapello County, will be found on section 15, Washington Township. He is a native of Preble County, Ohio, and was born Dec. 2, 1811. In 1830 he moved with his parents to Elkhart County, Ind., and in 1842 visited the Territory of Iowa with a view of locating, but did not remain. In December, 1844, he again visited Iowa, and purchased a claim of 320 acres in what is now Washington Township, Wapello County. On the 6th day of October, 1833, he married Rachel Beck, born Aug. 14, 1811, in Kentucky. To this union there were born eight children: Morris B., June 24, 1834; Mary E., now the wife of Chilon L. Dickson, born Sept. 8, 1839; Eli W., Feb. 24, 1843; Ira A., March 5, 1845; Sarah A., wife of William Clark, born Dec. 25, 1837, died June 11, 1867; Christopher A.; John F. and F. E. died in infancy. Mrs. Myers died Nov. 27, 1846, and on the 20th of January, 1848, Mr. Myers married Miss E. M. McNatt, born in Roane County, Tenn., March 9, 1824, moved with her parents to Elkhart County, Ind., in 1832, and to Wapello County, Iowa, in 1845. To this union twelve children were born: Rachel M., now Mrs. Acton, Dec. 29, 1848; Joseph N., June 8, 1850; Augusta I., now Mrs. Manro, May 12, 1853; George M., July 27, 1859; Luna A., now the wife of A. E. Hodgdon, June 16, 1863; Iva L., Dec. 10, 1865; Leota E., Oct. 27, 1867; Victor A., Aug. 5, 1870; Ellen J., Ida J., Louis A. and James E. died in infancy. E. W. enlisted in February, 1862, in Co. E, 17th Iowa Vol. Inf., and served three years.

Mr. Myers has been honored by his fellow-citizens with about all the township offices. He was ten years Justice of the Peace and four years a member of the County Board of Supervisors. For fifty years he has been a consistent member of the Methodist Episcopal Church. Politically he is a Democrat. The following is a portion of a very interesting reminiscence written by Mr. Myers for one of the local papers:

"My great-grandfather Myers came from Germany before the Revolutionary War, and settled in Pennsylvania, where my grandfather Myers was born. When he became a man he went to North Carolina and married Miss Fogleman, by whom he had two children—George, the elder, and Christopher, the younger. My father was born near Guilford Court House, N. C., March 8, 1776, just 111 years ago. When he arrived at the age of twenty-one he and his brother George left North Carolina and went across the mountains to Powell's Valley, Tenn., where he married my mother, Elizabeth Nation, who had been raised in South Carolina. They were married in 1802. They lived in Tennessee until 1811, when they moved to Preble County, Ohio, and stopped five miles east of Eaton, where I was born. My father bought 160 acres of land in the northeast corner of the county, and there moved in the fall of 1812, the year hostilities commenced between this country and Great Britain. His cabin stood on the very outskirts of the settlement. He now had seven small children to care for, the oldest being but about ten years of age, and that too in a heavily timbered country, a perfect wilderness. Here they had no church or school privileges, and were liable to be scalped by the Indians, who were then in large numbers in Ohio. Great Britain had hired these Indians to scalp the defenseless settlers, paying them a bounty on each white scalp, just as we now pay for a wolf scalp. As my parents were there the only chance was to go to work and clear up land and raise grain and flax, the one for food and the other for clothing. My mother at that time spun and wove linen and tow cloth for clothing for the entire family, and through all these trials and hardships was kept by a kind Providence. I will relate one or two incidents that took place during the War of 1812, as they were told me by my father and mother in after years. In 1813, during harvest time, when the men of the neighborhood were helping one of their number to reap his grain, the Indians drove the horses of one of my father's neighbors into his own stable, caught them, took them off about one mile and shot them. The colts would not follow their mothers, and their mothers kept up such a neighing for them that the Indians became frightened, and for that cause shot them. That same night the Indians came back and stole all the horses my father had, and as they took them away the next day they met a man by the name of Stoner and shot him. After going a few miles further they met a soldier by the name of Elliott, who was returning home on a furlough from Ft. Greenville. The Indians shot this soldier through the wrist, and then had a regular hand-to-hand fight with him with their tomahawks, around a beech-tree, and finally succeeded in killing him. It was thought there were three or four of the Indians and one white man in the company, and the soldier killed all of them but one. I have often seen this beech-tree with the marks of the tomahawks made in the fight. In the spring of 1830 my father sold out, and in the fall of the same year moved to Elkhart County, Ind., which was then a new country. The Indians were quite numerous there, but peaceably inclined. I lived with my parents until the fall of 1833, when I married and settled on Elkhart Plains and made a farm. In the spring of 1846 I sold out, and started for Wapello County, Iowa, where I landed on the 9th of September, and settled on the farm where I now live, about two miles north of Eldon. In November of that year my wife died, leaving me with five small children, in a strange land. The friends and neighbors were very kind to me in my affliction. I went to work, made rails, hauled them, and fenced my farm, and have now 250 acres under fence."

In 1851 Mr. Myers erected a brick dwelling, at a cost of $1,800, and in 1861 built his large barn at a cost of $2,200. He has now one of the best improved farms in Wapello County, and is surrounded by all the comforts of life. A view of his home is presented in this volume. For over forty years he has lived in this community, indeed the community has grown up around him. As a venerable patriarch, and one who has done much hard work and given much valuable aid to the county and the molding of the character of the people, his memory should be cherished and preserved. It will live in the minds of those who know him personally as long as they live, but the generations to come will know nothing of his labors, his trials, and good works, unless some means are taken to hand down to them a record of his life. This brief sketch and the accompanying portrait will therefore serve as a means to perpetuate his memory. As a fitting companion picture we also give that of his estimable wife.

BENNET S. SHAUG, M. D., a popular and successful physician of Eldon Village, is a gentleman skilled in his profession, an extensive reader, generally well informed, and possessed of a varied and valuable experience during the changes of a long and busy life. He is a native of Mason County, Va., and was born July 22, 1826, his parents being Dr. William Henry and Hannah (Sherwood) Shaug, natives respectively of Pennsylvania and Connecticut, the father born in 1792, the mother in 1801. Our subject received careful parental training, and during his boyhood days attended the common schools. After attaining manhood he left the parental roof, and going to Cincinnati, Ohio, secured employment in a drug-store for about six months, and then took a place as cabin-boy on a steamer of the Mississippi River, where he continued four months, and then crossing the Father of Waters, came into Iowa, stopping at Montrose for a short time and then, returning eastward, passed through Galena, Ill., to Farmington, remaining in the latter place until the 19th of April, 1847. He attended school here for a time, and at the opening of the Mexican War enlisted as a soldier under Col. Morgan, of Ohio, in Company K, 15th Regiment. He went with his regiment to New Orleans, whence they proceeded to Vera Cruz, where they were soon engaged in battle.

Our subject was soon afterward detailed as Hospital Steward at Castle Perote, and afterward went to the city of Mexico, where, after remaining three months, his regiment was ordered to Cerre Vaca, skirmishing all the time upon the march there, and remained there until peace was declared, our subject finally receiving his discharge at Covington, Ky., Aug. 4, 1848. He then returned to Farmington, Iowa, and commenced the study of medicine. He then came into Wapello County, and continued his studies under the instruction of Dr. C. W. Shaug, of Agency City, and after completing his studies commenced the practice of his profession in Corydon, Wayne Co., Iowa, where he remained until the fall of 1853, when he went to Keokuk and attended the Medical College. He then returned to Agency City, and from there went into Webster County, practicing at Homer until 1858. Thence he went to Mt. Sterling, Van Buren County, where he remained two years, and was very successful. From there he went to Adair County, Mo., and practiced until the spring of 1861, and thence returned to Farmington, where he was located until February, 1864. The Civil War being then in progress, he enlisted as a private in Co. B, 3d Iowa Vol. Cav., and marched toward the southeast with his regiment. At Memphis, Tenn., he was promoted Assistant Surgeon of his regiment, which position he held until the battle of Little Rock, Ark., in the fall of 1864, when he was made Assistant Surgeon of his camp at that place, and was transferred to the position of Hospital Steward, and served in this capacity until the close of the war, when he was mustered out at Atlanta, Ga., on the 9th of August, 1865, and received his discharge at Camp McClellan, Iowa.

After his return from the army Dr. Shaug resumed his practice at Farmington until 1881. He then purchased a stock of groceries, and opened up a store at Winchester, Iowa, and continued in trade until 1883, when he came to Eldon, which has been his home since that time. Dr. Shaug was married in August, 1852, to Miss May J. Myers, of Elkhart County, Ind. Of this union there have been born nine children, two living: La Fayette, a cigar-maker, now in Dallas, Tex., and Leonidas, who is with his parents in Eldon.

ISRAEL ZENTZ, a farmer and stock-grower on section 9, Richland Township, was born in Blair County, Pa., April 8, 1816, and is the son of Jacob and Elizabeth Zeitz, who both died in Blair County before Israel was old enough to have any recollection of them. On the death of his parents he was taken and reared by his Grandmother Zeitz, with whom he lived until he was about eighteen years old, when she died in Washington County, Pa. In 1843 Mr. Zeitz was united in marriage with Jane Greenlee, born April 1, 1815, daughter of John Greenlee, of Washington County, Pa. Five children were born of this union: Ebenezer (deceased), John G., Elizabeth, Finley H. and Leander, the latter also deceased. Mrs. Zeitz died in Wapello County, Feb. 16, 1874. Mr. Zeitz subsequently married Catherine Ruffcorn, widow of Cyrus Ruffcorn; her maiden name was Davidson.

In 1851 Mr. Zeitz moved from Pennsylvania to Champaign County, Ohio, where he remained until 1857, and then removed to Wapello County, where he has since continued to reside. He is the owner of 160 acres of fine land, all of which is under improvement. At present he makes a specialty of breeding graded Short-horn cattle, and it is said, has the best Clydesdale and Norman horses in the township. He has also three blood mares and a large number of Poland-China hogs. It will thus be seen that he believes in having the best stock, and that it is far more profitable. Everything about his farm is kept in the best of order. He is certainly a No. 1 farmer. Mr. and Mrs. Zeitz are members of the Presbyterian Church. Politically he is a Republican.

JACOB SEDORE, a prominent farmer and stock-grower of Keokuk Township, has been a resident of the Hawkeye State since 1846, and has materially assisted in the development of this section of Wapello County. He is a native of the populous and wealthy State of Ohio, was born March 24, 1841, and received his early impressions in life among the hills of the Buckeye State.

The first purchase of Mr. Sedore in the Hawkeye State was a claim of sixty-six acres in Wapello County. He possessed the true pioneer spirit which enabled him to overcome the difficulties encountered in the settlement of a new country, and was prospered in his labors. As time passed on he added to his first purchase until he became the owner of 525 acres, which included some of the best land in this county.

The subject of our sketch was one of a family of fourteen children. Of that number only four survive, and the record is as follows: Ann is the widow of Enoch Kassbeere, and is living in Montana; Harry is occupied in farming in this county, as is also his brother John; the remaining child is the subject of our sketch. The father died in about 1870, aged seventy-two years, and the mother eight years later, being at the age of her husband when he died. They were most excellent and worthy people, devoted members of the Christian Church, and carried out in their daily lives and conversation the principles which they professed. The elder Sedore always took an active part in educational and religious matters, and exercised an excellent influence over those with whom he associated. At his request he and his aged partner were buried side by side on the home farm.

The early education of our subject was quite limited, there being no school advantages within four miles of his early home, but he received careful training from his parents, and being naturally of an intelligent and inquiring mind, kept his eyes wide open to what was going on in the world around him, and thus obtained a useful fund of information in regard to matters of general interest. He has all his life been engaged in farming pursuits, and his pleasant homestead, acquired through his own industry and enterprise, comprises 260 acres of land, with a good frame dwelling and all necessary out-buildings for the shelter of stock and the storage of grain, a view of which we present in this volume.

Mr. Sedore was united in marriage with Miss Rebecca Richardson, in Wapello County, in 1863. Mrs. S. is the daughter of Era and Eva (Grant) Richardson, natives of Ohio. Of this union there were born the following children: Frances A., the wife of E. A. McGary, a farmer of Wapello County; Celia died in infancy; Melvina and Eva are at home with their parents; John E. is also at home and attending the district schools. The affectionate wife and mother departed this life about the year 1874, and Mr. S. was the second time married, to Miss Rachel E. Bailey. She is the daughter of Thomas and Margaret P. (Thompson) Bailey, natives of Ohio. Of this marriage there have been born four children—Aaron, Laura, Charles and Clara.

The farm residence is pleasantly located, convenient and comfortable, and its inmates are enjoying the good things of this life. Politically Mr. Sedore is a liberal Democrat, and possesses those staunch and substantial qualities which descended to him from an excellent line of the German and French ancestry.

EDMOND S. WYATT, a prosperous and highly respected farmer of Green Township, has been a resident of this section most of the time since the spring of 1855. He is the owner of 297 acres of tillable land, mostly improved, and under a good state of cultivation. He commenced life at the foot of the ladder, without a dollar in his pocket, and his possessions are the result of his own industry, acquired through years of labor and economy. In addition to other drawbacks, he had not even any education to assist him in his struggle for a livelihood, but learned to read and write after his marriage.

Mr. Wyatt is a native of Owen County, Ind., born in 1834. He is a son of Jacob and Sallie (Reynolds) Wyatt, natives respectively of Randolph County, Va., and Montgomery County, N. C., who removed to Indiana shortly after their marriage and were among the early settlers of that region. The father is still living and a resident of Llano County, Tex., engaged in farming. The wife and mother departed this life in 1859, at the age of forty-eight years.

At the age of twenty-one years the subject of our sketch left the parental roof and, crossing the Mississippi, came into Wapello County and settled in Green Township, arriving here in April, 1855. He purchased forty acres of land on section 22, and the following year sold it for the purpose of going to Allen County, Kan. He remained in Kansas, however, only six months, then, returning to this county, purchased back the forty acres which he had owned before. This he settled upon, and it has constituted his homestead since that time, although he has spent some time in traveling about. In 1864 he went overland to Colorado, and for about eleven months during the war was engaged in hauling provisions for the Government troops. For a period of four years, from 1871 to 1875, he carried on a general store at Ormanville. At the same time he retained his farm property, and in the different departments of business in which he was engaged was uniformly successful.

Mr. Wyatt was married, March 10, 1858, to Miss Zilpah Davis, of Clay County, Iowa, daughter of Willoughby and Polly (Ormand) Davis, natives of Tennessee. Of this marriage there have been born four children, two sons and two daughters, the record of whom is as follows: Mary Ann, born Nov. 17, 1858, is the wife of Dr. Torrence, of Ormanville; Aaron Noyes, born Aug. 12, 1859, is connected with a ruffler manufactory in Ottumwa; Willoughby, born Aug. 14, 1861, is at home with his parents; Sallie, born March 14, 1864, is the wife of John Phillips, of Green Township.

Mr. Wyatt is liberal in politics, and has an intelligent interest in the affairs of his county and township. He has been a School Director, and is a gentleman whose opinion upon matters of general interest is highly valued. He and his family are comfortably situated in life and enjoy the respect and confidence of the people of this locality.

L. G. TURNER, a highly respected citizen of Eldon, is a native of Pennsylvania, born in 1841, and the son of Gideon and Annie (Wixson) Turner, both natives of New York. They remained in Agency City during the later part of their lifetime, the father resting from his earthly labors in 1858, and the mother in 1852, at their home in Agency City. Our subject was an early pioneer of the Hawkeye State, coming to this section the second year after the admission of Iowa into the Union as a State. He settled at Agency City, and engaged in farming pursuits for the following twelve years and until near the opening of the late Civil War. Soon after the first call for troops to aid in the preservation of the Union, Mr. Turner proffered his services by enlisting in the 7th Iowa Cavalry. He was, however, unable to endure for very long the hardships and privations of a soldier's life, and after a severe illness and confinement in the hospital, he received his discharge on account of disability. He then returned to his farm, upon which he remained until 1870, and then coming to Eldon, engaged as clerk in a store.

Soon after the close of the war, in 1867, Mr. Turner was united in marriage with Miss C. M. Cross, a native of the Hawkeye State, and daughter of W. H. and M. L. Cross, natives of New York and Ohio. Of this union there were born three children: Nellie, who is at home with her parents; Fred W. and Lawrence E., who died in 1875, in early childhood. Mr. Turner is a Republican in politics, and belongs to the I. O. O. F. and G. A. R.

T. J. THOMPSON has been a resident of Wapello County since 1853, and now occupies a comfortable homestead in Highland Township, on section 17. After coming into Iowa he first settled at Dahlonega, and was engaged alternately as a farm laborer and in a steam sawmill. He settled upon his present homestead in the fall of 1854, and has brought about great improvements in its condition since he first took possession of it. He is now the owner of 130 acres of good land, and being a straightforward business man, honest and upright in his transactions, has met with success and secured the confidence and esteem of his fellow-citizens.

The subject of our sketch was born July 24, 1832, in Macoupin County, Ill., and is the son of John and Hannah (Landreth) Thompson, natives of Virginia. He was reared to farming pursuits, but at the age of forty-nine years learned engineering, and also served a short apprenticeship as clerk in a store of general merchandise at Franklin, Ill. He received a common-school education, and made the most of his opportunities. The father of our subject was born in 1801, and removed to Illinois in 1828, where he died at the age of sixty-two years, in 1863; the mother had closed her eyes on the scenes of earth in 1842. Their family included ten children, of whom our subject was the sixth in order of birth.

The marriage of Mr. Thompson and Miss Nancy

Ketteman of Indiana took place in 1853. The parents of Mrs. T. were Elias and Lydia (Redman) Ketteman, natives of Illinois. To our subject and wife were born seven children, four girls and three boys, as follows: Sarah Ann became the wife of John Shutelfield, of this township; Arthur is living in Cass County; Ida Belle married William Scott, of the same county; Elias, Clara, Emma and Le Roy are at home. Mr. and Mrs. T. are members of the Missionary Baptist Church. Mr. T. is Republican in politics, and has held the office of Justice of the Peace. He is engaged in general farming, and possesses all the appliances for the carrying on of agriculture in a first-class manner.

SILAS WARREN, one of the well-to-do merchants of the city of Chillicothe, is a native of this county, and was born Feb. 2, 1850. He is the son of Tillman and Elizabeth (Nye) Warren, the father a native of Ohio and the mother of Germany. The latter came to the United States when a young girl of thirteen years old, landing with her parents in New York City, whence they proceeded to White County, Ohio, where, in due time, the father of our subject made her acquaintance, and they were married on the 21st of September, 1837. Tillman Warren at once engaged in farming in Pike County, Ohio, until 1844, and then decided to seek his fortunes beyond the Mississippi. Coming to this county he purchased ninety-three acres of unimproved land, upon which he located, and at once began its cultivation. He was prospered in his undertakings, but only lived to labor for his family until 1855, when he was taken from the family who had ever regarded him with the highest respect and affection. The mother of our subject is still living. In earlier years she united with the Methodist Episcopal Church with her husband, and was his faithful helper in the useful projects which he set on foot for the good of his church and community. Their household included eight children, as follows: Mary J., the eldest, died in infancy; Richard L. enlisted as a soldier of the Union during the late war, in the 36th Iowa Infantry, and died in the hospital, at Helena, Ark.; William is clerk in a store at Eldon; Rhoda became the wife of A. W. Clark, a farmer of Cass Township; John A. is farming in Polk Township; our subject, Silas, was the next in order of birth; Catharine married Albert Cornwell, a highly respected farmer of Cass Township; George L. was born on the 5th of January, 1855, and is a butcher by trade. The living children of this family are all comfortably settled in good homes, and are useful members of the community.

Silas Warren, of this history, is essentially a self-made man. He commenced life a poor boy, and is a striking illustration of what may be accomplished by resolution, industry and perseverance. He was but five years of age when the father of the family was taken away, and as soon as old enough he assisted in the labors around the homestead. His education was necessarily limited, but he was a bright and intelligent lad, and kept his eyes open to what was going on in the world around him. He thus became possessed of a good fund of general information, and now ranks among the intelligent and useful men of his community. He was engaged in farming pursuits until 1877, and then learned the butcher's trade, which he followed for nine years with gratifying success. He then sold out his interest in this business, and removing to Chillicothe purchased a stock of general merchandise, and has been in trade since that time. He carries a stock of about $6,000, and his trade is prosperous and constantly increasing. He seems admirably adapted to the business, is courteous and obliging in his manners, and has taken the lead among the mercantile interests of this city. Mr. Warren has been prominent in the affairs of Columbia Township since his first arrival here. After occupying several of the minor offices, in the fall of 1886 he was elected Justice of the Peace on the Democratic ticket by a large majority, but moved out of the precinct, and consequently did not qualify.

The marriage of Silas Warren and Miss Fannie A. Forsythe was celebrated in Highland Township on the 4th of May, 1882. Mrs. Warren was born in Wapello County on the 3d of October, 1854, and is the daughter of James and Sarah (Perry)

Forsythe, natives of Ireland, who came to this country in 1845, locating near Elizabethtown, Pa., coming to Wapello County in 1851, where they became highly respected citizens, but are now both deceased. Mr. and Mrs. Warner became the parents of two children—Dora E. and James Tillman. The latter died when eleven days old. Mrs. Warren is connected with the Presbyterian Church. Our subject has been a liberal contributor to the church and Sunday-school, and is the staunch friend of education and all other measures calculated for the advancement and welfare of the community. He is Democratic in politics, a thorough-going business man, a valued member of society, and in all respects is entitled to rank among the best citizens of Chillicothe.

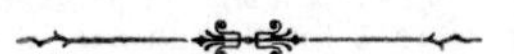

A. Z. SCOTT, of Highland Township, has been a resident of Iowa since 1863, when he settled in Mahaska County. After living there three years he removed to Keokuk County and two years later came to Wapello, making his location on section 6, which has since remained his home. He is the owner of 104 acres of choice land, in a good state of cultivation, and is held in high esteem by his neighbors and associates for his straightforward business methods and his upright life and character.

Mr. Scott was born in Guernsey County, Ohio, in 1826, and is the son of Charles and Susan (McCulla) Scott, his father a native of Ireland, and his mother of West Virginia. The former pursued the occupation of a farmer and miller. The parental household included fifteen children, eight of whom are living: Annis P. is the widow of Francis Patterson, of Cambridge, Ohio; David is farming in Keokuk County; George M. is a minister of the Methodist Protestant Church, and stationed at Oskaloosa; Charles is farming in Davis County, and Ross in Guernsey County, Ohio; A. Z., our subject, was the eighth in order of birth; John A. died in 1849 at Nevada City, Cal.; Wilson, of Cambridge, Ohio, has been route agent of the B. & O. R. R. for the past ten years; Sarah J. married George Brown, a merchant of Limaville, Ohio; Susan became the wife of Archie Shipley, express agent at Columbus, Ohio; three brothers died in the army.

The subject of our sketch was married on the 1st of January, 1847, to Miss Margaret J., the daughter of Zebedee and Mary Ann (Slaughter) Kendall, of Ohio, and they have become the parents of eleven children, as follows: E. P., born Nov. 24, 1847, is a resident of Keokuk County; S. C., born Feb. 19, 1849, is farming in Adams County; C. A., born Oct. 19, 1850, is also a resident of Adams County; T. M., born June 17, 1852, is in Cass County; Zebedee, born March 24, 1854, is living in Jewell County, Kan.; Nevada E. born June 1, 1855, died the following year; Zane, born March 3, 1857, died in 1859; A., born Feb. 14, 1859, became the wife of Andrew Chapman, of Cass County, Iowa; Annace, a twin of the former, married B. F. Harkins, of Jewell County, Kan.; Josiah, born Oct. 18, 1860, died in 1863; William, born Aug. 3, 1863, is living in Cass County; Susan M., born Feb. 25, 1866, was united in marriage with Marion Sammons, of Union County, Iowa; Grant, born July 15, 1867, is at home, as is also Margaret Jane, who was born Oct. 25, 1871. Mr. and Mrs. Scott are members in good standing of the Methodist Episcopal Church, and in politics Mr. Scott is a staunch Republican. The father of Mr. Scott was a soldier in the Revolutionary War.

THOMAS SWORD, of Ottumwa, occupying a position as Superintendent of the John Morrell & Co. Packing House, of this city, comes of good old Scotch ancestry, and was born among the hills of Roxburghshire, Scotland, on the 13th day of February, 1850. He is the only child of Thomas and Sarah (Bell) Sword. His father departed this life while our subject was yet quite an infant, and the latter thereafter made his home with an uncle, John Sword, by whom he was reared as a child of the family. He received his education in the district schools, and at the age of sixteen years left his native land and came to the United States. After landing he spent a short time on Long Island, and then went to London, Canada, where he started to learn the trade of carriage-making, but disliking the business, finally abandoned it. He was then employed by the firm of John Morrell & Co., and went with them, finally, to Chicago, Ill.; he came to Ottumwa in 1877. He has passed all the grades incident to his calling, having been foreman of the engineering department previous to his promotion to his present office. He now has charge of the entire establishment, and is performing the duties of his position with credit to himself and satisfaction to all concerned.

Mr. Sword was married, in London, Canada, on the 3d of April, 1877, to Miss Helen McKechnie, a native of the Dominion, and born Nov. 24, 1851. Of this union there have been born three children—Eva Bell, Thomas L. and Jessie Helen. They occupy a pleasant home on Thirty-second street, are highly respected by a large circle of friends and acquaintances, and in their home life are surrounded by all the luxuries of refined and cultivated tastes.

Mr. Sword is still a young man, possessing an intelligent mind, and is keenly observant of what is going on around him. He is well posted in local and general matters, and in politics is Democratic. He came to this county a poor boy, but by the exercise of industry and energy has raised himself to a good position as a man among men, and is now one of the most valued citizens of Ottumwa. Mr. and Mrs. S. are prominently connected with the Presbyterian Church.

T C. TAYLOR, a farmer and stock-grower on section 13, Richland Township, is a native of Washington County, Iowa, born Jan. 21, 1859, and is a son of Thomas and Sarah (Leucher) Taylor, the former a native of Maryland, and the latter of Kentucky. By trade his father was a blacksmith, and followed that occupation for many years, at times in connection with farming. In 1846 he moved from Cincinnati, Ohio, to Illinois, where he remained until 1850, and then went to Washington County, thence coming to Wapello County; he is now living a retired life. His wife, the mother of our subject, died Aug. 28, 1879.

T. C. Taylor and Emma Hayden, daughter of Samuel and Fanny (Forsythe) Hayden, were united in marriage in 1879. Mrs. Taylor was born in Missouri, Aug. 20, 1862, and of her marriage with our subject two children have been born—Harlan and Charles. Mr. and Mrs. Taylor are members of the Methodist Episcopal Church, and politically he is Republican.

A W. VANNOY. Among the leading farmers of Competine Township is the gentleman whose name heads this brief personal history. He resides on section 12, and is highly respected for his excellent character. Our subject was born Sept. 6, 1817, in Wilkes County, N. C., and is the son of Jesse Vannoy, a gentleman of French descent, and Mary (Kilby) Vannoy, who was of German ancestry. His father being a distiller, the son learned that business. At this occupation, together with that of farming, he labored until he was twenty-three years of age, when he bought a farm, which he operated until 1869. At that time he sold out and came West, starting on the 10th of April, with wagon and team, and traveling about seventy-five miles to the depot. They took the train at Johnson's depot, Tenn., securing tickets for Nashville, thence down the Cumberland River to Cairo, and then to St. Louis, when he decided to come to Ottumwa, having a sister living in Wapello County. He therefore proceeded on his western journey, landing in that city April 18, 1869.

Mr. Vannoy, while living in North Carolina, united with the church, and in 1851 commenced preaching the Gospel of Christ, and his great usefulness as a citizen of this community has been enhanced by his noble profession and the devotion he has ever displayed in behalf of both church and humanity. He has been a great Bible student and takes delight in turning its pages. He and his family are all members of the Missionary Baptist Church, and in 1870 he had charge of the Pleasant View Church.

Our subject was united in marriage, April 28, 1842, with Miss Aley Eller. To them have been born sixteen children, nine sons and seven daughters; four of the latter are now living: Anderson

RESIDENCE OF A. B. PHEL SEC. 29, COMPETINE TOWNSI

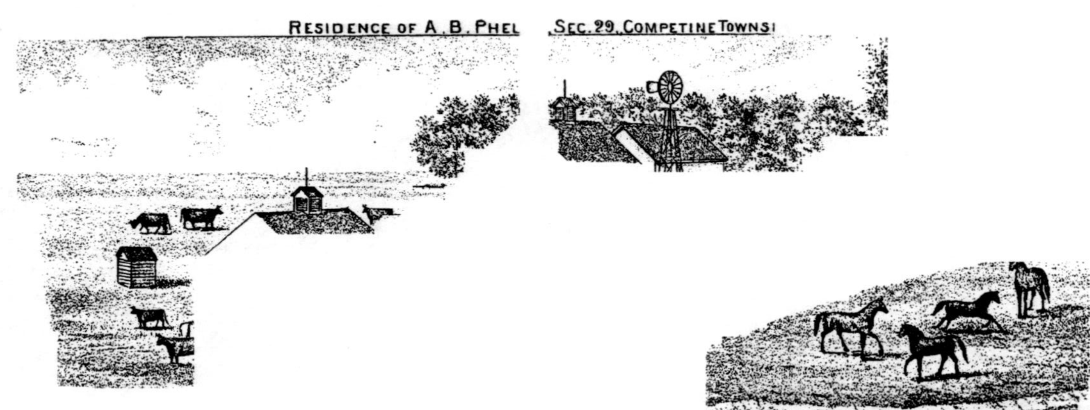

STOCK FARM AND RESIDENCE OF G:O.W. DICKINS, SEC. 17., COMPETINE TOWNSHIP

M. was born May 13, 1844; May A., Feb. 7, 1846; Sarah C., June 12. 1848; Nancy E., Jan. 18, 1850; George H., Nov. 13, 1851; Elza F., Jan. 11, 1856; Nancy Eveline, Aug. 22, 1857; Julia E., May 3, 1860; Frankie M., May 1, 1865; Allie C., Sept. 22, 1867; Jessie A., June 12, 1869; Nancy Eveline, Nancy E. and John F. are deceased.

A. B. PHELPS, a prominent and successful farmer of Competine Township, owns and occupies a fine homestead on section 29. He is a native of Gallia, Ohio, and was born Aug. 27, 1839. He is the son of B. B. and Jane Phelps, natives of Ohio, and the parents of ten sons and six daughters. The father departed this life Jan. 5, 1875, and the mother Dec. 27, 1871. The record of their family is as follows: John, a native of Ohio, now lives in Franklin County, Iowa; James H. was the second son, and lives in Hedrick, Iowa; Martha J. died Jan. 5, 1873; A. B., our subject, was the next in order of birth; Abigail B. was the second daughter; Josiah is the Sheriff of Franklin County; Sallie A. is a resident of Osborne County, Kan.; Benjamin F. died Jan. 5, 1852; the next in order of birth was a son, who died Jan. 27, 1847; Alonzo died Jan. 24, 1848; Harriet E. died Jan. 23, 1853, and was buried in Smith Cemetery, Jefferson County; S. V. lives in Clay County, Neb.; W. R. was a school teacher; Mary lives in Hedrick; Leonidas M. is a resident of Clay County, Neb.; Leora L. became the wife of H. McCormick, a farmer of Highland Township.

The parents removed from Ohio to Iowa in 1852, arriving here on the 13th of October. Their son, our subject, remained with them until the breaking out of the late war, when he enlisted as a soldier in Co. I, 1st Iowa Vol. Cav., serving four years and seven months. His regiment first went into camp at Burlington, and from there proceeded to Benton Barracks, Mo., and thence to Tipton, engaging in their first battle at Blackwater, where they captured 1,300 prisoners and six wagon-loads of arms. They drove the rebel General, Hindman, out of Missouri, and retired to Wilson Creek battle-ground on a forced march of 100 miles, and, afterward encountering the same General and his forces, routed them with half the number of troops which composed that detachment of the rebels. On the 3d of January, 1863, they again made a forced march of 100 miles, captured Ft. Smith, Ark., and returning in April joined the command of Gen. Davidson and proceeded to Little Rock, Ark., taking possession of that place in September. On the 1st of January, of the following year, under command of Gen. Steele, they marched on Camden, and thereafter proceeded through Arkansas to join the command of Gen. Banks. On the 19th of April they started with a forage train of eighty-two wagons, and on the way the entire outfit was captured excepting one mule. Mr. Phelps got back to camp by wading through swamps, and reached his command at Camden, from which place they started for Prairie Bluff with another train, which was captured at Marks' Mill with the 36th Iowa and 43d Indiana, with 400 veterans. These latter finally turned and drove the rebels back, with heavy loss on the side of the latter and without the loss of a man by the Union troops. At Camden they found Gen. Steele on the retreat. The regiment was put to the front, marching 200 miles, which they accomplished in five days. Our subject then came home on veteran furlough. The following month he returned to St. Louis, following the soldiers which had been engaged under Price's raid through Missouri, and returning to St. Louis in November following. From that place our subject with his comrades were again ordered to Little Rock, Ark., thence east across the Mississippi into Tennessee, proceeding directly to Memphis, and from there southwest again into Alexandria, La., where they joined the command of Gen. Custer and with him proceeded to Austin, Tex. They remained there until February, 1866, when they were mustered out and crossed the Gulf of Mexico to New Orleans, where our subject bade farewell to many of his comrades and proceeded to Davenport, Iowa. He received his final and honorable discharge on the 15th of March, having served a period of four years, seven months and sixteen days, and without missing a roll-call or being put upon extra duty. He participated in thirty-three engagements, and escaped without a wound.

The day of his discharge Mr. Phelps returned

home, and on the 18th of October, 1866, was united in marriage with Miss Elizabeth Dickens, of Competine Township, and the daughter of Martin Dickens. Mrs. Phelps was born July 9, 1841, and by her marriage with our subject has become the mother of three sons and three daughters, all at home and named as follows: Mary E., Orville O., Thomas M., Ella E. and Elza E. (twins), and Mattie J.

After his marriage Mr. Phelps located upon a farm, and in the pursuit of agriculture has met with more than ordinary success. He is now the owner of 480 acres, finely improved and under a good state of cultivation. He has a handsome farm dwelling, good barns and outhouses, costly farm machinery, and all the appliances necessary for carrying on agriculture in a first-class manner. He has been actively interested, since coming to this section, in everything pertaining to the welfare of his county and community, and has been the supporter and encourager of every worthy enterprise calculated to advance the cause of education, religion and morality. He and his good wife are connected with the Baptist Church, with their two eldest children, and he has been Deacon since 1878. He has been Treasurer of the School Board since 1877, and is now holding the office of Road Supervisor. In his business transactions Mr. Phelps has been upright and straightforward, and during his long residence in this vicinity has built up for himself a reputation as a good citizen, giving cheerfully of his time and means to whatever tends for the general welfare, and by his industry and enterprise affording a worthy example to the rising generation.

A lithographic view of Mr. Phelps' residence is shown on another page of this volume.

JEHU YOUNG, a representative man of Washington Township, is pleasantly situated on section 6, and engaged in farming and stock-raising. He has been successful in his undertakings in life and is essentially a self-made man, his present possessions being the result of his own industry and economy. Mr. Young is a native of the Buckeye State, having been born in Harrison County, Ohio, June 11, 1829. He is the son of Benjamin and Eva (Fisher) Young, whose household included seven children, five of whom are still living, and are recorded as follows: Elizabeth is the wife of James Brown, of Washington Township; Mary, Mrs. P. O. Overman, resides in South Ottumwa; Sarah is the widow of Timothy Holly, and lives with her sister, Mrs. Overman; Ellen married G. W. Stocker, a farmer of Washington Township; Jehu is the subject of our sketch.

Jehu Young came to this county about 1846, and the greater part of his life has been engaged in farming pursuits. His childhood and youth were passed under the parental roof, and he received a fair education in the pioneer schools. In 1853 he rented a farm of 159 acres, the greater part of which consisted of wild land, and set himself about its improvement and cultivation. In due time he succeeded in establishing a comfortable home, having occupied the same farm since that time. He has been honest and upright in his dealings, and enjoys in a marked degree the confidence and esteem of his neighbors and associates.

Oct. 11, 1852, Mr. Young was united in marriage with Miss Elizabeth McMillen, the daughter of James and Eliza McMillen. By her union with our subject she became the mother of two children, namely, Ben Franklin, born June 10, 1859, and Clara, April 18, 1861; the latter became the wife of John McIntyre, a farmer of Keokuk Township. The mother of these children departed this life in 1861, greatly mourned by her family and a large circle of friends and acquaintances. Her remains are laid to rest in the cemetery in Agency Township.

For his second wife our subject married the daughter of George and Elizabeth (Robinson) Harper. She is a native of Canada, and was born Feb. 28, 1849, and while yet a child came to this county with her parents. She was deprived of the affectionate care of her mother soon afterward; her father died in the year 1880, at the advanced age of eighty-eight years. Both he and his wife were members in good standing of the Presbyterian Church. Of the second marriage of Mr. Young there are four children, as follows: James, born May 9, 1865; Harvey, Dec.

20, 1868; Arthur, July 25, 1876, and Walter, July 25, 1883. The family residence is pleasantly situated, and its inmates are surrounded by all the comforts of life. Politically Mr. Young casts his vote with the Republican party; he is the friend of education, morality and religion, and in all respects is fulfilling his obligations as a good citizen.

S D. PIERCE, a prosperous boot and shoe merchant of Ottumwa, Iowa, illustrates in a varied experience in life what may be accomplished by perseverance under difficulties. Through a series of reverses, brought about by no fault of his own, Mr. Pierce has met with great losses, but is reaping the reward of his courage and resolution under adversity. He is now one of the leading merchants of the city, and by his straightforward business transactions and excellent personal traits of character, has secured in a marked degree the confidence and esteem of his fellow-citizens.

The subject of this brief history is a native of the Empire State, having been born in Providence, Saratoga County, Oct. 13, 1827, and his parents were Sewell H. and Eunice (Wells) Pierce, natives respectively of Vermont and Connecticut. Their household circle included ten children, five sons and five daughters, who are recorded as follows: Rebecca is deceased, also Solomon T.; Julia H. became the wife of William Kennedy, of Gloversville, N. Y.; Susan, the widow of James Wells, also resides in the latter town; Samuel D., our subject, was the fifth in order of birth; Francis S. lives in Pocahontas County, Iowa; Fannie and Rufus N. are in Ottumwa. The parents died in Fulton County, N. Y., the mother at the age of seventy-eight and the father at eighty years. The former was connected with the Presbyterian Church; the latter inclined to the Methodist doctrine, and connected himself with that society.

At the age of sixteen years the subject of this history was apprenticed to the trade of a tanner and shoemaker in Mayfield, which he continued for fifteen years in that place. He then removed to Fish House, in his native county, and thence, in 1847, to Little Falls in the same State. Here he became acquainted with and was married to Miss Nancy Petrie, the daughter of Reuben and Rhoda (House) Petrie, both natives of New York State. Subsequently Mr. Pierce with his young wife removed to Gloversville, where he embarked in the manufacture of gloves and mittens, and was thus engaged for the following two years. He then resolved to try his fortune in one of the Western States, and turning his face toward the setting sun, journeyed into Illinois and located in Lewistown, where he engaged in the manufacture of boots and shoes, and also in tanning the leather of which they were made. He remained in this locality for a period of seven years, was prospered in his labors and business transactions, and accumulated a handsome property.

In 1857 Mr. Pierce crossed the Mississippi over into Henry County, Mo., where he purchased a tract of wild prairie land and engaged in agricultural pursuits. He improved the greater part of his possession, brought the land to a good state of cultivation, and erected a substantial set of frame buildings. He then sold out to good advantage, and removing to Osceola, St. Clair County, in the same State, resumed his old business of boot and shoe making and tanning, to which he also added the manufacture of saddlery and harness. He became finely established here and was on the high road to prosperity at the breaking out of the late Rebellion. Being a Northern man with Northern views and sympathies, his customers withdrew their patronage, and he was forced to leave the country, sacrificing all his property, and thankful to escape with his life and the lives of his family. He then came to Wapello County, Iowa, and located in Ottumwa among strangers, without a dollar which he could call his own. He opened up a small shoe-shop, and in the humblest manner began what he trusted would prove the restoration of his fallen fortune. By close attention to business, and incessant industry, step by step he built up a business which to-day he may well be justified in viewing with pride and satisfaction. In the meantime, however, he suffered still further the loss of property, being burned out in 1868, by which he suffered a loss of $250, and nine years later was again caught by the fire fiend, which damaged him to the amount of $250. But notwithstanding these adverssties he is still enjoying a good business, and considers himself prepared for almost any future emergency.

The household circle of Mr. and Mrs. Pierce was completed by the birth of six children, as follows: Samuel M., of Ottumwa, was born Sept. 2, 1847; Mary L. is the widow of Joseph Gephart; George D. was born June 25, 1854, and resides in Ottumwa; Charles D., born Nov. 15, 1856, is deceased; Anna, born in June, 1864, died in infancy; Frank D. was born June 23, 1869, and is at home with his parents. The family residence is pleasantly located on West Main street, and Mr. Pierce and his family enjoy the friendship and association of the best residents of Ottumwa. In politics he is a stanch Republican, and socially belongs to the Masonic fraternity, the I. O. O. F. and the V. A. S.

PAGE WHITE, a prominent and highly respected resident of Adams Township, came to Wapello County in 1845, and entered 160 acres of land in this township, on section 35, which he improved and cultivated, and has occupied since that time. Mr. White was born in Clay County, Ky., Oct. 27, 1823, and is the son of Francis and Libby (Knowling) White, natives of the same State, whence they emigrated to Missouri, where the father died in 1844. Our subject, after his father's death, went to Missouri and brought his mother and her five children to this county, and maintained them until the latter had grown to years of maturity. He was the second child of the family, and was reared to farming pursuits, in the meantime receiving a fair education in the subscription schools.

In 1853 Mr. White was united in marriage with Miss Eliza Berry, who was born in Zanesville, Ohio, in 1836, and was the daughter of Joseph Berry, of Kentucky. Mr. and Mrs. White are the parents of eleven children, all of whom are living: Clara, the eldest, married James Arnold, of Green Township; Ella, Mrs. Charles Arnold, lives in Cass County, Iowa; Charles P. married Miss Ella Walker, and is operating his father's farm; Francis M. is in the employ of Sheppard & Co., of Ottumwa; Albert M. and Edward S. are at home; Robert Henry, Mary Elizabeth, Belle and Viola are at home.

The farm property of Mr. White includes 410 acres of finely cultivated land, and in addition to agricultural pursuits he has given considerable attention to stock-raising, making a specialty of hogs. He has been prominently identified with the business and industrial interests of this section since coming here, and has taken an active part in promoting its prosperity and advancement. He has been connected with the School Board at various times, once for a period of three years in succession, and was a member of the Board of Supervisors when the present county hospital was built. In 1883 he established a store of general merchandise on the south side of section 35, on the county line, where he still continues a good business, the location being six miles from the nearest town.

In 1850 Mr. White made an overland journey to California, and was engaged in mining for two years in the Golden State with satisfactory results. He came home by the way of New York and the Isthmus and, although he enjoyed the voyage, was very seasick, and suffered from the effects of it some time after reaching terra firma. Since that time he has remained closely at home, seldom going beyond the bounds of his extensive farm estate. Mr. White is Republican in politics, and Mrs. W. is a worthy member of the Baptist Church.

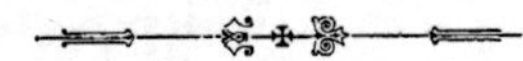

JOHN WILCOX, deceased, formerly of Eddyville, was born March 12, 1825, in Madison County, Ohio, of Scotch ancestry. His parents, Joel and Sarah (Williams) Wilcox, moved to Putnam County, that State, in 1826, and it was there that John was reared to manhood. The maiden name of the grandmother of our subject, on the father's side, was Elizabeth Cowan, and the maternal grandmother was, prior to her marriage, a Miss Mary McCarty. The parents of our subject emigrated to Oregon in 1847, all the family accompanying them except John, who remained in

Ohio. The journey was made thither overland, and the mother died during the same year, Oct. 18, 1847, at the Dalles, and was buried at Vancouver, Washington Territory. The father died November 10 of the same year, and was buried at the same place.

John Wilcox assisted in the labors of the farm, in the meantime attending the common schools. Nov. 9, 1843, he was married to Jemima Hopkins, a native of Ohio, and to their union eight children were born, six of whom are living at this writing: Eliza, wife of S. Bower, of Ohio; Elmira, wife of Samuel P. Wright, of that State; Martha, wife of Charles C. Woodward, also a resident of Ohio; Frank P. is a traveling salesman for D. McFerry, of Detroit, Mich.; Fremont is a telegraph operator at Toledo, Ohio, and the whereabouts of Kelly is unknown. The wife of our subject died in Putnam County, Ohio, Feb. 16, 1871.

The second matrimonial alliance of Mr. Wilcox took place Feb. 25, 1868, with Mrs. Mary Jane Mackay, a native of Aberdeen, Scotland, and widow of William Mackay, also a native of that country. Her maiden name was Drummond, and she is the daughter of John and Elizabeth (Gault) Drummond. She had been married previous to her union with Mr. Mackay, her first husband being Thomas Denham, by whom she had two children: Elizabeth, wife of George W. Taylor, of Washington, D. C., a clerk in the pension office, and John C., now a resident of Oskaloosa, Iowa, and engaged in the harness business. Of her union with our subject one child has been born, Della E., living at home and attending the High School; she will graduate therefrom this year (1887.)

In 1849 our subject moved to Mercer County, Ohio, where he continued to reside until 1854, and while there acted in the capacity of County Clerk. In 1855 Mr. Wilcox moved to Iowa and settled near Eddyville, this county, on a farm. There he continued to labor at his chosen vocation until the breaking out of the Civil War, when he enlisted as a private in Co. I, 7th Iowa Vol. Inf. It will be seen from the number of his regiment that he was one of the first to respond to his country's call, and he was mustered into service at Burlington, Aug. 2, 1861. He was promoted Corporal at Camp Walker, Sept. 22, 1861, and detailed with a company of ten men to do picket duty five miles from Columbus. He, with his squad of men, was charged upon by rebel cavelry, but repulsed the charge with a loss of five men to their opponents. Oct. 3, 1861, he was sent as an escort to rebel prisoners from Charleston Railroad to Bird's Point, and came near being captured, but eluded his pursuers, and arrived safely at the termination of his journey with his prisoners. Nov. 7, 1861, he participated in the battle of Belmont, Mo. Jan. 29, 1862, he was taken sick and sent to the hospital, but soon recovered, and February 13 of that year he participated in the ever memorable battle of Ft. Donelson, which lasted three days, and there commanded a company. April 2, 1862, at Pittsburg Landing he also commanded a company, and took part in the battle of Corinth, where he likewise was in charge of a company. Sept. 24, 1862, our subject resigned his position as Lieutenant in the army and came home. The reason of his resignation was that he was placed under a Captain whom he and many of the soldiers knew to be a coward, and under whom he refused to serve. Arriving home he organized a company of cavalry of which he was chosen Captain, and in May, 1863, he again went to the field and continued in the service until the close of the war. In fact our subject continued a soldier until May, 1866, when he received his discharge at Davenport. He was during these years Captain of Co. B, 7th Iowa Vol. Cav., and was wounded at the battle of Belmont; Nov. 7, 1861, he was promoted Second Lieutenant; Dec. 22, 1861, he commanded Company I, in the battles of Donelson, Shiloh and the seige of Corinth, and received his discharge in September, 1862. As stated, he at once commenced raising troops for the Government, and at his own expense soon had a full company which was transferred to the 7th Iowa Cavalry, and as stated, he was elected Captain of Company B, April 27, 1863. After Aug. 19, 1863, he served with his regiment in Nebraska, Kansas, Colorado, Wyoming and Dakota, and his company took part in all the expeditions against the hostile Indians. It occupied a prominent and important position in the Powder River expedition under Col. Moonlight, of the 11th Kansas District, and after this expedition our subject commanded a battalion with honor and credit, and was commissioned Major; he was a brave and honored soldier throughout the war.

After his return from the war Capt. Wilcox again engaged in the peaceful pursuits of life, and was thus occupied until 1868. His health being impaired by exposure while in the army, he was forced to give up farming, and in 1868 purchased the *Des Moines Valley Gazette*, published at Eddyville. This paper he edited for a number of years, and during the same time he was appointed Postmaster at Eddyville; his commission bearing date of May, 1869, and which he continued to hold until his resignation under the Hayes administration. He then attended the Soldiers' Home at Dayton, Ohio, for medical treatment, and there died June 3, 1881.

John Wilcox was a Republican in politics, and always took an active part in public affairs. The G. A. R. Post, of Eddyville, was named in his honor, and is known as the Wilcox Post. His education was obtained in the common schools in early life, and afterward supplemented by constant study, he being a great reader. His widow and daughter, who survive, are living in the fine residence which he left them on Third street, in Eddyville.

SAMUEL G. WILSON. This highly respected citizen of Wapello County is a native of Indiana, born in Montgomery County May 29, 1844, and the son of Newton B. and Hannah (Galey) Wilson, both natives of Kentucky. After their marriage they removed to Indiana, and were among the earliest settlers of that State. Their son, our subject, was there reared upon a farm until he had attained to manhood. The parents then removed to Iowa, and came into Wapello County on the 17th of October, 1865. They first settled near Blakesburg, and our subject remained with them for five years following, and engaged in general teaming. He then moved across the line into Monroe County, and located on a rented farm, which he occupied for six months, and has been renting cultivated land in various parts of the county since that time.

Our subject was married, Feb. 7, 1867, to Miss Savannah Galey, a native of Indiana, and a daughter of John and Eliza (Lane) Galey, the former a native of Kentucky and the latter of Virginia. Of this union there have been three children: Newton, born in 1868; Alverda, in 1872, and John, in 1878. Politically Mr. Wilson is Democratic.

The father of our subject departed this life Jan. 22, 1882, at the advanced age of seventy-five years. He was a blacksmith by occupation, industrious and prudent in his manner of living, and a devoted member of the Presbyterian Church. The mother is still living at Blakesburg, at the advanced age of seventy-one years, and is still connected with the Presbyterian Church, of which she and her husband became members in the earlier days of their marriage.

WILLIAM WIFEAT, a prosperous farmer of Green Township, is of Scandinavian origin, and was born in Sweden on the 6th of January, 1837. He is the son of John and Mary (Johnson) Wifeat, and emigrated from his native land to the United States in 1868, landing in New York City. After reaching American shores he proceeded directly westward, crossed the Mississippi, and going into Des Moines, Iowa, engaged in work on the Rock Island & Pacific Railroad, which was then in process of construction. He was thus employed for four months, and then came to Ottumwa, where he was variously employed for the following eight years. He had previously learned the trade of a shoemaker, and part of his time was spent in the manufacture of boots and shoes. In 1876 he resolved to change his occupation, and accordingly purchased forty acres of land in Green Township. This was only partly improved, and he industriously set about the cultivation of the soil.

In the meantime Mr. Wifeat had assumed domestic ties, having been married in 1860, to Miss Mary Johnson, a native of his own country, who was born in 1826. Mrs. W. is the daughter of John and Christina Angelia Johnson, also natives of Sweden, who spent their lives in their native country. Of this union there were born three children: Caroline died in 1870, when an interesting maiden of seventeen years; John August died the same year, at the age of eight years and three months; Mary married August Asplum; she is well educated and quite accomplished. Mr. W., his wife and daughter, are members in good standing of the Lutheran Church, and are highly respected in their community for excellent personal traits of character.

The farm estate of Mr. Wifeat includes eighty acres of finely cultivated land, a comfortable dwelling, good barns and outhouses, and all the appliances for carrying on agriculture in a first-class manner. Mr. W. started in life at the foot of the ladder, and has climbed up to his present position by slow degrees, having now fully established himself in the confidence and esteem of his fellow townsmen. He received a good education in his native Sweden, and since coming to this country has kept himself posted upon all matters of general interest, and possesses that fund of useful information which makes him an interesting man to converse with.

The father of our subject, in his early manhood, learned the trade of a shoemaker which, however, he did not follow for many years. He became a soldier in the Swedish army and spent thirty-three years in the service of his country, being in the Napoleon wars, and gaining a rich experience in his migrations over different parts of the North of Europe.

MRS. MARY J. HAWTHORN, widow of R. T. Hawthorn, and a highly respected resident of Competine Township, resides upon the homestead which was established by her husband over thirty years ago. It is pleasantly located on section 36, and includes 244 acres of finely improved land, a comfortable and handsome farm residence, good barns and out-buildings, and all the appurtenances of a first-class modern farm estate.

Mrs. Hawthorn is a native of Virginia, and was born June 29, 1825. She is the daughter of James and Elizabeth (Lively) Reed, also natives of the Old Dominion, and at the age of sixteen years was united in marriage with R. T. Hawthorn, who remained her affectionate and amiable companion for forty-three years, his death occurring on the 22d of April, 1884. R. T. Hawthorn was born in Virginia on the 5th of March, 1819. He spent his early years in Virginia, and received a fair education in the schools of his native county. In 1853 he and his wife emigrated to Iowa, and made their first location in Jefferson County, the journey from Virginia being made overland with teams, and they carried their household goods and provisions, partaking of their meals by the wayside, and sleeping in their wagons at night. The journey occupied seven weeks, and Mrs. H. could fill an interesting volume with the scenes and incidents of that journey, and of their subsequent life in the pioneer settlement of the Hawkeye State. After a brief period spent in Jefferson County, Mr. Hawthorn decided that it would be for his interest to make a removal, and accordingly purchased 153 acres of land, partly improved, in Wapello County. This was located on section 36, Competine Township, and constitutes the present homestead, where his widow resides, and where their children were reared to years of maturity. Immediately after his purchase Mr. Hawthorn commenced the improvement and cultivation of the land, and was prospered in his labors. As time passed and his means accumulated he added to his territory, until the estate now embraces 244 acres, all finely improved and under a good state of cultivation.

The household circle of Mr. and Mrs. Hawthorn was completed by the birth of ten children—four daughters and six sons. The record is as follows: Elizabeth M. was born Sept. 17, 1843, became the wife of George W. Dickens, and departed this life in 1874; H. T. was born April 17, 1846, and is a resident of this county; James P. was born Sept. 4, 1848; Margaret A., born June 5, 1852, died July 22 of the same year; Samuel R., now of Clay County, Neb., was born Sept. 19, 1854; Mary J., born March 27, 1857, is the wife of S. H. White, a farmer of Wapello County; Ellen H., born Oct. 30, 1859, died Sept. 24, 1860; David F., born Aug. 10, 1861, died March 1, 1862; John A. C. was born Jan. 22, 1863; Templeton C., Aug. 7, 1866. Mr. and Mrs. H. were connected with the Baptist Church for many years.

R. T. Hawthorn was widely and favorably known

in this section of the State. His high moral principles, honesty and uprightness in all the concerns of life, and his excellent personal traits of character, had endeared him to a large circle of friends and acquaintances. He was a man of enterprise, industry and energy, and contributed his full quota toward developing the resources of this section of the Hawkeye State. He was the stanch friend and supporter of education, religion and morality, and was always to be found on the side of justice and right. In all respects he fulfilled the obligations of a good citizen, and his name is held in kindly remembrance.

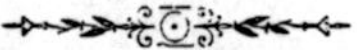

THOMAS D. McGLOTHLEN, a wealthy and highly respected citizen of Columbia Township, has been a prominent resident of this section for a period of forty-two years, and during that time has firmly established himself in the confidence and esteem of his fellow-citizens. He is a gentleman of fine abilities, and as a leader among the influential men of his locality is entitled to due credit for what he has accomplished and the influence which he still brings to bear in aid of whatever pertains to the progress of intelligence, education and morality.

The subject of our sketch was born in Wayne County, Ind., in 1816. He is the son of Charles and Jane (Davis) McGlothlen, and was reared upon the farm of his parents. When he was a child of three years old, they removed from Indiana to Missouri, where they remained for two years, and then moved back into Indiana, and lived there twenty-seven years. Their son Thomas, our subject, came to Wapello County in the spring of 1845, and purchased 120 acres of unimproved land. He industriously set himself about redeeming the soil from its original condition, and was prospered in his undertakings. As time passed on he added to his original possessions, and is now the owner of 419 acres of as finely cultivated land as is to be found along the Mississippi Valley.

The marriage of Thomas D. McGlothlen and Miss Sarah Meek, of Kentucky, was celebrated in Fountain County, Ind., in 1836, when our subject was twenty years of age. Of this union there were born two children: Rebecca J., now the wife of Clayborn R. Raveal, of Wapello County, and Mary Isabelle, who married Adam Bell, also of this county. The first wife of our subject survived her marriage only about five years, dying in 1841, and two years later he was again married, to Miss Martha Taylor, also of Kentucky, born in Hardin County. This lady became the mother of eleven children, of whom the record is as follows: Nancy Maria died in February, 1846; Charles died when an infant of three months old, in 1845; Jacob L. is living at Eddyville; Ellen married Temple Harris, of this county; John W. met his death by sunstroke, in July, 1881, at the age of twenty-seven years; Sarah E. is the wife of Joseph McCombs, of this county; Thomas B. is engaged in the dairy business at Des Moines; A. J. is living near Barnard, Nodaway Co., Mo.; George is at home with his parents; Frank is engaged with the Western Supply Coal Company, at Kirkville, Iowa, and Adolphus P. is connected with a creamery near Eddyville.

Since coming to this vicinity Mr. McGlothlen has been actively interested in public matters, and his talents have received due recognition. In the fall of 1862, after occupying other prominent positions among the councils of his townsmen, he was elected to the Iowa Legislature, in which he served acceptably for two years. He has been a member of the Board of Supervisors, and the incumbent of other minor offices. The residence of Mr. McG. and his family is one of the finest farm dwellings in this vicinity. His barns and out-buildings in every way correspond with the residence, and his farm implements and machinery are of the most improved designs. In near proximity to the house is a valuable spring of living water, which extends to the pasture land and which the proprietor values at thousands of dollars. The homestead in every respect gives evidence of the intelligence and the cultivated taste of its proprietor, and forms one of the most attractive spots in the landscape of Wapello County. In addition to the ordinary pursuits of agriculture, Mr. McGlothlen has given much attention to the breeding of fine stock.

L. F. Newell

"OAKDALE" (700 ACRES) RES. OF L. F. NEWELL (BREEDER OF SHORTHORN CATTLE & NORMAN HORSES) SEC'S. 5 & 6, WASHINGTON TP

Mr. G. and his wife are members in good standing of the Christian Church, and number among their friends and associates the best class of people in this vicinity. Our subject commenced life a poor boy, at the foot of the ladder, and has climbed up to his present position solely by the exercise of his own natural talents. In his early years he applied himself to hard labor, and is now enjoying the fruits of his early toil, being surrounded by all the comforts of life and many of its luxuries.

The father of our subject departed this life in the fall of 1850, at the ripe age of seventy years. He was a farmer by occupation, and trained his son to those habits of industry and economy which have been the secret of his success in life. The mother survived her husband until 1864, dying at the age of eighty years. She was a good woman in every sense that the term implies, and left behind her a record of womanly virtues and kindly deeds.

L. F. NEWELL. Emerson says all history is only biography. So we find this is especially exemplified in the community in which Mr. Newell resides. Its history is only the biography of the lives of a few men, chiefly among whom is our subject. He is a farmer and stock-dealer residing on section 6, Washington Township, and was born in Warren County, Ind., Jan. 25, 1841. He is a son of William and Jemima (Foster) Newell, both of whom are natives of Ohio. His father moved from Indiana to Wapello County, Iowa, as early as 1847, and died in Washington Township, Jan. 5, 1860; his mother died Feb. 5, 1860. Both were highly respected pioneers of this section.

When his parents moved to Wapello County, the subject of this sketch was but six years of age. He was consequently educated in the district schools of this county, grew up here, and embarked in an active and what has been a successful business career. On the 6th day of February, 1862, he married Martha E. Page, a native of New Hampshire, who was born March 22, 1841. She is the daughter of David and Martha (Davis) Page, both of whom died near Fairfield, Iowa. Mr. and Mrs. Newell are the parents of three children: Ida M., born April 13, 1863; Carrie E., Oct. 25, 1864; Frank W., Dec. 10, 1866.

Mr. Newell owns 700 acres of land in Washington, Pleasant and Agency Townships. On the home farm he has one of the best dwellings in the township, and everything about the place is kept in the best order, and we are pleased to present a full page view of it as a splendid representation of the farm homesteads of Wapello County. In his farming operations he makes a specialty of thorough-bred Short-horn cattle and Norman horses, keeping the best grades of all kinds of stock. He has also devoted much attention to shipping, and for twenty years has been quite an extensive shipper of stock, in which business he has been quite successful. He is a thorough business man, and withal a public-spirited one. There is no enterprise tending to build up the township, county or State, but in him finds a friend. He was President of the Wapello County Agricultural Society one term, and served two terms as Treasurer of the same. He has also been connected with, and active in the management of the Agency District Fair, and was one of the Directors of the State Agricultural Society for three years. He and his wife are members of the Methodist Episcopal Church, and in politics he is a Republican.

Mr. Newell's success has not been a success solely in the accumulation of wealth, but in doing good to others, in serving others well, and in winning their respect and esteem. He has ever strictly observed that most important factor in the public or business life of anyone—honesty. He is a careful, conscientious business man, ever adhering to the dictates of his conscience in matters both of a public and private nature. Such a man is an excellent representative of a community, and we take pleasure in presenting his portrait.

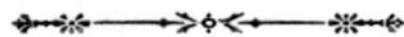

M. H. SPRAGUE, one of the successful and enterprising business men of Eddyville, was born in Washington County, Ohio, Oct. 9, 1852, and is the son of Joseph S. and Henrietta M. (Laughery) Sprague, the former a native of Muskingum County, Ohio, and the latter of Noble County, the same State. M. H. Sprague was educated in the common schools and at Beverly Academy, Ohio. He followed teaching and attended college between times, and graduated from the Columbia Medical College with honors in 1880, having previously studied medicine under the preceptorship of Dr. W. B. Hedges. After receiving his diploma he at once engaged in the practice of his profession at Coal Run, Washington Co., Ohio, and remained there for about eighteen months. He then removed to Beverly, the same county, and practiced there for about eighteen months. Dr. Sprague came to this State from Beverly, Ohio, and took up his residence at Eddyville, where he purchased the drug-store and business of D. W. McManas, in which he is at present engaged, carrying a full line of drugs and medicines. He is also occupied in the practice of his profession at that place, and in both departments of his vocation is meeting with success.

Dr. Sprague was married to Miss Ella Leonard, March 29, 1877. She is a native of Washington County, Ohio, and a daughter of Joseph and Betsey (Danely) Leonard. Her father was born in Fairfax County, Va., Feb. 17, 1804, and her mother was a native of Washington County, Ohio, born June 10, 1808. Dr. and Mrs. Sprague have two children: M. Leora, born Dec. 21, 1878, and Lillian C., May 21, 1882. The father of our subject departed this life at Eddyville, Aug. 25, 1885, aged fifty-four years, three months and twenty-two days; his widow survives, and is a resident of Eddyville. He was a member of the Christian Church, to which denomination she also belongs. Socially our subject is a member of the Masonic fraternity.

Joseph S. Sprague, father of our subject, was born May 1, 1831, in Muskingum County, Ohio. He removed to Washington County, that State, while young, and there resided for many years. Nov. 7, 1852, he married Miss Henrietta Laughery, with whom he lived happily until his death. Commencing poor in life, he resolved to make his word as good as gold and, when he had comparatively nothing, he could borrow money or buy property almost without limit. He was a gentleman who feared debt and always advised his children to live within their means. He lived the free and enjoyable life of a farmer, and was one of the most energetic and thorough-going men in the county. He awoke one night about four weeks prior to his death, and said he wanted his business matters all attended to as he was going to die shortly, though at this time he was in good health. During his illness he manifested a desire to die; once he remarked "I want to go to that beautiful world where there is no sin or suffering." He united with the Christian Church early in life, and remained a devoted worker in the cause. No person had more confidence in prayer, and his favorite place of prayer was in the woods alone, and in perfect solitude. In life he was active, sociable in disposition, desiring to make friends of everybody. Although residing in Eddyville only about eight months, he formed a large circle of friends, and often spoke of their kindness to him. He left a family of four children, who were all present during his sickness, and who will never forget "Father." His remains were interred in the Eddyville Cemetery, in a vault thoroughly made of cement, so as to resist the action of water or other elements. His remains will be preserved for ages.

J C. McCLUNG, one of the useful and valued residents of Dahlonega Township, where he is pleasantly located on section 9, became a resident of Wapello County on the 3d of November, 1847. He first purchased a claim, and afterward rented 160 acres which were only partially improved, and upon which he at once began to labor with highly satisfactory results. He now has a finely improved farm with a good residence, barn and out-buildings, and while passing down the hill of life is enabled to enjoy the fruits of his early toil.

Mr. McClung was born in Kentucky, March 19, 1808, and was the son of Samuel and Mary (Cloyd) McClung, both natives of Rockbridge County, Va. His maternal grandfather became a resident of Kentucky at an early period in its history, and was the friend and companion of Daniel Boone. When our subject was but a small child his parents removed to Clark County, Ind., where they remained three years, then going into Jefferson County, same State, resided there ten or twelve years. They then moved across the Mississippi to Marion County, Iowa, living there two years, and thence went to Montgomery County, where they remained until 1847, and then came to this vicinity. Our subject then came to Wapello County. On the 15th of April, 1831, he was united in marriage with Miss Mary Chandler, of Kentucky. They became the parents of two children, of whom Mary Jane died in 1853, at the age of seventeen years, and Samuel is living in Highland Township. Mrs. Mary McClung departed this life Sept. 16, 1834, at the age of twenty-four years, and in May, 1837, Mr. McClung, for his second wife, married Miss Mary E. Scott, a native of Jefferson County, Ind., whose father was of Irish birth and parentage, and her mother of Pennsylvania. Of this latter marriage of Mr. McClung there were born eight children, as follows: Rebecca E. was the wife of W. H. Kitterman, and died in Shawnee County, Kan., Dec. 28, 1860; James, the eldest, is mining in Colorado; John lives in Schuyler County, Mo.; Susan married G. T. Redman and lives in Highland Township; Martha married L. S. Wilson, Nov. 22, 1868; M. H. manages the home farm, and R. B. is a clerk at Ottumwa. The family homestead consists of 320 acres of land, all improved and under a good state of cultivation. Mr. and Mrs. McClung are worthy members of the Christian Church, and highly respected as useful factors of the community

JOHN McCARTY, of Highland Township, owns and occupies 160 acres of good land on sections 29 and 32, where he has established a comfortable homestead, and in the pursuit of agriculture he has met with fair success. He was born in Pennsylvania in 1809, and is the son of Joseph and Catharine (Livingston) McCarty, natives of the above-named State. They removed to Virginia when John was a lad of twelve years old, locating in Lexington, Rockbridge County, where they remained until 1821, thence went to Ross County, Ohio, where our subject remained fifteen years, then started for the farther West, and coming into Iowa, decided to settle in Wapello County. He first purchased a farm on section 19 of Highland Township, which he occupied for six years and which he afterward disposed of, securing the place which is his present homestead.

The marriage of John McCarty and Miss Catharine Anthony took place Oct. 4, 1832, in Ohio. Mrs. McC. is also a native of Pennsylvania, and the daughter of Jacob and Mary E. (Davis) Anthony, natives respectively of New Jersey and Ireland. Their household circle was completed by the birth of seven children, as follows: Jemima is at home; Elmina married A. Gleason, and they live in Missouri; William is a jeweler of Saline, Mo.; H. B. lives in Montgomery County, Mo.; Mary S. and S. Q. are at home; Clara is the wife of Jasper Grey, of this county. The family residence is comfortable and convenient, and the barns and out-buildings of the homestead denote thrift and prosperity. Mr. McCarty is highly respected by all; he has served as Township Clerk, and been otherwise identified with public affairs. He is Democratic in politics, and in all respects is considered a good citizen and valued member of the community.

I. S. RIGGS, one of the leading lumber merchants of Eddyville, is the proprietor of a business which was established by Messrs. A. W. Riggs and T. C. Spellman in 1875. These gentlemen continued it for two years, and were succeeded by A. Hormer & Co., of Keokuk, who operated it until 1880, and then sold out to the present proprietor. The latter, however, has had the management of the business for the past eleven years, and consequently at the time of purchase was well qualified to continue it successfully and profitably. In addition to his lumber-yard he is also the owner of valuable town property and his residence adjoining his place of business. His transactions extend over this section of the State, and he handles about fifty carloads of lumber annually. He also has a lucrative trade in pumps, plasterer's materials, and other similar commodities.

Mr. Riggs was born in Warrick County, Ind., in

1854, and is the son of A. W. and Martha (Spellman) Riggs, who removed from that State to Iowa in 1855. At the age of twenty years, in 1874, our subject was united in marriage with Miss Ella McWilliams, a native of his own State, and the daughter of Nathan and Ellen McWilliams. She was born in 1853, and by her marriage with our subject became the mother of two children, Birdie and Walter. Mrs. Riggs remained the affectionate companion of her husband for six years, and departed this life in April, 1880. Mr. Riggs was a second time married, to Miss Nanny McMahon, of Missouri, and they have two children, a son, Clyde, born May 23, 1881, and Mabel Lee, Nov. 25, 1886. Their home is pleasantly located, and they enjoy the confidence and esteem of a large circle of friends and acquaintances. Mr. Riggs is a member of the I. O. O. F. as P. G.; and the A. O. U. W.

BENJAMIN THOMAS, a resident of the Hawkeye State since the spring of 1865, is pleasantly located in Keokuk Township, on section 33, and successfully engaged in agricultural pursuits, and is also giving much attention to the raising of good grades of the various kinds of farm stock. Mr. Thomas is a native of the Buckeye State, having been born in Fayette County, Ohio, on the 20th of March, 1808. He is the son of John and Catharine (Putnam) Thomas, natives of Virginia, who removed to Ohio after their marriage and located upon a farm at an early period in the history of that State.

The subject of our sketch remained under the parental roof until he was fifteen years of age, and then went to Portsmouth, Ohio, where he was engaged in chopping at a salary of $8 per month. He was thus occupied for two years, and then started with a drove of 860 head of hogs from Portsmouth to Richmond, Va., which trip occupied two months. After his return to Ohio he engaged in farming pursuits for the following six years. He then returned to the old homestead in Ohio, where he took charge of his father's farm for two years afterward. In the meantime, on the 11th of July, 1833, he was united in marriage with Miss Patience Thompson, the daughter of Francis and Hessie (Templeton) Thompson, who were natives of Virginia. Of this union there were born three children: Minerva J., the wife of Mumford Jones, a farmer of Kansas; William J., engaged in agricultural pursuits in Green Township, this county, and Elizabeth A., who died in infancy.

After his marriage Mr. Thomas and his wife remained in Ohio for the following ten years, during which time he was engaged in farming and carrying on a cooper-shop, and then went to Brown County, Ill. The mother of these children closed her eyes to the scenes of earth on the 11th of March, 1851, and was buried near Versailles, Brown County, Ill. Mr. Thomas then removed from Brown to Knox County, and thence, in March, 1865, to Jefferson County, Iowa. Here he purchased a small farm which he cultivated for nearly three years, then sold out and moved into Wapello County. In the spring of 1868 he purchased eighty acres of unimproved land, upon which he established his present homestead. In the meantime he was the second time married, to Mrs. May Willis, the widow of R. P. Willis, who died June 11, 1847. She was the daughter of Benjamin and Lydia Eggers, both natives of Ohio. Of their last marriage there were born the following children: Matthew A., a farmer of Keokuk Township; Mary Patience, deceased, and buried in Brown County, Ill.; Benjamin F. is operating a farm in this county; Mary P. married Anson A. Brooks, a farmer and miner; Eliza W. is at home; Annie E., deceased, was buried in Adams County, Ill.; George E. is at home.

At an early age the subject of our sketch became greatly interested in religious matters and in the salvation of his fellow-men. He began to deliver brief addresses in public, and in 1843 was ordained as a local minister of the United Brethren Church. He was thus earnestly engaged until his health began to fail, or until about 1871. In the meantime, in 1860, he took a trip overland to Colorado, starting in March, the journey occupying about six months. He resumed his ministerial duties after returning, but in 1871 was obliged to abandon them. His labors in this direction were greatly blest, and he witnessed many conversions, with the comforting assurance that he had been instrumental in saving souls. Mr. and Mrs. Thomas are both members of the United Brethren Church, and politically our subject is a stanch Republican.

NATHANIEL PRESCOTT, a resident of Green Township since 1864, operates a snug farm on section 9, and is carrying on his farm pursuits and business transactions in that commendable manner that has gained for him the respect and esteem of his neighbors. He was born in Ireland in 1815, and is consequently well advanced in years, though still retaining his mental faculties and that energy of purpose which characterized him in his early youth. Mr. Prescott is the son of Robert and Jane (Agers) Prescott, both natives of Ireland. Five years after the birth of our subject they emigrated to America, and located on a farm in Muskingum County, Ohio, where they lived until 1840. They then removed to Pennsylvania, and for nine years following Nathaniel Prescott was engaged in boating on the Delaware River as Mate and Captain. In 1850 he returned to Ohio, where for the following five years he was engaged in farming pursuits. From there he went to Covington, Ind., and became a clerk in the dry-goods store of his uncle, being thus employed for two years. He then returned to Ohio, and from there again proceeded westward, to Scotland County, Mo., where he rented a farm until 1864. He then came into Wapello County, and located in Green Township, purchasing eighty acres of land, and upon which he established a permanent home. At the time he came into possession of this farm the land was in its original condition, but he industriously set about its improvement and cultivation, and met with that success which is the reward of enterprise and perseverance.

The marriage of Nathaniel Prescott and Miss Melissa Jane Gander was celebrated in Ohio in 1857. Mrs. P. is the daughter of John and Catharine (Schull) Gander, both natives of Virginia, and by her marriage with our subject has become the mother of four children: John William is employed in a foundry in Ottumwa; Addie also lives in that city; Emma Jane became the wife of William Rhodes, a plasterer, and lives in Ottumwa; Susanna is at home.

Mr. Prescott is highly esteemed in his community, and a member in good standing of the I. O. O. F. In politics he is a Republican, and he takes an active interest in all matters calculated to promote the welfare of his county and community. The father of our subject spent his last years in Ohio, and died there at the age of eighty-five years. The mother, after becoming ninety-five years of age, was fatally burned by falling into a fireplace when no one was near to assist her.

ISAAC SHIELDS, a self-made man, and one who has attained success in life through individual effort and economy, is at present a resident of the thriving little city of Eddyville. He was born in County Cavan, Ireland, in 1819, and is a son of James and Eliza (Niel) Shields, natives of the Emerald Isle. James Shields was a farmer by occupation, and followed his calling in his native country until his demise, in 1881, while in his eighty-ninth year. He was a member of the Presbyterian Church.

Our subject crossed the briny waters, and landed on the soil of our free Republic in 1848, settling soon thereafter at Pittsburgh, Pa. There he continued to reside for three years, engaged as clerk in the wholesale grocery business of Edward Hazelton. He then went to Harrison County, Ohio, and after a residence there of four years, during which time he was also merchandising, he came to this county and took up his residence near Eddyville, the date of his settlement being 1852, and engaged in farming, being thus occupied for about ten years. During the year 1863 he moved into the village and established his present residence, and has since made this his home, living a retired life.

Mr. Shields was first married July 20, 1849, and the lady chosen as his life companion was Miss Rebecca Sherrod, a native of Ohio. She died Jan. 29, 1857, after having borne him six children, two of whom are yet living—John G., a resident of Mahaska County, and Lemuel B., a farmer of Decatur County, this State. Our subject was a second time married, July 2, 1863, Miss Sarah Heacock being the other contracting party. She was born in Ohio, and is the daughter of John G. and Rachel (Peterson) Heacock, the former a native of Pennsylvania and the latter of Ohio. Mr. and Mrs. Heacock were both members of the Methodist Episcopal Church. Of this latter union three children have been born: William H., now in Minnesota; Eddie and Rachel E., both living at home.

Both Mr. and Mrs. Shields are members of the Methodist Episcopal Church. Our subject is the proprietor of six lots in Eddyville, and also owns 320 acres of good farming land in Decatur County. He has been a member of the School Board and also of the City Council of Eddyville.

Isaac Shields began life a poor boy, but by economy and industry has succeeded in accumulating a sufficiency to enable him to retire from active labor and pass the sunset of life in peace and quiet. He is a Republican in politics, and has always advocated the freedom of the races, and fifty years ago assisted the British Government in the freedom of the slaves on the Island of Jamaica.

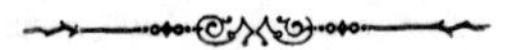

COLUMBUS N. UDELL, M. D., a prominent and successful physician of Blakesburg, was born in Guernsey County, Ohio, on the 15th of February, 1842. He is consequently in the prime of life, and, it is hoped, has many years of usefulness before him. His father, Dr. N. Udell, is a graduate of the College of Physicians and Surgeons, at Keokuk, and located in Appanoose County in 1848. His practice extended over Southern Iowa into Northern Missouri, and he located at Cedarville, whence, in 1884, he removed to Concordia, Kan. He has been President of the Des Moines Valley Medical Association, and member of the State and American Associations. He was born in Pennsylvania in 1817, and in early manhood was married in Monroe County, Ohio, to Miss Eliza Payne. They became the parents of five children, of whom our subject was the eldest: Alice A. became the wife of E. E. Swearingin, of Concordia, Kan.; Addison S. is a clerk in the wholesale drug-store of Blake, Bruce & Co., of Ottumwa, this State; John H. is engaged in mercantile pursuits in Concordia, Kan.; Ida E. married Kos Harris, an attorney at law, of Wichita, Kan. The wife and mother departed this life in 1883. She was a lady widely known and highly respected in this vicinity for her goodness of heart and sympathy with the afflicted and distressed. She was a consistent member of the Presbyterian Church, and at her death was mourned by a large circle of friends and acquaintances.

Dr. Udell, Sr., is still living, in Concordia, Kan., and has been a man of more than ordinary ability. He is an extensive reader, and keeps himself well posted on all matters of general interest, both in connection with his profession and in public matters. In 1855 he was elected to the State Senate of Iowa, in which he served with credit for three terms, and since early manhood has been a useful member of the community wherever his lot in life has been cast.

The subject of our sketch was only six years old when he came to Iowa with his parents. He received his early education in the pioneer log schoolhouse, and subsequently took a practical course of study at Hiram College, at the time the late President Garfield was President of that institution. At an early age he became greatly interested in the contents of his father's library, and began to read medicine under the supervision of the latter. In the winter of 1867–68 he attended the College of Physicians and Surgeons at Keokuk, and in the spring of the latter year hung out his shingle at Milledgeville, Appanoose Co., Iowa, subsequently graduating, and has been in active practice for a period of nineteen years, eight of which have been spent in Blakesburg, where he located in 1878. He is a member of the Des Moines Valley State and American Medical Association, and occupies an enviable position among his brethren of the profession in this locality.

Dr. Udell enlisted, in 1862, in the 3d Iowa Cavalry, served in that regiment for seventeen months, and then re-enlisted as a veteran in the 8th Iowa Cavalry, and served in this until the close of the war. He was engaged in the battles of Pea Ridge, Franklin, Nashville, Tenn., and the Hood raid through the same State; he was also at Pulaski, Columbia, Florence, Ala., Buzzard's Roost, Lost Mountain, and a great many small skirmishes. He enlisted as a private, and was discharged as Second Lieutenant.

Dr. Columbus N. Udell and Miss Harriet C. Wilson were married in Centerville, Iowa, Dec. 16, 1868. Mrs. U. is the daughter of T. O. and Mary (Capp) Wilson, natives respectively of Virginia and Ohio, who emigrated to Iowa in 1856. Dr. and Mrs. Udell have become the parents of seven children, viz.: Myrtle O., Orren O., Lola P., Roy C., Valena H., Zarelda M. and Mary G. Our subject and his family occupy a handsome residence, which in all respects is indicative of refined tastes and ample means. They enjoy the friendship and esteem of a large circle of acquaintances, which embrace the best class of people in the city.

A. W. RIGGS, engaged in the milling business at Eddyville, is a native of Connecticut, and was born in 1826. He accompanied his parents to Ohio when he was quite young, and in 1837 went with them to Indiana. There he continued to reside, engaging the while in agricultural pursuits, until he came to Henry County, this State, the date of his settlement being 1855: He came to this county in 1865, and here learned the business in which he is at present engaged.

Mr. Riggs is a son of S. B. and Almira (Short) Riggs, natives of Derby, Conn. The father was a shoemaker by trade, but followed farming during the latter years of his life. Mr. Riggs was married, in 1849, to Martha A. Spelman, a native of New York, and a daughter of O. Spelman, and to their union were given eight children, six of whom are now living, namely: Eva, wife of Andrew Baker, of Mahaska County; I. S., engaged in the lumber business at Eddyville; James H., editor of a paper at O'Neill, Neb.; Cora B., wife of J. H. Meredith, an attorney at law of the same place; E. S., living at home, and has part interest in our subject's mill; George D., residing in O'Neill, Neb., and engaged at the printer's trade.

Mr. Riggs takes an active interest in educational matters, and has been a member of the School Board of Eddyville for a number of years, and also Alderman. His good wife departed this life in 1869, aged thirty-nine years. He was again married, in 1873, to E. C. Armstrong, a native of Ohio. The milling business in which our subject is at present engaged was established in 1865 by Mr. Riggs and a gentleman by the name of Spelman. At that time there were only two pair of buhrs in the mill, but in 1880 it was rebuilt by our subject, and he now has four pair of buhrs, and is meeting with success in conducting the business.

JAMES H. VAN WINKLE has been a resident of the Hawkeye State for a period of forty-three years. He was born in Perry County, Ind., in 1835, and is the son of James and Matilda (Henton) Van Winkle, who were both natives of Nelson County, Ky. Upon coming to Iowa they located in Jefferson County, whence they removed to Wapello, where the father died in January, 1876, aged eighty-three years, and the mother in 1862, at the age of sixty-two. Our subject removed with his parents into Highland Township, this county, in 1844, and settled with them on section 31. He remained under the parental roof until 1874, and then became the owner of a tract of land on section 6, which he still occupies. His farm consists of 102 acres, finely improved, and in a good state of cultivation, and in his later days he is enjoying the fruits of his early industry.

Mr. Van Winkle was married, in 1866, to Miss Lettie J. Davis, the daughter of David T. and Lorinda (Baker) Davis, both natives of Kentucky. Her father was born in Madison County, in 1810, and was the son of Isaac and Jane (Jamison) Davis, both of Virginia. Mr. D. left his native State in 1833, and came to Van Buren County, Iowa, where for six years he was engaged in farming. His wife, Miss Lorinda Baker, was also a native of Madison County, Ky., and became the mother of nine children, of whom one died in infancy. The record of the others is as follows: Alexander died in 1882, aged forty-seven years, leaving a family of six children: Lettie J. is the wife of our subject; Jasper is farming in Oregon; David M. is farming in Wayne County, Iowa; Sarah E. is the wife of Dr. J. W. Bates, of Oregon; William H. is farming in Davis County, Iowa; Maggie married Reuben Lanman, of Davis County; Isaac is teaching and farming in the same county.

Mr. Van Winkle was the eighth of a family of eleven children, and in early life was trained to those habits of industry and economy which have been the secret of his later success. He has been prominent in the affairs of his township for many years, is warmly interested in educational matters, has held the various school offices, and is consulted upon matters pertaining to the general welfare of his community. Mr. and Mrs. V. are members of the Missionary Baptist Church.

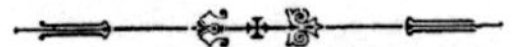

I. N. ROGERS, a prominent and prosperous citizen and business man of Eldon, Iowa, was born in Belmont County, Ohio, in 1821, and is a son of Michael and Rachel (Sherwood) Rogers, natives respectively of Massachusetts and New York. They removed to the State of Ohio after their marriage, and located upon a farm in Belmont County, removing thence into Guernsey, when their son, our subject, was about eighteen years old. Here the father established a store of general merchandise, and engaged his son, I. N., as clerk. They operated together for a period of ten years, after which, in 1849, our subject started west, crossed the Mississippi, and engaged in mercantile pursuits in Burlington, Iowa, until 1851, and after the beginning of the late war. He then became a suttler of the 1st Iowa Cavalry, remaining with this regiment for two years, and finally going to Southwest Missouri he established himself in business at Clinton, removing thence to Bloomfield, this State, where he was occupied for ten years in the hardware trade. Mr. Rogers came to Eldon in the spring of 1884, and although his residence has been comparatively brief he has already established a prosperous trade. His stock comprises a full line of hardware and stoves, the latter of which he makes a specialty.

The marriage of Mr. Rogers and Miss Sarah M. Gillett, of New York, was celebrated in 1843, in Guernsey County, Ohio. Mrs. R. is the daughter of Comfort and Caroline (Dodd) Gillett, and by her marriage with our subject has become the mother of six children, as follows: Carrie is the wife of J. E. Tolfree, of Springfield, Mo.; Albert is a locomotive engineer, having his home in Wymore, Neb.; Walter P. is a cattle dealer of Nebraska; L. E. is a dentist of Ottumwa; Forrest died in May, 1884, at the age of thirty years; Herbert is a clerk in his father's store at Eldon.

Mr. and Mrs. Rogers are members in good standing of the Congregational Church, and Mr. R. belongs to the I. O. O. F., with which he has been connected for many years. He has been a prominent man in the public affairs of Wapello County, and takes an active interest in every enterprise calculated to promote the welfare of this locality. During his residence in Missouri he was Treasurer of Henry County for two years. His early education was obtained in the common schools of his native town, and when he started out in the world he had nothing to depend upon but his own industry and perseverance. He is now accounted one of the best citizens of Eldon, and is rapidly accumulating a large circle of friends and acquaintances.

Michael Rogers, the father of our subject, was a resident of Bloomfield during the latter years of his life and closed his eyes upon the scenes of earth at the advanced age of eighty-six years. The wife and mother died in Licking County, Ohio, aged about sixty-five years.

C. W. NICKLIN, engaged in general merchandising at Eldon, Iowa, established his business here in 1883, and in July, 1886, took in as a partner Mr. J. A. Trott, the business now being carried on under the firm name of Nicklin & Trott, their stock including dry-goods, groceries, boots and shoes, hats and caps, etc. Mr. Nicklin is a native of Tyler County, W. Va., and was born in 1857. His parents were William W.

and Elizabeth (Smith) Nicklin, natives of the same State. The subject of our sketch was reared on a farm until fourteen years of age, and then attended the academy at Troy, Iowa, taking a three years' course, after which he commenced teaching school, which he followed for four years continuously in Van Buren and Davis Counties. He became a resident of Eldon in 1875, arriving here on the 17th of June. He was employed as a clerk by Mr. Hunnel, engaged in that business until Dec. 1, 1883, when he went into business for himself, as stated.

Mr. Nicklin was married, July 14, 1883, to Miss Jennie M. Kelley, of Muscatine County, Iowa, and they have become the parents of one child, Myrtle, now aged two and one-half years. Mr. Nicklin is Republican in politics, and a member of the Congregational Church, of which he is Treasurer. He also belongs to the I. O. O. F. and K. of P. He is a straightforward and energetic business man, and in all respects is considered one of the valuable citizens of this community. He has served as a member of the School Board and is a friend of temperance and morality, exerting his influence as opportunity occurs for the promotion of every good and worthy object.

The parental family of our subject consisted of ten children, of whom eight are still living, all comfortably situated in life and most of them in homes of their own, being variously engaged. One brother is in the dry-goods business in Ottumwa; one occupies a similar position in Fairfield, and another is a farmer of Van Buren County, where the father is still living on a farm.

DAVID H. MICHAEL, a general farmer and stock-raiser of Center Township, owning 240 acres of valuable land and residing on section 1, came into this county in 1846, and is to-day living upon the land which he settled upon at that time. He is a native of Tennessee, having been born in Franklin County in 1819. His parents were Barnabas and Sarah (Johnston) Michael, natives of North Carolina and Virginia respectively. The former was descended from German ancestry. The same year our subject was born, Feb. 14, 1819, the elder Michael moved into Illinois, locating in Montgomery County, and was a very early settler of that section. D. H. was there reared on a farm, educated in the subscription schools, and at the age of sixteen moved with his parents to Indiana, locating about twenty-five miles north of Indianapolis. Here the son remained, assisting his father for two years longer, when, at the early age of seventeen, he left the parental roof, and went into the world to work for himself. We next find him engaged in the milling business, where for the following four years he labored in the mill, doing both grain and lumber work.

In 1844 our subject went to Knox County, Mo., where he engaged in farming until 1846, at which time he came to Wapello County and located upon his present property, and with the exception of two years passed in Ottumwa, when serving as Sheriff of Wapello County, has made this his home. In 1853 he was elected to the above-named office on the Democratic ticket, and served two years. In politics he has been a Republican since 1861. He has served his community in numerous official positions, among them being a member of the Board of Supervisors for five years. He has a splendid farm, well improved, and is regarded as one of the leading men of the county. He is a radical Prohibitionist, and takes an active part in all public affairs.

Mr. Michael was married, April 21, 1839, to Elizabeth Shaul, a native of Hamilton, Ind., and a daughter of Peter Shaul, a native of Virginia, whose father was a native of France. By this union two children were born, namely, Sarah, who became the wife of Harvey Mulford, who was a member of the 17th Iowa Infantry, and was killed at the battle of Champion Hills; his widow died in 1876; Lee J., the other child, is living at Ottumwa. Mrs. Michael died in February, 1843, and he was subsequently married, in 1844, to Zarilda Shaul, a sister of his first wife. Two years later he was called upon to mourn her loss. In 1848 he was married to Jane Hull, a native of Mahoning County, Ohio, and a daughter of John Hull, a native of Pennsylvania. To them have been born six children, namely, Ferris J., who died at the age of five years; O. H., who was killed at the age of twenty-eight by an explosion of mining powder; the explosion occurred while drilling for the purpose of developing a mine at Gunnison, Col.: Hiram F., now living at Emporia, Kan.; B. F., living at home; H. W., residing in Custer County, Neb.; L. J. was a soldier in the late war, enlisting in August, 1862, in Company B, 36th Iowa Vol. Inf. He served in that regiment about twelve months, and then went into a colored regiment and was finally promoted to the rank of Captain, serving three and a half years. Mr. M. and his wife are members of the Methodist Episcopal Church, of which he is a Steward.

DR. E. C. PYLE, physician and surgeon, has been a resident of Ottumwa for a period of two years, and successfully engaged in the practice of his profession. He occupies a high standing in the Hawkeye State as one of the best read and most skillful practitioners in the Mississippi Valley. Dr. Pyle is a native of Philadelphia, Pa., his birth occurring on the 7th day of June, 1824. He is the son of Joseph and Mary (Berkhart) Pyle, both natives of the same State. His father was reared a Quaker, and descended from ancestors who came over from England with William Penn. Joseph Pyle was a preacher for many years among the Friends, but finally wandered away from his first teaching, and was excluded from the community. He was afterward solicited to acknowledge his error and return to the Friends, but having rather resented their former action, he declined to return to them.

When our subject was a lad of twelve years old his parents removed from Pennsylvania and joined a Quaker settlement in Richmond, Ind., where he grew to manhood, reared in the Quaker faith, and educated in the subscription schools. He was a bright and studious boy, and in early youth began to mark out his plans for the future. Since he began to think seriously upon this future it had been his wish to become a physician like his brother-in-law, J. A. Salter, but this plan his mother had always opposed. He was determined, however, to adopt the profession, and at the age of eighteen commenced studying with this end in view. He started out as an allopath, but, after becoming acquainted with the principles of the homeopathic system, he identified himself with the latter, and has practiced under its methods since that time. After completing a thorough course of study, the young physician commenced the practice of his profession in Richmond, Ind., and was uniformly successful from the start. He has always been opposed to severe measures in treatment and to nauseating medicines, and in the course of his practice has largely resorted to magnetism, with flattering results.

Dr. Pyle was married in Long Island, N. Y., in 1848, to Miss Phœbe Wiggins, and they became the parents of three children: Mary E. is the wife of A. M. Beaty, of Wilson County, Kan.; Joseph A. is a resident of Centerville, Iowa, and Frank H., of Ottumwa. Mrs. Phœbe W. Pyle remained the companion of her husband for only seven years, departing this life at Richmond, Ind., in 1855. She was a descendant of Quaker ancestry, and adhered religiously to the faith of her childhood. After the death of his wife Dr. Pyle removed to Keokuk, Lee County, where he practiced his profession and also engaged in real-estate business for one year. He then returned to Richmond and remained until 1862, thence went back to Lee County, and the following year was united in marriage with Miss Ada Wickersham, of Keokuk, who by her union with our subject became the mother of three children. Of these only two are living—Charles, a physician of Mt. Sterling, Iowa, and Harry A., a jeweler of Ottumwa.

In 1866 Dr. Pyle went into Kansas, where he resided until 1875. He then spent two years in Centerville, Van Buren County, this State, and in 1884 became a resident of Ottumwa. He has administered to the ailments of mankind without money and without price, being one of those rare characters to whom the consciousness of doing good is ample reward. He is a strict temperance man, never having taken a drink of whisky in his life, and is also a total abstainer from tobacco in any form.

Dr. Pyle has long been a prominent member of the I. O. O. F., having been connected with the order for a period of thirty-eight years. He passed all the subordinate Chairs in Indianapolis, and represented Woodward Lodge No. 128 in the convention at Richmond. He now belongs to Lodge No. 230, at Ottumwa; he has always taken a deep interest in the success of the order and has been one of its most valued members.

THOMAS TOOTHAKER, a self-made man, a successful farmer and stock-raiser, and one of the old pioneers of Wapello County, who yet lives to tell of the trials incident to its early settlement, he having been a resident of the county since 1850, is following his avocation on his fine farm on section 19, Green Township. Mr. Toothaker was born in Licking County, Ohio, June 21, 1820, and is a son of Nathaniel and Catherine (Campbell) Toothaker. The father was a native of Ohio, and the mother of Scotland. The latter came to this country when quite young, and died when Thomas was about seven years of age, in 1827, and is buried in Delaware County, Ohio. The father died Oct. 21, 1872, having attained the venerable age of seventy-five years and eleven months. They were both members of the Methodist Episcopal Church for about fifty years, and were devoted Christians, always taking an active part in church affairs, and respected by all who knew them.

The early life of our subject was passed on his father's farm, and in attending subscription schools. In 1842 he left the parental homestead to do for himself, and going West located in Van Buren County, Iowa. There he rented a farm and continued to follow his calling in that county until 1850, in the meantime entering ninety acres of land in Wapello County. He subsequently settled on his homestead in Wapello County and has there been a resident until the present time. He developed his present farm from its original natural condition, and has brought it to a high state of cultivation.

Nov. 19, 1844, Mr. Toothaker was united in marriage with Miss Mary Ann Kisinger. She was born April 19, 1819, in Jefferson County, Va., and is a daughter of George and Nancy (McCormick) Kisinger. Her father was born in Maryland, and her mother in Virginia. He was a member of the Methodist Episcopal Church, and she was raised a Quaker, and they were both respected and honored citizens of the community in which they lived. The father died Feb. 7, 1872, while in his eighty-sixth year, and his last resting-place is at Burlington, Iowa; the mother died in 1852, aged fifty-six years, and is buried at Pittsburg, Iowa. Thomas Toothaker and wife are the parents of seven children: George and Nathaniel (twins) are farmers, and reside in Pottawatomie County, Kan., both are married and have families; Catherine is the wife of Joseph Draper, a farmer of Ringgold County, Iowa; Martha J. is living at home; James is a farmer by calling, and a resident of Pottawatomie County, Kan.; Benjamin is also a farmer, and resides in Ringgold County, Iowa; Mary E. lives at home; she is a teacher and graduate from the schools of Ottumwa. Two of the eldest sons and Benjamin were also teachers.

Mr. and Mrs. Toothaker of this notice are members of the Methodist Episcopal Church, and both take an active interest in advancing the cause of the Master. Our subject started in life with comparatively nothing, and by industry and economy, coupled with good judgment, he has succeeded in accumulating a competency, which enables him to pass the sunset of life in peace and quiet, and retired from the active labors of life. They have given their children a good education, and look back upon their past with but few regrets. In politics Mr. Toothaker votes with the Democratic party.

PETER REAM resides upon section 1, Agency Township, where he is engaged in general farming and stock-raising, and owns 122 acres of good land, all of which is under cultivation. He is a native of Stark County, Ohio, born Feb. 1, 1823, and is the son of Peter and Barbara A. (Smith) Ream, who were natives of Pennsylvania. In 1853 his parents moved to Indiana, where his mother died in 1855, and his father about 1858. The latter was a Methodist

Episcopal minister, and a man of more than ordinary ability.

While living in Indiana, in 1852, Peter Ream and Sarah E. Shuman were united in marriage. She was born in Cumberland County, Pa., Sept. 28, 1834, and was the daughter of Jonas and Hannah (Bender) Shuman. Her parents moved from Pennsylvania to Ohio in 1837, and lived there till 1847, when they moved to Indiana, where her father died in 1856. He was a farmer and stock-grower, and a man who enjoyed the respect and confidence of all who knew him. Her mother still made that State her home, but in 1871, while on a visit to Ohio, to see a sister who was at the point of death, she herself took sick, and died Jan. 7, 1872. Her remains were taken back to Indiana and buried by the side of those of her husband in the old cemetery at Akron.

Two children were born to Mr. and Mrs. Ream, both of whom died in infancy. They raised a girl, Catharine Shuman, who subsequently married Joseph Watson, and is now living in Ohio. Louisa Ream was also reared by them; she married Charles Naftger, but is now deceased. They also adopted a boy who took their name, and is now married and living in Canton, Ohio. Mr. and Mrs. Ream came to Wapello County in 1884. They are probationers of the Methodist Episcopal Church. Politically he is a Republican.

CONRAD STOCKER, an enterprising farmer and stock-raiser of Keokuk Township, and pleasantly located on section 4, on a farm of ninety-nine and one-half acres, is carrying on the different departments of his business intelligently and successfully, and enjoys in a marked degree the esteem and confidence of his fellow-townsmen. Our subject is a native of Tuscarawas County, Ohio, and was born Nov. 18, 1820, his parents being Daniel and Christina (Steiger) Stocker, natives of Pennsylvania and of German ancestry. They removed from their native State across the Father of Waters to Iowa, in 1846, about the time it was admitted into the Union as a State. Their first location was in Monroe County, whence they removed, in 1861, to Wapello, settling in Keokuk Township.

About this time the Rebellion began to assume alarming proportions, and Conrad, who had been reared to sentiments of patriotism, proffered his services for the defense of the Union, enlisting in the 7th Iowa Infantry. Their first rendezvous was at Burlington, where Mr. S. was mustered into the United States service. The regiment was then sent to St. Louis, where they were equipped for service, and were soon afterward ordered to Bird's Point, remaining there in camp for the next two months. While at Bird's Point Mr. Stocker was detailed as nurse at Mound City Hospital, where he served one year, after which he was sent to his regiment, which was stationed at La Grange. They soon afterward proceeded to Iuka, and from there went into winter quarters at Pulaski, Tenn. Here Mr. S. suffered with an attack of rheumatism, and rather than be sent to the hospital, at his request, was detailed to the pioneer corps and put into the wagon-shops, where he assisted as well as he could in repairing ambulances and wagons for the spring campaign. When that time arrived, in company with Richard Hayes, our subject took charge of a wagon train which was bound for Kingston, Ga. At this point the train was divided, and a part sent on to Rome, and soon afterward Mr. S. was sent to his regiment, which was then in front of Atlanta. His term of enlistment having expired, he received his descriptive roll from Capt. Benjamin, and started northward just as the battle opened, getting away just in time to escape the dangers of that terrible siege. He was sent to Louisville, Ky., where he received his honorable discharge, after giving to his country his faithful services for a period of three years. While in the service he was always found at his post ready to do his duty, and received the marked approval of his superior officers.

When a little over eighteen years old, Feb. 17, 1839, Mr. Stocker was united in marriage with Miss Mary C. Ginther. Their wedding took place in Ohio, and they have lived happily together for a period of forty-eight years. They became the parents of thirteen children, four daughters and nine sons, the record of whom is as follows: Daniel, the eldest, is deceased; Louisa married Joseph Bader of this county; William is deceased; Mary became the wife of W. A. Hackett, of Appanoose County, Iowa; James is in Seward County, Neb.; Thomas J. lives in this county; John M. is a resident of Ottumwa; George W. resides in this county; Harry L. is in Ottumwa; Joseph A., in Carroll County; Rosanna died in infancy; Edward M. is at home; Sarah I. and Alfred died in infancy.

The family residence is a model of convenience and comfort, and Mr. S. and his family are fully enjoying the good things of this life. He has been energetic, industrious and frugal, and is reaping the just rewards of his labors. Mr. and Mrs. S. are members in good standing of the Main street Methodist Episcopal Church of Ottumwa, and politically our subject affiliates with the Republican party. Socially he belongs to Clautman Post No. 69, G. A. R.

PETER NELSON, a resident of Chillicothe, in this county, is a fine representative of that enterprising, honest and industrious Scandinavian element which has so materially assisted in the development of the resources of the West. He was born in Sweden on the 15th of January, 1848, and is the son of Jennisen and Betty (Loda) Nelson, natives of the same country. They emigrated to America in 1868, landing in New York City and coming directly to Ottumwa, Iowa. Here, two years later, Peter, our subject, and his brother, John, purchased lot No. 8, in block 7, and in 1871 erected a comfortable dwelling-house for their parents. This was one and a half stories in height, and contained nine large rooms, and in it the father and mother were comfortably established, and their wants carefully looked after by the affectionate sons. Here the father died in 1869, and was buried in Monterville Cemetery in Polk Township; the mother lives in Chillicothe.

Peter Nelson, of our sketch, in 1872, sold out his interest in the homestead at Ottumwa and removed to Chillicothe, where he engaged as foreman of section 19 on the C., B. & Q. R. R., running east from Chillicothe, which position he occupied for ten years thereafter. In the fall of 1881 he took charge of the track-laying on the O. & K. from Comstock to Carver, and also the placing of switches, continuing with this company for two years, after which he abandoned his connection with railroads. During these years he had been economical as well as industrious, and accumulated sufficient means to purchase a tract of land comprising forty acres lying just outside the limits of Chillicothe, and valued at $75 per acre. Upon this he subsequently erected a handsome frame dwelling, and in 1885 established the creamery with which he is at present occupied. This is fitted up with all modern improvements, with engine, steam vats, patent churns and butter-worker, and is considered one of the best establishments of its kind in this section of the State. It has a capacity of 10,000 pounds of butter per month, which its proprietor ships to New York, Chicago, Denver, and other important points. The excellence of his products commends them at once wherever they are used, and from this Mr. Nelson reaps a handsome income.

The possessions which our subject now enjoys are the result of his own industry and enterprise, and his entire property has been accumulated since he came to this country. He is a gentleman of intelligence, and keeps himself well posted upon all matters of general interest. He takes a just pride in being the citizen of a country which places within the reach of the poor man the same opportunities of advancement which it accords to the more fortunate, and is as patriotic in his thoughts and feelings as the genuine American-born citizen.

The marriage of Peter Nelson and Miss Annie Johnson took place on the 14th of August, 1869, at Munterville, Iowa. Mrs. Nelson is a native of the same country as her husband, and came to this country when quite a child, in 1852, with her parents, whose family consisted of seven children. She remained under the parental roof until her marriage with our subject, receiving careful home training and a fair education in the public schools. Her mother departed this life at Ottumwa in 1880, and her father died in Sweden. After first coming to this country her mother located in Chicago, where her two eldest sons died of cholera. She was widely known and universally respected for her excellent personal traits of character, her rare virtues, and kind, womanly sympathy for the afflicted and distressed.

Mr. and Mrs. Nelson became the parents of five children, as follows: Otto P., born July 21, 1871, died Sept. 31, 1872; Lillie F. was born in Chillicothe, April 11, 1874; Michael died in infancy; Clara Z. was born in Chillicothe, July 1, 1877; Lewis P. was born Nov. 11, 1879, and died just one year from the day of his birth. Mr. and Mrs. Nelson are members in good standing of the Lutheran Church, and socially our subject is a member of the I. O. O. F. His excellent qualities have been duly recognized by his fellow townsmen, who elected him a member of the Board of Aldermen in 1883, and he has held other important positions in matters pertaining to the welfare of his community. Their handsome and attractive home is one of the pleasantest spots in the township, and both Mr. Nelson and his family are held in the highest respect by the community. His property lies in Cass Township on section 36, and invariably attracts the eye of the traveler passing through this vicinity. His business and other transactions are carried on in a straightforward and systematic manner, and the whole premises gives evidence of the thrift, prosperity and good judgment of the proprietor.

JAMES McMULLIN, a farmer and stock-grower on section 24, Richland Township, was born in Columbiana County, Ohio, Dec. 25, 1836, and is a son of Ananias and Mary McMullin. The former was born in the State of New York, and was a stone and brick mason, removing with his parents to Ohio at a very early day. About 1842 he moved to Parkersburg, Va., and from there to Pomeroy, Ohio, where he continued to work at his trade. In 1852 he moved to Henderson County, Ill., where he remained until 1866, at which time he came to Wapello County, where he has since continued to reside. His wife died in Henderson County, Ill., in October, 1857. Our subject also came to Wapello County in 1866, and purchased 160 acres of land, where he has since continued to reside. In October, 1861, he enlisted in Co. H, 11th Ill. Vol. Cav., commanded by Capt. John C. Knowlton. He was in the battle of Corinth, and was discharged at that place on account of disability contracted while in the service.

On the 14th day of September, 1865, Mr. McMullin married Martha Neighbors, daughter of William and Melinda Neighbors. Of this union there were five children—Charles M., Effie M., William A., and Robert and Emma (deceased). The mother died in February, 1875, and Mr. McMullin subsequently married Margaret Johnston, widow of Solomon Johnston, and daughter of Walter Story. Her father was an engineer, and ran the first engine that ran on the railroad from Baltimore to Wheeling, W. Va. He was a master mechanic, following railroading for twenty-one years, and was killed Nov. 25, 1857, while overseeing the work of getting upon the track a locomotive that had been ditched. To this last union of our subject three children have been born—Walter S., James M. and Allie M. Mr. McMullin is the owner of 160 acres of good land, which is well improved. He and his wife are members of the Methodist Episcopal Church.

F. L. REINHARD, a highly respected citizen of Wapello County, occupies a comfortable homestead in Green Township, located on section 28, the property of his father. He is one of the younger citizens of the county, and was born here in 1855, his parents being Henry and Elizabeth Reinhard. He is engaged in general farming and has eighty acres of fairly cultivated land, upon which is a good dwelling-house and all necessary out-buildings convenient for the storage of grain and the shelter of stock. He has a good supply of farm implements and, occupied with his peaceful pursuits, is fulfilling the duties of a good citizen, and as time and opportunity afford, casting his influence in favor of temperance, education and morality.

Mr. Reinhard was married, in December, 1881, to Miss Sarah J. King, also a native of Wapello County, and the daughter of Cyrus D. King, of Center Township. Of this union there have been born two children: Cyrus Henry, who died in September, 1883, aged seven months, and Verdon George, born July 22, 1885. Mr. and Mrs. R. are members in good standing of the Methodist Protestant Church, and Mr. R. belongs to the I. O. O. F. He is also a member of Green Township Protective Society, and of the society called "Hobobs." Mrs. R. is a member of Rebecca Lodge. In addition to his general farming operations Mr. Reinhard is giving considerable attention to the breeding of fine stock, making a specialty of Canadian-French horses, and is in possession of one especially fine animal, which weighs 1,500 pounds.

Mr. Reinhard takes an intelligent interest in the affairs of his township and county, and has been President of the School Board, beside occupying other positions of trust among the councils of his townsmen. He is still a young man, full of enterprise and plans for the future, and if permitted to live a long life, will contribute his share toward its labors and the fulfillment of its duties.

DR. A. C. OLNEY, of Eddyville, ranks among the pioneer settlers of Iowa, having come to Wapello County with his parents in 1846. He was born in Morgan County, Ohio, Oct. 13, 1817, and is the son of Oman and Tryphena (Cheadle) Olney, his father a native of Marietta, Ohio, born June 23, 1795, and his mother of Barnard, Windsor Co., Vt., born Oct. 27, 1798. They removed from Ohio to McLean County, Ill., in 1830, and thence in 1846, to this county, where they remained the balance of their lives. The father of our subject died March 16, 1872, at the ripe age of seventy-five years, and the mother July 16, 1867, aged sixty-nine years.

The subject of our sketch passed the years of his early childhood and youth in his native State, and pursued his primary studies in the common schools of Morgan County, Ohio. After coming to Illinois he entered Knox College at Galesburg, and was a graduate of the first class which was turned out of that institution. This was in June, 1846. After completing his studies here he went into Henry County, Iowa, and taught school during the winters of 1846–47. Thence he removed to Jefferson County, Iowa, where he commenced the study of medicine in the office of Dr. W. W. Cottle, late of Fairfield, this State, and commenced the practice of his profession four years later at Chillicothe, in this county. Wishing, however, to perfect himself still further in the intricacies of his calling, he went to Keokuk and entered the College of Physicians and Surgeons, which was then called the Iowa University. From this institution he graduated on the 9th of February, 1853, and returning to Chillicothe resumed his practice, and continued there for the following twenty-five years. He became prominent in the affairs of that vicinity, and was especially interested in educational matters, being at one time County Superintendent of Schools. He removed to Ottumwa on the 1st of January, 1878, and followed his profession until June, 1881, in the meantime being County Physician and Coroner of Wapello County for a period of four years. On the 1st of June in the year last mentioned he removed to Eddyville, and in this city, as elsewhere, soon became prominent in his profession, and a worthy and valued citizen. At the present time he is City Physician, with which position he has been honored for five years past.

Dr. Olney was united in marriage with Miss Eliza Ann Saunders on the 4th of April, 1817. Mrs. O. was a native of Wood County, Va., born Sept. 30, 1817, and departed this life in Chillicothe Feb. 4, 1870. Of this marriage there were born six children, of whom the record is as follows: George W. is a farmer of Ringgold County, Iowa; Tryphena L. is engaged as a milliner and dressmaker in Chillicothe; Susan M. married Ely Bailey, a railroad man, and they make their home in Chillicothe; Eliza Ann, Mrs. Jason Welsh, also lives in the latter-named city.

Dr. Olney was married the second time, on the 23d of October, 1870, to Miss Frances A. Daines. The present Mrs. Olney was born in Carroll County, Ill., Oct. 7, 1839, and is the daughter of Caleb and Charlotte Daines; she was reared and educated in Illinois. Our subject and wife occupy a handsome residence in Eddyville, located on Third street, and enjoy the esteem of a large circle of friends and acquaintances. The Doctor has been successful in his practice in this county and ranks among the leading physicians. He is a member of Chillicothe Lodge No. 115, I. O. O. F., and the Wapello Medical Society, also the Des Moines Valley Medical Association, and is a permanent member of the Iowa State Medical Association. The Doctor never fails to vote the Republican ticket.

S. R. MITCHEL, M. D., an esteemed member of the medical profession of Ottumwa, is a native of Springfield, Ill., and was born on the 14th of April, 1826. He is the son of Payton and Elizabeth (Briggs) Mitchel, the father a native of Hampshire County, Va., and the mother of Kentucky. They were married in the latter State in 1812, and at an early day emigrated to Springfield, Ill., where they remained until 1827, thence went into McLean County, settling at Danvers, and engaged in agricultural pursuits. They located upon a tract of unimproved land, which they improved and cultivated successfully, and established a comfortable homestead, where they lived the remainder of their days. They were people highly respected in their community, and prominently connected with the Cumberland Presbyterian Church.

Dr. Mitchel was reared on the farm of his parents and received a fair education in the common schools, which was supplemented by attendance at Kellogg's Institute, in Tremont, Tazewell County, Ill., where he took a three years' course, in the meantime pursuing his studies with unremitting interest and attention. He had first intended to become a civil engineer, but the state of his health compelled him to abandon this project, and he concluded to devote himself to the study of medicine. He accordingly entered the office of Dr. E. K. Cruthers, of Bloomington, and in the winter of 1853–54 attended a full course of lectures at Rush Medical College, Chicago, and soon afterward entered upon the practice of his profession at Bowling Green, Ill.

In 1855 Dr. Mitchel went to Franklin County, being one of a few who assisted in the organization of the county, and was elected as the first Clerk of the Court. He was subsequently elected County Judge, serving a term of two years, and transacting all the business of the county. In the spring of 1862, during the progress of the late Civil War, he was appointed Acting Assistant Surgeon of the United States Army, and was connected with the service until 1864. While in this locality he took occasion to attend a course of lectures at the St. Louis Medical College, from which he graduated March 4, 1864. That same year he came to Ottumwa, and entered upon the practice of his profession, which he has followed continuously in this city for a period of twenty-two years.

The marriage of Dr. S. R. Mitchel and Miss Fannie Stoddard took place in Franklin County, Iowa, in the fall of 1862. Mrs. M. is a native of Litchfield, Conn., and was born in 1837. Of her union with our subject there were born six children, only three of whom survive, viz., Clara, Mary and Fannie. Mrs. Fannie Mitchel, after remaining the faithful companion of her husband for twelve years, departed this life on the 12th of February, 1874. She was a highly esteemed Christian lady, and an earnest and sincere member of the Episcopal Church, in which she had been reared.

JEFFERSON WILLIAMSON, M. D., the subject of this sketch, was born in Adams County, Ohio, March 31, 1827. He received a thorough common-school education, which was supplemented with a two years' course under Prof. Robert Buck, of West Union, Ohio. His medical preceptor was Dr. H. G. Jones, and his degree of M. D. was taken at the Medical Department of the Western Reserve College at Cleveland, Ohio, class of 1852. In May following he was united in marriage to Miss Sarah N. Jones, of Wilmington, same State, and in November of that year (1852) they came to Iowa, and have made Ottumwa their home to this date. Their only child, Maggie, was married to Mr. A. J. Colt, Sept. 21, 1881.

Dr. Williamson is one of the leading physicians of Southern Iowa and is well known to the profession throughout the State. He has remained stead-

ames McAdam
Davis Caldwell

fastly in the practice and at the same time has been an earnest student, not alone of medicine, but in the broader fields of science and philosophy as well. His contributions to medical science may be found in the current journals and in the published transactions of the Iowa State Medical Society. Among the subjects treated may be mentioned articles on insanity, ovarian cysts, uterine fibroids, and perineal rupture.

Dr. Williamson was Vice President of the State Society in 1865 and President in 1873. He is a member of the American Medical Association, and an officer of the International Medical Congress to be held in Washington, D. C., in September, 1887. He is President of the Ottumwa Loan and Building Association, and also President and Medical Director of the Iowa Mutual Aid Association. He takes an active interest in all matters affecting the public welfare. In politics Dr. W. is a Republican, and prior to the organization of that party was an Abolitionist. He is an independent thinker and a forcible writer.

PARIS CALDWELL, a prominent citizen of the county, is a farmer and stock-grower on section 14, Center Township. The desirability and value of Mr. Caldwell's place is largely enhanced by its close proximity to the business center of the city of Ottumwa. His farm comprises 120 acres, about fifty-four of which are in the corporation. He is one of the few pioneers of 1843 that are yet left in Wapello County. He was born in Ohio County, Va., March 13, 1818, and is a son of John and Sarah (Mulligan) Caldwell. The former was a native of Scotland, and died when Paris was but eleven months old.

The subject of this sketch came from his native State to Burlington, Iowa, in 1841, where he remained seven months, and then went to what is now Davis County, Iowa, and remained there until May, 1843, when he came to Wapello County, made claim to the land on which he now resides, and which he afterward purchased from the Government. For two years after coming to Wapello County he lived a bachelor's life. He was then united in marriage to Margaret Hackney, daughter of William and Ellen Hackney, of Virginia. She was born Dec. 22, 1824, and died Nov. 26, 1863. To this union there were eight children born: John R., who married Clara J. Jordan, and now lives in Kansas City, Mo.; Sarah R., deceased; Clara A. is the wife of Edward Graves, living in Joplin, Mo.; Mary F., deceased; Anna L. is the wife of Newton Annison, living on her father's place; Charles S., deceased; Joseph S., living at St. Joseph, Mo.; Cassius C., deceased. Mr. Caldwell, after the death of his first wife, contracted a marriage with Mrs. Walker, widow of William Walker. She was born Oct. 8, 1825, and died Sept. 17, 1877. To this union there was one child born, Blanche, now living with her father.

Mr. Caldwell is a member of the Masonic fraternity, and politically is a Republican. When he first came to Iowa it was yet a Territory, and so remained for five years. For fourteen years after his arrival, there was not a mile of railroad in all the State. The only means of conveyance was by water or by the slow going ox-team, or that of the not much faster horses. The Indians yet existed in great numbers, and that portion of the territory now comprised in the county of Wapello was almost unknown, there being only the Indian agency at what is now called Agency City. The changes that have since taken place it is hardly possible for man to realize. In not one of the ninety-nine counties of the State but what the seat of justice is penetrated by the railroad, the markets of the world are brought to our very doors and the news of the world is given to us day by day, almost as soon as the events occur.

Mr. Caldwell is one of those men we find so thickly scattered over Iowa, and who undoubtedly form the best element of her society, and who were reared under the beneficent influences of the schools, and refinement of the society of the older settled States. Such men are well equipped to go forth and open up a new empire. They could lay its foundations broad, deep and solid, so that the colossal edifice of a great commonwealth might be reared upon it without hazard to the highest pinnacle to which Government or human society reaches.

To those people, Iowa to-day largely owes her greatness, and to this class the subject of this sketch belongs. As one of the representative pioneers of the county, we place the portrait of Mr. Caldwell in this volume.

JAMES McADAMS, of Cass Township, is prosperously engaged in farming and stock-raising on section 6, where he owns and occupies an attractive homestead, and as a citizen enjoys the confidence and esteem of his fellow-men. He is a descendant of stanch and warm-hearted Irish ancestry, and is himself a native of Erin's Green Isle, having been born near Belfast in the year 1807. His parents were William and Hannah (Brown) McAdams, who passed their entire lives in their native Ireland. Our subject remained in his native country until 1835, and then resolved to emigrate to the New World. He accordingly set sail, and after a voyage of several weeks, landed in New York City, whence, after one week he proceeded to Philadelphia, and thence to Baltimore, where he remained for six months. He then went into the agricultural district of Somerset County, Pa., where he engaged in farming for a few seasons, and from there proceeded to Ohio, where, after a few months spent in various pursuits, he engaged as a boatman on the Mississippi and Ohio Rivers until 1861. The Civil War then being in progress, he embarked on a Government vessel and was wounded while on duty, from which wound he has never fully recovered.

Mr. McAdams made his first visit to Wapello County in 1855, and then entered 400 acres of land, which he has since brought to a fine state of cultivation. The homestead now comprises 300 acres, and the residence and other farm buildings are substantial structures fully in keeping with the character and enterprise of the proprietor. Mr. McAdams has given considerable attention to stock-raising, and keeps a goodly number of high grade animals.

The marriage of James McAdams and Miss Emma Hover took place on the 10th of January, 1864, in Cass Township. The wife of our subject was born Feb. 18, 1846, in Indiana, and was the daughter of Daniel and Sarah (Dougherty) Hover, the former a native of Pennsylvania, and the mother of Irish ancestry. Mr. and Mrs. McAdams became the parents of nine children, a record of whom is as follows: William was born Feb. 25, 1866; James F., Sept. 10, 1867; Mary M., May 11, 1869; Daniel, Jan. 10, 1871; Elvira died in infancy, John F. was born June 17, 1875; Florence, Oct. 10, 1877; Thomas died in infancy; Lewis J. was born June 11, 1886. The family are regular attendants of the Christian Church, of which our subject and his wife are members in good standing. Mr. McAdams is the friend and encourager of education, morality and religion, and is in all respects fulfilling the duties of a good citizen. He has added materially to the business and industrial interests of this section, and has set an example worthy of imitation by the young men of Wapello County.

This gentleman, though born across the ocean, was one of the early pioneers of Wapello County. He has given the best efforts of his life to the building up of the community in which he now lives, and developing the agricultural resources of Wapello County. As one of her most highly respected citizens, we take pleasure in presenting his portrait in connection with this brief outline of his life

WILLIAM N. B. SPURLOCK, a well-to-do farmer of Pleasant Township, Wapello County, and also a minister of the Christian Church, in which denomination he has been Elder since 1846, was born in Bedford County, Ala., in 1817. The parents of our subject were Matthew and Lucretia (Sellers) Spurlock. Matthew Spurlock was an Elder in the Christian Church, and was also a preacher in that denomination for a number of years, and followed the latter profession until his death. That event occurred in Iowa, and he and his good wife lie buried side by side in the cemetery at Abingdon.

The subject of this brief notice formed a matrimonial alliance with Miss Elizabeth Ann Mason, Oct. 4, 1839. She was the daughter of Samuel and

Mary (Spear) Mason, and was born in Spencer County, Ind., May 1, 1820. Her father was a farmer, and both himself and wife departed this life in Indiana. Mr. and Mrs. Spurlock have had born to them eleven children: Inez T., born May 8, 1840, is married and lives in Cloud County, Kan.; Loranza, born March 4, 1841, died April 3 of the same year; Sarah J., born Feb. 22, 1842, departed this life while a resident of Missouri; Mary A., born May 18, 1844, is the wife of George Forney, and they are living in Ottawa County, Kan.; Lucretia E., born Feb. 18, 1847, died March 17, 1869; George W., born Aug, 9, 1848, is a Benedict and lives in Eagle Grove, Wright County, this State; Lutitja A., born Dec. 11, 1851, is the wife of John Edwards, and they reside in Republic County, Kan.; Burnetta A., born June 4, 1854; was united in marriage with Daniel Smith, and they are living in Livingston County, Mo.; Columbus F. was born June 2, 1857; Delcina C., born July 17, 1860, became the wife of Albert Davis, and they are living in Bladensburg, this county; Ira M., born Aug. 24, 1866, died Nov. 2, 1870. Mr. Spurlock is the proprietor of three acres of land, on which he has erected a good and substantial building, and devotes his attention to the raising of small fruit. He is also engaged quite extensively in the manufacture of sorghum. In politics he votes the Republican ticket.

E M. FAUSNAUGH, of the grocery and provision firm of Fausnaugh & Hall, at Eddyville, is a native of the Buckeye State and was born in 1842. He is the son of Adam and Amelia (Cadwalader) Fausnaugh, the former a native of Pennsylvania and the latter of Ohio. Our subject came to this county in June, 1854, and located in Eddyville, where his mother had settled a year previous. E. M. was educated in the public schools of Eddyville, and there remained until seventeen years of age.

In 1860 our subject left the parental home and made a trip to Oregon with an ox-team. He was five and a half months on the road, and he remained nine years in Oregon, Washington Territory and Idaho, engaged in mining and trading and also in working in a store. Returning to this county in 1869, he continued to live here until 1873, when he went to Colorado, and was there engaged in mining for about a year. He then returned, and in 1877 went to California, and after an absence of about a year in that State he returned to Eddyville and accepted a position as Deputy Postmaster. This he held until 1879, when he was appointed Postmaster, and continued in that position until September, 1885, when he engaged in the business in which he is at present. The firm of Fausnaugh & Hall do a general grocery, provision and queensware trade, and their place of business is on Bridge and Second streets, the dimensions of their room being 24x60 feet.

Mr. Fausnaugh was united in marriage with Adeline Porter, in 1871; she is a native of Ohio. Our subject's father departed this life in 1849, in Ohio, and his mother is yet living and resides at Marshalltown, Iowa; she is sixty-seven years of age.

E L. ELLER, Postmaster of Competine, and also engaged in mercantile pursuits, has been a resident of this section since 1852. He is a native of North Carolina and was born Jan. 10, 1846, his parents being John and Jane (Montgomery) Eller, natives of the same State as their son, the father born in 1822, and the mother in February, 1827. They are still living, and reside near Harvard, Neb., where the father is engaged in farming.

The subject of our sketch was the eldest of a family of eight children, five sons and three daughters. He came with his father to Iowa, and they made their first location in Jefferson County. He remained under the parental roof until he arrived at the age of twenty-three years, and then set out to do for himself. He proceeded southwest into Kansas and pre-empted 160 acres of land in Wilson County, cultivating his claim in summer and teaching school in winter, and remained there about eighteen months, when he traded his land for town property at Altoona, Kan. In 1881 he returned to the home of his father in Jefferson County, Iowa, and after a residence of two years there came into Wapello County, and engaged in mercantile pursuits in Competine Township. He was appointed Postmaster in 1883, and has filled the duties of his position with credit to himself and satisfaction to all concerned.

On the 10th of November, 1881, our subject was united in marriage with Miss Emma V., daughter of V. D. and Sarah (Van Valtenberge) Peck, natives of New York. Of this union there have been born two children: Rolla, Aug. 2, 1882, who died in October, 1885, and a boy unnamed, born Nov. 12, 1886. Mr. and Mrs. Ellen are connected with the Mission Baptist Church. Politically he is strongly Republican, and a member in good standing of the A. F. & A. M.

HON. F. M. EPPERSON, of the firm of Manning & Epperson, of Eddyville, is engaged successfully with his partner carrying on a trade in general merchandise. The business was established in 1871, and they carry a stock of $12,000, their trade extending throughout the greater portion of this section of the State. Mr. Epperson has been prominently identified with the interests of this community since coming here in February, 1861, and is one of its most valued citizens.

The subject of our sketch is a native of Pulaski County, Ky., and was born Nov. 14, 1841. He is the son of Andrew and Lockey (Coomer) Epperson, both natives of East Tennessee, and after first coming into Iowa settled in Marion County, upon the site of what is now the town of Bussey, and there engaged in farming. The following year, in the month of August, the Rebellion having then begun to assume alarming proportions, he enlisted as a soldier in the Union army, becoming a member of Co. D, 36th Iowa Vol. Inf. With his regiment he participated in the various battles and skirmishes in which it became their duty to engage; was with the Yazoo expedition, and at the battles of Helena, Ark., Little Rock and Camden, and in the spring of 1864, during the engagement at Mark's Mill, Ark., was captured by the rebels and confined ten months at Camp Ford in Tyler, Tex. He was exchanged in February, 1865, and was granted a furlough of thirty days. He then rejoined his regiment at St. Charles, Ark., where it was re-organized, and Mr. Epperson was made Orderly Sergeant and served as such during the remainder of his term of enlistment. He served until the close of the war, being mustered out at Devall's Bluff, Ark., in August, 1865.

After returning from the army Mr. Epperson engaged as clerk in a store at Eddyville until 1871. He then formed a partnership with Mr. E. Manning, and they have continued to operate together until the present time. In 1879 they started a bank in connection with their business, which is still continued and has proved a good investment. Mr. Epperson has had the control of the entire business since its beginning. In the fall of 1879 he was elected to the Eighteenth General Assembly of the State of Iowa, and re-elected to the same position two years later. He became prominent in matters of legislation, and was appointed Chairman of the Committee on Appropriations, beside holding other responsible places. He has been School Treasurer of Eddyville for eight years, also City Treasurer, and is at present a member of the City Council. He takes a lively interest in public matters, both local and general, and is one of the most valued citizens of the community.

The subject of our sketch was married to Miss Louise O'Hara, on the 8th of June, 1875. Mrs. E. is a native of Wisconsin, and the daughter of Samuel and Louisa (Mayham) O'Hara, both natives of New York. Of this union there have been born three children: Frank, June 13, 1876; Elbert, Feb. 5, 1882, and Arthur, Nov. 3, 1886.

The father of our subject died in Kentucky at the age of sixty-eight years. He was a farmer by occupation, a man of energy and industry, and established a comfortable home for his family in the Blue Grass State. The mother died when her son, F. M., was a lad of ten years. He received his early education in the common schools at Beech Grove, in his native State, and was reared to farming pursuits. His early life peculiarly fitted him for the duties of later years, and developed in him those qualities which have constituted a thorough business man and an honorable and upright citizen. Mr. E. in politics is Republican, and socially is a member in good standing of the A. F. & A. M., having reached a high position in the order.

JOHN M. RUPE, engaged in farming and stock-raising on section 27, Keokuk Township, was born in this county, Sept. 9, 1845, and is a son of L. Z. and Mary M. (Smith) Rupe, natives of Ohio. John M. Rupe spent the early years of his life on a farm, assisting in the labors thereon, and in attending the district schools. He supplemented his common-school education by an attendance of two terms at McElroy's Seminary, and was engaged in teaching during the winter of 1860–61.

Feb. 18, 1863, our subject enlisted in Co. E, 36th Iowa Vol. Inf. After the regiment had started on the Little Rock, Ark., expedition, he was taken sick with the measles, with which he was confined for about three weeks. After his recovery he was placed on provost duty and also guarded prisoners for about eight months. He was then sent from Little Rock to Ft. Smith, but the boat stuck on a sand-bar and lay there for three weeks, during which time they were constantly menaced by rebels firing at them behind the trees. After they had freed their boat from the bar and were once more fairly on their way to Ft. Smith, they struck a second sand-bar, and again were three weeks confined there. They then succeeded in getting their boat off the bar, and went back to Little Rock. From the latter city our subject went to St. Charles, after which he returned with his regiment to Little Rock, and then went to Camp Price. Thence the regiment was sent to Davenport, where it was discharged Sept. 6, 1864.

Returning home, Mr. Rupe engaged in farming and stock-raising, and the following year, May 20, 1865, he was married to Mary J. Gee, a daughter of Solomon and Hannah (Donnelson) Gee. Her father was a member of the same company and regiment as our subject, and died from disease contracted while in the army, in 1862. Her mother is living at Ottumwa. Mr. and Mrs. Rupe have become the parents of six children: Thayer, born June 14, 1867; Wayne, Dec. 16, 1868; Drake, Dec. 2, 1870; Guy, July 8, 1878; Lewis, born Oct. 26, 1874, died Sept. 29, 1886, and is buried at Mars Hill Cemetery, this county; Pearl, born July 5, 1885. Mr. Rupe has held various offices and is a member of the G. A. R., belonging to Clautman Post No. 69, of Ottumwa. Mr. Rupe is at present the proprietor of 120 acres of good farm land, all of which is under an advanced state of cultivation. In politics he is a Greenbacker.

L. P. TORRENCE, M. D., a successful and popular physician of Green Township, is a native of Palmyra, Mo., born in 1847, and the son of Dr. John and Sarah (Sprott) Torrence, natives respectively of Pennsylvania and Virginia. His father is still engaged in the practice of his profession, and stands high among the profession in his locality. He is at present consulting physician in St. Peter's Hospital, at Quincy, Ill. In 1832 he removed from his native State, settling upon a farm near Palmyra, Mo. His son, our subject, was there educated in the public schools, and afterward took a course in the Christian University at Columbia, Mo. He also spent two terms in the Eclectic Medical Institute of Cincinnati, Ohio, from which he graduated in 1870, and commenced the practice of his profession at Rockport, Ill., remaining there only one year, when he received an appointment in the city hospital of Quincy, Ill., where he was occupied for nearly three years as ward nurse, finally becoming resident physician.

At the expiration of his engagement here, Dr. Torrence spent the winter of 1875–76 in attendance at the American Medical College, of St. Louis, and then located at Ash Grove, Davis Co., Iowa, where he remained until 1883, when he came to Ormanville, and since that time has been successfully engaged in the practice of his profession, and takes his recreation in superintending the cultivation of forty acres of valuable land near the city limits, of which he has been the owner for some years. He also owns ten acres within the corporation.

Dr. Torrence was united in marriage with Miss Mary A. Wyatt, in June, 1879. Mrs. Torrence is a native of Wapello County, and the daughter of Edward S. and Zylphia (Davis) Wyatt, and by her union with our subject has become the mother of three children—Olive, Mary and John. They occupy a handsome residence, and number among their list of friends and acquaintances the best citizens of Green Township. The Doctor is Democratic in politics, takes an interest in the affairs of his township and county, and whenever opportunity affords, contributes of his time and means for the promotion of worthy enterprises.

HON. CHARLES DUDLEY, deceased, one of the pioneer settlers of Wapello County, came to Iowa in 1843, while it was yet a Territory, and took up 167 acres of land on section 30 in Agency Township. He was born Sept. 16, 1813, whence he removed to Illinois in 1836, then to Louisa County, Iowa, and from there came to this county. In early manhood he was married in Hancock County, Ill., Dec. 29, 1838, to Miss Jeanette Daubenheyer, and of this marriage there were two children, both now deceased. Edward J. served as a Union soldier during the late war, and died in 1867. Mrs. Jeanette Dudley departed this life Sept. 5, 1844.

Mr. Dudley was again married, Dec. 17, 1846, to Miss Polly A. Dennison, a native of Illinois, born in Scott County, Dec. 11, 1827. By her union with our subject she became the mother of ten children, only five of whom are living: Charles S. lives in Polk County, Neb.; Sarah J. married George L. Nye, of Wapello County; Mary E. Wilton and Kate E. are also in this county; Frank W. is at home. In 1870 a terrible accident occurred, which resulted in the death of their three children, the house having taken fire, and the escape of these impossible. The children burned to death were, Lewis T., Thomas D. and Orrin O., the remains being buried in one coffin.

Mr. Dudley in earlier years took an active part in politics and held various local offices. He served as County Coroner, and was elected by the Republicans to the Thirteenth General Assembly in 1866, serving six years, and has been Justice of the Peace for many years. He took an active stand against the use of whisky, and did everything in his power to advance the temperance cause. He was an extensive reader, keeping himself well posted upon all general and local matters, and was actively interested in the cause of education. He belongs to the Free-Will Baptist Church, of which he was Deacon for many years, and was an active worker in the Sabbath-school, always ready to lay aside personal interests for the good of others. As a business man he was honorable, upright, prompt to meet his obligations, greatly beloved by his family, and held in the highest esteem by his neighbors and acquaintances. Mr. Dudley was possessed of considerable means when he came to this county, which he made good use of, and disbursed in a judicious manner. Mr. Dudley departed this life Aug. 25, 1880, leaving a widow and five children to mourn his loss. Mrs. Dudley is living in Agency City, where she has a comfortable home, and is greatly esteemed by a large circle of acquaintances.

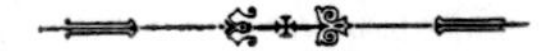

ERNEST B. VOGEL, farmer and stock-grower, residing on section 18, Center Township, is a native of Hesse Cassel, Prussia, born Nov. 16, 1824. He is the son of William and Mary (Rosemeier) Vogel. When Ernest was but five years of age his parents emigrated to America, and located in Zanesville, Ohio. His father was by profession a teacher in the public schools. After living in Zanesville a short time he bought a farm near Taylorville, on the Muskingum River, where he carried on farming until his death, which took place in 1856, near Taylorville; the mother died in the same place in 1858.

In 1855 the subject of this sketch removed from Ohio to Davis County, Iowa, where he remained eight years. He then moved to Wapello County and purchased a farm in Dahlonega Township, where he lived ten years. In 1873 he moved to the city of Ottumwa, where he resided four years, at which time he purchased the place where he now resides, consisting of thirty acres of land which has lately been annexed to the city of Ottumwa. He has a neat and comfortable home, and a fine orchard, in which is grown all the fruit adapted to this climate. In stock business he makes a specialty of graded Norman horses and graded cattle. His farm is principally in grass.

May 30, 1852, Mr. Vogel was married to Elizabeth Burckhalter, a native of France, born May 4, 1833, but who came with her parents to America when but an infant. Both of her parents are now deceased. Mr. and Mrs. Vogel are the parents of three children: Callie L. is the wife of Baxter Pickell, living in Albia, Iowa; Adelia F. is the wife of Albert Nickerson, living in Hot Springs, Ark.; Ianthe M. lives with her parents. Mrs. Vogel is a member of the Lutheran Church. When Mr. Vogel came to this country he was not possessed of much means, but by dint of industry and energy he has succeeded in accumulating a comfortable competency for himself and family. Besides his farming operations he is interested in the cutlery works at Ottumwa. He is a member of the Masonic fraternity, and in politics is a Democrat.

J. A. MAJOR, a resident of the Hawkeye State since 1848, owns and occupies a comfortable homestead in Polk Township, on section 31, and is busily engaged in general farming and stock-raising. He is a native of Ohio, and was born in Auglaize County, Dec. 26, 1827, being the son of Hamilton and Charity (Obdyke) Major; his father was a native of Maryland and his mother of New Jersey. After their marriage they located in Ohio, whence they removed in 1848 beyond the Mississippi to the Hawkeye State, where the father purchased the property which now constitutes the homestead of his son, our subject. Hamilton Major was born on the 26th of December, 1791, and departed this life on the 22d of June, 1849, in Polk Township, and within the home which he had established for his family. He was a useful citizen, possessed of a good fund of general information, and always ready to aid in any enterprise designed to improve the condition of his county or township. The mother died Feb. 14, 1881; she had lived a consistent Christian life, having been a member of the Methodist Episcopal Church since early youth.

Hamilton Major and wife were the parents of ten children, all of whom, with one exception, are still living: William Bell, a farmer of Clarke County, Iowa, was born Oct. 5, 1821; Lydia M. was born June 7, 1823, and became the wife of E. S. Hinkle, of the State of Nebraska; Marietta, born May 9, 1825, married Mr. George Pierce, a farmer of Monroe County, Iowa; Rachel, born Aug. 27, 1826, became the wife of W. S. Dowty, a farmer of Auglaize County, Ohio; J. R., our subject, was the next in order of birth; Peter was born Feb. 28, 1830, and is engaged in agricultural pursuits in Monroe County, Iowa; Albert, born July 21, 1831, is a farmer of Wapello County; Margaret J., born Jan. 4, 1834, married Stephen Osborn; Hamilton, born Oct. 14, 1835, died about 1880; Aaron M., born Jan. 27, 1838, is living in Trinity County, Cal

The subject of our sketch has followed farming pursuits, excepting a short period, during which he was engaged in the grocery trade at Macedonia, Pottawattamie Co., this State. He was married, in June, 1864, to Miss Louisa Sheppard, a native of Illinois, born in Lacon, June 29, 1841, and the daughter of David and Sarah (Powell) Sheppard, natives respectively of Ohio and Virginia. They afterward removed to Iowa, and the mother died in Lee County in 1853. The father is still living, located on a farm in Otoe County, Neb.

Mr. and Mrs. Major have become the parents of five children, as follows: Matilda was born Dec. 5, 1864; Sarah E., Jan. 20, 1870; William A., July 23, 1872; Lewis, Nov. 5, 1877; Ada May, Sept. 12, 1879. The family residence is pleasantly located, and its inmates are surrounded by all the comforts of life. The farm includes eighty acres of choice land, under good improvement and with an excellent set of farm buildings. The possessions of Mr Major are the result of his own industry, as he commenced at the foot of the ladder in life and has climbed up without any assistance save the good-will of his neighbors, which he acquired by his honesty of purpose and straightforward methods of doing business. He has always been prompt to meet his obligations, and wherever opportunity afforded has assisted in the enterprises which have been set on foot for the advancement of the interest of his community. Politically he affiliates with the Democratic party, and uniformly casts his vote in support of its principles.

EPHRAIM McMILLIN, comfortably located on section 9, of Keokuk Township, is the possessor of a valuable farm estate, and is successfully engaged in agriculture and stock-raising. He comes of an excellent Pennsylvania family, and was born in Fayette County, that State, on the 21st of September, 1827, the son of James and Elizabeth (Hess) McMillin, who were the parents of ten children, as follows: Ephraim, our subject, was the eldest born; Leah is the widow of Jesse Miller, and resides in Agency Township; Delilah, deceased, was the wife of Sanford Davis; Nancy died in infancy; Rebecca is the wife of John Saylor, of this county; Sarah married A. R. Wilcox, and is now deceased; John and Franklin are also residents of this county; Eliza married Mr. George Viley, and Elizabeth, deceased, was the wife of John Young.

James McMillin, the father of our subject, ranks among the pioneer settlers of the Hawkeye State, having come to Iowa in 1839, while it was yet a Territory. He first located in Jefferson County, from which he removed four years later to Wapello County, being among the earliest settlers of this county. He entered 229 acres of Government land in Keokuk Township, upon which he erected a log cabin and commenced opening up a farm. In April, 1849, he came to his death by drowning, his body being recovered after a search of ten days. After the death of her husband the bereaved mother kept her family together as best she could, and assisted and directed her sons in the management of the farm and the establishment of a permanent and comfortable home. In due time the property was divided among the children, and those who survive are all comfortably settled in life. The faithful and affectionate mother survived her husband until 1862, and then finally closed her eyes to the scenes of earth, mourned by all who knew her. She was a devoted member of the Christian Church, and left behind her a record of kindly deeds and generous womanly sympathies for all who were afflicted or in distress, and whom she always aided to the best of her ability.

The subject of our sketch came with his parents to Iowa, and received his early education in the subscription schools. He remained under the parental roof until his marriage, which occurred in 1855, the maiden of his choice being Miss Rachel Bower, a native of his own State. Of this union there were born three children—Sarah Alice, Elizabeth, and one who died in infancy. Mrs. McMillin departed this life in 1867.

The second marriage of Mr. McMillin, which occurred in 1872, was with Miss Nancy Saylor, who was born in Keokuk Township, in 1848, and was the daughter of Godfrey and Phœbe A. (Anderson) Saylor, natives of North Carolina. Of this marriage there are two children—Estella May, born May 7, 1878, and James E., Nov. 30, 1880. Mrs. McMillin died on the 2d of December, 1880. She was highly esteemed in this community, a devoted member of the Christian Church, and possessed of most amiable and excellent qualities. Her name is held in kindly remembrance by a large circle of friends and acquaintances. Since coming to this township our subject has been prominent in its local affairs, and has held the various offices within the gift of his townsmen. He is Democratic in politics, and uniformly casts his vote in support of the principles of that party.

CHARLES C. WARDEN, M. D., now living a retired life in Ottumwa, was the first physician to permanently locate in Wapello County. Coming here at the time the wily red man took up his march toward the setting sun, he has been an eye-witness and an active participant in all the startling events that have since transpired in the county, State and nation. Dr. Warden is first in number of the family of Richard and Eliz-

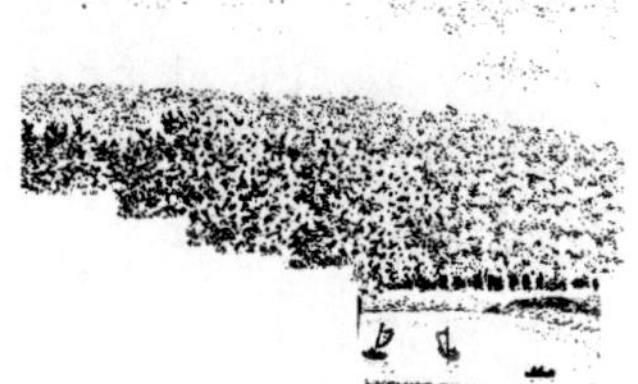

abeth (Chunn) Warden. He was born in Maysville, Mason Co., Ky., Nov. 20, 1816. Of the parental family one brother and two sisters are yet living: Richard H., at present and for many years connected with the Ottumwa *Courier*; America, wife of J. B. Belmot, of Ottumwa, and Eliza A., married to John Peterson, and resides in Williamsburg, Clermont Co., Ohio.

The father of our subject was a man of considerable culture, and a native of Hanover County, Va., but went to Kentucky when a youth, and was there married to Elizabeth Chunn, also a native of Virginia. In about 1834 the parental family moved to Clermont County, Ohio, where the elder Warden purchased a tract of land, a portion of the Nicholas land grant, and at once cleared a farm. He died there in August, 1835. Richard Warden lived long in the State that had reason to be proud that it was the home of Henry Clay, and he was a loyal follower of that eminent statesman. Religously he was for many years a consistent member of the Methodist Episcopal Church, and his wife was also a member of that denomination. She died Dec. 23, 1867, and both had enjoyed the love and respect of all who knew them.

Much of the early life of Dr. Warden was spent in farming. He also assisted his father in clearing up the land in Clermont County, Ohio, being at that time about eighteen years of age. He was educated in the common schools of Kentucky and Ohio, which was supplemented by a short term at an academy in Greensburg, Ind., to which place he moved in 1837, just after reaching his majority. On moving to Greensburg he embarked in the drug trade, and soon commenced the study of medicine, having as a preceptor Dr. Fogg of that place. He continued his studies for about two years, and then entered the Ohio Medical College at Cincinnati, after which he entered into partnership with the above-mentioned physician, which was terminated by the death of Dr. Fogg about six months afterward. This was in the winter of 1842-43. In the spring of 1843, being broken in health, he determined on a trip West, and came to Ottumwa, this county, then just laid out by the Appanoose Rapids Improvement Company. Here he found friends, among whom was Rev. Martin Jemison, who prevailed upon him to remain for a time, though he had no intention of making it his permanent home. When it became known that he was a physician, he was frequently called upon to prescribe and, without effort on his part, his practice increased, and he kept deferring his return to Indiana until finally he abandoned the idea altogether, and thus became a permanent resident of the present city of Ottumwa, and, as stated, the first physician to locate in Wapello County.

Dr. Warden actively engaged in the practice of his profession for thirteen years, then retired from it, other business demanding his attention. In 1851 he engaged in the mercantile trade, which he continued until 1882, when he sold out and has been living a retired life. He also engaged in farming to some extent. In the early day a medical society was organized, embracing the physicians of Wapello County, of which organization Dr. Warden was President for some years. He was also a member of the State Medical Society. An event which may have had much to do with the Doctor's choice of Ottumwa as a permanent home, was his marriage, June 13, 1846, with Martha Williams, a native of Ohio, born in Cincinnati, Sept. 28, 1828, and a daughter of Washington Williams. Of this union there were twelve children, seven of whom are now living—Frank C., Laura C., Charles H., Hester, Sallie, Lucy T. and Martha T.

As might be inferred from the foregoing, the life of Dr. Warden has been an active one. In politics, like his honored father, in early life he was an old-line Whig, ever ready to follow the lead of Henry Clay. His first vote was cast for Gen. Harrison, and his recollection of that exciting political campaign in which log cabins, coons and hard cider were prominent, is vivid indeed. On the death of the old Whig party, the Republican party sprang into existence, with which organization our subject has since continued to act. Though never an office-seeker, Dr. Warden has held several official relations. For twelve years he was Chairman of the School Board of Ottumwa, and for four years was a member of the Board of Trustees of the Agricultural College at Ames, two years of which time he was Chairman of the Board. That he is a consistent and steadfast friend of education the time spent in these offices certainly testifies. Much credit is due to our subject for the present efficient schools of Ottumwa, to which he gave much time and thought for so many years, without hope of reward other than the consciousness of doing good and building for the future.

Dr. Warden has reached his threescore years and ten, and can look back upon a well-spent life. For forty-three years he has been a citizen of Ottumwa and, as remarked in the beginning of this sketch, has witnessed all the changes that have been made in transforming a wilderness into a thickly settled country, the home of an industrial class of people, and in all he has taken an active part. To him and others "who have borne the burden and the heat of the day" is the present generation largely indebted for what it enjoys.

JOHN LOBER, one of the pioneer settlers of Adams Township, is a prosperous dealer in dry-goods and groceries at Blakesburg, and is contributing his full quota to the business interests of this town. Mr. L. is a native of Bavaria, and was born May 18, 1826, being the son of George and Abelona Lober, natives of the same country, who spent their entire lives there, and where their remains are buried. In early life our subject was apprenticed to the trade of a shoemaker, at which he served three years, and in 1849 set out for America, and after a voyage of forty-one days he landed in Baltimore with two five-franc pieces in his pocket. He thus practically commenced life in the New World at the foot of the ladder, without means or influence to assist him in the struggle before him. From Baltimore he proceeded to Wheeling, Va., where he worked for a few years at his trade, and in May, 1855, started for the West, and made his first location in Blakesburg, Iowa. Here he opened a small shoeshop, which he carried on for twenty-two years, and then embarked in his present business. The firm carries everything required in an ordinary household, and keeps a generous stock of first-class goods.

Mr. Lober was married in Wheeling, Va., in 1851, to Miss Dora Weldman, who was born in Switzerland in 1830. They became the parents of three children: John F.; Amelia, the wife of A. C. Bigby, of Arkansas City, Kan., and Louisa, who married Perry Cloyd, of this county. Beside the store and valuable town property, Mr. Lober owns 174 acres of good land, and enjoys a handsome income from the business of himself and son. From the start he identified himself with the interests of his adopted county, and has been the encourager and supporter of everything calculated to advance its interest. He has witnessed with interest and satisfaction the growth and development of this region, and is a forcible illustration of what industry and perseverance may accomplish.

J. W. NICHOLS, a prominent resident of the city of Ottumwa, is a magnetic healer by profession, and well and favorably known throughout this city and vicinity. He is a native of New Haven County, Conn., and was born April 15, 1830. His parents were Joseph and Betsy (Smith) Nichols, natives of the same State and county as their son. The parental family comprised two children only—Ranson S., a brass caster of Thomaston, Conn., and J. W., our subject. Joseph Nichols died in the same year that his son, our subject, was born. Mrs. N., for her second husband, married William Johnson, and of their union there was born one son—Charles K., now of Mahaska County, Iowa. After her second marriage the mother of our subject removed to Iowa and located in Mahaska County, where she passed the remainder of her days, dying April 18, 1880, at the age of seventy-three years. She was reared in the Episcopal faith, but afterward became a devoted member of the Methodist Episcopal Church.

Young Nichols having been deprived of a father's care when an infant of six months old, was reared by his step-father, who removed with his wife and her little son to Berkshire County, Mass., when the latter was four years old. The latter remained there until he attained to years of manhood, receiving a common-school education, and on the 12th of April, 1852, was united in marriage with Miss Sarah E. Watkins, who was born in that county on the 3d of January, 1836. After their marriage they removed to Connecticut, and in 1856 they journeyed westward into Iowa and located in Richland Township, Mahaska County, engaging in farming pursuits. Subsequently Mr. N. purchased a steam sawmill and operated the same for ten years. The household was brightened by the birth of two children, and Mrs. Sarah Nichols, after having been the partner of her husband for only six years, closed her eyes to the scenes of earth on the 23d of September, 1858.

Mr. Nichols was again married on the 2d of March, 1859, to Miss Elizabeth A. Ryan, a daughter of Jesse B. Ryan, of West Virginia. He emigrated to Iowa at an early period in the history of the State, first locating in Mahaska County. Thence he removed to Cass County, Neb., where he is at present living. In early manhood he was married to Miss M. Sterms, and they became the parents of six children, as follows: Ingaba J. became the wife of William Godby, and is now a resident of Kearney, Neb.; James R. lives in Cedar Rapids; Elizabeth A., wife of our subject; Jacob S., in Cass County, Neb.; Thomas H. B., in New Sharon, Iowa; and Nancy E. married Paris Van Cleave, of Marquette, Hamilton Co., Neb. Mrs. Nichols was born in Virginia, June 6, 1840, and by her marriage with our subject has become the mother of four children, viz: Josephine M., born Oct. 10, 1861; Frank, born Sept. 15, 1865, is now deceased; Sarah E. was born Sept. 10, 1866, and Charles E., June 8, 1880. They occupy a handsome home, and number among their warmest friends the cultured people of the city.

Dr. Nichols became a resident of Ottumwa in 1869. He was poor in pocket and no prospect of business or work. He was willing, however, to engage in any honest labor, and his first day's work in the city consisted in sawing two cords of wood. Not being accustomed to such work he went home, lay down to rest and fell asleep. His arms pained him very much and he dreamed that in rubbing his hands over them the pain immediately ceased. Upon awaking his arms still pained him, he passed his hands over them and the pain in reality left them. After practicing upon himself in this manner for some time with uniformly good results, the cess to his friends and neighbors, and in due time his operations in this line became so successful and extensive that he found he must either abandon it entirely or make a business of it, and he decided upon the latter course. He did not understand it at first, and was at a loss to know from whence his powers came, being disposed to treat the whole matter with ridicule, and Paul Castor, the famous magnetic healer, as well. At this time the latter, then a resident of Ottumwa, was taken ill and sent for Dr. Nichols, who commenced treating him with excellent results, and continued for fifteen months. He is now often employed by Dr. Castor to assist in the treatment of patients in his institution at Ottumwa.

Dr. Nichols states that he does not himself understand the secret of his powers, but knows that he has effected remarkable cures. He now does an extensive business, and travels through Iowa, Missouri and Illinois, engaged in practice which for the most part has been unsought by him. He is a gentleman of rare intelligence, an extensive reader, and keeps himself thoroughly posted on all the important questions of the day. Socially he is connected with Empire Lodge No. 269, A. F. & A. M., and also with Clinton Chapter No. 9, of Ottumwa, in which he has served as Deacon for eight years. He is a straightforward business man, honest and upright in his transactions, and a worthy and valued citizen.

DANIEL DENNISON, deceased, one of the honored pioneers of Wapello County, was born in Kentucky in 1797, and was the son of William and Margaret Dennison. The parental family included the following children—William, Madison, Elizabeth, Catharine, Mary, John, Alexander and Daniel, our subject being the sixth in order of birth. William Dennison emigrated from Lexington, Ky., to Illinois in 1818, the same year that it was admitted into the Union as a State. He had been a soldier in the Revolutionary War under Gen. St. Clair, and died in 1838.

The subject of this history removed to Illinois in 1836, and seven years later came to Iowa. In

Township, and commenced the improvement of a farm, living with his family in a tent until he could roll up logs enough for a cabin. This latter served their purpose for a number of years, and being prospered in his labors he afterward erected a good frame house, and upon the homestead thus established passed the remainder of his days. His wife, before her marriage, was Miss Sallie S. Riggs, and they became the parents of six children, all of whom are living, the youngest being forty-two years of age: Parthena is the widow of Thomas Foster; Polly A. is the widow of Hon. Charles Dudley, a sketch of whom will be found in another part of this work; William S. is in Kansas; Margaret E. became the wife of Jacob T. McMinn, of Wapello County; Hanna E., Mrs. William N. Milligan, lives in Ringgold County, this State; Sarah L. married Edward F. Bartholomew of the same county.

Mr, and Mrs. Dennison were members in good standing of the Christian Church for many years, and carried out in their daily lives the principles of the religion which they professed. They were held in the highest esteem by their neighbors and associates, and endured with their fellow-pioneers the privations and hardships incident to the settlement of a new country. They were widely and favorably known throughout this county for their kindly and charitable deeds, and were blest with many years, the father dying in 1870, at the age of seventy-three years, and the mother in 1877, aged seventy-two.

W. F. FOSTER, a farmer and stock-grower, will be found on section 31, Agency Township. He was born in Wapello County, Iowa, Nov. 25, 1846, and is a son of Thomas and Parthena (Dennison) Foster. (See sketch of Thomas Foster on another page of this work.) The subject of this sketch was reared on a farm and obtained his education in the common schools of this county. On the 6th day of October, 1874, he was united in marriage with Hattie C. Linder, also a native of this county, born Sept. 26, 1853, and the daughter of Joseph and Mary (Reat) Linder. Her parents reside in Agency City. Four children have been born to our subject and wife: Charles S., Russel (deceased), Mary P. and Walter L.

Mr. Foster is the owner of 188 acres of land, including the farm on which he resides, and also has 340 acres in Washington Township. On the home farm he has a good dwelling, a barn, 43x55 feet, with 20-foot posts, and all the necessary out-buildings. He is a breeder of Short-horn cattle, which he makes a specialty; his Short-horn bull was sired by the 22d Duke of Airdrie, No. 16,695. He has some fine roadsters, and also breeds Poland-China hogs. Mr. and Mrs. Foster are members of the Methodist Episcopal Church, and politically he is a Republican.

CHARLES W. DERBY, one of the honored pioneers of Wapello County, is a native of New England and born in Addison County, Vt., on the 23d of June, 1816. He is the son of Jonathan M. and Clarissa (Baker) Derby, natives respectively of New York and Vermont, who settled in the latter State after their marriage, and after the birth of their son, our subject, emigrated to Ohio, locating in Licking County at an early period in the history of that State. The parental family consisted of twelve children, ten of whom lived to mature years, but only two are now living —George, of Seward County, Neb., and Charles W. of our sketch. The father of our subject came to Wapello County, Iowa, in about 1847, and located on a farm, where he remained a few years, afterward removing to Mahaska County, and died there on the 6th of October, 1864, aged seventy-eight years. The mother had previously passed to her rest, on the 6th of August, 1861. They were worthy people, useful members of society, and actively connected with the Presbyterian Church.

Charles W. Derby, of this sketch, emigrated with his parents to Ohio when a mere child, and received his education in the pioneer log school-house. He remained under the parental roof until he arrived at years of manhood, and on Aug. 30, 1838, was united in marriage with Miss Jane Longwell. Mrs. D. was born in Licking County, Ohio, Feb. 13, 1823, and was the daughter of Adonijah and Mary (Clark) Longwell, the father a native of Virginia, and the mother of Irish birth and parentage. They became the parents of eight children, four of whom are deceased: Clark is living in Licking County, Ohio; Jane, in Wapello County, Iowa; Eliza is the wife of Noah Bush, and lives in Licking County, Ohio; Mary, Mrs. James Parker, is deceased. Mr. and Mrs. Longwell died in Ohio. The former was a member first of the Presbyterian, and then of the Baptist Church.

The family circle of our subject and his wife was completed by the birth of nine children, two of whom are deceased: Melissa is the wife of Daniel Cummings, of Butler County, Kan.; Nelson lives in Wapello County, Iowa; Clark is in Peabody, Kan.; John M., and Nancy, Mrs. William Peck, are residents of this county; George W. is in Kansas; Ina married Cyrus Van Cleave, an attorney of this county.

In 1845 Mr. Derby came with his family to Iowa, making the trip overland with teams, cooking by the wayside and sleeping in the wagon at night. They came into Wapello County, and Mr. E. entered a claim in Adams Township on section 18. Upon this there was not even a log cabin, and his first duty was to put up a dwelling for his family. There was plenty of wild game, and they feasted on venison and turkey, but were obliged to go a long distance to mill, the nearest one being at Benton's Point, in Van Buren County, about sixty miles away. During the first seasons in which he raised crops for the markets he was obliged to haul his grain to Keokuk, and our subject experienced with his fellow pioneers all the hardships, privations and difficulties incident to the settling up of a new country. During their long residence here they have been interested witnesses of the progress and development of the Hawkeye State, and have contributed their full share toward its advancement and prosperity.

Upon his arrival in this county Mr. Derby found himself with a cash capital of $6.25, and he has received no legacy since then to assist him on the road to prosperity. He is now the possessor of 116 acres of land, lying near Blakesburg, with a comfortable residence, and all the necessary appurtenances of a first-class agriculturist. His possessions have been the result of his own industry and enterprise, and he is considered one of the representative men of Wapello County who have come honestly by the competency which they are enjoying as they go quietly down the sunset hill of life.

Before the outbreak of the late war Mr. Derby was an anti-slavery man, and strongly opposed to the peculiar institution. After the first call for troops he enlisted in the 37th Iowa Infantry, which was then known as the "Graybeard" regiment, and served until the close of the war in a courageous and conscientious manner. Politically he is a stanch Republican, and uniformly casts his vote in support of the principles of his party.

L. A. CHAMBERLIN is manager of the Kirkville Supply Company, Kirkville, Iowa, of which company T. J. Potter is President, O. M. Ladd, Vice President and Treasurer, and S. A. Corey, Secretary and Cashier. The company are dealers in dry-goods, boots and shoes, clothing, hardware, groceries, furniture, stoves, tinware, lumber, etc., and transact a very large business annually. L. A. Chamberlin was born in Summit County, Ohio, July 30, 1842, and is a son of Joel G. and Mary A. (Bartlett) Chamberlin, the former a native of Ohio, and the latter of Vermont. In 1851 his father went to California, and died there of cholera; his mother died in Summit County, Ohio, in 1855.

Since eighteen years of age, the subject of this sketch has made his own way in the world. He received a fair English education in the common schools of his county and neighborhood, and at the age of twenty enlisted as a private soldier in Co. B. 41st Ohio Vet. Vol. Inf., participating in the battles of Stone River, Mission Ridge, Peachtree Creek and other engagements. At Peachtree Creek he was shot through the hand, and discharged at Cleveland, Ohio. In 1869 he emigrated to Monroe County, Iowa, and remained there till 1874, at which time he moved to Kirkville, this county, where he has since remained. For twenty years he engaged in the manufacture of cheese on the associated dairy plan, and made the first cheese ever made in this country on that plan.

Mr. Chamberlin was married, Dec. 3, 1865, to Rhoda F. Babcock, who was born Aug. 16, 1845, in Ohio, and is the daughter of David and Alvira (Wright) Babcock. Her parents both died in Ohio. Two children were born of this union—Afton R., Sept. 26, 1869; and Minnie E., Jan. 14, 1872. Mr. Chamberlin owns 140 acres of farm land in Ohio, 160 acres in Colorado, and eleven acres in the village of Kirkville. He is a thorough business man, and in the management of the extensive business of the Kirkville Supply Company renders satisfaction not only to the company, but to its patrons as well. He is a member of the A. F. & A. M., and politically is a Republican.

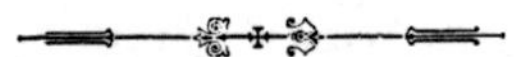

M C. ISRAEL resides upon section 11, Washington Township, and is engaged in farming and stock-raising. The home farm consists of 400 acres of mostly improved land, there being upon the premises a good dwelling-house, fine barn, and all necessary out-buildings. He is a native of Butler County, Ohio, born Nov. 20, 1820, and is a son of Thomas and Christina (Deem) Israel, the latter of whom died in Indiana. The father came from Indiana to Wapello County in 1860, remained two years, and then returned to Indiana, where he has since died. He was a native of Virginia, and the mother of Kentucky.

In 1844 the subject of this sketch was united in marriage with Ruth Brownfield, a native of Pennsylvania, who was born Jan. 16, 1825, and is the daughter of Robert and Sarah (Price) Brownfield. Her father died in Van Buren County, Iowa, where her mother now lives. Eight children were born of this union—J. A., S. E., Mary, Robert T., Hiram J., Margaret A., John and George P. Of this number S. E., Margaret A. and John are deceased.

In 1849 Mr. Israel, with his family, came to Van Buren County, and in 1854 to Wapello County, Iowa, where he has since continued to reside. He ranks among the best farmers in Wapello County, and is a man who takes an interest in all public affairs, and has held the offices of County Supervisor and Township Trustee; politically he is a Democrat. Mr. Israel and wife are members of the Missionary Baptist Church.

GEORGE W. THOMAS, a highly respected citizen of Green Township, occupies a comfortable homestead on section 27, and is engaged in general farming and stock-raising. He has been a prominent man in his community, possesses many excellent traits of character, has been upright and straightforward in his business transactions, and mostly successful in his undertakings in life.

Mr. Thomas comes of an excellent family, and was born in Washington County, Pa., July 17, 1807. His parents were Nathaniel and Anna (Townsley) Thomas, also natives of the Keystone State. His father was a soldier in the War of 1812, and when not in the service was engaged in agricultural pursuits. He departed this life in 1853, at the advanced age of eighty years, having spent his latter days in his native State; the mother had preceded him to the better land several years before. Both parents were members in good standing of the Presbyterian Church, and carefully trained their children in principles of morality, honesty and integrity.

Our subject was reared to farming pursuits, and when a lad twelve years old removed with his parents from his native State to Clermont, Ohio. The country was wild and unbroken, and they were among the earliest settlers of that region. His father entered a claim, improved and cultivated the land, and lived there until the spring of 1851, and when not busy with his farming operations was engaged as a cabinet-maker, which trade he had learned when quite a youth, and at which he continued until the spring of 1857, when he started for the farther West and, crossing the Father of Waters, purchased 160 acres of land, which he cultivated until the spring of 1885, when he retired from active labor and went to live with his children.

G. W. Thomas was united with Miss Eveline Bell, in 1829. Mrs. T. was a native of Maryland, and the daughter of John Lee Bell, and of her marriage with our subject were born four children, as follows: Francis Marion is a carpenter, and lives in Ottumwa; Oliver Perry is a painter by trade, and is also a resident of Ottumwa; George Milton is a resident of Davis County, Iowa; Minerva Jane is the wife of William Gadd, of South Ottumwa. Mrs. Eveline Thomas departed this life Aug. 30, 1882, at the advanced age of seventy-four years, and her remains are buried in Zion Cemetery in Green Township.

Mr. T. is Democratic in politics, and for a number of years was Postmaster at Point Isabel, in this county. He is conscientious in the discharge of his duties as a citizen, and although now over seventy-nine years of age, has never failed to cast his ballot at election time since he became a voter. His first vote was for Henry Clay. After the dissolution of the Whig party he became a Democrat.

D. T. FOSTER is a native of Wapello County, Iowa, born Nov. 19, 1849, and is a son of Thomas and P. J. (Dennison) Foster. (See sketch of Thomas Foster.) He now resides on section 8, Washington Township, and the owner of 250 acres of good land, with all modern improvements. D. T. Foster was reared upon his father's farm and educated in the common schools of his native county. In 1872 he was united in marriage with Miss S. A. Nimocks, a native of Jefferson County, Iowa, born Nov. 2, 1850, and a daughter of R. and Amy (Thomas) Nimocks, who reside in this township. Five children have been born to them—Nellie M., Mamie B., Millard T., Arthur D. and William R.; the latter died in infancy.

Mr. Foster is a man who is active in all public affairs. He was Deputy Auditor of Wapello County for two years, has held the office of Township Clerk two terms, and has been a member of the School Board of Washington Township, being President and Secretary of the same. He and his wife are members of the Methodist Episcopal Church. Politically he is a Republican.

PHILIP HOREN, a highly respected citizen of Wapello County, is the possessor of a fine farm estate located in Keokuk Township, on section 32, where he is successfully engaged in farming and stock-raising. Our subject is a native of Ireland, his birth taking place in that country Sept. 29, 1845. He is the son of Charles and Johanna (O'Connor) Horen, and at the age of seventeen years emigrated from his native land to the United States. He landed in New York City, and after making a short stay there went into Massachusetts, and was a resident of the city of Worcester, that State, for the following seven years. He then resolved to visit the country beyond the Mississippi, and in 1869 came into Monroe County, Iowa, where he engaged in farming pursuits successfully for about four years. He then came to Wapello County, and purchased 160 acres of land and began its improvement and cultivation. After he had brought it to a fine condition he sold eighty acres at a good profit, and in 1885 purchased 120 acres adjoining. He has since added to his landed property until he is now the possessor of 240 acres, 200 under fence and forty in timber. The greater part of this is finely improved and supplied with a good set of farm buildings, and under the wise direction and management of Mr. Horen has become one of the most attractive in this section of the county. Mr. H. is progressive and liberal in his ideas, and carries on his farming and stock-raising operations after the most approved methods. He has kept his eyes open as to what was going on around him in the world, and is possessed of a valuable fund of information, both in regard to agriculture, stock-raising, and other matters of general interest.

Mr. Horen was married, in 1870, to Miss Maggie Sullivan, whose parents, John and Julia (Danaty) Sullivan, were natives of Ireland. They subsequently emigrated to the United States, and are now residing in this township. Mrs. H. was born on the 5th of October, 1853, and by her marriage with our subject has become the mother of six children—two daughters and four sons—as follows: Charles, the eldest, was born Jan. 14, 1871; John, Nov. 11, 1873; Michael, Jan. 11, 1876; Helen, Nov. 13, 1879; Josephine F., Oct. 13, 1882, and Philip, Jan. 24, 1885. Mr. H. has been prominent in the affairs of his community since coming here, and has held the various township offices. He is Democratic in politics, and both he and Mrs. H. loyally adhere to the Catholic faith.

EDWARD JOHNSTON, a farmer and stock-grower on section 5, Richland Township, was born in County Antrim, Ireland, Oct. 5, 1822, and is the son of Edward and Margaret (Crone) Johnston, both of whom were natives of Ireland and died in that country. When twenty-three years of age Edward came to America, crossing the ocean in a sailing-vessel, and being on the water six weeks and three days. He landed at New York City, remaining there a short time, and then went to Pittsburgh, Pa., where he staid until 1850, when he came to Iowa, traveling by steamboat down the Ohio and up the Mississippi Rivers to Burlington, at which place he remained about four months, and then came by stage to Wapello County.

Mr. Johnston was married, March 11, 1850, to Mary Carnes, a native of Harrison County, Ohio, born March 25, 1831, and a daughter of Joshua and Nancy (Cook) Carnes. Her parents moved from Ohio to Iowa in 1849, and died in Columbia Township, this county. The father was a native of Maryland, and the mother of Virginia. Mr. and Mrs. Johnston are the parents of ten children: Julia A., born Jan. 1, 1852, is the wife of George Vermilion, and now resides in Richland Township; Nancy E., born April 2, 1853, was married to George Carlyle, and is now living in Nebraska; William H., born near Kirkville, June 3, 1854, married Martha E. Cox, and lives in Mahaska County; Lizzie C., born March 16, 1857, is the wife of Walter Brown, and lives in Pennsylvania; George H., born Sept. 12, 1859, is living at home with his parents; Arra B., born June 7, 1861, died Aug. 26, 1864; Joshua M., born June 30, 1863, died July 21, 1864; John E., born Sept. 15, 1864, married Lottie Pellen, and lives in Kirkville; Jed B., born July 9, 1866, lives at home; Isaac H., born June 7, 1868, lives at home.

When Mr. Johnston first came to Wapello County he purchased 160 acres of land in Green Township, for which he paid $700, and on which he remained three years, and then sold for $1,150. He then bought 160 acres in Richland Township, of which only forty acres have been improved; he has since purchased eighty acres adjoining, and has all under a high state of cultivation. His land and improvements cost him $5,200. Mr. Johnston is a No. 1 farmer, and has been very successful in all his undertakings. He has never aspired to office, and only takes such interest in politics as every good citizen should manifest. Politically he is a Republican, and religiously he and his good wife are members of the Methodist Episcopal Church.

RICHARD D. ROSSER, Superintendent of supplies for a coal mining company in Richland Township, was born in South Wales, March 12, 1841. He is a son of David and Margaret (Thomas) Rosser, both of whom are deceased. The parents were also natives of South Wales. The subject of this notice emigrated to the United States in 1868, and settled in Trumbull County, Ohio. Remaining in the latter county for some four months he removed to Braidwood, Ill., and was there engaged in mining. From the latter place he came to this State, in 1878, and in 1881 took charge of a mine in Van Buren County. This he successfully conducted until 1882, when he removed to this county and engaged with the Wapello Coal Mine, and has thus been occupied until the present time. The capacity of the mines in which he is employed is about 800 tons per day.

Mr. Rosser was united in marriage with Miss Jane Williams, April 5, 1859. She was born in

Alvin Lewis
Lucinda Lewis

1840 in South Wales, where her parents died, having been residents there all their lives. Mr. and Mrs. Rosser have become the parents of twelve children, but all of them have crossed the river to the other shore with the exception of one, William. Mr. Rosser is the proprieter of a residence and lot in Braidwood, and also owns a house and lot in Cleveland, Iowa. In religion he and wife are members of the Congregational Church. Socially our subject belongs to the A. F. and A. M., the I. O. O. F. and the K. T., and in politics is a stanch and active Republican.

ALVIN LEWIS. The subject of this biography, who has long been familiar upon the streets of Ottumwa, and who is held in the highest respect and esteem, ranks among the earliest pioneers of Wapello County. He is a native of Champaign County, Ohio, and was born Oct. 6, 1811, his parents being William and Dianah (Nina) Lewis, who were among the earliest settlers of the county of his birth, where they took up a claim, improved and cultivated a farm, and reared a large family of children, thirteen in all. Of these only two are living, William and Alvin, of this county. The parents passed to their final rest several years ago, leaving behind them a goodly record of worthy lives filled with kindly deeds and Christian charity. They were both prominently connected with the Baptist Church, and were highly respected in the community where they resided a larger portion of their lives.

Mr. Lewis of this history was the youngest child of his parents, and was deprived of their affectionate care while a mere child. He was reared and kindly cared for by his sister Mary, who became the wife of Richard Rutledge. His first school days were passed in a log cabin, with puncheon floors and slabs for seats, into which light was admitted through greased paper for window-panes. The structure was warmed by a large fire-place which extended across one end of it. But, having known nothing different, the pupils of those days were quite content with their advantages, and usually made the most of them. Books were scarce and high-priced, and one small volume often went through the family from the eldest to the youngest, the frequent changes of the present day in school-books being then unknown, and the old pioneers probably obtained fully as much practical and serviceable knowledge from those well-worn text-books as do many of the more fashionable students of to-day from their high-priced and scientific volumes.

At the age of sixteen years Alvin Lewis left the home of his sister, and was apprenticed to learn the plasterer's trade, for which he was to serve three years in consideration of his board and clothes. This business he followed for twenty-eight years thereafter, doing many a hard day's work and receiving what would now be considered but indifferent pay. After he had attained his majority Mr. Lewis, not quite satisfied with his condition in his native State, decided to cross the Mississippi and investigate the territory beyond it. He came into Iowa in 1837, and first located in what is now Van Buren County. He opened up a farm there when there was only one white man in the vicinity north of him and one west—Samuel Clayton and James Duffield. The country was full of Indians, and they could be seen any day prowling around the outskirts of their claims, although they were peaceable and did not offer any violence.

Two years later, in 1839, Mr. Lewis sold his land, returned to Ohio for a time, and then, in 1842, recrossed the Mississippi, and came into Wapello County. He entered a claim and camped upon it for about two weeks before the land came into market, and was here also among the first settlers in the Des Moines Valley. His claim finally proved to be located in township 32, range 13 west (now comprised in Dahlonega Township), on section 5, and he lived upon it the first year in a tent. He broke the first sod north of the river which was disturbed by actual settlers in Wapello County. His claim comprised 320 acres, which he industriously improved and cultivated, and in due time received abundant reward and a handsome income from his labors. At the time of his coming here the county had not been organized, and the surveyors tarried for a time at his homestead. After a residence of fifteen years upon the farm, which

Mr. Lewis by unremitting industry and perseverance had brought to a very valuable condition, his health failed and he was obliged to retire from active labor. He then moved into Ottumwa, of which he has since been a resident.

After his first visit to the West, having occasion to stop for a time in Monmouth, Warren Co., Ill., Mr. Lewis became acquainted with Lucinda, the daughter of Thomas Pearce, to whom he was married in August, 1839. Mrs. Lewis, at the time of her marriage, was the widow of William Haines, who died of cholera at Pekin, Ill., in 1832. She had two children by her first marriage: Martha Ellen, who became the wife of John Gossage, of Dahlonega, and is now deceased; Mr. Gossage went to California in 1858, during the gold excitement, and died two or three years later. He left two sons, who are editors and publishers of a newspaper in Rapid City, Dak. The younger daughter, Matilda C., became the wife of Gen. J. M. Hedrick, but is now a widow, and resides at the old Hedrick homestead in Ottumwa.

Mr. and Mrs. Lewis have had no children of their own, but have taken several homeless ones into their hearts and home, and have performed by them the offices of father and mother. Mrs. L. is a highly respected Christian lady and connected with the Methodist Episcopal Church. Mr. L., although not a member of any religious denomination, has always contributed liberally to the causes of morality and education, having been particularly interested in the building up of the school system of this vicinity. He has also been intimately identified with the business and industrial interests of this section, and there are few worthy enterprises which have not received his sanction and more substantial aid from his abundant means. He is a Republican in politics, casting his first vote for Henry Clay. The first public speech that he attended was delivered by Abraham Lincoln, of whom he was a great admirer and with whom he enjoyed a friendly acquaintance. He recalls many a pleasant conversation with the martyred President, and often repeats many of his puns and witticisms.

When Mr. Lewis came into Wapello County he was possessed of only about $200, and had nothing further to rely upon but his own perseverance and energy to carry him through the battle of life. He is now possessed of a fine property, consisting of one of the most valuable farm estates in this county. He has a fine farm residence, good barns and outhouses, valuable machinery and farm implements, and all the appliances for carrying on agriculture after the most approved methods. This, in addition to his city property, affords him a handsome income, and those who know him best rejoice the most that he has been thus richly rewarded for his earlier toils and the steady pursuit of an upright and honorable course of action in all his dealings with his fellow-men. He is held in the same veneration and respect which is tacitly accorded to the brave band of pioneers who first came into the wilderness and marked out a path for the advance of civilization, and as a representative citizen of the county, and a respected and honored resident of Ottumwa, the publishers of this ALBUM are pleased to present the portrait of Mr. Lewis in connection with this sketch, as also that of his estimable wife.

CASWELL DENNIS, a prosperous farmer of Highland Township, has been a resident of Wapello County since the fall of 1864. He was born in East Tennessee in 1817, his parents being Thomas and Charity (Beason) Dennis, both natives of North Carolina, from which they removed to Tennessee at an early period in the history of that State. Thomas Dennis was of Irish birth and parentage, and his mother descended from English ancestors. Mr. Dennis, of our sketch, removed from his native State in 1841, to Shelby County, Ind., and for two years was engaged there in farming, thence removing to Schuyler County, Mo., where he lived until August, 1864, when he came to this county. He first located in Competine Township, but after two years purchased eighty acres on section 15 of Highland, which constitutes his present homestead. He has added to his original purchase until he now owns 102 acres, which are finely improved and in a good state of cultivation.

The parental household of our subject included

twelve children, of whom Mr. Dennis is the only one living. He was married in his native State to Miss Cyrene Yadon, a native of his own State, and the daughter of William and Margaret (Capps) Yadon, natives of the same State. Of this union there were born six children, as follows: William A., the eldest, died in infancy; Silas M. is engaged in the grocery trade in Ottumwa; E. J. became the wife of J. R. Alexander, a carpenter of Kansas City, Mo.; Sarah E. married J. W. McCormick, of Highland Township; Mary M. became the wife of William H. Stevenson, engaged in the grocery business in Ottumwa; John B. is an employe of the First National Bank of Iowa. The mother of these children departed this life in 1873, aged forty-three years, having been born in 1830.

The second wife of our subject was Miss E. J. Capps, of Indiana, to whom he was married in 1874. She was born in 1833, and is the daughter of William and Anna Capps. Mr. Dennis is one of the law-abiding citizens of Highland Township, and a member in good standing of the Regular Baptist Church.

J. N. DAVIS, of Highland Township, owns and occupies a snug homestead on section 31, where he has sixty acres of valuable land, and at present is engaged in dairying. Mr. Davis is a native of this county, and was born in 1854. His parents were Abraham and Electa (Stearns) Davis, natives of New York. The father died in 1856, at the age of forty-five years; the mother still lives in Center Township.

Our subject was raised on a farm, receiving his primary education in the public schools, and completed his studies at the Business College in Ottumwa. He was married in 1884, to Miss Lulu Whitsett, a native of Kansas, and the daughter of William Henry and Martha Jane (McGlasson) Whitsett, natives respectively of Ohio and Iowa. Mrs. Davis was born in Jefferson County, Kan., in 1860. Her father was a tinsmith by trade, and departed this life in 1862, at the age of thirty-two; the mother is still living, and a resident of Poweshiek County, Iowa. Mrs. Davis is a lady of much intelligence and of good education, having been a teacher in this vicinity for several years before her marriage. Mr. and Mrs. Davis are active members of the Methodist Episcopal Church. Mr Davis is Steward of the church and Superintendent of the Sunday-school, and Mrs. Davis is a teacher in the school.

WILLIAM ROBERTSON, a highly respected resident of Highland Township, was born in Perry County, Ind., in 1827, and is the son of George and Annie (Ketterman) Robertson, natives respectively of Kentucky and Maryland. The former came to Wapello County in 1847, and located with his family on a tract of land in Highland Township. This consisted of 120 acres, and forms the present homestead of our subject, he having resided upon it continuously since that time. The father died in 1861.

William Robertson and Miss Elizabeth Van Winkle, of Indiana, were united in marriage in 1854, and became the parents of seven children, the record of whom is as follows: George D. lives in Highland Township on a farm; James F. is also a resident of the same township; W. H. is engaged in farming on his father's homestead; Mary Matilda became the wife of Lincoln Dimmitt; Isaac E., Emery and Thomas are at home. Mr. Robertson has been greatly prospered in his farming pursuits, and added to his original purchase until he is now the possessor of 643 acres, mostly improved, and a large part under cultivation. His fine residence was erected at a cost of $3,000, and his barn of $1,000. The family is surrounded by all the comforts of life, and many of its luxuries, and both within and without the home gives evidence of cultivated tastes and ample means.

In addition to the general routine of farming, Mr. Robertson has given considerable attention to the breeding of fine stock, and has a herd of graded cattle which will compare with those of any other gentleman in this section. He commenced life a poor boy, at the foot of the ladder, and has climbed up to his present position solely by the exercise of his own industry and perseverance, and he has his reward in the profound respect and esteem of his fellow-citizens, and the competency which is the result of honest toil and wise management. Mr. Robertson is Democratic in politics, and conscientiously casts his vote in support of the principles of his party. Since coming to this locality he has been prominent in the councils of his fellow-townsmen, and has been honored with the various offices in their gift. Mrs. Robertson and Mary Matilda are members of the Methodist Episcopal Church; G. D., W. H. and I. E. are connected with the First Baptist Church of Ottumwa. The entire family is widely and favorably known throughout this section.

J E. HOUGHLAND, Claim Agent at Eldon, this county, is a native of Lee County, Iowa, born in 1844. His parents were Elza and Sarah (Adair) Houghland, natives of Ohio and Indiana, respectively, the former being born in Washington County, and the latter in La Fayette, Tippecanoe County. After their marriage they first settled in La Fayette, Ind., whence they removed to Ft. Madison, Iowa, in 1838. The city was then an humble hamlet, consisting of a few scattering houses, and the place upon which they settled is now occupied by solid, substantial brick business blocks. Elza Houghland was a carpenter by occupation, and also officiated as a local preacher of the Methodist Episcopal Church. He spent the remainder of his days in Ft. Madison, and died in 1857, at the age of fifty-five years. The wife and mother survived him until Sept. 8, 1884, and departed this life at the home of her son in Eldon.

The subject of our sketch came into Wapello County and located at Eldon in 1879. He had previously been a resident of Washington, Iowa, where he was engaged as a wholesale and retail dealer in groceries for a period of three years, after which he went to Brighton, Iowa, where he engaged in the hardware business for six years, and then came to Eldon. During the first years of his residence here he was employed as a carpenter and builder, and pursued this vocation until the spring of 1883, when he commenced the manufacture of brick and tile. While in Washington he was associated with his brother, William D. Houghland, and they continued in the manufacture of brick and tile until the spring of 1884. Our subject opened an office for his present business Dec. 16, 1885, as pension claim agent.

Mr. Houghland was married, Sept. 27, 1871, to Miss Emma McCoy, of Cadiz, Ohio, daughter of William and Esther McCoy, and they have become the parents of three children—Ida D., Thomas C. and Nellie E. Mr. H. is prominently connected with the affairs of this locality, and identified with nearly every movement tending to the promotion of morality and education. He belongs to the A. F. & A. M., is Secretary of the School Board, also of the G. A. R. Hall Association, and a member of the Board of Directors of the Building and Loan Association; he is also a large stockholder in the last-mentioned associations. Mr. Houghland is also Notary Public, general insurance agent, and western land agent.

During the progress of the late Civil War Mr. H. enlisted as a soldier at Ft. Madison, July 14, 1862, in Co. E, 19th Iowa Vol. Inf., serving two years as a private, and was then promoted Color-Bearer. He participated in the siege and capture of Vicksburg and all the engagements and skirmishes of that campaign. He was taken prisoner at Sterling Farm, La., and confined ten months at Camp Ford, near Tyler, Tex. After returning from the war he was appointed to the position of guard at the Penitentiary at Ft. Madison, in 1866, and afterward promoted to turnkey, his duty being to receive and discharge men through the gates, and escort visitors through the various wards and departments of the institution. He owns and occupies a handsome residence in the town of Eldon, and is classed among the best residents of this locality.

William D. Houghland, the brother of our subject, and formerly associated with him in partnership, is a native of Tippecanoe County, Ind., born in 1832. He came to Iowa with his parents when a child, and accompanied them when they located at Ft. Madison. He was married, in 1855, to Miss Jeannette Mallet, a native of the Hawkeye State, and daughter of Tompkins P. and Cassandra (Pope) Mallet, natives of Ohio, and became the parent of three children, as follows: Carrie Belle is the wife of George Kent, of St. Paul, Minn., who is engaged as a butcher and carries on a provision store; Katie Lee is a dressmaker in St. Paul, and Gracie Ellen, the youngest, is in the same city with her sisters. Mr. William D. Houghland was the second time married, in 1878, to Miss Aldora Belle Graham, of Mt. Pleasant, Iowa, the daughter of J. H. Graham. They occupy a pleasant home in the village of Eldon, and are highly respected members of society.

During the progress of the late war Mr. H. also enlisted as a soldier, in the 19th Iowa Infantry, serving six months, when, on account of ill-health, he was discharged and returned home. During this time he was in various skirmishes and engagements with his regiment, but escaped unharmed. He is connected with the G. A. R., the K. of P. and the I. O. O. F. Mr. and Mrs. H. are members in good standing of the Congregational Church.

J. H. GRAHAM, a prosperous druggist of Eldon, established his business here in September, 1885. He has been a resident of Wapello County since 1878, when he located in Eldon, and was engaged as a clerk for one year; he was afterward a real-estate and insurance agent. He has been a resident of the Hawkeye State since 1845, making his first location at Troy, in Davis County. In the spring of 1855 he removed to Mt. Pleasant, where he remained for six years, then returned to Troy, and engaged in the drug business for the following ten years. He then went to Van Buren County, and at Selma engaged in mercantile pursuits for five years. Thence he went to Brighton, and was engaged as general agent for the State to introduce to the people of Iowa that famous publication "Johnson's Encyclopedia," and was thus occupied until he established his present business at Eldon.

Mr. Graham is a native of Ohio, born in 1825, and the son of Andrew and Ruth (Carson) Graham, natives respectively of South Carolina and East Tennessee. He was reared upon a farm in Champaign County, Ohio, and educated in the public schools of that vicinity. He was an ambitious and energetic youth and made good progress in his studies and in the favorable opinion of his associates and fellow-citizens. He served as Justice of the Peace in that locality for several years and was honored with various other offices in the gift of his townsmen.

The marriage of Mr. J. H. Graham and Miss Elizabeth M. Patterson was celebrated in Ohio in 1845. Mrs. G. is a native of the same State as her husband, and they have become the parents of five children, as follows: William W. is a resident of Ottumwa; Aldora became the wife of William Houghland, of Eldon; Mary E. is at home; Charles L. is engaged in the drug house of Graham & Cook, of Nebraska, and Harvey A. is clerking for his brother William in Ottumwa. Mr. and Mrs. G. are members in good standing of the Congregational Church, and Mr. G. is connected with the A. F. & A. M. and also with the I. O. G. T., of which his wife and daughter are also members.

Andrew Graham, the father of our subject, was a soldier in the War of 1812, and at the close of his military services resumed his occupation as a farmer. He spent his latter days in Ohio, and departed this life in 1845, at the age of sixty-eight years. The faithful wife and mother passed to her final rest in 1845, aged sixty years.

SEBASTIAN LEELING, a highly respected resident of Columbia Township, is a fair representative of that useful German element which has contributed so materially toward developing the resources of the West. He was born in Bavaria in 1822, and the year after attaining his majority set sail for the New World. His parents were Sebastian and Elizabeth (Frank) Leeling, both natives of the same country as their son, and spent their entire lives there. The mother died when our subject was a lad twelve years of age; his father survived her, and departed this life at the ripe age of seventy years.

After our subject had decided to emigrate to the United States he boarded the steamer "Westphalia" at Bremen, and after a voyage of forty-seven days landed in the city of New Orleans in the month of February, 1844. He at once proceeded to Ohio, and engaged as a laborer in Cincinnati, where he remained for eighteen months. At that time the Territory of Iowa had applied for admission into the Union as a State, and was holding out great inducements to the young and enterprising emigrant. Young Leeling determined to visit the country beyond the Mississippi and see for himself what there was for him there. He first located in Van Buren County, purchasing a tract of unimproved land, and for ten years thereafter he labored to redeem the soil from its original condition, with fair success, but, believing he could do better in another locality, came into Wapello County, purchased 160 acres of land, and established the homestead which he now owns and occupies. A part of this had been improved at the time he took possession of it, but he has added greatly to its original value. In 1870 he erected a fine farm dwelling at a cost of $3,000, and a barn at $700. He now has all the appliances of a first-class agriculturist, and as a farmer and business man is considered a fine representative of a more than ordinarily intelligent community.

Mr. Leeling was married in 1849, in Missouri, to Miss Caroline Hugus, who was born in Westmoreland County, Pa., in 1831. She was the daughter of Jacob and Ann Maria (Crider) Hugus, and by her union with our subject became the mother of ten children, who are recorded as follows: John is engaged in farming in this county; George died in the fall of 1882, at the age of thirty-one years and nine months; Samuel is a farmer, also of this county, together with his brothers Clemence H. and Charles; Mary is the wife of Gideon Dott; Gidius lives in this county; Paul E., Hue and Elizabeth are at home. The parents feel a just pride in this fine family of children, the family circle having been invaded only once by the grim destroyer. The family are faithful adherents of the Catholic Church, and parents and children together combine to form one of the most pleasant and happy households in the land.

Mr. L. has been prominent in the affairs of his township, and has been the encourager and supporter of every measure having for its object the advancement of education and morality. He started in life without means or any substantial aid, and his present possessions are the result of his own industry and good management. Aside from the ordinary pursuits of agriculture he has given considerable attention to stock-raising, and sells annually fifteen to twenty head of fine cattle.

WILLIAM M. DIMMITT, of Dahlonega Township, became a resident of Wapello County, Iowa, in the spring of 1845. He is a native of Indiana, and was born in 1822, on the farm of his father, where he was reared to years of manhood. His parents were William and Susanna (Elliott) Dimmitt, both natives of Tennessee, and reared near the city of Knoxville. Our subject, with his parents, removed from Indiana to Iowa with an ox-team, and they were twenty-six days on the road. They at once came into this county, and settled on section 10, in Dahlonega Township, where our subject purchased a quarter-section of land on section 10, and proceeded to open up a farm, and occupied it for the following six years, thence removing to section 3, where he now lives.

Mr. Dimmitt was married on the 1st of January, 1850, to Miss Matilda Padgett, who was born in Fountain County, Ind., in 1829. By her union with our subject she became the mother of eight children, as follows: William H., of Dahlonega Township; R. C., also of that township; Mary, the wife of John Long of Keokuk County; John, a farmer of Madison County; Pilana, the wife of Frank Giltner of this township; Clydena died at the age of nine months; Mattie and Freddie are at home.

The homestead of our subject comprises 245 acres of land, mostly improved, with a comfortable farm dwelling, good barns, and all the appliances of a first-class farm estate. Of late he has been quite extensively engaged in buying and feeding stock, turning out about fifteen head of fat cattle annually. His possessions are solely the result of his own perseverance and industry. He commenced life at the foot of the ladder, with no one to depend upon but himself, and in his latter years is a marked illustration of what may be accomplished by resolution and enterprise. He is a highly esteemed business man, and in all respects is fulfilling the obligation devolving upon him as a valued member of society. Politically Mr. D. is a Republican, and uniformly casts his vote in support of the principles of that party.

The father of our subject was one of the early settlers of Indiana, and departed this life in Dahlonega Township in 1855. The mother survived her husband only two years, dying in 1857. The father of Mrs. Dimmitt, George Pagett by name, was a native of Kentucky, and in early manhood was married to Miss Catherine Booker. He died in 1836, in Worthington, Ind., and the mother twelve years later, in 1848, in Fountain County, the same State.

O. M. JONES, a native of Shenandoah, Va., has been a resident of Highland Township since 1870, and is well and favorably known in this community as possessed of qualities which constitute an honest man and good citizen. The birth of our subject took place in 1813, and his parents were Thomas and Nancy (Wood) Jones, both natives of the Old Dominion. About ten years after the birth of their son they removed to Ohio and settled in Gallia County, where they lived for ten years. Thence they went to Fulton County, Ill., where for a period of forty years our subject engaged in farming pursuits, and in 1870 came to Wapello County, Iowa, and located in Highland Township on section 16, which constitutes his present homestead. His farm includes 205 acres of valuable land, to which he has added many improvements since it came into his possession.

Mr. Jones was united in marriage with Miss Mary Cozad, a native of Illinois, who by her union with our subject became the mother of the following children: Nancy married Thomas Livingstone, of Page County, Iowa; Sarah, Mrs. Elias Shaw, lives in Fulton County, Ill.; Mary Ann became the wife of Henry Oviatt, of Fulton County, Ill. The mother of these children departed this life on the 1st of February, 1844, and for his second wife Mr. Jones married Miss Caroline Buffum, a native of Ohio, who bore him six children, as follows: Thomas L., during the late war, enlisted in the 103d Illinois Infantry, and was killed at the battle of Lookout Mountain, June 22, 1864; Richard died at home June 22, 1862, at the age of sixteen years; Sarah became the wife of Amaziah Shaw, and lives in Kansas; George W. is a resident of Fulton County, Ill.: Isaac N. lives in Wayne County, Iowa; Betsy A. married John Wycoff, of McDonough County, Ill. Mrs. Caroline Jones departed this life Jan. 25, 1870, and for his third wife Mr. J. married Miss Eliza Summers, in August, 1870. Of this marriage there were born three children—Allen W., Lemuel W. and Benjamin C., all at home.

Mr. Jones is a member of the Missionary Baptist and his wife of the Christian Church. Our subject takes an intelligent interest in the affairs of his township, and has served as School Director for a period of twelve years. He has been engaged in farming pursuits the greater part of his life, although he followed milling for three years in Illinois. He was only two years old when his father died, and was reared by his stepfather, who trained him to habits of industry by which he became fitted for the later duties of life, which he was enabled to grapple with success.

THOMAS W. HOLLINGSWORTH, a highly esteemed farmer and stock-raiser of Green Township, owns and occupies a valuable homestead on section 11, where he is successfully managing the various departments of his chosen calling. The subject of this history is a native of Clarke County, Ohio, and was born Nov. 10, 1843. His parents were J. W. and Nancy (Maholem) Hollingsworth, the father a native of Virginia and the mother of Ohio. The parental household consisted of five children, three sons and two daughters, of whom the record is as follows; Sarah E., now deceased, became the wife of Michael Baum; T. W., the subject of this sketch, was the second child;

Frances married D. L. Gephart, a resident of Great Bend, Barton Co., Kan.; H. C. is Superintendent of Schools at Centerville, Iowa; J. P. is operating the old homestead for his father.

The parents of our subject came to Wapello County, Iowa, in 1844, and J. W. Hollingsworth assisted to build the first cabin on the present site of the city of Ottumwa. He was thus fully entitled to be ranked among the pioneer settlers of this region. He came to Iowa when horses were a luxury and oxen in great demand. He was a miller by trade and was also engaged in agricultural pursuits. As a stirring, energetic citizen, industrious and enterprising, he commanded the respect and esteem of his neighbors, and became one of the leading citizens of this community.

The subject of our sketch has spent the greater part of his life in farming pursuits. His early advantages were quite limited, but he was possessed of more than ordinary intelligence, and keenly observant of what was going on around him in the world. He thus obtained a good fund of information which served him well, and he has always kept himself well posted in matters of general interest. He remained under the parental roof until the breaking out of the late Civil War, and then proffered his services as a soldier to assist in the preservation of the Union. He accordingly became a member of Co. E, 36th Iowa Vol. Inf., and was mustered into service at Davenport, in February, 1864. His regiment was at once ordered to Little Rock, Ark., and after remaining there in camp three or four weeks, set out on the Camden expedition, and participated in all the battles of that campaign until they were mustered out at Devall's Bluff, Ark. Mr. H. then returned to Davenport, where he received his honorable discharge on the 21st of August, 1865.

After our subject had been transformed from a soldier into a citizen, he resumed his farming pursuits upon his purchase of 100 acres of land on section 11, which constitutes his present homestead. On the 24th of November, 1868, he was united in marriage with Miss Sarah Baird. She was born in Zanesville, Ohio, Jan. 8, 1844, and is the daughter of James P. and Rebecca (Davis) Baird, natives respectively of Virginia and Ohio. They are still living, and are residents of Prairie City, Iowa.

Mr. and Mrs. H. have become the parents of three children: Laura B. was born Feb. 14, 1872, and is the only one living; the eldest born and the youngest died in infancy. Our subject and his wife are prominently connected with the Methodist Episcopal Church, and socially Mr. H. belongs to Clautman Post No. 69, G. A. R., of Ottumwa. Politically he is a staunch Republican, and uniformly casts his vote in support of the principles of that party. He is classed among the representative farmers of Wapello County, and in all respects is fulfilling the obligations of a good citizen.

H. C. HUMBERT is a farmer and stock-grower on section 26, Agency Township. He was born in Somerset County, Pa., April 22, 1827, and is a son of Jacob and Hester (Crener) Humbert, both natives of Pennsylvania. His father died May 16, 1871, and his mother Dec. 25, 1886, in her native State, in the eightieth year of her age. The subject of this sketch married Lydia Dietz, in February, 1852; she is a daughter of Adam and Elizabeth (Long) Dietz, the former of whom died in Pennsylvania in June, 1852, and the latter Nov. 5, 1875. For many years her father was a teacher in the public schools and was also a veterinary surgeon.

In 1857 H. C. Humbert came to Wapello County, where he has since continued to reside, with the exception of two years spent in Nebraska. In 1862 he enlisted, and was made Captain of Co. E, 22d Iowa Vol. Inf., and served eighteen months, being discharged on account of disability contracted while in the service. He was in the battle of Black River Bridge and in the siege of Vicksburg. While yet a resident of Pennsylvania, he held a Captain's commission in the uniformed militia of the State for five years. He was subsequently commissioned Major of the 16th regiment of the Pennsylvania State Militia, and served as such for four years, a part of which time he was absent on the staff of Gen. Ross.

Capt. Humbert has been honored by his fellow-citizens with many local offices. At present he

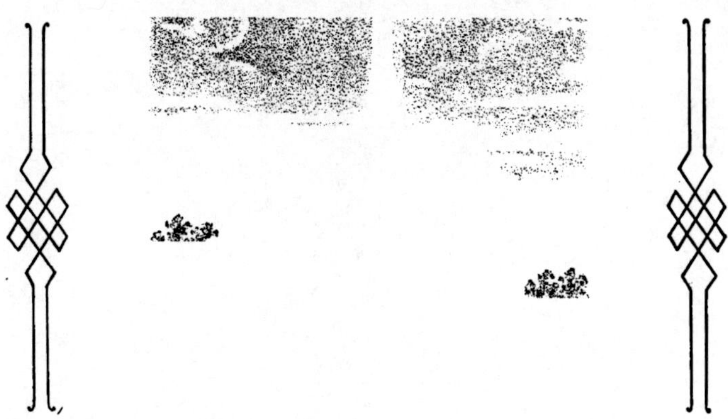

is President of the School Board of his district, of which he was Secretary for some years. He was also Coroner of the county one term. Capt. Humbert owns a farm of forty acres of well-improved land, and for some years has made a specialty of raising White Cochin and Partridge Cochin chickens.

Capt. H. is a member of the G. A. R. and A. F. & A. M. Religiously he is connected with the Methodist Episcopal Church; his wife is a member of the Free-will Baptist. Politically our subject is a Republican. He is well known to the citizens of Wapello County, and in every enterprise calculated for the public good he is in the front rank. No man in the county enjoys the respect and confidence of his fellow-citizens in a greater degree.

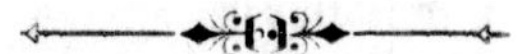

MICHAEL HECKART, a prominent and successful farmer of Green Township has been a resident of this locality since the fall of 1850, and the possessor of a valuable homestead of 200 acres located on sections 22 and 28. He purchased it from the Government when first coming to the township, and since that time has been continuously engaged in its improvement and cultivation. Under his wise and judicious management it has become one of the handsomest and most valuable bodies of land in this section, and with its fine residence, good barns and outbuildings and valuable domestic animals, presents one of the most attractive spots in this section of Iowa.

The subject of this biography is a native of Dauphin County, Pa., and was born in 1822. He is the son of Jost and Mary E. (Schneider) Heckart, both natives of Dauphin County, Pa. The former served as a soldier during the War of 1812, and departed this life in 1858. The mother of our subject survived the partner of her youth for a period of twenty-three years, and folded her hands for her final rest in January, 1882, at the advanced age of eighty-seven years, having made her residence with our subject during the latter part of her life. Jost Heckart was a farmer and millwright, and carried on these joint occupations successfully and profitably. Both parents were connected with the Presbyterian Church, and were highly esteemed members of society.

Michael Heckart, at the age of sixteen years, in 1838, moved with his parents to Ralls County, Mo., where the father purchased a farm. He was an enterprising and ambitious youth, and had been trained to habits of industry by his careful and conscientious parents, consequently he was well fitted, even at that early age, to begin the struggle of life for himself. He at once engaged at carpenter work, at which he served a thorough apprenticeship, and when not occupied at his trade accepted employment at farming pursuits. He remained in Missouri for a period of twelve years, and then went up North into Iowa, making his location in Green Township, Wapello County, which has been his home since that time.

April 6, 1848, while living in Ralls County, Mo., Mr. Heckart was united in marriage with Miss Mary M. Moyer, a daughter of Adam Moyer, a native of Pennsylvania, where Mrs. H. was also born, April 7, 1828. Mr. and Mrs. Heckart became the parents of eleven children, the record of whom is as follows: John A. is a carpenter by trade and a resident of Adams Township; he married Sadie Spangler; Frances became the wife of Frank Price, and after his death she married J. Sproal Randolph, of Adams County, Iowa; Mattie E. is at home; Libbie married Marion Higdon, of Colorado; Mollie became the wife of Charles Richey, also of that State; William is engaged as a carpenter and farmer in Nebraska; he married Carrie Howk; Rebecca is the wife of Charles Reinhard, of this county; Joseph is also a resident of this county; Adala and Charles are at home. Mrs. Mary Heckart departed this life May 14, 1883, lamented by a large circle of friends and acquaintances, and her remains are interred in Pleasant Ridge Cemetery.

For his second wife Mr. Heckart, in September, 1884, married Miss Rosa, daughter of F. L. Backman, of Green Township, and of their union there has been born one child, a daughter—Ruth. Mr. Heckart is a member of the Presbyterian, his wife of the Protestant Methodist Church, to the support of which they contribute liberally and cheerfully. Mr. H. is a Democrat in politics. In addition to his general farming operations he is devoting considerable attention to the breeding of fine stock, which includes horses, cattle and hogs. He has two fine stallions, "Temberline" and "Blackhawk," which are models of symmetry and beauty, and all his animals are high grade, among them being some of the finest and most valuable exhibited by any stock-breeder in this section of the Hawkeye State.

R. M. GIBBS, one of the representative farmers and stock-raisers of Cass Township, is the owner of a valuable farm estate on sections 25 and 36, where for many years he has been industriously engaged in cultivating the soil, and building up for himself an honored position among his fellow-citizens. Our subject was born in Athens County, Ohio, on the 4th of December, 1831, and is the son of Wareham and Eliza-beth Gibbs, both natives of Vermont. They were there married, and removed to Pennsylvania about the year 1817, whence, in 1822, they went to Athens County, Ohio. There the father became a prominent citizen, in due time being elected Sheriff of the county several terms, and holding other important positions. He finally became engaged in coal-mining, and opened up the first mine of this description in the Hocking Valley in about 1836. His transactions extended over a large amount of territory, and he became the owner of a line of boats which navigated the Hocking Canal, and were used for transporting the product of his mine to different points. The elder Gibbs operated in this manner until 1847, and then resolved to seek the farther West. Crossing the Mississippi and coming into Wapello County, this State, he entered 160 acres of land in Cass Township, and began to improve a farm, with the intention of establishing a permanent home. Here also he met with abundant success, and as time passed on added to his first purchase until he became the owner of 320 acres, all in one body.

In addition to his own personal interests Mr. Gibbs also took an active part in the progress and development of the township, and was the supporter and encourager of every enterprise calculated for its advancement. He contributed toward the establishment of schools and religious societies, and was prominently connected with the Methodist Episcopal Church. He early became identified with the Masonic fraternity, of which he remained an honored member until his death, which took place in 1863, being called while still actively engaged in the duties and labors of a busy life. His first wife, the mother of our subject, preceded her husband to the better land about thirty years, her death occurring in 1833. Of their union there had been born seven children, five sons and two daughters, as follows: Cortland, deceased; Eliza, the wife of Benjamin Hoskinsons; Harriet and Harris, deceased; Homer was wounded at the battle of Poison Springs, and captured by the rebels, and died in Camden (Ark.) prison; George, a soldier of the Mexican War, under Gen. Taylor, was killed while in the service; R. M., our subject, was the youngest of the family. After the death of his first wife, Wareham Gibbs was again married, in 1835, to Mrs. Spencer, a widow, and they became the parents of three children: Charles is in Oregon; Elias, a ranchman of Medicine Lodge, Kan., and John, who died in infancy. This last lady died in 1842, and the last years of Mr. Gibbs were spent with his children.

The subject of this history was trained to habits of industry by his excellent parents, and at an early age began life on his own account. His school education was extremely limited, but he was possessed of a bright and observing mind, and obtained a fund of useful information in keeping his eyes open to what was going on around him, and perusing carefully the few books and papers which came in his way. He was also possessed of excellent judgment, and while yet a young man had saved his earnings, so that in 1850, when only nineteen years of age, he became the purchaser of fifty-two acres of land, to which he added as time passed on, buying and improving, and then selling each time to good advantage. He purchased his present homestead in 1865, it then consisting of 110 acres. Besides this he owns eighty acres in Columbia Township, all of which is under a fine state of cultivation.

On the 7th of November, 1852, after our subject had made his first purchase of land, and there was a good prospect of his being able to provide for a family, he was united in marriage with Miss Loscania Olney, who was born in McLean County, Ill., and was the daughter of Oman and Triphena (Cheadle) Olney. Her father was a native of Nova Scotia, and her mother of Vermont. They are both now deceased, the father at his death being about seventy-two years of age, and the mother sixty-nine. They were kind and judicious parents, useful members of society, and active workers in the Methodist Episcopal Church.

Of the marriage of Mr. and Mrs. Gibbs there were born ten children, three sons and seven daughters: Ursula died at the age of ten years; Eliza became the wife of Dr. N. J. Hyatt, and lives in Van Wert, Iowa; Sarah married William Sylivan, a farmer of Custer County, Neb.; Chloe married Edward Marshall, roadmaster on the A., T. & S. F. R. R., and they live in Colorado; Charles is deceased; Sherman is a resident of Washington Territory; Edward died when seven years old; Clara is deceased; Lena is at home with her parents, and Alta at school.

Mr. Gibbs for many years has been prominent in the general and political affairs in this section, and is a stanch Republican, in which party he exerts a strong influence in this vicinity. He has been Chairman of the Republican Central Committee for a number of years, and has always occupied a position in the front rank as the supporter of public improvements, and every measure tending to the development and progress of his township and county. He has been honest and outspoken in his views, which have always been held in respect even by those who have been compelled to differ with him. He has also been foremost in the establishment of educational facilities, and is in all respects the stanch supporter of morality and good order. Mrs. Gibbs is a member of the Methodist Episcopal Church of Cass Township, and has contributed liberally and cheerfully to its maintenance and growth.

In addition to general farming, Mr. Gibbs has given especial attention to the breeding of high-grade cattle, of which he has a fine herd which will compare favorably with any that can be exhibited in this section of country. The homestead, in all its appointments, denotes thrift and prosperity, and is one of the attractive spots to which the attention of the traveler throughout the country is invariably turned. To such men as Mr. Gibbs is Wapello County indebted for her present position among the wealthy and intelligent communities of the great commonwealth of Iowa.

WILLIAM H. LEWIS, a highly esteemed citizen of Ottumwa, is a gentleman of fine abilities, well read and intelligent, and occupies a prominent position among the better class of citizens of this locality. He has been a resident of Ottumwa since 1857, first occupying himself at his trade of plastering, and subsequently became a successful contractor, which business he followed until the spring of 1876. He then moved upon a farm in Center Township, and followed agricultural pursuits until 1882, when he returned to Ottumwa and was elected to the office of Justice of the Peace. The duties of this position he fulfilled with great credit to himself and satisfaction to his constituents; he is now retired.

The subject of this history was born in the little city of Urbana, Champaign Co., Ohio, Aug. 30, 1832. He is the son of William and Ruth (Pearce) Lewis, and his father was a native of Kentucky, in which State he was born on the 15th of May, 1810; the mother was a native of Ohio. The parental household included five children, who are recorded as follows: William H., our subject, was the eldest born; Louisa is deceased; Theophilus enlisted as a soldier in the late war and was killed in battle near Oldtown, Miss., in 1862; George died in infancy; Clara died in California about 1877. When our subject was about thirteen years of age his father removed into Illinois, and there the mother's decease occurred in 1845.

When he had arrived at the age of fifteen years young Lewis was apprenticed to the trade of a plasterer in Peoria, Ill., where he remained four years. He then went to the rapidly growing town of Pekin, where he was at once busily engaged at his trade, and the father received the contract in his department for some of the largest buildings then in process of construction. On the 10th of September, 1857, in Kappa, Ill., he was united in wedlock with Miss Mary A. Jones, and soon afterward removed to Ottumwa, Iowa. Mrs. L. is the daughter of Charles, Jr., and Mary (Vining) Jones, natives of Massachusetts. She was born in November, 1840, and by her union with our subject became the mother of five children, as follows: Josephine L. was born Nov. 14, 1858; Jennie A., Oct. 13, 1862; Walter A., Oct. 19, 1864; Clara A., Feb. 11, 1867, and Arthur, Aug. 12, 1875.

Mr. Lewis has given his children the advantages of a liberal education, and his daughter, Miss Clara, is an artist of considerable merit, and has painted a portrait of her father which does great credit to her skill and genius. The family residence is pleasantly located, and in all respects is indicative of the cultivated tastes and the education of its inmates. Mr. Lewis is an extensive reader, and is the encourager and supporter of education, temperance and morality. In politics he is a Republican, and socially belongs to the I. O. O. F. of Ottumwa.

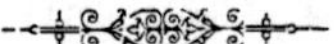

A. A. JENISON is a retired farmer, living in Kirkville. He was born in Ripley County, Ind., June 2, 1831, and is a son of Elias and Polly (Gookins) Jenison, natives of Massachusetts, but who moved to Indiana at an early day. The father died in that State and the mother in Ottumwa. Ripley County at this time was but little more than a wilderness, and it can well be reasoned that the advantages enjoyed by the subject of this sketch were very meager indeed. Like many others he was early trained in work. In 1854 he came to Iowa and located in Mahaska County, where he lived until 1881, when he came to Kirkville, and has since lived a retired life. He yet owns the farm of 180 acres in Mahaska County, together with sixty-three acres of land in Wapello County, thirteen of which lie in the village limits of Kirkville.

In 1857 Mr. Jenison was united in marriage with Drucilla Dashiell, born in Dearborn County, Ind., in 1833, and a daughter of John and Amelia (Duncan) Dashiell. Her parents were both natives of Maryland, and died in Dearborn County, Ind. Of this union there were two children: Mary, born Dec. 14, 1860, died in infancy, and E. M., born April 16, 1866. Mr. and Mrs. Denison are members of the Methodist Episcopal Church, and in politics he is a Republican.

JONATHAN HECKART, of Green Township, owns and occupies a homestead located on section 28. He has been a resident of Wapello County since the fall of 1849, and during a residence of over thirty-five years has been a witness of remarkable and pleasing changes in this section of country. At that time Iowa had been only a few years before converted from a Territory into a State, and although emigration was rapidly opening up farms and homesteads throughout the State, there was still an abundance of wild and uncultivated land. Mr. Heckart, in common with his brother pioneers, settled upon a new farm and industriously set about its improvement and cultivation. That he succeeded admirably his present surroundings amply indicate. His possessions consist of forty acres of land, a good residence, and everything pertaining to a first-class farm estate. He is now retired from the more active labors of life, and in the consciousness of a life of honesty and integrity, is passing his later days in peace and contentment.

Mr. Heckart is a native of Dauphin County, Pa., born in 1816, and is the son of Jost and Mary (Schneider) Heckart, both natives of the same State and of staunch German ancestry. Our subject emigrated from his native State at the age of twenty-one years, and proceeding southwest made his first location in Ralls County, Mo. He remained there for the following twelve years, working at the trade of a carpenter, at which he had previously served an apprenticeship of two and one-half years under the instruction of his father in Pennsylvania. In the meantime, during his residence in Missouri, he was married, in 1842, to Miss Mary Ann Thomas, of Kentucky, who bore him one child, a daughter named Nancy Thomas, who died in infancy. His young wife only remained his companion for the short period of two years, dying in September, 1844, at the age of twenty-six years.

Mr. H. was married the second time, Feb. 8, 1849, to Miss Harriet E. Carman, of Harrison County, Mo. Of this union there were born ten children, the record of whom is as follows: John Collins died at the age of eight years; Mary Ann died in January, 1883, at the age of thirty-one years; Ava J. is at home; Lucy E. is the wife of William J. Davis, of Washington County, Iowa; Susanna is at home; Sarah Ellen died in infancy; Martha Alice died in early childhood; William Henry is at home; Joseph Siegel died at the age of seven years, and Isaac Newton also died in childhood. Mr. and Mrs. H. are prominently connected with the Presbyterian Church, and in politics our subject is a stanch Republican. He and his son William jointly own and operate a saw and grist mill at Ormanville, this county, the proceeds of which yield them a handsome income.

Joseph Heckart, the brother of our subject, during the progress of the late war enlisted in the 15th Iowa Infantry, in which he served four and one-half years. He was known to have engaged in the battle of Atlanta, and during the siege disappeared from the sight of his comrades and was never afterward heard from by his family or friends. Another brother, Henry, enlisted in a Missouri regiment and was wounded, but recovered, and returned home at the close of the war.

A. DANGUARD, member of the firm of John Hausmann's Union Brewery, and located in the city of Ottumwa, was born in Baden, Germany, Feb. 3, 1849. In accordance with the custom of his native country, he was placed at school at an early age and completed his studies at the college of Manheim. At the age of eighteen years he emigrated to America and made his first location at Freeport, Ill., where he learned the printer's trade in the office of the *Deutcher Anzeiger*, William Wagner proprietor, with whom he remained until December, 1867. He then came to Iowa and secured employment in the office of the Council Bluffs *Press*. Three years later he established the Sioux City *Courier*, which he sold the following year, and then coming to Ottumwa, established the *Journal* of this city, which he operated until 1885, and then sold to John A. Wagoner, the present proprietor.

Mr. Danguard was married, in 1876, at Sioux City, to Miss Katie Murchrath. Mrs. D. was born in Dubuque, Iowa, in 1856. They are established in a pleasant home in Ottumwa and enjoy the esteem of a large circle of friends and acquaintances. Mr. D. belongs to the "Ottumwa Turnverein," a branch of the North American Turener-Bund, also Burlington Lodge No. 132, K. of P., having filled various positions in the same, and is one of the most valued members. He is a gentleman of good address and fine intelligence, and numbers among his friends and associates the cultured people of his community.

H. M. HUGHES, "the Village Blacksmith" of Eldon, is a native of Davis County, Iowa, born in 1851. His parents were John L. and Martha (Loftus) Hughes, natives respectively of Virginia and Ohio, the former born in 1822, and his wife Martha, the following year. They became the parents of seven children—W. T., J. P., H. M., S. J., O. B., J. M. and R. G. They came to Iowa in 1848, and settled in Davis County. They are still living on a farm a short distance from Eldon, and enjoying in their later years the fruits of early toil and industry. They are most worthy and excellent people and highly respected in the community where they reside.

H. M. Hughes learned the trade of blacksmithing soon after attaining his majority, and a few years later came to Eldon and established his present business, in which he has been uniformly successful. He is a skilled workman and has built up a large and profitable patronage, besides fulfilling all the duties of a good citizen. In 1881 our subject was united in marriage with Miss Emma, the daughter of James Higdon, and a native of the Hawkeye State. Of this union there have been born three children—Frank, Ethel and Hurles. They occupy a comfortable homestead and enjoy the friendship and confidence of a large circle of acquaintances.

Mr. and Mrs. H. are connected with the Methodist Episcopal Church, and Mr. H. is Township Trustee. He owns some valuable property in Eldon and occupies a place among its worthiest citizens. He is a member in good standing of the I. O. O. F., and takes an interest in everything pertaining to the welfare of his county and community.

CALEB FOSTER, a farmer and stock-grower, will be found on section 6, Richland Township. He was born in New Brunswick, Oct. 7, 1822, and is the son of George and Jerusha (Wortman) Foster, the former a native of England, and the latter of New Brunswick. His father came to America when about twenty-one years of age, and settled in New Brunswick, where he was married, and where the subject of this sketch was born. In 1824 the family moved from New Brunswick to Ohio, where the father of Caleb engaged in farming and teaching. His parents both died in Ohio.

In 1847 Caleb Foster moved from Ohio to Mahaska County, this State, and remained there until 1850, when he removed to his present farm, on which he has since continued to reside. On the 9th day of July, 1846, he was married to Melila J. Pickens, the daughter of Alpha and Jane (Anderson) Pickens, both of whom are now deceased. Nine children were born of this union—Alfred, J. C., V. A., Jerusha (deceased), Mary E. (deceased), M. J., Agnes, Benjamin B. and George. Mrs. Foster died Sept. 8, 1870, and Mr. Foster was subsequently marrried to Hannah Loveless, widow of T. A. Loveless, and daughter of James and Ann Murray. She was born in Buffalo, N. Y., March 25, 1828. To this union one child was born, J. B., now deceased. Mr. Foster owns fifty-five acres of well improved land, where he now resides, and also owns 117 acres in Mahaska County, which are likewise well improved. He is a member of the Methodist Episcopal Church, of which body his wife is also a member. In politics he is a Republican.

B. FRITZ, a prominent and representative citizen of Blakesburg, Wapello County, is a native of Austria, born in the beautiful Province of Tyrol, on the 15th of October, 1826. He is the son of Benedict and Virneck (Yocum) Fritz, the latter of whom died in her native country at the age of about forty years, when her son, our subject, was a lad ten years old. He still remembers her as a careful and affectionate mother, devoted to the religious faith of her fathers, that of the Catholic Church. She was buried near the old home in Tyrol, and is held in sacred remembrance by the son, who, although so young when she passed away, can recall her devoted and loving care. The father of our subject died in his native country in about 1859, and was also a Catholic, as were most of the people of that part of the country. Their children were carefully trained in the doctrines of that church.

The parental household of our subject consisted of several children, five sons and two daughters. Joseph came to this country with the subject of our sketch, and died in Columbus, Ohio, in 1884; Benedict of this history was the second son; Christian is engaged in farming near Des Moines, Iowa; Anthony, a baker by trade, is in his native land; Priscilla died in the old country in about 1873; the second child died in infancy.

Mr. Fritz left his native country for the United States in the spring of 1853. The voyage occupied thirty-six days, and after landing in New York City he proceeded to Cleveland, Ohio, where his brother Christian had previously located. Upon arriving he found that the latter had left there, and not being able to find out his whereabouts, went to Columbus, and there engaged as a house-painter, in which he was occupied for the following eight months. About this time came the glowing reports about the quantity of gold to be found in California, and Mr. F. being seized with the fever, started on the 5th of January for San Francisco via New

York, and thence by steamer, arriving on the Pacific coast on the 2d of February, 1854, and proceeded straight to the mines in Placer County, Cal., where he was engaged in searching for the shining ore for the following three years. He was successful in his enterprise, and in the year last mentioned returned eastward as far as Iowa, and coming to Wapello County, purchased 160 acres of land in Adams Township, on section 17, obtaining possession of it in October.

In the meantime, however, on the 20th of September, Mr. Fritz secured unto himself a partner and helpmeet in the person of Miss Annie Miller, a native of his own country. She was born May 7, 1831, and was the daughter of Martin Miller. Of this union there were eight children, as follows: Louise B., born July 13, 1858, became the wife of Moses Abernethy, a merchant and hotel-keeper of Blakesburg; William T. was born Jan 15, 1860, and is now the manager of his father's farm in Adams Township; Henry, born Nov. 25, 1862, is employed as a clerk by his brother-in-law, Mr. Abernethy; Matilda, born May 5, 1861, died March 20, 1864, and is buried in the cemetery at Blakesburg; the next daughter, also named Matilda, was born Aug. 7, 1864, and married Mr. Frank Hardy, a farmer residing near Blakesburg; George, born Oct. 10, 1866, is now attending the Business College of Bryant & Stratton, at Chicago; Franklin, born Sept. 26, 1868, is attending the district school; and Gertrude C. was born Feb. 14, 1871.

Mr. Fritz is the owner of about 1,000 acres of land. He is extensively engaged as a dealer in live-stock and is also interested in mercantile pursuits. In addition to this he owns and superintends a gristmill. In his various business pursuits he has been remarkably successful and has accumulated a handsome competency. On departing from his native land he was possessed of a very small amount of this world's goods, and that little was spent on the journey. But he had been reared to habits of industry, and had served over four years in the German army, and thus became familiar with hardship and privation, so that he was well fitted for the emergencies of the future. He has been richly rewarded in his efforts to become a man among the men of this great Republic, and occupies an enviable position as a representative citizen, enjoying the fullest confidence and respect of those among whom he has lived for so many years. Although his course has been seemingly very successful, he, too, has been visited by afflictions, the greatest being the death of his wife, to whom he was devotedly attached; she departed this life at her home on the 25th of August, 1884. She was an affectionate wife and mother, a faithful friend and counselor, and devotedly attached to the religion of the Catholic Church. Her remains were laid to rest in the cemetery near Blakesburg, and she is kindly remembered by a large circle of friends and acquaintances.

Mr. Fritz has provided liberally for his children, giving each the advantage of a good education, and has generously assisted them in starting in life. He is now retired from active labor and can look with satisfaction over the years of a life in which he has striven to perform his duty to those within his influence and to fulfill the obligations of a good citizen. He is a staunch adherent of the Democratic party, and uniformly casts his vote in support of its principles.

HARVEY DICKENS, a successful farmer and stock-grower of Competine Township, is pleasantly located on section 32, and in the several departments of his calling is meeting with well-merited success. He has been a resident of the Hawkeye State since 1846, the year that Iowa was transformed from a Territory into a State, and is a native of Wyandotte County, Ohio, his birth occurring on the 27th of March, 1839. Upon his arrival in the State Mr. Dickens came at once into Wapello County, and has been a resident of this section since that time. He was accompanied by his father on the journey here, and lived with him until he was twenty-four years of age. Thereafter for four years he made his home with his brother Malachi, and in 1866 made a trip across the plains to Pike's Peak, Col., and went to work on the Union Pacific Railroad for about three months, and at the expiration of this time, being satisfied with his experience West, returned home.

Mr. Dickens then engaged in the buying and selling of stock, and was thus occupied for about five years. He had been successful in his operations, and purchased 295 acres of improved land on section 32, which constitutes his present homestead. Since taking possession of his farm he has been continuously making improvements, until it forms one of the most attractive spots in the landscape of the county. He has a comfortable frame dwelling, with all necessary out-buildings for the shelter of stock and the storing of grain, and is considered one of the most skillful farmers and stock-raisers in this locality.

The marriage of Harvey Dickens and Miss Mary McDowell took place on the 8th of October, 1875. Mrs. D. is the daughter of John and Mary (Fisher) McDowell, both natives of Indiana, but now living in Pleasant Township, Wapello County. The household of our subject and his wife has been blest by the birth of eight children, three of whom are living: Nellie was born Dec. 30, 1877; Elizabeth, Jan. 13, 1879, and Alice, Jan. 12, 1883.

Politically Mr. Dickens is strongly Republican, and uniformly casts his vote in support of the principles of that party. He and his wife are members in good standing of the Christian Church, and are highly respected in their community for their upright and praiseworthy lives and generous, kindly deeds.

E. H. WRIGHT, a resident on section 2, Washington Township, is a farmer and stock-grower, and the owner of 180 acres of well-improved land. He was born in Scott County, Ill., Dec. 1, 1832, and is a son of Jacob and Rebecca (Groce) Wright, both of whom were natives of Kentucky. His parents moved from Kentucky to Illinois about 1825, and in 1847 went to Jefferson County, Iowa, where his mother died in 1876. His father, who was a farmer by occupation, is now living a retired life in the latter-named county.

The subject of this sketch was reared upon a farm, and in 1857 was united in marriage with Eunice Everett, a native of Ohio, born Dec. 9, 1839, and the daughter of Edward and Eliza A. (Langdon) Everett. Her mother died in Iowa, and her father in Kansas. To this union ten children have been born, four of whom are now living —Franklin, Mattie, Edward and Effie. Mary B., Rebecca A., Amanda J., Thomas H., Eliza A. and Hattie are deceased. Mr. and Mrs. Wright are members of the Predestinarian Baptist Church. In politics he is a Democrat.

REV. M. F. HOKASON, who is well and favorably known throughout this section, is a native of Sweden, and was born at Runobe, that country, Sept. 7, 1811. There he was educated in the common schools but later attended a special school, where none but males were admitted. In 1847 he emigrated to America and located in Jefferson County, Iowa. Here he labored in the cause of his Master as an exhorter, but was subsequently licensed to preach the Gospel by the Ohio Synod, and afterward was licensed by the Northern Illinois Synod, and ordained in October, 1853. He had studied diligently, having his heart thoroughly in the work, and thus after two years of preparation was ordained a minister of Christ. He is a gentleman possessing far more than ordinary ability, and is not only highly esteemed for his labors of love, but is respected by all throughout the county who have the pleasure of his acquaintance. He has labored with great energy, and has accomplished a great deal for his people and has been a guiding star to them.

Our subject was married, in Jefferson County, Iowa, on the 27th of November, 1848, to Miss Ann Elizabeth Anderson, who, like himself, was a native of Sweden. They have had no children of their own, but adopted Minnie O. Hokason when she was an infant of fourteen months. In 1856 Mr. Hokason came to Wapello County, where he lived for three years, and the following eight years were passed in Boone County, when he returned to this county, where he has since made his home. When he first came here, which was in an early day, the broad, undulating prairies were covered with a rich and verdant growth of tall prairie grass, the

John S. Wolfe

dead monotony being unbroken by the beautiful groves which are now seen on every hand. He has taken an active part in the development, not only of the social and spiritual conditions of the people, but of the rich material resources of the county. Politically he is a Republican.

COL. JOHN S. WOLF, of Ottumwa, is contractor of the Iron Range Railroad, and the able manner in which he discharges the duties of his responsible position meets the approval and appreciation of the traveling public. He has had a large experience in railroad matters, having been long connected with the building and constructing department, and is well acquainted with all that appertains thereto.

Mr. Wolf is a native of Dauphin County, Pa., and was born in Harrisburg on the 7th of October, 1820. He is the son of Samuel and Elizabeth (Spicer) Wolf, the former a native of Pennsylvania and the latter of Maryland. The parental family included ten children, of whom the record is as follows: Samuel served as a private in the Mexican War, and in the late Rebellion was a Captain in the Union army, and was killed at the battle of Atlanta; Henry, a soldier of the Union, returned from the war unharmed, and is now a resident of Janesville, Iowa; Hiram was in the Buck-Tail Regiment from Pennsylvania, and was wounded at Dranesville; he recovered, however, returned home in safety, and is now living at Duluth, Minn.; Maria was married to William Maddin, of Dauphin, Pa., and is now deceased; Mary Ann departed this life in Cumberland County, Pa., aged between three and four years; Hezekiah died in infancy, in Lancaster County, Pa.; Elizabeth married David Miller, who is connected with the nail factory at Duncannon, Pa.; Sarah became the wife of Harvey Mell, who was a soldier in the late war and is now connected with the nail mills of Harrisburg, Pa. The father of our subject was a soldier in the War of 1812, but was not engaged in any battle. He lived to the advanced age of seventy-five years, and died in Dauphin County, Pa., which was the place of his birth.

The subject of this history was reared and educated in his native town, and after he arrived at years of manhood was married, in Dauphin County, Pa., to Miss Margaret L. Deobler, a native of his own county, and daughter of Henry and Mary (Shafer) Deobler, natives of the same county. Mr. Deobler was a soldier in the War of 1812, and the parental household included eight children, three of whom are living, as follows: Elizabeth, the wife of Henry Ehrman, of Benton's Port, Iowa; Margaret, the wife of our subject, and Fannie, who married Rev. D. Speck, of Baltimore, Md. The parents of Mrs. Wolf spent their entire lives in their native State. In early life they were both connected with the Lutheran Church, but in later years Mrs. D. joined the Methodist Church. She was an earnest Christian lady, and held in high esteem by all who knew her.

During the earlier years of his railroad life Mr. Wolf assisted in the construction of the Pennsylvania Central. His field of labor in this line has been quite large, extending through Ohio, Indiana, Wisconsin, Illinois, Missouri, Kentucky, Mississippi, Kansas, Iowa and Minnesota. Soon after the close of the war he came to Ottumwa as contractor on the B. & M. R. R., operating along the line from Ottumwa to Council Bluffs, and on the branch of the C., B. & N., and other roads. In an experience of forty years he has operated on some of the principal roads in the United States, and has gathered a rich experience in his peculiar calling, and is highly esteemed in railroad circles for his rare ability as a railroad man. Personally Mr. Wolf is of fine physique, of powerful frame and graceful carriage. He is genial and courteous in his manners, and has the polished air of a man who has seen much of the world. In politics he is a staunch Republican, and uniformly casts his vote in support of the principles of his party. He is a member of the Masonic fraternity of thirty-five years' standing. He possesses a well informed and intelligent mind, and is well posted in the affairs of the country. He always fully availed himself of all privileges of instruction to which he found access, and a distinguishing characteristic of his is the possession of quickness of mind and talent.

Mr. and Mrs. Wolf became the parents of ten

children, of whom the record is as follows: Louisa is the wife of George C. Hammond, of Cedar Rapids, Iowa; Samuel served as a soldier in the 20th Iowa Infantry, participated in the siege of Vicksburg, and died at New Orleans in 1863, of disease contracted in the army; Joseph is a railroad contractor; John S. is a farmer, of Cedar Rapids, Neb.; Sarah is the wife of L. D. Groon, a banker of Cedar Rapids, Neb.; Fannie married A. Q. Chase, of Springfield, Ohio, engaged with the Champion Reaper and Mower Manufactory; Trevis died in Ottumwa at the age of fifteen years; Prudence became the wife of Mathias Wilbur, a merchant of Colorado Springs; Harry is a resident of Ottumwa; Grant is conducting a farm in Wapello County. The children of Mr. and Mrs. Wolf were carefully educated and trained in those principles which have constituted them worthy citizens and an honor to their parents.

In presenting the portrait of Col. Wolf, which we do in this connection, we give our patrons the portrait of one of the best-known citizens of the county, and in many ways one of her representative men.

WILLIAM WILSON, a prosperous farmer and dairyman of Wapello County, will be found industriously engaged in his chosen calling on section 10, Center Township. He is a native of Monroe County, Ind., and was born April 27, 1843, being the son of Henry and Nancy J. (Farmer) Wilson. (See sketch of P. S. Wilson elsewhere in this volume.)

The subject of this sketch came to Iowa in company with his parents, when a child six years of age, and in 1861 was married to Miss Elizabeth Hardesty. Mrs. Wilson was born in Lee County, Iowa, March 24, 1845, and is the daughter of Thomas and Elizabeth (Stevenson) Hardesty. Of her marriage with our subject there have been born two children—Eldorado L. and Thomas W.

Mr. Wilson is the owner of 160 acres of good land, has a tasteful and substantial dwelling, and probably the best barn in Wapello County. This latter is 35x86 feet in area, with a stone basement, sixteen-foot corner posts, and cost $1,700. He also has another barn in which to feed his cattle, and for milking purposes, with room for forty animals. He has at present about fifty head of cows, of good common stock and all good milkers. He also has sixteen head of work horses and brood mares. Politically our subject is a Democrat, and a law-abiding citizen, who takes an intelligent interest in the welfare of his county and community.

A view of Mr. Wilson's homestead is shown on another page in this ALBUM.

J. M. HULL, a prominent and highly respected resident of Chillicothe, is largely identified with the milling and farming interests of this section, and one of its most energetic and prosperous business men. Mr. Hull was born in Culpeper County, Va., on the 18th of October, 1817, and is the son of J. B. and Jane (Willey) Hull, whose families were among the first in the Old Dominion, and widely known throughout that locality for their high character, and extensive landed estates and other property. The mother of our subject was a native of England, born in 1793, and came with her parents to the United States three years later. They landed in Philadelphia, Pa., and from there removed to Virginia, where, in Culpeper County, she became acquainted with J. B. Hull, and in 1814 became his wife. Mr. Hull was a millwright by trade, and followed that occupation until his removal West. He came to Iowa in 1854, and purchased property in Chillicothe, where he located and which remained his home until his death on the 26th of September, 1881, he having survived his wife for a period of twenty years, the mother's death taking place also in Chillicothe, in 1861. Both were active members of the Methodist Episcopal Church, to which they contributed liberally and cheerfully of their means, and were in all respects useful and honored members of society. Their household circle included six children, of whom the record is as follows: William, the eldest-born, lives on the old homestead in Virginia; J. M., our subject, was the second son; Mary J. became the wife of William Bashaw, now deceased, and is a resident of Blakesburg, this county; Catharine married Mr. J. Wesley Stockweather, of Blakesburg; Lucia C. became the wife of Samuel Blair, and resides at Oskaloosa; Elizabeth B., now deceased, was the wife of J. W. Lockhart.

The subject of our sketch was united in marriage with Miss Lucretia Partlow on the 23d of December, 1847. Mrs. Hull was born in Culpeper County, Va., on the 8th of May, 1826, and was the daughter of John L. and Martha (Lillard) Partlow, also natives of the Old Dominion, who spent their entire lives there, where the mother died in 1880, and her husband two years later. They were faithful adherents of the old-school Baptist Church, and Mr. Partlow held the various offices of his township and county. He was a man of considerable ability, and highly respected by his neighbors and associates.

Mr. and Mrs. Hull have become the parents of ten children, as follows: John E., born Oct. 13, 1848, died in Chillicothe on the 7th of January, 1886; Josephine, born Jan. 15, 1850, became the wife of Irvin Butin, a druggist and jeweler of Fredonia, Kan.; Mary L. and Benjamin died in infancy; Flora J., born Aug. 18, 1854, is the widow of Zenus Park, and a resident of Fredonia, Kan.; Martha died in infancy; B. Almira was born Jan. 1, 1859, and became the wife of R. A. Waddell, of Kirksville; James William was born Nov. 26, 1860, and is now a practicing physician of Brainard, Neb.; Emma C., born Feb. 7, 1863, is teaching school in Fredonia, Kan.; Jennie L., born April 6, 1865, is also a teacher.

Mr. Hull, of our sketch, removed from his native State to Iowa in 1855, and locating in Wapello County, purchased a sawmill which he has operated until the present time, in connection with a gristmill. A great change has been brought about in the condition of this section since Mr. Hull became a resident of Chillicothe, which was then a little hamlet struggling into a village. He soon became prominently connected with the affairs of the young community, and was acknowledged as a leader from the beginning. He was soon elected a member of the Board of Supervisors, and in 1857 was elected to the office of Justice of the Peace, which he has now occupied for a period of over twenty years. With his excellent wife he identified himself with the Methodist Episcopal Church, and they have been among its strongest and most liberal supporters. Our subject is an honored member of the I. O. O. F., and in every respect has fulfilled the obligations of a good citizen, and a valued member of society. His children have received careful home training and the advantages of a good education, and in early life were taught those principles of honor and honesty which are so essential to the character of the upright citizen and to those who are appointed to the leadership among the affairs of a community and county.

JAMES GIBSON, deceased, a late resident of Competine Township, was a native of Kentucky, and born on the 5th of June, 1817. He became a resident of Iowa in 1863, established the homestead in Competine Township which his widow now occupies, and departed from the scenes of his earthly labors on the 15th of December, 1877. At the age of nineteen years the subject of our sketch removed with his parents from his native State to Indiana, locating there in 1836. His father entered a tract of land in Marion County, and James assisted him in the development of a farm, and remained an inmate of the parental household until his marriage.

On the 27th of December, 1844, Mr. Gibson was united in wedlock with Miss Nancy B. Hunter, a native of Ohio, who was born April 16, 1825. Mrs. G. is the daughter of Reuben and Mary (Brazier) Hunter, and her parents remained residents of Indiana until 1861. They then proceeded further westward to escape the ague, and located in Mercer County, Ill. They sacrificed their property in Indiana for the benefit of their health, and passed away with comparatively little means. They possessed, however, that brave pioneer spirit which was fully armed to successfully battle with all difficulties, and they soon found themselves upon their feet again and prepared for a journey still further westward. In 1863 they crossed the Mississippi into Iowa, and coming into Wapello County, located in Competine Township, upon the farm which is still the home of Mrs. Gibson. The land then was but little removed from its original condition, but Mr. Gibson possessed abundant energy, and set about the cultivation of his purchase with the perseverance and industry which had characterized him from early youth. Here he and his wife lived happily and contentedly with their children until the Death Angel visited their fireside and took away the main support and comfort of the family.

Mr. and Mrs. Gibson became the parents of thirteen children, seven sons and six daughters: Mary, born Dec. 12, 1846, became the wife of Isaac Bare, a farmer of Smith County, Kan.; Francis M. was born Oct. 1, 1848; Elizabeth, born Nov. 20, 1849, married George True, of Smith County, Kan.; Reuben, born Sept 12, 1851, is also a resident of the last-named county; Andrew was born March 4, 1854, and is living near his brothers and sisters in Kansas; Eliza J., born Aug. 20, 1856, married Benjamin Davis, now deceased; Ellen A., born Aug. 28, 1858, became the wife of Fletcher Pribble, and is now deceased; Alexander, a resident of Wapello County, was born Jan. 20, 1860; Charles A. was born March 12, 1861; Nancy C., May 10, 1862; Delilah M., May 17, 1864; James T., Sept. 12, 1866, and William P., Sept. 28, 1870.

Mr. Gibson was a lifelong member of the Methodist Episcopal Church, and contributed liberally and cheerfully to its support. Mrs. G. is still connected with that denomination, and has reared her children to those moral and religious principles which will constitute them good citizens and fully worthy of the respect and esteem of the community which holds in such reverence the name of their honored and worthy sire.

CYRUS D. KING, Superintendent of the County Hospital, located in Highland Township, was born in Somerset County, Pa., July 18, 1831, and is the son of Enis and Barbara (Wymer) King, the father a native of the same county as his son, and the mother of German birth and parentage. Mr. King lived in his native county until he was thirteen years of age, and then emigrated with his parents to Iowa. They settled on the old Agency farm, which they occupied for five years, and then removed to a farm near Round Point, where the father entered 320 acres of fine farming land. This our subject assisted in improving and redeeming from its original condition, and remained upon it with his parents until the outbreak of the late war, when he enlisted as a Union soldier, in August, 1862. He served as a private in the 22d Iowa Infantry for two years, and was in the battles of Jackson, Miss., Champion Hills, Black River, the siege and capture of Vicksburg, and the second battle of Jackson, where he was sunstruck, and also otherwise injured by being thrown against a forge while working as a blacksmith in the service. He received his final discharge on account of disability, and after a tedious journey reached his home. After recovering from his injuries he purchased a small farm in Highland Township, where he engaged in agricultural pursuits for the following six years. He then removed into Green Township, and lived there seven years, and is now the owner of 200 acres of valuable land.

In 1876 Mr. King was placed in charge of the old Poor Farm, where he lived until the new County Hospital was erected two years later, and then took possession of the latter. This building is 75 x 40 feet in dimensions, and four stories in height, built of brick, and contains thirty-six sleeping-rooms. It now shelters fifty-three persons, twenty women and thirty-three men, and the surrounding farm belonging to it includes 240 acres. During the seven years Mr. King has had charge of this institution he has conducted it with ability and success, and has proved himself admirably adapted to the discharge of his difficult and responsible duties.

The subject of our sketch was married, in May, 1852, to Mrs. Nancy G. (Moss) Robert, the daughter of Henry and Amelia (Walker) Moss, and widow of George W. Robert, by whom she had two children—Amelia A., the wife of Alexander Giltner, of Agency, and who died in April, 1876, at the age of thirty-two years, and George W., a resident of Competine Township. Henry Moss was born in North Carolina, and his wife, Amelia, in Tennessee. Mrs. King was born Dec. 31, 1826, and came to Iowa with her parents in 1835. They were ferried across the Mississippi River on a cake of ice, and settled in Van Buren County, being the first to locate there, with two other families who accompanied them, and they did not know of any settlement west of them. Here Henry Moss lived for a number of years and improved a farm, finally removing to Wapello County, and opened up another farm here, upon which he spent the remainder of his days. When the survey was made his land was located in Pleasant Township, where he died in 1860, at the age of fifty-eight years, being buried at Round Point Cemetery, where the faithful wife and mother had been laid to rest soon after coming into the (then) Territory. Mr. Moss was a man of strong character, hospitable, liberal and generous, and had the faculty of attaching to himself strong friends wherever he made his home. He was a soldier in the Blackhawk War before coming to Iowa, and subsequently lived in Morgan County, Ill., before crossing the Father of Waters. He was connected with the Regular Baptist Church, and in his daily walk and conversation faithfully lived up to his religious principles, which had been the rule of his life from early youth.

Of the union of Mr. and Mrs. King there were born four children, as follows: John H. is a resident of Ottumwa, and acts as turnkey in the jail; Elisha E. is Assistant Superintendent of the County Hospital; Sarah, Mrs. Lawrence Reinhart, lives on a farm in Green Township; Mary E. became the wife of Milton S. White, of Sullivan County, Mo. Mr. and Mrs. K. are active members of the Methodist Episcopal Church, and socially our subject belongs to the I. O. O. F. and G. A. R. He is a Republican in politics, and in all respects is fulfilling the obligations of a good citizen.

At the outbreak of the late war Mr. King, laying aside personal interests and plans, started at the earliest opportunity to proffer his services in assisting to preserve the Union. He belonged to the 22d Iowa Infantry, and with his comrades skirmished all through Maryland under command of Col. Stone, who was afterward elected Governor of Iowa.

The father of Mr. King was a very religious man, and a member of the Methodist Episcopal Church. He was one of the first to organize a society in this county, and meetings were held in his house before even a school-house was built. He was a blacksmith by trade, and our subject, during his earlier years, also followed the same in connection with farming. Enis King departed this life at Agency City in 1872, having arrived at the age of seventy-eight years. His wife, the mother of our subject, died in 1866 at the same place. John King, the eldest brother of our subject, was the first person buried in the cemetery at Agency.

JOHN KIELKOPF, a prosperous German farmer of Highland Township, was born in Wurtemberg in 1832, and is the son of Martin and Catharine (Rose) Kielkopf, natives of the same country, his father being a farmer by occupation. Mr. K. emigrated to the United States April 25, 1857, taking passage on a sailing-vessel, and being forty-seven days on the ocean. He landed in New York City, and immediately proceeded westward to Ottumwa, Iowa, where he located upon a rented farm and occupied it for two years. He then moved into Monroe County, where he bought eighty acres of land, and lived there six years. He then sold out, and coming into Wapello County purchased eighty acres on section 5, in Highland Township, which he has occupied since that time. He has greatly improved the original condition of his purchase, and now has a good farm, with a comfortable residence and all necessary outbuildings.

The subject of this sketch was married in 1862, to Miss Catharine Ritter, a native of his own country, and who became the mother of twelve children, as follows: Elizabeth, born March 20, 1864, became the wife of Peter Kling, of Highland Township; Katie, born Sept. 7, 1866, and John, Oct. 30, 1868, are at home; Clara, born May 12, 1870, married Frank Damer, of Highland Township; Emma, born April 19, 1872; William, Nov. 23, 1875; Charlie, Oct. 18, 1879, and Phillip, Sept. 19, 1882, are at home with their parents; Phillipine, born in 1865, died in October of the same year; Leonard was born Oct. 3, 1884; Jacob died when a few months old; George, born Nov. 9, 1877, died Nov. 6, 1882.

Mr. and Mrs. K. are members of the Lutheran Church, of which Mr. K. is a Trustee. Beside the home farm, which consists of 140 acres, Mr. K. has sixty acres elsewhere. When he came to this county he was poor in purse, but rich in energy and determination, and has been amply rewarded for his years of labor and frugality. He takes an intelligent interest in all matters pertaining to the welfare of his community, is the friend of education and progress, and at present is a member of the Board of School Directors.

The father of Mr. K. was a prominent man in his native Province, and departed this life in 1870, in the country of his birth; the mother died in 1858. Both parents were members of the Lutheran Church, and possessed in a marked degree those worthy traits of character which are peculiar to the German nationality.

ASA LESTER GRAVES, residing at the end of W. Second street, Ottumwa, is a gardener and fruit-grower. He was born in Franklin County, Ind., Feb. 13, 1822, and is a son of A. C. and Elizabeth (Webb) Graves. His father was of Scotch and English extraction, and his mother of French and Irish descent. His father came from Massachusetts to Indiana in 1816, where he married Elizabeth Webb, and in 1832, in company with his wife and six children, moved to Missouri, near where Kansas City now stands. In 1838 the family moved to Quincy, Ill., and lived there until 1840, when they moved to Des Moines County, Iowa, where, in 1854, the father died. He was a tanner and currier by trade. His wife, Elizabeth, the mother of our subject, is still living, residing in Missouri with her daughter, Mrs. E. J. Christy, and is now eighty-six years of age.

On the 22d day of May, 1844, in Des Moines County, Iowa, A. L. Graves, the subject of this sketch, was united in marriage with Julia A. Moffet, born Sept 17, 1826, and the daughter of Levi and Elizabeth (Keck) Moffet. Her father was of Scotch-Irish, and her mother of German descent. They moved from Pennsylvania to Des Moines County, Iowa, in 1834. Her mother died March 29, 1838, and her father in March, 1854. Her father was a fuller by trade, but the latter years of his life were spent in the milling business. He built the first gristmill in the State of Iowa. It was erected in Des Moines County, on the Skunk River.

Mr. and Mrs. Graves were the parents of seven children: Elizabeth A., born Sept. 13, 1845, is now the wife of Joseph E. Langford, who lives in Ottumwa; Henry E., born Oct. 9, 1847, married Clara A. Caldwell, and lives in Jasper County, Mo.; John M., born in Ottumwa, March 26, 1852, married Leonora E. Pierce, and now lives in Gunnison County, Col.; George A., born in Ottumwa, Jan. 22, 1854, married Marietta McQuigg, and now lives in Jasper County, Mo., engaged as a railroad engineer; Julia L., born July 22, 1856, now the wife of R. W. Roberts, lives in Ottumwa; Rofeno A., born Oct. 5, 1858, is the wife of Prof. O. L. Miller; Carrie E., born March 8, 1864, married A. L. Pedrick; he is engaged in the grocery business in Ottumwa.

In 1849 Mr. Graves made a trip across the plains to California, by ox-teams, with a company made up at Augusta, Iowa. His wife's brother, E. R. Moffet, was also of the party. He spent nearly two years engaged in mining, and succeeded in accumulating about $3,000, which gave him his first start in the world. He made the trip home, from San Francisco via the following route: He went to Acapulco, Mex., thence to the city of Mexico, then to Vera Cruz, thence by sailing-vessel to New Orleans, thence by the Mississippi River home. Mr. Graves had many hard and perilous experiences in roughing it on the plains. He also spent about four years in prospecting in Colorado, and one year in Arkansas and Texas. He also had some railroad experience, being engaged as a railroad contractor for about a year and a half on the C., B. & Q. R. R., in company with his son-in-law, Mr. Langford.

In 1851 Mr. Graves moved with his family to Ottumwa, where he has since continued to reside. He owns twenty-seven acres of valuable land in the city limits, has a good brick dwelling-house, fine barn, and is well and comfortably fixed. A view of the place is given in this volume. At an early day Mr. Graves held the office of Commissioner of School Funds. He is a member of the Masonic fraternity, and politically is a Democrat.

WILLIAM H. FARMER, located on section 9, Center Township, is industriously engaged in agriculture and stock-growing, and ranks among its valued citizens. He was born in Putnam County, Ind., Feb. 6, 1835, his parents being P. S. and Elizabeth (Devore) Farmer, both natives of Kentucky. The father moved from Indiana with his wife and four children to Van Buren County, Iowa, in 1849, and the following year came into Wapello County, which remained his home until the close of his life, his decease occurring in January, 1868. The mother of our subject survived her husband four years, dying also in this county in 1872. Their remains are buried in the Burns Cemetery in Center Township.

Mr. Farmer remained under the parental roof until he attained his majority. In 1856, at the age of twenty years, he married Miss Ellen M. Whitcomb, who was born in Lorain County, Ohio, Sept. 26, 1838, and was the daughter of David and Lucy (Prouty) Whitcomb, both natives of Vermont, who removed to Ohio at an early period in the history of that State. In 1843 Mr. Whitcomb came to Iowa and located in Richland Township, this county. In the fall of 1845 he sent for his family, consisting of his wife and seven children. Here they established a comfortable home, where the parents spent the remainder of their days, the mother dying Sept. 16, 1863, and the father on the 6th of September, 1876. They were buried in the Ottumwa Cemetery.

Of the marriage of Mr. and Mrs. Farmer there were eight children, as follows: Flora M., born Aug. 18, 1857, became the wife of Frank Bizer, and lives in Center Township; Fred C. was born March 18, 1862, and also lives in this township; Sadie E. was born March 14, 1864, and Lucy A., March 8, 1866; Emma W., born Feb. 16, 1872, died May 5, 1874; the next one died in infancy; Nellie H. was born Jan. 27, 1877, and Willie S., Jan. 22, 1880.

The homestead of Mr. Farmer comprises 100 acres of good land, upon which is a comfortable farm dwelling, a good barn and other improvements. He also owns twenty-five acres of coal land. He has been prominent in the affairs of his township since coming here, and has held the offices of Constable and Supervisor. He is now President of the School Board, and has always been the stanch friend and supporter of every measure calculated to benefit his county and township. In politics he is a Democrat.

PRIER S. WILSON, an intelligent farmer and stock-grower of Wapello County, may be found on section 10, Center Township, about one mile northwest of Ottumwa. He was born in Monroe County, Ind., July 21, 1838, and is a son of Henry and Nancy J. (Farmer) Wilson, both of whom were natives of Kentucky, but who had lived in Indiana from their childhood. In 1849, the family, consisting of the father and mother and two children, left Indiana for Iowa, coming through with teams. The mother died about 1865; the father is still living in Ottumwa. By trade, his father was a plasterer, but followed farming for many years, and is now engaged in the real-estate business.

Mr. Wilson, of this sketch, was united in marriage with Mrs. Mary Stephenson, Nov. 9, 1859. Mrs. Wilson was the widow of Newton Stephenson, and daughter of Thomas and Elizabeth Reveal. Five children were born of this union—Nancy J., Laura E., Albert D., Emra M. and Thomas H., deceased. Mrs. Wilson died Feb. 2, 1877, and on the 1st day of December, 1878, Mr. Wilson contracted a second marriage, with Mary J. Willis, widow of Isaac Willis, and daughter of Daniel Sheeler.

Mr. Wilson is the owner of 200 acres of improved land, with three good dwelling-houses, one good barn, and all necessary out-buildings, everything about his premises being in good repair. At this time he is quite extensively engaged in the dairy business, milking from fifty to sixty cows regularly. His milk is sold to dealers in the city of Ottumwa, and he furnishes the trade of that city with about ninety gallons per day. In politics Mr. Wilson is a Democrat, and in all respects a worthy and reliable citizen.

When Mr. Wilson came to Iowa he had but little of this world's goods, and his accumulations are the result of his industry and application to business. Most of his farm is good bottom land, well adapted to corn and grass, particularly the latter. The main C., B. & Q. R. R., with its Rock Island Division, passes through his farm, of which we are pleased to be able to present a lithographic view in connection with this sketch.

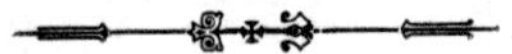

SAMUEL T. CALDWELL, deceased, was born in Marshall County, Va., in 1824, and was the son of Van and Elizabeth Caldwell. He was reared on a farm and came to Iowa while it was yet a Territory. This was in 1837, and on his arrival here he located in Van Buren County, with his parents. He followed the vocation of a farmer until he attained the age of about thirty-five years, when he embarked in mercantile pursuits and met with more than ordinary success in that venture. He was likewise connected in the banking business, and continued an active business career until his death, which took place in 1878, at the age of fifty-four years. Mr. Caldwell also represented his district in the State Legislature for two terms, and was greatly honored and respected by all who knew him.

Of his union with Mrs. Adeline Grant two children, both daughters, were born; he had also two daughters by a former wife. The record is as follows: Cora E. resides with her mother at Eddyville; Della is a teacher in the public schools at Ottumwa, and Kittie and Frankie are living at home. The widow of our subject, Mrs. Adeline Caldwell, is residing at Eddyville in a fine, two-story frame residence, located on Church street. She was a daughter of Oliver Grant, and was born in Meigs County, Ohio. Her mother's maiden name was Jones. The father of Mrs. Caldwell was born in Bangor, Me., and his wife in Ohio. While a resident of Maine he was engaged in milling, but on coming to this State, in 1853, he located in Mahaska County, and there engaged in farming, and was thus occupied for about eight years, when he removed to Eddyville and there died, the date being May 27, 1884. His widow still survives, and is living with her daughter, Mrs. Caldwell.

J R. PICKLER, who has been a resident of Ottumwa since the fall of 1861, is prosperously established in the grocery trade and enjoys an extensive patronage. He does business in a straightforward and systematic manner, is highly respected by his associates in the business community, and has built up for himself an enviable record as an honest man and a good citizen.

The subject of this history was born and reared in the wilds of Indiana, in Washington County, near Salem. The date of his birth was May 9, 1830, and his parents were John and Lydia (Grace) Pickler, both natives of North Carolina. They first removed from their native State southwestward to Kentucky, whence, later they proceeded north to Indiana, being among the early pioneers of the Hoosier State. They settled upon a heavy timber tract, peopled principally by wild animals and wild Indians. They opened up a farm in the wilderness, and in due time established a comfortable home.

The parental family of our subject included seven children, of whom four are still living, as follows: Lydia became the wife of John Overman, of Center Township; Patsy married Thomas H. Mitchell, of Indiana; John is a resident of Southern Illinois; the subject of this sketch completes the fourth. John Pickler departed this life in Indiana in about 1840. The mother afterward became a resident of Iowa, and died in Wapello County in 1880.

The subject of this history was reared under the parental roof, and remembers with surprising distinctness many of the scenes of his earliest childhood. He recollects going with his father to mark out a path through the forest by "blazing" the

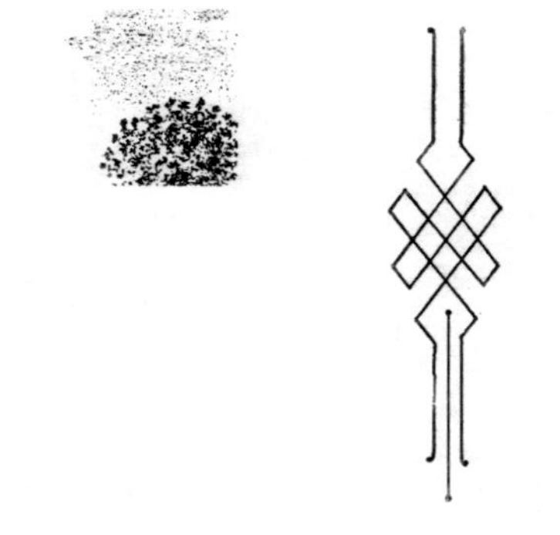

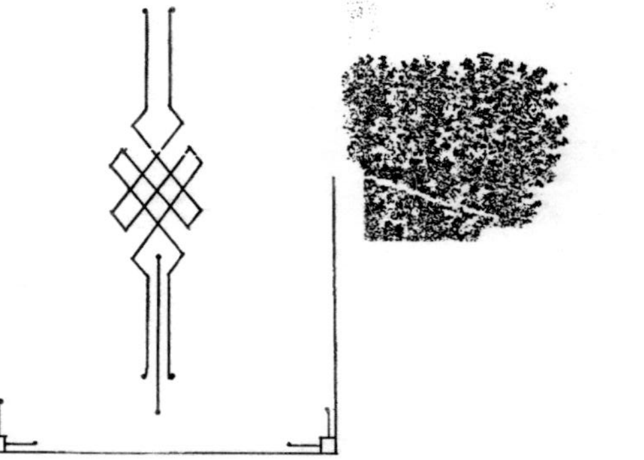

RES. OF DAVID GEPHART, SEC. 1, CENTRE TP.

RES. OF GEO. F. CAPELL, OTTUMWA, IA.

trees, for a mile and a half, to the "Deboal House." The first building in which he pursued his studies was a log cabin, 16x20 feet in area, with puncheon floor, and slabs for seats and desks. The pupils were ruled with an iron rod, and the system of study pursued in those primitive days was widely different from that followed at present.

When he had arrived at the age of twenty years Mr. Pickler left his native State to seek his fortune beyond the Mississippi. He first came into Davis County, Iowa, and engaged in farming pursuits. Three years later, in 1853, he was united in marriage with Miss Elizabeth Ball, a native of his own State, and the daughter of William and Elizabeth Ball, natives of Kentucky. In the fall of 1861 Mr. P., with his wife, abandoned farming pursuits and removed to Ottumwa, where Mr. Pickler established himself in the grocery trade, which he has pursued continuously until the present time. He has been prospered in his undertakings, and is in the enjoyment of a competency. With his family he occupies a handsome residence on East Main street, where they are surrounded with all the comforts and many of the luxuries of life.

Of the union of our subject and his wife there have been born the following children: Rosella, the wife of J. B. Joslyn, of Ottumwa, and John W., Thomas H., Frank and Etta, all residents of this city and living with their parents.

A handsome lithographic view of the business block of Mr. Pickler accompanies this sketch.

FRANCES LAYNE, widow of Jacob Layne, and who, since his demise, has continued to reside on the old homestead on section 3, Adams Township, where, with her children, she has been actively engaged in its cultivation and improvement, is a native of Montgomery County, Ind., and was born Dec. 22, 1828. Mrs. Layne is a daughter of Daniel and Nancy (Detherge) Easley, natives of North Carolina, both now deceased.

Mrs. Frances Layne was married to Jacob Layne, July 9, 1849, and the following year they came to Iowa, and purchasing 160 acres of land in Adams Township, this county, located upon it. Their union was blest by the birth of five children: Elizabeth, deceased; Daniel, deceased; Sophronia, wife of H. Hepler, and living in Adair County, Iowa; Sarah J., wife of Philip Ross, a successful farmer of Polk Township, and Ira, who lives with his mother and is engaged in the cultivation of the farm. Jacob Layne was a native of Kentucky, a farmer by occupation, and was killed by a runaway team May 15, 1878.

Our subject is at present the owner of forty acres of good farm land, with substantial improvements upon it. She is a laborer in the cause of the Master and holds fellowship with the Christian Church, and is respected and honored for her many good deeds and loving disposition, as well as comforting words and generous heart.

GEORGE F. CAPELL, builder and contractor, residing at Ottumwa, is a native of the county of St. Lawrence, N. Y., and was born on the 6th of February, 1848. His father, William P., and his mother, Mary (Cook) Capell, daughter of Maj. Cook, of Revolutionary fame, were both natives of New Hampshire. They were married at Parishville, St. Lawrence Co., N. Y., and reared a family of six children, the record of whom is as follows: Mary A. became the wife of Alonzo Johnson, of Portland, N. Y.; Sarah E. married David Richardson, and Martha E. became the wife of James G. Taylor, all residents of St. Lawrence County, N. Y., and also William H.; Emma A. became the wife of Frank Hulbard, and they are living at Chicago; George F., our subject, was the youngest of the family.

In early life the father of our subject was an old-line Whig, but upon the birth of the Republican party entered its ranks and voted with that party until his death, which occurred in St. Lawrence County, N. Y., in January, 1870. His wife still survives him, and is a member of the Presbyterian Church. George F. Capell was educated in the district schools, and early in life worked at the trade of his father, that of a cabinet-maker, which he mastered under his instruction.

In 1869 Mr. Capell came West and located at

Ottumwa, where he has spent the major portion of his time until the present, engaged at his trade and in building and contracting. In February, 1879, he was married to Miss Emma Spencer, daughter of Capt. H. A. Spencer, of Bloomfield, Davis Co., Iowa. Mrs. Wilson was born in the city in which she was married, in June, 1849, and by her marriage with Mr. Capell has become the mother of one child—George V. Mr. Capell is a member of the V. A. S. and Modern Woodmen of America. He has done much toward the upbuilding of the city in which he resides, and is one of her foremost and most highly respected citizens. Mr. Capell was the contractor and builder of the South Ottumwa public school building, which is a model of convenience and beauty.

A view of his own tasteful dwelling is given on another page in connection with this brief history.

GERHARD OSTDEICK is a brickmaker and farmer residing in the city of Ottumwa, in Hammond's subdivision. He has been running his brick manufactory for seventeen years, and has made an average of 1,000,000 bricks per year. Many of the business blocks of Ottumwa are erected with brick manufactured by him. He is a native of Prussia, born Oct. 18, 1840, and in 1846 came to America with his parents. They landed in New Orleans and came up the Mississippi River to Lee County, Iowa, where Gerhard lived until 1869, when he came to Ottumwa and engaged in the manufacture of brick. Ferdinand Ostdeick, the father of Gerhard, was a teacher in the parochial schools of Lee County for twelve years, after coming to the United States, and also followed the occupation of a farmer. He died in St. Paul, Lee County, in 1873; the mother died in 1885.

Nov. 27, 1866, Gerhard Ostdeick and Mary E. Steiger were united in marriage. She was born in Indiana in 1845, but was of German origin, her parents being John and Mary M. (Smith) Steiger, who yet survive, and are living in Lee County, near Ft. Madison. To this union there were born eight children—Catharine, Mary, Philomena, John, Callie, Elizabeth (deceased), Barbara and Hermon (deceased). At the present time Mr. Ostdeick is in partnership with his brother Hermon in the manufacture of brick. In addition to his property in this city he has 300 acres of farm land in Pottawattamie County, which is under a high state of cultivation. He and his wife are members of the Catholic Church. In politics Mr. Ostdeick is a stanch Democrat.

M. M. LANE, a well-known and highly respected resident of Dahlonega Township, has been a resident of Iowa since 1856. He was born in Tompkins County, N. Y., Oct. 18, 1810, and is the son of E. and Dollie (Rodgers) Lane, who were the parents of twenty children. His father was a native of New York City, and his grandfather, Doxsy Lane, was a blacksmith by trade and served in that capacity in the Revolutionary War, having had the honor of shoeing the horse of Gen. Washington many times. He was of English birth and parentage, and came to this country during the colonial days. The mother of our subject was of German descent, and a native of New Jersey.

When Mr. Lane of our sketch was a child of six years old his parents moved to Ohio, settling in the town of Thompson, which is situated in the Western Reserve. The following spring, in 1818, our subject went from his parents' home to live with a man named Matthew Warner, with whom he remained until he was seventeen years old. He then went to Harpersfield, in the same State, and apprenticed himself to learn the trade of bricklaying and stone-masonry with James Woodworth of that place, and served three years. In the spring of 1831 he returned East as far as Erie County, Pa., where he engaged at his trade, and in the meantime formed the acquaintance of Miss Caroline Woolley, to whom he was united in marriage on the 1st of January, 1832. Mrs. Lane was born in Otsego County, N. Y., in 1815, and is the daughter of Peter S. and Mary Woolley, both natives of the Empire State. Of this union there were born six children, as follows: Lysander is living in Dahlonega; Wilsey C. is farming in Marshall County, Kan.; Nancy Amanda married Mr. E. Springer, who is engaged in real-estate business in Garnett, Kan.; Michael M. is a practicing physician of Waynesville, Mo.; he served three years in the 18th Iowa Volunteers during the late war as a drummer; Mary died in 1846, aged five years, and Perry in 1843, at the age of two years.

Mr. Lane lived in Erie, Pa., until 1854, and then removed to Macoupin County, Ill., whence, two years afterward, he went to Morgan County in the same State and lived there nine years, following his trade until 1856. He then came to Wapello County, and purchased 100 acres of land in Pleasant Township, which he occupied for a few months, and then traded it for a stock of merchandise in Dahlonega. He then engaged in trade for two years, and sold out his stock to George Godfrey. After this he went into the hotel business at Dahlonega, and after two more years engaged in the grocery trade until the fall of 1883, when he removed to his farm on section 17, where he still lives.

Mr. Lane has been prominently identified with the public affairs of his township since coming into this vicinity. He was Postmaster at Dahlonega for fourteen years and Justice of the Peace three terms. He is Democratic in politics and takes much pride in the fact that he voted for Gen. Jackson for President twice. Mr. and Mrs. L. are members of the Christian Church, and enjoy the society and friendship of the best people in this locality. They held the fifty-fifth anniversary of their marriage Jan. 2, 1887.

W M. WHEATON, a prosperous farmer of Highland Township, is pleasantly located on section 36, where he is the owner of 270 acres of finely improved land. He is a native of the Green Mountain State, his birth occurring in 1843, and is the son of Lucius and Maria (Moore) Wheaton, also natives of Vermont. He was reared on a farm in his native State, which remained his home until 1868, when he emigrated to Iowa and became a resident of Wapello County, settling first in Agency Township, where he cultivated rented land for a year, and then purchased his present homestead in Highland Township.

Before coming to Iowa, after the outbreak of the late Civil War, young Wheaton enlisted as a soldier in Co. D, 1st Vt. Vol. Cav., and served three years and seven months. He was with Gen. Kilpatrick and Custer in the campaign of the Shenandoah Valley, being at the battle of Gettysburg and other engagements in which his regiment participated. He was also present at the second battle of Bull Run. On the 7th of October, 1863, he was captured by the rebels under Gen. Mosely, taken to Libby Prison, and confined there until the following January. He was then transferred to Annapolis, Md., and was absent from his regiment for nearly one year, rejoining it finally at Harrisburg, Va., and while skirmishing under Gen. Sheridan was again captured, and confined in Libby Prison until the following February, when he was exchanged. In 1862 he was detailed as Orderly for Gen. Howe, and served in that capacity for several months.

After his honorable discharge from the army, Mr. Wheaton, after a brief sojourn in his native State, turned his face westward as heretofore stated. In the meantime he had been united in marriage with Miss Sybil Hatch, of Vermont, the wedding occurring in October, 1865. Mrs. W. is the daughter of James and Rebecca (Rutter) Hatch, and was born Sept. 12, 1844. By her union with our subject she has become the mother of four children, all at home—James, Carrie, William and Harry. Our subject and his family occupy a fine residence, which he erected in 1882. His barn and outbuildings correspond with the dwelling, and the farm machinery, with all other appurtenances, indicate the supervision of a first-class agriculturist.

The father of our subject departed this life on the 10th of July, 1861, while in the prime of life, being only forty-seven years of age. The mother survived her husband seventeen years, dying in 1878, aged sixty-five. The latter was a member of the Presbyterian Church, and passed her declining years at the home of her son in Elk River, Minn. The parental household included four children, of whom only three are living: Charles, a lawyer, and Harry, a merchant, both residing in Elk River, Sherburne Co., Minn., and W. M., our subject.

The mother of Mrs. Wheaton, before her marriage, was Miss Rebecca Rutter, of English descent, and both parents were natives of Vermont. Mr. Hatch was a harness-maker by trade, and also engaged in agricultural pursuits, and departed this life in August, 1883, at the age of seventy-four years. The mother is still living in Vermont, and is a member of the Baptist Church. The parental family consisted of five children, only two of whom are living—Mrs. Wheaton, and her brother, Martin B. Hatch, who is engaged in farming in his native State.

WILLIAM HIRST, a farmer and stock-grower, will be found on section 21, Richland Township. He is a native of Yorkshire, England, born Sept. 19, 1819, and is a son of Thomas and Phœbe Hirst. Thomas Hirst in his younger days was a weaver by trade, and afterward a farmer. He and his wife both died in England. In his native country William learned the trade of a shoemaker, which occupation he there followed for some years, and there married Eliza Kershaw, who was born in 1822. With his wife and two children, Mr. Hirst came to this country in 1851. They were five weeks in crossing the ocean on a sailing-vessel, and made their first location in Steubenville, Ohio, where they remained three years, and where Mr. Hirst worked at his trade of shoemaking. From Ohio they moved to Burlington, Iowa, and from there they came to Wapello County, in 1851, where they have continued to reside, Mr. Hirst alternating shoemaking with farming. The parents of Mrs Hirst came to America about 1843, and located at Steubenville, Ohio, where her father engaged at his trade of a cloth manufacturer. Both her parents are now deceased.

Mr. and Mrs. Hirst became the parents of seven children: Sarah A., the wife of William Hayes, lives in Nebraska; Ruth is deceased; Thomas is at home; James married Nancy McGee, and now lives in Dakota; Martha is the wife of Thomas Kirkpatrick, and lives in this county; John married Esther McGee, and lives in Ottumwa; Abraham Lincoln is at home; William is deceased. Mrs. Hirst died in 1862, and Mr. Hirst was again married, in 1865, to Mrs. E. J. Marshall, who was born in Ohio, Dec. 19, 1838, and the widow of William Marshall. By this union there has been one child, Rosilla, who lives with her parents. Mr. Hirst is the owner of a fine farm of 160 acres, all of which is under improvement, and on the place are a good house and barn and all necessary improvements. In politics he is a Republican.

F. M. KELSEY, a farmer and stock-raiser on section 36, Richland Township, was born in Putnam County, Ind., July 9, 1843, and is a son of Joseph and Rebecca (Stephens) Kelsey. The family moved from Indiana to Davis County, Iowa, in 1850, and about 1860 moved to Mercer County, Mo., where the father died Jan. 5, 1865. After his death his widow came to Iowa, and died in this county Jan. 30, 1873.

F. M. Kelsey, the subject of this sketch, was reared upon a farm, and received only the advantages of a common-school education. In 1862 he enlisted in Co. B, 27th Mo. Vol. Inf., under Capt. Henry Shook, and served until June, 1865. After its organization the regiment was stationed at St. Louis, Mo., for a time, and was then sent to the front. It was in the siege and capture of Vicksburg, the battles of Lookout Mountain and Mission Ridge. It accompanied Sherman on his famous march from Atlanta to the sea, and was then sent by steamer to Buford, S. C., from which place it was sent to Raleigh, N. C., and thence to Washington City, where it was at the close of the war. The members of the regiment were paid off and discharged at St. Louis. Mr. Kelsey was among the fortunate ones who passed through the service without injury, except sunstroke.

After his discharge our subject returned to Iowa, and in 1865 was married to Emily J. Brown, daughter of Williamson and Jane (Rich) Brown. Her father died in Indiana in 1875, but the mother still lives on the old homestead in that State. Mr. and Mrs. Kelsey are the parents of four children—Ollie E., Charles H., Samuel R. and Andrew M. Mr. Kelsey is the owner of eighty acres of good land on the home farm, on which is a good house and barn and other first-class improvements. He has ninety acres of farm land, with good house and barn, on section 36, of Richland Township. For three years Mr. Kelsey was Superintendent of the Poor Farm of Wapello County, his management being very satisfactory. He and his wife are members of the Methodist Episcopal Church. In politics Mr. K. is a Republican.

HARVEY ELLER, a highly respected farmer and stock-grower of Competine Township, is the possessor of a valuable tract of land on section 16, and in the various departments of his business is meeting with more than ordinary success. He is a gentleman of enterprise and energy, carrying on his farming operations in a skillful manner, and in his stock-growing operations exhibits some of the finest animals in this section of the Hawkeye State. Mr. Eller is a native of Wilkes County, N. C., and was born March 24, 1819. He is the son of Simeon and Fannie (McNeil) Eller, the former born in Ashe County, N. C., Sept. 8, 1796, and the latter in Wilkes County, the same State, about the year 1798. The father of our subject was of German, and the mother of Scottish ancestry. Their household consisted of eleven children, eight sons and three daughters, as follows: Harvey, of our sketch, was the oldest; Polly Whitington resides in North Carolina; J. C. lives in Clay County, Neb.; Nancy, Mrs. Vannoy, died in April, 1847, and is buried in her native State; William moved to Nebraska in 1873, and there died; James is a farmer and merchant, and remains in his native State of North Carolina; Jesse F. was a Captain in the Confederate army, and is now engaged in agricultural pursuits in Virginia; David was also a soldier during the late war, and died in the Confederate army, the date of his death and the place of his burial are unknown; Anderson, a farmer and blacksmith, resides in Wilkes County, N. C. The mother of these children died in October, 1857. Thomas Eller was conscripted into the Confederate army, and killed at Chancellorsville. The youngest daughter, America Ann, first married William Whitington, afterward Mr. Weaver, and resides in Ashe County, N. C. The Eller family were prominent in the social and political affairs of North Carolina, and well known throughout that section for their straightforward business methods, kindly sympathies, and the efforts which they made to promote the general welfare of their fellow-citizens, being strong supporters of education, morality and religion.

The early life of Harvey Eller was passed in his native county, on his father's farm. The father was also engaged in distilling and blacksmithing, and his son operated with him after he became of suitable age until his marriage. This event took place in November, 1841, the maiden of his choice being Miss Mary Caroline Vannoy. After their marriage young Eller continued farming pursuits in Wilkes County for the following eleven years. In view of his strong temperance views and his anti-slavery principles, and having listened to a forcible speech by Phillip S. White upon these subjects, in due time Mr. Eller concluded to "pull up stakes" and go away from a vicinity where his principles of right were being constantly subjected to outrage, and accordingly he loaded his wife and seven small children into a wagon, and started for the country beyond the Mississippi. They landed in Jefferson County, Iowa, on the 10th of December, 1852, after a tedious journey of eight weeks. In 1855 he removed to Wapello County, and purchased a tract of wild land on section 5, in Competine Township, which he cultivated and occupied for the following ten years, when he sold out and purchased 240 acres on section 16. He afterward sold eighty acres of this, and continued to improve and cultivate the remainder, which he has brought to a fine state of cultivation, and it is provided with a good farm residence and out-buildings.

Of the union of Mr. and Mrs. Eller there were born fifteen children, of whom the record is as follows: William H. is an attorney of Blair, Neb.; he enlisted as a soldier during the late war, being a member of the 19th Iowa Volunteers; B. C., another son, is a farmer of Clay County, Neb., he was also a soldier, a member of Co. K., 9th Iowa Vol. Cav.; Jennie, Mrs. Hook, lives in Highland Township; Nancy, Mrs. Troxel, resides in Clay County, Neb.; Mary O., Mrs. Phelps, died in 1881, in Hampton, Franklin County, this State; James A. is a farmer of Clay County, Neb.; Jesse F. is engaged in the real-estate and brokerage business at Clay Center, Neb.; Israel Curtus is a practicing attorney and Clerk of the Court of Washington County, Neb., his residence being at Blair; Martha E., the wife of G. W. Dickens, lives in Competine Township, this county, on section 17; John was drowned in 1875, in Competine Creek; T. A. is a farmer of Clay County, Neb.; J. H. is a hardware merchant of Clay Center, the same State; E. C. operates a farm in Clay County, Neb.; Maggie, Mrs. Davis, is a resident of Wapello County; O. R., the youngest son, is living with his parents. A grandson of Mr. Eller, L. D. Phelps, is the son of Mary O. (Eller) Phelps.

The parents of Mrs. Eller were Jesse and Polly (Kilby) Vannoy, and were natives of North Carolina, the maternal grandfather being a drummer boy during the Revolutionary War. Our subject and his wife are prominently connected with the Baptist Church, and Mr. Eller politically is strongly Republican, and an ardent advocate of prohibition.

FREDERICK METZGER, a first-class farmer and stock-grower, residing on section 2, Center Township, was born in Wittenberg, Germany, Nov. 12, 1839. He is a son of John M. and Barbara (Bloodhart) Metzger, who came to America with their family in 1854, and located in Muskingum County, Ohio, where the father bought a farm and engaged in farming. There Frederick remained until 1867, when he removed to Davis County, Iowa, where he engaged in farming three years. In 1870 he moved to Wapello County, and in 1878 to Floyd County, where he remained until 1881, and then came back to Wapello County, where he has since continued to reside.

In 1863 Mr. Metzer was united in marriage with Miss Carrie Harsh, who was born in Ohio, Oct. 25, 1843. Mrs. M. was the daughter of Gottlieb and Phœbe (Burkhart) Harsh, and her parents were of German origin.

Mr. and Mrs. Metzger are the parents of nine children—Charles F., deceased; William C., Lizzie, Jennie, Edward, Albert, Clara, Harry and Carrie. Our subject is the owner of 160 acres of good land, on which is a desirable house and substantial barn, together with other improvements. Under a part of the land has been discovered a fine vein of coal, the whole farm probably, being underlaid with coal. Mr. Metzger religiously is a member of the Lutheran Church, and in politics is a Democrat. Mrs. Metzger died Feb. 7, 1884, at their residence, and is buried at Mt. Zion Cemetery, about six miles south of Ottumwa.

When Mr. Metzger began life he had but little of this world's goods, but by industry and economy, he has succeeded in accumulating a comfortable competency for himself and family. A fine view of the residence, barns, stock and coal mine is shown on another page of this work.

DAVID GEPHART, an enterprising farmer and stock-grower of this county, will be found on section 1, Center Township, where he is prosperously engaged in the varied duties of his chosen calling.

Mr. Gephart is a native of Berkeley County, Va., and was born Aug. 27, 1820, being the son of Barnett and Sarah (Falk) Gephart. His father was a native of Pennsylvania, and his mother of Virginia. The former died Jan. 23, 1829, in Virginia. After his father's death his mother moved with her family to Pickaway County, Ohio, where she died in about 1867.

In early life David Gephart learned the trade of a carpenter, which he followed for many years. In 1849 he left Ohio, and coming to Iowa he worked at his trade in connection with farming until 1857. He then quit the carpenter business and has since followed that of farming exclusively. In 1846, when the war with Mexico broke out, he enlisted as a private in Co. I, 2d Ohio Vol. Inf., and served one year, being mustered out June 27, 1847. On the 5th day of June, 1851, he was united in marriage with Miss Sophia E., daughter of Charles F. and Mary Blake, and they have become the parents of the following children: Agnes, now the wife of Joseph Kitchen, lives in Knox County, Neb.; Mary, Mrs. William Carpenter, lives in Wapello County; Arthur married Miss Rosalind Dutton, of Oskaloosa, Iowa, and they live in Ottumwa; Franklin, Walter, Anna and Xelis are single and live at home. Mrs. Gephart died Sept. 31, 1871.

The subject of this biography is the owner of 165 acres of good land where he resides, and twenty acres near Ottumwa. On the home farm is a fine brick dwelling-house, good barns and all necessary out-buildings. His place is well fenced, and the farm is in a high state of cultivation. He is a member of the Masonic fraternity, and in politics is Democratic.

A fine lithographic view of the handsome residence and out-buildings on the farm of Mr. Gephart will be found on another page of this work.

BENJAMIN L. REES, a locomotive engineer, and a resident of Kirkville, was born in Lancaster County, Pa., March 21, 1849. His father was John Rees, and the maiden name of his mother was Rachel A. Brooks. The father went from Pennsylvania to Ohio in 1852, and lived there for twenty years, or until 1872, when he passed to the land of the hereafter. His good wife is yet living, and resides near Columbus, Ohio. Mr. Rees of this notice, in 1869, hoping to better his financial condition, left Ohio, where his parents were residing, and came to Louisa County, this State. He remained there only a few months, and then went to Muscatine County, where, in 1871, he was married to Miss Eliza Bond. Miss Bond was born in Liverpool, England, Feb. 4, 1851, and is a daughter of John Bond, who, with his good wife, departed this life at St. Louis, Mo.

The subject of this notice, by his union with Miss Bond has become the father of five children—Hattie A., Birdie M., Emma A. (deceased), and two who died in infancy. Whatever education our subject possesses he acquired in the common schools and by study at home. He is the proprietor of a good dwelling and two lots, situated in Bissell's addition to Kirkville. The company for which Mr. Rees is at present working is engaged in mining on the O. K. R. R., twelve miles from Ottumwa and one mile from Kirkville; he is now engaged as an engineer and is held in high esteem by his employers. Prior to accepting the position which he at present occupies he was engaged as an engineer on the "Q" road, running an engine for two years, and also having acted in the capacity of fireman on that road for a number of years. He is a thorough master of his trade, and a gentleman well liked by all who have the pleasure of making his acquaintance. The only order to which he belongs is that of the A. F. & A. M.

ROBERT McCORMICK, a pioneer settler of Highland Township, located here in 1848, upon the homestead which he still occupies and which is pleasantly situated on section 16. His first purchase consisted of ninety acres in its original condition, which he industriously cultivated and improved and to which he subsequently added until he now has 174 acres (ten of which are in timber) finely improved and under a good state of cultivation. He has been honest and upright in his transactions, and during a period of nearly forty years has built up for himself a reputation as an honest man and a good citizen.

The subject of this history was born in Gallatin County, Ky., in 1825, and is the son of John and Nancy (Cox) McCormick, natives respectively of Maryland and Kentucky. When he was a lad ten years old his parents removed to McDonough County, Ill., and settled upon a farm, where our subject lived until 1848. He then crossed the Father of Waters, and coming directly to Wapello County, located on the farm where he now resides.

Mr. McC. was married in 1847, to Miss Charlotte Miller, of Breckenridge County, Ky., and they became the parents of ten children, of whom the record is as follows: Louis C. lives in Cass County, Iowa; Martha became the wife of Joseph Gray, and died in 1879; Jesse D.; Henry married Leorah Phelps, and lives in this county; Parthenia is at home; Catharine is married to Robert Cresswell, of Ottumwa; Sarah E., Jane, Flora E. and Nancy Irene are at home.

Mr. McCormick has been connected with the

School Board of this township for sixteen years. He is a member of the Predestinarian Baptist Church, and politically is a Greenbacker. In addition to general farming he makes a specialty of raising hogs for the market and has attained quite a reputation in this direction. The father of our subject departed this life in 1880, at the advanced age of ninety-three; the mother had passed to her long home in 1837, aged forty-eight years.

JAMES M. RIGGS, one of the most prosperous farmers of Wapello County, was a pioneer settler of Iowa, coming here in 1844, when he was a little lad of six years old, from his native State of Virginia, where he was born in Marshall County, on the 11th of April, 1839. He is the son of Edmund and Susanna (Rush) Riggs, natives respectively of Virginia and Pennsylvania, who were married in the latter State. In 1844 they emigrated to Iowa, locating first in Van Buren County, where they remained for two years, engaged in agricultural pursuits. They then came into Wapello County and located on a piece of Government land in Washington Township, three miles west of the present site of Eldon village. Before their removal, however, the father had entered his claim and erected upon it a log cabin 16x18 feet, into which he removed his family in the spring of 1846. He then entered industriously upon the improvement and cultivation of his land, and with the assistance of his wife and son, soon commenced the raising of produce and stock. Here, also, the devoted family endured all the hardships and privations of pioneer life. Their milling was done principally at Bonaparte, many miles away, which, with the distance and the uneven roads, occupied a week's time in carrying and bringing the grist for the family. But they had come to stay, and no obstacle which presented itself had any weight in moving them from their resolution, and in due time they received the reward of their labors. The barren fields gave place to waving grain and pasture land, and fine farm stock soon took the place of the wild animals that originally roamed over the prairies and through the forests. In due time the household was completed by the birth of five more children, and now included four daughters and two sons, of whom two are deceased: Mary married John A. Kerr, in 1848, he died in 1852, and she then married E. Rush, who died in 1855, of cholera; she then became the wife of H. J. Thomas, of Wapello County; John is also a resident of this county; Martha A. married D. Malon Railsback, of Galatin County, Mont., and James M., our subject, completes the list of those living.

Edmund Riggs, the father of our subject, departed this life on the 22d of June, 1875, the affectionate wife and mother having preceded him to the better land on the 4th of December, 1857. They had led earnest Christian lives, and their names are held in kindly remembrance by all who knew them. Mr. Riggs was a gentleman of enterprise and energy, of sound judgment and intelligence, and the strictest integrity. In politics he was originally an old-line Whig, but after the disestablishment of the old party became a Republican, and uniformly cast his vote in support of its principles.

James M. Riggs was reared in Wapello County and received his early education in the pioneer schools. In 1874 he went to Montana and spent the greater part of his time there for the following ten years. In the meantime, on the 21st of December, 1882, he was married in Wapello County to Mrs. Anna (Walkins) Williams, the widow of David Williams. Mrs. Riggs is a native of Pennsylvania, and was born in 1840.

The subject of our sketch is the possessor of 156 acres of farming land, eighty of which are in a good state of cultivation. The farm is all enclosed, and is provided with a comfortable residence, good barns and all necessary out-buildings. From his boyhood Mr. R. has been an interested observer of the changes which have been succeeding each other as his adopted State has developed into her present position of wealth and independence, and these changes he has viewed with the unselfish satisfaction which has characterized the feelings of the genuine pioneers who cheerfully gave their labor

Israel Young
Catharine Young

and their lives for the development of the resources of the country and the consequent good of their children unto later generations.

ISRAEL YOUNG, one of the honored pioneers of the Hawkeye State, crossed the Mississippi from the State of Indiana in 1843, while Iowa was still a Territory, and has been a resident of this section since that time. He has been an interested witness of the remarkable changes which have taken place since that time, and to the best of his ability he has contributed his quota to aid the march of civilization and progress. He is now one of the highly respected citizens of Ottumwa, and is passing the later years of his life in the enjoyment of the fruits of early industry and economy.

The subject of this history was born on a farm near Franklin, Warren Co., Ohio, on the 23d of November, 1816. He is the son of Jacob and Elizabeth (Price) Young, the father a native of Maryland and the mother of Lancaster County, Pa. They were married at Emmitsburg, Md., and in 1810, journeyed westward into Warren County, Ohio, where they located, and were among the earliest settlers of that region. They there became the parents of ten children, of whom the subject of our sketch is the third in order of birth.

Israel Young was reared and educated in his native county, his home life being spent in the log cabin which constituted his parents' dwelling, and his studies being pursued in another cabin called a school-house. At the age of twenty-two years, in 1838, he started for the West with teams and accompanied by his brother. They crossed the Mississippi into Jefferson County, Iowa, and there our subject located a tract of land. Very few settlers had ventured into this region at that early day and only the smoke of the rude cabin here and there disturbed the primitive calm of the prairie. In a short time Israel Young returned to Indiana, where he remained until 1843, and then, crossing the Father of Waters the second time, once more came into Jefferson County, and located near the Wapello line. He now industriously commenced to improve the land in his possession, and in due time was rewarded by its fertility and beauty. In the course of four years he considered that he was in a condition to invite a companion to share his cabin home, and accordingly, in 1847, was united in marriage with Miss Catharine Hughell, who was a native of his own county, where she was born on the 8th of June, 1812. Mrs. Young was a daughter of Joseph Hughell, of Washington County, Pa., who removed from his native State to Kentucky, and served as a soldier in the War of 1812. He was a daring and courageous man, and was identified with the Rangers, who obtained such celebrity in that region during the agitation between the colonies and the mother country. Mr. Hughell, in early manhood, was married to Miss Phœbe Pugh, in 1803, in Warren County, Ohio, and they became the parents of seven daughters and one son, all of whom excepting two are now living. The record is as follows: Phœbe became the wife of Alex McCleese, deceased; Mary was born in Iowa, became the wife of George Wilson, now deceased; Catharine is a resident of Ottumwa; Martha married Eden Cramer, of Oregon; Clarissa J. married William Freeman, of Stockton, Cal. Mr. and Mrs. Hughell came to Jefferson County, Iowa, in 1838, and spent the remainder of their lives in this State. They lived together as husband and wife for nearly seventy years and, strongly attached in their lives, in death were not long divided. They were active members of the Methodist Episcopal Church, in which Mr. Hughell was a Class-Leader for more than fifty years. They retained their mental faculties and physical strength to a remarkable degree, and when they were both about ninety years old they made a journey together from California to Iowa by themselves.

Mr. and Mrs. Young, after their marriage, settled in Des Moines Township, and resided upon one farm for a period of forty years. They became the parents of four children, of whom the record is as follows: David, now a resident of Southern Missouri, served as a soldier in the late Rebellion, and returned home unharmed; Samuel is in Montana; Julia A. is in Cloud County, Kan., and is the wife of Curtis Alderson, who served in the late war, was captured by the rebels and confined in Andersonville Prison, and is now living in Kansas, and Joseph is in Pottawatomie County, Kan.

Mr. Young removed from Des Moines to Wapello County, in 1886, locating in Ottumwa, where they have won the confidence and esteem of a large circle of friends and acquaintances, who will be pleased to see their portraits in connection with this brief personal sketch. Mr. Young is Democratic in politics, and in all respects is fulfilling the duties of a good citizen.

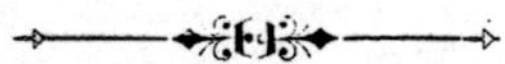

THOMAS E. SHEARS, engineer of the water-works at Ottumwa, was born in Brooklyn, N. Y., Jan. 1, 1852, and is the son of Joseph and Mary A. Shears, natives of Oxfordshire, England. The old folk came to the States when quite young, and were married in Brooklyn, N. Y., in 1849. In 1856 they removed to Aurora, Kane Co., Ill., where the father followed his trade, that of a brickmason. He subsequently engaged in building and contracting, but at present is working for the C. & N. W. R. R., and is located in Dakota. At the breaking out of the late Civil War, the father of our subject, who was at that time an engineer of the C., B. & Q. R. R., in company with several others, enlisted. They were sworn into the 89th Illinois Infantry, which was known as the "railroad regiment," there being so many railroad men belonging to it. On account of so many engineers leaving the C., B. & Q. R. R. to join this regiment, the company was scarce of men, and it was through their influence that our subject's father and several others were released from service. The parents of our subject had a family of three children: T. E., the subject of this notice; George F., professor in surgery at Hahnemann College, and Sarah J., wife of Charles Fritz, of Aurora, Ill., and a carriage-maker by vocation.

The subject of this notice was reared to manhood at Aurora, Ill., and it was in the schools of that city that he received his education. He first started out to do for himself by clerking in an insurance office at Aurora, which position he filled with credit to himself and his employers. When seventeen years of age he was engaged as an employe of the C., B. & Q. R. R., as fireman. When twenty years old he was promoted to the position of engineer, and in 1874 he was transferred to Iowa and placed on the Iowa division of that company. This necessitated a change of his residence, and was the principal cause of his removal to Ottumwa. In the fall of 1880 Mr. Shears was elected engineer of the water-works at Ottumwa, and has since held that position, giving entire satisfaction to all interested in the faithful performance of his duty.

Mr. Shears was married, in 1876, at Galesburg, Ill., to Miss Mary Lamphere, daughter of Hon. G. C. Lamphere, of Galesburg. Our subject is a member of the Masonic fraternity, holding fellowship with Ottumwa Lodge No. 16, and also Clinton Chapter No. 9, of Ottumwa.

A CROSSON, one of the old settlers of Mahaska and Wapello Counties, and a gentleman well known by the citizens of this county, and respected for his sterling traits of character, settled at Eddyville in 1855, and has continued to reside there ever since, with the exception of about three years, during which time he lived at Keokuk. Mr. Crosson was born in Fayette County, Ind. in 1833, and is the son of James and Catharine (Dix) Crosson, the father a native of Ohio, and the mother of Pennsylvania. Our subject was reared to manhood on a farm and received what education he possesses in the public schools and in the seminary at Connersville, Ind. When he was twenty years of age he apprenticed himself to learn the trade of a brickmason, and has followed that occupation off and on until the present time. In the winter of 1855-56, he taught a winter school in Mahaska County, and the next winter taught school in Wapello County. He is a thorough master of his trade and has done considerable contracting and building, having worked in various parts of the State. He erected the livery stable of McNeil & Co., and the Novelty shops, and several other buildings at Oskaloosa, and also erected a large block of buildings in Grinnell, Iowa, in 1861. He was appointed Postmaster at Eddyville, Sept. 1, 1885. In 1876 he was nominated on the Greenback ticket for State Representative, but was defeated.

Mr. Crosson was married, in October, 1856, to Miss Elizabeth Stannus, a native of Ohio, and a daughter of George and Sarah Stannus. Of this union five children were born: Frank Stannus, at present a contractor and builder in New Mexico; Albert Lincoln, editor of a paper in Black Hawk, Col., known as the Black Hawk *Times*; Marion Elsworth, living at home and engaged in the study of law; Laura May is residing at home, and Assistant Postmaster of Eddyville; Erminna Jane is living at home and attending school. From 1858 to 1861 our subject was engaged in clerking in a store at Keokuk, the firm with which he was engaged being Stannus Bros. During the war he was Assistant Provost Marshal of his district. Mr. Crosson comes of a family noted for its longevity, his father having been born in 1795, and dying in 1860, and his mother having lived to attain the venerable age of eighty-seven years.

H. I. LENTNER, of Highland Township, and a citizen held in the highest esteem by his community, is a native of Ohio, and the son of George M. and Mary Lentner, natives of Delaware and Ohio respectively. He was born in 1835, and at the age of sixteen years accompanied his parents across the Mississippi. Coming into Wapello County, they made their first location in Dahlonega Township, on section 12, where they remained until the spring of 1864. They then removed into Highland Township upon a tract of land on section 35, which constitutes the present homestead. The farm was only partly improved, and they labored industriously for a number of years, bringing it to a good state of cultivation.

The subject of this history was married in August, 1862, to Miss Elizabeth Godfrey, of Wapello County, and of their union there were born four children—William Tyler, Grace D., Norton G. and Rhoda. During the late Rebellion Mr. Lentner served his country as a soldier in the Union Army, enlisting Aug. 7, 1862, in the 36th Iowa Infantry, and served until the close of the war. He endured courageously with his comrades all the privations and hardships of a soldier's life, and participated in the various battles of his division, being at Ft. Pemberton, Helena, Little Rock, etc., and escaping unharmed through many dangers. After his return home he engaged in agricultural pursuits upon the old homestead, where he has since resided, carrying on the peaceful pursuits of a farmer's life and fulfilling all the duties of a good citizen.

SENECA CORNELL, attorney at law, and editor and publisher of the *Des Moines Valley Journal* at Eldon, Iowa, is a native of Jefferson County, Iowa, and was born in 1858. His parents are Washington and Sarah (Wilson) Cornell, natives of Ohio, who came to Jefferson County, Iowa, in 1849, and are still living in the city of Fairfield. The subject of this biography was reared upon his father's farm, receiving careful parental training, and his primary education in the public schools. He remained with his parents until the age of eighteen years, when he entered Parson's College, in 1876, and pursued his studies there for the following four years. He then took up the study of law in the office of Senator J. F. Willison, of Fairfield, and remained under the instruction of the latter for two years following. He was admitted to the bar in Bloomfield, May 5, 1882, and soon afterward came to Eldon and commenced the practice of his profession. He has been remarkably successful as an attorney and counselor, his transactions extending from Wapello into Van Buren, Jefferson and Davis Counties, and he practices in the United States Courts when occasion requires. Mr. Cornell, in connection with J. J. Conger, established the *Des Moines Valley Journal* Oct. 2, 1886. It is a seven-column folio, Democratic in politics, and published every Thursday. It is conducted in a fearless and outspoken manner, and bids fair to become a successful and influential paper.

The marriage of Seneca Cornell and Miss Ella.

daughter of Paul and Sarah (Gilbert) Castor, was celebrated Nov. 25, 1885. Mrs. Cornell is a native of Wapello County, born in Ottumwa, and by her marriage with our subject has become the mother of one child, a son, George A., now deceased.

Washington Cornell, the father of our subject, is now living in retirement at Fairfield, Jefferson County. The parental family consisted of eleven children, of whom Seneca was the sixth in order of birth; four are deceased. Those surviving are as follows: G. W., a resident of Jefferson County, is a farmer; Laura is the wife of Joseph Veerman, of Van Buren County; the next was Seneca, our subject; Oscar is engaged in farming near Larned, Kan.; Sylveuus is carrying on agriculture in Jefferson County, Iowa; Alvah U. is engaged in the grocery trade at Fairfield; Chloe is the wife of William Miller, of Fairfield. The family are well and favorably known in this vicinity as the supporters and encouragers of everything which tends to the promotion of temperance, morality and the nobler elements of life.

PATRICK H. RIORDAN, the subject of this biographical notice, and a resident of Ottumwa, was born near the town of Killarny, County Kerry, Ireland, Dec. 13, 1844. His parents emigrated to the United States in December, 1853, and took up their residence at North Adams, Mass. There young Riordan attended the public schools, and in early life displayed a zeal for the acquisition of useful knowledge, reading by candlelight, after the labors of the day were ended, such works as the local libraries afforded.

Early in life our subject became a hand in the woolen factory of S. Blackington, of North Adams. He continued to labor in this manner until rebel shot and shell had been thundered against Sumter, when, although but sixteen years of age at the time, he at once determined that as soon as practicable he would shoulder his musket in defense of the country he had adopted. About a month after the battle of Bull Run our subject carried his resolution into effect, and bidding adieu to mother and father, and receiving their blessing, he left the old home, paid his own transportation to New York, and on the 12th of September, 1861, enlisted as a private soldier in the Union Army, and was assigned to the 63d New York Infantry. He participated in the battles of Yorktown, Fair Oaks, and the seven days' battle before Richmond, and was conspicuous for his gallantry at the battle of Antietam. After the latter battle he was promoted Second Lieutenant, and subsequently commanded his company until after the battle of Fredericksburg, in which last engagement, while leading his men in a charge upon the enemy, he was struck by a bullet from the enemy's gun, which disabled him, and in consequence of which he received an honorable discharge and was breveted Captain of the United States Volunteers. The wound which he received while in the army was in his left shoulder, and after his discharge he returned home to Massachusetts, where he worked at mill work until 1873.

During the year last named Mr. Riordan came to this State and attended the State University, from which he graduated in 1875, in the law department. He was admitted to practice in the courts of Iowa during that year, and in April, 1881, was admitted to practice in all the United States courts. He resided in Dubuque for two years, when he came to Ottumwa, where he has continued in practice until the present time. Mr. Riordan has always cherished a deep and affectionate love for his mother land, and is heartily in sympathy with any cause that is calculated to strike the fetters from the oppressed people of his native home. He is President of the Ottumwa Land League, and in the last five years has through his own exertions collected and forwarded $650, through the liberality of the citizens of Ottumwa, to the oppressed people of the Emerald Isle. In an article published in Congressman Finerty's paper, of Chicago, the Congressman says: "Capt. P. H. Riordan, of Ottumwa, a gallant ex-officer of Gen. Meagher's famous Irish Brigade of the army of the Potomac, has been nominated for the office of Representative in the Iowa Legislature. We don't know which party the Captain belongs to, nor do we care. Any Irish-American soldier who charged up the heights of Fredericksburg with Meagher, is deserving of the vote of any decent American citizen of whatever party." Mr. Riordan received the Democratic nomination for Representative, in September, 1885, and polled 2,880 votes. His opponent received 2,935.

Capt. Riordan received a beautiful sword from the citizens of North Adams, Mass., for gallant and meritorious conduct while fighting in defense of his country. It was received on the 14th of February, 1863. On the Captain's leaving Dubuque for Ottumwa, appropriate resolutions were passed by the Land League of which he was a member, regretting that his business called him to another part of the State, and he was elected an honorary member of the League.

THOMAS BROWN, who owns and occupies a comfortable homestead on section 20, Richland Township, is prosperously engaged as a farmer and stock-grower. He was born in Ireland, Oct. 25, 1825, and is a son of Samuel and Letitia (Cannon) Brown, both of whom were natives of Ireland and died in their native land. Thomas was reared upon a farm, and received but a limited education. In 1845 he came to America, and locating at Philadelphia worked at his trade of blacksmithing, which he had learned before leaving Ireland. In 1855 he came to Wapello County, Iowa, and worked at his trade and farming alternately until a few years ago, when he quit 'smithing, and has since devoted his attention to farming alone.

Mr. Brown was married in Philadelphia, Aug. 10, 1849, to Miss Mary Gilmore, also a native of Ireland, born in 1825. Her parents came to America and located in Philadelphia, but only remained one year, when they returned to Ireland, and there both have since died. Mr. and Mrs. Brown are the parents of ten children—Letitia (deceased), James, Mary L., Jennie (deceased), Samuel H., John (deceased), Austin, Martha A., James H. and Myrtle.

The farm of our subject comprises ninety acres of land. On the place is a good house and barn and all necessary out-buildings. Mr. Brown has held the offices of School Director and Road Supervisor, and with his wife is a member of the Christian Church. In politics our subject is a Democrat.

JAMES W. NORRIS, deceased. The subject of this biography deserves more than a passing notice. He was a native of Sandwich, N. H., and was born Aug. 10, 1815. His parents were Samuel and Anna (Bean) Norris, and when a mere boy he removed with them from his native town to Compton, Canada, where they spent about six years. They then, on account of some property troubles, returned to the Old Granite State, where our subject remained until he was a youth of sixteen years. He then, with the consent of his father, went to Boston with his uncle, who was a merchant of Meridian and had gone to Boston to trade. The latter placed him on board a sailing-vessel, by which he journeyed to New Orleans, and thence by river to Marietta, Ohio. He soon afterward entered the college at that place and completed the education which he had begun in the common schools of his native State. The means for this he obtained by his own labor. He was studious and improved every opportunity to avail himself of useful knowledge, and after the completion of his course at Marietta, went to Danville, Ky., and spent several months in a law office with a skilled lawyer of that locality. He then journeyed north into the Prairie State, locating at Bloomington, and in due time was admitted to the bar, and became the friend and associate of some of the first men of Illinois. He enjoyed an intimate friendship with Abraham Lincoln, and practiced with him on the same circuit. He was also a great admirer of Henry Clay, of whom he was an active and valuable supporter at the time the latter was a candidate for the Presidency of the United States.

In 1841 or 1842 Mr. Norris went to Chicago, Ill. where he published the first directory of the city, in 1844. He was also the founder of the Chicago *Evening Journal*, which has been a regular visitor at the homes of so many in the Northwest for a period of forty years. Five years later Mr. Norris, in company with six young men, started for the gold fields of California. They were equipped with a mule-team and a colored driver, and supplied not only with everything to make them comfortable, but many of the luxuries of travel. While crossing the Skunk River in Iowa one of the mules was drowned, and in going through Dahlonega Township, this county, there appeared to the astonished eyes of James Norris, his father coming toward them on horseback. The latter persuaded our subject that it would be folly to proceed on the expedition, and wished him to go to St. Joseph, Mo., with him to distribute Bibles. To this James consented, and upon returning located in Ottumwa, Iowa, where he again entered upon the practice of his profession. In due time he was intrusted with an important bill for collection, and the only way in which it could be settled was to levy on a ten-acre tract of land, which eventually came into his possession, is now included in the city limits, and is very valuable.

In 1850 Miss Martha R. Spaulding came to Ottumwa on a visit to her brother, Rev. B. A. Spaulding. This lady was highly educated, and our subject was united with her in marriage July 27 of the following year. They subsequently went to Eddyville, where Mr. Norris established the Eddyville *Free Press*, which is still in existence and boasts the age of thirty-four years. After a time, wishing to change his location, he returned to Ottumwa and purchased the *Courier*, which he conducted as editor and proprietor, and materially assisted in the organization of the Republican party. He remained connected with this paper until after the war, and in 1867 visited Europe and attended the Paris Exposition, reaping a rich experience from his observation of foreign customs and manners and the commodities and works of art of the world as exhibited there.

During the war Mr. Norris was made Postmaster of Ottumwa by the appointment of President Lincoln. He was a staunch Republican in politics and a strong temperance man. A few years later, moved by his detestation of the liquor traffic, he established a prohibition paper, which he named the *Daily Vindicator*, which was afterward suspended. He subsequently purchased a half interest in the Ottumwa *Democrat*, his idea being that he could better subserve the prohibition party, and eventually became the sole proprietor, but conducted the paper only a short time. Both he and his wife were connected with the Congregational Church. This excellent man died in Ottumwa on the 3d of March, 1881, leaving a wife, but no family.

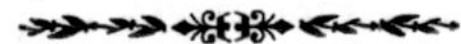

GEORGE RILEY, Jr., one of the editors and publishers of the Ottumwa *Press*, is managing his department of this journal with ability and success, and assisting to bring it to the standard of a first-class paper of the Hawkeye State. Mr. Riley is a native of Owego, Tioga Co., N. Y., and was born Sept. 11, 1855. He is the son of George and Loranda (Chittenden) Riley, the former being a native of the State of New York, whose ancestors came from the North of Ireland. The mother was also a native of New York, and descended from an old New England family; she departed this life in April, 1886. The father is still living in Owego, and pursuing his trade as a blacksmith.

The subject of our sketch was reared in the county of his birth, and remained there until 1877. He received his primary education in the public schools, and later attended an academy, whence, after pursuing a thorough course of study, he went into the office of the Owego *Record*, and served an apprenticeship of four years at the printer's trade. In 1876 he removed to Newark Valley and established the *Tioga County Herald*, which he conducted for six months, then sold out and returned to his native town. He worked at his trade in the latter place and Elmira until the opening of the year 1877, when he went to New York City and engaged with the Union Printing Company, and also as reporter upon a daily paper, and was thus engaged until he took charge again of the Owego *Record*, on the 1st of January, 1879. He remained here this time until December of the following year, doing special reporting for several daily papers, in which he gave ample proof of the ability which has since characterized him as a newspaper man. In December, 1880, Mr. Riley started West, and coming to Ottumwa purchased an interest in the *Press*, and has been connected with the paper since that time, being associated with his brother-in-law, Edwin A. Jones.

When Mr. Riley first came West he had not thought of locating in this city, but at several times went out to hunt a location, invariably drifting back to Ottumwa. His purchase of the Ottumwa *Press* has proved a fortunate investment, because he is admirably adapted to the position which he has assumed upon it. It is one of the most readable journals in Wapello County, and bears fair comparison with the newspapers of the Hawkeye State.

The subject of our sketch was united in marriage with Miss Ida A. Jones, in June, 1880, in Owego, and his wife accompanied him in his first journey to the West. They have become the parents of one child, a son—George. Mrs. R. is a finely educated and accomplished lady, and prominently connected with the Baptist Church of Ottumwa. Politically Mr. R. is a stanch Republican, and carries out in the management of the paper his independent political ideas. Mr. and Mrs. R. occupy a pleasant home, and number among their friends and associates the most cultured people of this locality.

JAMES H. HATCH, a farmer and stock-grower living on section 12, Center Township, is a native Hawkeye, born in Appanoose County, Sept. 19, 1859, and is a son of George and Mary E. (Betterton) Hatch, the former a native of England and the latter of Pennsylvania. They reside upon a farm in Center Township. Our subject passed his early life upon a farm and in attendance at the common schools of his native State.

Mr. Hatch was united in marriage with Fannie M. Booz, daughter of J. G. and Mary A. W. (Townsend) Booz, the former of whom was born in Pennsylvania and the latter in New Jersey. She was born Nov. 16, 1864, in Center Township. Two children have been born to them—Amy Beatrice, March 8, 1885, and a son, Chester, Dec. 13, 1886. Mr. Hatch is living on a farm of 142 acres, belonging to C. F. Blake, of Ottumwa. The farm is well improved and is numbered among the best in Center Township. Politically Mr. Hatch is a Republican. His wife is a member of the Episcopal Church.

LINSAY H. PAGE, deceased, came into Iowa in 1852, was born in the State of Kentucky, and died near Batavia, this county, in 1864. He was reared and educated in his native State, and after arriving at years of manhood went to Logan County, Ohio, and in due time was there married to Miss Axie Harris. Of this union there were born seven children, three only now living: James J., a Mormon Elder of Salt Lake City, Utah; Isaac H., of Nebraska, and Mary E., the wife of David Railsback, of Ottumwa. Mrs. Axie Page died in Ohio, and the subject of our sketch married for his second wife Miss Annie Smith, and they became the parents of three children: Lettie E., the wife of Edward Burnett, of Michigan; William H., living near Catawba, Ohio, and John T., of Albia, Dane Co., Wis.

Mr. Page removed from Ohio to Indiana in 1850, and two years later crossed the Father of Waters and came into Wapello County, Iowa, settling upon a farm in Richland County, where he engaged in agricultural pursuits. He was a man of excellent character, an active member of the Union Baptist Church, and highly respected in the community where he resided. After his decease Mrs. Page returned to her home in Logan County, Ohio, where she still resides.

JOHN MORROW HEDRICK, a late resident of Ottumwa, was born in Rush County, Ind., Dec. 16, 1831, and died of paralysis Oct. 3, 1886, at his home in this city. His disease was no doubt induced by the severe wounds he received in the army during the Rebellion. His father was John W. Hedrick, a native of Kentucky, a farmer of much intelligence, and a sterling citizen. His mother's maiden name was Mary Morrow. She died many years ago, but the father still survives, at the advanced age of seventy-eight years.

Our subject was reared upon a farm, and emigrated to Wapello County, Iowa, with his father's family in 1845, and remained with his father upon the farm till the age of twenty, when he engaged as a clerk in a dry-goods store, and upon arriving at his majority became a partner in the firm. The General continued in the mercantile business nearly all the time till he entered the army as First Lieutenant of Co. D, 15th Iowa Vol. Inf., Sept. 20, 1861. While the regiment was in rendezvous at Keokuk, Iowa, he was promoted to the captaincy of Company K, of the 15th, and in the first day's battle at Shiloh his regiment was to the front in Gen. Ben. Prentiss' command, and there he was quite severely wounded and taken prisoner. He was six months in various prisons of the South, and finally parolled Oct. 18, 1862, and came to his home in this city, where he remained until exchanged, and then joined his regiment at Lafayette, Tenn., Feb. 9, 1863. He was soon thereafter promoted Major of the regiment, and on the 22d of April following was commissioned Lieutenant Colonel. In the spring of 1864, on account of Iowa allowing her soldiers at the front to vote, the Republican State Convention designated the General as a delegate to the National Convention, sitting that year in Baltimore, which convention renominated the lamented Lincoln for President, the General being an earnest supporter of his nomination.

On the 22d of July, 1864, in the fierce fighting of that day, before Atlanta, Ga., Gen. Hedrick received a fearful wound in the hip, the ball passing around near to the spine, and while being borne from the field he received another ball through his arm. His wounds proved nearly fatal, and when he was able to be around he went on crutches for many months. Unable to take the field he was detailed for duty in the War Department at Washington, and remained there from March, 1865, to September, 1866. He was a member of a court martial there which tried many of the important cases noted in the history of those days. Upon the fall of Atlanta the Colonel of the regiment, W. W. Belknap, was promoted Brigadier General, and Hedrick was promoted Colonel, his commission dating Aug. 20, 1864. He was soon after commissioned Brevet Brigadier General for conspicuous gallantry upon the field of battle. In 1866 he was appointed Postmaster of Ottumwa, and held that office until he resigned to take the position of Supervisor of Internal Revenue for Iowa, Nebraska, Minnesota, Colorado and Dakota, in 1870. He held this position until 1876, and until a revision of the corps of Internal Revenue officials, when Supervisors were superseded by revenue agents. While Supervisor he was detailed to take charge of the great whisky fraud cases of Milwaukee and Chicago, which at that time attracted the attention of the whole country. His marked ability, indomitable energy, fearless fidelity to duty, and sterling integrity, brought him into wide and extended notice throughout the Northwest, especially at that time, and he was highly complimented by the Secretary of the Treasury for his eminently satisfactory discharge of so important a service.

In 1866 the Ottumwa (Iowa) *Courier*, a daily and weekly newspaper, passed into the hands of several stockholders, and the General was chosen as its editor, and so remained until August, 1869, when the ownership of the paper was vested in the General and A. H. Hamilton as joint owners. From that time forward the editorial charge was in the hands of both its owners until Jan. 1, 1878, when he sold his interest to the said Hamilton. He was a delegate at large from Iowa to the Chicago convention, in 1868, which first nominated Gen. Grant for President, and was one of the committee appointed by the convention to notify Gen. Grant of his nomination.

On retiring from the *Courier* the General gave his attention chiefly to his own affairs, but was ever alive and to the forefront in all public enterprises for the advancement of the growth and prosperity of Ottumwa. Some eight years ago he built a street railroad in the city, which proved profitable to him, as well as a great convenience to the public. He always gave liberally to all public enterprises, his large gifts of this character amounting to thousands of dollars. He was especially the citizen of all others to represent Ottumwa abroad

RESIDENCE OF DAVID COBLER, SEC. 20,

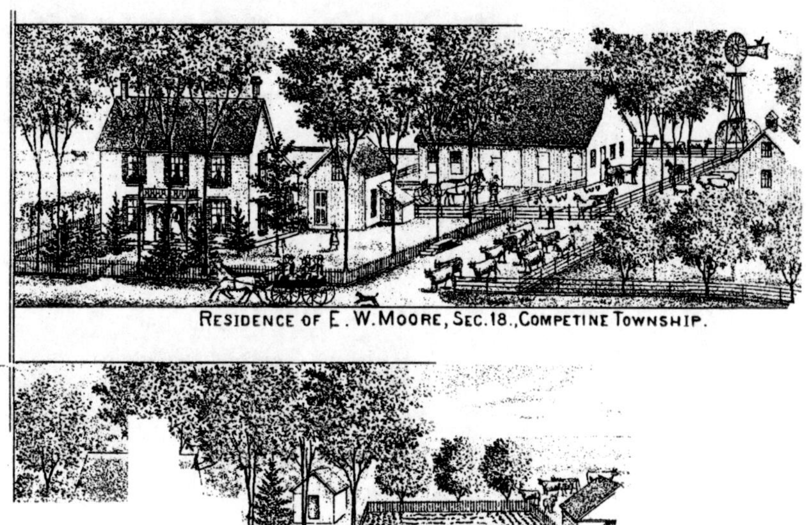

RESIDENCE OF E. W. MOORE, SEC. 18., COMPETINE TOWNSHIP.

in railroad projects, and he gave months of his time without compensation in this direction, for the public good, having no other interest save one in common with other citizens. He was peculiarly the citizen above all others who finally secured for Ottumwa that great railway thoroughfare—the C., M. & St. P. The life of the General since the close of the Rebellion was intimately and most prominently interwoven with the material advancement of city and county. Reared on a farm, he took great interest in agriculture, and was President of the county agricultural society, and paid liberally to promote its interests. No citizen was more universally missed by the people of his county and city, and none more sincerely mourned at his death.

The General was married, July 3, 1853, to Matilda Caroline Haines, a most estimable lady, who still survives. The living children of this marriage are Mrs. Kate M. Ladd, Howard L., Charles M., Harry McP. and Carita B.

WILLIAM COLE, at present a retired farmer and a resident of Kirkville, Iowa, was born in Marietta, Washington Co., Ohio, Sept. 28, 1810, and is a son of Abijah and Susan (Cathcart) Cole. His father was a native of Connecticut, a tanner and shoemaker by trade, and died in Wyandotte County, Ohio, in 1850. His mother died in April, 1823, in Washington County, Ohio.

Before reaching his majority, William Cole learned the trade of a stonemason, which occupation he followed for fifteen years in his native State. In 1833 he was married to Miss Elizabeth B. Patton, born in Washington County, Ohio, Jan. 9, 1813, and the daughter of Thomas Patton. Of this union there were born ten children, who are recorded as follows: Ann A. is the wife of H. C. Kirkpatrick, and lives at Winchester, Kan.; Irene D., the wife of D. H. Cline, lives in Oskaloosa, Kan.; William W. married Miss Julia Darey and lives in Kansas; T. E. married Miss M. J. Picker, and lives in Richland Township; John L. was next in order of birth; Mary E., the wife of M. E. Holloway, lives in Mahaska County; Susan M. is deceased; three others died in infancy. Mrs. Elizabeth Cole departed this life Sept. 19, 1881, and was buried in the Kirkville Cemetery.

Mr. Cole is the owner of fifty-six acres of land in Richland Township, together with three dwelling-houses in Kirkville. He has held the office of Justice of the Peace for six years, and politically is a Greenbacker.

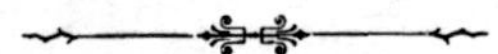

NELS ABRAHAM, a prosperous Swedish farmer of Green Township, was born March 25, 1836, and emigrated to America from his native land when a young man twenty-two years of age. His parents were Charles and Hannah (Peterson) Abraham, who spent their entire lives in their native country, engaged in agricultural pursuits. After reaching American shores Mr. Abraham proceeded to Illinois, and located in Rock Island County, and at Moline was engaged for about seven months in the plow factory of John Deere. He then removed to Henry County, where he was engaged as a coal miner for a year, and thence came to Ottumwa in 1870, being employed the following five years on the C., B. & Q. R. R. All this time he had in view the pursuit of agriculture like his father before him, and had saved what he could of his moderate wages, and now found himself the possessor of sufficient means to purchase a small farm. He found a tract of eighty acres in Green Township, with which he was well pleased, but upon which no improvements had been made. Like any other man naturally interested in his own possessions, he turned his whole attention to the improvement of his little farm, in which he was eminently successful.

In the meantime Mr. Abraham had assumed family and domestic ties, having been married, in January, 1871, to Miss Anna Knoto, a native of his own country, and the daughter of Peter and Berta (Anderson) Knoto. Of this union there were born three children: Charles Alfred, Sept. 23, 1871; Selma, Dec. 9, 1873, and Emma Mary, March 6, 1875. Up to 1886 the little family lived contentedly in a log cabin patiently waiting for better things in the future. In the fall of that year Mr.

Abraham erected a comfortable and shapely frame house, 28x14 feet, with an L 12x14 feet, in which they are now established, and living in a style corresponding with their means.

The possessions of Mr. Abraham have been acquired solely by the exercise of his own energy and industry. In his own country he followed the trade of a miller to a certain extent, but is now giving his whole attention to the cultivation of his land, and the raising of good grades of cattle and other stock. Mr. and Mrs. Abraham are members of the Lutheran Church, and politically our subject uniformly casts his vote with the Republican party.

IRA PHILLIPS, a prominent business man and highly respected citizen of Ottumwa, is closely identified with the business and industrial interests of this section, and is President of the Phillips Coal and Mining Company, whose operations extend over a large portion of this locality, and give employment to numbers of working-men. Mr. Phillips is a native of Madison County, Ohio, and was born on the 28th of May, 1830. When he was a lad of twelve years old his parents removed from his native State to Van Buren County, Iowa, while the latter was a Territory. He here grew to manhood, and received his early education in the pioneer schools, which were conducted in the humble log cabin. He was carefully trained to habits of industry and economy by his excellent parents, and in early years imbibed those principles of honor and integrity which have made his life successful and secured for him the respect and esteem of his associates.

Mr. Phillips was married in Van Buren County in 1854, to Miss Emily, the daughter of Sylvester Henry, who came to Van Buren County in 1838, Mrs. Phillips at that time being a child of three years old. They located upon a tract of wild land, improved a farm, and established a comfortable home upon the site of what had formerly been a wilderness. Of the union of Mr. and Mrs. P. there were born two children: Ora, who died in Van Buren County in 1874, and Henry, now of the firm of Ira Phillips & Co., of Ottumwa.

The subject of our sketch became a resident of this city in 1875, and since that time has been extensively engaged in the coal business. During his long residence in this locality his name has become familiar as that of a man honest and upright in his transactions and of the highest moral principles. In politics he is a staunch Republican, and keeps well posted upon the affairs of the county and State at large. He is an extensive reader and a man of decided views. Of strong temperance principles, he took a firm stand against the sale and manufacture of whisky in this State, and arrainged himself promptly upon the side of the Prohibitionists.

The property of the Phillips Coal and Mining Company consists of valuable engines and hoisting machinery and all the appliances required for successful mining. The works are in a prosperous condition and form a valuable factor in the industrial interests of this section.

B. J. HARMAN, a prosperous farmer and stock-grower on section 5, Pleasant Township, was born in Harrison County, Ohio, May 15, 1828, and is a son of George and Juda (Whitmore) Harman, both of whom are natives of Pennsylvania, but who moved to Ohio at an early day. On the 30th day of September, 1842, the family arrived in Jefferson County, Iowa, and there wintered, and in May of the following year moved to Wapello County, the elder Harman taking up a claim adjoining the farm on which his son now lives. He died on his original homestead, Nov. 4, 1864, at the age of sixty-seven years. He was a man well known to all the early settlers of Wapello County, and enjoyed the respect and esteem of all who knew him. His wife survived him over six years, dying Jan. 15, 1871.

B. J. Harman came to Iowa in company with his parents and remained with them until twenty-two years of age. On the 21st day of November, 1851, he was united in marriage with Catherine A. Dickens, born in Ohio, Jan. 19, 1831, the daughter of

Martin and Elizabeth (Staley) Dickens. Her mother is dead, but her father yet survives, and is living in Competine Township. One child blest this union, James A., born June 30, 1852, now living in Appanoose County, this State. Mrs. Harman died Nov. 21, 1854, and in 1858 Mr. Harman married Sarepta Cobler, a native of Indiana, who was born April 29, 1841, and the daughter of Lewis and Nancy Cobler. Her mother is deceased, but her father is living in Dahlonega Township. Of this union there were three children: Harvey, born April 26, 1860; Nancy C., Nov. 11, 1861; Clara B. Aug. 24, 1866.

Mr. Harman is the owner of 195 acres of fine farm land, all of which is under a high state of cultivation, there being on the place a good frame dwelling, barn, and every convenience that tends to make it a fine stock and grain farm. Mr. and Mrs. Harman are members of the German Baptist Church, of which he has been a minister for a period of twenty years. Politically Mr. H. is a Democrat, and has served his township as Assessor.

SAMUEL BUSH, a highly respected resident of Chillicothe, Iowa, is a native of Ross County, Ohio, and was born in 1810, being the son of Michael and Susanna (Bowers) Bush, both natives of Virginia. They removed from their native State to Ohio soon after their marriage and were among the pioneer settlers of that region. There, their son Samuel was reared and educated, remaining under the parental roof until he had attained to years of manhood. He removed to Iowa in 1839, while it was yet a Territory, settling near Stumptown, Van Buren County, and remained there until 1843, when he settled upon a tract of land about one-half mile from the present site of Chillicothe, upon which he has lived since that time, the primitive condition of it having given way to town lots and residences. In 1866 he established the hotel business in which he has since been continuously engaged, and in an experience of nearly thirty years has acquired a considerable degree of perfection in the office of "mine host," his house being the resort of the best class of travelers through this section.

Samuel Bush was married, at the age of twenty-three years, in his native State, to Miss Christina Campbell, also a native of Ohio, and who became the mother of two children: Elizabeth, the wife of John Cottrell, and Susanna, now deceased. This lady did not long remain his companion, departing this life in 1837. Mr. Bush was a second time married, in 1839, to Miss H. M. Michael, of Virginia. Of this marriage there were born nine children, only three of whom are now living, viz.: Francis M., a merchant of Chillicothe; Charles, a conductor on the C., B. & Q. R. R., a resident at Creston, and Louisa, at home with her parents. The eldest son served as a soldier in the late war. Mr. Bush had one son, Zacharia Taylor, who went to California and has not been heard from for many years. It is not known by the family whether he is living or dead.

J. A. WAGNER, editor and publisher of the *Journal and Freie Presse* of Ottumwa, Iowa, is conducting one of the best papers in Wapello County in a creditable and intelligent manner, and has built up a subscription list which is increasing steadily as time passes. Mr. Wagner is a native of this county, and was born in Agency City, Sept. 7, 1861. His parents were John and Elizabeth (Lader) Wagner, natives of Germany, where they were reared and married. They emigrated to the United States in 1856, and proceeding directly westward crossed the Father of Waters and located in the village where their son, our subject, was born. John Wagner was a woolen manufacturer, and pursued his trade after coming to Iowa, in Agency City and Ottumwa. He then opened a grocery store on Birch street, and has been conducting this business since that time, being now located at the corner of Main and Birch streets. The mother is also living, and they are among the most highly respected residents of this vicinity.

The subject of our sketch was reared in Ottumwa, received a fair education in his native language, and at the age of thirteen years entered the office of the *Journal* to learn the printer's trade.

In 1877 he went to Sigourney, where he remained nearly two years, and then, setting his face westward, located at Columbus, Neb., where he was engaged in the office of a German publication for a period of seven months. He then returned to Ottumwa, and engaged with McClellan Bros., job printers, until October, 1881, when he purchased an interest in the *Journal and Freie Presse.*

Mr. Wagner is a prominent man among the excellent class of German citizens in this locality, and one of the officers of the Turnverein. He is also a member of the Printer's Union, and a gentleman whose opinions are greatly respected, and his judgment often appealed to in the consideration of matters of importance. The parental family of our subject consisted of six children, of whom he was the third in order of birth. All these are living but one, and are named: Mary A., John A., Lizzie, Carrie and Katie.

J. E. LANGFORD, of Ottumwa, is a manufacturer of artificial building stone, for checkered sidewalks, cellar floors, door-steps, window-sills, hitching-blocks, carriage-steps, fountains, vases, tombstone bases, sewer and drain pipe, well-tubing, roofing, pitch, window arches, etc., and dealer in home and foreign cement, plaster Paris, lime, hair, sand, fireclay, clay pipe, fertilizer, etc. The factory is located at the corner of Clay and Lincoln streets, and besides this Mr. Langford is the owner of forty-nine acres of land in and adjoining the city limits of Ottumwa, near the fair ground, on which he has a fine brick residence, with well-kept lawn, a good barn with stone basement, and various out-buildings. Everything about the place is neat and tasteful, and denotes the thrift and industry of its proprietor.

J. E. Langford was born in Tioga County, N. Y., Feb. 10, 1826, and is a son of J. E. and Sarah (Swartwood) Langford, who both died in Tioga County, his mother in 1831, and his father in 1862. On the death of his mother, the subject of this sketch went to live with a cousin Swartwood, where he remained until he was eighteen years of age, during which time he was employed at all kinds of general work and attended the country schools of the neighborhood. He then went to work with two of his half-brothers, James and Daniel Pierce, and remained with them until 1849, when he engaged with Captain Smith of a whaling-ship and went to sea, being out two years. They crossed the Equator four times in 72 north latitude and 51 south latitude. They captured thirty-two whales while out, the longest measuring seventy-four and one-half feet from tip to tip. They brought home 3.650 barrels of oil and 45,000 pounds of black whalebones. Their return was in 1851, and for the next two years Mr. Langford followed farming and clerking in a store. In 1853 he commenced railroading with James Thompson on the second track of the New York & Erie Railroad. He next was employed on the Lackawanna & Pittsburgh Railroad, near Scranton, Pa.; from there he came west and worked on the old Mississippi & Racine Railroad, and while engaged on this road built a levee opposite St. Louis, Mo. He next was employed on the Chicago, Alton & St. Louis Railroad, at Joliet, Ill., and from there, in 1862, he went to Lake Superior and assisted in building a railroad from Escanaba to the Lake and to the iron mines. He then came to Iowa and filled a contract on what was then known as the Burlington & Missouri River, now the Chicago, Burlington & Quincy Railroad. In 1870 he worked on the Burlington & Southwestern Railroad. In 1871 he came to Ottumwa and assisted in building the water-works for the city, which contract was finished in 1876.

Since his first contract work in 1853, Mr. Langford has been engaged continuously on public works of some kind. Few men could get more work out of a set of men than Mr. Langford, yet he was always liked and respected by those whom he had in his employ, endeavoring to treat them as he would wish to be treated. He was united in marriage, Aug. 14, 1866, in Wapello County, Iowa, with Miss E. A. Graves, daughter of A. L. and Julia (Moffett) Graves. Her father was a native of Indiana and mother of Pennsylvania. Both are living in the city of Ottumwa. Mr. and Mrs. Langford are the parents of five children: J. E., born Nov. 19, 1867; Estella, Feb. 4, 1871; Earl,

March 12, 1875; Leola, April 29, 1879; Nettie, June 23, 1881. Mr. Langford is a member of the I. O. O. F. A handsome lithograph view of the family residence is shown on another page.

JAMES T. LAYNE, one of the early settlers of Iowa, is pleasantly located in Adams Township, on section 15, where he is enjoying his later days in that comfort and quiet which are the just rewards of industry, economy and enterprise. Mr. Layne was born in Montgomery County, Ind., Oct. 31, 1835, and is the son of Jarlton and Sarah (Easley) Layne, both natives of Kentucky, who emigrated to Iowa while it was still a Territory, locating first in Montgomery County. Their marriage occurred in Indiana, and they became the parents of seven children, one of whom is deceased: James T., of our sketch, was the eldest born; Franklin M. lives in Turner County, Dak.; Walter H. is the Sheriff of Cherokee County, Kan.; Joseph S., Hayman D. and Nancy A. (Mrs. William Gaily) live in this county.

In 1849 the father of our subject removed with his family from Montgomery to Wapello County, and with the assistance of his sons opened up a farm in Polk Township, where he passed the remainder of his days. Mrs. Sarah Layne departed this life in 1842, greatly mourned by her husband and surviving children. Mr. L. is still living, at the advanced age of seventy-five years. He is Democratic in politics, and in his younger years held the various local offices of his township. With his wife he was connected with the Baptist Church. His second wife was Miss Sarah Edgman, and they became the parents of four children, three of whom are living. After the death of this lady he was married to Mrs. Delilah McDole, who is still living.

James T. Layne, of this biography, received his education in the log school-house of his native county, and remained under the parental roof until he attained to years of manhood. He was then married, in November, 1856, to Miss Sarah Doggett, a native of his own State, and they became the parents of two children: George W., now living in Kansas, and Franklin M., of this county. Mrs. Sarah Layne departed this life in 1861, having lived a worthy and useful life, and greatly esteemed by her family and friends; she was a member in good standing of the Baptist Church. Mr. Layne was married the second time, March 9, 1862, to Miss Minerva Drummond, a native of Clarke County, Va., and of this union there were born the following children: Elizabeth, Mrs. Anderson, lives in Monroe County, Iowa; Fannie became the wife of Asa Hepler, of Adair County, Iowa; Irvine, Liva, Joseph, Maude and Lloyd are at home.

Mr. Layne came to Wapello County in 1849, when the country was thinly settled and wild game abounded in plenty. In 1876 he purchased his present farm of 298 acres, which he has industriously cultivated and improved, and now has one of the most attractive homes in this section of the county. The farm residence is a model of convenience and comfort, and the barns and out-buildings are of first-class description. The possessions of our subject are the result of his own industry and enterprise, as he came here comparatively poor and has received no assistance from legacies or influential friends. He has held the various local offices of his township and takes an interest in local and general matters, keeping himself well posted in regard to what is going on around him in the world.

WILLSON KENNEDY, a well-to-do and prosperous farmer residing on section 14, Green Township, where he is meeting with success in the prosecution of his calling, was born in Rockbridge County, Va., Jan. 7, 1820. The parents of our subject, William and Rhoda (Wilson) Kennedy, were also natives of the same State. Willson Kennedy was brought up to the calling of a farmer's son in his native county and there lived, assisting in the maintenance of the parental family, until 1846.

During the year last named our subject came to this State, and five years later, in 1851, came to Wapello County, where he made claim to a tract of Government land in Green Township. Locating on this land he at once entered upon its improvement and cultivation, and by energy and economy has not only brought his land to a high state of cultivation, but has been enabled to place improvements upon it. Three years ago his pleasant little home was swept away by the fiery element, but he contemplates the erection of a new house soon, into which he will move his family and pass the remaining years of his life on the old homestead. In politics he is Republican, and has held the offices of School Director and Road Overseer.

In 1850 our subject was united in marriage with Miss Elsy Wortman, a daughter of John and Rebecca (Cain) Wortman, both natives of New Jersey. Seven children have been born of this union: Mary R., deceased; Wilmot, deceased; Charles H., a resident of Green Township, and a farmer by calling; Wayne, a farmer of Keokuk Township; Pluma V., deceased; Amanda E., wife of John Emery, a well-to-do farmer of Keokuk Township, and James A., who is living with the old folk, and assists the father in the cultivation of the farm. Our subject and wife are members of the Methodist Episcopal Church, and are honored citizens of the community in which they reside.

DANIEL EASLEY, deceased, one of the early pioneers of Wapello County, was a native of Stokes County, N. C., and was born April 20, 1792. After arriving at years of manhood he was married to Miss Nancy Deatheridge, Nov. 17, 1815. Mrs. E. was born Sept. 1, 1795, in North Carolina, whence she removed with her parents to Kentucky in about 1812. In 1824 Mr. and Mrs. Easley went to Montgomery County, Ind., where they lived until 1850, and then crossed the Father of Waters into Wapello County, Iowa, where they established a permanent home and passed the remainder of their days. They became the parents of eleven children, five now living, of whom the record is as follows: Daniel is a resident of Wayne County, Iowa; Catharine became the wife of James LaFollett, of Montgomery County, Iowa; Frances is the widow of Jacob W. Layne, and a resident of this county; Isaac lives in Missouri; Angeline married John H. LaFollett, of this county. The father of this family died Sept. 18, 1876, the mother having preceded him to the better land Nov. 9, 1871. They were people greatly respected in this vicinity for their high moral principles and consistent Christian lives, and were prominent members of the Baptist Church.

In early life Mr. Easley was an old-line Whig, but after the abandonment of that party by the organization of the Republicans he cordially endorsed the principles of the latter, and subsequently identified himself with them. He was prominently identified with the affairs of his township, held the various local offices, and was the encourager and supporter of every measure calculated to advance its prosperity.

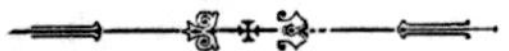

HON. EUGENE FAWCETT, deceased, a former highly respected resident and business man of Wapello County, was born in Belmont County, Ohio, March 22, 1845, and received his early education in the public schools of the Buckeye State. He remained with his parents until he attained to years of manhood, and then, during the progress of the late Civil War, enlisted in the army as a telegraph operator, and remained until the close of the war. He then went to Panama as correspondent of the New York *Tribune*, and subsequently officiated in the same capacity for the New York *Herald* and San Francisco *Chronicle*, and was appointed Superintendent of the Aspinwall Telegraph Company. After being thus occupied for several years he returned to the United States on account of failing health, and settled temporarily in Chariton, Iowa, where, for a short time, he conducted the editorial department of the Chariton *Patriot*.

In 1869, having previously taken a thorough course in the study of law, Mr. Fawcett came to Ottumwa and formed a partnership with William McNett, Esq., and subsequently, in September, 1872, went to Santa Barbara, Cal., where he soon built up an extensive and lucrative practice. He also became prominent in the public affairs of that section, and after filling other prominent positions was elected Judge of the District Court of Southern California. While holding this position he was a member of the Constitutional Convention of California, and there was a motion made to debar him of his seat, the opposition claiming he was not eligible on account of holding the office of Judge. A heated discussion grew out of this, but Judge Fawcett was sustained in his position.

Judge Fawcett departed this life Jan. 9, 1880, after establishing a record as one of the most able jurists who have adorned the bar of Wapello County, as well as that of the Pacific slope. He was a close student, a deep thinker, and keenly observant of what was going on around him. His commanding presence and fine physique, added to his eloquence as an advocate, deepened the impression which he invariably made as to his marked abilities, force of character, and more than ordinary genius.

A. W. BELL. The subject of this biography, one of the honored pioneers of Iowa, came to the State with his parents in 1846, and has been a resident of Wapello County since that time. He now owns and occupies a valuable homestead in Cass Township on section 6, where, for many years, he has been successfully engaged as a farmer and stock-raiser.

Mr. Bell was born in Marion County, Ind., on the 28th of November, 1831, and is the son of Nathaniel and Celia (Wright) Bell. Nathaniel Bell is a native of Ohio, and the mother of our subject was born in Randolph County, N. C. They became the parents of nine children, six daughters and three sons, five of whom are still living: Lucia became the wife of Thomas Griffith, who is now a retired farmer and living in Richland; Adam, our subject is the fourth in order of birth; B. F. is a farmer and stock-dealer of Center Township; T. J. is engaged in mining in Nevada, he has been a prominent citizen of that State for a number of years, and in the fall of 1886 was candidate for Governor; Helen graduated from the Medical Department of Ann Arbor University in 1882; after receiving her diploma she spent one year in the Female Hospital of Boston, Mass., and has now opened an office in Denver, Col., where she is successfully engaged in the practice of her profession.

In 1846 the parents of our subject removed from Indiana to Wapello County, Iowa, and the father entered 320 acres of land on sections 4 and 9 in Center Township. It was but slightly improved and he at once began its cultivation. He was successful in his operations, and at the time of his death had one of the most valuable farm estates in this section of the county. He departed this life on the 7th of January, 1879, leaving a good record as an honored citizen and a valuable member of the community. The wife and mother had preceded him to the better land on the 24th of December, 1875. They were both devoted members of the Christian Church, with which they became connected early in life, and their loss to the church and to the community was one not easily repaired.

The subject of this history spent the early part of his life on the farm with his parents, and after he had attained his majority was united in marriage with Miss Nancy E. Goodwin, their wedding taking place on the 22d of February, 1853. Mrs. Bell was born in Putnam County, Ind., July 22, 1835, and was the daughter of Rolla and Hannah (Gardner) Goodwin, natives respectively of North Carolina and Kentucky. Mr. and Mrs. Bell became the parents of two children: Minerva C. was born Dec. 11, 1853, and became the wife of John Jordan, a prosperous farmer of Cass Township; Alfred died in infancy.

After his marriage Mr. Bell, with his wife, located in Appanoose County, where he entered 160 acres of unimproved land. They only occupied this, however, about eighteen months, and then, returning to Wapello County, located upon the farm which they now occupy. This consisted of 170 acres partly improved, and our subject moved upon it in 1857, and industriously set himself about its cultivation. He had formed many plans for the future, and was looking forward with hope and encouragement when the family was visited by a sad calamity in the death of the wife and mother, which took place July 22, 1858. Mrs. Nancy Bell was a lady greatly beloved by her friends and acquaintances, and a sincere believer in the Christian religion. She was kind and affectionate in her family relations and always ready to sympathize with the afflicted and distressed. Her name is held in kindly remembrance by those who knew her best and appreciated to the fullest extent her excellent qualities of mind and heart.

On the 2d of January, 1860, Mr. Bell was the second time married, to Miss Mary I. McGlothlen. This lady was born in Fountain County, Ind., March 2, 1839, and is the daughter of Thomas D. and Sarah (Meek) McGlothlen, both natives of Indiana, and a sketch of whom will be found elsewhere in this volume. This union was blest by the birth of six children, of whom the record is as follows: Jefferson, the eldest, who was born Dec. 22, 1862, died Aug. 22, 1863; Addie M. was born Dec. 4, 1863, and became the wife of Harvey Shayhan, a resident of Ottumwa; Lucia J., born Dec. 28, 1865, married Mr. D. P. Fagerstrom, station agent at Stanton, Iowa; T. B. was born March 12, 1868, and Nellie V., Feb. 28, 1871; W. T., born Jan. 12, 1873, died April 25, 1879.

In 1862 Mr. Bell took a trip to Nevada, and while there occupied himself in chopping and hauling wood, at a net profit of $100 per month. After fourteen months thus employed he returned to Wapello County and resumed his farming operations. He also operated a threshing-machine and sawmill for a number of years, and then engaged with his brother, B. F. Bell, in buying and shipping stock east to Chicago and west to Nevada and Salt Lake City, which he followed for about seven years, and from which he received a handsome income. In the meantime he also added to his landed possessions, and is now the proprietor of 300 acres, all improved and under a good state of cultivation. He has a fine set of farm buildings, and the homestead, with all its appointments, forms one of the most attractive features in the landscape of the county. In connection with his farming operations our subject has been running a custom sawmill on Bear Creek in Polk Township, which has proved, like most of his undertakings, a fortunate investment.

The possessions of Mr. Bell are the result solely of his own enterprise and industry. He has been prominent in the affairs of his community and has held the various offices of trust within the gift of his townsmen. He has been upright, generous and manly in all his dealings, taking a lively interest in every measure pertaining to the intellectual, moral and religious advancement of his township. His children have received careful home training and the advantages of a good education, and are thus fitted to take up his mantle in the years when he shall have been gathered to his fathers. Mr. and Mrs. Bell are members in good standing of the Christian Church of Cass Township, and are looked up to by all as worthy and valued factors in the moral and industrial elements of this section.

W. R. MOORE, deceased, formerly an esteemed resident of Highland Township, was born in New York State in 1814, and removed westward in 1837, locating first upon a farm near Lansing, Mich., which he improved from a tract of wild and uncultivated land. Thence he removed to Iowa in 1867, and became the proprietor of a farm of 160 acres in Wapello County, upon which he spent the remainder of his days, departing this life May 17, 1873. Both he and his wife were members in good standing of the Baptist Church.

W. R. Moore and Miss Lucy M. Morton were married May 19, 1845. Mrs. M. was the daughter of Bishop and Elnora Morton, natives respectively of New York and Massachusetts, and of this marriage there were born the following children, only one of whom is a resident of this county: Ella J. married A. Fuller, a coal inspector for the C., B. & Q. R. R. Co., and they live in Chicago; Jennie C. married William Bushnell, also of the Garden City, and Elmer.

Elmer E. Moore, son of our subject, was born in Clinton County, Mich., in 1849, and came to Wapello County with his father. In early manhood he was married to Miss Laura Spencer, their wedding taking place in May, 1872, and they became the parents of one child, who died in infancy. Mrs. Laura Moore survived her marriage only one year, and died at the age of twenty-three. In 1876 Mr. Moore was united in marriage with Miss Ada Reynolds, of Michigan, and the daughter of Richard and Betsey Reynolds. Mr. and Mrs. Moore

A. D. Book

have three children—Clyde, Bessie and Charlie. They are pleasantly located upon a farm of 160 acres, all improved, and beside the ordinary duties of agriculture Mr. M. is giving considerable attention to the raising of a good breed of cattle. He is highly esteemed among his fellow-townsmen, has been prominent in matters relating to the general interest, and was Constable in 1886. In politics he is a stanch Republican, and uniformly casts his vote in support of the principles of his party.

ANDREW D. WOOD, M. D. The late Dr. A. D. Wood, of Ottumwa, was born in Scipio, N. Y., in 1809, and departed this life in the city of his adoption in 1862. He was one of the early pioneers of Wapello County, and one of the first representatives of his profession to locate here. During a long residence here, his professional skill and excellent personal character secured for him a large circle of friends, whose confidence and esteem he enjoyed to a marked degree.

Dr. Wood was reared to manhood in his native town and entered upon the study of medicine at Auburn, N. Y., under the instruction of Dr. Morgan, a prominent physician of that city who, for many years, had charge of the medical department of the State Penitentiary. After the completion of his first course Dr. Wood entered Fairfield Medical College near Utica, N. Y., and graduated in the class of 1830. He had been a close student, was thoroughly interested in the intricacies of his profession, and ambitious to excel. He was consequently eminently fitted to enter upon his peculiar duties and responsibilities.

The year following his graduation Dr. Wood was united in marriage with Miss Eliza Ann, the daughter of Jabez Pease, who served in the War of 1812, and after returning to New York was numbered among the most useful and prominent citizens of Seneca County. His father served as a soldier of the Revolution and was a favorite aide on the staff of Gen. Washington.

Mrs. Wood was born in Seneca County, N. Y., in 1812, and inherited from her parents their noble and striking traits of character. She was eminently fitted to be the companion of her husband, and they set out in life with high hopes for the future, making their first home at Port Byron, where the young physician commenced the practice of his profession. They remained in Port Byron for nearly three years, whence, in 1850, they removed to Iowa and located in Ottumwa. Here Dr. Wood was at once recognized as possessing more than ordinary ability as a man and as a physician. He was straightforward in his business methods, careful and faithful in his practice, and took a lively interest in everything pertaining to the welfare of the city and community at large. In politics he was Democratic, and voted conscientiously to support the principles of his party. Of the demise of this lamented citizen and physician, the Ottumwa *Courier* at the time wrote as follows:

"We are pained to announce the death of Dr. A. D. Wood. He died in this city on the morning of Oct. 12, 1862, of consumption, in the fifty-fourth year of his age. He leaves a widow and seven children to mourn their loss.

"While the death of Dr. Wood was not altogether unexpected, yet it fell heavily on family and friends. He had been declining for some years, and some weeks ago very rapidly sank under the disease, but more recently had, apparently, sufficiently recovered to give hope that he might be spared during the winter, and probably longer, but his disease, insidious in its ravages, took him off on Sabbath morning last. So far as his future was concerned, death had no terrors to Dr. W., yet he seemed at times to dread that suffocation, which he feared might accompany dissolution.

"The subject of this notice came to this place in 1849, and established himself in his profession. He stood prominently at the head of the profession in this part of the State, and in the surgical department of his profession he was very eminent. The afflicted under his care knew that whatever of skill and attention could be brought to bear in their cases would be rendered by Dr. Wood. In his profession he was prompt, energetic and skillful; to the fraternity, he was kind and obliging, seeming to the younger members more as a tutor than a competitor. Socially no man was his superior—nature had stamped him with a noble spirit and a great mind.

"At the time of his death, we think he had not a personal enemy anywhere. The community sincerely mourns the deprivation of his skill, and society the loss of his high social qualities. To say that his family were devoted to him was but too feelingly manifested by the deep grief with which they received the sad reality of his death. The death of such a man is no less a loss to the community than to society and his family. The family of the deceased have our most lively sympathies in this their affliction."

Of the union of Dr. and Mrs. Wood there were born eight children, as follows: George D. is a resident of Waco, Tex., and an Alderman of that city; Mary became the wife of Kinsey Jordan, of Ottumwa, and died in 1872; Helen I. is the wife of E. R. Oliver, a jeweler of Ottumwa; Charles L. is in Pensacola, Fla.; Clara A. married James L. Serviss, a railway conductor; Julia F. is the wife of K. Jordan, of Ottumwa; Robert P. is in Montana; one child died in infancy. Mrs. Wood occupies a handsome residence within the city limits, and her home is the resort of the cultured people of the city.

We give in connection with this sketch a fine lithographic portrait of Dr. Wood, which will be looked upon with interest by the many friends and patrons to whom his pleasant countenance in the past was ever a pleasure and a satisfaction.

EDWARD G. WOLF, a prosperous farmer and stock-grower, residing upon section 6, Center Township, was born at Cedar Rapids, Linn Co., Iowa, Aug. 6, 1861, and is the son of Col. John S. and Mary L. (Doubler) Wolf, both of whom are natives of Pennsylvania. The father is a railroad contractor, and at present is engaged on the Duluth & Iron Range Railroad. He has had contracts with nearly every railroad from Pennsylvania to the Northern Pacific, and has been engaged in the business for about forty-one years. He came west as a contractor, and is at present residing in the city of Ottumwa. The subject of this sketch is living on and working a farm of 165 acres, the property of his mother. The farm is one of the best in the township, with good buildings and all the improvements of a well-regulated grain and stock farm.

Edward G. Wolf was married, Nov. 1, 1883, to Miss Lillie M. Miller, who was born in the city of Ottumwa, May 16, 1864. She is the daughter of Jacob and Christina (Aldrich) Miller, the former of whom was for many years engaged in the mercantile trade and also in operating a farm. His death took place in Ottumwa some years ago. Her mother is now living in Nebraska. Mr. and Mrs. Wolf have one child, Franklin T., born April 3, 1885. In politics Mr. Wolf affiliates with the Republican party.

G. W. BLACKMAN, a successful farmer and stock-raiser on section 36, Cass Township, was born Aug. 28, 1811, in Dedham, Mass. He is the son of Moses and Hannah (Wentworth) Blackman, who were the parents of six children, as follows: Hannah is the widow of Jonathan Andrew, formerly of Bradford, N. H.; Lewis is a farmer, residing in Wayne County, Iowa; Harriet, the late wife of Joseph Barker, is deceased; our subject is next in order of birth; John is a farmer in Wayne County, Iowa, and Elizabeth is deceased.

The father and mother of our subject removed with their family from Massachusetts to Ohio, in 1833, and settled in Vinton County. The father purchased 430 acres of land there, on which he erected a beautiful residence, and at the time of his demise, 1844, he had one of the best improved farms in Vinton County. He died at the age of sixty-three years, loved and mourned by a host of relatives and friends. His wife, the mother of our subject, died in about the year 1870, at the ripe old age of ninety-two years. She was a member of the Baptist Church, a loving Christian mother and wife, and a good neighbor.

The subject of this notice lived with his parents until he was sixteen years old, when he was apprenticed to learn the carpenter's trade, which he followed for a number of years. In 1833 he was married to Miss Elvira Palmenter, born May 1, 1815, in Hillsboro, N. H., and a daughter of Nathaniel and Rhoda (Carr) Palmenter, both of Irish ancestry. By this union two children were born, both of whom died in infancy, and the good wife and mother departed this life Aug. 12, 1844. She was a member of the Methodist Episcopal Church, and is buried in Vinton County, Ohio. On Dec. 31, 1844, our subject was married to Miss Melissa Mayhew, daughter of William and Lorilla (Gibbs) Mayhew. She was born in Athens County, the State of Ohio, and her father and mother were natives of New York. Her father died when she was a small child, and her mother departed this life about 1860. Both were members of the Methodist Episcopal Church. Of the union of our subject with Miss Mayhew there were seven children, namely: Marinda E., born June 20, 1848, became the wife of Isaiah Van Winkle, a farmer of Ringgold County, Iowa; William P., born Feb. 17, 1850, is also a farmer of the latter county; Charles P., born March 28, 1853, is a resident of Chillicothe, this State, and a plasterer by trade; Lewis A. was born April 25, 1855; Christa, Aug. 11, 1858; Phœbe L., born Aug. 22, 1860, became the wife of Charles Stuber, a farmer of Columbia Township, this county, and Elma was born Jan. 10, 1873. All the children were born in Ohio except the last-named, who first saw light in this county.

In 1858 Mr. Blackman built a steam sawmill in Vinton County, Ohio, and there carried on milling in connection with his farming and carpentering until 1861. During that year he sold his mill and engaged in digging and delivering iron ore to the Vinton furnace, and subsequently became manager of the ore department of the company, and held that position for two years. In 1865 he sold his farm in Ohio and moved to this county, purchasing seventy-five acres of land, and subsequently increasing his landed area until he is now the proprietor of 115 acres of good farming land, on which he has erected substantial buildings. He immediately located on his farm, on coming here, and at once entered upon its cultivation, also working at his trade until 1882. During that year he abandoned carpenter work, and since that time has devoted his time and energy to the cultivation of his land and the raising of high-grade cattle, in which he is assisted by his son. Mr. Blackman has held various township offices, and is at present serving a three years' term as Township Trustee. His wife is a member of the Methodist Episcopal Church, and socially our subject belongs to the Masonic fraternity. Politically he is a Democrat, and cast his first presidential vote for "Old Hickory."

ALBERT CONWELL, a successful farmer and stock-raiser of Cass Township, occupies a comfortable homestead on section 2, and is considered one of the representative men of this locality. He comes of a good family, and was born in Tuscarawas County, Ohio, on the 22d of February, 1846. His parents were John and Katie (Griffin) Conwell, a sketch of whom appears on another page of this volume. He came with his parents to Iowa in 1852, and spent his early years on the farm of his parents, who were among the pioneers of this region. He attended the common schools of Cass Township, and received careful home training from excellent parents, which fitted him to become a useful and valued member of society.

Mr. Conwell resides only a short distance from the old homestead, where he lived with his parents until his marriage. The maiden of his choice was Miss Catharine Varner, to whom he was united in wedlock on the 11th of April, 1877. Mrs. Conwell was born in Wapello County, June 21, 1852, and is the daughter of Tillman and Elizabeth (Nye) Warner, her father a native of Ohio, and her mother of German birth and parentage. She is a lady highly respected in this community, and a member in good standing of the Methodist Episcopal Church. Our subject in politics is a stanch Republican, and uniformly casts his vote in support of the principles of his party.

The homestead of Mr. Conwell includes seventy-eight and one-half acres of land, most of it under a fine state of cultivation, with ten acres of valuable timber. The residence is a handsome frame structure, and the barns and out-buildings are of first-class description. The possessions of our subject have been accumulated solely by his own industry, and, being yet a comparatively young man, the prospects for his further prosperity and usefulness as a member of society are remarkably good. He is ever ready to lend a helping hand to every enterprise calculated to advance the moral and intellectual development of his community.

E. M. ARENSCHIELD, M. D., has been a resident of Eldon, Iowa, since April 4, 1883, and occupies a high position in the medical profession in this locality. He is a close student and a skillful physician, and during the comparatively brief period of his residence here has built up a good practice and secured a large patronage among the best residents of the city.

Dr. Arenschield is a native of Rock Island County, Ill., born in 1860, and the son of C. J. and Harriet (Robinett) Arenschield, natives respectively of Germany and Ohio. His father was a farmer by occupation, and emigrated from his native country to the United States in 1835, settling in Ohio about the time of the opening of the Mexican War. He enlisted as a private in a company of mounted riflemen, and was under the command of Gen. Scott until the termination of the war. He was wounded in the knee by a horse falling upon him while acting as a scout, which was the only accident which he encountered during his term of service. After being mustered out he returned to Ohio and resumed farming there until 1856, when he removed to Rock Island County, Ill., where he still lives. He was married, in 1852, to Miss Harriet Robinett, and they became the parents of six children, of whom four sons are now living: C. O. is a farmer in Rock Island County, and now thirty-two years of age; W. L. is engaged as a contractor and builder at Geneva, Neb.; the subject of our sketch was the next in order of birth; A. S. is a fireman on the Southwestern Railroad.

Dr. Arenschield remained under the parental roof and attended school until he was sixteen years of age. He then went to Moline and entered upon a course of study at the High School there, from which he graduated in 1879, and then commenced the study of medicine with Dr. Hunter, of Hampton, Ill. The following year he entered the Medical Department of the Iowa State University, and after a three years' course graduated from that institution, and entered upon the practice of his profession at Eldon, of which city he has since been a resident. He was soon afterward appointed local railroad surgeon for the C., R. I. & P. R. R., which position he occupies at the present time. He is also Surgical Examiner for the Fidelity and Casualty Insurance Company of this place. In June, 1883, he established his office here, and has devoted himself closely to his profession in this place since that time.

Dr. Arenschield was married, June 26, 1884, to Miss Lillian A. Williams, a native of Ottumwa, and daughter of Judge Williams, well known in this section of the State as one of the ablest men occupying the position of advocate and counselor. Of the union of Dr. and Mrs. Arenschield there has been born one child, a daughter, Ione T., now one year old. They occupy a handsome residence, and besides this the Doctor owns a store building. He is highly respected in this community as the friend of temperance, morality and good order, and in all respects is fulfilling the obligations of a worthy citizen.

The father of Dr. Arenschield served as a soldier of the Union in the late war, enlisting in August, 1862, in the 89th Illinois Infantry as a private. He was soon promoted Corporal, next Sergeant, and in March, 1864, received a commission as Second Lieutenant. The following October he was promoted First Lieutenant, and served as such under the command of Logan and Thomas until the close of the war. He participated in the various engagements of his regiment, being at the battles of Stone River, Chickamauga, and through the Atlanta campaign, receiving but one wound, by a piece of shell, in the shoulder. He was a Whig until the abandonment of the old party by the organization of the Republicans, when he indorsed the principles of the latter, and has since voted with them. He began life as a poor boy, with a limited education, having never had but twenty-one days' schooling. But he was possessed of an inquiring mind, and was keenly observant of what was going on around him, and by this means obtained a good fund of general information. He was strongly opposed to the institution of slavery, and at all times and in all places was the encourager and supporter of everything tending to morality, temperance, and the general welfare of the community.

JAMES BURLEY, a prosperous farmer and stock-grower of Adams Township, is a native of the Buckeye State, being born in Perry County, Ohio, on the 12th of August, 1836. His parents were Lee and Rachel (Iliff) Burley, natives of Pennsylvania. The mother died about 1873, at the age of sixty-eight years. She was a most worthy and excellent Christian lady, and a devoted member of the Methodist Episcopal Church. Her remains are buried in Iliff Cemetery, in Perry County, Pa., and her name is held in kindly remembrance. The father is yet living in Perry County, Ohio, having arrived at the advanced age of eighty-three years. He removed there from his native State when a lad of nine years old, and settled among the early pioneers of that region, having now been a resident there for the long period of seventy-five years. He is a member of the Baptist Church, and still takes an intelligent interest in what is going on in the world around him.

The parental household of our subject consisted of nine children, seven of whom are yet living: Jane is married, and residing in Marshall County, Illinois; John V. is engaged in farming pursuits in Perry County, Ohio; James, of our sketch, was the third in order of birth; Hannah, unmarried, resides with her father in Perry County, Ohio, and also Rebecca; Thomas served as a soldier in the late war and died in Salsbury prison, South Carolina; Harriet married Jacob McKeefer, a farmer of Page County, Neb.; William M. is a merchant in Cookville, Perry Co., Ohio.

James Burley left the parental roof at the age of twenty-one years, and proceeding westward crossed the Mississippi and came to Afton, Iowa, where he located for seven months, and thence went to Chillicothe, Mo. In this latter place he remained eighteen months, following his trade of potter, and from there went to Mound City, Ill. He then returned to the old homestead in Ohio, and thence proceeded again to Marshall County, Ill., where he remained until 1862, and until after the beginning of the late war. After the repeated call for troops he returned to his native State, enlisted in the navy, and went on board the gun-boat "Brilliant," which acted as convoy on the Cumberland and Tennessee Rivers. There, with his comrades, Mr. Burley took part in the siege of Ft. Donelson, and participated in the various other engagements of his regiment, until the expiration of his term of service. Then, having felt that he had contributed his full quota toward the success of the Union army, he returned once again to Ohio and engaged at his trade.

The subject of our sketch was united in marriage with Miss Catherine Keohler, in Ohio, in 1866. Mrs. Burley was the daughter of Jacob and Mary (Myers) Keohler, natives of Maryland, and was born in Perry County, Ohio, on the 24th of May, 1846. After their marriage, Mr. and Mrs. Burley decided to make their permanent location in the Hawkeye State, and settled in Lucas County for the first year, thence removing to Ottumwa, and from there to Dahlonega, where Mr. Burley followed his trade for the next five years. From there they went to Blakesburg for eighteen months and thence to Sugar Creek, where Mr. Burley purchased twenty-eight acres of land, which they occupied for two years. He then sold this and purchased seventy-five acres in Adams Township. This is now finely improved and under a good state of cultivation, and in connection with his successful prosecution of agriculture he is also carrying on a pottery. Mr. Burley is complete master of this latter business, and manufactures several thousand pieces of ware each year, which yields him a comfortable income.

Of the union of Mr. and Mrs. Burley there have been five children, the record of whom is as follows: Ada May, born Sept. 10, 1867, died on the 10th of October following; Jasper T., born Jan. 28, 1869, died Sept. 25, 1875; Cordia, born Oct. 3, 1871; Etta C., Sept. 17, 1874; Loretta, Dec. 28, 1877. The family residence is a model of convenience and comfort, and Mr. Burley and his family are enjoying the good things of life, and performing acts of neighborly kindness as they have opportunity. Mr. Burley, politically, is a stanch Republican, and has held the office of Township Trustee for several years.

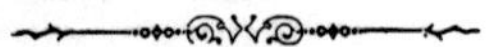

J. F. BLAKE, an attorney at law and highly respected citizen of Eldon, has been a resident of this vicinity since January, 1884. He is a native of Lowell, Mass., born in 1855, and the son of Lyman and Zeruah (Rollins) Blake, both natives of Orange County, Vt. He remained under the parental roof and was sixteen years of age when his parents came West to Wisconsin, in which State they located and remained for five years. During this time our subject took a course of study in the State Normal School at River Falls, and afterward engaged as a teacher in Pierce and St. Croix Counties, Wis., for two years, when he crossed the Mississippi and came to Ida County, Iowa, and alternately occupied his time in teaching and reading law, pursuing his studies under the instruction of C. W. Rollins, with whom he remained two years. He then went to Cedar Rapids, and entered the law office of Capt. Colyer, with whom he remained one year. He then came into Wapello County, settling at once in Ottumwa, and removed thence to Eldon.

Mr. Blake was admitted to the bar in March, 1882, at Ottumwa, and has built up a large practice, extending into the counties of Jefferson, Davis and Van Buren. He was married in September, 1881, to Miss Rachel W., daughter of Abram and Anna (Lee) Tabler, of Indiana, and they have become the parents of one son—Harold L., born Nov. 29, 1882. Mr. Blake owns 160 acres of land in Nebraska.

The death of Mr. Lyman Blake, the father of our subject, was attended with very painful circumstances, he being instantly killed by an engine on the railroad track in Eldon, of which town he had been a resident for only a few months, but in that brief time had made many friends. Lyman Blake was born in Washington, Orange Co., Vt., in October, 1820. He removed from his native place to Lowell, Mass., in 1843, and two years later was united in marriage with Miss Zeruah Rollins. They became the parents of eight children, only two of whom are now living.

Mr. Blake was engaged in business in Lowell, Mass., for a period of twenty years, owning and operating a general variety store and two livery-stables, and at the same time was extensively engaged in the sale of wood, giving employment to from thirty to forty men. He accumulated a large property and occupied a beautiful residence in Lowell. In about 1861 he received a kick from a horse, which broke three of his ribs and confined him to his bed for several months. During this time he was compelled to leave the management to his book-keeper and found, upon his return to business, that, owing to dishonesty or mismanagement, his finances were wrecked. He disposed of his business, sold his residence, and paying the last cent to his creditors, went back to Vermont to regain his health if possible. After a period of five years he came West, locating in Pierce County, Wis., and assumed the management of a flourmill. He was thus occupied for five years, and then removed to Iowa. He was strictly moral and temperate in his habits, and a kind and loving father and indulgent husband, a member of the Methodist Episcopal Church, and counted among his list of friends and associates the good and influential members of the community in which he lived.

JOHN T. PERDUE, of Ottumwa, occupies a prominent position as Clerk of the Courts of Wapello County. He is a native of Stark County, Ohio, and was born on the 9th of November, 1850, his father being Benjamin R. Perdue, at present a resident of Oskaloosa, this State. In 1862 our subject removed from his native State with his parents to Oskaloosa. He was educated in the public schools of that city, and received careful training at the hands of wise and judicious parents. After he had completed his primary studies, he entered the Business College of Oskaloosa, from which he graduated in 1873. Three years later he was appointed Superintendent of the business of W. C. Perdue & Co., at Muchachinock, and was afterward located at Cedar Mines, where he took charge of the coal company's store which was operating there. He was thus occupied until 1880, when he came to Dudley, this county, and became associated with the mercantile firm of Bosworth & Co., with which he was connected for the following two years. In the meantime, notwithstanding he was busily employed with the concerns of his business matters, he had kept himself well informed upon local and general political affairs, and in 1884 was nominated by the Republican party for County Clerk, to which position he was elected and re-elected in 1886, against a Democratic majority of 400 in 1884, and 200 in 1886, coming out 168 votes ahead of his ticket.

In 1879 Mr. Perdue was united in marriage with Miss Orpha J. Ramsey, in Prairie City, Iowa. Mrs. P. is the daughter of John Ramsey, of Jasper County, Iowa, and was born in Ohio, Oct. 22, 1854. They became the parents of three children—Mary K., Frank R. and Varner V. Their comfortable and homelike residence is located on Albany street, and they enjoy the friendship of a large circle of acquaintances.

Mr. Perdue belongs to the Masonic fraternity as a member of Albia Lodge No. 76; Zerubabel Chapter No. 71, and is a member of Malta Commandery of Ottumwa, No. 31. He is also a member of Wapello Lodge No. 72, K. of P., and of Mahaska Lodge No. 16, I. O. O. F. He is a gentleman of more than ordinary ability, an extensive reader, and thoroughly well informed upon all matters interesting to an intelligent and enterprising citizen.

A. J. CREAMER, a prosperous farmer and stock-raiser of Pleasant Township, and located on section 35, is a native of Coles County, Ill., born June 5, 1847, and the son of H. and Amanda (Laughlin) Creamer. (See sketch of H. Creamer on another page of this work.) The subject of this history was reared upon a farm and educated in the common schools, and after attaining to years of manhood, was united in marriage, in 1869, with Miss Samantha Bartholomew. Mrs. Creamer was born in Jefferson County, Ohio, Aug. 21, 1847, and is the daughter of A. J. and Margaret (Scott) Bartholomew. Her father was born in Maryland, and is yet living in Sheridan County, Kan. The mother, born in Ohio, died Jan. 5, 1870. Four children came to bless this union: Leona J., born Jan. 2, 1870, died Sept. 30, 1880; Winona A., born Jan. 29, 1872; Jessie A., in Washington County, Ark., June 29, 1874; Clarence M., July 8, 1878. Mr. Creamer enlisted as a Union soldier May 4, 1864, in Co. K, 47th Iowa Vol. Inf., under Capt. Norris, and was mustered out Sept. 28, 1864. The regiment did garrison duty while in the service.

Mr. Creamer is the owner of 156 acres of good land, all of which is under a high state of cultivation. He is a breeder of Short-horn cattle and other fine stock, and is considerably engaged in shipping. Mr. and Mrs. Creamer are members in good standing of the Methodist Episcopal Church. Socially our subject belongs to the G. A. R., and politically he is a Republican.

JAMES W. HOLLINGSWORTH, one of the earliest pioneers of Wapello County, was born in Virginia, July 31, 1812. He is the son of Thomas and Rachel (Jones) Hollingsworth, the former a native of Pennsylvania and the latter of Virginia, and of English and Welsh ancestry respectively. His father was a soldier in the War of 1812, and by occupation a miller. He died at the age of seventy years, while his mother lived to the ripe old age of eighty-eight.

Mr. H. left Virginia in 1835, going to Maryland, where for one year he was engaged in milling. He then went into Ohio, locating in Greene County, where he engaged in the milling business for the following eight years. Thence he came to this county and settled on section 14, of Green Township, in 1844. Since then he has been a respected resident here, and an interested witness of the wonderful transformation in the country about him.

Our subject was married, in 1839, to Miss Nancy

Maholam, a native of Ohio, and daughter of William Maholam, of Ireland. To them have been born a family of five children, all, with the exception of one, now living: Sarah became the wife of Michael Baum, of Green Township; she died in 1882, at the age of forty-two years; Thomas is a farmer of Green Township; he served his country in the late war for three years, being a member of the 36th Iowa Infantry; Frances A. is the wife of D. L. Gephart, now of Great Bend, Kan; Henry Clay is living at Centerville, where he is Principal of the High School, and James P. is managing the home farm.

Mr. Hollingsworth has been an enterprising, public-spirited man, and has served his community in various official positions. In politics he is a Greenbacker. He owns 160 acres of good land, which he has cultivated in a systematic manner, rotating his crops so that the soil is always vigorous. His farm is also well stocked with high grades of the various domesticated animals.

There were six children in the family of which our subject is a member, only two of whom are now living: Joseph is a retired miller at Great Bend, Kan.; Isaac died at the age of fifteen; our subject was next in order of birth; Mary J. died in 1885, aged sixty-two years; Catherine died at the age of eighteen, and Putnam G. was killed at the battle of Manassas. Mr. H. is a member of the Methodist Episcopal Church.

T. E. COLE is running a creamery on section 8, Richland Township, where he manufactures about 5,000 pounds of butter per month. He was born in Washington County, Ohio, Nov. 14, 1842, and is a son of William and Elizabeth Cole. His father was a stonemason by trade, which occupation he followed for many years, much of the time being spent in farming. He is now living a retired life in Kirkville, Iowa. The mother died in 1881.

The subject of this sketch came with his parents to Wapello County, in 1854, and has since continued to make this his home. He was reared upon a farm and educated in the district schools of this county. In 1863 he enlisted in Co. C, 47th Iowa Vol. Inf., served out his full time, was paid off, and discharged at Davenport, Iowa. In 1866 he was united in marriage with Miss M. J. Picken, born in Harrison County, Ohio, Aug. 11, 1840, and the daughter of Alexander and Rachel (Conaway) Picken. Her father now resides in Mahaska County, this State; her mother died in that county in 1856. Mr. and Mrs. Cole are the parents of four children: Minnie M., born May 20, 1868; Ohma L., born Jan. 17, 1870, died Feb. 22, 1875; Bruner W., born Jan. 12, 1872, and Thomas W., Dec., 25, 1874. Mr. Cole is a member of the G. A. R., and politically is a Republican.

PETER BRIDENSTINE is a retired farmer, living in Kirkville, Wapello County. He was born in Maryland, April 30, 1808, and is a son of Martin and Catherine (Springer) Bridenstine, both of whom were natives of the same State as their son. The family moved from Maryland to Ohio at a very early day, when that now populous State was a vast wilderness. The father died in Ohio at the age of eighty-four years, ten months and twelve days, and the mother died also at an advanced age. There were five children in the family, of whom Peter was the fifth son.

The early life of our subject was spent on a farm, in Maryland and Ohio, with the privilege of a few months' attendance at the common school during the winters. In 1830 he was united in marriage with Miss Catherine Mason, daughter of John and Catherine (Brandeberry) Mason, who were also among the early settlers of Ohio, and who died in that State.

In 1848, in company with his wife and six children, Peter Bridenstine left Ohio and came to Iowa, locating in Mahaska County, where he remained until 1880, when he came to Kirkville, whence, after one year he returned to his farm in Mahaska County, remained one year, and returned to Kirkville, where he has since resided. Mr. and Mrs. Bridenstine are the parents of eleven children:

John W., deceased; Martin L., married and living in Oregon; Mary C., the wife of George Nedrow, of Van Buren County, Iowa; Martha A., the wife of William Lorance, in Kansas; Mason was a soldier in the 7th Iowa Infantry, and was killed at the battle of Belmont; L. S. is married, and lives in Audubon County, Iowa; David served as a soldier in the War of the Rebellion, and was accidentally killed by a railroad engine, near Kirkville, Iowa, in 1885; Sarah E. died in infancy; Isaac W. is engaged in the coal works at Kirkville; Rachel A. is the wife of Adam Echlebarger, and lives in Nebraska. Mr. Bridenstine is the owner of five lots in Kirkville, with three dwelling-houses. He has never aspired for office, but served one term as Justice of the Peace while a citizen of Mahaska County. He, with his excellent wife, is a member of the Methodist Episcopal Church, and politically he is a Republican.

SOLOMON BLYSTONE, a successful farmer residing on section 27, Green Township, where he follows the general routine of a farmer's life, was born in Crawford County, Pa., Sept. 3, 1826. He is a son of Isaac and Elizabeth (Heckernelle) Blystone, natives of Pennsylvania. The mother departed this life Jan. 6, 1856; the father is yet living, and resides at Meadville, Pa.

The subject of this notice was reared to manhood in his native State, and there commenced his early education in the common schools. He subsequently attended Allegany College at Meadville, and, during the winters, taught school, spending his summers at farm work, until September, 1861. During that year he came to this State, and located at Point Isabell, Green Township, this county, where he worked at his trade, shoemaking, for about five years, and entertained travelers who came by the stage; he was also Postmaster at this point, and subsequently purchased his present farm of eighty acres, on which he located and where he has since continued to reside, engaged in its improvement and cultivation.

Mr. Blystone was united in marriage with Miss Louisa Peters Nov. 8, 1849. She is the daughter of Adam and Elizabeth (Bear) Peters, natives of Pennsylvania. The former died Feb. 12, 1864, and the latter in 1870. Mr. and Mrs. Blystone have become the parents of seven children, as follows: Maggie E., who lived to attain the age of maturity, became the wife of E. E. Harris, and departed this life May 19, 1871, aged twenty years; John M., born June 22, 1853, died Feb. 2, 1864; Richard, born June 22, 1855, died Jan. 6, 1861; Ida M., born Feb. 6, 1857, died Feb. 10, same year; Joseph, born Oct. 11, 1859, was fatally injured on the C., B. & Q. R. R., at Albia, May 25, 1886, while engaged in switching; his foot caught in a frog and he was thrown under a moving train, his right arm being severed from his body, and he receiving other injuries which resulted in his death; he left a wife and one child—a little boy, three months old—who are yet living, and reside at Ottumwa; William F. Blystone was born Aug. 17, 1862, and is living on the old homestead, assisting our subject in the cultivation of the same; the youngest child died in infancy unnamed.

Mr. Blystone is Democratic in politics, and has held the offices of Justice of the Peace, Assessor, Secretary and Clerk of the School Board, and Township Clerk. Religiously he is a member of the United Brethren Church, and has been a licensed preacher for that denomination upward of twelve years. Prior to that time he had been a local preacher in the Methodist Church. His good wife also belongs to the United Brethren Church.

THOMAS H. BARRITT, favorably known in Highland Township, is a native of Champaign County, Ohio, and was born in 1825. His parents were Abner and Rebecca (Diltz) Barritt, natives of Ohio and Kentucky respectively. Our subject was reared on a farm in the Buckeye State, and in 1860 turned his steps westward, and coming into Wapello County, Iowa, settled near the town of Dahlonega, upon a tract of rented land, which he cultivated for one year, and was variously engaged for the following eleven years. In the fall of 1865 he purchased eighty acres on section 17, Highland Township, where he established a permanent home and has continued to live since that time. He is engaged in general farming, and is possessed of all the conveniences for carrying on agriculture in a first-class manner.

Thomas H. Barritt was married in 1849, to Miss Mary V. Potter, a native of Pennsylvania, and the daughter of Capt. James and Matilda (McNoten) Potter, natives of the same State. Of this union there have been born seven children, of whom the record is as follows: Edgar H. is farming in Nebraska; Albert V. is an agriculturist, and lives in Gove County, Kan.; Belle became the wife of John Cole, a druggist, and they live in Dakota; Jennie married Thomas Funk, of Walnut Grove, this county; Tillie, the widow of Elmer Jones, is at home with her parents; her husband was a telegraph operator, and died July 11, 1883, at Martinsburg, Iowa; Ralph and Walter W. are farming in this county. The farm residence of Mr. Barritt is pleasing and attractive in appearance, and the family enjoy the respect of their neighbors and acquaintances in a marked degree. Mr. Barritt is possessed of a good fund of general information, and is a pleasant conversationalist.

The father of our subject served through the entire War of 1812, under Gen. Harrison, and received a Captain's commission. He spent his declining days in his native State, and died in July, 1843, at the age of seventy-five years. His faithful and affectionate wife survived him until 1874, and departed this life when eighty-four years of age. The father of Mrs. Barritt also was a Captain in the War of 1812.

HENRY ZULAUF, proprietor of the Ottumwa Woolen-Mills, is a native of Germany, and was born Jan. 6, 1851. He came to America with his parents when a child of five years old, and they proceeded directly westward into Iowa, and made their first location in Agency City. They came to Ottumwa in 1864, where our subject was employed in his uncle's mill for a brief period, later engaging in the drug business, which he afterward abandoned for the grocery trade. This he only followed for a few years, and in 1877 became interested in the woolen-mill which he now owns, and which he has operated successfully from the start.

Mr. Z. is a young man of more than ordinary ability, and has built up a business of which he may well be proud. He is held in high esteem by a large circle of friends and acquaintances, and is a member of Ottumwa Lodge No. 16, A. F. & A. M., Clinton Chapter No. 9, and Malta Commandery No. 31, K. T. He is straightforward and enterprising in his business methods, and is already becoming a leading citizen of this locality.

DR. J. B. KROUT, of Competine Township, a practicing physician and surgeon, during a residence of one year in this vicinity, has built up for himself a good reputation as an educator, an excellent business man, and a valued member of society. He is a native of Baltimore County, Md., and was born July 27, 1856, his parents being Jacob and Sarah L. (Rule) Krout, who are now residents of Reno County, Kan. The parental household of our subject included ten children, as follows: Mary A., born Oct. 16, 1848, is the widow of Rev. T. V. Dye, and resides in Morrow County, Ohio; J. N., born Aug. 24, 1850, married Mary H. Dennis, and is engaged in teaching school in Reno County, Kan.; Elizabeth E., born July 12, 1852, is the wife of L. Dennis, and a resident of Morrow County, Ohio; William H. died in infancy; J. B., our subject, was the next in order of birth; George F., born March 31, 1859, married Miss Kelly, and is carrying on farming in Morrow County, Ohio; Charles A., born March 12, 1862, is a teacher in the place above mentioned; Hiram E., born March 12, 1866, a farmer of Reno County, Kan., married Susan Henderson; Vincent D., born Feb. 28, 1869, is a teacher in Morrow County, Ohio; Ida M., born Sept. 19, 1871, resides in Reno County, Kan.

The parents of Dr. Krout removed from Maryland to Ohio in 1857, when he was an infant of a year old. He began attending school at the age of seven years, and after completing his primary studies, attended the Union School at Woodview and the High School at Mt. Gilead, Ohio. He was a bright boy and fond of his books, and at the age of eighteen years had fitted himself for a teacher, which vocation he followed until 1878. He then crossed the Mississippi, visiting Iowa and Kansas, and in the spring of 1879 returned to Iowa with a view of making it his permanent home. He settled in Keokuk County, and entered upon his former occupation as a teacher, in the meantime taking up the study of medicine and pursuing it industriously for many months, and then entering the College of Physicians and Surgeons at Keokuk, he completed the regular course, and graduated on the 2d of March, 1886. Dr. Krout commenced practice at Marysville, and although young in the profession, there is evidently a bright future before him.

The subject of our sketch was married, Aug. 15, 1880, to Miss Allie M. Dinsmore, daughter of William and Mary (Hampson) Dinsmore, of Fremont, Iowa. Mrs. Krout was born in January, 1858. Of her union with Dr. Krout there has been born one child, Emma L., the date of whose birth was May 30, 1881. Both the Doctor and Mrs. Krout are members in good standing of the Baptist Church at Marysville, and the former belongs to the A. F. & A. M.

MICHAEL BAUM, a highly respected farmer of Green Township, is the possessor of a fine estate located on section 10, and presenting a scene of thrift and prosperity as well as beauty. The farm comprises eighty acres of finely cultivated land, upon which is erected a beautiful residence, a fine barn, and all the other appliances of a first-class agriculturist.

Mr. Baum is a native of Vermilion County, Ill., and was born Nov. 11, 1834. He is a son of Benjamin and Mary (Weaver) Baum, natives of Ohio. His father was born Sept. 6, 1811, in Clermont County, and died on the 24th of March, 1866. He was a devoted member of the Methodist Episcopal Church, and a true Christian in his daily walk and conversation. The family came to this county in 1848, and two years later Benjamin Baum purchased 160 acres of land on section 15, and eighty acres on section 27, in all 240 acres, and at the time of his death his farm was finely improved and under a good state of cultivation. Upon this he had erected a comfortable residence, a good barn, and other necessary out-buildings. The mother of our subject is now living, at the age of seventy-five years, with her son-in-law, Mr. Mendenhall. To this devoted and affectionate couple were born the following children: Susan became the wife of Ivy Mendenhall, a farmer of Green Township: Michael, our subject, was the second child; John is deceased; Joseph F. is engaged in farming and milling; Mary J. married John Lawrence; D. H. is operating a sawmill, and Marion V. is in Kansas.

The subject of our sketch spent his earlier years upon the farm of his father, and attended the common schools in winter until about 1854. He then went to learn the carpenter's trade, and after serving a thorough apprenticeship, was occupied at this for the following nine years. On the 3d of January, 1860, he was married to Miss S. E., the daughter of J. W. and Nancy (Mabolam) Hollingsworth, natives respectively of Virginia and Ohio. Of this union there were four children: Virginia C., born Oct. 3, 1860; William, Nov. 10, 1862; Charles C., Jan. 7, 1868, and Nellie L., Sept. 23, 1871.

In 1863 Mr. Baum purchased a farm of eighty acres which constitutes his present homestead, and since that time has been mainly engaged in its cultivation and improvement. On the 11th of March, 1882, he met with a severe affliction in the death of his wife. Mrs. Baum was an amiable and intelligent lady, and highly respected by all who knew her for her excellent personal traits of character. She was a consistent Christian and a devoted member of the Methodist Episcopal Church. Her remains are resting in Zion churchyard.

Mr. Baum has been prominently identified with the business and industrial interests of this county since first coming here. He has taken an active interest in everything tending to its welfare and advancement, and has been the encourager and supporter of every worthy public enterprise. He is

Democratic in politics, and has held the various township offices, fulfilling the trust imposed in him faithfully and conscientiously, having the same care for the interests of his township as he does for his own.

J. C. BURNS, a prominent farmer and stock-grower of Competine Township, is finely located on section 9, and has been a resident of the Hawkeye State for the last ten years. He is the son of Henry and Cynthia (Moler) Burns, natives respectively of Ohio and Indiana. The parental household included two children: John C., our subject, born July 9, 1858, and George, born in 1860; the latter died three years later in Knox County, Ill. Henry Burns was born in 1837, and the greater part of his life was employed in farming. In 1862, after coming to Iowa, the late Civil War being then in progress, he enlisted as a soldier in the 23d Iowa Infantry, and lost his life in the war, being killed by a cannon-ball at Cumberland Gap, Tenn. After his enlistment his wife returned to Knox County, Ill., and here, with her only son (our subject), remained until the latter was a youth of nineteen years. Then, wishing to see something more of the western country, John C. Burns crossed the Mississippi and came into Iowa, arriving in Wapello County on the 7th of November, 1875. He and his step-brother embarked in the stock business for the year following, after which our subject engaged in farming.

Mr. Burns was united in marriage, Jan. 30, 1879, with Miss Ella Harris, the daughter of Joseph and Orpha J. (Callom) Harris, who were both natives of Indiana. Mrs. Burns was born Sept. 27, 1860, in Wapello County, and after her marriage with our subject they located upon a tract of prairie land, where Mr. B. had erected a good frame house, and other necessary farm buildings. They became the parents of three children: Harry E., born Dec. 3, 1880; Ralph T., Nov. 12, 1882, and Freddie, born July 8, 1885, and died Feb. 8, 1886. The mother of Mr. Burns died at Knoxville, Ill., Dec. 20, 1886. The little household of our subject is surrounded by all the comforts of life, and the homestead presents a picture which may well be envied by many who have larger possessions and more brilliant prospects. Since purchasing his farm Mr. Burns has been engaged in the breeding of Jersey cattle, and has met with fine success. In 1884, at the Keokuk County Fair, he took the first prize on all classes and sweepstakes, and first prize on the best cow of any age or breed. In Mahaska County he took the three first prizes and two second, with the three herds in competition. In Wapello County, three first prizes and three second, also with three herds in competition, and in Jefferson County the same.

Mr. Burns and his wife are connected with the Baptist Church, and in politics our subject is a stanch Republican. He has held various offices in his township, and is highly esteemed by his fellow-citizens as a straightforward business man and a skillful and intelligent agriculturist.

WILLIAM BROWNFIELD, M. D., a resident of Wapello County since 1854, first settled in Ashland, soon after coming into Iowa. He is a native of Fayette County, Pa., born in 1820, and a son of Zedock and Rebecca (Marker) Brownfield, natives of Pennsylvania, his father being a tanner by occupation. The mother died when her son, our subject, was a small boy, in 1828.

Dr. Brownfield commenced life a poor boy, but with a rich fund of determination and energy. At the age of twenty-one years, after having served a thorough apprenticeship as a farmer's boy, he left his native State and went to Greensburg, Decatur Co., Ind., where he lived until August, 1854, occupied mostly in painting. He had already decided upon the practice of medicine, and for some time previously had employed his leisure time in study. From Greensburg, Ind., he removed to Iowa, and first engaged in the practice of his profession at Ashland, after which he became a resident of Eldon. Since coming to this vicinity Dr. Brownfield has been a prominent citizen and highly esteemed, not only for his straightforward business methods but his many excellent traits of character. He has been a Justice of the Peace for eight years, was a member of the School Board for several years, and has served as City Councilman. The Doctor owns fifty acres of land in this county, and also valuable real estate in Eldon.

Dr. Brownfield was married, March 29, 1848, to Miss Mary Whitlaw, of Madison County, Ky., daughter of John and Mary (Byrum) Whitlaw, natives of North Carolina. Of this union there were born eight children, three only of whom are living: Rebecca R., born Feb. 23, 1849, became the wife of Henry Springer, and lives in Ottumwa; John T., born Aug. 19, 1851, died in 1855; Mary E., the wife of Aaron A. Cain, was born March 22, 1853, and is living in the Indian Territory; Willie E., born Jan. 24, 1858, is a locomotive engineer, and makes his home with his parents. Dr. B. is connected with the A. F. & A. M. and the I. O. O. F.

The maternal grandfather of Mrs. Brownfield was a soldier of the Revolutionary War, as were also his seven sons, and her paternal grandfather was a soldier in the War of 1812.

A. N. CAIN, a farmer and stock-grower of Washington Township, owns and occupies a fine homestead on section 11, and is successful in his agricultural and business operations. He was born in Guilford County, N. C., Jan. 8, 1831, and is a son of Morrison and Rhoda (Satterfield) Cain, both of whom are natives of North Carolina. In 1832 his parents moved to Indiana, where they remained till May, 1854, when they came to Kirkville, Wapello County, where his mother died in 1857, and his father in 1864.

The subject of this sketch came to Wapello County in 1852, where he has since continued to reside. In 1856 he married Ruth B. Goff, who was born May 5, 1835, in Pennsylvania, and is the daughter of Peter and Rebecca (Brownfield) Goff, both natives of the same State. Her parents moved to Iowa in 1849. Her mother died in 1875 and her father in 1879. Mr. and Mrs. Cain became the parents of six children, as follows: Ella B., born Aug. 7, 1857, is the wife of Marshall M. Whited, living in Kansas; Mary M., born Aug. 3, 1863, is the wife of William M. Evans, living in Kansas; Grace L. was born June 25, 1867; Alvesta N., April 20, 1875. The deceased are George P., who was born April 14, 1859, and died June 11 of the same year, and Rhoda I., born Sept. 26, 1872, and died Sept. 18, 1873. They have two adopted sons: Charles W. Pitman, who became an inmate of the household at the age of five years, and who remained with them until twenty-one, is now living in Kansas; the other is Walter Springer.

The homestead of our subject consists of 250 acres of good land, finely cultivated, and with a fine set of frame buildings. He is a good citizen in all respects, a member of the Baptist Church (as is also Mrs. Cain), and belongs to the I. O. O. F. Politically he uniformly casts his vote in support of the principles of the Republican party.

J. V. JONES, a highly respected farmer of Adams Township, is pleasantly located on section 5, and engaged in the ordinary pursuits of agriculture. His farm estate consists of 111 acres, upon which he has erected a comfortable residence, a good barn and all the necessary out-buildings, and possesses all the machinery and equipments of a first-class agriculturist.

The subject of our sketch is a native of Indiana, and was born in Montgomery County on the 5th of July, 1836. He is the son of J. B. and Rebecca (Carman) Jones, natives respectively of Virginia and Kentucky. They removed from Indiana in 1856, when their son, our subject, was a young man of twenty years, and crossing the Mississippi came into Wapello County, where the father purchased 200 acres of good land in Adams Township. The journey was made overland with teams and occupied twenty-one days. The father of our subject proceeded to the improvement and cultivation of his purchase and in due time had established a comfortable home, upon which the parents now reside.

The subject of this sketch remained under the home roof until he attained his majority, having received his education in the subscription schools of his native State. His father had been one of the pioneer settlers of Indiana, and upon coming to this section was amply fitted for the duties which subsequently devolved upon him in the young State of Iowa, and transmitted to his son those qualities which have to-day constituted one of the valued citizens of the community. Young Jones, at the time of attaining his majority, had a good knowledge of farming pursuits, and had decided upon these as his future occupation in life, and had selected his future location at the time of his marriage. This latter interesting event in the life of our subject occurred on the 4th of January, 1866, the maiden of his choice being Miss Barsheba Draper, the daughter of J. W. and Margaret (Ralston) Draper, both natives of Virginia. They subsequently removed to Indiana, and Mrs. Jones was born in Carroll County, that State, on the 23d of October, 1838. Seven years later her parents crossed the Mississippi and came into Wapello County, Iowa, bringing their family with them.

Mr. and Mrs. Jones have become the parents of three children: John B. was born Oct. 11, 1866, and died Oct. 8, 1869; his remains are buried in the cemetery near Blakesburg; Robert Lee was born March 7, 1869, and Emma T., Sept. 12, 1878. Mr. and Mrs. Jones are members in good standing of the Christian Church, and politically our subject is a liberal Democrat. He has held the various township offices within the gift of his fellow-citizens, and in all respects is a useful member of the community.

J. P. HOLLINGSWORTH. Among the very few active business men of to-day, who are natives of this county, is our subject, born April 9, 1857. His father, James Hollingsworth, is represented elsewhere in this volume. J. P. was united in marriage, Nov. 3, 1880, to Miss Laura Alice Carson, also a native of this county. Her father, John A. Carson, was an early settler of this county, and lived here until his death, which occurred in 1885, at the age of fifty-nine years. He was a farmer, and with his wife, a respected member of the Methodist Episcopal Church. The latter died here in 1872, at the age of fifty. They were the parents of the following eight children: Carry was a soldier in the late war, serving three years as a member of the 26th Iowa Infantry; Andrew J. is living in Kansas; Sarah is the wife of John Rupe, of Kansas; Mary, who is living in the same place, is the wife of James Rupe; Richard is living in Ottumwa; John in Kansas; Laura Alice is the wife of our subject; Elizabeth is the wife of Edward Swiggard.

Mr. and Mrs. Hollingsworth are the parents of two children, whom they have named Fred Austin and Edward J. In politics Mr. H. is a Republican, and as a citizen is held in high esteem.

RICHARD BUTCHER, a wealthy and prominent business man of Eddyville, has been a resident of this locality since the spring of 1843, and has occupied a prominent position among the business and industrial interests of Wapello County. Mr. B. is an Englishman by birth and parentage, and first opened his eyes to the light in 1818. His parents were John and Margaret (Thompson) Butcher, natives respectively of Ireland and Scotland, and they transmitted to their son the excellent and estimable qualities of both races in a marked degree. Being ambitious for their future and not satisfied with their condition or their prospects in their own country, they resolved to emigrate to the New World, and accordingly in 1821 set sail for the United States. They first settled in Belmont County, Ohio, and here young Richard at an early age engaged as clerk in a store at St. Clairsville, where he remained until he was nineteen years old.

Our subject then went to Wheeling, W. Va., where he was employed as a dry-goods clerk until 1840. He then set his face to the farther West, and going into Illinois located in Vermont, Fulton County, where he engaged at chopping cord-wood for two years following. He then crossed the Father of Waters, having traveled on foot until he reached the Eastern bank of the Mississippi, and coming into Iowa located in Eddyville and engaged as a clerk for J. P. Eddy, who had formerly been an Indian trader but was then carrying on general merchandising. Mr. Butcher continued with the latter for one year and then went into business for himself, which he has continued until the present time. He has been uniformly prosperous in his undertakings and has accumulated valuable property. He owns 1,200 acres of land in this county and is possessed of considerable real estate within the city limits of Eddyville. At the present time he is quite extensively engaged in the purchase and shipping of wool, which yields him a handsome income.

The subject of our sketch is Democratic in politics and uniformly casts his vote in support of the principles of that party. He is credited with having fulfilled all the obligations of a good citizen with perhaps one exception, and that is that he has never married. He is the oldest business man in the county, having been established in trade for a period of forty-four years, and during that time has built up for himself an enviable reputation as an honest man and a public-spirited and enterprising member of the community.

The father of our subject departed this life at the age of thirty-three years in Belmont County, Ohio. He belonged to the laboring classes, and during the varied experiences of an industrious and useful life, earned for himself an honest name—all the inheritance which he was able to leave to his children. His death occurred in about 1825, and that of the mother in about 1834. Their family consisted of five children, of whom the subject of our sketch was the eldest born, and one is deceased. Of those living, Sarah became the wife of George Neff of Belmont County, Ohio; William is occupied in farming pursuits in California; John died in about 1880, near Red Rock, Iowa, and Thompson still lives in Belmont County, Ohio.

TIMOTHY RIORDAN, a Justice of the Peace of Ottumwa, comes of starch, warm-hearted Irish ancestry and parentage, and was born in the city of Cork, Ireland, on the 6th of January, 1829. He was reared and educated in his native city, and at the early age of fourteen years made up his mind to emigrate to America. He accordingly set sail in 1843, and after a prosperous voyage landed at New Orleans, whence he proceeded to Cincinnati, and thereafter traveled over a large portion of the State of Ohio. He then determined to cross the Mississippi and see what there was for him in the country beyond, and in 1855 found himself in the then small village of Ottumwa, where he decided to locate until he could find something that suited him better. He was wide-awake and ambitious, and had improved his opportunities for study and observation, and soon after coming here secured a position as check clerk for the C., B. & Q. R. R. Co., which position he occupied for several years, and in due time was appointed Justice of the Peace, the duties of which office he is fulfilling in a manner creditable to himself and satisfactory to all concerned.

In 1854, during his residence in Ohio, Mr. Riordan was married to Miss Hannah Levering, a native of his own country, and of their union there have been born seven children, all living, and named as follows: Mollie, Daniel J., Susan and Margaret (twins), James A., John T. and Allen B. Mr. Riordan is Republican in politics, and since coming to Wapello County has kept himself well posted upon all public matters, and by his courteous manner and intelligence has secured a large circle of friends and well-wishers.

JAMES J. BOX, M. D., a prominent and successful physician of Eldon, Iowa, came to this vicinity in 1883, and although his residence here has been comparatively brief, he has fully established himself in the confidence and respect of his fellow-citizens. He is a close and intelligent student, and by diligent attention to his calling, has already secured a good practice with a bright outlook for the future.

Dr. Box is a native of Morgan County, Ill., and the son of John and Delilah (Bratton) Box, natives respectively of Kentucky and North Carolina. They emigrated to Morgan County, Ill., in 1820, while Illinois was yet a Territory, and settled upon a claim of unimproved land, which they industriously cultivated, and upon which they remained for the following thirteen years. John Box then "pulled up stakes," and setting his face westward, crossed the Mississippi with his family into the portion of Iowa which then belonged to the Territory of Wisconsin. They located one and a half miles north of the present site of Ft. Madison, and the father of our subject became prominent in the public affairs of this section, and was a member of the Territorial Legislature which convened at Belmont, Wis. He served one term, when Iowa was stricken off as the Blackhawk Purchase, and in 1838 was elected to the Territorial Assembly of Iowa, at its first session, serving until 1840. He introduced the bill for the division of Lee County, which then embraced an area equal to five counties, and was apportioned into Des Moines, Lee, Van Buren, Henry, Jefferson and Louisa. At the expiration of his last term of office, John Box engaged in mercantile business at Ft. Madison for a number of years, and then moved back upon the old farm and remained there until 1852. He then resumed business as a merchant for eight years following, and then retired to Floris, Davis County, where he spent the remainder of his life, his decease occurring Feb. 30, 1874. He was a straightforward business man, honorable and upright in his transactions, a member in good standing of the Christian Church, and contributed liberally of his means for the promotion of education, temperance and religion.

The subject of our biography was reared upon the farm, and remained with his parents until he was a young man twenty-three years of age, and had decided upon his profession in life. He attended the first school taught in Iowa and afterward went to Ft. Madison, and studied medicine in the office and under the instruction of Drs. Eads and Baker, with whom he remained three years. He commenced the practice of his profession at Drakesville, Davis Co., Iowa, and remained there until the fall of 1858, when he removed to Floris, and pursued his practice there until the 15th of August, 1883, at which time he came to Eldon, where he has since remained. Dr. Box started out in life without financial assistance, and the handsome property of which he is now the owner at Floris has been accumulated solely by the exercise of the talents which nature bestowed upon him, and his heritage of industry and determination.

Dr. Box was married, Dec. 7, 1852, to Miss Eva A. Bryson, a native of Kentucky, and they have become the parents of seven children, the record of whom is as follows: The eldest son, J. C. Box, M. D., is a practicing physician at Floris, Davis County; William A. is at Eldon; Cordelia A. died at the age of sixteen months; Emma became the wife of F. E. Truax, of Drakesville; Charlie E. is a dentist of Medicine Lodge, Kan.; Marquis D. and Mary Belle are at home. The Doctor and his wife are members in good standing of the Christian Church. They occupy a handsome home in Eldon which is the resort of the cultured people of the city. Dr. Box is Democratic in politics, and socially belongs to the I. O. O. F.

HARRY C. PETERS, a successful and efficient druggist of Ottumwa, Iowa, is a native of Zanesville, Ohio, and first opened his eyes to the light on the 23d day of October, 1856. He is the son of Charles C. and Mary J. (Oden) Peters, natives respectively of Ohio and Virginia. They were married in Zanesville, Ohio, on the 21st of December, 1855. The father of our subject was a paymaster of the Baltimore & Ohio Railroad in an early day, and his grandfather, John Peters, a prominent citizen of Zanesville, and a banker. Charles C. Peters left Ohio in 1859 and came to Ottumwa, Iowa, where he purchased a large tract of land in Center Township and opened up a farm. In 1863 he became interested in the dry-goods trade, and operated as a member of the firm of Devin & Peters, which subsequently became Peters & Co., Mr. D. having sold his interest. Five years later he lost heavily by the fire of 1868, but recovering himself continued business up to 1872. Three years later he went to Keokuk and associated himself with the firm of R. F. Bower & Co., with whom he still remains. He served for several years as Alderman of the Fourth Ward, being elected on the Republican ticket.

The household of Charles C. Peters included six children, two sons and four daughters, five of whom are living, the record being as follows: Harry C., of our sketch, is the eldest; Kate M. became the wife of R. N. Morrell, of Ottumwa; Maggie

W.; Annie W. and Fannie D. (twins) are at home. The faithful and affectionate wife and mother departed this life on the 20th of September, 1875. She was a most estimable Christian lady, and highly respected in the community where she lived. She was a devoted member of the Methodist Episcopal Church, and in her daily walk and conversation lived up to the principles of her religion.

Harry C. Peters received his early education in the Hawkeye State, and remained under the parental roof until he had attained to years of manhood. He was united in marriage with Emma Boulton on the 29th of December, 1880. Mrs. Peters is a daughter of G. W. Boulton, of Ottumwa, and was born in Green Bush, N. Y., Jan. 28' 1860. Of this union one child has been born, George Boulton, now deceased.

Mr. Peters is a young man of industry and enterprise, and takes an active interest in everything pertaining to the welfare of his county and community. While attending strictly to his business affairs, he still finds time to encourage and support the various worthy enterprises of this locality to which his attention may be called. His good business talents are well known and appreciated, and he is looked upon as one of the future leading business men and citizens of Wapello County.

PETER UTECHT, deceased, was a highly respected resident of Ottumwa. He located in this city as early as the year 1858, and remained a resident here until the date of his death, in 1884. He was a native of the Empire of Germany, and was born in 1834. He received careful parental training and grew to manhood in his native country. At the age of twenty years he decided to seek his fortune in the New World, and accordingly set sail from the "Faderland," landing in New York City on the 30th of April, 1854. From there he proceeded to Buffalo, and in 1856 went to Peoria, Ill. He sojourned there but a short time, subsequently visiting Leavenworth, Kan., and in 1858 retraced his steps northeastward into Wapello County, Iowa. Being pleased with this locality he concluded to make it his home, and secured employment as clerk in the drug-store of Mr. John Pomroy, with whom he remained for three years. He was industrious and economical in his habits, and saved his money, so that at the expiration of this time he was prepared to embark in business for himself. He was prospered in his undertaking, and pursued it for a period of twenty-three years and up to the time of his death.

Mr. Utecht was married in Eddyville, Iowa, Dec. 24, 1863, to Miss Mary I. Ryan, of Jefferson County, Ohio. Mrs. U. was the daughter of John and Sarah J. Ryan, and was born March 19, 1846. Her father was a native of Baltimore, Md., and her mother of Ohio. The parental household consisted of six children, as follows: Carrie A. is the wife of Frank Flanders, of Ottumwa; the others, at home, are Willie E., Laura A., Mamie B., Orra, Maude and Byron C.

In politics Mr. U. was independent in thought and action, and cast his influence in support of those whom he believed to be the best men, irrespective of party. He was a member of the Masonic fraternity, and his funeral services were conducted with the impressive ceremonies of that order. He was a valued citizen of this community, and his name is held in kindly remembrance.

Mrs. Mary Utecht, the widow of our subject, is a highly respected lady, and has wisely kept her little household together, training her children in those principles which were the groundwork of their father's good name and the secret by which he gained the respect and esteem of all who knew him.

The lithographic portrait of Mr. Utecht, on another page, we trust will be recognized as a faithful likeness of a worthy and honored citizen.

AMOS O. BILBY, a pioneer resident of the Hawkeye State, crossed the Mississippi in 1847, prepared with his brother pioneers to meet and overcome the difficulties always incident to the opening up of a new section of country. The time had been brief since Iowa had been transformed from a Territory into a State, and log cabins were still more plentiful than frame dwellings. One of the first duties of our subject after coming here was the erection of this style of dwelling upon his tract of eighty acres of unimproved land, and after this was accomplished he vigorously set about the tilling of the soil. He was a man of great industry and perseverance, and his possessions to-day are indicative of the success which followed his efforts. He is now pleasantly located on section 35, in Keokuk Township, and is engaged in the joint operations of farming and stock-raising.

Mr. Bilby was born in Hunterdon County, N. J., Aug. 19, 1814, and was the son of Peter and Mary (Belles) Bilby, both also natives of New Jersey. When their son was a little lad six years old they emigrated to Indiana, and locating in Franklin County, lived there until 1829. They then removed into Shelby County, the same State, and our subject remained with his parents until he attained to years of manhood. In 1834, at the age of twenty years, he was married to Miss Malinda J., the daughter of John and Nancy (Shipp) Hoagland, of Kentucky. The wedding occurred on the 31st day of October, and soon afterward Mr. B. entered a small farm in Shelby County, Ind., which they occupied until 1847. It was in about its original condition when Mr. Bilby took possession of it, and after making valuable improvements he sold it to good advantage and then started for the far West. His intended location was Monroe County, Iowa, but having an old friend in Wapello County, he came here for a visit, and being pleased with the outlook in this vicinity decided to locate here. He then returned to Indiana after his family, and after a short delay started with them for their new home. The trip occupied three weeks' time, and they made their home that winter with an old friend, Hiram Lewis. In the meantime his wife was taken ill and remained so until July of the following year. After her recovery Mr. Bilby entered eighty acres of unimproved land in Keokuk Township, and built a log cabin into which they removed, and he commenced the improvement and cultivation of his farm. They occupied this humble home until 1854, when our subject built a more pretentious residence of hewed logs, 18x24 feet in dimensions; he now feeds his team from a corn-crib built of the logs which formed a part of the first cabin. Later, in 1862, Mr. B. put up a good frame dwelling, two stories in height, 18x32 feet in dimensions. He has always been a wide-awake business man, ready to avail himself of any opportunity for turning an honest penny, and in 1850, finding that he had a little spare time on his hands, he engaged in running a freight line from Keokuk to Ottumwa, thus securing cheap transportation for his own farm produce and becoming of material assistance to his neighbors.

The homestead of Mr. Bilby includes 160 acres of finely improved land, with a tasteful and substantial residence, a good barn, and all other necessary buildings required by a first-class agriculturist. The household circle of our subject and his wife has been completed by the birth of eleven children, the record of whom is as follows: George W. is a ranchman near Pueblo, Col.; John F., a resident of Appanoose County, Iowa, and a graduate of the Keokuk and St. Joseph Medical Colleges, is now a practicing physician; Peter M., M. D., is a graduate of the Keokuk College of Physicians and Surgeons, and is engaged in the practice of his profession at Floris, Iowa; Caroline M. died Jan. 12, 1866, and her remains were buried in Peden Cemetery, Davis County, Iowa; Francis M. died June 15, 1850; Nancy L., born March 8, 1855, is the wife of Sherman Ewing, and resides on a farm in Graham County, Kan.; Amos M., M. D., a graduate of the Medical College of Iowa, is a practicing physician of Mitchell, Dak.; Mary I., born Feb. 12, 1857, died in infancy; Arene J. was born Dec. 13, 1858, and became the wife of Albert T. Brooks; they are now living on the old homestead; Eliza L. was born Feb. 3, 1862, and married James A. Johnson, a farmer of Cowley County, Kan.; one child died in infancy unnamed. The faithful and affectionate wife, and the devoted mother of these children, after remaining the companion of her husband for a period of forty-five years and seventeen days, departed from the scenes of earth on the 17th of November, 1879. She was a devoted member of the Baptist Church, with which she became connected in 1884, but after coming to Iowa cast her lot with the Methodists. Mr. B. is also a member of the Methodist Episcopal Church, of which he has been Steward, Class-Leader and Sunday-school teacher for thirty years.

Since coming to the Hawkeye State Mr. Bilby has been intimately identified with its industrial and agricultural interests. He has been the friend and supporter of education, religion and morality, and organized the first public school in this district in 1849. Six of his eight children have been teachers. They are possessed of excellent educations and are more than ordinarily intelligent. Mr. B. has held the various offices of trust in his township, and politically is a firm supporter of the principles of the Democratic party. A handsome lithographic portrait of Mr. Bilby is shown on another page.

THEOPHILUS BLAKE, Sr., deceased, one of the pioneer settlers of the Hawkeye State, came to this county in the spring of 1845, and entered a claim upon which the town of Blakesburg now stands, of which town he was the founder and which was named after him. When first coming here he judged that the location would be favorable for a village, and very soon afterward began marking off town lots from his purchase and reserved the balance for a farm. He built the first storehouse in this section, and was the leader in every measure adopted for its welfare and advancement. As the settlers came in and the little colony began to assume the proportions of a village, the township organization was effected and Mr. Blake was elected Justice of the Peace, which office he held for several years.

Theophilus Blake, Sr., was born in Vermont, in 1799, where he was reared and received his early education. After arriving at manhood he went to Canada, and was there married to Miss Mary Adams, a native of the Dominion and one year her husband's junior. After marriage they moved to Auburn, N. Y., and in 1836 turned their faces still further westward, going to Licking County, Ohio, whence, nine years later, they came to Iowa, the year before it was admitted into the Union as a State. This trip was made overland with teams. A great amount of rain fell during this season and they were six weeks in making the journey. Of their subsequent settlement we have spoken in the previous paragraph. They became the parents of eleven children, and were accompanied by eight olive branches on their journey to Iowa: Frank is now a resident of Shelby County, Iowa; Charlotte and Mary are deceased; Samuel lives in Missouri; Theophilus in this county; William H., during the late war, enlisted in the 3d Iowa Cavalry, Co. K., serving four years, and after the close of the war died from the hardships and exposure which he had encountered while in the service; Marcia lives in Shelby County, Iowa; James enlisted in the 2d Iowa Infantry, Co. K, and was killed at Ft. Donelson. Mr. and Mrs. Blake were both members of the Baptist Church, highly esteemed in this community, and passed their declining years in the enjoyment of the esteem and confidence of those friends whom they had gathered around them in the years when hardship, toil and privation had formed between them a common bond of sympathy. Theophilus Blake, Sr., departed this life in September, 1864; the mother survived her husband for sixteen years and died Feb. 1, 1880.

Theophilus Blake, Jr., son of the foregoing, and a resident of this county, was born in Licking County, Ohio, on the 29th day of October, 1836. He was a lad nine years old when his parents came overland to Iowa, and his early education, begun in Ohio, was completed in the pioneer log schoolhouse of Iowa. He remained under the parental roof until his marriage to Miss Margaret Thompson, which took place May 15, 1859. Mrs. Margaret Blake was born in Indiana, Jan. 2, 1838. By her marriage with our subject she became the mother of eight children, three of whom are now deceased. Those living are—Olive, Bertha, Sada, Lewis and Moses.

Mr. Blake, with his father, was also a pioneer settler of Wapello County, and distinctly remembers many of the incidents during their long and tedious journey hither from Ohio, the wild and desolate appearance of the uncultivated prairie, and the entire lack of conveniences and comforts which the people of the present day uniformly demand. He recalls the time when the embryo town of Blakesburg was platted and the journeys to mill at Bonaparte, Van Buren County, sixty-five miles away.

At one time this journey was performed by one of his brothers who, on account of the weather and other incidents, was detained for three weeks, thirteen days of which the family had no bread or bacon, the latter being considered almost indispensable to the health of the pioneer family. In 1851, which was a very wet season, the mills were washed away. A man in their vicinity, named Holliday, was the possessor of a hand-mill, and the people of this section were obliged for some time to depend upon this meager substitute, which ground very slowly, and some times ten or fifteen men would be standing and waiting their turn at the mill.

Mr. Blake with his brothers and sisters were carefully trained to habits of industry and principles of honor, and in their worthy lives are doing full credit to the teachings of their excellent parents.

BENJAMIN JAMES BOULTON, late of the firm of Boulton Bros., wholesale confectioners of Ottumwa, Iowa, was born in Great Yarmouth, county of Norfolk, England, on the 12th of March, 1831. He is the son of Benjamin and Mary (Ward) Boulton, natives of the same country. He remained under the parental roof until the age of nineteen years, receiving what education he could by attendance at the common schools of his native town until eleven years old, at which time he was bound out to learn the trade of a baker and confectioner, and served a term of six years. He received the munificent salary of one shilling per week, for the first two years, and his wages were then increased to fifty cents a week. He had been reared to habits of economy, and disbursed his money in the most judicious manner possible, much of it being devoted to the purchase of good and instructive books, whereby he might become better fitted to cope with the business world and become a man among his fellows.

At the age of twenty years, not being satisfied with his condition or his prospects in his own country, young Boulton determined to emigrate to America. He accordingly set sail, and in August, 1851, found himself walking the streets of New York City. His stay there was comparatively brief, and he proceeded to Canandaigua via Albany, where he found employment in a bakery, and remained steadily at one place until 1854, when he purchased an interest in the business. He assisted in operating this, however, only one year, going, in 1855, to Dubuque, Iowa, where he set up in business for himself, and continued there for the following four years. He was not quite satisfied with this place as a permanent location, chiefly on account of stringent times, brought on by the panic of 1857, and in 1859 started out to see something more of the Hawkeye State. Coming into Ottumwa he at once concluded that he could not do better, and very soon afterward made arrangements to engage here in the wholesale bakery business. There was at that time a good field for an energetic man, and he started out with encouraging prospects, Ottumwa then being the terminus of the C., B. & Q. R. R., and consequently a large demand for this kind of goods.

Mr. Boulton put in the first cracker machine ever operated in this city, in 1861. It was quite a novelty, and was well patronized. He also manufactured the first candy and fancy goods of that line made in Ottumwa. Retail dealers from all points in that vicinity came after loads of crackers and other bakery goods, and Mr. B. soon found himself on the high road to a competency. He was straightforward and upright in his business transactions, courteous in his demeanor toward his patrons, prompt to meet obligations, and in due time received ample reward for the toils and difficulties of his earlier years. He came to this country a poor boy, comparatively without friends, and commenced business without pecuniary assistance. He is now the possessor of a handsome property, and occupies a leading position among the citizens and business men of Ottumwa. In politics he is a Republican, and socially is a member of Laramie Lodge No. 230, I. O. O. F. He has passed all the chairs, and was elected Deputy Grand Master in 1864–65. He has been an Alderman in the Fourth Ward of the city. The family attends the Episcopal Church.

The marriage of Benjamin James Boulton and Miss Rachel Belle Hobbs was celebrated April 9,

1861, in Ottumwa. Mrs. B. is a native of Indiana, and was born Feb. 21, 1845. She is of Scotch parentage and ancestry, and a daughter of William Hobbs, who came to this county before the War of 1812, and enlisted as a soldier with the Federal forces.

Of the union of Mr. and Mrs. Boulton there have been seven children, whose record is as follows: Ettie Mary, born Oct. 19, 1862, died Dec. 20, 1866; James H. was born Nov. 6, 1865; George Loren, Dec. 18, 1867; Laura, Oct. 25, 1869; Annie, Dec. 14, 1872; Esther L., Sept. 6, 1875, and Lela, Aug. 21, 1881. The family residence is pleasantly located, and is the resort of the cultured people of Ottumwa.

CHARLES G. LEWIS, M. D., is numbered among the older physicians of Ottumwa. He is a native of Ohio, born in Champaign County, Oct. 25, 1832. His father, George Lewis, was a native of Virginia, and a farmer by occupation; he died in Ottumwa in the seventy-fifth year of his age. His mother, Sophia (Wooley) Lewis, was a native of New Jersey; she also died in Ottumwa, at the age of seventy-six years. There were seven children in the parental family, four of whom are now living: John F. and C. G., of Ottumwa; Martha, now the wife of David W. Warner, of Van Buren County, and George M., who also resides in the latter-named county.

Charles G. Lewis passed his early life on a farm, and received his literary education in the common schools. In 1840, when but eight years of age, he came to Iowa with the family, and lived with them in Van Buren County. At the age of seventeen years he commenced reading medicine, with Dr. P. Walker as preceptor. He afterward attended the medical department of the Iowa State University, from which he graduated in 1859, after which he located at Libertyville, Jefferson County, remaining there until 1862, when he was commississioned Assistant Surgeon of the 30th Iowa Infantry and served about six months, when he was compelled to resign his commission on account of hemorrhage of the lungs. Returning to Libertyville, he continued in practice there until 1866, when he came to Ottumwa, where he has since continued to reside, giving attention to the practice of his profession.

Dr. Lewis has been twice married; first, in 1860, to Maria C. Walker, daughter of Dr. P. Walker, his preceptor. She died in 1861, and on the 10th of September, 1869, the Doctor married Anna Ball, daughter of Joseph and Margaret Ball. She was born in Virginia in 1840, but at the date of her marriage was residing in Jefferson County, Iowa. By this union two children have been born—Fred Arthur and Charles B.

The Doctor is a member of the Wapello County Medical Society, of which he has served as President and Secretary. He is also a member of the Des Moines Valley Medical Society, the Iowa State Medical Society, and the American Medical Society. Dr. Lewis is regarded by the profession and the people at large as a safe physician. Politically he is a stanch Republican, but takes no very active part in political affairs, his time being given to the practice of his profession.

JOSEPH SLOAN, agent for the C., M. & St. P. and W. St. L. & P. R. R., and residing at Ottumwa, was born in Will County, Ill., on the 7th day of July, 1844. There he grew to manhood and received his primary education. In 1866 Mr. Sloan engaged in the railroad business, becoming an employe of the Chicago & Alton Railroad, eight months, as night operator at Pontiac. He remained with that company eight years, as agent, and then hired his services to the company with whom he is at present engaged, and has been in their employ since that time. Mr. Sloan was married, in 1873, at Alton, Ill. Socially he is a member of the G. A. R., and also of the Masonic fraternity.

G. M. COWGER, M. D., one of the well-known and highly esteemed professional gentlemen of Wapello County, resides at Marysville. He is a native of Rush County, Ind., where he was born Dec. 10, 1837. His parents, J. D. and Sarah

(Downey) Cowger, were natives of Ohio and Kentucky respectively. To them were born a family of nine children, five of whom were sons. The father died Aug. 12, 1885, and his remains were interred at Marysville. The mother is still living, and although at the age of seventy-seven is enjoying good health.

Dr. Cowger was reared principally on a farm in this county, where his father moved in 1846. At that time he purchased 320 acres of raw prairie land, upon which he moved and began its improvement. This, of course, required hard work by every member of the family. There are three brothers and four sisters of his father's family now living: D. H. is a farmer, living in Washington County, Kan.; Henry lives in Competine Township, and is also engaged in farming; Sarah is married, and lives in this county; Lucinda, now Mrs. Bradon, lives in Keokuk County, this State; Amanda is now the wife of Charles Thompson, and lives in Norton County, Kan., and Priscilla, now Mrs. Houdyshell, lives in Rice County, Kan.

During the trying days of our country's peril, Dr. Cowger enlisted in her defense. He was a member of Co. E, 17th Iowa Vol. Inf. The first engagement was at Iuka, the next at Ft. Gibson, Miss., and the next at Raymond, the same State, being with Grant in his famous battles on his way to Vicksburg. May 14, 1863, he took part in the engagement at Jackson, Miss., where he was wounded in the left hip, which was so severe as to require the amputation of the left leg, above the knee, which was done on the morning of the 15th, and in the afternoon of the same day the Confederates captured the city of Jackson. He was thus taken prisoner, and remained in charge of the enemy there for four weeks. He was then put in a stock car with others, taken to Richmond, Va., and consigned to old Libby Prison, a place second in its inhuman treatment only to Andersonville. He remained there for two months, when he was exchanged and sent to Annapolis, Md., and there remained until the 22d of December, 1863, when he was discharged and sent to his home in Wapello County.

After his return home our subject began the study of medicine, since which time he has been greatly devoted to his profession, and is regarded as one of its most worthy members. He studied under Dr. E. H. Downey, of Jefferson County, Iowa, for two years, but has always been quite a student, trying to make the most of his honored profession. He is a member of the Baptist Church, of the I. O. O. F., and, as might be expected, of the G. A. R.

Dec. 11, 1873, Dr. Cowger and Rebecca Goodman were united in marriage. To them have been born three children, namely: Argolia, who was born Feb. 28, 1875; Chester, Sept. 14, 1878, and Nellie, March 27, 1884.

A. F. JOHNSON is successfully engaged in farming and stock-raising on section 32, Polk Township, where he has established a comfortable homestead, and is receiving as the reward of industry and economy the good things of this life, which he has fairly earned. Our subject is a native of Scandinavia, and was born in Sweden, on the 24th of April, 1826, his parents being John P. and Annie (Auguston) Johnson. The father died in his native land at the age of fifty-three years, and the mother at the age of seventy-five, also in the country of her birth. They were the parents of five children—Christina, John A., E. P., Eva and A. F.—all of whom are in Sweden except the subject of our sketch.

In 1868, Mr. Johnson, having then become the father of a family, was not satisfied with his condition or his prospects in his native land, and resolved to emigrate to the New World. He was a bookbinder by trade, and had followed this since he was a boy of thirteen years old until he left his native Sweden. In the meantime he was married, in 1861, to Miss Louise Jenson, also a native of Sweden, born Nov. 26, 1825, and the daughter of Nels and Sisley Jenson. Of their union there were two children: A. T., born Jan. 5, 1862, and Ernst Ludwig, Jan. 5, 1865. They sailed from the port of Stockholm on the 11th of May, 1868, and landed at Castle Garden, New York City, on the 8th of June following. They proceeded directly westward, crossed the Mississippi, and coming into

Monroe County, Iowa, purchased fifty acres of land, which they occupied for two years, and then selling out, removed to Eddyville, where they located for eighteen months, and then Mr. Johnson, visiting Wapello County, was so well pleased with the appearance of the country in this vicinity that he resolved to locate here, and accordingly purchased thirty-five acres in Polk Township. This he occupied for two years, when he sold it and purchased seventy-five acres in another part of the township, and lived upon this ten years. He then sold forty-five acres of this, and purchased 120 on section 32, in the same township, which he has occupied since that time, and which he has brought to a fine state of cultivation. Upon it he has erected a good farm residence, an excellent barn, and all necessary out-buildings convenient for the shelter of stock and the storing of grain.

The wife of our subject, Mrs. Louise J. Johnson, departed this life on the 2d of September, 1886, after having been the faithful and affectionate companion of her husband for a period of twenty-five years. She is buried in Munterville Cemetery, Polk Township, and her memory is held in tender remembrance by her family and a large circle of friends and acquaintances.

Mr. Johnson has been straightforward and upright in his transactions, and his present possessions have been accumulated solely by the exercise of his own industry. He enjoys in a marked degree the confidence and respect of his fellow-townsmen, and all the family are connected with the Lutheran Church. Politically Mr. J. casts his vote with the Republican party.

JOHN HARDEN is the proprietor of Harden's Hotel in Agency. He is the fourth of a family of nineteen children of William and Susan (Boone) Harden, the father a native of Pennsylvania and the mother of Maryland. Both died in the first-named State, the mother in 1875 and the father in 1882. John Harden was born in Somerset County, Pa., Jan. 14, 1820. He was reared on a farm and received but a limited education. He was married, in Pennsylvania, in 1848, to Mary J. Beard, daughter of John Beard. In 1855 he left his native State and came to Wapello County, where he remained one year, and then moved near Libertyville, Jefferson County, where he lived until 1866, and then returned to this county and located at Agency City, where he has since continued to reside. Mrs. Harden died at Agency in 1871, and on the 20th day of July, 1872, Mr. Harden contracted a marriage with Mary A. Stephens, widow of James Stephens, and daughter of Charles F. Harrow. Our subject's family comprised the following children—George, Jesse, John, William, Polly, Catherine, Susan, Alexander, Elizabeth, Lavinia, Lydia, Isaac, Sally, Margaret, Caroline, Perry and James K.; two died in infancy. At the present writing Mr. Harden is an invalid, and has been such for eight years. He is a member of Magnolia Lodge No. 24, I. O. O. F. Politically he is a Democrat.

E. H. SAGE, M. D., a successful physician of Agency City, and occupying a good position among the profession in this locality, was born in Jackson County, Ind., April 3, 1838, and is the son of James and Rebecca (Powell) Sage. When a lad of eight years of age he went to Clark County, Ind., to attend school, and in 1852 came with his parents to Fairfield, Jefferson Co., Iowa, where he pursued his studies under the tutorship of an English gentleman of fine education and abilities.

The father of our subject was a practicing physician, and from him he received his early instruction in matters pertaining to his profession. After his marriage our subject also pursued his studies with his father-in-law, Dr. William Hilton, and in 1874 attended the Medical College at St. Louis, from which he graduated the following year. He commenced practice with his father-in-law at Chillicothe, Mo., in 1868, and subsequently went to Ft. Smith, Ark., and in 1870, came to Agency City, which he has since made his home, and continuously followed his practice.

The subject of our history was married in

Agency City, in 1866, to Miss Mary C. Hilton, and they became the parents of two children, one of whom, Nellie V., is deceased; Drury H. is six years old. Mrs. Mary C. Sage departed this life in September, 1886, greatly mourned by her family and a large circle of friends. She was an amiable and accomplished lady, and an ornament to the society of which she was a highly esteemed member.

Dr. Sage is a member of the Eclectic State Medical Society of Iowa and Missouri, and is Examining Surgeon of the V. A. S. He possesses acknowledged ability in his profession, and is widely and favorably known throughout this section. He is a member in good standing of the I. O. O. F., in Magnolia Lodge No. 24, having passed the chair, and is also a Scribe of the V. A. S.

ROBERT WEST is the senior member of the firm of West & Wing, engaged in the butcher business at 103 South Court street, Ottumwa. His trade is quite extensive, selling weekly six beeves, six hogs, two calves and four sheep. He was born in Vermillion County, Ind., May 3, 1835, and is the son of James and Isabel (Gray) West. His parents moved from Indiana to Wapello County in 1847, where his father's life terminated in 1851; his mother's decease occurred in 1853. They were both natives of Kentucky.

At the age of eighteen Robert West commenced business for himself, renting a farm and working the same until 1855, when he bought 120 acres of unimproved land, on which he made some improvements and then sold. He then purchased another farm, which he improved and held until 1858, when he sold a part of the same and commenced to feed and ship stock, in which business he continued until 1874, when he commenced his present business, which he has since followed with success.

In 1854 Mr. West married Eliza Godfrey, and to this union four children have been born: Lewis G., now living in Wyoming Territory, engaged in the cattle business; James K., now in Nebraska on a cattle and sheep ranch; Maggie, who is the wife of John B. Dimmit, and lives in Madison County, Iowa; Jennie lives with her parents. In addition to his other property Mr. West owns a half interest in seven and a half acres inside of the city limits of Ottumwa. Politically he affiliates with the Republican party.

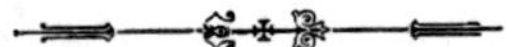

I. E. PAGE, a merchant living and doing business in the town of Kirkville, Richland Township, carries a stock of general merchandise, the average value of which is about $8,000, and has a large and satisfactory trade. Mr. Page is a native of Clarke County, Ohio, born Jan. 10, 1843, and is a son of James C. and Keziah F. (Harris) Page, the former of whom was a native of Kentucky, born May 6, 1795, and died July 31, 1886. The mother died in 1864.

The subject of this sketch grew to manhood in his native State, and on the breaking out of the Civil War enlisted as a private in Co. F, 44th Ohio Vol. Inf., at Springfield, Ohio, Sept. 17, 1861. He re-enlisted at Knoxville, Tenn., in Co. F, 8th Ohio Vol. Cav., Jan. 4, 1864, and served until the close of the war. He was with the regiment in all of its battles and marches; was captured in Virginia, and taken to Libby Prison in January, 1865, exchanged in February, joined the regiment in March, and was discharged in August of the same year.

On the 25th of February, 1864, Mr. Page was united in marriage with Sarah C. Neer, a native of Ohio, born July 25' 1844, and a daughter of Isaiah and Eliza A. Neer. Her father died in Ohio in 1879, and her mother is yet living, in Wapello County. Mr. and Mrs. Page are the parents of four children; Anna C., born Dec. 5, 1864, is now the wife of David Waters, and lives in Kirkville; Keziah F., born Feb. 15, 1867; Fred C., April 20, 1873; Ernest D., born March 29, 1882, died Jan. 27, 1884.

In addition to his stock of merchandise Mr. Page is the owner of his business property and also a dwelling-house in Kirkville. He held the office of Deputy Treasurer for a term of two years, at which time he lived in Ottumwa. Mr. Page came

to Kirkville from Ohio in 1870, and has since continued to reside here, with the exception of the two years mentioned. He and his wife are members of the Methodist Episcopal Church, while he is a member of the Masonic fraternity, and also of the I. O. O. F. In the latter body he is at present filling the office of Deputy Grand Master of his district, and Noble Grand of his Lodge. Politically he is a Republican.

SAMUEL BUCHANAN, a highly esteemed resident of Keokuk Township, is a native of South Carolina, having been born in York District in 1808. When he was a little lad of seven years old his parents removed to Indiana, where he attained to years of manhood, their home being in Clark County until 1832. They then removed to Parke County, where they remained until 1844, and from there removed to Jasper County, Ill. Our subject had been reared to farming pursuits, and had carried on agriculture on his own account before going to Illinois, and after locating there also opened up and improved a farm. In 1854 he determined to go still further West, and accordingly crossed the Father of Waters, and coming into Wapello County, Iowa, settled first in Cass Township, where he leased a coal bank, and operated it for four years. He then rented a farm in Keokuk Township, and locating upon it followed his former occupation until the beginning of the late Civil War, in 1861. At this time he laid aside his personal interests and proffered his services to aid in the preservation of the Union, becoming a member of Co. D, 15th Iowa Vol. Inf. He was mustered in on the 1st of February, 1862, and participated with his comrades in the various engagements which followed. At the battle of Shiloh he received a wound by a cannon-ball striking a tree near him and tearing off a limb which struck him on the head, and left a wound which disabled him for further service. He accordingly received his discharge, June 19 of that year, and returned home.

After his return Mr. Buchanan again located upon his farm, but was unable to do any work for a period of three years following. As soon as he had recovered sufficiently to attend to business he commenced to prospect for coal in this county, and wherever he found it leased the land under which it lay, opened the mines, and did a successful business in coal lands until 1872. He then purchased a tract of land on the southwest quarter of section 23, Keokuk Township. This consisted of 160 acres, and he at once located upon it and commenced the improvements, which he has been carrying on since that time in a successful and creditable manner.

The subject of our sketch was married to Miss Sarah Toller in 1832. Mrs. B. was a native of Kentucky, and by her union with our subject became the mother of five children, as follows: Nancy Jane married Jasper Poston, a resident of Cass Township, who is now deceased; George W. is a carpenter and superintendent of a coal business in What Cheer, Iowa; Margaret married Stephen Wilkins, of Keokuk Township: Sarah Ann became the wife of Z. Edgington, a coal miner; Amanda, Mrs. Isaac Clark, is a resident of Decatur County, Iowa. Mrs. Sarah Buchanan departed this life in Keokuk Township in 1863, at the age of fifty-six years, and is buried in Mars Hill Cemetery. She was a highly esteemed lady, and a member of the Methodist Episcopal Church.

Mr. Buchanan was married the second time, in 1872, to Miss Lucinda Shaw, a native of Indiana, and of this union there were born six children: Wesley Allen, Eliza Luella, Martha and Corda are at home; Samuel died at the age of one year; Amy Cloretta is the youngest born. Mr. and Mrs. B. are members in good standing of the Methodist Episcopal Church.

The subject of our sketch has been prominent in the affairs of his community for many years. He served four years as Justice of the Peace, has been Township Trustee, and was, for a number of years, Constable of Cass Township. He was census-taker in 1880, and during his connection with the church here was for a number of years Steward and Class-Leader. Politically Mr. B. is an uncompromising Prohibitionist, and an earnest worker in the temperance cause. He uniformly casts his vote with the Republican party, is well read and intelligent, and keeps himself posted upon matters of general interest.

The homestead of Mr. Buchanan comprises 200 acres, is equipped with a good residence and all necessary farm buildings, and he has all the appliances for the successful carrying on of agriculture. He commenced life at the foot of the ladder, and his present possessions are the result of his own industry and perseverance. He is fulfilling all the obligations of a good citizen, and has his reward in the confidence and esteem of his friends and neighbors.

JOSEPH R. MYERS, a resident of Ottumwa, and Deputy Sheriff of Wapello County, was born in Elkhart County, Ind., April 14, 1837. He came with his parents to Iowa in 1842, and continued to reside with them until he had attained to the age of manhood, receiving a good education in the meantime in the primitive log school-house of the locality in which he lived. The first undertaking in which Mr. Myers was directly interested that he remembers, was that of closing out a stock of goods which his brother owned, and had left in his hurry to visit the land of gold. This stock of goods, our subject, together with his father, took to Agency, where they closed it out, and soon after Joseph R. became an employe as merchant's clerk. In 1863 he went to Helena, Mo., and was employed as an assistant suttler in the army until the following spring. His employer was ex-Sheriff S. Chaney, who was suttler of the 4th Iowa Cavalry, and our subject continued in his employ until the close of the war. While the C., B. & Q. R. R. was in force of construction, our subject lost all of his savings, and returning to Agency he engaged as clerk at $45 per month, being thus occupied two years. He then embarked in the lumber, grain, live-stock and agricultural implement business, in company with J. M. Murray and E. H. Sage, which relation continued for about six years. On account of the failure of crops, our subject disposed of his interest as partner, and became an employe of the firm of Sage & Co., with whom he continued for about two years. Mr. Myers' next move was to engage in the live-stock business with Mr. Fullen, which relationship existed for a year, and then our subject was employed by a packing-house at Ottumwa, and was in their employ for some three years, in which capacity he labored as buyer.

In March, 1885, Mr. Myers was appointed Deputy Sheriff by J. W. Workman, and has continued to hold that position until the present time. Mr. Myers was married at Agency City in 1854, Miss Julia A. Springer, a native of Indiana, becoming his wife. Of their union there are two daughters yet living, Leonora, wife of John Davis, a resident of Agency City, and Cora H., wife of George Bryan, of Ottumwa, who is a night trainmaster on the C., B. & Q. R. R. Mrs. Myers died in 1859, and in 1865 our subject formed a second marriage, Miss Emma H. Dillon being the other contracting party. She was born in Ohio, and by her marriage with our subject has become the mother of three children—Gertrude, Charlie and Guy; the latter died at the age of three years.

Socially Mr. Myers is a member of Magnolia Lodge No. 24, I. O. O. F., and has passed through the chairs and also represented his lodge in the Grand Lodge. In 1867 Mr. Myers was instrumental in the organization of several lodges in this section of the county. He has always taken an active interest in the welfare of the society, and has probably done as much for the order as any man in the county. He and his good wife are members of the Methodist Episcopal Church. He is one of the old settlers of Ottumwa, and during the many years that he has lived here has always been identified with every undertaking that was calculated to advance the interests of the city or the welfare of its people.

RICHARD B. SUTTON, well known in Ottumwa as "Dick" Sutton, and proprietor of Dick's Hotel, is one of the most genial of "mine hosts" to be found anywhere within the boundary lines, not only of Wapello County, but of this State. He was born in Jessamine County, Ky., within eighteen miles of Lexington, April 15, 1845, and is a son of David P. and Isabella (Reynolds) Sutton, natives respectively of Virginia and Kentucky. David P. Sutton, when a young man, went to Kentucky, where he was married, and built the first frame building in Mt. Freedom, Jessamine County, and was appointed the first Postmaster in that place, the post-office being located at his residence. This first frame building was also used as a hall and a general store, the people for miles around trading with him, and he received pay for his goods only about once during each year. He nevertheless did an extensive trade, and was exceedingly successful, and at his death, which took place in 1850, had accumulated a fine property.

David P. Sutton was the father of seven children—four daughters and three sons: Mary J. became the wife of B. J. Smith, and they are living in Bloomington, Ind.; Margaret married Tobias Slocum, and they are also living in Bloomington; Martha was united in marriage with William Andrew, and they reside in Ohio; Richard is living in Ottumwa, and is the subject of this notice; George H. resides in St. Louis, and is a railroad conductor; and David P. lives in Shelbyville, Ill. The mother of these children was married a second time, John Coley being the other contracting party, and of this union two children were born—Benjamin F., a farmer of Woodford County, Ky., and John W., deceased. Mr. Coley departed this life in 1854, during the terrible cholera scourge of that year. Soon after the death of her husband Mrs. Coley returned to Lexington for the purpose of educating her children, and died there in 1856–57. Three of the children were sent to the Orphan's Home.

Soon after the death of his mother our subject, together with his brothers, George and David P., went to Evansville, Ind., where they were received into the family of an uncle, and adopted as his children. Richard continued to reside with his uncle until sixteen years of age, when he was employed on the river during the winter seasons, and during summers was occupied in accompanying a show. In 1874 he went to Moberly, Mo., where he opened a restaurant in the depot, and did quite a good business. In August, 1877, he came to Ottumwa, and here, in company with Robert J. Cannon, opened a restaurant, conducting the same successfully for one year. Our subject then bought the right of city bill poster, and subsequently assumed control of the Lewis Opera House, and while thus employed he received two gold-headed canes for his efficiency. July 3, 1884, Mr. Sutton gave up the management of the Opera House, with the intention of going to Chicago, but abandoned the idea, and remained at Ottumwa.

Richard Sutton was united in marriage with Fannie Keeler at Albia, Iowa. She was born in Montreal, Canada, and after a tour throughout the country the newly married couple returned to Ottumwa, where our subject rented a small hotel with fifteen rooms, and engaged in the capacity of "mine host." He has subsequently increased the capacity of his house to fifty rooms, and is doing a good business. He is manager of the Turner Opera House at the present time and has a lease of the same for two years.

J. T. CARNES, builder and contractor, residing at Ottumwa, and a gentleman of prominence in that place, was born in Clinton County, N. Y., Feb. 15, 1834, and a son of Thomas and Ann (Cavender) Carnes, of Scotch lineage, but natives of Clinton, N. Y. The father was a farmer by occupation, and followed his calling successfully for many years. They were both members of the Presbyterian Church, and respected by all who knew them. Five children were born of the parental union, three sons and two daughters, and of the number three are yet living: John T., the eldest, is the subject of this biography; James is a farmer by occupation and resides in Ida County, Iowa; Edward Worthington is Railroad Superintendent of the Minneapolis, St. Paul & Manitoba Railroad; Mary M. and Catherine are deceased. After the death of Mrs. Ann C. Carnes, the father of our subject was a second time married, to Mrs. Mary Hultz, widow of Joseph Hultz, and daughter of Judge William Hultz, a carriage-maker of Ottumwa. The father died in 1864, after having lived a useful and Christian life, and being for many years a member of the Christian Church.

The subject of this sketch was reared in Fairfield County, Ohio, and received his education in the common and High School at Carroll Village. In 1850 he removed to Montgomery County, Ind., and was there a resident until he attained the age of twenty-four years. In February, 1858, he left Indiana for the undeveloped West, and located in what is now Franklin County, Kan. Here he engaged his services to old Ottawa, an Indian chief of the Ottawas, and subsequently formed a partnership with him and they did quite a trade with the Indians. Our subject was thus occupied for about eighteen months, and while in that portion of Kansas formed the acquaintance of John Brown, better known as Pottawatomie Brown, who was a strong advocate of Free State principles, and who did what he could to make Kansas a free State. To the reader familiar with the history of that State, we need not state that there were dark days in her history, and the subject of this notice can pride himself on being associated with that element which, in the early history of Kansas, made such a formidable stand for right, and which has subsequently became successful throughout the entire land. Returning from Kansas to Crawfordsville, Ind., he remained there for a time, and in 1865, at Warsaw, that State, he was married to Miss Mary A. Keitner, a native of Mahoning County, Ohio. During the fall of the year our subject was married, he came back with his young bride to Ottumwa, and settling down has continued to make this place his home until the present time.

Soon after coming to this State our subject formed a partnership with Zacharia Pickett, under the firm name of Pickett & Carnes, architects and contractors, and they have erected some of the finest structures in Ottumwa, among which are the Adams and Garfield school buildings, the First National Bank, Richards' Block, Gurley's Baker Block, the Wood Block, the Madison Block and the Potter Block. The partnership was dissolved in the fall of 1885, and Mr. Pickett, at the present writing (1886) is on a visit to San Diego, Cal. In politics Mr. Carnes is Republican and cast his first vote in Kansas Territory, and at a time when it was almost worth a man's life should he let it be known how he voted. Mr. and Mrs. Carnes are both members of the Methodist Episcopal Church, with which our subject has been connected for many years, and has always taken an active interest in the promotion of the cause of the Master. He and his wife have become the parents of three children—Cora E., Jessie M. (deceased) and Edward K. Socially Mr. Carnes is a member of the Masonic fraternity, holding fellowship with Ottumwa Lodge No. 269, and also Clinton Chapter No. 9.

JOHN L. MILLER, of Ottumwa, has been a resident of the Hawkeye State since 1855, and has worthily occupied his place among the industries of the city of Ottumwa. He is a native of Germany, and was born in Hainstadt, Odenwald, June 30, 1835. His parents were John and Eva C. Miller, and he was their only child. He was deprived of the protecting care of his father when little past infancy, and at the age of fourteen was apprenticed to learn the tailor's trade, at which he served four years, and then determined to try his fortunes in the New World. In 1854 he emigrated from his native land, and landed in New York City on the 16th of May of that year, remaining in the Metropolis about six months, then went to Buffalo, and the following year crossed the Mississippi and came into Iowa. He located in Keokuk County and two years later, in 1857, visited New Orleans, where he was united in marriage with Miss Caroline A. C. Fleer, on the 14th of March, 1858. Mrs. Miller was a native of the same county as her husband, and born July 5, 1838.

Soon after marriage, our subject and wife came to Ottumwa, Iowa, and during the progress of the late war, Mr. Miller enlisted as a soldier in the Union service, becoming a member of the 36th Iowa Infantry. He was mustered in at Keokuk, and sent with his regiment to St. Louis, and thence to Helena, Ark., where he was on detached service for eight months. His regiment was then ordered to Little Rock, and Mr. Miller received instructions to report to Dr. Park, Surgeon-in-Chief, by whom he was detailed to hospital service for one year. Soon afterward all detached men were ordered to their regiments by Gen. Steele. Mr. Miller after reporting at headquarters, was ordered to report to Dr. Sawyer, Surgeon-in-Chief of the division, who appointed him Acting Hospital Steward at Camden. He then returned to St. Charles, and from there was detailed for duty at the general hospital, where he remained three months. Thence he went to the hospital at Devall's Bluff, where he remained until September, 1865, the close of the war. He was then sent to his regiment to be discharged with his comrades, having served three years, and receiving the approval of his superior officers.

After his return from the army Mr. Miller joined his family in Ottumwa, and engaged in farming, which occupation he followed for nine years. His health then failing, he abandoned this to engage in the grocery business, which he conducted until 1884. At this time, on account of the illness of his wife, he did not engage in any business for over ten months, giving to her his entire time and attention, day and night, until she was relieved from suffering by death on the 19th of June, 1885. Mrs. Miller was a highly esteemed Christian lady, and was greatly mourned by her husband and a large circle of friends and acquaintances. She was prominently connected with the German Methodist Episcopal Church for many years, and in her daily walk and conversation exemplified all the Christian virtues. Her remains were interred in the cemetery lot belonging to her husband, No. 58, block 2. Mr. and Mrs. Miller were the parents of one child, which died in infancy.

LEONARD KNOX, one of the thrifty farmers and stock-raisers of Columbia Township, has been a resident of Iowa since the fall of 1847, coming here when a young child with his parents from Logan County, Ohio, where he was born on the 30th of January, 1843. He is the son of Peter and Mary H. (Peach) Knox, the father a native of Greenbrier County, Va., and the mother of Logan County, Ohio. His father was a man of fine abilities, who, during the summer seasons was engaged in agricultural pursuits, and in winters taught school in Ohio until the time of his removal to this State. After crossing the Mississippi he purchased 312½ acres of wild land in Columbia Township, this county, and became one of the most thrifty and well-to-do farmers, and his land at the time of his death was under a fine state of cultivation. He departed this life on the 7th of December, 1878, and by his death the community lost one of its most valued members.

During the earlier years of his life Peter Knox was identified with the old Whig party, but afterward affiliated with the Republicans. He was elected to the offices of County Treasurer and Recorder, and in 1863 was the successful candidate on the Republican ticket for Representative in the General Assembly of the State of Iowa. Two years later he was re-elected, on the Republican ticket, and did good service for his constituents during his connection with the Legislature. He was a kind and indulgent parent, and at his death was greatly lamented by those who had known him best. The parental household consisted of nine children, of whom the record is as follows; Jessica became the wife of W. M. King, a farmer of Columbia Township, residing on section 27; Leonard is the subject of this sketch; Elizabeth, now deceased, was the wife of B. F. Gordon, a farmer of Monroe County, this State; Mary died at the age of three years; William and J. W. died in infancy; Ellen became the wife of W. M. Peatman, a real-estate agent of Centerville, Appanoose County; Emma May and Elsie are deceased. The mother of these children makes her home with her children. She is now sixty-six years of age, a well-preserved old lady, who is beloved by her family and held in the highest respect by a large circle of friends and acquaintances.

Leonard Knox lived with his father on the farm and attended the school of that vicinity until he had attained the age of nineteen years, and then, the late war being in progress, he enlisted as a Union soldier in the 36th Iowa Infantry, and participated in all the engagements of his regiment and the other vicissitudes of war until the close. At the battle of Mark's Mills, in Arkansas, he was captured by the rebels and taken into Texas, where he was confined in the rebel prison at Tyler, where he remained from the 25th of April, 1864, until the 25th of February following, in the meantime suffering all the privations, exposure and hardship incident to the life of a captive in the rebel prison. He was finally exchanged and sent to New Orleans, whence he was allowed to return home on a furlough of thirty days. At the expiration of this time he rejoined his regiment at St. Charles, Ark., whence they marched to Devall's Bluff and were discharged on the 24th of August. Mr. Knox then returned home to his peaceful farm pursuits, and in due time became possessor of a good tract of land, where he established a comfortable and permanent home. His farm estate now consists of 173 acres, with a commodious two-story residence, good barns and out-buildings, and everything necessary for the carrying on of agriculture in a first-class manner. His farm implements and machinery are after the most improved pattern, and his orchards, stock and beautiful fields proclaim at once the supervision of an intelligent and enterprising mind.

The marriage of Leonard Knox and Miss Mary E. Sackett took place Nov. 8, 1865. Mrs. K. was born in Huntington County, Ind., on the 30th of November, 1845, and is the daughter of Alexander and C. C. (Gilbert) Sackett. Mr. and Mrs. K. have become the parents of five children, viz.: F. E., born Oct. 22, 1866; W. E., May 3, 1868; the third child, a daughter, died in infancy; Elsie D. was born Sept. 18, 1875, and Kate B., Aug. 1, 1880.

In 1872 Mr. Knox, believing that he could advance his interests by a removal to Kansas, rented his farm, and going to the "Grasshopper" State, purchased 300 acres of railroad land in Ellsworth County. In addition to this he pre-empted 160 acres, and opened up a farm. He remained there until the following year, and was then elected one of the County Commissioners, which office he filled with credit to himself and satisfaction to all concerned. He lived in Kansas until 1874, and then, disposing of his landed interests, removed back to the old farm in Wapello County, becoming satisfied in his mind that the Hawkeye State was a good enough place in which to spend the remainder of his days. He is a man who takes pride in his work, and in the status of his community and county. He is actively interested in public and political matters and has held various offices in his township. Politically he is an uncompromising Democrat, and whenever possible is a regular attendant of the various county and State conventions of his party The sum and substance of his history is that he is an honest man and a good citizen, and fulfills all his obligations to the best of his ability.

SAMUEL RANDALL, of Green Township, who is held in high respect as a citizen and business man, is a native of Maryland, and was born in 1822. His parents were Joshua and Dorothea (Jones) Randall, both natives of Maryland. While an infant his parents removed from their native State to Wheeling, W. Va., remaining there, however, but a short time. Thence they went to Pittsburgh, Pa., and resided two or three years, and from there moved to Cincinnati, Ohio, where the subject of our sketch was reared and educated. Joshua Randall was a cooper by trade, and removed to Dayton, Ohio, and after a brief residence at Middletown, that State, returned to Queen City, where the mother departed this life in 1839, at the age of forty-two years. About two years after this sad event Samuel, our subject, went to Darke County, Ohio, and was employed as a farm laborer until the spring of 1848. The Mexican War being then in progress, he enlisted as a soldier and served six months. He then returned to Darke County and learned the carpenter's trade, in which he was occupied for three years, or until 1854. He then determined to try his fortunes in the Far West, and accordingly crossed the Mississippi into Wapello County, and entered eighty acres of land on section 9, in Green Township. The land was unimproved and uncultivated and he set himself diligently to till the soil. He was successful in his undertakings, and was soon rewarded by the picture of smiling meadows and growing grain, and in time had established a comfortable homestead, with a good dwelling, barns and outhouses, and in his later days is enjoying the fruit of his early labors and frugality.

Mr. Randall was married, in 1851, to Miss Hester

Beny, of Ohio, a daughter of James and Mary (Reid) Beny. Of this union there have been born eight children, the record of whom is as follows: John is a farmer of Green Township; Dorothea is the wife of William Hendrick, also of Green Township; James is occupied in farming in this vicinity; Mary is the wife of Munford Cloyd, of Adams Township; Thomas, George and Charlie are at home. Mr. Randall has been prominent in the affairs of his township, serving as School Director, Road Supervisor, Township Clerk and Assessor. He is Democratic in politics, and was elected Justice of the Peace in the fall of 1886. He commenced life a poor boy, and made his way independent of any assistance except his own strong hands and courageous heart.

The father of Samuel Randall died in 1878, at the age of eighty-four years, and the mother at the age of forty-two. They were both connected with the Methodist Episcopal Church and left behind them a record of good deeds. The elder Randall had been quite an extensive traveler, having been over the greater portion of seventeen States, and during his residence of thirty-five years in this county built up for himself a reputation as an honest man and a good citizen, the encourager and promoter of education, temperance and morality, and left a good influence upon all those with whom he associated. His name is still held in kindly remembrance by those who knew him best and valued him according to his just deserts.

WILLIAM H. MIX, of Eldon, Iowa, a highly respected citizen of Wapello County, crossed the Mississippi in 1867, and settled in the Hawkeye State. He first located in Van Buren County, where he lived until 1872, engaged in mercantile pursuits. He then removed to Eldon, and established the business which he is now operating successfully and profitably. His stock consists of general merchandise, and by his straightforward dealings he has secured a large and steadily increasing patronage.

The subject of our sketch was born in Warsaw, Wyoming Co., N. Y., in 1840, and is the son of Charles K. and Caroline (Worden) Mix, also natives of the State of New York. His grandfather was of French nativity, and came to America with La Fayette during the Revolutionary War as a soldier under the colonial Government. After independence had been established he settled in Connecticut, being the only representative of his family in this country and from whom descended the various members of the present family.

William H. Mix left the parental roof at the age of twenty years for the purpose of traveling over different States, but soon afterward Ft. Sumpter was fired upon by the rebels, and patriots all over the country were proffering their services for the preservation of the Union. Young Mix at once abandoned his personal plans and interests, and enlisted as a soldier in the 2d New Hampshire Infantry, April 21, 1861, serving with this regiment two and a half years. He was then promoted First Lieutenant, and held his commission for three years, in the meantime having been sent to the frontier near the Mexican line. He was in the first battle of Bull Run, and at Williamsburg was wounded in the neck. He also participated in the battle of Fredericksburg, the seven days' battle at Champion Hills, and at Gettysburg, where he was wounded in the left breast. He was in the battle of the Wilderness and at the mine disaster at Petersburg, where he was wounded in both legs, captured by the rebels and taken to Columbia, S. C., being confined in that city. His release was finally procured, and he recovered from his wounds, being able to rejoin his regiment and go to Mexico, as before stated. At the close of the war he received an honorable discharge, and returned home, after which he set his face westward, and came to the Hawkeye State.

Mr. Mix was married, in Portsmouth, N. H., March 8, 1863, to Miss Susan Yeaton, of Portsmouth, N. H. Of this union there were born three children: Winnifred C. and Katie Y., now attending school in Boston, and Moses K., at home. Mr. Mix was the second time married, in April, 1877, to Miss Josephine Nichols, a native of Jasper County, Iowa, and of this union there were also three children—Elmer S., William Edgar and Franklin H. They occupy a handsome residence located on Railroad avenue, and their large circle of friends and acquaintances embraces the best class of citizens in this community. Mr. M. is still connected with the Free-Will Baptist Church, of Dale, Wyoming Co., N. Y., and socially is a member of the G. A. R. Post No. 73, of Eldon.

ESQUIRE DANIEL CARL, a pioneer settler of Wapello County, is a native of Pennsylvania, and was born in Perry County April 27, 1819. His parents were David and Catharine (Snyder) Carl, of German descent, and natives of Chester County, Pa., the father born Nov. 12, 1792, and the mother Nov. 16, 1793. They were married in Perry County, Pa., and David Carl carried on the business of carpenter and miller combined. The parental household consisted of five sons and three daughters, the record of whom is as follows: Isaiah, born Jan. 30, 1814, lives in Niagara County, N. Y.; John, born May 27, 1816, is in Livingston County, Mich.; Daniel is the subject of our sketch; Rebecca, born Feb. 21, 1822, died in about 1853; Jacob, born March 18, 1825, is in Livingston County, Mich; Elizabeth, Mrs. Knapp, born April 14, 1828, lives in Michigan; Henry, born May 21, 1831, served as a soldier in the late war, in a Michigan regiment, and was killed in front of Richmond; Mary A., Mrs. Hildebrand, was born Feb. 8, 1834; Andrew J., born Jan. 18, 1837, was also killed at Richmond.

In 1826 Mr. Carl removed with his family from Pennsylvania to Seneca County, N. Y., thence he went to Michigan and located in Livingston County, which remained his home until his death, in 1858. Soon after his marriage came on the War of 1812, and Mr. Carl served as a soldier until the close of that struggle. Mrs. C. survived her husband twenty-seven years, and died in Livingston County, Mich., at the advanced age of ninety-two years. They were both members of the Presbyterian Church. Mr. Carl was a Jackson Democrat, a prominent man wherever he made his home, and held various local offices.

Daniel Carl was only seven years of age when his parents removed from Pennsylvania to the Empire State. He received a common-school education in Seneca and Morgan Counties, N. Y., and in 1842 enlisted in the regular army, at Lockport, N. Y., in the 4th United States Artillery, joining his regiment at Buffalo Barracks. The following June they were sent to Governor's Island, N. Y., thence to Ft. Monroe, and from there to Mexico. There they participated in the battles under Gen. Taylor, where our subject completed his term of enlistment, and was mustered out in the latter part of January, 1847. He then came into Wapello County, Iowa, and located in Adams Township on section 18 where he took up a tract of land and improved a farm. He occupied this for about ten years, in the meantime having removed his family hither and in 1856 moved to Blakesburg, where he has since resided.

Daniel Carl was united in marriage with Miss Elizabeth Tinsley, in this county, on the 29th of February, 1848. Mrs. Carl is the daughter of Thomas and Sarah (Robertson) Tinsley, who were among the early settlers of this county. She was born in Shelby County, Ky., July 30, 1825, and has become the mother of five children, viz.: William H., born in Shelby County, Iowa, Jan. 31, 1849; Mary E., Mrs. Daniel Lewis, was born March 16, 1851, and now lives in Central City, Col.; Harvey, born Dec. 9, 1853, is also in Colorado; Lucinda married George W. Hull, and lives in Denver; Thomas, born March 10, 1859, is a resident of Shelby County, Iowa.

In politics Mr. Carl is a stanch Democrat, and has held various offices of trust in his township, having been Justice of the Peace for over twenty-eight years. He has been Notary Public for twelve years, and is Treasurer of the school fund. During the early days of his settlement here he experienced all the vicissitudes of pioneer life, going long distances to mill and to market, and when these privileges were destroyed by reason of high water, the mills being carried away, lived like his neighbors—upon ground corn and a limited amount of bacon. He has received his reward, however, in beholding the growth and development of his adopted State, and feels a just pride in being a resident of the great commonwealth, which has become one of the most wealthy and populous districts

P. G. Ballingall

Mrs. M. J. Phillips

along the Mississippi Valley. In common with the other pioneers who are passing away he is held in peculiar veneration and respect for what he has accomplished as a factor of the industrial and agricultural interests of Wapello County.

HON. PETER G. BALLINGALL, prominent among the representative men of the county, and one of the leading hotel men of the State, at present a resident of Ottumwa, was born in Glasgow, Scotland, March 3, 1830. He is the son of P. and Martha (Smith) Ballingall, both of whom were also natives of Scotland. The father was born in Ayers and died in 1832 in his native land. The mother was born in Glasgow. They became the parents of one child only, the subject of this sketch. After the death of the father, the mother contracted a second marriage, with James Hodge, who was born in Edinburgh, Scotland. This union resulted in the birth of nine children, only three of whom are living: David, a resident of Ottumwa, who was born in Glasgow; N. J., the widow of W. P. Phillips, who was born in Philadelphia, Pa., and died in 1805, in that city; the third is Martha K.

At the age of seven years our subject, in company with his mother and stepfather, came to America, landing at Quebec after a voyage of several weeks. In crossing the Atlantic the entire family were seized with illness, one brother dying and receiving an ocean burial. From Quebec the family went to Montreal, and thence to Port Hope on the banks of Lake Ontario. After a short sojourn there his mother, brother and himself walked fourteen miles to Brighton, and from there proceeded to Helderman Four Corners, where our subject earned his first money selling matches. Before he was eleven years old he walked from Coburg, seventy-three miles below Toronto, to Chicago, by a roundabout way, which involved a distance of seven or eight hundred miles. After arriving he was employed in various capacities at different hotels, and proved himself peculiarly adapted to this calling. He advanced from one position to another, and in the course of time was appointed Receiver of the Lake House, which position he filled acceptably until 1855. Upon leaving he was presented with a fine gold watch, the letter accompanying it being signed by some of the most prominent men in the city.

After leaving the Lake House Mr. Ballingall spent three months in traveling, going through most of the Southern States, and while off the coast of Cape Hatteras was driven by a storm to the Bermuda Islands. After reaching terra firma again and visiting the East, he came to Chicago and opened the Briggs House, whence, after a few months he came West to Galesburg and became proprietor of the Haskell House. The following year he closed out his interest in this and visited Minnesota, where he purchased a tract of land, and thence, in the fall of 1856, came to Keokuk, Iowa, as manager of the Ivins House. The following year he removed to Bentonsport and opened the Ashland House, thence to Fairfield, and from there to Agency City, where he opened the Revere House. Here he met with a serious loss, having his valise stolen, with a valuable collection of rare coins and the watch that had been presented to him in Chicago. In the summer of 1859 he still moved on with the terminus of the railroad, to Ottumwa. Since coming here he has been the life of the town, having gathered from his removals and his experiences a valuable fund of information and making many useful and pleasant acquaintances with public men. During this time also he exhibited the great energy of character which is one of his chief peculiarities. In connection with his hotel operations he had at one time seventeen Government licenses for separate and distinct branches of business, all of which he made successful. For nine years he was proprietor of the stage line from Ottumwa to Bloomfield, and during that long period, through sunshine and storm, never missed a trip. In 1870 the railroad crowded his stage line off the track and he withdrew his stock. Since that date he run a line to Sigourney, a distance of thirty-two miles, until the completion of the Chicago, Milwaukee & St. Paul Railroad, when that, too, was withdrawn.

In 1864 Mr. Ballingall erected the Ballingall House on the corner of Main and Green streets, which he operated for ten years. He then leased this but retained the management of the Depot Hotel. As this work goes to press he is contemplating the rebuilding or remodeling of the Ballingall, and making it one of the handsomest and most convenient public houses in the West.

While never an aspirant for official position Mr. B. has frequently been honored by his party and his fellow-citizens with local office. For many years he has been a member of the State Democratic Central Committee, and has contributed liberally of his time and money to advance the interests of his party. He was a member of the General Assembly of Iowa in 1883. Previous to this, however, he was elected Alderman of the city of Ottumwa and re-elected several terms after. He originated many of the improvements of the city, and urged them with a zeal that insured success. In the spring of 1873 he was nominated for Mayor, but was obliged to decline the honor on account of pressing private business. He had also been nominated for Senator on the Democratic ticket, and ran over 100 votes ahead of his ticket, and against a party majority of over 200, was beaten by only 109 votes. On the 18th of March, 1873, he was presented with another fine gold watch and chain of superb workmanship, elegantly engraved with the following inscription: "Hon. P. G. Ballingall, by his guests at Soldiers' Reunion at Des Moines, 1870, and other friends in Iowa, in token of esteem." Prior to this a chain manufactured to order in New York was presented him by "The Citizens of Ottumwa." Both these gifts are exceedingly valuable in more respects than one.

Later, Mr. Ballingall visited the West for rest and recreation, spending about six weeks on the Pacific coast, and upon his return interested himself in organizing the militia of Iowa. In this, as in the greater part of his undertakings, he distinguished himself and was appointed Major of the 5th Regiment in 1876, being promoted two years later to Colonel. He was soon afterward presented with a gold-mounted sword by the Sheridan Guards. The following year he was elected Major-General, but the Governor assuming a supervisory power to revise the returns, placed his competitor in the place to which he was legally elected by the organized citizen soldiery. The officers and soldiers of the different brigades testified in many ways to their belief in his just claims by banquets in his honor, and notably in one case by the presentation of a magnificent badge set with precious stones.

As a hotel man Mr. Ballingall has taken an interest in everything pertaining to the business, and was principally instrumental in securing the present law for the protection of landlords. He was elected the first President of the Hotel Keeper's Association in 1878, and has been annually re-elected since that time. In 1881 he was presented with another valuable gold chain, consisting of forty-six flat links, on either side of which is the name of a hotel and its landlord. This costly gift was manufactured by Tiffany, of New York City, at a cost of $400, and presented by the Association.

In the three last National Democratic Conventions Col. B. had charge of the Iowa delegation, and in appreciation of his services the delegates at Chicago presented him with a cross and star set with diamonds, engraved with the coat-of-arms of the State of Iowa. The Wapello County Agricultural Society selected Col. Ballingall for its first President, and he devoted much time and means for its advancement. Indeed there are few public enterprises in which he has not been actively interested and has contributed generously of his time and means. He is naturally industrious and has been an incessant worker, frequently devoting from fifteen to nineteen hours a day to his business affairs and public enterprises.

In the spring of 1886 Col. B. made a trip to Europe, visiting England, Ireland, Scotland, Wales, France, Italy, Austria, Prussia, Bavaria, Holland, Belgium, and minor Provinces, and at this time (January, 1887) he is making a trip around the world, sailing from San Francisco, and intending to visit Australia, China, Japan, and all other points of interest in the Old World. On his return from his first trip to Europe a banquet was given in his honor at the Ballingall House, which was participated in by hundreds of his fellow-citizens, without regard to party or creed.

The subject of our sketch is a brilliant illustration of what may be accomplished by energy, industry and resolution. He was thrown upon his own resources at an early age, and has arisen to his present position by the exercise of his own native talent, and has not only succeeded in acquitting himself with honor, but has been the means of giving employment to hundreds of people by the public enterprises which he has inaugurated, which required the erection of buildings, the institution of public improvements, and the distribution of money. Amid all the honors which have been heaped upon him he has preserved his natural simplicity of character and never consciously commits a questionable act in order to gain public applause. The portrait of Mr. Ballingall, which accompanies this sketch, will be heartily welcomed and appreciated by his many friends, as well as that of his sister, Mrs. Phillips.

JAMES McCLURE, a prosperous farmer and stock-grower on section 5, Richland Township, was born in County Armagh, Ireland, in 1818, and is a son of Robert and Jenny (Johnson) McClure, both of whom were natives of Ireland, and there died when our subject was quite young. In 1845 James left his native country for America. He crossed the ocean in a sailing-vessel, and was twenty-eight days in making the voyage. He landed at New York City, from which place he went to Pittsburgh, Pa., and there remained until 1867, when he came to Wapello County, and purchased the farm on which he now resides. He bought 150 acres of land, for which he paid $5,000. During the greater part of the time he resided in Pittsburgh he was engaged in mercantile business and in peddling dry-goods and jewelry through the country.

After settling in this county, in 1867, Mr. McClure was united in marriage with Margaret M. McCullough, born in Westmoreland County, Pa., March 18, 1834, and the daughter of David and Mary (Rice) McCullough. Her mother died in Kirkville, July 29, 1865, and her father in the same place, Sept. 29, 1872. Mr. and Mrs. McClure have one child, Mary J., born June 29, 1868. The farm upon which Mr. McClure resides is one of the best in Richland Township, and is well improved in every respect. Mr. and Mrs. McClure and daughter are members of the Presbyterian Church. Politically he is a Republican.

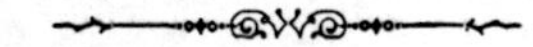

WILLIAM COWLEY has been a resident of the Hawkeye State for over thirty years, and has witnessed its development and progress with the interest of a worthy and enterprising citizen. He is now a resident of Eddyville, having come here in the spring of 1856. His first employment in this vicinity was in the sawmill of John Leggett, where he spent one summer, and then purchased a lath machine, which he ran until the following winter and then engaged as clerk in the store of Butcher & Cox. The firm afterward dissolved partnership, and Mr. Cowley continued in the employ of the senior member until he was given the management of the business, a position which he still occupies. They are principally engaged in the buying and shipping of wool, and in money-loaning. Mr. Butcher being a bachelor, has for some years made his home with our subject, and their relations are of the most pleasant and amicable character.

Mr. Cowley was born in Montgomery County, Ind., March 25, 1831, and is the son of Mathew and Nancy Cowley. His father died when he was a young boy, and he removed with his mother to Illinois, where they spent the winter, and thence to Wapello County, in the spring of 1844. They settled seven miles east of Agency, and purchased 160 acres of land, which they sold soon afterward, and our subject returned to Mercer County, Ill., where he had previously lived. In this latter place he made his home with his brother-in-law, James Duncan, until 1854, when he returned to Iowa and spent the following winter of 1855 in Polk County, thence coming to Eddyville as previously stated.

Mr. Cowley received his early education in the log school-house of his native State. As may be supposed his early advantages were limited, but he kept his eyes open as to what was going on in the world around him, and now bears fair comparison with many men who have taken a course in a collegiate institution. He was at one time employed as a raftsman on the Mississippi River, and floated lumber from Stillwater, Minn., to St. Louis, Mo., for a period of four years, being most of the time in the employ of Hanks Bros., of Albany, Ill.

The marriage of Mr. Cowley and Miss Anna Thompson took place on the 21st of June, 1860. Mrs. C. was born in Ohio, and by her union with our subject became the mother of one son—Grant, who was born June 26, 1864, and is now a prosperous jeweler of Eddyville. Mr. Cowley was elected Assessor in 1870, which position he filled for seven successive years, and has held most of the minor offices of his town and township. For four years past he has been Justice of the Peace, and was at one time Mayor of Eddyville. Socially he is connected with the A. F. & A. M., has been Secretary of his lodge for a number of years, and Master for four years, having held some office since first becoming connected with the fraternity. Our subject, in politics, is Republican, and takes an active interest in all matters pertaining to the general welfare of his county and community. Beside his town residence he owns 195 acres of land in Monroe County, and is in good shape to extract a large amount of enjoyment from the good things of life.

E D. SOMERS lives in the city of Ottumwa, and is book-keeper and manager of the agricultural warehouse of John Fuller. He was born in Hancock County, Ill., March 25, 1855, and is a son of Albertus and Caroline Somers, the former a native of Germany and the latter of Vermont. In 1859 the family moved from Hancock County, Ill., to Davis County, Iowa, where they remained two years, and then moved back to Hancock County. In 1867 they again returned to Davis County, Iowa, remaining there one year, and then moved to Jones County, Iowa, where they remained ten years. The father is now living, and doing business in Minneapolis, Minn.; the mother resides in Ottumwa.

The subject of this sketch is one of a family of six children, and is second in order of birth. The others are: Ella E., who was married to J. N. Ellis, but is now deceased; Charles G., now living in Anamosa, this State; Susan B. is the wife of Charles E. Fliesbach, and has one child; they live in Sigourney, Iowa; America A. is the wife of W. R. Kizer, and lives in Ottumwa; James A. is married, and also resides in Ottumwa.

E. D. Somers was married, April 26, 1877, to Hester A. Jenkins. The father of Mrs. Somers is deceased, but her mother survives, and makes her home in Hancock County, Ill. Mr. Somers is a man of good executive and business abilities, and in his political affiliations he is a Republican.

JAMES REESMAN owns and occupies a comfortable homestead on section 36, Highland Township, and is engaged in general farming and stock-raising. He has been a resident of the Hawkeye State since the fall of 1839, coming here when a young man of twenty years old. His birthplace was in Pennsylvania, and the date thereof 1819, his parents being David and Sarah (Shaffer) Reesman, who were natives of the same State. After the birth of our subject they removed to Pickaway County, Ohio, where the father engaged in milling and farming, and whence, in the fall of 1839, they removed to Iowa and settled in Lee County. They remained there until their death, in 1851. Our subject settled in Dahlonega Township, this county, on section 1, where he had entered ninety acres of land, and was engaged in its improvement and cultivation until 1856, when he sold out and moved into the town of Dahlonega, engaging in mercantile pursuits. After three years he removed to Agency City, and the following year, 1860, came to Highland Township and located on section 36, which is his present homestead. He here purchased 130 acres of land, which he has brought to a fine state of cultivation. With his family he occupies a comfortable farm residence, has a good barn and other out-buildings, and all the appliances of a first-class agriculturist.

The marriage of James Reesman with Miss Eunice E. Neal was celebrated in the fall of 1842. Mrs. R. was the daughter of Jesse and Nancy (Strickland) Neal, and was born in Tennessee. By her union with our subject she became the mother of one child, a daughter, Frances M., who died in 1848, at the age of five years, and was buried at Farmington, Iowa. After remaining the faithful and affectionate companion of her husband for a period of forty-four years, Mrs. Eunice Reesman closed her eyes to the scenes of earth on the 26th of February, 1886, at the age of sixty-three years, and is buried in Ottumwa Cemetery. She was a most excellent and worthy lady, and a devoted member of the Christian Church, with which Mr. R. has also been connected for many years.

The father of Mr. Reesman, who was born July 4, 1790, followed the trade of a miller the greater part of his life and died in 1867; the mother had departed this life three years previously, in 1864, having attained the age of seventy-two years. They also were connected with the Christian Church, and their remains are buried in McDonald Cemetery, near Farmington, Iowa.

W. H. CROSS, engaged in real-estate business in, and a prominent citizen of Eldon, erected the first hotel in this city and has been engaged in various departments of business since coming here. He is a man of great energy, and his busy mind is most of the time actively engaged in financial schemes, most of which have proved profitable and reflected credit upon himself as an energetic business man of good judgment and wise management.

The subject of this biography is a native of the Empire State, born in 1818, and the son of Harry and Lovisa (DeWolf) Cross, both natives also of New York. Their son, our subject, remained under the parental roof until 1846, some time after he attained his majority, and then decided to seek a home in the Far West. He accordingly crossed the Mississippi, making his first location in what is now Monroe County, where he followed farming pursuits for two years. He then removed to Wapello County, making his residence at Eddyville, and engaged as stage agent for Fink, Walker & Co., with whom he remained until 1851. He then engaged in the livery business for the following five years, when he returned to Eddyville and established in the same business there, at which he was occupied until 1869. He then secured possession of a hotel in Eldon, the business of which he conducted for seven years, and was then elected Justice of the Peace and held this position for three years. He then became interested in a coal shaft near town, which yielded no profit, Mr. C. barely escaping considerable loss.

Mr. Cross was united in marriage with Miss Maria L. Smith, of Ohio, in 1841, and they became the parents of ten children, the record of whom is as follows: Edgar and Mason died in childhood; Melissa is the wife of L. G. Turner, of Eldon; Phœbe married J. V. Nelson, of Altoona, Iowa; Walter Lovel is engaged in teaming in Eldon; Gertrude is the wife of J. M. Myers; Lawrence W. is at home; Harry L. is yardmaster of the C., R. I. & P. R. R.; Billie A. was killed by the cars near Pella, in November, 1881; Minnie died in 1866.

Mr. and Mrs. Cross are prominently connected with the Methodist Episcopal Church, and our subject is a member of the I. O. O. F., with which he has been connected since 1849. He is a charter member of Eldon Lodge No. 28, which was organized in 1872, principally through his instrumentality.

JOHN M. MURRAY, Assistant Postmaster at Ottumwa, was born in Oskaloosa, Iowa, Jan. 25, 1845. His father, William Murray, was a native of Virginia, but in early life moved with his parents to Coshocton County, Ohio. In about 1840 he removed to Iowa, where he lived the remainder of his life, excepting about four years, when he resided in Missouri. He was a resident of Wapello County a greater portion of the time, and was engaged in farming, being thus occupied until his death, which event occurred in 1884, when in the sixty-seventh year of his age. His wife, Mrs. Selina J. Murray, survives him. Eight children were born of their union, three of whom died in childhood, and five are yet living.

John M. Murray is the oldest living. He resided with his parents until 1862, receiving his education in the common schools and also in the

High School at Oskaloosa. During the year last named he went to Agency City and clerked in a general store, following this occupation the major portion of his time until the fall of 1869, when he engaged in business for himself.

In 1877–78 our subject spent considerable time traveling, engaged as purchasing agent for J. J. Hatfield, of Ottumwa, a dealer in wool. In January, 1879, Mr. Murray was appointed Deputy County Clerk, under W. C. Thompson, and held the position with great credit to himself, as well as his employer, until February, 1882. From this time he was employed in the National and First National Banks of Ottumwa, Iowa, until Aug. 17, 1885, when he received the appointment of Assistant Postmaster.

John M. Murray was united in marriage with Miss Ludie R. Sage, daughter of James and Rebecca Sage, March 19, 1868. She was born June 17, 1851, and of her union with our subject six children have been born—Laura F., Prudie B., Mina M., Le Gene, Poe and Maggie M.

Socially Mr. Murray is a member of Empire Lodge No. 269, A. F. & A. M., and holds the office of Past Master. He is also a member of Clinton Chapter No. 9, R. A. M., and was Secretary of the same for one year. He is likewise a member of Malta Commandery No. 31, K. T., and was Secretary of that commandery for two years.

GRIMES POMEROY, a highly respected citizen of Center Township, owns and occupies a comfortable homestead on section 34, and is successfully engaged in general farming and stock-raising. He is a native of Wayne County, Ohio, and was born July 7, 1820, his parents being Thomas and Annie (Kregel) Pomeroy, who were natives of Pennsylvania and removed to Ohio in early youth.

The subject of our sketch remained under the parental roof until he was eighteen years of age, assisting in the duties of the farm in summer and attending the common schools during the winter. In the fall of 1839 he determined to see something of the western country, and crossing the Father of Waters came into Lee County, Iowa, where he lived until the fall of 1854, in the meantime being engaged in manufacturing fanning-mills. He then purchased a small farm of sixty acres, which he retained possession of until 1855, when he sold out and moved to Ottumwa. In the spring of 1854 he purchased 120 acres of the farm which he now owns and occupies. The land was in its original condition, but he vigorously set about its cultivation. He prospered in his labors, and as time passed on added to his possessions until he now owns 250 acres of land, besides three dwellings in the city of Ottumwa, valued at $2,000.

When young Pomeroy left the parental roof his father gave him about $100 in bank notes, the value of which in those days was very unreliable, and, when he arrived at his journey's end, he found that his money was below par, and that he must depend entirely upon his own resources. But he went to work with a will, determined to establish for himself a comfortable home, and to so build his character that he would be a man among men and occupy a worthy position as a citizen.

The marriage of Mr. Pomeroy occurred in 1846, the maiden of his choice being Miss Martha Johnson. She became the mother of three children, and died in the fall of 1851. She was a highly esteemed lady, and a member in good standing of the Christian Church. The record of their children is as follows: Susan became the wife of Peter Dunberger, a farmer of Allen County, Kan.; the other two children died in infancy. The mother of these children is buried near Ft. Madison, in Lee County.

The second wife of our subject was Miss Ellen I. Thrush, to whom he was married in the fall of 1853. She was the daughter of Robert and Hannah Thrush, and by her union with our subject became the mother of eight children: Martin is in Jackson County, Kan.; Levi, Flora, Rosanna, James, Crage, Ellen and Maggie are at home. Mrs. Pomeroy died Jan. 31, 1884, and is buried in the Shawl graveyard.

During the progress of the late war Mr. Pomeroy enlisted in Co. D. 15th Iowa Vol. Inf., and with his regiment participated in the battles of Shiloh,

Corinth, and the seige and capture of Vicksburg, and after two years' service in the army received his discharge on account of disease contracted while there. Mr. Pomeroy prides himself upon being a "Simon-pure" Republican, and is a member of Cloutman Post No. 69, G. A. R., of Ottumwa. He is considered one of the most skillful and intelligent farmers of this section, and has given much attention to the raising of all kinds of stock.

The father of our subject died in March, 1840, and was buried near Ft. Finley, Ohio. He was a good man in every sense of the word, and a consistent member of the Methodist Episcopal Church. In 1841, after the decease of her husband, the mother of our subject joined her son in this State, and remained with him until her decease, in the fall of 1843. She was buried in the family lot near Ft. Madison, Lee County, and is kindly remembered as an earnest Christian and a devoted member of the Methodist Episcopal Church.

GEORGE W. BOULTON, of the late firm of Boulton Bros., of Ottumwa, was born at Great Yarmouth, England, on the 11th day of December, 1834. He is the son of Benjamin J. and Mary (Ward) Boulton, also of English parentage and ancestry. Mr. Boulton, Sr., was a carpenter by trade and one of the finest builders and contractors of his native place. He was a man of great energy of character, and fine abilities, and prominent in the public affairs of his community, and both parents were active members of the Episcopal Church. Of their union there was born a large family, only three of whom are living, and are residents of Ottumwa: Esther, the wife of George W. Herbert, deceased, lives in this city; Benjamin J. is a resident of Ottumwa, and also George W., of our sketch. Benjamin Boulton, the father, died in his native England in 1849. Three years later Mrs. Boulton emigrated to America with her daughter, and became a resident of Albany, N. Y., where her life terminated Dec. 6, 1868. Her remains are buried at Green Bush.

The subject of this sketch was reared in his native country and received his early education in the English schools. In 1851 he emigrated to America with his brother, B. J., and they located at Albany, N. Y., where he was apprenticed to the barber's trade, and conducted a shop devoted to this business for several years. In connection with it he also engaged in trade in gentlemen's furnishing goods. In 1858 he returned to England, and was there united in marriage, Feb. 2, 1859, with Miss Eliza Palmer Fill, a daughter of Capt. Thomas P. Fill, who commanded a merchant's vessel. Mrs. Boulton was born in the same town as her husband, Great Yarmouth, England, on the 11th of February, 1837. Two weeks after marriage Mr. and Mrs. B. set sail for the United States, and after their arrival located in Green Bush, N. Y., where they remained for the following seven years. Mr. B. then concluded to go into the western country, and after crossing the Father of Waters came into Ottumwa, Iowa, in December, 1866. He was pleased with the appearance of things in the Hawkeye State and, his brother Benjamin having preceded him to this city and being engaged as a baker and confectioner, the brothers went into partnership under the style and title of Boulton Bros., and operated successfully thereafter. They became engaged extensively in wholesale transactions, and as time went on and their trade increased, they were obliged to extend their facilities and move into larger quarters. The last building they occupied was fifty feet deep and three stories high, and their trade extended throughout Iowa and into adjoining States. They gave employment to five men, and our subject was constituted general superintendent and manager. In October, 1886, they having accumulated a handsome competency, retired from active business, and are now enjoying the fruits of their early enterprise and energy.

Mr. Boulton came to America a poor boy, landing on our shores with a capital of $2.50. He had been trained to habits of industry by his excellent parents, and was willing to work at whatever his hands could find to do. He has been an upright and conscientious citizen, and in politics is strongly Republican and cast his first presidential vote for Abraham Lincoln.

The household circle of our subject was completed by the birth of six children, as follows: Emma, the wife of H. C. Peters, a druggist of Ottumwa; May S., Benjamin J. and Grace W. are at home; two died in infancy and are buried in Green Bush, N. Y. The family residence is pleasantly located, and within and without is indicative of cultivated tastes and ample means. The friends and associates of our subject and his family comprise the cultured people of Ottumwa, and they are most worthily filling their places as worthy members of society.

JOHN W. MILLER, a prominent factor in the business interests of Ottumwa, was among the early settlers of Wapello County, and has watched the rapid growth of the Hawkeye State with interest and satisfaction. He is a native of Clay County, Ind., and was born on the 8th of July, 1839, his parents being Abraham and Elizabeth (Yocum) Miller, the former born in Hardin County, Ky., in 1811, and the latter in Montgomery County, the same State, on the 4th of March, 1812. The grandfather of our subject, Jacob Miller, was the founder of Millerstown, Hardin County, and one of the early settlers of the State.

Abraham Miller removed, in 1829, from Kentucky to Indiana, locating near Brazil, now the county seat, of which the lady whom he afterward married, was also a resident, their wedding occurring in 1837. Here Mr. Miller entered a tract of land, and opened up a farm in the midst of heavy timber, after years of laborious toil and sturdy perseverance. He remained there until the fall of 1850, and then went still further west into Schuyler County, Ill., locating on what was called the bottom of Crooked Creek. This stream, during the time of high water, often overflowed its banks, and the pioneers experienced great difficulty in securing their crops. Mr. Miller here labored under great disadvantages on this account, for the space of three years, and then abandoned the struggle. Nearly everyone in that vicinity was afflicted with sickness, the sick outnumbering the well by a large majority. He then removed into McDonough County, and located eleven miles east of Macomb, and subsequently, in about 1869, came into Wapello County, Iowa, and after a useful life of industry and kindly deeds, departed from the scenes of earth in about 1871.

Mr. and Mrs. Abraham Miller became the parents of seven children, of whom the record is as follows: John W. of our sketch, was the eldest born; Nancy E. became the wife of James Patterson, of Bureau County, Ill.; Elijah P. is a resident of New Philadelphia, Ill.; Barbara C. is deceased; James P. and Alexander A. reside in Fulton County, Ill.; Albert J. is deceased. Mrs. Miller had been previously married to James Walch, who died of cholera in 1833, and of this union there was born one son, Jacob R., now a resident of Fulton County, Ill. The mother is still living, and resides in New Philadelphia, Ill., with a son. She is blind, but otherwise well and hearty, and is a most estimable lady, having been for many years a devoted member of the Christian Church.

The subject of our sketch was reared in a log-cabin among the wilds of Indiana, and received his early education in the pioneer school, which was also conducted in the same kind of structure, with puncheon floor, and slabs for seats and desks, the light being admitted through window-panes made of greased paper, and the chimney constructed of mud and sticks. He removed with his parents to Illinois, and subsequently went to Iowa. He was early trained to habits of industry, and as soon as old enough assisted in the duties on the farm, in the meantime procuring such books as he could, and pursuing his studies at home during his leisure time when not at school. He remembers the first religious meeting which he attended, which was conducted in a barn, barns and school-houses being then commonly used for religious purposes. As the result of his studious habits he developed into a teacher, and conducted the first colored school in this county, the people having built a house expressly for that purpose. He was an enterprising and ambitious young man, and starting out from home was employed for a time as insurance and book agent. He then engaged in business as joint proprietor of the Star Mills, at Ottumwa, under the firm name of Wilson & Co., his partner being A. K. Wilson, of Ottumwa. They conducted the

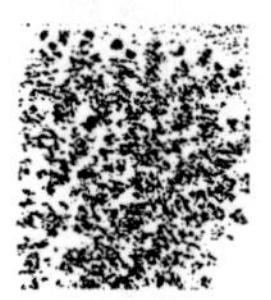

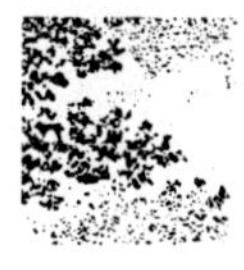

business for three or four years, and then dissolved. Mr. Miller then engaged in trade in second-hand furniture and other commodities, being the pioneer in this business in the city of Ottumwa, it proving quite a novelty in those days.

John W. Miller was united in marriage with Miss Nancy A. Yarnell, on the 13th of March, 1869, in Ottumwa. Mrs. Miller is a native of Wayne County, Ohio, and was born in August, 1845. She was bereft of a mother's affectionate care while an infant, and was reared by the family of Peter Troxel, coming to Iowa in 1868. By her union with our subject she has become the mother of five children, viz., Harry N., Blanche E., Grace E., Ralph E. and Mabel C.

During the progress of the late war Mr. Miller enlisted as a soldier in the 72d Illinois Infantry, which rendezvoused at Chicago. He was soon afterward taken ill with the measles, and on the 28th of February following was discharged on account of disability. Mr. Miller in politics is a stanch Republican, and strongly in favor of prohibition, and the enforcement of the laws. He is straightforward and upright in his business transactions, and highly esteemed for his excellent personal traits of character. Both he and Mrs. Miller are connected with the Methodist Episcopal Church of Ottumwa, to the support of which they contribute of their means in a liberal manner. They are pleasantly located in a handsome home, and surrounded by all the comforts of life.

J. M. SWOPE, a resident of Wapello County of thirty years, and a successful and well-to-do farmer, residing on section 35, Cass Township, was born Oct. 13, 1831, in Monroe County, W. Va. Mr. Swope is a son of John and Nancy (Riffe) Swope, the father a native of West Virginia and both of German descent. They became the parents of the following children, seven of whom lived to attain the age of man and womanhood: Rachel became the wife of Christopher Sodghill, and both are deceased, their demise having occurred in this county; Michael, Rebecca and Malinda died in infancy; David R. came to this county with our subject and died in 1877; Adeline became the wife of Robert Cummings, and departed this life in Virginia; J. M., our subject, was the next in order of birth; Martha is living on the old homestead in Virginia; Amanda died when quite young and while the family were yet residents of Virginia; Mary M. is the wife of J. H. Shumate, a stock-dealer and also Postmaster in Eskridge, Wabaunsee Co., Kan.; W. L. yet lives on the old homestead where he was born, in Virginia. The father died in 1877, in Monroe County, W. Va., aged eighty years, and his good wife departed this life a year later, aged seventy-eight years.

It was during the year 1856 that the subject of this notice left the parental roof-tree and went forth in the cold, unfriendly world to do for himself. He came West in company with his brother, David R., and family, and located at Chillicothe, this county, on the 10th of November of that year. The journey was made overland, and required forty-six days to complete it. During the winter of 1856 he attended school at Chillicothe, and in the spring of 1857 he and his brother rented 160 acres of land, on which they worked with a will, for it was there they expected to get their first start. It was during that spring that Mr. Swope purchased his first land, the same being forty acres, it being located on section 35, and including a portion of his present farm. In the fall of 1857 he moved on his land and began farming for himself, having in the meantime, April 16, 1857, become a Benedict. The lady whom he chose as his companion for life was Miss Alvina R. Myers. She was born June 12, 1839, in Ohio, and is a daughter of G. F. and H. R. Myers, natives of that State. A biography of her father is given elsewhere in this work.

The union of our subject with Miss Myers was productive of the birth of seven children, viz: Willie, who died in infancy; Rebecca M., born July 6, 1860, departed this life Oct. 3, 1862; John F., born Feb. 13, 1863, died March 24, 1880; Emma L., born Dec. 10, 1865, is living at home, as likewise is George M., born March 24, 1869, and Robert C., Dec. 21, 1874; Lloyd H. was born Feb. 13, 1880, and eleven days later his mother passed from earth to a better home beyond. She was a member of the Methodist Episcopal Church, a loving wife, a kind mother, and a generous friend, and is buried in the cemetery at Chillicothe.

Mr. Swope has added to his original purchase and is now the owner of 165 acres of well-improved land, on which he has a good dwelling, barn, and other necessary out-buildings. What he has he has made by hard work and economy. He has been Township Assessor and Collector several terms, and is respected for his integrity and fair dealing. He is a Democrat in politics, and socially is a member of the Masonic fraternity, holding fellowship with Lodge No. 74, of Eddyville.

HOMER D. IVES, deceased, was formerly a prominent attorney of Eddyville, and had established himself as one of the brightest members of the profession in this locality. He was born in North Haven, Conn., in 1814, and departed this life Oct. 14, 1867, on board the steamer Rob Roy, while on his way home from St. Louis. The subject of our sketch was the son of William and Mary (Bray) Ives, natives of Connecticut. He received his primary education in the common schools of his native State, and after arriving at a suitable age entered Yale College, from the law department of which he graduated, and subsequently came to Iowa, in 1843, making his first location in Keosauqua, and commenced the practice of his profession. After a few months he removed to Eddyville and opened an office, in the duties of which he employed himself until his decease. He practiced in the courts of Marion, Mahaska, Wapello and Monroe Counties, and at one time was on one side of every case in three or four counties around, and built up for himself an enviable reputation as an advocate and counselor.

The marriage of Mr. Ives and Miss Mary Eastman was celebrated in the spring of 1849, at Eddyville. Mrs. Ives is a native of New York, and the daughter of Oliver and Laura (Ward) Eastman, also natives of the Empire State. Of her union with our subject there were born the following children: Mary V., the wife of Dr. Todd, of Los Angeles, Cal.; Carrie E., married to W. A. Hunter, station agent for the C., R. I. & P. R. R. at Eddyville; Wilfred H. is a farmer of St. John's County, Kan.; Jennie W. has for the past three years been a teacher in the graded schools of Moline, Ill., and Nina B. is engaged in teaching music at Brookfield, Mo.

Mr. Ives was a public-spirited citizen, always willing to contribute of his time and means for the advancement of any enterprise calculated to promote the mental, moral or educational advancement of his community. He became very successful in his business, and besides acquiring considerable town property was the owner of over 200 acres of valuable land in Wapello and Monroe Counties. Mrs. Ives occupies the residence in Eddyville, and is a lady highly esteemed for her excellent personal traits of character. The family is well known and highly respected throughout the community, the children being of bright and promising characters, and giving ample evidence of having inherited the talents and genius of their estimable parents.

B. W. SCOTT, a prominent and successful attorney of the city of Ottumwa, is a native of Ohio County, Ky., born near the town of Hartford, Jan. 17, 1854. His parents were George W. and Nancy C. (Keith) Scott, natives of the same State. When our subject was yet a boy his parents moved to Indiana and settled in Perry County, where he received his early education in the common schools. He remained at home until he arrived at the age of twenty years, and then entered the office of Judge C. H. Mason, under whom he studied law for the following three years, teaching school in the meantime to assist in meeting his expenses. He was admitted to the bar in 1878, and three years later was admitted to partnership with his former preceptor, the style of the firm being Mason & Scott, and they operated in company until September, 1885, when Mr. S. concluded to seek the western country. He traveled through Illinois, and in the spring of 1886 came into Iowa, locating in Ottumwa. He opened an office and began practice, and within a comparatively brief space of time has established himself in the confidence and esteem of his fellow-townsmen and his brethren of the profession. He makes a specialty of criminal practice, and is considered an advocate of more than ordinary merit.

The marriage of Mr. Scott and Miss Mary E. Marshall, of Perry County, Ind., was celebrated on the 29th of March, 1879. Mrs. C. is the daughter of W. W. Marshall, who served in the Union army during the late war, and was killed near Helena, Ark. Mr. and Mrs. S. have become the parents of one child, Charles M.

Mr. Scott is Republican in politics, and while in Indiana took a prominent part in local and general political matters, being Chairman of the Republican Central Committee, and "stumped" the county in the interest of his party in 1884. He is a young man of more than ordinary ability, and while in Indiana served as Deputy Prosecuting Attorney. In his special line he is a most able advocate.

LIEUT. WILLIAM P. SHARP, a resident of Ottumwa, and an honored pioneer of Wapello County, came to this region at an early period in its history, and has watched with intense interest and pleasure the progress of the remarkable changes which have taken place since. When a young man he crossed the Father of Waters and gazed with wonder and admiration upon the beautiful country, with its great possibilities, which lay before him. Mr. Sharp is a native of Wooster, Wayne Co., Ohio, and was born Oct. 9, 1825, his parents being James O. and Margaret (Crosby) Sharp, both natives of Pennsylvania. They removed from their native State to Ohio in 1815, and were among the early settlers in that locality. The cabins of the pioneers were few and far between, and they made the journey thither with teams, cutting their way through the heavy timber. Amidst this timber they also settled, erected a rude cabin, and commenced to clear a spot of ground. By incessant industry they soon brought a few acres to a condition of cultivation, and established a comfortable home.

James O. and Margaret Sharp were the parents of three children, as follows: Mary became the wife of Thomas L. Wisner, who was the County Clerk of Wells County for twenty years; Sarah was the wife of Ayers Knight, of Defiance County, Ohio, and died in 1877, and William P., our subject. James Sharp departed this life in 1838, at the age of forty years. His wife, Margaret, survived him ten years, passing to her final rest in 1848. They were most worthy and excellent people, highly respected in the county where they resided, and active members of the Baptist Church.

William P. Sharp of our sketch was reared in his native county, receiving careful parental training and a fair education in the pioneer schools. The school buildings at that day and in that section consisted of log cabins with puncheon floors, and slabs for seats and desks, supported by poles fastened in the wall. He was fond of his books, and after completing his primary studies, entered Edinburg Academy at Edinburg, where he took a thorough course, becoming qualified as a teacher, and followed this occupation for some time afterward. At the age of eighteen years he was employed as a clerk in a general store in the town of Congress, Wayne County, which position he occupied for two years following, when he returned to his father's homestead and remained for about three years

The marriage of William P. Sharp and Miss Sophia Helfer was celebrated in 1846, at the residence of her parents in Ashland County. Mrs. Sharp was a daughter of Christopher and Lydia Helfer, natives of Pennsylvania, who emigrated to Ohio at an early day and shared in common with their fellow pioneers, the privations and hardships incident to the early settlement of that State. In 1848 Mr. Sharp with his wife removed from Ohio to Indiana, and located in Bluffton, Wells County. There he pursued the occupation of a clerk in a general store for two years, after which he returned to his native State and engaged in the sale of boots and shoes. He then returned to his former residence in Indiana, remaining there until 1856, when he removed to Danville, Iowa, and two years later came into Ottumwa. Mr. Sharp then started a boot-and-shoe store in the city, and was engaged in this department of trade until 1862, after the Rebellion had necessitated an urgent call for troops for the preservation of the Union, when

Mr. Sharp, laying aside his personal interests, volunteered his services to his country, and enlisted in Co. H, 36th Iowa Vol. Inf. They first rendezvoused at Keokuk for two months and then proceeded to Benton Barracks, St. Louis. They were soon ordered to Helena, Ark., and Mr. Sharp was detailed for guard duty. He only served about one year, as the exposure and hardship incident to a soldier's life undermined his constitution, and becoming unable to fulfill his duties, he was compelled to abandon his post and return home, receiving his discharge on account of disability. He has never recovered from the effects of army life, and still suffers from the hardships which he endured. During his brief experience as a soldier he received the encomiums of his superior officers for duty bravely performed.

Mr. Sharp was employed as a traveling salesman for about twenty years, and in that time has made many trips from Boston to St. Louis, while transacting a large amount of business in the intervening cities. Mr. Sharp went into the army a Democrat, and now may be classed as an independent Republican. His aim is to vote for the best man and the best measures without regard to party. Socially he belongs to the I. O. O. F., with which he has been connected for a period of thirty-seven years. He became a member of the Wooster (Ohio) Lodge No. 42, in 1850, and upon his removal to Indiana withdrew from this, and was transferred to Bluffton Lodge No. 142, afterward becoming a member of Charity Lodge No. 56, at New London, and after coming to Ottumwa he joined Ottumwa Lodge No. 9, and has been a delegate to the sessions of the Grand Lodge of the United States. He was Grand Master of the State of Iowa, in 1868–69, Grand Patriarch in 1872–73, and Grand Representative in 1871–72.

Mrs. and Mrs. Sharp became the parents of five children, only two of whom are living: Oscar H., a jeweler of Centerville, Appanoose County, and Mary, the wife of Charles E. Boude, ticket agent of the C., R. I. & P. R. R.; three children died in early childhood. The family residence is pleasantly located at No. 437 East Fourth street, and during a residence of twenty-eight years in Ottumwa Mr. and Mrs. Sharp have occupied an enviable position in the community, and enjoy, in the highest degree, the respect of a large circle of friends and acquaintances.

CAPT. JOHN PUMROY, deceased, a former resident of Ottumwa, and one of the earliest settlers of Wapello County, was a native of Westmoreland County, Pa., the date of his birth being July 15, 1815. While a young man he went from his native State to Wooster, Ohio, and in 1825 crossed the Mississippi and came into Lee County, Iowa, before it became a State. The following year, on the 27th of October, he was united in marriage with Miss Eve Ann Booer, who was born on the 4th of August, 1817. Of this union there are two children living: Mary A., the wife of A. D. Boyer, of Lincoln, Neb., and James, whose residence at present is not known. After remaining the companion of her husband for sixteen years, Mrs. Eve Pumroy departed this life Sept. 26, 1852.

In 1845 Mr. Pumroy removed into Wapello County, locating in Ottumwa, where he established a drug business, and built the corner block which is now occupied by the dry-goods store of W. W. Ennis & Co. After becoming a resident of this city he made the acquaintance of Miss Sarah Z. Burge, to whom he was married in 1852. She was a native of Genessee County, N. Y., born in 1824, and the daughter of John and Polly W. (Morgan) Burge. In 1833, when his daughter, the wife of our subject, was a little girl eight years old, Mr. Burge removed from New York to Ohio, and from there, in 1840, crossed the Mississippi and came into Van Buren County, Iowa. Twelve years later he went to Oregon, accompanied by his wife, and they both died in that State, Mr. Burge in March, 1872, and Mrs. B. three years later, in 1875.

Mr. Pumroy of our sketch was a very intelligent man, an extensive reader, and thoroughly posted upon the current events of the day. Upon the breaking out of the Rebellion, he enlisted in Co. M, 9th Iowa Vol. Cav., which he had himself raised, and of which he was commissioned Captain by Gov. Kirkwood. They first rendezvoused at Davenport, Iowa, for a short time, and were then sent to Benton

Barricks, St. Louis, where they soon received marching orders, their destination being Little Rock, Ark. Here the health of Mr. Pumroy failed, and he contracted the disease of which he died at Bright Haven, six weeks afterward.

Capt. Pumroy was of a nervous temperament, generous and whole-souled, quick to form an opinion and courageous in its expression. During the earlier years of his life, while the Whig party was in existence, he was a firm adherent to its principles and a great admirer of Henry Clay. Upon the abandonment of the old party by the organization of the new, he cheerfully indorsed the platform of the latter and uniformly cast his vote for its principles and candidates. He was warmly attached to his home and friends, and in his family relations, it was said, never an impatient or unkind word passed his lips and that he was most generous in providing for them.

Capt. Pumroy occupied a high position in the Masonic fraternity, under the auspices of which he was buried with all the honors which it could confer. He was a member in good standing of the Christian Church, and his death was greatly lamented by a large circle of friends and acquaintances. He left a widow in good circumstances, who is at present living in Ottumwa in a pleasant home, and enjoying the esteem and friendship of many of the cultured people of the city.

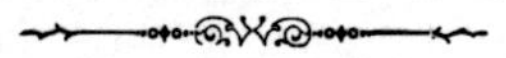

AARON MELICK, Justice of the Peace and a resident of Ottumwa, is a native of Knox County, Ohio, and was born April 8, 1835. He is the son of Timothy and Maria (Noffsinger) Melick, both natives of the same county as their son. They were the parents of two children, Sarah Belle, now deceased, and Aaron, our subject. Timothy Melick spent his entire life in his native State, and died there in 1839, when his son Aaron was a child of four years old. The latter remained with his mother until he was sixteen years of age, attending the district schools, where he received a fair education. His mother subsequently married James Britton, and in 1851 they came to Iowa and located in Johnson County.

In 1852 the subject of our sketch removed from Johnson to Wapello, Louisa County, and went into the office of the *Louisa County Times*, the first paper printed in that county. He there learned the trade of a printer, and in 1855 returned to Ohio, where he was united in marriage with Miss Mary E. Bellville, the daughter of Nicolas Bellville, of Union County, that State. Mrs. Melick was born in that county in 1841, and five years after marriage removed with her husband to Iowa, where he assumed charge of the *Jeffersonian Blade*, at Albia, Monroe County, under the proprietor, Mr. Noffsinger. In the spring of 1862, the war being then in progress, Mr. Noffsinger enlisted in the 8th Iowa Infantry, and Mr. Melick then went into partnership with George Heckenlooper, who is now in the Treasury Department at Washington, D. C. Mr, Heckenlooper also enlisted in the service in the 22d Iowa Infantry, and Mr. Melick then took in for a partner Josiah T. Young, who was afterward Secretary of State for two terms. He also enlisted in the army, becoming a member of the 36th Iowa Infantry, and then Mr. Melick moved the office into Eddyville, this county. Here he established the Eddyville *Star*. A few years later he sold out, and subsequently, in company with C. C. Bitner, established the *Independent*, which they afterward sold to H. N. Clement.

Mr. Melick was afterward appointed Postmaster by President Lincoln, the appointment being confirmed after the assassination of the latter. Mr. Melick held this office four years, and was then elected Mayor of the city. After serving his term he came to Ottumwa in 1872, and for a short time was associated with Samuel Evans, and was next employed on the *Courier* as city editor. He remained with the publishers of that paper for several years, and then took charge of the *Daily Democrat* until 1883, when he abandoned the newspaper business and engaged in keeping a hotel and restaurant.

In the spring of 1885 Mr. Melick was elected City Clerk of Ottumwa, and in the fall of 1886 was elected Justice of the Peace on the Democratic ticket, which office he continues to hold, and the duties of which he is conducting with great credit to himself and satisfaction to his constituents. Socially Mr. Melick belongs to the Masonic fraternity, being a member of Eddyville Lodge No. 74, demitted and joined the Ottumwa Lodge No. 269. Mr. and Mrs. Melick have become the parents of four children, three daughters and one son: Annie M. became the wife of William H. Pangborn, deceased; Stella B., Winnie and Griffin are at home.

DAVID RAILSBACK, a resident of Ottumwa, and a pioneer settler of the Hawkeye State, came to Iowa with his parents while it was yet a Territory, in 1841. They located in the northern part of Van Buren County, and remained there until the 1st of May, when they went into Washington Township, Wapello County, where the father purchased a claim of that well-known old pioneer, James Jordan, consisting of 320 acres, upon which he located and opened up a farm. He first moved his family into an Indian wigwam until he could roll enough logs together to build a cabin. When this was completed, with the exception of the floor, he moved his family into it, and they commenced pioneer life in good earnest, and for several years thereafter endured their full share of the hardships and privations incident to the settlement of a new country. He pursued the improvement and cultivation of his farm industriously and laboriously for many years, and in due time received an abundant reward. He was a man of great energy and enterprise, and took pride in seeking to do the best he could under all circumstances, and consequently his crops and stock were among the best in that region. He was the first man to bring a Shorthorn bull into the county, from which the greater part of the fine cattle in this vicinity have sprung.

The subject of this sketch was born in Marion County, Ind., on the 27th day of March, 1839, and is the son of Edward and Francina (Hunt) Railsback. The parental family consisted of fourteen children, four of whom are living, as follows: Clarrisa is the wife of David Bear, of Davis County; Mary, the wife of Jacob Rutherford, of California; Mahlon, of Montana, and David, our subject. The mother of these children departed this life in 1845, and for his second wife Edward Railsback married Miss Rebecca Langdon, of which union one child was born, now deceased. Mrs. Rebecca Railsback died a short time afterward, and Mr. R. was married the third time, taking for his wife Miss Catharine Houtman, who became the mother of the following children: Olive, the wife of James Brown; Jacob, Jasper, Allen, and Nina (now Mrs. Jones). The father of our subject died in 1859. He was a member of the Whig party, which, at the time of his death, was being merged into the new Republican organization, the latter having sprung into existence three years previously.

David Railsback was reared in the pioneer log cabin, received a limited education, and as soon as old enough began to assist his parents in the duties around the homestead. At the age of twenty-two years, in 1861, the Civil War being then in progress, he enlisted as a soldier of the Union in Co. E, 3d Iowa Vol. Cav. The 2d battalion of the regiment was detailed in Northern Missouri, where they were engaged in circumventing the bushwhackers, and our subject participated in the various engagements and skirmishes which his regiment encountered until 1864, the expiration of his term of service. He then veteranized in the same regiment, and at the battle of Big Pine Grove, Ala., was wounded in the right hip by a rifle-ball, from which he never recovered, and which will probably cause him annoyance and suffering as long as he lives. He did not, however, allow this to disable him permanently, but as soon as possible recovered from the first effects of the wound and rejoined his regiment, remaining with his comrades until the close of the war, when he was mustered out at Atlanta, receiving an honorable discharge. On account of his wounds he now receives a pension of $12 a month.

Returning home at the close of the war, Mr. Railsback was married in Wapello County, on the 10th of December, 1865, to Miss Mary E. Page. Mrs. Railsback is a native of Ohio, and the daughter of L. A. and Achsa (Harris) Page, natives of Ohio, who crossed the Mississippi and came into Wapello County at an early period in the history of this State. Their daughter, the wife of our subject, was born July 17, 1842. Mr. and Mrs. R. have become the parents of four children—William E. L., Achsa F., Clarissa May and Lillie Belle. Mr. and Mrs. R., with their son William and daughter Clarissa, are members of the Christian Church. Politically Mr. R. is a Greenbacker. He has been identified with the industrial and business interests of the county for many years, has watched its growth with interest and pleasure, and in all respects has fulfilled the obligations of an honest man and a good citizen.

CHARLES HALL, of the law firm of Coen & Hall, at Ottumwa, a firm well and favorably known for its trustworthiness and proficiency, was born at Carthage, Hancock Co., Ill., Dec. 7, 1856. He is a son of George W. and Mary Ann (McHary) Hall, the former a native of Delaware and the latter of Kentucky. The father of our subject was a physician by profession, and a graduate of Jefferson Medical College of Philadelphia. Subsequently he was Professor of Keokuk Medical College for several years, and is at present engaged in the practice of his profession in St. Louis, Mo.

Charles Hall graduated at St. Louis High School, and supplemented his education by a course of study at Cornell University, at Ithaca, N. Y. He also graduated from the Law School at St. Louis in 1881, and was admitted to practice in all the counties of that State and Iowa. In 1882 our subject came to Ottumwa, where he hung out his shingle and engaged in the practice of his profession, in which he has been constantly engaged to the present time, meeting with more than ordinary success. He is a young man of far more than ordinary ability, and, judging from the past has an exceedingly bright future before him. During the year 1884 Mr. Hall was elected City Solicitor of Ottumwa, and in 1886 was re-elected to the same position.

Our subject is a Democrat in politics, and in 1885 was elected Chairman of the Democratic Central Committee. Socially he is a member of the Masonic fraternity, belonging to the Chapter and Commandery, and also the K. of P. and A. O. U. W. Mr. Hall was married in Carthage, Ill., to Miss Eva Carlton, daughter of Dr. J. W. Carlton, and they have one child—Edith.

RITZ, of Eldon Village, is a dealer in general merchandise, and also the proprietor of Eldon Mills, and in his joint occupations is meeting with that success which is the just reward of enterprise and perseverance. Mr. Ritz came to this county in 1884, and at once located in Eldon. He is a native of Switzerland, born in 1844, and is the son of J. U. and Annie (Newcomb) Ritz. He came to America with his parents when a child of five or six years old, and they first located in Greene County, Ohio, making their home there for several years. They then removed to Bloomfield, Iowa, and afterward to Davis County, thence to Van Buren County, and located upon a farm, where they remained until 1868. Our subject then went to Portland, Iowa, where he made his home until 1877, and engaged in general merchandise. He afterward removed to a farm in the same county, where he lived until the fall of 1878, and then moved to "Stumptown," now Selma, Van Buren County. Here he again engaged in general merchandise, which occupied his time until he came to Eldon, and purchased the stock and trade of J. G. Randall, and has continued the business at the same place since that time, but still has an interest in the Selma business.

Mr. Ritz was married to Miss Margaret McIntosh, of Van Buren County, in 1868, and of this union there were born five children—Clarence, Ira, Henry, Ethel and Cora. Mr. Ritz is a member in good standing of the A. F. & A. M., and the I. O. O. F. The subject of our sketch was the eldest of seven children born to his parents, and was a poor boy when he came to this country. He received a limited education in the district schools, but made the most of his opportunities and kept a watchful eye on what was going on around him. His success in life has been the result of his own energy and industry, and for the many excellent qualities of his character he is held in the highest esteem by his fellow-townsmen. His parents are still living, and reside at Selma, Iowa.

G. M. LENTNER, a pioneer of the Hawkeye State, came to Wapello County in 1851, three years after the admission of Iowa into the Union as a State. The country was but thinly settled, and only here and there curled the smoke from the lowly cabin of the adventurous emigrant. Mr. L. was a native of Delaware, born in Essex County in 1807, and the son of Jacob and Lydia (Russell) Lentner, natives of Pennsylvania and Delaware respectively. He was reared to farming pursuits, and obtained such education as the schools of that early period afforded. When he was a lad of nine years old he went to Athens County, Ohio, with his parents, and lived there until 1851. They then came to Wapello County, settling in Dahlonega Township, where our subject remained until the spring of 1864. He then removed into Highland Township, and purchased 120 acres of land on section 35, which constitutes his present homestead and where he still lives.

Mr. Lentner, of our sketch, was married, Dec. 10, 1829, to Miss Ann McGonigal. She died Nov. 10, 1830, leaving one child, Sarah Ann, who is now the widow of William Stillwell, and resides in Ohio. Mr. Lentner was again married, in 1831, to Miss Mary Imes, a native of Ohio, and the record of their children is as follows: Elizabeth died at the age of four years; Henry J. is a resident of Highland Township; Louisa F. is the wife of Dr. Hinsey, of Ottumwa; Jacob is a farmer of Highland Township; Rhoda was married to William T. Scott, who became a soldier of the Union and died in the service; she departed this life Sept. 12, 1876; Hester Matilda is the wife of Sanford Kirkpatrick.

Mr. Lentner was a natural mechanic, and during his earlier years exhibited with pride many of the products of his skill and handiwork. His somewhat limited education has been supplemented by a course of instructive reading, and he has been a keen observer of what was going on around him. By this means he possesses a rich fund of information upon matters in general, and is a remarkably interesting talker.

The father of our subject was a soldier in the War of 1812, and during times of peace was engaged in agricultural pursuits. He reached the ripe old age of seventy-three years, and died about 1848. His faithful wife, the mother of our subject, preceded her husband nearly thirty years to the land of the hereafter, dying in 1819.

E. E. McELROY, of the firm of Chambers & McElroy, of the city of Ottumwa, in company with his partner, is successfully conducting the business of attorney and counselor at law. Mr. McElroy is a native of Fayette County, Ohio, and was born on the 16th of February, 1849, his parents being T. G. and Esther (Kerr) McElroy, natives of the same county. He was reared on a farm, where he remained until sixteen years of age, receiving his primary education in the district schools, which was supplemented by an attendance at the High School of Greenfield, and afterward at the Academy of South Salem, Ohio. From these he entered Cornell University at Ithaca, N. Y., from which he graduated in the class of 1872. He then entered the law department of the State University of Iowa City, from which he received the degree of LL. B., and license to practice in all the courts of the State, and began the practice of his profession at Ottumwa, on the 18th of August, 1873. He operated alone for the space of sixteen months, and then entered into partnership with W. E. Chambers, and Feb. 18, 1884, they admitted a third partner, Mr. S. A. W. Carver, a former student in the office, into the firm. The firm of Chambers, McElroy & Carver continued in business until Feb. 1, 1887, when Mr. Carver retired, and moved to California, leaving as his successor the old firm of Chambers & McElroy. Beside other important trusts the firm is attorney for that powerful corporation, the C., M. & St. P. R. R.

Mr. McElroy is still on the sunny side of forty, and is possessed of more than ordinary ability. He

B. Randel

is a gentleman of fine address and gives strict attention to the duties of his profession. He was married in Greenfield, Ohio, in 1873, to Miss Belle Hamilton. She was a native of that State, and the daughter of Thomas and Elizabeth Hamilton, and by her union with our subject became the mother of five children—Clifford, Carl, Walter, Ralph and Evalyn. Mrs. McElroy departed this life May 10, 1883, and our subject was subsequently married to Miss Elizabeth A. Milner, of Polk County, Iowa. They have one child—Edna. Their home is one of the resorts of the cultured people of Ottumwa, and is surrounded with much that constitutes the abode of cultivation and and refinement. Our subject and his wife are regular attendants of the Presbyterian Church, and are held in high esteem by a large circle of friends and acquaintances.

BENJAMIN RANDEL, a prominent and influential farmer and stock-grower of Center Township, owns and occupies a fine estate situated on section 12. He has been a resident of the Hawkeye State since 1865, locating first in Ottumwa, and then removing to the farm which he now occupies. This consists of 220 acres of finely improved land, upon which is a comfortable brick residence, a shapely and substantial barn, and all the out-buildings necessary to a well-regulated grain and stock farm. Beside the homestead in Center Township he has three other farms in the county, his landed possessions in all aggregating about 500 acres. He formerly owned 2,000 acres, but two years ago divided up 1,500 among his children. Beside having been one of the largest landowners in Wapello County, he has materially assisted in its industrial and agricultural interests, and as an honest man and a good citizen has contributed his full quota to its growth and development.

The subject of this history was born in Hamilton County, Ohio, June 16, 1812. His parents were Benjamin and Ollie (Williamson) Randel, the father a native of Vermont and the mother of Virginia. Benjamin Randel, Sr., followed farming as a business, and served as a private soldier in the War of 1812, under Gen. Harrison. He died in Ohio many years ago. Mrs. Ollie Randel afterward came to Iowa, and died at the home of her son, our subject.

The parental family removed from Ohio to Franklin County, Ind., at an early period in the history of the latter State, and there Benjamin Randel was reared on a farm and educated in the pioneer schools, which, as is well understood, were not to be compared with the institutions of learning of the present day. The edifice in which he pursued his primary studies was built of logs, with puncheon floor and benches, greased paper for window-panes, and heated by the broad, old-fashioned fireplace. The teacher was not expected to give instruction in or to know anything more than the rudiments of a common English education. At the age of fifteen years young Benjamin commenced to learn the trade of a potter, with John P. Williams, who lived in Blooming Grove. He followed his trade until 1850, and then resolved to interest himself in agriculture. He purchased 280 acres of land near Greensburg, Ind., and had it apportioned off into "out-lots," of five acres each. These Mr. Randel sold so that he realized about $150 per acre, and most of the money thus received he invested in lands in Wapello County, Iowa, which was undoubtedly one of the best things that ever happened to this county, for it not only secured an enterprising and energetic business man, but a valuable citizen to this section.

The marriage of Benjamin Randel and Miss Maranda Lathrop was celebrated in 1832. Mrs. Randel was a native of Canada, and born March 30, 1811. She was the daughter of Erastus and Delia (Ingles) Lathrop, both of whom were natives of Connecticut, but afterward became residents of Canada and then of Vermont. They removed from the Green Mountain State to Indiana in 1815, having left Canada during the War of 1812. Erastus Lathrop served as a soldier in that war, and retired with the rank of Colonel. Both parents died in Indiana.

Mr. and Mrs. Randel became the parents of ten children, the record of whom is as follows: J. M. married Miss Martha Terhoon, and resides in Mississippi; E. L. married Miss Rachel Draper, and resides in Center Township, this county; Margaret J. is the wife of William Meek, and they are living in

Monroe County, this State; Martha died in infancy, and William at the age of sixteen years; Holliday enlisted as a soldier of the Union, in the 129th Indiana Infantry, and died in Nashville, Tenn., from disease contracted in the army; John N. married Miss Adelia Brown, and lives in this county; Elmira is the wife of Thomas Spillman, and they are living in Ottumwa; Morris E. and Harriet are deceased. Mr. and Mrs. Randel are both members in good standing of the Methodist Episcopal Church. Politically our subject is a conscientious Republican, and in Indiana was one of the Associate Judges of Decatur County.

A fine portrait of Mr. Randel is shown on another page of this work, also a view of his home.

E. S. KENT, a liveryman at Nos. 111 and 113 West Second street, Ottumwa, has been in this business since 1881. He has twelve head of horses, a fine hearse, and gives special attention to the undertaking department. As a liveryman he is pleasant and accommodating, and has a fine patronage. Our subject was born in Greene County, Pa., Aug. 24, 1845, and is a son of John and Eliza (Shields) Kent, the father being a farmer by occupation. In 1874 the parents came to Iowa and remained one year, then returned to Pennsylvania, where they staid one year, and in the spring of 1876 came back to Iowa, remaining eighteen months, and then returned to Pennsylvania, where they have since remained.

The subject of this sketch was reared upon a farm, receiving his education in the common schools of Pennsylvania. In 1868 he came to Iowa, worked on a farm by the month for Mr. Buckner, and then rented the same in company with his brother Hiram, for one year. In 1870 Mr. Kent was united in marriage with Elizabeth C. Stevens, who was born in Wapello County, in 1848, and is the daughter of Benjamin and Mary Stevens. Mr. Stevens was a carpenter and machinist by trade, but for many years was engaged in farming. He is now deceased; his wife yet survives, and is living in this county. Mr. and Mrs. Kent have become the parents of seven children: Orie E., deceased; Maggie, deceased; Hudson E., at home; Maud, deceased; Mamie, Freddy and Hosie.

Mr. Kent held the office of Deputy Sheriff from the 14th of April, 1884, to March 16, 1885, when he resigned the office, having been elected to that of City Marshal of Ottumwa, in which latter office he served one year. As an official Mr. Kent gave entire satisfaction to the people generally. He is a member of the Masonic fraternity, and politically is a Democrat.

W. S. CRIPS, of Ottumwa, is successfully engaged with his brother in operating a transfer line, in connection with which he is also carrying on the largest livery and feed business in the city of Ottumwa. He is a thorough-going business man, energetic and straightforward, and is reckoned as one of the leading men in the business affairs of the city. Our subject is a native of Ross County, Ohio, and was born March 22, 1847, his parents being W. H. and Martha (Jones) Crips, natives respectively of Pennsylvania and Ohio. The father was of German descent and parentage, and possessed the sturdy and honest attributes of his ancestors in a marked degree. The mother, a native of Ohio, is now living in Center Township.

W. S. Crips became a resident of this county in 1850, coming here with his father. The latter purchased a farm in the township where he now resides, and our subject remained under the parental roof until he was twenty-five years of age, receiving careful parental training at home and a fair education in the district schools. After leaving school he engaged in farming pursuits and as a stock-dealer, driving and shipping cattle for a period of one year, after which he abandoned this branch of business and confined his attention to farming. In November, 1878, he persuaded his father to lease the farm to a tenant, and then purchased the transfer line which was owned and operated by T. E. Muir. He proved himself especially adapted to this business and met with success from the start. In June, 1881, he added to it the livery and feed business, and is on the high road to prosperity.

Now, in connection, he is running the only bus line in the city, formerly run by Con Lewis.

The subject of our sketch was united in marriage with Miss Rosa L. Jeffries, of South Ottumwa, in 1874. Mrs. Crips is the daughter of B. W. Jeffries, of Kentucky, and was born in Center Township, this county, Aug. 12, 1857. She has become the mother of two children, a son and daughter: B. W., born March 12, 1876, and Mary E., May 19, 1881. Mrs. C. is prominently connected with the Main street Methodist Episcopal Church, and socially Mr. C. is connected with the K. of P. They occupy a handsome residence, pleasantly located, and are surrounded by all the comforts of life and many of its luxuries.

GEORGE D. HACKWORTH, deceased, was one of the early pioneers of Wapello County, coming to this section as early as 1845. He located in Center Township and engaged in farming pursuits, building up for himself a record as an honest man and a good citizen, and the encourager and supporter of every worthy enterprise calculated to advance the interests of this community. Our subject was a native of Virginia, born March 8, 1810. When a young man Mr. Hackworth removed to Ohio, where he met the lady of his choice, and they were married there in 1832. In August, 1845, they started west across the Mississippi, and coming into Wapello County, Iowa, located upon a farm in Center Township, and became engaged in agricultural pursuits.

Upon coming to this county the native talents and ability of Mr. Hackworth received ready recognition, and he was at once selected as a leader in the affairs of this section. He was soon afterward elected County Surveyor, and superintended the work of determining the township lines, and laid off several additions to the town of Ottumwa. In 1874 he was elected County Auditor, which position he filled for two years. He afterward went to Kansas and died in 1877. The partner of his early manhood and the mother of his children had preceded him to the better land in 1856, in Center Township. They were both devoted members of the Methodist Episcopal Church, and contributed liberally of their means to charitable purposes and the support of worthy objects. They enjoyed the confidence and respect of a large circle of acquaintances who hold their names in kindly remembrance.

WILLIAM SHADFORD, a furniture dealer and undertaker of Agency City, is an old resident of this section, and is the senior member of Shadford & Son. He was born in York County, England, Aug. 13, 1808, and is the son of John and Mary (Collinson) Shadford, the latter of whom died when her son, our subject, was a little lad of ten years old. Ten years later John Shadford emigrated to America, and proceeding to Pennsylvania remained there for a brief time, and then went into Lorain County, Ohio, where he established a comfortable home and passed the remainder of his life, dying in the winter of 1854, and having in the meantime married his second wife.

The subject of our sketch, while a boy, was apprenticed to the blacksmith's trade, at which he served seven years, and emigrated to America in 1862. The late Civil War being then in progress, he proffered his services in aid of the Union cause by enlisting in the 19th Iowa Infantry, but was rejected on account of his age. He determined, however, to try it again, and shortly afterward enlisted in the 37th Infantry, and was promoted First Sergeant, in which capacity he served until the close of the war, being on guard duty most of the time.

William Shadford was married to Miss Ann Duggleby, March 30, 1839. Mrs. Shadford was a native of the same country as her husband, and was the daughter of John and Jane (Dollie) Duggleby, who lived and died in their native England. Mr. and Mrs. Shadford became the parents of seven children, as follows: John C. married Miss Nancy Palmer, and they live in Ross County, Ohio; Charles M. departed this life in Cleveland, Ohio. Charles D. married Miss Margaret Clinton, of Fairfield, Iowa, and they are living in Agency City; Mary J., Mrs. G. L. Littler, lives in Moline, Ill.;

Elizabeth A. is the wife of P. W. Wilcox, and they live in Mendota, Ill.; William D. died in 1856; J. G. B. is married, lives at Leaf River, Ill., and is a minister of the Methodist Church.

Our subject is the owner of valuable property in Agency, is a member in good standing of the I. O. O. F., and belongs to the Methodist Episcopal Church. In politics he is a Republican. He is a straightforward and upright business man, and in all respects is entitled to a place among the first citizens of Agency.

THOMAS J. LAFFERTY, deceased, and a late resident of Eddyville, was born in Harrison County, Ohio, Oct. 15, 1826, and gave his life to the service of his country, dying on the 14th of October, 1876, from injuries and exposure received during his service in the army. Mr. Lafferty was the son of Samuel and Elizabeth (Mansfield) Lafferty, the father a native of Ohio and the mother of Pennsylvania. When he was a youth of fifteen years old, Mr. Lafferty crossed the Mississippi with his parents while Iowa was yet a Territory, and they located in Jefferson County, near Fairfield. There our subject was reared upon a farm and remained until 1846. His parents then removed to the vicinity of Des Moines, where the father departed this life in 1848; the mother's death took place in Sacramento, Cal., in 1884, at the age of seventy-four years. Our subject remained near Des Moines until 1848, and then returned to Harrison County, Ohio, where he was united in marriage with Miss Lucy R. Caves, a native of that county, and the daughter of John and Frances (Ross) Caves, who were both natives of Virginia, but were reared in Alabama..

The household of our subject and wife consisted of five children, the record of whom is as follows: Virginia became the wife of Gale Tone, of Ohio; Frank is engaged in the grocery business at Oskaloosa; John A. resides at home; Ella is the wife of William Redick, of Flint, Mich., and Hattie is a teacher and makes her home with her mother, who resides at their late residence at Eddyville, and is a lady highly esteemed and respected in that community.

Immediately after his marriage in 1848, Mr. Lafferty came with his wife to Keokuk, Iowa, where they lived until 1861. They then removed to Eddyville, where Mr. Lafferty engaged in the livery business for the following year, and then in 1862 was appointed Provost Marshal. which office he occupied for seven years. In the meantime, the late Civil War being in progress, Mr. Lafferty raised a company of volunteers, and with them was mustered into service at Davenport, Dec. 30, 1863. He received the commission of First Lieutenant of Co. I, 9th Iowa Vol. Cav., and served until July, 1864, being then discharged for disability on account of injuries received by being thrown from a horse. He then returned to Eddyville, and engaged in the marble business, which he continued until he was obliged to give it up, owing to ill-health. He was a man of great courage and perseverance, and attended to his business affairs long after many a man would have abandoned them.

E. T. SAGE, Postmaster of Agency, has been a resident of the Hawkeye State since 1851, and during a period of over thirty years has acquitted himself as one of the most valuable citizens of this locality. Mr. S. is a native of Jackson County, Ind., and was born Jan. 31, 1829, his parents being James and Rebecca (Powell) Sage, natives of Indiana and North Carolina, respectively, the latter of whom emigrated to Indiana with her parents in early youth, and was married to the father of our subject in Jackson County. Their household circle included ten children, six of whom are living, as follows: E. T., our subject, was the eldest born; Nancy J., now Mrs. George Miller, lives in Louisville, Ky.; Dr. E. H. Sage is engaged in the practice of his profession at Agency, and Dr. D. M., in Howard County, Iowa; Kate F. became the wife of William Owens, of Louisville, Ky.; Luda is married to J. M. Murry, Deputy Postmaster of Ottumwa.

The father of our subject was one of the prominent men of Jackson County, Ind., and besides filling many other responsible positions, was County Commissioner for many years. In 1852 he came to Jefferson County, Iowa, and settling in Fairfield, engaged in agricultural pursuits. He was very active in educational matters and gave his children the advantages of the best schools in this region. He experienced all the hardships and difficulties of the pioneer settler, especially in Jackson County, Ind., and possessed the peculiar faculty of adapting himself to circumstances, which enabled him to encounter the difficulties of life with manly courage and resolution. He was prominently connected with the Methodist Episcopal Church, in which he was Class-Leader for many years, and departed from the scenes of his earthly labors May 15, 1860. His wife died Dec. 11, 1871.

Mr. Sage of this biography received careful parental training and a fair education in the pioneer schools of Indiana, which were conducted in a log cabin with pucheon floor, slabs for seats and desks, and greased paper for window-panes. He remained under the parental roof until twenty-one years of age and then, coming to Iowa, located in Jefferson County, where he purchased 110 acres of land and opened up a farm. Three years later, in 1854, he was married to Miss Elizabeth J. Lydick, who was born in Knox County, Ohio, and came to Iowa when a child. Mr. Sage remained upon his farm for a period of twelve years and then, coming to Agency, embarked in agriculture. In the course of time he was appointed Assessor, and became Postmaster of Agency under the Cleveland administration, in August, 1885.

The children of our subject and wife are three in number: L. S., of Falls City, Neb.; Charles H., of Endicott, Neb., and Florence K., the wife of Thomas Kirkpatrick, of Westphalia, Kan. Mr. and Mrs. S. are members of the Methodist Episcopal Church of Agency, and are highly esteemed in this community for their excellent personal traits of character and the qualities which have made them useful and valued citizens. Mr. Sage has been identified with the growth of the State for many years, and has lived to see the wild prairie transformed into fertile farms and beautiful homesteads. During his long residence here he has become widely and favorably known, and is as much esteemed for his straightforward business methods as for his kindly and hospitable character. He is an honored member of the A. F. & A. M., belonging to Olive Branch Lodge No. 21, and of Magnolia Lodge No. 24, I. O. O. F., having passed all the chairs of the latter.

JAMES J. SMITH, attorney at law of Ottumwa, is a native of the Hawkeye State, and was born in Iowa City, Johnson County, Feb. 12, 1854. He is the son of Andrew and Mary (Donohue) Smith, of Irish ancestry and parentage, who came to America in 1850, locating first in Ohio, from which State they subsequently removed to Illinois. Two years later they crossed the Father of Waters and came into Iowa City, subsequently locating upon a farm, where the father became one of the largest stock-raisers in the State of Iowa. They were the parents of two children—J. J., our subject, and his sister Katie. Andrew Smith retired from the active labors of his farm and stock-raising in 1885, and became a resident of Ottumwa, where he is at present living. He is a man of remarkable intelligence, an extensive reader, and keeps himself thoroughly posted upon all important general matters. He is held in the highest respect in this county, where his name is familiarly known.

The subject of our biography received his primary education in the schools of Iowa City, after which he entered the State University, first taking a collegiate course of four years, and graduating from the law department in 1879. That same year he came to Ottumwa and commenced the practice of his profession. He had been a close student, ambitious to excel, and for his close attention and industry has obtained the reward of a high position among his professional brethren in this section.

He has a fine law library, and possesses an intimate acquaintance with the views and opinions of the men who became eminent in the profession from the beginning to the present in the history of this country. Politically he is an uncompromising Democrat, and has done his party good service by his stump speeches prior to important elections.

The marriage of James J. Smith and Miss Mary T. Shields was celebrated on the 29th of September, 1885. Mrs. Smith comes from an excellent family and is a niece of the late Gen. James T. Shields, one of the heroes of the late war. Mrs. S. is a native of Ireland and came to this country when a child, residing with her uncle, Gen. Shields, up to the time of his death, the greater part of her education having been received here. Of this union there has been born one child, a son, James L.

WILLIAM A. McINTIRE, Superintendent of the Public Schools of Wapello County, and at present a resident of Ottumwa, is a young man of whom much may be said regarding the zeal he has manifested in educational matters in this county and State. Mr. McIntire was born in Wapello County, April 11, 1849. The father of our subject, William Clark McIntire, was born and reared to manhood in Clarke County, Ohio, where he became acquainted with Miss Eliza A. Myers, who afterward became his wife. They were married in 1843, and immediately thereafter removed to this State and located in Keokuk Township, this county. Soon afterward he took up a claim of Government land, and at once locating upon it engaged actively in its improvement and cultivation, and continued in that vocation until his demise, Jan. 30, 1881. He was an old Jacksonian Democrat, well posted in politics, and at one time was elected a member of the Board of Supervisors.

William C. McIntire was a pioneer, and on first coming to the State domiciled his family in a little log cabin and endured all the hardships incident to a new country, but was possessed of that energy which conquered adversity and brought him success. He always took an active interest in educational matters, and bestowed upon his children a good education. The family consisted of six children, four sons and two daughters: Caroline C. died when five years of age; Joseph died Jan. 6, 1886, at thirty years of age; John is now living on the old homestead; Frank is a member of the firm of Harper, Chambers & Co., wholesale and retail dealers in hardware; Harriet F. became the wife of D. G. Davis, who is deceased, and she is now living at Los Angeles, Cal. The mother of our subject died July 31, 1882. She was a member of the Methodist Episcopal Church, and a sincere Christian, loved and respected for her many good traits of character. These two were the persons who came to Iowa, like many others, poor in pocket, but with a determination to get on in the world, and by strict economy, hard labor and good judgment, succeeded, and at their death left 340 acres of finely cultivated and valuable land to their children.

The subject of this notice was reared on his father's farm and received his early education in the primitive log school-house of that day. He continued to reside upon the old homestead until twenty-one years of his life had passed, in the meantime having had the privilege of attending the High School at Ottumwa two years. In 1870–71 he attended the Agricultural College at Ames, Iowa, and on finishing the sophomore course, engaged in teaching school in Taylor County. In the fall of 1877 he was elected to the office of Superintendent of Schools of this county. In 1879 he was defeated for the position, but in the fall of 1881 was elected again, and re-elected in 1883, and also in 1885. In 1883 he prepared and introduced a course of study for the country schools of the county. He has done much to advance the cause of education throughout the county as well as State. He is a close student and highly respected wherever he is known.

In 1882 our subject introduced a four years' graded course of study in the County Normal Institute, since which time the Institute has rapidly grown in favor and importance. The schools throughout Wapello County are progressing finely under his supervision, and it is doubtful if any county in the State has a better system of public schools than is to be found here, and when the reader is aware of the fact that the schools have attained their high degree of perfection through the supervision of Mr. McIntire of this notice, too much credit cannot be given him.

Mr. McIntire was married in the county of his nativity, March 26, 1874, to Miss Clara M. Goldsberry. She was born in Ross County, Ohio, July

15, 1849. Socially our subject is a member of the K. of P., holding fellowship with Wapello Lodge No. 12.

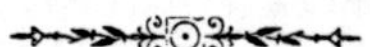

WINFIELD S. COEN, senior member of the law firm of Coen & Hall, of Ottumwa, is a native of Perry County, Ohio, where he was born April 9, 1847. He is the son of Samuel Coen, of Lancaster County, Pa., whose birth took place on the 4th of August, 1815, and he was an infant of a year old when his parents removed to Perry County, Ohio, where he was reared to manhood, and united in marriage with Miss Mary A. McCormick, who was a relative of Cyrus H. McCormick, of Chicago. She was born on the 2d of March, 1814. After the birth of our subject they emigrated West and located in Monroe County, Iowa, where the father died on the 25th of December, 1883. His wife had preceded him to the better world on the 11th of April, 1869. The parental household consisted of five children, three of whom are living, viz., James, an attorney at law at Albia, this State; John, a farmer of Monroe County, and Winfield S. of our sketch.

Mr. Coen of this biography received his early education in the common schools of Monroe County, Iowa, which were conducted in the pioneer log house. Although his advantages were comparatively limited, he was industrious and very fond of his books, and employed his leisure time in acquiring valuable knowledge. In 1864, although only seventeen years of age, he proffered his services as a soldier of the Union, enlisting in Co. A, 5th Iowa Vol. Cav., the first scenes of his military experience being in Middle Tennessee and Georgia. He was engaged with his comrades in active service against the rebel raids of Wheeler and Forrest, and participated in the battle of Franklin, and after the hard campaign around Nashville was engaged with his regiment in following up the troops of Gen. Hood, and afterward participated in the famous brigade charge at Pulaski, Tenn., charging the rebels and burning the bridges along the route, being under rebel fire much of the time. Mr. Coen received a wound in the foot while his regiment was four miles west of Pulaski, on account of which he received an honorable discharge on the 14th of July, 1865.

After his return from the army, Mr. Coen proceeded to Monroe County, Iowa, and engaged in farming pursuits, which, after two years, he was compelled to abandon on account of his wound. He then engaged in teaching school in this county, and was thus employed until 1875, when he took up the study of law. In August of that year he was admitted to the bar, and was soon afterward associated in partnership with his brother, the style of the firm being Coen & Coen, having their office in Albia. They operated together until February, 1881, when Winfield S. came to Ottumwa, where he managed an office alone for the following four years. He then associated himself with his present partner, and they have built up a solid and lucrative practice.

Mr. Coen is a close student, well read in his profession, and has always taken an active interest in local and State politics, being, at the time of this writing, a candidate for Prosecuting Attorney of Wapello County. Socially he is connected with the G. A. R. and I. O. O. F.

Mr. Coen was married on the 1st of January, 1878, to Miss Martha E. Harbison, of Albia, Iowa. Mrs. Coen was born on the 18th of September, 1846, and is the daughter of the late William Harbison. Of her union with our subject there have been born three children—Walter S., Thomas F. and John R. They are pleasantly located on Main street in this city, and number among their friends the first citizens of Ottumwa.

D. T. MILLER, attorney at law and loan agent of Ottumwa, has been a resident of the Hawkeye State since his early childhood. He was born in Licking County, Ohio, on the 2d of May, 1843, and when only a few years old his parents removed to the Buckeye State across the Mississippi into the young and rapidly growing State which has since been the home of our subject. They first located in Keokuk County, in the town of Sigourney, where their son was reared to manhood, having in the meantime received a liberal education. After completing his primary course he entered the Iowa State University, and was in that institution during 1863.

The Civil War being then in progress, in February of the following year Mr. Miller enlisted in Co. G, 15th Iowa Vol. Inf., as a private. With his comrades he joined the regiment at Vicksburg, going with them subsequently to Huntsville, Ala. and afterward participating in the siege of Atlanta. He was also in the engagement at Big Shanty, Kennesaw Mountain, Peachtree Creek, and participated in other engagements and skirmishes, and was also with Gen. Sherman on his march to the sea. He was present at the surrender of Savannah, Ga., and with his regiment marched through the Carolinas, being at the capture of Columbus, S. C., and one of the first men to enter the city, which entrance was effected on the 15th of February, 1865. He was afterward detailed to accompany a foraging excursion, from which he returned in time to assist in the capture of Fayetteville, N. C., thence going to Bentonville, the same State, and engaging under Gen. Sherman in his last battle. The brigade thence was ordered to Washington for grand review, where our subject, with his comrades, was mustered out, and received his final discharge at Davenport, Iowa.

At the close of his military career, Mr. Miller entered the office of C. H. Mackey, in the meantime attending Normal School. He afterward, while engaged as a teacher, pursued his law studies under the instruction of W. W. Cory, of Ottumwa. He was admitted to practice in the courts of Iowa, in September, 1872, and entered upon his profession, to which he has since added his business of loan agent. He is an energetic man, a close student, and attends strictly to business. He keeps well posted in the affairs of his State and county, and is a man whose judgment is considered more than usually reliable. Politically he is a stanch Republican and actively interested in the support of the principles of his party. Socially he is connected with Ottumwa Lodge No. 16, A. F. & A. M., and Clinton Chapter. He is a member of the I. N. G., and also of Cloutman Post No. 64, G. A. R., being Post Commander.

The marriage of D. T. Miller and Miss Mary Griswold was celebrated in Keokuk County on the 2d of October, 1872. Mrs. Miller is a daughter of W. H. and Sarah (Onderkonk) Griswold, both natives of Lock Berlin, N. Y., and was born on the 18th of April, 1850. Of this union there have been born two children—Maude and Sidney G. They occupy a pleasant residence in Ottumwa, and their home is replete with the evidences of refined and cultured tastes.

PAUL ARNOLD, a representative farmer and stock-grower of Columbia Township, is comfortably located on section 34, where, beside his agricultural pursuits he is giving considerable attention to the raising of fine stock. Mr. Arnold has been a resident of the Hawkeye State since 1852, and at one time was the owner of 577 acres of land in the above township, a part of which he has given to his children. He now owns 387 acres, has a fine farm dwelling, with good barns and out-buildings, and has attained to his present position by the exercise of his own industry and economy.

The subject of this history was born in Washington County, Ohio, March 6, 1826, and is the son of John and Sarah (Althey) Arnold, both natives of West Virginia, who moved to Ohio in about 1820, and engaged in farming pursuits. The country was new at the time of their going there, and they labored industriously for the establishment of a home. They were successful in their undertakings, and at the death of the father, which took place while he was still in the prime of life, being forty-six years old, he was the owner of 140 acres of valuable land, finely improved and under a good state of cultivation. A portion of this farm was afterward divided into suburban outlots in the town of McArthur. The parental household included ten children, of whom our subject was the third in order of birth. He remained under the home roof until he arrived at years of manhood, and on the 18th of March, 1849, was united in marriage with

RESIDENCE OF A. J. JENKINS, SEC. 26. CASS TOWNSHIP.

RESIDENCE OF R. H. TINDELL, SEC. 27, RICHLAND TP.

RESIDENCE OF P. S. WILSON, SEC. 10. CENTRE TP.

Miss Mary Speed. Mrs. Arnold was born in Athens County, Ohio, on the 9th of November, 1829, and was the daughter of George and Mercy (Robinett) Speed, both natives of Ohio. A few years later they removed to Wapello County, Iowa, where Mr. Arnold purchased 160 acres of land, which he added to from time to time, as before stated. They became the parents of seven children, the record of whom is as follows: Sarah E. was born March 8, 1850, in Vinton County, Ohio, and became the wife of David Canfield, a farmer of Cloud County, Kan.; G. F. was born April 16, 1852, in Vinton County, Ohio, and is living in Wapello County, engaged in agricultural pursuits; Amon S. was born April 13, 1855, in Wapello County, Iowa; John, a farmer of Cass Township, was born March 31, 1857; James G., Aug. 15, 1861; Amanda, born Sept. 1, 1864, became the wife of Andrew Stodghill, a farmer of Columbia Township; Charles, born Sept. 2, 1866, is engaged in farming in Wapello County. John received forty-six acres of land from his father. George and Amon each received seventy-eight and one-half acres, and are established in comfortable homes. The others will probably be similarly provided for upon their marriage.

When Mr. Arnold first landed in Iowa he was the owner of two old horses and a wagon to match, and had a cash capital of $19.50. His present possessions are the result of his own industry, and he is a striking illustration of what may be accomplished by resolution and perseverance. He is essentially a self-made man, and his straightforward, upright course through life has secured him the confidence and esteem of the people of this community. He has held the various township offices, and in his political views assimilates with the Republican party. He has given his children a good education, and has had their interests steadily in view from the time the little family began to gather about his hearthstone. Although having passed the meridian of life, he has been so temperate in his habits that his health has been preserved unimpaired, and he is strong and capable, doing all his own work and attending to his business concerns. He is now feeding 600 head of sheep, and seventy head of cattle, turning his attention mostly to stock-raising, and deriving a handsome income from his investments. To such men as Paul Arnold is this county indebted for the proud position which it holds among other prosperous communities of Iowa.

WILLIAM McNETT, senior partner of the firm of McNett & Tisdale, of Ottumwa, is a prominent factor in the business interests of this city, and is one of its most thorough-going and enterprising citizens. Mr. McNett is a native of the Prairie State, having been born at Mt. Morris, Ogle County, on the 10th of March, 1845. He received his early education in the schools of Ogle and Stephenson Counties, and later, attended Rock River Seminary, leaving there in 1864. In the meantime he worked upon a farm during the summer seasons and pursued his studies through the winter. In 1867, at the age of twenty-two years, he entered the office of Thomas Turner, of Freeport, and under his instructions pursued the study of law, and was admitted to practice on the 27th of May, 1868, his certificate being signed by Judges Lawrence, Breece and Walker of the Supreme Court of Illinois. In June following, Mr. McNett came to Marshalltown, Iowa, and commenced the practice of his profession. Five years later he practiced in the Supreme Court, and soon afterward was admitted to the United States Court.

Mr. McNett has been a resident of Ottumwa since 1869. He soon afterward formed a partnership with Henry Clement, of Eddyville, and Mr. Fawcett, of Ottumwa, he being the junior member of the firms. This last firm dissolved in 1872, and for the following ten years Mr. McNett practiced alone, the present partnership being formed in April, 1882. The firm of which our subject is a member is one of the strongest in the county. Mr. McNett commenced life at the foot of the ladder, and may be properly termed a self-made man. He is a close student, and has followed the intricacies of his profession with untiring perseverance and determination; he is considered one of the best advocates in the county, and occupies a leading position in legal transactions. Though having an intelligent interest in public matters he has given very little time to practical politics other than to make a few speeches during the busiest part of a campaign. He is still young, with great possibilities within his reach, and those who are interested in his welfare will rejoice at his ultimate success.

William McNett and Miss Mary Stoddard were united in marriage on the 24th of July, 1872. Mrs. McN. is a native of Clarke County, Ohio, and the daughter of John Stoddard. She is an estimable and accomplished lady, and of her union with our subject there have been born five children, two sons and three daughters—Nellie, Blanche, Walter, James W. and Mary. Blanche died in 1880. Mr. and Mrs. McN. are connected with the Congregational Church of Ottumwa, and socially Mr. McNett is a member in good standing of the Masonic fraternity.

The father of our subject was a native of Pennsylvania, born July 20, 1803. He soon afterward removed with his parents to Maryland, where he was reared and educated. The mother, Susan (Knodle) McNett, was a most estimable lady, and, with her husband, was prominently connected with the Lutheran Church, of which the latter was a member for a period of fifty years. They were familiarly known in the locality where they resided as most excellent and worthy people, of kindly and generous impulses, and given to deeds of charity. They have left behind them the record of worthy lives, replete with virtues and excellent influence, which will be felt for many years to come.

M. S. DARROW, Chief Train Despatcher of the Middle Division of the C., B. & Q. R. R., at Ottumwa, Iowa, is a native of the Green Mountain State, having first opened his eyes to the light in St. Albans, on the 21st of November, 1850. He is a son of M. S. and Harriet B. (Wheeler) Darrow, who emigrated to Wisconsin, and settled in Janesville, when our subject was a small child. It was in the common schools of this latter place that young Darrow received his early education, and at the age of fourteen began the study of telegraphy, being soon afterward employed by the C. & N. W. R. R. Co., with whom he remained for the space of eighteen years. When but twenty-one years of age he was appointed to the responsible position of train despatcher, with headquarters at the Kinzie street depot, Chicago, performing his duties in a prompt and satisfactory manner.

In 1882 our subject came to Ottumwa, where he received the appointment of Chief Train Despatcher of the C., B. & Q. R. R., which position he still retains. Having been "in the harness" since he was fourteen years old, he may properly be termed a thorough railroad man. Although still young, he has the entire confidence of his employers, and bids fair to rise still higher in his profession.

M. S. Darrow was married in 1876, at Ft. Atkinson, Wis., the lady of his choice being Miss Louise M., daughter of Dr. W. M. Smith of that place. They have become the parents of one child, a son, William W. Our subject and his wife occupy a prominent place in the social circles of Ottumwa, and are honored and respected by all who know them. Politically Mr. D. is a firm adherent of the Democratic party, for the support of whose principles he casts his vote whenever opportunity occurs.

W. G. CROW, successfully engaged as a dealer in general merchandise in the village of Eldon, came to Iowa in 1844, and established his present business in 1886. He is a native of East Tennessee, born in Jefferson County in 1837, and the son of John and Betsey J. (Manson) Crow, both natives of the same State as their son.

Mr. Crow came to Iowa with his parents, and they settled in Appanoose County. He had his home in that vicinity until 1870, when he came to Eldon, Wapello County, and engaged as a fireman on the C., R. I. & P. R. R., and was thus occupied for fourteen months, when he was given charge of an engine, and was employed as engineer until Dec. 20, 1880. In April of the following year he purchased a half interest in the store of George Earhart, continuing in partnership with him until

February, 1886, when he put up the brick building which he now occupies. This is 24 x 80 feet in dimensions, and consists of two stories and basement. He chopped the wood, burned the brick and hauled all the material used in its construction, and besides this it cost him the sum of $5,000. It fronts on Elm street, and is one of the handsomest business blocks in the county. It is finished in ornamental brick, after the most modern style, and all the material used in its construction is of the best quality.

Mr. Crow was married, on the 1st of January, 1857, to Miss Marinda Thomas, a native of Bartholomew County, Ind., and a daughter of Henry S. Thomas, of Bedford, Ind. They are prominently connected with the Methodist Episcopal Church. Mr. Crow is a Republican in politics, and served as a soldier in the Union army from the spring of 1864 until the close of the war. He is a member of the I. O. O. F. and Centerville Encampment, and also belongs to the G. A. R.

The father of Mr. Crow departed this life March 10, 1881, at the age of seventy-two years. The mother had previously died, in 1857, at the age of forty-four. They were upright and conscientious people, and members in good standing of the Methodist Episcopal Church.

H. C. JENNINGS, a highly respected resident of Competine Township, is pleasantly located on section 10, and successfully carrying on farming and stock-raising. He has been a resident of the Hawkeye State since 1851, and during this time has gathered about him a large circle of friends and associates who tacitly render him the respect and esteem which is due him as an honest man and a good citizen. Our subject is a native of Kentucky, and was born on the 10th of May, 1825, his parents being Peyton R. and Nancy Jennings, the former also being a resident of the Blue Grass State. The grandfather of our subject became a resident of Kentucky while Daniel Boone was there, and secured a tract of land in Owen County. While out hunting horses one day he was captured by the Indians, scalped and tomahawked and left for dead. He revived, however, and lived to become the father of four children.

The early years of Mr. Jennings of our notice were spent upon his father's farm, and he received a very limited education in the schools of his native county. After arriving at years of manhood he was united in wedlock with Miss Lavina A. Lamb, a native of his own State, and the daughter of John and Sarah L. (Grace) Lamb, also of the Blue Grass region. In 1851 Mr. Jennings left his native State and proceeded northwestward and across the Mississippi into Iowa. After reaching Wapello County he purchased forty acres of land in Competine Township, and commenced in earnest the establishment of a home for himself and family. As time passed on he became successful in his farming and business transactions, and added to his possessions until he is now the owner of 240 acres, all of which are enclosed and under a good state of cultivation. He has a comfortable farm residence, good barns and out-buildings, and all the appliances of a model farm estate.

The household circle of our subject and his wife has been completed by the birth of twelve children, four sons and eight daughters, of whom the record is as follows: John W., a resident of Glenwood, Iowa; Edward lives in Kansas; Lewis P. is at home; Peyton R. is deceased; Alice became the wife of Samuel Spicer, of Abingdon, Iowa; Lena L. married Marion Foster, of Ringgold County, Iowa; Sarah L., Mrs. Noble Hays, resides in Ness County, Kan.; Nora is deceased; Mary F., Amanda, Laura and Nancy are at home with their parents. They are a bright family of children, of whom the parents may be justly proud, and have been reared in those principles which will make them valued members of society. The fine stock operations of Mr. Jennings have proved uniformly successful. He is thoroughly in love with this branch of his business and maintains a just pride in his judgment of what is required for the care and comfort of animals and in developing those qualities which shall render them handsome and valuable. Among his herd are some of the finest animals to be seen in this section, and he has attained quite a reputation in this section as a breeder and dealer. Politically Mr. J.

is a staunch supporter of the Democratic party, and religiously he belongs to the Christian Church. Mrs. J. is connected with the Baptist denomination.

JOSEPH LOCKWOOD, M. D., physician and magnetic healer, having his office at Ottumwa, was born at Whiting, Addison Co., Vt., Jan. 12, 1831. He is a son of Asahel and Axie (Pond) Lockwood, his father being a soldier in the War of 1812. During the year 1857, accompanied by his family, he emigrated to Decatur County, this State, where he died at the advanced age of eighty-one years in 1882. He was also a soldier in the late Civil War, enlisting as drummer and serving until the close. His wife died in 1863. Of their union there were born seven children, five of whom are yet living: Elizabeth, the wife of H. D. Richardson, and Horatio G. are living in Decatur County; John Q. resides at Corydon, Wayne County, this State; Joseph is our subject; Emily is the wife of Dr. C. P. Mullinix, and they live at Leon, Decatur Co., Iowa.

Joseph Lockwood was educated in the Green Mountain State, and there reared to manhood. In September, 1854, he came West, expecting to find a broader field in which to labor, and hoping to better his financial condition. He first located in Wisconsin, then went to Illinois, and in 1855 came to Iowa. Even while a young man Dr. Lockwood claims to have possessed healing qualities, which were discovered by his ability to assist many indisposed persons, and relieve them of their many ills and pains. In 1871 he publicly commenced practice, and has since followed the same, meeting with remarkable success. He claims to have cured many cases where regular practicing physicians of all the different schools gave them up, and to-day has numerous patients throughout the country who will testify to this fact.

In 1863 Dr. Lockwood came to Ottumwa, where he has since resided. He is a gentleman of considerable ability, although his education was somewhat neglected in early life. He is well posted in the affairs of county, State and nation, and takes an active interest in all matters calculated to advance the community in which he lives.

Dr. Lockwood was married at Bloomfield, Davis Co., Iowa, to Miss E. Hinkle, and of this union there were born two children—James H. and Harvey D. Mrs. Lockwood died in 1868, and the Doctor formed a second matrimonial alliance, with Miss Lizzie M. Barton. This lady died in 1882. The maiden name of our subject's present wife was Nanic Taylor, a native of Brown County, Ill., and of this latter union one child, Buelah Bell, has been born. Socially Dr. Lockwood is a member of the Masonic fraternity, and a gentleman of considerable prominence in the community in which he resides.

A handsome lithographic view of the Doctor's residence is shown on another page of this work.

WILLIAM PAGE, a highly esteemed farmer of Keokuk Township, is a native of the Buckeye State, having been born in Pickaway County, on the 3d of March, 1822. He is the son of William and Elizabeth (Roberts) Page, both natives of Virginia, the former of whom died when our subject was a mere child. Young William was then placed upon a farm, where he was reared until seventeen years of age, at which time his mother also departed from the scenes of earth, and he was left to fight the battles of life alone.

After the death of his mother young Page was variously employed at farm work in the neighborhood where he had always lived, until he attained to his majority, and then, changing his occupation, was employed on a flatboat, which plied the Wabash River from La Fayette to New Orleans, and afterward ran on the Wabash, Ohio and Mississippi Rivers, upon different boats, for the following four years. He then returned to farm pursuits, in which he was occupied until 1852, and then started overland for California, where he remained until the death of his brother, in Indiana, whither he had removed when he was boy of thirteen years old.

After remaining for a time in La Fayette, Ind., Mr. Page returned overland to California, being on the road from March until the last of August. He started with a team from Independence, Mo., and after arriving in California sold his team and entered the mines, engaging in a vigorous search for the precious metals. He was thus occupied for the following two years, when he returned to Indiana, and, on account of his sister, purchased a farm there, placed her upon it, remained with her a few months, and then returned to California, where he remained till 1860. He then returned East as far as Iowa, and purchased a farm near Floris, in Davis County. This consisted of 240 acres, and he occupied it until December of the following year, when he was once more seized with the gold fever, and started again for the Pacific Slope via New York and Aspinwall. This journey occupied twenty-three days, and Mr. Page this time continued in California until 1865, and then returned to Davis County, in April of that year, just after the assassination of President Lincoln. He went onto his farm near Floris, where he remained three years, and thence removed to a farm on Loop Creek, in Davis County, which he occupied a year, and then purchased a tract of land on sections 14 and 15, of Keokuk Township. This consisted of 240 acres, and he determined upon a final settlement, and vigorously set about its improvement and cultivation. He was successful in his labors, and established a comfortable home. On the 6th of October, 1885, Mr. Page had the misfortune to lose his handsome property by fire, by which he was the loser to the amount of between $3,000 and $4,000.

The marriage of William Page and Mrs. Margaret C. (Monroe) Anderson was celebrated on the 6th of March, 1866. Mrs. P. was born in Trimble County, Ky., and is the daughter of William and Phœbe (Parkham) Monro. In early youth she was married to John Anderson, and became the mother of three children: Lucy A. is the wife of Julius M. Morrison, of Dallas, Tex.; O. W. died in Leadville, Col., in 1881, at the age of twenty-six years; he was engaged there in mining, and was found dead in a cabin, presumably from heart disease; Phœbe E. died at the age of eighteen years, at the home of her mother in this county. Of the marriage of Mr. and Mrs. Page there have been born two children: Mary, at home with her parents, and William Milton, attending the Normal School at Dexter, Iowa.

The homestead of our subject is pleasantly located, and he is successfully engaged in the ordinary pursuits of agriculture, at the same time giving much attention to stock-raising. His residence, barns and out-buildings are constructed in a tasteful and substantial manner, and the farm in all respects constitutes one of the attractive spots of Keokuk Township. Mr. Page has accumulated his property solely by his own efforts, having commenced in life at the foot of the ladder, with a limited education and without capital. He has been an industrious worker, a good manager, and a wide-awake business man, and in his later years is receiving the reward which is his just due. In his early life he affiliated with the Whig party, but since the party organization of the Republicans he has cheerfully indorsed the principles of the latter, and has uniformly cast his vote in support of them. He is fulfilling his obligations as a good citizen and enjoys the confidence and esteem of his neighbors and associates.

John Anderson, the first husband of Mrs. Page, was born in Indiana, on the 5th of March, 1828. He served in the Union army during the late war, in which he enlisted during the first year of the conflict, in December, 1861. He was a member of Co. C, 7th Iowa Vol. Cav., and was killed by the Indians at Cottonwood Springs, Neb., where his remains were interred. He was a good man in every sense of the word and a member of the Baptist Church

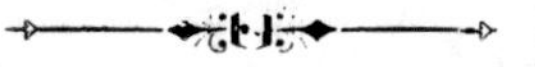

THOMAS GOODALL, a well-known and respected resident of the city of Ottumwa, was born in Glasgow, Ky., Jan. 15, 1815. He is the son of Thomas and Mary (Baker) Goodall, and removed from his native State to Hancock County, Ill., at the age of nineteen years. He remained in Carthage, that county, for two years following, engaged in learning the carpenter's trade, and in 1836 came to Iowa and took up a claim in Van Buren County. He occupied this for twenty-four years, in the meantime laboring industriously for its improvement, so that it became a valuable farm. In 1859 he removed to Ottumwa, and engaged in wagon-making until 1884.

The father of our subject was a slave-holder in Kentucky, but his son, notwithstanding his surroundings, never looked with favor upon the peculiar institution, and determined to escape from the boundaries of a slave-holding State as soon as possible. In the meantime his father had sold the home farm and purchased another in Kentucky which was unimproved. He sent Thomas and a younger brother to his purchase to prospect for water, that being a very important consideration in that region. They went to the place designated by the father, and after digging awhile found a good spring. Thomas said to his brother, "If father sees this spring he will never leave here and we'll not get to go West." So they covered up the spring carefully so that not a sign of it could be seen, and returning to their father told him there was no water on the place and persuaded him to move to Illinois, which was done and the boys were satisfied. The parents died in Van Buren County, the father in 1855, aged seventy-five years, and the mother in 1864, at the age of eighty.

Thomas Goodall and Miss Jane Cox were married in December, 1840. Mrs. Jane Goodall was a native of Virginia and the daughter of Jefferson Cox, and by her union with our subject became the mother of three children: William H., now of Mitchellville, this State, served in the late war for three and one-half years in Co. K, 2d Iowa Vol. Inf.; at the charge of Ft. Donelson he received a gunshot wound in the arm which, however, did not seriously disable him, and he remained with his comrades until the close of the war; W. B. is a wholesale druggist, engaged with Blake, Bruce & Co., of Ottumwa; Mary E. became the wife of Robert Ball, a contractor and builder, of Mitchellville. The mother of these children departed this life in Van Buren County, in March, 1854, and in June, 1856, our subject was married to Miss S. E. Tindell, a native of Tennessee, and the daughter of Nathan and Margaret (Ross) Tindell, natives respectively of North Carolina and Tennessee. Of this marriage there were born the following: Fred T., a druggist of Ottumwa; Frank died Sept. 12, 1860, aged one year; Alice died in 1862, at the age of thirteen months; Hattie died in 1864, aged one year and eight months; James E. died in September, 1867, aged two years and five months; Hattie B. died in April, 1886, aged seventeen years, three months and seventeen days; Mattie M. is at home.

Mr. Goodall owns a good residence on Fifth street, and also has property in another part of the city. The greater part of his life has been spent in farming pursuits, and his energy and industry have served him well so that in his later days he is enjoying the fruits of his early toil and the just reward of a well-spent life.

W A. JORDAN, who departed this life May 26, 1873, became a resident of the city of Ottumwa in 1862, and nineteen years ago established the business in which his widow still retains an interest. He was one of the representative citizens of Wapello County, and contributed his full share toward the advancement of the business and industrial interests of this section. The subject of this history was born in Ohio, Aug. 20, 1820, whence he removed with his parents to Indiana in about 1840. Subsequently he came to Iowa, locating in Richland, Keokuk County, where he carried on general merchandising until 1862. In this latter year he came to Ottumwa and established the business in which he was engaged until the time of his death.

The business block belonging to the estate is a four-story brick building, and was built in 1873 at a cost of $22,000. Mr. Jordan was a thorough-going, straightforward business man, and remarkably successful in his business transactions. He started in the world a poor boy, and his accumulations were the result of his own industry and wise judgment. He obtained a fair education in his early years, and for several terms taught school in Indiana.

The marriage of W. A. Jordan and Miss Maria McGrew was celebrated June 21, 1846. Mrs. J. was the daughter of William W. and Margaret (Milligan) McGrew, both natives of Pennsylvania, and there engaged in agricultural pursuits. Our subject and wife became the parents of twelve children, all of whom are living, and recorded as follows: Walter B. is a wholesale merchant of St. Paul, Minn.; J. W. and J. C. are in Ottumwa, carrying on the business of their father; A. C. is a merchant of Chicago; Charles L. and G. W. reside in Ottumwa; Mary L. became the wife of Ira A. Myers, of Ottumwa; Ada married B. W. Ladd, of Montana; Ida became the wife of G. F. Hall, of this city; Kittie and Inez V. are at home with their mother; Eva is at school. Mrs. Jordan occupies the family residence at 448 North Court street. She is a highly esteemed lady and a member of the Methodist Episcopal Church.

A. W. CLARK, a worthy agriculturist of Wapello County, which calling he has followed the most of his life, may be found on his little farm on section 2, Cass Township, daily engaged in the general routine of mixed husbandry. He was born July 30, 1837, in Jackson County, Ohio, and is a son of William and Elizabeth (Hartley) Clark, both of whom were born and reared in the Buckeye State, whence they emigrated to Iowa in 1851. The father was of German and the mother of Irish extraction, and they became the parents of eight children, recorded as follows: Absalom is a farmer in Harrison County, Mo.; Hiram is a carpenter and resident of Cass Township; A. W. was next in order of birth; Eliza, the widow of Isaac Strang, resides in Decatur County, Iowa; Isaac is also a resident of that county; Priscilla is the wife of M. H. Beltz, a farmer living in Nodaway County, Mo.; Aaron and William died in infancy.

When the father of our subject came to this county in 1851, he purchased an eighty-acre tract of wild land on which he located with his family, and he and his children at once began its improvement. He was born Jan. 4, 1806, and died Dec. 23, 1870. At the date of his demise he had one of the finest improved farms in his neighborhood. He was a member of the Methodist Episcopal Church, and always took an active part in church matters. The mother survived him, and is at present making her home with her daughter, Mrs. Eliza Strang, of Decatur County.

The early years of the life of our subject were passed on the old homestead, assisting in the labors on the farm, and attending the common schools. He remained with his parents until 1858, when he engaged to work for a Mr. Martin, and was with that gentleman about a year. On the 25th of December, 1859, he was married to Miss Rhoda Warren, who was born Aug. 2, 1842, and is a daughter of Filmore and Elizabeth (Nye) Warren. Her father was born and reared to manhood in Ohio, and the mother was born in Germany, lived there until she was thirteen years old, and then came to this country with her parents and settled with them in Ohio. Of the union of Mr. and Mrs. Clark there have been four children: Emma E., born Dec. 21, 1869, died Oct. 24, 1870; George M. was born Nov. 1, 1872; Frank, March 11, 1877, and Minnie May, Oct. 12, 1879.

In 1876 Mr. Clark purchased forty acres of improved land where he is at present residing. He has good buildings on his place, and in addition to the cultivation of the cereals, is devoting a portion of his time and attention to the raising of stock. He and his wife are members of the Methodist Episcopal Church, of which he is Steward, and is also active in Sunday-school matters connected therewith. Politically he votes with the Democratic party.

DAVID BURTON. For upward of thirty-four years the subject of this notice has continued to reside within the boundaries of Wapello County and during that time has been actively identified with its agricultural development. Mr. Burton is at present engaged in the independent calling of a farmer, which he has followed thus far in life, and is pleasantly situated on his fine farm on section 5, Center Township. He was born in Sussex County, Del., Oct. 21, 1810, and is the son of Samuel and Sarah (Spears) Burton, natives of that State but of English descent. The mother departed this life when in her thirtieth year, and is buried in Sussex County.

She was a member of the Methodist Episcopal Church, a kind mother, a loving wife, a generous neighbor, and a good Christian woman. The father died at the age of forty, and is also buried in Sussex County. He was likewise a Christian, and held fellowship with the Church of England.

David Burton was but six months old when his mother died, and he went to live with his uncle, John Burton, in whose household he continued to reside, engaged in farming and attending school until 1825. During that year he went to Philadelphia and served an apprenticeship to the blacksmith trade. After four years of hard labor, during which time he had completely mastered the trade, he returned to Delaware and went to work on a farm at $5 per month. He was thus occupied for about ten months, receiving his wages in the meanwhile for the purpose of preparing himself to take an important part in the greatest event of his life, which was that of his marriage. The lady whom he chose to accompany him through the years of his future was Miss Ann Vessels, a daughter of John and Pernalpha (Fisher) Vessels, natives of Delaware. Of the union of our subject with Miss Vessels nine children have been born: Samuel H. died in infancy; William is a farmer of Center Township, this county; Hester is the wife of Elijah Walker; Sarah E., deceased, was the wife of Ezekial Walker; Samuel A. lives in Polk Township; Matilda J., wife of Elias Park, a resident of Davenport, Iowa; George R. is a farmer in Center Township; Mary L. and David T. died in infancy.

The subject of this sketch came to Wapello County in 1852, and purchased 200 acres of partly improved land. On this tract he settled with his family, and with his sons began its improvement, adding thereto from year to year until he is at present the proprietor of 307 acres, all under fence and the major portion under an advanced state of cultivation. His farm is within five and one-half miles of Ottumwa, and is a valuable property, having upon it a good residence and other necessary farm buildings.

The parents of Mrs. Burton were both active members of the Methodist Episcopal Church. Her father died at the age of fifty, and her mother when forty years old, and they are both buried in Sussex County, Del. Mrs. David Burton is a member of the Methodist Episcopal Church. In politics our subject is a Republican. He is a self-made man, and what he has of this world's goods has been accumulated through years of honest toil and economy.

JOHN H. LAFOLLETTE, a pioneer settler of Wapello County, came to Iowa in the fall of 1850. He purchased eighty acres in Adams Township, and opened up the farm which he still owns and occupies, and which now embraces 266 acres, under a good state of cultivation. He has been remarkably successful in his farming and business transactions, and, besides the homestead, owns 240 acres in Union and 164 acres in Guthrie County. He was born in Putnam County, Ind., June 5, 1828, and is the son of Joseph and Hester (Hinton) Lafollette, both natives of Kentucky, where they were reared and married about the time that Daniel Boone became famous for his exploits in that region.

Joseph Lafollette was born in 1801, and died about 1877, in Putnam County, Ind., whence he removed after his marriage. He was one of the pioneer settlers of that State, and opened up a farm in the wilderness. His wife, Hester, was born in January, 1799, and accompanied her husband to Indiana, cheerfully enduring with him the hardships and privations of pioneer life. They became the parents of ten children, all of whom lived to mature years, and seven of whom still survive: David is in Salem, Ore.; Nancy became the wife of Martin McHenry, of Montgomery County, Ind.; John H. lives in this county; Charles is in Polk County, Ore.; Jeremiah lives near St. Joseph, Mo.; Christiana is the wife of Thomas Hamilton, of Putnam County, Ind.; Mary C. married Samuel Harshbarger, and they live on the old homestead in Indiana. The father of our subject died in 1877, at the age of seventy-six years, and the mother about 1872. The latter was a member in good standing of the Baptist Church.

The great-great-grandfather of our subject came to America from France with Gen. La Fayette, and

John Kreckel Me. R.

served with the latter in the Revolutionary War, where he was killed and left upon the field. His son, the great-grandfather of our subject, settled in New Jersey, whence he subsequently moved to Kentucky, where, later, the father of our subject was born. From this branch of the family in France sprang the Lafollettes of America.

John H. Lafollette, of our sketch, received his early education in the log school-house of his native county, which was built and furnished after the fashion of those times, and which has been described on various other pages of this work. To reach this temple of learning he was obliged to travel two miles in the severe winter weather, being guided through the forest by "blazed" trees. In 1850, after attaining his majority, he crossed the Mississippi and came into Wapello County, where he purchased land and opened up the farm which constitutes his present homestead, first building a log house, 16 x 18, which is yet on the place. The following year he was married in this county, on the 8th of May, to Miss Angeline Easley, who was born in Montgomery County, Ind., and was the daughter of Daniel and Nancy (Deatheridge) Easley, who were early pioneers of the Hoosier State, and in the spring of 1850 came to Adams Township, this county. Of this marriage there were born eight children, viz.: Joseph, a natural mechanic and artist, of Ottumwa; Pary, the wife of Henry Jones, of Union County, Iowa; Hester, who married J. T. Kent, of Oregon; Daniel, of Wapello County; Jeremiah, a merchant of Ottumwa; John and William Henry, at home.

When our subject and his wife came to this county there were but few settlers, and very little of the land was improved, but they have witnessed with interest and satisfaction the remarkable changes which have taken place around them since that time. They have also contributed their share toward the progress and development of this vicinity. Our subject came here poor in pocket, and his present possessions are the result of his own industry and enterprise, ably assisted by the good judgment, encouragement and industry of his good helpmeet and partner. Mr. Lafollette has been prominent in the affairs of his township, and held various local offices. He has been the encourager and supporter of everything calculated to advance its interests, and in all respects has fulfilled his obligations as a good citizen.

REV. JOHN KRECKEL, a highly respected resident of Ottumwa, is a fine representative of the reliable and substantial German element which has done so much toward the development of the resources of the New World. Our German citizens have almost invariably been people of enterprise, industry and honesty, and have been identified with the better class of the community. They have opened the way for agriculture and manufactures, and in all respects have fulfilled their duties as upright and conscientious citizens.

The subject of our sketch was born in Nassau, Germany, June 5, 1826. He is the son of John and Margaret (Groth) Kreckel, natives of the same country. His maternal grandfather was of Irish birth and parentage. Our subject emigrated to the United States in 1842, settling in Lancaster, Pa., whence, after a few months he went to Baltimore, and entered St. Mary's College, pursuing a course of study for eighteen months. From there he went to Cincinnati, Ohio, where he entered the Jesuit College, pursuing his studies there until 1849, when he graduated. He was ordained for the Priesthood Nov. 17, 1853, and was appointed to a charge at Ottumwa. He proceeded by boat to Dubuque, and from there to Ottumwa by stage, arriving here Feb. 11, 1854. He has had charge of all the churches of Wapello, Polk, Marion, Warren, Appanoose, Jasper and Wayne Counties. When he first came to this section there were only eight families in Des Moines, and Maj. Cavanaugh, then a bachelor. He has aided in the organization of nearly all the church (Catholic) societies of this district and also in the erection of the church buildings, superintending the erection of the first church building in the Irish settlement west of Des Moines.

The parents of our subject emigrated to Lancaster, Pa., with their son, where they died. His father was engaged jointly in mercantile pursuits and farming. During the wars of Napoleon he served as a soldier, being at the battle of Waterloo where the Emperor was overthrown. He died in Lancaster at the age of seventy-five years. His wife, the mother of our subject, departed this life when the latter was a lad of ten years old.

The subject of this history has experienced many changes during a long and useful life, and has greatly improved his opportunities for doing good. As a pioneer evangelist he had much to encounter, and he labored diligently to perform the task which was set before him. Much was expected of him, and it is conceded by all that he performed his part well. We are pleased to present in connection with this brief outline of his life, the portrait of Rev. Kreckel, together with a view of his church building and surroundings.

EDWIN A. JONES, of Ottumwa, an expert member of the printer's craft, is business manager of the office of the Ottumwa *Press*, with which he has been connected as part owner since a youth of sixteen years old. He is a young man of great promise, possesses the pen of a ready writer, and is in every respect admirably fitted for the position which he holds with such ability and success.

Mr. Jones is a native of Bradford County, Pa., and was born July 5, 1865. His parents were Edwin A. and Jane (Jones) Jones, natives respectively of Pennsylvania and Wales. The father died in Bradford County, Pa., on the 15th of October, 1865, when our subject was an infant of a few months old. The mother is still living in Ottumwa, of which she has been a resident since December, 1880.

The subject of our sketch was educated in the common schools of Owego, N. Y., whither his mother had removed when he was a lad of seven years old, and after a residence in that place of seven years, they crossed the Mississippi, making their first location at Ottumwa, and Edwin A. engaged in partnership with his brother-in-law, George Riley, Jr., to purchase the *Press*, which they have operated since that time. Mr. Jones learned the printer's trade since coming to Ottumwa, and after a very brief apprenticeship, seems, apparently, naturally adapted to the art preservative. He commenced under the most favorable auspices, and has a host of friends who wish him all the success to which he is entitled by reason of his enterprise, industry and perseverance.

LEWIS J. BAKER, M. D. Among the medical fraternity of Ottumwa, who, through years of study and practice, have become proficient in the profession, we take pleasure in mentioning the name of Dr. Baker, who located in this city in 1882, and has since practiced here. Dr. Baker was born near Waynesburg, Greene Co., Pa., May 13, 1850, and is the son of George Baker, also a native of that State. The father was owner and operator of a woolen-mill for a number of years, but during the latter part of his life he followed the occupation of a farmer. The grandfather of our subject, J. W. Baker, was born in 1854, and was a soldier in the Revolutionary War, and his father, great-grandfather of our subject, was born in England, and emigrated from that country to the United States and here died. George Baker departed this life in his native State April 24, 1881, aged seventy-six years. Charity (Sharpe) Baker, mother of our subject, was born in Pennsylvania in 1807, and is yet living there, having reached the venerable age of eighty years. Of her union with George Baker ten children were born, five of whom died in childhood, and the other five are living at this writing (1887), Lewis J. Baker being the youngest.

Our subject's early life was passed on the farm in his native county, receiving his education at the public schools, the Academy at Carmichael's, and select school in Beallsville, Pa., supplemented by teaching, being engaged in the latter vocation for thirteen months. In 1871 he began reading medicine, and in 1875 graduated from Jefferson Medical College, Philadelphia, soon after which he located at Bellaire, Ohio. In 1878 he removed to Pittsburgh, Pa., where, in addition to his practice he was engaged in the manufacture of facings, and was thus occupied until 1882. During that year he came to Ottumwa, and since then has devoted his entire time to the practice of his profession.

In 1876 Dr. Baker was united in marriage with Miss Emma D. Shugert, who is a native of Pennsylvania, being born near Pittsburgh. In politics our subject is Republican, and socially he is a member of the Knights Templars and Odd Fellows.

G. E. SHARP, a prosperous farmer and stock-raiser of Cass Township, owns and occupies a fine homestead on section 34, and in his business and farming transactions has been very successful. Our subject is a native of Chatham County, N. Y., and was born May 14, 1825. He is a son of Jacob and Nancy (Westfall) Sharp, both natives of the Empire State and of substantial German ancestry. Their household embraced five children, one son and four daughters, as follows: Maria is the wife of Stephen Miller, a retired farmer of Sandwich, Ill.; Betsey is married to Scott Byers, and Caroline is the wife of Andrew Miller, both being residents of Sandwich; Christina became the wife of Briggs Finch, and resides in Green Springs, Ohio; G. E., our subject, was the fourth in order of birth.

When Mr. Sharp was about four years of age he went to live with his grandfather, where he made his home for the following twelve years. At the age of sixteen he started out for himself, working at whatever his hands could find to do. He was faithful and industrious, and wherever he staid he gained the good-will of his employer so that he could always go back to a place after leaving it. He was prospered in his labors and preserved his health and strength, and after arriving at years of manhood was married to Miss Phœbe Lewis, the daughter of Samuel Lewis, a native of Vermont. Of this union there were born three children: Jacob, the eldest, located in Colo, Storey Co., Iowa, and came to his death by being run over by a railroad train near the center of the State. Our subject, at that time, lived two miles west of Chillicothe, and it is said that young Sharp, after the accident, crawled on his hands and knees for nearly half a mile to the nearest house, where one leg was amputated and it was decided that he would also have to lose the other. But he died while the second operation was being performed, on the 28th of January, 1878, leaving a wife who gave birth to a child about seven months after the accident. The feelings of the present wife of our subject on the loss of this young husband were expressed in the following lines:

"Unveil thy bosom, faithful tomb,
Take this new treasure to thy trust,
And give these sacred relics room
To slumber on in silent dust.
Nor pain, nor grief, nor anxious fear
Invade thy bounds; no mortal woes
Can reach the peaceful sleeper here,
While angels watch the soft repose."

Jane, the second child, and Lavina, the third and last, died in infancy. The mother of these children departed this life in 1851, and was buried in Pennsylvania.

After the death of his first wife, our subject removed to De Kalb County, Ill., and three years later was married to Miss Maria Finch, the daughter of Samuel Finch, of De Kalb County. Mr. Sharp then engaged in farming pursuits, and two years later was again bereaved by the death of his second wife, who died in 1856, and was buried in De Kalb County, Ill. For his third wife Mr. Sharp married Miss Abbie Eastman, on the 16th of October, 1859. This lady was born on the 10th of May, 1838, and is a daughter of Josiah and Angeline (Bullock) Eastman, the father a native of New Hampshire, and the mother of New York.

Mr. Sharp remained in De Kalb County until the spring of 1866, and then removed to Marshall County, Iowa, where he was engaged in farming until 1875. He then purchased 110 acres of land in Cass Township, this county, located on section 34, which he has since occupied. He has greatly improved the condition of this land since it came into his possession, and has a fine farm dwelling, good barns and outhouses, and all the appurtenances of a first-class farm estate. Of his last marriage there were born the following children: Jefferson J. was born on the 5th of February, 1861, in De Kalb County, Ill.; G. Monroe, Nov. 24, 1865, in Kendall County, Ill.; Edson G., Oct. 2, 1870, in

Marshall County, Iowa; Minnie B., Sept. 21, 1872, in the same county. They have also taken within their household circle a child by the name of Cora Hendricks, whom they purpose rearing to womanhood. The date of her birth was Dec. 15, 1883. Mr. and Mrs. S. are members in good standing of the Christian Church.

The subject of this history is essentially a self-made man, and his possessions are the result of his own industry and wise judgment. In his earlier years he labored incessantly with the hope of future results to strengthen him on his way. He is now enjoying the reward of his earlier toils and sacrifices, during which he built up for himself an honest name and an enviable reputation. He is thoroughly esteemed by the citizens of Cass Township, and has held nearly all the offices within their gift. He has ever been the ready friend and supporter of every measure calculated for the welfare of his community, and in all respects has fulfilled the obligations of a good citizen.

ANDREW SEIFERT, deceased, a former highly respected citizen of Eddyville, was a native of Germany, born in Veda Brunswick, in 1832, and departed this life on the 26th of November, 1880, at the age of forty-eight years. He was the son of Andrew and Mary (Boettcher) Seifert, also natives of Germany, and when a youth of sixteen years emigrated to the United States with his father. After reaching the shores of the New World they proceeded directly westward, crossed the Father of Waters, and located in Ft. Madison, this State, where our subject lived until 1858. In the meantime he learned the trade of a harness-maker, and in the year last mentioned removed to Keokuk and worked at his trade in the Gate City for two years. In October, 1860, he came to Eddyville, and established the first harness-store in the place, making this his home until his earthly labors were ended.

Mr. Seifert was married, Oct. 16, 1860, to Miss J. V. Grucer, a lady of German birth and parentage, and the daughter of Gotlob and Caroline (Kinzelman) Grucer, also natives of Germany. Of this union there were born four children: Arthur Albert, who is now carrying on the harness-store for his mother; Eda, a teacher in the Adams school at Ottumwa; Oscar Hugo, who lives with his mother and attends the harness-shop, and Alma, at home. Mr. Seifert was an enterprising business man, a valued citizen, and prominently connected with the Protestant Church. He also belonged to the I. O. O. F. and the A. F. & A. M. Mrs. S. is connected with the Presbyterian Church. The residence of Mrs. Seifert and her family is a tasteful structure, pleasantly located, and that in connection with the harness business constitutes a valuable property. The family are well known and highly respected, and number among their associates and friends the best people of the community

W. S. McLAIN, who is engaged in the livery business at Kirkville, was born in Muskingum County, Ohio, Oct. 3, 1842, and is the son of Jacob and Harriet (Davis) McLain. The family moved from Ohio to Farmington, Iowa, in 1849, and there remained two years, coming from thence to Wapello County in 1851. The father died in Kirkville, Dec. 1, 1871; the mother is still living and resides in Richland Township.

The subject of this sketch was reared upon a farm and educated in the common schools of his adopted State. When the war for the Union commenced, he offered his services to his country, and on the 22d day of September, 1861, enlisted as a private in Co. D, 15th Iowa Vol. Inf., and served as a private and non-commissioned officer during the war. With his regiment he participated in the battles of Corinth, Iuka, siege of Vicksburg, and Atlanta, Ga. In this last battle, on the 20th of July, 1864, he received a gunshot wound just below the right elbow. The ball passed through the arm and came out just above the joint. After being wounded he was taken prisoner, sent to Andersonville, and for eight months and a half endured all the horrors of that loathsome prison. He was then sent to Vicksburg, Miss., for a charge. In June, 1865, he was mustered out, and discharged at Davenport, Iowa. The wound received in his arm rendered it almost useless for heavy labor.

In 1866 Mr. McLain was married to Emma J. Fenton, a native of Wapello County, born Nov. 6, 1846, and the daughter of John and Lucinda (Kirkpatrick) Fenton. Her father died in this county, and her mother is now living in Bates County, Mo. But one child was born to Mr. and Mrs. McLain, Fannie B., July 23, 1867; she died March 30, 1870. Mr. McLain is the owner of two lots and a good, comfortable house in Kirkville. His wife is a member of the Methodist Episcopal Church. Politically he affiliates with the Greenback party.

I. H. ENNIS, a highly respected resident of Ottumwa, was one of the pioneers of Wapello County, and has been a resident of this city since 1869. After the varied scenes of a long and busy life he is now living retired from active labor, while in memory he often reviews the scenes of his early manhood and can tell many an interesting tale of by-gone years to those of the present generation who have the happiness of listening to him.

The subject of this history is a native of Worcester County, Md., and first opened his eyes to the light at the beginning of this century, in 1809. His parents were Boaz and Mary (Marshall) Ennis, natives of the same county as their son, and descended from staunch old English ancestry. Boaz Ennis was a man of fine education, a teacher by occupation, many of the prominent men of the State having been pupils under him. He was the master of several languages, and possessed a remarkable memory. Politically he was a Jeffersonian Democrat, and although never an aspirant for any office, contributed of his time and means liberally to establish and maintain the principles of the party of his choice.

The parental household of our subject included five children, of whom Mr. Ennis of our sketch is the only surviving member. The mother is connected with the Episcopal Church, and their son quaintly observes that, although his father was not identified with any religious denomination, he prayed more than most of the members of churches. After an honest and goodly life, Boaz Ennis rested from his earthly labors in 1834, at the age of seventy-four years. His wife survived him for a period of twenty-four years, and folded her hands for her final rest in 1858, having arrived at the advanced age of nearly ninety-four years.

I. H. Ennis was reared to manhood under the parental roof, and received a careful education, principally under the instruction of his father. In early manhood he was united in marriage, Nov. 5, 1834, with Miss Elizabeth Williams. She was a native of Worcester, Md., and born in 1806. After their marriage Mr. Ennis engaged in farming. In 1850 he went to Rock Island, Ill., remaining a short time only, however, at that point, and then going to Davenport purchased a stock of boots and shoes, opened a store, and was there engaged in trade for several years. He then decided to come into Wapello County, and July 28, 1869, first visited Ottumwa, and decided to establish a permanent home in this city. He had heretofore been very successful in his business transactions, and since becoming a resident of Ottumwa has been living a retired life.

Mr. Ennis is a gentleman of more than ordinary intelligence, and has kept himself well posted in regard to political and general matters connected with this county and State. Before the abandonment of the old Whig party he was one of its stanchest supporters, but upon the organization of the Republican party he cordially indorsed its principles, and has uniformly voted with it since that time. During his business career he was strictly upright and honorable in his dealings with his fellow-men, prompt in meeting his obligations, and courteous in his demeanor to those with whom he was associated, and thus acquired the esteem and respect of his community. He has generously identified himself with the business and industrial interests of this section, and has been a pleased and interested witness of the changes for the better which are constantly taking place in his adopted State and county. Before coming to this section he was a witness of the first railroad train in the United States which ran from Baltimore to Ellicott Mills, Md., and crossed the Mississippi years before the question of a railroad in this section had ever been agitated.

Mr. Ennis and his faithful and affectionate wife

have lived together in peace and harmony for a period of fifty-two years. Their union has been blest by the birth of five children, of whom one is deceased. The record is as follows: Dr. Edgar H. is a graduate of Griswold Medical College, at Davenport, Iowa, and is now a practicing physician of Deep River, Poweshiek County; Sidney M. died at the age of thirteen years; William W. is a druggist of Ottumwa; John B., attorney at law, is a resident of St. John County, Kan., and engaged as a speculator in real estate; Mary E. is the wife of W. W. Cory, attorney at law of Ottumwa. The children of Mr. and Mrs. Ennis have been finely educated, receiving all the advantages which the cultivated tastes and ample means of their parents could afford.

SAMUEL B. EVANS, Postmaster at Ottumwa, and editor and proprietor of the Ottumwa *Democrat*, is a native of Jefferson County, Tenn., his birth occurring July 31, 1837. His ancestors are numbered among the earliest settlers of Eastern Tennessee. His father, Samuel Anderson Evans, was a soldier in the Seminole Indian war, and a lawyer by profession. His death took place in Keokuk County, Iowa, in 1881, he having attained nearly threescore years and ten. The grandfather of our subject, Samuel Evans, served in the War of 1812, and his great-grandfather, Andrew Evans, was a soldier in the Revolutionary War, and participated in the battle of King's Mountain. The mother of our subject, Sarah (Mitchell) Evans, was a daughter of Berry Mitchell, a soldier of the War of 1812. She also died in Keokuk County, Iowa, in 1865. Samuel A. and Sarah (Mitchell) Evans were the parents of four children, of whom Samuel B., our subject, is the eldest; Gideon is a printer, and resides at Ottumwa; Margaret lives at Richland, Keokuk County, where Nancy, now the wife of J. D. Hayworth, also resides.

The subject of this notice came with his parents to Iowa when but five years old, and resided with them in Davis County until 1849, when the family moved to Keokuk County. At the age of sixteen years he entered a printing-office and served an apprenticeship to the printer's trade, and afterward worked as a "jour," accumulating a small sum of money. He now found himself, at the age of manhood, with a good trade, a small amount of capital, and but an intermediate education, and, realizing that an education was more desirable than capital, he entered a branch of the Iowa State University, located at Fairfield. This was in 1855. Three years later, in 1858, in company with John R. Farra as partner, he founded the *Democrat* at Sigourney. Mr. Farra soon sold his interest to Mr. J. B. Shollenbarger. The paper was edited by Mr. Evans, assisted by Judge J. M. Casey, and in 1860 it supported Stephen A. Douglas for the presidency. When the Civil War broke out Mr. Shollenbarger enlisted in the cause of the Union.

In the fall of 1861 Mr. Evans suspended publication of the *Democrat*, moved to Ottumwa and, with Judge E. L. Burton as partner, established the *Mercury*. But Mr. Evans, like his forefathers, could not be content at home when the country needed his service in the field. So, leaving his paper in charge of Judge Burton and Judge H. B. Hendershott, he enlisted, in August, 1862, and was mustered into service with Co. B, 33d Iowa Vol. Inf. He was appointed Commissary Sergeant of the regiment, and held that rank until 1864, when he assisted in organizing the 4th Arkansas Cavalry, a regiment of loyal whites, and was promoted First Lieutenant, with which rank he was mustered out in June, 1865. He participated in the Yazoo Pass expedition, the battle of Helena, the Little Rock and Camden expeditions, including the battle of Jenkin's Ferry, besides numerous skirmishes, and was never wounded or taken prisoner.

On returning from the field of bloody conflict our subject resumed the editorial chair of the *Mercury*, and attended to its duties until 1868, when he sold it to Samuel Burton. He next, in connection with others, founded the Ottumwa *Democrat*, which he conducted until 1881, when he sold it. Soon after disposing of the *Democrat* he took charge of the archæological expedition into Mexico in the interest of the Chicago *Times*. His researches took him into several of the States of Mexico, and he succeeded in making some discoveries acknowledged by the Mexican Government to be of great importance. One of these was the Tezcuco calendar stone, found in the pyramid at the ancient city of Tezcuco. The original stone is now in the Government Museum of Mexico, and fac-similies are in the Smithsonian Institute at Washington and also at Ottumwa. He was three months in Old Mexico, and during his stay there, through the influence of Gen. U. S. Grant and the American Minister, Judge Morgan, the Mexican Government permitted him to excavate at any place, and gave him a guard of troops whenever he desired. His guides were Indians, and he lived with them during his sojourn. After leaving Old Mexico our subject continued his researches in New Mexico for a like period of time, and there became interested in some mines, which interest he still owns, and to which he gave his personal attention until 1884. Returning to Ottumwa in August, 1884, he again became editor of the *Democrat*, and in February, 1886, once more became its proprietor.

Politically Mr. Evans has at all times adhered to the Democratic party. In 1872 he was a delegate to the National Convention, held at Baltimore, and voted for Horace Greeley. In 1876 he was an alternate delegate at large to the National Convention held at St. Louis, and supported Samuel J. Tilden. In 1880 he was delegate to the National Convention at Cincinnati, and was also one of the Vice Presidents of the convention, and after the declination of Samuel J. Tilden our subject supported Thomas F. Bayard for the presidency. Mr. Evans was appointed and commissioned Postmaster at Ottumwa by President Johnson in 1866, but during the fight between the President and the Senate his nomination, with many others, was withdrawn. During the year 1866 he also served several months as Deputy Collector of Internal Revenue.

Mr. Evans was appointed Postmaster at Ottumwa by President Cleveland July 14, 1885, and confirmed by the Senate without opposition in March, 1886. In 1874, when the Iowa Legislature established the Fish Commission, Mr. Evans was chosen President of the same, and it was largely through his influence that the commission was created, thereby largely benefiting the people. He may well be proud of his labors while acting in that capacity, and also of the results achieved.

The most important event of our subject's life took place Dec. 19, 1866, on which date Sarah E. Potter became his wife. She is the daughter of John and Nancy Potter, and was born in Carroll County, Ohio, in November, 1845. Five children were given to this marriage—Margaret, Sarah Edith, Lucy, Samuel McDonald and Bertha, all of whom are living with the exception of Samuel McDonald.

Socially Mr. Evans is a member of the I. O. O. F. and G. A. R. As a citizen he has always been ready to assist in any enterprise whereby the public could be benefited, especially if the enterprise in any way tended to benefit the wide-awake city of Ottumwa, of which our subject is one of the most prominent citizens.

DOMINICK SCHLAGETER, a prominent and well-to-do farmer and stock-raiser, residing on section 12, of Polk Township, is a German by birth, having been born in Baden, March 19, 1821. His parents, Jacob and Anna (Wasmer) Schlageter, were farmers in their native country, where they lived lives of usefulness, and died there, their remains being buried in their native soil. Our subject at the age of thirty, determined to seek his fortune in the New World, and accordingly boarded a vessel for New York, where he landed Aug. 4, 1851. He made the journey in a sailing-vessel, and experienced a stormy voyage, being forty-four days in making the trip. Our subject remained in New York for a year, and in 1853 came to Ottumwa, where he made his home until the 10th of May, 1854, when he moved to the farm he now occupies, and where he owns 200 acres of well-improved land, with good residence and excellent farm buildings. He has become prominently identified with the community of which he has been so long a member, and is regarded as one of the solid men of the county.

Mr. Schlageter was united in marriage with Caroline Matt, in Baden, Germany. This lady was born Jan. 1, 1829, and is the daughter of Jacob and Mary (Gersback) Matt, both of whom died in Germany. Mrs. Schlageter has borne her husband the following children: Mary R. is the wife of Benhart Hoffman, of Ottumwa: John A. died in Leadville, Col., where Joseph M. is now living; Carrie D. is at home; Seth L. died in Denver, Col.; Fred E. is living at Leadville, that State; Lucy L. is the wife of L. O. Johnson; Minnie C. is deceased, and Andrew D. lives with his parents.

Our subject is, as he always has been, active in local affairs, taking an interest in the progress and welfare of the community. He is at present serving his fifth term as Justice of the Peace, and has held the office of Assessor and various others of his township. Politically he is a Democrat, and both himself and wife are members of the Catholic Church.

IVY MENDENHALL, a successful farmer and stock-grower of Green Township, is comfortably located on section 16, and is pursuing the peaceful vocation of a farmer with satisfactory results. Mr. Mendenhall is a native of the Buckeye State, and was born in Greene County, on the 9th of November, 1823. His parents were Malachi and Elizabeth (Starr) Mendenhall, natives respectively of Ohio and Virginia. After their marriage, they located in the former State, and in 1835 removed from there to Vermilion County, Ill., where they entered a tract of land, being among the early settlers of that part of the State. Here the father remained until his death, which occurred Feb. 12, 1879, after he had attained the ripe age of seventy-seven years. He was an earnest Christian gentleman, generous in his impulses, charitable and benevolent in disposition, and left a good record of an honorable and upright life. The mother is yet living, and makes her home on the old homestead in Vermilion County, Ill., aged eighty-five years.

The subject of this history was reared upon his father's farm and obtained his early education in the subscription schools. He remained with his parents until he was about twenty-nine years old, and then, in 1852, left the old homestead, crossed the Mississippi, and came into Polk County, Iowa. He was a resident there for eighteen months, and in the spring of 1853 came to this county, where he was variously employed for the following three years. In 1856 he purchased a small farm of sixty acres, fifteen of which was timber land, and engaged in its improvement and cultivation. He was fairly prospered, and as time passed on was enabled to add to his first purchase until he is now the owner of 145 acres.

The marriage of Ivy Mendenhall and Miss Susan Baum took place Aug. 30, 1855. Mrs. Mendenhall is the daughter of Benjamin and Mary (Weaver) Baum, and was born April 27, 1833. By her marriage with our subject she became the mother of three children, only one of whom is now living, Lewis C., born July 27, 1859. Wesley and William are the names of those deceased. The father of Mrs. Mendenhall died in Wapello County at the age of fifty-five years. Her mother is still living and has arrived at the age of seventy-six years; she is a bright and intelligent old lady, and retains her mental faculties in a marked degree. Both parents are prominently connected with the Methodist Episcopal Church.

Since coming to this township, Mr. Mendenhall has taken an active part in politics, and at every opportunity has done all within his power to support the principles of the Democratic party, of which he is a stanch adherent. He has been an incumbent of the various township offices, and has fulfilled the important duties intrusted to him with credit to himself and satisfaction to his fellow-townsmen. He started in life at the foot of the ladder, possessing nothing but willing hands and a clear head, and has climbed up to his present position solely by the exercise of his own native qualities of resolution and perseverance.

JACOB P. REES, a skillful mechanic of Ottumwa, is a carpenter and joiner by trade, and has been a resident of this State and city since 1871. He is an adept at his profession, and has superintended the erection of some of the finest buildings in this city. He is a thorough-going business man of excellent abilities, and has accumulated a handsome property by the exercise of

his natural industry and mechanical genius. Mr. Rees was born in Butler County, Ohio, on the 22d of October, 1822, and is the son of William and Naomi (Finley) Rees, the former a native of North Wales and the latter of Pennsylvania.

William Rees, father of our subject, emigrated from his native country to America when a youth of fifteen years, locating in Pennsylvania, and was afterward married in Indiana County, that State, two children, John and Thomas, being born there. Mr. Rees, at an early day and before the War of 1812, took a flatboat and with his family proceeded to Ohio, and at the breaking out of the war mentioned, he enlisted in the ranks, but only served a short time. After his return from the army he located in Butler County, Ohio, where four more children were born: William, who enlisted in the 10th Indiana Volunteer Battery, and was killed in Texas at the last battle; George, now in California; J. P., our subject, and one who died in infancy. In the fall of 1831 William Rees removed with his family to Montgomery County, Ind., and engaged in farming for the following twenty-one years. Then, in 1852, he again set his face westward, and crossing the Mississippi, came into Des Moines County, Iowa, where he located and remained the balance of his days, closing his eyes on the scenes of his earthly labors in 1862. His first wife, the mother of our subject, had died in Butler County, Ohio, and he was the second time married, Miss Sarah Pritz becoming his wife, by whom he became the father of one daughter, Elizabeth, now a resident of Missouri.

Jacob P. Rees was reared in Indiana and received his education in the common schools of the Hoosier State. He was there married, in 1845, to Miss Eliza Price, having already served a thorough apprenticeship at the carpenter's trade, and when not engaged at his trade, occupied himself in farming pursuits. After his marriage he was employed as a contractor and a builder, and took an honest pride in the excellence of his work. He remained with his family in Indiana until 1871, when he came to Ottumwa, as before stated.

The family circle of Mr. and Mrs. Rees was completed by the birth of five children: Henry C., during the progress of the late war, served as a soldier of the Union in the 5th Indiana Cavalry; he remained in service until the close of the war, returned home unharmed, and is now living in Ottumwa, engaged as a carpenter; James P. and Edward B. are also in Ottumwa; Anna became the wife of Frank Akens of this city, and Roscoe is engaged as a railroader at Omaha. The boys, like their father, are all natural mechanics, having inherited his talents and genius in a marked degree. Mr. and Mrs. R. are highly respected in their community and worthy members of the First Methodist Episcopal Church of Ottumwa. Politically Mr Rees is an uncompromising Republican, and cast his first vote for Gen. Harrison for President.

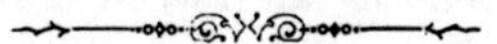

M. L. KIRK, of Ottumwa, senior partner of the firm of Kirk & Walker, successfully engaged as lumber dealers, is a native of Trumbull County, Ohio. He was born on the 22d day of April, 1838, and is the son of William and Elizabeth (Rose) Kirk, natives respectively of Pennsylvania and Ohio. They were married in the latter State, and after the birth of our subject, removed from Trumbull to Morrow County, where the father departed this life in 1854. Two years later Mrs. Kirk came with her children to Iowa, and settled at Ft. Madison, where she reared her family together and provided them with a liberal education. She is a lady of great energy of character, a devoted member of the Methodist Episcopal Church, and for her efforts in keeping her little family together deserves the highest praise. She now resides at Ft. Madison, and enjoys the esteem of a large circle of friends and acquaintances.

The parental household included eight children, four of whom are living: John S., during the late war, enlisted in Co. D, 7th Iowa Vol. Inf., participated in the various engagements of his regiment during the conflict, and at the close returned home with a Captain's commission, and is now a resident of Havana, Ill.; the next was our subject, M. L.; Harriet became the wife of Frank Sherwood, of Ft. Madison, who served as a soldier of the Union in the 7th Iowa Regiment, and returned home unharmed at the close of the war; Lovina married Jacob Votaw, of Hamilton County, Tex.

The subject of this sketch was a youth of sixteen years old when he crossed the Father of Waters and came into the Hawkeye State. He remained at home until 1863, and then enlisted in the United States Navy, under Admiral Porter, on the Mississippi. He was on detail service, and participated in the battle of Ft. Pillow, and was in the engagement at Paducah, Ky., remaining in the service until the close of the war. He then returned home, and afterward went to Pella, where he engaged in the lumber trade for five years, thence going to Mt. Sterling, Ill., pursuing the same occupation with a partner, the name of the firm being Kirk & Co. He came to Ottumwa in 1874, and formed a partnership with Mr. Walker, that same year. The firm is a popular and reliable one, and their operations extend throughout Iowa and into the States adjoining.

Mr. Kirk was united in marriage, in 1866, at Ft. Madison, with Miss Amanda Sherwood. Mrs. K. is the daughter of Ira and Hannah Sherwood, and was born in Pennsylvania in 1843. By her union with our subject she has become the mother of two children—Clarence and Katie. They are pleasantly located in this city, enjoying all the comforts of life and many of its luxuries. Mr. K. in politics is Republican; socially he is a Master Mason, and also a member of Pella Lodge No. 55, G. A. R., Capt. Cloutman Post.

WILLIAM S. LYMAN is a farmer and stock-grower on section 18, Center Township. He was born in Randolph County, Ill., March 6, 1855, and is a son of W. W. and Ada (Shattuck) Lyman. His father was engaged in the mercantile trade in Connecticut for many years, and moved from that State to Illinois in 1844, and is still living, being now a resident of Ashley, Washington Co., Ill.

When twenty-one years of age the subject of our sketch moved from Illinois to Monroe County, Iowa, where he remained seven years, and in 1883 came to Wapello County, and soon after took charge of the stock farm of Charles F. Blake, of Ottumwa, where he is now living. This land is situated on section 18 of Center Township, and is one of the best stock farms in the country. Among the fine stock are two fine imported thoroughbred Norman stallions, "Captain" and "Desire," and two imported brood mares, together with a large lot of fine grade Short-horn and grade Holstein cattle. The farm consists of 800 acres of fine land, and has a large, comfortable dwelling-house, and all modern improvements of a well-regulated stock farm. Mr. Lyman owns a one-half interest in all the stock upon the farm. He is a thorough stock farmer and understands well the care of all kinds of stock.

In 1882 Mr. Lyman was united in marriage with Miss Sadie Carroll, a daughter of Noble and Sarah (Chandler) Carroll, who are now living in Ottumwa. They have one child, Edna, born on the 29th of June 14, 1884. Politically Mr. Lyman is a Republican.

GEORGE Z. COWAN has been a highly esteemed resident of Wapello County since 1861, and a resident of Center Township since 1869. He owns and occupies a fine farm estate on section 1, and in his pursuits of agriculture and stock-raising is meeting with success. He is a native of the proud and wealthy Buckeye State, having been born in Holmes County, Oct. 15, 1850, and was the son of William P. and Rachel (Commer) Cowan, natives respectively of Virginia and Ohio. At the age of five years he crossed the Mississippi with his father and mother, and with them located first in Tipton, Cedar County. This was their home for the following eight years, his father being engaged in the drug business until 1865. They removed from there to locate upon a tract of land in Center Township, which they had purchased and which was situated on section 14. The first consisted of seventy-eight and one-half acres, and by subsequent purchase was increased to 237 acres. Upon this Mr. Cowan has erected a handsome farm residence, with a good barn, and all conveniences for the storage of grain and the shelter of stock.

George Z. Cowan and Miss Martha Alice Crips were united in marriage Nov. 9, 1874. Mrs.

Cowan is a native of Wapello County, and by her marriage with our subject became the mother of five children, as follows: Julian Lee, George William, Fannie Lorelle, Jennie Lena and Winnifred P.

Upon leaving his native State, the parents of Mr. Cowan first came into Tipton, Cedar Co., Iowa, in 1855, and there our subject was reared and educated during his earlier years. After completing his primary studies he attended the Notre Dame Academy at South Bend, Ind., where he remained, pursuing his studies for three months, and at the age of fourteen years engaged in clerking in his father's drug-store, being thus occupied for five years following. Since engaging in agricultural pursuits in Center Township he has also given much attention to the breeding of fine stock, especially horses. He established his breeding stables in 1868, and has made extensive preparations to continue this business. His herd of cattle consists of high-grade Short-horns, and his sales of these have amounted to $1,300 per year. He is also raising Poland-China hogs, his first purchase of these being procured from Dr. Magie, of Oxford, Ohio. Of these he sells $1,000 worth per year. He has exhibited some of the finest animals in the county at the fairs of this locality and taken many premiums.

Mr. Cowan has been prominent in the affairs of his township and county, and as a level-headed man his advice has been consulted upon matters of general importance as being a wise and safe counselor. He has been Supervisor and School Director, and politically is an uncompromising Democrat. He is liberal in his religious views.

JOHN G. HOWARD, Jr., a highly esteemed resident of Ottumwa, is a native of the Hawkeye State, and was born in Keokuk, Oct. 16, 1854. He is the son of John G. and Elizabeth A. (Godfrey) Howard, natives respectively of Kentucky and Massachusetts. They were married in the former State, and in 1819 emigrated to Iowa, being among the early settlers of Lee County. They became the parents of twelve children, three of whom are living: George W., of Denver, Col.; Debbie, the wife of James T. Lee, of Council Bluffs, and engaged in the tea business, and our subject, John G. John G. Howard, Sr., was a staunch Republican in politics, and a man of good abilities, who kept himself well posted in affairs of general interest. His wife, the mother of our subject, departed this life July 4, 1870. She was a most estimable Christian lady, and a member of the Unitarian Church.

John G. Howard, Jr., was educated in the common schools of his native county, and reared to habits of industry and honesty, and after leaving the parental roof was engaged in mercantile business. In 1882 he was appointed to his present position as Agent with the Consolidated Tank Line Company, which was established in August of the year mentioned, and was first known as the Keokuk Oil Tank Line, under which it was operated eight months, and then changed to the Iowa Tank Line Company, L. J. Drake being then the general manager at Keokuk, Iowa, his headquarters first being at Des Moines, and he was then appointed general manager of Iowa, Nebraska and Dakota, with headquarters at Omaha. When the name was changed, Nebraska and Dakota were taken in. The factory is 60x100 feet in dimensions, with a front of 250 feet, and has a storage capacity of 2,500 barrels. Their sales extend throughout the States mentioned. The tanks were constructed with great care, and are considered perfectly safe; they are located on Samantha street, between McLain and Hope streets, in the west part of the city.

REV. BEN. E. S. ELY, a prominent citizen of Ottumwa, is a native of Philadelphia, Pa., and the son of Rev. E. L. Ely, D. D., and Mary A. (Carswell) Ely, natives respectively of Connecticut and Pennsylvania. The father was a minister of the Presbyterian Church, and presided over one congregation in Philadelphia for a period of twenty-seven years. He was made Moderator of the General Assembly of the Presbyterian Church of America, and was its stated clerk for a space of twelve years. He was reared in the town of Lebanon, Conn., and was a graduate of

Yale College. His grandfather, Zebulon Ely, was also a Presbyterian minister, and was Pastor at Lebanon for forty-one years. He was born Feb. 6, 1759, in Lyme, Conn., and died in 1824. His son, the father of our subject, was born June 13, 1786, and died in 1861, in the Quaker City.

Rev. Ben. Ely was a student of Delaware College, and at the early age of twenty years was admitted to the practice of law. He had been a close student under the instruction of Hon. James Todd, of Philadelphia, and was finely qualified as an attorney and counselor. Soon afterward he went to California, and followed his profession in the Golden State for a period of ten years. He was elected to the California Legislature in 1858. Not long after this, however, he abandoned the profession of the law to take up that of the ministry, and in 1862 was ordained and became Pastor of the church at Healdsburg, Sonoma County. He was afterward located at Stockton, and from there moved east to Chicago, and took charge of Grace Presbyterian Church, now the Sixth Church. After severing his connection with this charge he became connected with the Willow Creek Scotch Presbyterian Church, with which he remained until June, 1881, when he was called to the charge of the First Presbyterian Church of Ottumwa, where he has remained until the present time.

While in California Mr. Ely was City Attorney of Sacramento, and introduced the first prohibitory liquor law, which passed the Assembly but failed in the Senate. He was greatly interested in the temperance movement, and did everything in his power to promote sobriety, being a leader of the movement in that section. He has been a member of five General Assemblies of the Presbyterian Church in the United States, and in the winter of 1885–86 was elected Moderator of the Synod of Iowa.

Our subject was first married, Sept. 29, 1849, to Miss Elizabeth McElroy, a native of Christian County, Ky., and they became the parents of seven children, three of whom are deceased: Elizabeth died in infancy in 1849; Ben. E. S., Jr., is Pastor of the Presbyterian Church of Washington, Iowa; George Montgomery died at the age of nineteen years; Laura Elizabeth is the wife of Prof. E. L. Curtis, of the Theological Seminary of the Northwest, of Chicago, Ill.; Rose is a teacher at Sioux Falls, Dak.; Charles Wadsworth is deceased; Mary Anita is at home. Mrs. Elizabeth Ely, the mother of these children, died Aug. 16, 1871, at the age of thirty-eight years. Mr. Ely was a second time married, March 25, 1873, to Miss Abbie Aurelia, daughter of Portius Moore, of Massachusetts. Mrs. E. was born in Chicago, Ill., and by her marriage with our subject is the mother of one child, Francis Argyle.

BENJAMIN REED, a highly respected citizen of Green Township, is a native of Pickaway County, Ohio, born May 2, 1806. His parents were Dorman and Nancy (Penniwell) Reed, both natives of Delaware, who went to Ohio after their marriage and were among the early settlers of Pickaway County. His father served forty-five days in the War of 1812, under Gen. Harrison. Both parents were of Scotch and Welsh descent, and inherited from a worthy ancestry the excellent qualities peculiar to both nations. The parental family consisted of ten children, of whom the subject of our sketch was the eldest born. He was reared to farming pursuits and was trained to habits of industry and economy, and into his youthful mind were instilled those high moral principles which were characteristic of his parents and ancestors.

At the age of twenty-one years Benjamin Reed commenced farming upon his own account in Vigo County, Ind., being located near Terre Haute, where he remained seven years, cultivating rented land. Previous to this, however, when a boy of thirteen years old, his parents had removed to Darke County, Ohio, and were living there while their son was farming in Indiana. At the expiration of the time mentioned he returned to Darke County, and locating upon a tract of rented land, operated it for five years, and from there, in 1840, went to St. Clair County, Mo., near Monagan Springs, and entered forty acres of land, most of which was improved and under a good state of cultivation. He occupied this for five years, and then, recrossing the Father of Waters, again went into Indiana, locating in Gibson County, where he remained until the fall of 1845. He then retraced his steps westward and came into Iowa to Wapello County, settling in Green Township, where he has since resided. At the time of coming here he entered forty acres of land, upon which he erected a log cabin. He was prospered in his agricultural pursuits, and added to his possessions as time passed on and his means accumulated, being now the owner of 359 acres, mostly improved and fenced

In early manhood Mr. Reed was married, in 1829, to Miss Margaret Reed, of Ohio, and of their union there were born five children, as follows: Silas died in childhood; Sarah, born Dec. 5, 1832, is the wife of Andrew Murker, of Lucas County, this State; Nancy married Joshua Cloyd, and is living in Adams Township; Anthony died at the age of twenty years. Mrs. Margaret Reed departed this life in October, 1843. Mr. Reed was the second time married, in 1844, to Miss Delilah Lathom, a native of Gibson County, Ind., and a daughter of Jonathan L. and Delilah (Potter) Lathom. Of this marriage there were born ten children: Marita died in infancy; Mary Ann became the wife of Isaac Read, a merchant tailor of Nebraska; Amanda married Willoughby Orman, and died Oct. 4, 1869; Elizabeth became the wife of Merritt Nicols, of Green Township; M. L., born Oct. 13, 1853, married Sarah Loper, and is engaged in farming in Green Township; Alice Jane, born Feb. 6, 1846, is the wife of William Kent, of Adams Township; Delilah, born Sept. 9, 1858, is the wife of Lawrence Kent, of Monroe County, Iowa; Benjamin F. was born Feb. 9, 1861, and lives at home; Thomas J., born March 14, 1862, is also at home; Maria May, born Jan. 28, 1856, is the wife of A. J. Hicks, of Green Township. They have also raised two orphan grandchildren: William Orman, born June 8, 1867, and Amanda Jane, Sept. 24, 1869.

Mrs. Reed is a member in good standing of the Christian Church. Mr. Reed has been Supervisor, Township Trustee and School Director. He is Democratic in politics, and takes an intelligent interest in the welfare of the community, contributing of his time and means in support and encouragement of every worthy enterprise. At the organization of the county, Mr. Reed and James Hollingsworth were the only men in Green Township. Mr. Hollingsworth was made the first Clerk and Mr. Reed the first Trustee. There were then no roads to Ottumwa, and he had to pick his way through the timber. He traveled over a great deal of the Western country, and from the outlook at that time he did not think it possible it would ever be settled up to any great extent for purposes of farming, and as he wanted to go into the stock business, he thought this section would make a good range for his cattle. But he was mistaken in his calculations, as the appearance of this section at the present day indicates. The pioneers began to come in one after another, and in due time the land around him was taken up by the enterprising pioneers, until the choicest portion of it had been entered and settled upon. It was not many years before the humble cabins began to give way to more pretentious dwellings, and comparing the present with the past, the changes which have occurred in a comparatively brief time seem more like a dream than a reality.

B. D. WOLF, a prosperous member of the agricultural community of Columbia Township, owns and occupies a comfortable homestead on section 32, and beside his ordinary farm work, has attained quite a reputation as a breeder of fine stock. Our subject was born in Athens County, Ohio, on the 19th of March, 1815, and is the son of Christopher and Rhoda (Dorr) Wolf, natives respectively of Westmoreland County, Pa., and New York.

Christopher Wolf removed from his native State to Ohio, where he formed the acquaintance of the lady whom he afterward married, their wedding taking place about the year 1804. They settled in Athens County, and the father of our subject became one of the most extensive farmers of that region. He also engaged in milling, and shipped the first boat-load of produce that was sent down the Hocking River from Athens to Louisville, Ky., about 1824. He was one of the early pioneers of

Athens County, and became a useful and highly respected citizen. He lived there until 1840, and then sold out his farm and milling interest and removed to Hocking County, where he purchased another tract of land, which he occupied until the time of his death. He possessed a large estate there, aggregating about 900 acres of land. The affectionate wife and mother departed this life on the 9th of May, 1843, the father surviving her only until the following September. Mrs. Wolf was a consistent member of the Methodist Episcopal Church, a lady highly esteemed for her excellent traits of character, and at her death was greatly mourned by a large circle of friends and acquaintances.

The parental family included ten children, of whom the record is as follows: William and Lida are deceased; Andrew has been a practicing physician of Vinton County, Ohio, for forty years; Mathew is a farmer of Hocking County, Ohio; our subject was next in order of birth; Rhoda died in infancy; Edmund is engaged in farming and sheep-raising in Vinton County, Ohio; Joseph is deceased; Elizabeth became the wife of Wilford Stires, a farmer and stock-dealer of Hocking County, Ohio; Jonathan is deceased.

B. D. Wolf, of our sketch, on the 19th of November, 1836, married Miss Eliza Johnson, who was born in Hocking County, Ohio, March 3, 1813. They remained in the Buckeye State until 1856, and then removed to Iowa. The early years of our subject had been spent on his father's farm and he also assisted about the mill. After coming West he located in Wapello County, purchasing about 887 acres of land, and was engaged in its improvement and cultivation, until he now has one of the finest farms in Columbia Township. Our subject and wife became the parents of seven children, as follows: Josiah, a farmer of Monroe County, Iowa, was born Nov. 19, 1838; Hiram, born April 29, 1840, enlisted as a soldier during the late war in the Union army, and in 1863, with a number of his comrades, was captured by the enemy and taken to Andersonville Prison where, after great suffering and privation he died, and was buried in one of the trenches, the bereaved and afflicted parents never having been able to recover his body; Elizabeth was born Aug. 14, 1842, and became the wife of Benjamin Chisman, a farmer of Columbia Township; Henry, another son who had enlisted in the army, died in the hospital at Nashville, Tenn.; he was born on the 7th of October, 1844, and, with his brother Hiram, was a member of the 8th Iowa Cavalry; Eliza, born Dec. 18, 1846, is the wife of J. W. Nye, a farmer of Monroe County, Iowa; Mary L. was born Jan. 28, 1851, and married Samuel Nye, a farmer of Columbia Township; S. P. was born April 6, 1847, and is farming in Columbia Township.

Mrs. Eliza Wolf died Oct. 3, 1873, and was buried in the cemetery of Columbia Township. She was a faithful and affectionate wife, a loving mother, and highly esteemed by her neighbors and acquaintances. The second wife of our subject was Mrs. Elizabeth Eyre, to whom he was married April 30, 1874. This lady was born in Brown County, Ohio, Sept. 22, 1818, and is the daughter of William and Sarah (Wilson) Maholam, natives of Ireland and Virginia respectively. The father is deceased, but the mother yet survives, and is living in Green Township, at the ripe old age of ninety years. Mrs. Wolf is a member in good standing of the Methodist Episcopal Church.

Mr. Wolf gave his children the advantages of a good education and divided up a portion of his large landed estate among them, giving to each a good farm, and has yet 230 acres left for his own use. The family residence is one of the finest farm dwellings in Columbia Township, and the barns and outhouses are of the best description, conveniently arranged for the shelter of stock and the storing of grain. Everything in and about the premises betokens a cultivated taste and ample means. Mr. Wolf takes great pride in his stock, which consists of high-grade Short-horn cattle, which he is crossing with Herefords, and exhibits some of the finest animals in the Mississippi Valley. His horses are principally Normans, and models of symmetry and strength.

Politically our subject is a stanch Republican and a great admirer of the lamented Lincoln. In his social life he has hosts of friends who respect him alike for his rare business qualities and straightforward dealings, and his kindness and hospitality as a friend and neighbor. Mr. Wolf, however, amid all his prosperity and the comfort and society of friends will never cease to mourn for his two sons who fell in the Rebellion. They were unusually bright and promising young men, admired and beloved by all who knew them, and of whom great things were expected in the future. The manner of their taking-off is a perpetual sorrow to the hearts who loved them.

REUBEN MYERS is a farmer and stock-grower on section 8, Washington Township. He was born in York County, Pa., March 29, 1815, and is a son of Abraham and Catherine (Conn) Myers, both natives of Pennsylvania, and of Holland-Dutch descent. When Reuben was but two and a half years of age, his parents moved from Pennsylvania to Preble County, Ohio, where they lived until 1830, when they moved to Fountain County, Ind., where the father died May 23, 1849. The mother then moved to Jasper County, Ind., and there died Oct. 28, 1854.

Reuben Myers and Sallie Moore were married in Indiana Sept. 15, 1836, by ex-Bishop William Brown. She was born in Ross County, Ohio, May 7, 1819, and is a daughter of Edward and Kitty (Foster) Moore, who were also natives of Ross County, but who moved to Warren County, Ind., in 1826. Her mother died in 1849, and her father in 1869. In 1843, with his wife and two children, Mr. Myers came to Wapello County, Iowa, and settled on the farm he now occupies, purchasing the claim of a squatter, and afterward purchasing from the Government. He was one of the first judges of election in Wapello County, and served with James Acton and Robert Wright. In the early days he was appointed and served as Road Commissioner, and has since held the office of Township Trustee. Mr. Myers is the owner of 104 acres of good land, nearly all of which is under cultivation.

Mr. and Mrs. Myers have become the parents of five children: John F., deceased; T. J.; Mary C., deceased; M. J., now the wife of G. W. Creath, and James E., deceased. In politics Mr. Myers is a Republican, and he and his wife are members of the Methodist Episcopal Church. They are of that number of pioneers who are fast passing away, and to whom credit is due for all that we now enjoy in this beautiful land. They have experienced trials and privations, but now, in their old age, are blest with plenty, and are surrounded by many friends who love and respect them.

On the 15th day of September, 1886, our subject and wife celebrated their golden wedding, on which occasion there was a large number of friends present and many valuable presents given. Of the guests, John F. Moore, of Mahaska County, Iowa; Elizabeth Moore, of Warren County, Ind., and Jacob Myers, of Wapello County, were present at their wedding, which took place in Indiana fifty years ago. Among others present were Rev. R. B. Allender, of Bloomfield, Iowa; Rev. J. B. Hill and wife, of Agency; Rev. S. S. Martin and wife, of Agency; Rev. J. C. Kendrick and wife, of Eldon; Rev. T. J. Myers, the son of our subject, and wife, who now reside in Burlington, and Dr. B. W. Searle and wife, of Ottumwa. While the gifts were valuable the kind expressions of love and esteem were valued more by this worthy couple than all else beside.

W. J. BASTIAN, Vice President of the Ottumwa Cutlery Company, and a resident of that city, is a native of Greenfield, Mass., where he first saw light Dec. 13, 1851. His parents, John and Kate (Class) Bastian, were natives of Germany, and came to this country while quite young. They were married at North Hampton, Mass., in 1848, and became the parents of four children, our subject being the eldest. The remaining children are Frank; Carrie, wife of John Andrews, of Ottumwa, and Henry. The father learned his trade, that of a cutler, in his native country, and after coming to the United States, engaged as an employe of John Russell, of Greenfield, Mass., with whom he continued to work until his demise in 1861. Mrs. Bastian still survives her husband, and is residing in Ottumwa with her son, W. J.

The subject of this sketch was reared to manhood

in the county of his nativity, and received his education in the schools of Greenfield. It was in that city that he first engaged to learn the cutlery business, which he followed until January, 1879, when he came to this State. Arriving here he located at Ottumwa and established his present successful business. He is a young man of more than ordinary business ability, and is meeting with success in conducting the enterprise in which he is engaged. He was married, Oct. 12, 1880, to Miss Ina Antrobus. She was born in Wapello County in 1861.

The Ottumwa Cutlery Company, of which Mr. Bastian is Vice President, is the product of a business established in January, 1879, by Rose & Bastian. The business, under the firm name of Rose & Bastian, continued until 1882, when it was merged into the Ottumwa Cutlery Company, with the following Directors: J. T. Hackworth, C. F. Blake, W. F. Rose, S. H. Harper and W. J. Bastian. The following are the officers: W. T. Harper, President; W. J. Bastian, Vice President; C. F. Blake, Treasurer, and W. E. Chambers, Secretary. They manufacture table and butchers' cutlery, and their office is located at Nos. 214, 216 and 218 South Tisdale street. They employ a corps of ninety men, and the size of their building, which comprises two stories, is 150x38 feet. They have a salesman constantly on the road, and do an annual business of $100,000.

TIMOTHY TERREL, a farmer and stock-grower on section 29, Richland Township, was born in Harrison County, Va., Jan. 3, 1814, and is a son of Timothy and Elizabeth (Nixon) Terrel. His parents moved from Virginia to Ohio in 1819, where the mother died in 1830; the father survived her ten years, passing from the scenes of his earthly labors in 1840.

The subject of this sketch was reared upon a farm and received his education in the pioneer log school-houses of Ohio. In 1838 he was united in marriage with Amy Arnold, who was born in Rhode Island, June 3, 1819. Her parents moved from that State to Ohio about 1822, where both of them subsequently died. Mr. and Mrs. Terrel are the parents of three children: Hiram married Delila Bonham, and is now living in Colorado; Solomon married Rena Berry, and now lives in Pottawattamie County, Iowa; Huldah lives with her parents.

In 1848 Mr. Terrel moved from Ohio to Wapello County, Iowa, and for thirty-eight years has been a resident of this county. He is the owner of forty acres of good farm land, with a house and barn and all necessary out-buildings, a view of which is presented on another page of this work. Mr. Terrel and wife are consistent members of the Methodist Episcopal Church, and politically he is a Republican.

JAMES HAWLEY, deceased, formerly a resident of Ottumwa, and respected for his sterling traits of character, was born on the 4th of June, 1803, at Albany, N. Y., where he spent his early years and received a good common-school education. When thirty years old he engaged in the merchantile business at Red Creek, Wayne Co., N. Y., where he continued for five years, meeting with success in his enterprise, after which he removed to Lyons in the same county.

In 1839 our subject was elected on the Whig ticket to the office of County Clerk, which position he held for three years, when failing health demanded a change of climate, and he removed to Chillicothe, Ohio. There he embarked in the dry-goods trade, and after a highly successful business career, was induced by some of his friends to move to Washington County, Ky. There he also engaged in business, but not meeting with the success anticipated, he, in 1848, started West on an exploring tour, having in his mind's eye a desirable locality for engaging in business. Coming to this State and happening to be in the city of Ottumwa, and viewing all the advantages afforded by that city, he concluded it was the most favorable he had seen, and thither he removed and commenced business in a small frame building. His success was such that the second year of his stay there he erected

Thomas Hardestey
S C McCullough

the first two-story brick building in the Des Moines Valley. On the arrival of his family at Ottumwa Mr. Hawley, not having a home for them, moved into and took charge of the first hotel in Ottumwa. In the latter enterprise, as well as in his mercantile pursuits, he was, during several years of active business life, successful.

On the 20th of September, 1831, Mr. Hawley was united in marriage with Miss Juliette Jones, of New York, by whom he had three children, two sons and a daughter, both sons having passed to the home of the hereafter. Upon the death of our subject, Oct. 21, 1882, resolutions were passed by the City Council, and many citizens and friends lamented the death of one who, while living, was kind and courteous to all, and never known to turn a deaf ear to true charity. Through life Mr. Hawley was a Republican in politics, and twice was honored with the office of Mayor of Ottumwa. He was also President of the First National Bank of Ottumwa for eighteen months. Mr. Hawley was not a man of ponderous intellect, but he possessed that energy which, when he made up his mind to accomplish a given object, generally carried him through, and this was one of the principal causes of his success in life. His home was a happy one, and affection was crowned everywhere within its walls. He left a widow, two sons and a daughter, but, as stated, the sons have gone to meet him on the other shore, and there now remain only wife and daughter, who will meet him by and by on the other side of the river.

THOMAS HARDESTEY, who is residing at Ottumwa, is a native of North Carolina and was born in 1811. His parents were Samuel and Hannah (Hoover) Hardestey, natives of the above-named State. Thomas was reared in his native State, and in 1834, after a sojourn in Indiana, removed westward, crossed the Mississippi, and coming to Iowa purchased a quarter-section of land near Fairfield, Jefferson County. This he improved, selling it at a profit, and moved to Kirkville, in 1844, and occupied the farm, which he there opened up, until 1886. He then came to Ottumwa, and purchased six and one-half acres in the suburbs of this city, where he has erected a comfortable residence, located his family, and is spending his declining years.

The career of Mr. Hardestey as a pioneer has been one eminently worthy to the community in which he resided so long, as well as successful from a financial point of view. He became one of the largest land-owners in this section of the State, having divided among his children 900 acres of land, retaining eighty for himself. After coming to this new country, as he did at an early day, he steadily advanced, meeting formidable obstacles and discouragements with great fortitude, and not only acquired great possessions, but gained for himself the respect and confidence of those who knew him.

The subject of our sketch was married, in 1841, to Miss Maria Stevenson. She was the daughter of John and Elizabeth (Cole) Stevenson, was born in Indiana, and by her union with our subject became the mother of seven children, whom we record as follows: William, a broom-maker by trade, is carrying on business at Ottumwa; Elizabeth is the wife of William Wilson, a farmer of Center Township; Mary married Daniel Dana, who is farming in Richland Township; Samuel is also an agriculturist of Richland Township, and Hannah, a resident of the same, is the wife of Heber Parker, also engaged in farming pursuits; Louisa married Albert Fairchild, of Richland Township, and Lincoln is at home.

Mr. Hardestey removed to Indiana from his native State in 1832, and was among the early settlers of that region. He there engaged as a farm laborer, and his first trip across the Father of Waters landed him at Flint Hills, now the city of Burlington, which was included in the Black Hawk purchase. Thence he went to Ft. Madison, where he engaged at carpenter work, and where he lived for the following nine years.

The wife of our subject departed this life in January, 1868, at the age of forty-six years. She was a lady highly esteemed for her many excellent qualities of character, and was the true helpmeet of her husband's amid his early toils and struggles to maintain his family as became a worthy and honorable citizen. Since coming to this locality Mr.

Hardestey has been prominently connected with its business and industrial affairs and has held the various township offices. Aside from his business of general farming, he has given considerable attention to stock-raising, and in all his undertakings has met with that success which is the just reward of enterprise and perseverance. His entire career presents a forcible illustration of what courage and resolution may accomplish under difficulties. In politics our subject is a true Democrat. A lithographic portrait of Mr. Hardestey appears on another page of this work.

SAMUEL CLINTON McCULLOUGH, M. D., a prominent and successful physician and surgeon of Ottumwa, and whose portrait is given in connection with this sketch, is a native of Morgan Station, Montgomery Co., Ky., and was born on the 9th of June, 1816. He is the son of John and Sarah (Morgan) McCullough. His father was a native of Bourbon County, Ky., and his mother was a daughter of Ralph Morgan, of Shepherdstown, Va., who built Morgan's Station, in Montgomery County, Ky., being the fifth station which was built in the State. It was first captured by Simon Girty, with a force of whites and Indians, and was subsequently captured twice by the Indians, most of the men being killed; the women and children were killed while en route to Miamitown, in Ohio. Mr. Morgan died at the old fort. He was a Colonel in the Revolutionary War, and a son of Sir William Morgan, of Shepherdstown, Va.

The paternal grandfather of our subject was born in Washington County, Pa., and while an infant his parents removed to North Carolina, where they both died while he was a small boy. He was then apprenticed to learn the tanner's trade. When about sixteen years old he enlisted in the Regular Army, and served under Gen. Washington for five years and six months, and participated in the battle of River Reason, where he was pierced through the body with a bayonet. He recovered sufficiently, however, to be present at the storming of Stony Point, where he received a similar wound through the hip, but also recovered from this, and lived to receive his honorable discharge with his comrades. After the war he went to the city of Charleston, S. C. The charms of the soldier's life, however, still had their influence over him, and after arriving at the latter city he once more enlisted to engage in the last siege of the city of Charleston, where he met with an accident which caused the loss of one of his thumbs, and he then accepted his final discharge and went to Kentucky. In the meantime he had been married, and after rearing a large family, living a part of the time in Bourbon and latterly in Montgomery County, he removed with a portion of his family to Indiana, locating in Ripley County, where he spent the remainder of his life.

John and Sarah McCullough, the parents of our subject, reared a family of fourteen children, eight of whom are still living as follows: Van R. is a resident of Walla Walla Valley, Ore.; James A. and Hugh B. are in Lyon County, Kan.; John M. lives in Coffee County, the same State; Ralph M. resides in Decatur County, Ind., and the sixth is Samuel Clinton, our subject. Four of these sons served as Union soldiers in the late war, and escaped unharmed, serving the full time from the commencement to the end. Rawley, now deceased, enlisted during the first year of the war, and through exposure and privation contracted a disease of which he subsequently died; Keziah is living at McCoy Station, near Greensburg, Decatur Co., Ind.; Drusilla lives in Coffee County, Kan. The parents of Mr. McCullough, after a long residence in Indiana, removed to Coffee County, Kan., where they both died. John McCullough, the father, was a soldier in the War of 1812, being one of the first to enlist, and was under the command of Gen. Harrison, serving until the close.

The subject of our sketch removed from his birthplace with his parents to Jefferson County, Ind., when he was a child of six years old. He was early trained to habits of industry, and began to assist in the labors around the homestead as soon as he could be of any use. The tract of land upon which his parents had settled consisted of 200 acres of heavy timber, mostly black walnut, and the labor of clearing this land and bringing it to a condition for successful agriculture can more easily be imagined than described. In this labor Samuel C. assisted in the summer seasons, and during the winter walked two and one-half miles through the timber to pursue his studies in the log cabin which was dignified by the name of a school-house. The term of his educational advantages was limited to three months in the year, but, notwithstanding the difficulties under which he labored, he succeeded in acquiring a fund of useful knowledge, being fond of study and ambitious to excel. When only ten years of age he had already selected his calling in life, and began the study of medicine. Four years later he went to Cross Plains, Ind., and entered the office of Dr. James McCullough, his uncle, under whose instruction he remained for the following three years. Then, although only seventeen years old, he began the practice of his profession, and was remarkably successful. Eight years later he went to St. Louis, Mo., and became the pupil of Prof. Joseph N. McDowell, with whom he remained for five years, and became proficient in medicine and surgery, receiving his certificate from the Medical Department of the State University of Missouri, the document being signed by Dr. McDowell, Drs. Charles W. Stevens, Robert Leffingwell, J. B. Johnson, John S. Moore, Thomas Barbour and Richard Barrett, who composed the faculty of that institution.

Dr. McCullough now returned to Madison, Ind., and by special invitation went to Delaware, Ripley Co., Ind., where he engaged in practice for the following thirteen years. During this time this locality was visited by the cholera scourge of 1849, lasting five years, and our subject passed through the midst of it unharmed, and was remarkably successful in his treatment of those who suffered from the awful epidemic. Dr. McC. continued there until 1856, and then, crossing the Mississippi, came into Iowa, locating in Fayette County, in the town of West Union, where he spent the winter and spring of 1856-57, and then came into Wapello County, locating in Kirkville. He here followed the practice of his profession up to 1864, when he came to Ottumwa, and has since that time been successfully engaged in practice in this locality.

Dr. McCullough has made two fortunes since the commencement of his practice. Several years ago he had a large amount of property destroyed by fire, and after he had recovered from this disaster and was on his feet again on the high road to prosperity, he again suffered great loss by other means. He has occupied a prominent position among his professional brethren since coming here, and was one of the organizers of the Wapello County Medical Society, at Ottumwa, and also the Des Moines Valley Medical Association. He is a close student, and keeps himself well posted upon the new discoveries of the day, reducing them to practice as his judgment directs.

In early manhood Samuel Clinton McCullough was united in marriage in Delaware, Ripley Co., Ind., to Miss Harriet L. Huggins, a native of Ripley County, Ind. Of this union there were born six children, two of whom are still living: Sarah S., the wife of Greene A. Denham, of Williamsburg, Ky., and Mary A., who is unmarried. Mrs. Harriet L. McCullough departed this life at Kirkville, Iowa, in 1858. The Doctor was married the second time on the 1st of January, 1860, to Miss Annie W. Wilson, of Callensburg, Clarion Co., Pa., who became the mother of seven children, as follows: Theodore W. is local editor of the Rapid City *Journal*, in Dakota; John M. is a wood-worker by trade, and a resident of Ottumwa; Frederick A. is connected with the car-works of the Ft. Scott & Gulf Railroad at Kansas City, Mo.; Allen is a printer by trade; Emma K., a graduate of the High School of Ottumwa, is engaged in teaching; Herman A., also of this city, is a clerk in the grocery of Henry Throne; the youngest is Ralph M., at home.

In politics Dr. McCullough is exceedingly liberal in his views and largely independent, aiming to vote for the best men irrespective of party. He affiliated with the Whigs until the abandonment of the old party.

S. A. W. CARVER, of the prominent law firm of Chambers, McElroy & Carver, with headquarters at Ottumwa, Iowa, is fully worthy of his association with his eminent partners, who form one of the strongest combinations for the transaction of legal business in this county. Mr. Carver is a native of Wapello County, and was born on the 6th of March, 1859. He is the son of John H. and Margaret J. (Bartow) Carver, the former born in Ohio and reared in Pennsylvania, and of whom, in connection with his excellent lady, a sketch appears in another part of this volume.

The parents of our subject came to this county in 1849, three years after Iowa was admitted into the Union as a State. Here our subject received his early education in the district schools and assisted in the lighter duties about his father's farm. Later, he entered the High School at Kirkville, and afterward attended Iowa Wesleyan University at Mt. Pleasant, Iowa, where he graduated in the class of '83. Thence he came immediately to Ottumwa and entered the office of Chambers & McElroy as a student of law. In due time he was admitted to the bar and, according to previous arrangement, was taken as a partner into the firm, since which time he has been successfully engaged in the practice of his profession. He is a gentleman of fine abilities, a close student, and ambitious to excel in his profession.

The marriage of Mr. Carver with Miss Stella F. Winans took place in June, 1884. Mrs. C. was born in Bentonsport, Iowa, in 1861, and is the daughter of E. H. Winans, a minister of the Methodist Episcopal Church. Of this union there has been born one child, a son Chesney W. Mrs. C. was a student at Iowa Wesleyan University, Mt. Pleasant, at the same time as her husband, and there the acquaintance was made which resulted in their marriage. Mrs. C. graduated in the class of '82, having received a musical education, and is at present teaching this art. She also occupied the position of a teacher in Hedding College at Abingdon, Ill., for two years.

CAPT. W. H. C. JAQUES, of the firm of Williams & Jaques, of Ottumwa, is, with his partner, successfully engaged in the practice of law. The firm is a strong one, each member being well read in his profession, and they occupy a prominent position in the legal fraternity of Wapello County. The subject of this biography is a native of Abingdon, Va., and was born on the 29th day of October, 1841. When a child of eight years old he came to Iowa with his parents, William and Mary Jaques. They located in Jefferson County upon a farm, and engaged in agricultural pursuits. William Jaques was also a bricklayer by trade, and alternated his duties of the farm with working at his trade as opportunity permitted.

Our subject, in the meantime, became a farmer and learned the trade of his father. He attended the district school three months out of the year up to 1862, until the outbreak of the Rebellion necessitated a call for troops for the preservation of the Union. Our subject, then a young man of twenty years, determined to proffer his services to his country, and accordingly enlisted as a private in Co. D, 19th Iowa Vol. Inf., serving with his comrades through the campaign in Southeast Missouri and Northwest Arkansas, in the fall of 1862, and in 1863 in the campaign around Jackson and at the siege of Vicksburg, then, on account of illness while at New Orleans, to which place his regiment had gone, was sent home on sick furlough in the fall of 1863. He was disabled for a long period but finally recovered and started to return to his regiment, which was then at Brownsville, on the Rio Grande, but while on his way there he was commissioned Second Lieutenant of the 56th United States Cavalry, then at Helena, Ark., and joined his new regiment in February, 1864. He soon rose to the rank of First Lieutenant, and afterward served on the staff of Gens. McCook, Thayer Carr and Col. Bentzoni while they were in command of the Eastern district of Arkansas, as aid-de camp and Assistant Adjutant-General, until promoted Captain of Company B, of the same regiment. After serving awhile with his company, he was detailed as a member of the court martial at Little Rock, Ark., which was appointed to conduct the trial of Capt. Green Durbin, Assistant Quartermaster, a trial that lasted for over three months. While acting as one of the members of this court he first conceived the idea of studying law, realizing then of what importance and benefit the knowledge of this might become to him. After a little over four years' service in the army, the war having now practically closed, he was mustered out with his regiment in September, 1866, receiving the marked approval of his superior officers.

Immediately upon returning home Capt. Jaques entered the law department of Harvard College, intending to take a full course, depending for his expenses upon the money which he had loaned a wealthy planter near Helena, Ark., to take him through. By the partial failure of the cotton crop of 1866, this man became a bankrupt, and every dollar that Capt. Jaques possessed was irretrievably lost, and he was compelled to leave college the following spring. He then came directly to Ottumwa, and entered the office of Judge Williams, one of the leading jurists of Southern Iowa, as a law student. Here he pursued his studies with desperate diligence, and was admitted to the bar that same year. In 1868 he began the practice of his profession at Ottumwa, which he has followed continuously in this city since that time. He is now admitted by all to be one of the leading attorneys of Wapello County. He has taken an intelligent interest in general and political matters, although the only office he has ever been a candidate for was that of Circuit Judge, in 1884. Then, in a total vote of over 25,000 he was beaten by 140 votes.

As an attorney Capt. Jaques is careful and painstaking in the preparation of a case for trial or for argument. He seems to work upon the supposition that his side is the weaker one, and carefully views at every point the possibility of defeat. The result of this care is that he is seldom defeated. As an advocate he is forcible, agreeable and persuasive, and possesses considerable natural talent as an orator. His extensive reading and a practice of eighteen years in connection with one of the ablest attorneys of this section, has proved a rich and invaluable experience. He is still in the prime of life, and there is no doubt that there are greater successes awaiting him.

The marriage of Capt. Jaques with Miss Flora Williams was celebrated on the 29th of August, 1869. Mrs. J. is a sister of Judge Williams, and of this union there have been born four children—Stella W., J. Ralph, Edna and Mabel. They occupy a handsome residence in Ottumwa, and their hospitable home is the resort of the culture and refinement of the city.

MAJ. A. H. HAMILTON, proprietor of the Ottumwa *Courier*, was born Jan. 19, 1827, within the present limits of Cleveland, Ohio. He is a son of Justus and Salinda (Brainard) Hamilton, his father being a native of Massachusetts and his mother of Connecticut. The parents moved to Ohio at an early day, and locating near Cleveland became acquainted with each other and were there married, becoming the parents of four children: Augustus H., the eldest, is the subject of this notice; Delia is living on the old homestead in Cleveland, Ohio; Edwin T. is present Judge of the Court of Common Pleas at Cleveland, Ohio; Albert J. is engaged in the manufacturing business at Cleveland. The mother of these children was a member of the Presbyterian Church, and the father of the Unitarian. The mother died in 1859, and the father in 1864.

The subject of this biographical notice received the advantages afforded by the common schools, and supplemented his education by a literary course at Allegheny College, Pa. He was practically through his course in that institution when his uncle, who had been elected Sheriff, requested his return home that he might enter his office as Deputy. While living at Cleveland he read law with Williamson & Riddle, and was there admitted to the bar. Believing the West afforded a broader field of operation, and hoping to better his financial condition, he, in June, 1854, came to this State, and after visiting various portions, in August of that year located at Ottumwa. On his arrival here he opened an office, and at once engaged in the practice of his profession, and was thus occupied until August, 1862, being associated about eight years with Hon. Morris J. Williams.

The pressing need of the Government for men in the field, during 1862, induced our subject to give up a large practice, and he enlisted in the 36th Iowa Infantry, receiving the appointment of Adjutant of the regiment. He served in the latter office for about one year, when he was commissioned Major of the regiment. In 1865 our subject was commissioned Lieutenant Colonel, but was never mustered in, on account of there being a lack of men to justify it. Maj. Hamilton participated in nearly all the engagements of his regiment, and was captured at Mark's Mills, Ark., April 25, 1864. He was imprisoned at Camp Ford, near Tyler, Tex., and retained there until July 23 of the same year, when, in company with Capt. Allen W. Miller, of Company C, and Capt. John Lambert, of Company K, his regiment, he escaped. They traveled a distance of 700 miles on foot, without arms, and poorly clad, and arrived at Pine Bluffs, Ark., on the 24th of August. During the journey the trio suffered terrible privations, subsisting at one time for eighteen days on raw green corn. They were compelled to resort to all possible means to avoid detection. During the many weary days of their journey these three brave men slept in the shade of the forest, or under such shelter as they could find, but not a single day was passed indoors. They traveled nearly always by night, and their experience sounds like the ante-war stories of escaping slaves, rather than white men, in this boasted land of freedom. For weeks at a time their ragged and dirty clothes were wet through, and their escape was indeed a marvelous one, considering the dangers to which they were subjected. The Major's brave comrades died from the effect of their exposure. Capt. Miller reached his home in Iowa, but died in September, 1864, from slow fever, which produced insanity. Capt. Lambert returned to his regiment, but was not fitted for duty, and died Jan. 6, 1865. Maj. Hamilton rejoined his regiment after a period of rest, and subsequently was much of the time in command. He was mustered out Aug. 24, 1865, and the regiment was disbanded September 7 of that year, at Davenport.

In 1869 Maj. Hamilton became associated with Gen. Hedrick in the publication of the *Courier*, and Jan. 1, 1878, became sole proprietor. In the publication of this paper he has since continued. He has been favored by his fellow-citizens with a number of local offices. He was elected second Mayor of Ottumwa, and served several years as a member of the Common Council. In 1866 he was elected a member of the State Senate to fill a vacancy, and was re-elected in 1868 to a full term. In 1870 he was appointed Postmaster at Ottumwa, and continued to hold that office until July, 1885. Mr. Hamilton has been prominently identified with the public interests of Ottumwa. In the construction of the St. L. & C. R. Ry., now the Wabash, he was appointed agent by the company to secure subscriptions, and succeeded in raising $50,000 in Wapello County. In the building of the Cedar Rapids, Sigourney & Ottumwa, now the C., N. & St. P. R. R., he was very active, and for a time was one of its Directors. In educational matters our subject has always taken a great interest, and was for many years a member of the School Board at Ottumwa. In fact there has been no public enterprise that he has not aided by voice, pen or money.

Aug. 19, 1856, Maj. Hamilton was united in marriage with Elma C. Coffin, a native of Springfield, Ohio. Six children were born of this union, three yet living—Mary E., Justus A. and Emma S. The deceased are, Edwin M., who died in infancy; Henry A. died in the third year of his age, and Charles H., who was drowned at the age of nine years, June 16, 1875.

WILLIAM B. ARMSTRONG, of Ottumwa, occupies the position of local freight and passenger agent on the C., B. & Q. R. R., and is fulfilling the duties of the office in a satisfactory manner. He is a native of Pike County, Pa., where he was born Aug. 10, 1830. His parents were William and Mary (Pellett) Armstrong, his father in early life being a farmer by occupation and afterward extensively engaged in milling. When our subject was a small child his parents removed to Sussex County, N. J., and there William B. was reared and received a fair education in the common schools. His grandfather held a Major's commission in the Revolutionary War, and enjoyed the acquaintance and confidence of Gen. Washington. He was a man of great force of character and fine abilities, and represented his district in the State

Legislature. He was afterward proffered a judgeship, which he declined to accept. He was a remarkable man in many respects, and in all his dealings with his fellow-men strictly adhered to the principles of honor and honesty.

The parents of our subject had a family of eight children, three only of whom are living: Obadiah P., of New Jersey; William B., our subject, and John B., a farmer of Sussex County, N. J. They were Scotch Presbyterians in religious belief, and their children were carefully trained to principles of high morality and integrity.

William B. Armstrong of our sketch received a liberal education, and in 1851, determining to see something of the western country, started out and, crossing the Father of Waters, located first in the city of St. Louis, Mo., where he was employed as clerk in a commission house. The following year he went to Athens, where he continued his occupation as clerk, and there, for the first time, became engaged in railroading, being the first local agent appointed for the Keokuk, Ft. Des Moines & Minnesota Railroad. He was thus employed for a period of eleven years, and in 1861 came to Ottumwa, acting in the same capacity for the Des Moines Valley Railroad, with which he remained until 1872, when he resigned to accept the position of General Agent of the B. & M. R. R. In January, 1872, this road was consolidated with the C., B. & Q. Mr. Armstrong is a practical railroad man, and has now had an experience of twenty-five years in this line. From a small beginning the business has extended until now there are seven miles of switch track near their depots in Ottumwa, and the company itself will not deny that its success in a large measure is due to the intelligence and fidelity of its employes, of whom the subject of our sketch ranks among the first and most faithful.

In the spring of 1862, Mr. Armstrong, in company with his brother, Capt. B. C. P. Armstrong, who died in the army near the close of the war, recruited, and B. C. P. Armstrong enlisted in Co. M, 9th Iowa Vol. Cav., of which the latter was First Lieutenant, and subsequently received the commission of Captain. Mr. Armstrong remained at home, believing it to be a duty to look after the families of those who were absent, and was consequently not engaged in active service on the field of battle.

The subject of our sketch was united in marriage with Miss Virginia Thorne, at Athens, Mo., in 1858. Mrs. Armstrong is a native of Kentucky, and the daughter of Arthur and Eliza Thorne, of Athens, Mo. Of this union there were born four children, three of whom are living, as follows: William is ticket agent of the C., B. & Q., at Ottumwa; Mary is the wife of John C. Fetzer, of Omaha, Neb.; Anna T. is at home with her parents.

Mr. Armstrong is a member of the Masonic fraternity, Blue Lodge Chapter and Commandery, being a charter member, and was the first Treasurer of the commandery. In politics he is a stanch Republican, and has held various local offices. He has been a member of the City Council of Ottumwa several terms, and was Treasurer of the city several years, and School Director six years. Since first locating here he has been identified with the business interests of the city, giving his active support toward the cause of education and morality, and has been the encourager of every worthy enterprise having for its object the welfare of his adopted city.

JOSEPH L. HARMAN, of the firm of Harman & Tisdale, in company with his partner is conducting the insurance business successfully in the city of Ottumwa and vicinity, their operations extending throughout the State. Mr. Harman is a native of Highland County, Ohio, and was born on the 21st of July, 1840. He is the son of David M. and Hester (Lawrence) Harman, the father a native of Virginia and the mother of English ancestry and parentage. Their son, our subject, was reared in his native county, and received his education in the district schools. He remained under the parental roof until he had attained to years of manhood, and then, the late Civil War being in progress, he enlisted, in 1862, in Co. I, 4th Ind. Vol. Cav., which was detailed to do duty in Kentucky and Tennessee. He remained in the service for two years following, and then on account of failing health received his discharge and returned to his home in Ohio.

After he had recovered his health young Harman again enlisted in the service of the Union, becoming a member of Co. B, 175th Ohio Vol. Inf. This regiment he had assisted in raising, and received the commission of First Lieutenant of his company. They were ordered to Columbia, Tenn., to guard the Nashville Railroad, and were then ordered to Franklin, in the battle of which the regiment joined, whence they marched to Nashville. Capt. Heistand being detailed for other service, the command devolved upon Lieut. Harman. They participated in the fight, and came out unharmed, and our subject remained with his regiment until the close of the war, soon afterward, being mustered out with his comrades at Nashville.

After the close of the war Lieut. Harman, in the fall of 1865, came to Ottumwa, where he has since resided. In 1876 he established his present business. He represents the principal companies of the United States, the Hartford and Phœnix, of Connecticut; the North American, of Pennsylvania; the Fire Association, the Pennsylvania, and the American of Philadelphia, and the Home, Continental, Niagara, and Glen Falls, of New York; the Fireman's Fund, the Union, of California; the St. Paul, of St. Paul, and the Royal, City of London, and Lancashire, of Liverpool; and the Norwich, the Williamsburg City, the Western, and the Fire Association. Mr. Harman is considered an enterprising business man, and is peculiarly adapted to his present undertaking. He is highly esteemed among the business men of this community, and socially belongs to Capt. Cloutman Post No. 69.

Lieut. Harman was married, in 1867, to Miss Maggie Zollers, of Ottumwa, and of their union there have been born two children—Lillie and Frank. They occupy a handsome home in the city, and are surrounded by all the evidences of refinement and cultivated tastes.

SAMUEL H. BURTON, City Engineer of Ottumwa, and Surveyor of Wapello County, is a native of Waterloo, Seneca Co., N. Y., where he was born on the 29th day of January, 1841. He is the son of John and Elizabeth (Hooper) Burton, the former a native of Manchester, England, and the latter of Saratoga, N. Y., and a grand-daughter of Gen. Clark of Revolutionary fame. The parents of John Burton emigrated to America when he was a mere boy. He received careful parental training, a fine education, and became an attorney at law. He was a skillful practitioner and prominent in the public affairs of his adopted country.

The subject of our sketch was reared in the county of his birth, obtained his primary education in the district schools, and subsequently entered Waterloo Academy, from which he graduated in 1859. He entered upon the study of law in the office of Judge E. L. Burton, came to Ottumwa on the 1st of January, 1862, and was admitted to the bar the following year. Soon afterward the publisher of the Ottumwa *Democrat*, Capt. Evans, enlisted in the army, and Judge Burton, the proprietor of the paper, solicited our subject to fill the editorial position vacated by Capt. Evans. In the fall of the same year he was elected County Surveyor, serving two years, and also remained editor of the *Democrat* until 1869. In 1875 he was appointed to fill a vacancy as County Surveyor, which position he has since held.

Mr. Burton is a practical civil engineer, and is well posted in regard to the duties of his position. He was married in Wapello County, in 1863, to Miss Julia, the daughter of Lyman Day, of Waterloo, N. Y. Of this union there were born six children, three of whom are living—Mabel, Gracie and Mary. Mrs. Burton departed this life in 1875. She was a highly respected Christian lady, and prominently connected with the Episcopal Church, of which our subject was a member.

For his second wife Mr. Burton was united in marriage with Mrs. Rhoda (Garbery) Armstrong, who by her marriage with James Armstrong, now deceased, became the mother of one child, a daughter, Edna. Of her marriage with our subject there has been born one child, a son, Frank. They occupy a pleasant residence in the northern part of the city, and enjoy the friendship of a large circle of acquaintances.

Mr. Burton has been identified with the interests of Wapello County for a period of twenty-four years. During that time he has witnessed with

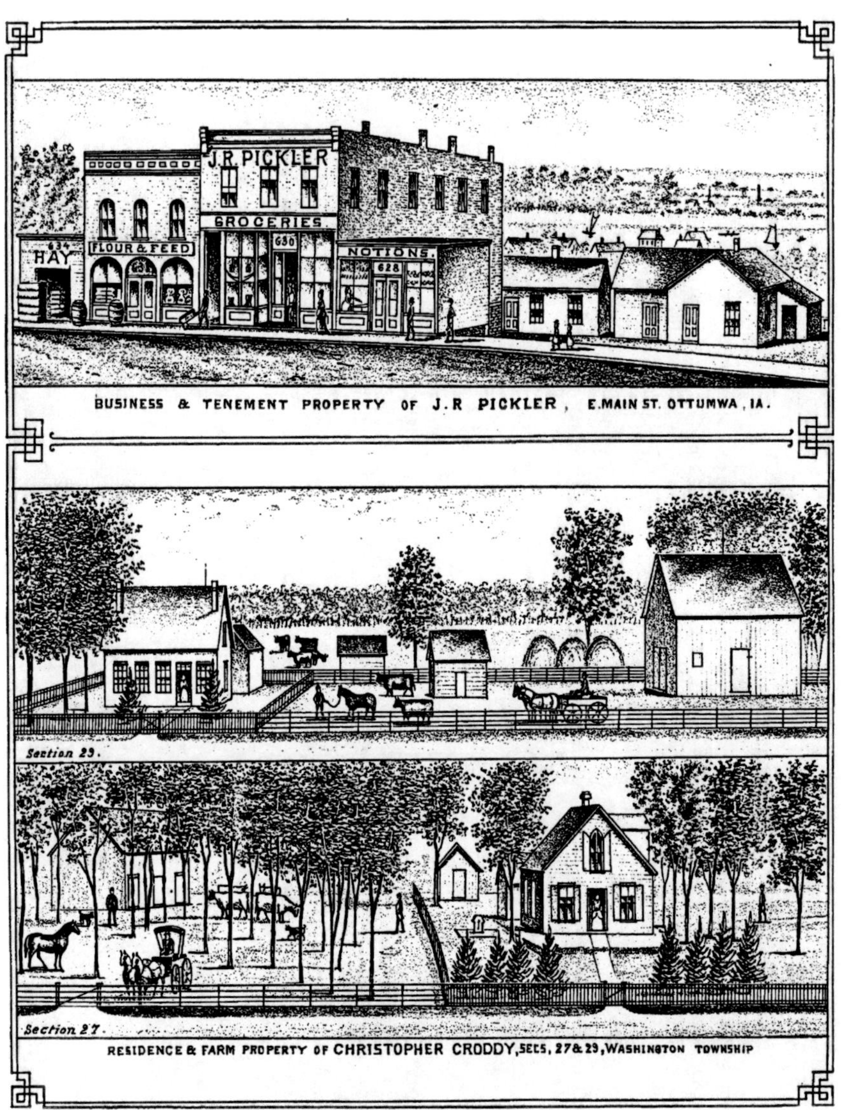

BUSINESS & TENEMENT PROPERTY OF J.R PICKLER, E. MAIN ST. OTTUMWA, IA.

RESIDENCE & FARM PROPERTY OF CHRISTOPHER CRODDY, SECS. 27 & 29, WASHINGTON TOWNSHIP

pleasure the march of progress and the many changes of this locality, and he, in common with all other good citizens, feels a just pride and satisfaction in the prosperity of the Hawkeye State. He is Conservative in politics, decided in his views, and possesses an intelligent and well-informed mind.

C. CRODDY, a farmer and stock-raiser on section 27, Washington Township, was born in Rockbridge County, Va., Aug. 31, 1828, and is a son of John and Mary (Shafer) Croddy, both of whom are of English ancestry. His mother died in Virginia, April 18, 1833. In 1843 his father moved from Virginia to Indiana, where he remained until his death, which occurred Aug. 29, 1846. He was a boat-builder by trade.

The subject of this sketch was reared upon the farm and educated in the common schools of his native State. In 1849 he married Miss M. J. Goodwin, a native of Indiana, born March 25, 1833, and the daughter of B. D. and Lillie (Hildreth) Goodwin. Eight children were born to this union: John J., deceased; Benjamin F., deceased; Algera A., deceased; Alice J., now the wife of James T. Mael, and living at Eldon; J. J., C. T., C. L., and one who died in infancy.

In 1855 Mr. Croddy came with his wife and three children into Wapello County, where he has since continued to reside. He owns 198 acres of well-improved land. He has held several of the different township offices, is a member of the Masonic fraternity, and in politics is a Democrat. A handsome lithographic view of Mr. Croddy's country and city property is shown on another page of this work.

HEMAN P. GRAVES was among the pioneers of Ottumwa, Iowa, and was born in Ashfield, Franklin Co., Mass., on the 1st day of May, 1810. His ancestors were of the old Puritan stock who first settled at Cape Cod, and afterward scattered over the State and throughout the country. The father of our subject, Dorus Graves, married Thankful Parker, and they settled at Ashfield, Mass. There ten children were born to them and five of the number are yet living: Naomi is the wife of Darius Beardsley, who was born in Ithaca, N. Y.; Dorus, Jr., is living at Ottumwa, Wapello County; Heman P. is the subject of this notice; Orra is a resident of Van Buren County, and the widow of Sylvester Henry; Charles is a resident of Ashfield, Mass. The father and mother always lived at Ashfield. They were both church members and highly respected by all who knew them. He was a woolen manufacturer by occupation.

The subject of this notice was brought up to the trade of his father, and in 1831, when twenty-one years of age, left his native State and went to Jersey Shore, Lycoming Co., Pa., where he embarked in the mercantile business as traveling merchant. He came to this State in the fall of 1836, when the same was yet a Territory, and located at Benton's Port, Van Buren County. There, in the heavy timber, he took up a tract of Government land, and locating upon it vigorously entered upon the task of its improvement and cultivation. He was married in 1838, to Miss Harriet Reid, a native of Palmyra, Mo., who was born in 1820. In the fall of 1844 our subject moved his family to and located in Ottumwa, and took charge of the first store at that place, owned by Richard & Coles. He remained with that firm for some three years, at the expiration of which time the business was purchased by Mr. Richards, and our subject remained with him for twelve years, since which time he has been interested in looking after his own affairs.

Mr. and Mrs. Graves are the parents of four children, two of whom are yet living: Maria, wife of James S. Harlan, a resident of Corydon, Wayne Co., Iowa, and Julia, wife of David Spear, of Princeton, Mo. Mrs. Graves departed this life in 1847. She was a member of the Methodist Episcopal Church, and a sincere Christian. For his second wife our subject married Miss Lydia A. Goddard, the union occurring in 1852. She was born in Urbana, Ohio, in 1825. Of this latter union there are three living children—Flora, May Belle and William F.

In politics Mr. Graves is and has been a Republican ever since the organization of that party. For six years he held the office of Justice of the Peace, and has also been the incumbent of other offices of minor import. When he first came to Ottumwa there were only seven small log cabins here and one little frame residence. He has lived to see the small hamlet develop into a city of 12,000 inhabitants, and in addition thereto he has witnessed the broad uncultivated acres brought to a high state of cultivation, and made to bloom and blossom as the rose. What a change! When he came to this State there were plenty of Indians, but their faces are to be seen no more, and old Black Hawk, with whom our subject was intimately acquainted, has long since passed to the happy hunting-ground. There are but few living in the State who have been residents of the same longer than our subject, and it is by such biographical history as this that their names will be perpetuated. Mr. and Mrs. Graves are both members of the Methodist Episcopal Church, to which denomination our subject has belonged for many years.

MRS. K. G. CONWELL, the widow of John Conwell, of Cass Township, owns and occupies an attractive homestead on section 3. John Conwell was a farmer and stock-grower, and one of the most highly respected men of this community. He was born in Ohio about the year 1810, and was the son of William and Mary (Sampson) Conwell, both natives of Kentucky. On the 29th of February, 1833, he was united in marriage with Miss Kitty G. Griffin, their wedding taking place in Tuscarawas County, Ohio. Mrs. Conwell was born in Charles County, Md., on the 23d of January, 1812, and was the daughter of Samuel and Elizabeth (Robey) Griffin, also natives of Maryland. They removed to Ohio soon after the birth of their daughter, where they passed the remainder of their lives.

Mrs. Conwell was the fourth child of a family of six, and after her marriage lived with her husband upon a farm in Ohio until about the year 1852. Mr. C. then sold his property, and coming to Iowa purchased 280 acres of wild land in Wapello County, and commenced the improvement of the farm which constitutes the present homestead. He was prospered in his business and farming transactions, and at his death had accumulated sufficient property to furnish a comfortable support for his family.

The death of John Conwell occurred on the 17th of November, 1872, at his home in Cass Township. He was a useful member of the community, and the encourager and supporter of every measure calculated to increase its prosperity. He took an active and intelligent interest in public matters, was the friend of education, and especially interested in the Methodist Episcopal Church of this township, to whose support he contributed cheerfully and liberally. He held the various offices within the gift of his fellow-townsmen, and was honored and esteemed by all on account of his straightforward business methods and his kindly Christian character.

Of the union of Mr. and Mrs. Conwell there were born twelve children, six of whom are living: William, Elizabeth and Samuel are deceased; Mary became the wife of Nelson Johnson, who is a farmer by occupation; Lot is conducting a farm in Cass Township; John W., in Monroe County, Iowa; Albert in Cass Township; Martha and Ruth died in infancy; Thomas is at home; Sarah J. married William Warren, of Eldon, this county; the youngest child died unnamed.

Mrs. Conwell reached the seventy-fifth year of her age on the 23d of January, 1887. She is a well preserved, bright and intelligent lady, a kind friend and neighbor, and a devoted member of the Methodist Episcopal Church.

JOHN KIRKPATRICK, a farmer and stock-grower, living in the village of Kirkville, this county, was born in Guernsey County, Ohio, Aug. 25, 1808, and is the son of Thomas B. and Mary (Henthorn) Kirkpatrick, the former a native of Ireland and the latter of Pennsylvania. The father was by occupation a farmer, and a man of more than ordinary ability, and was for seven years one of the Associate Justices of Guernsey County, Ohio. He was born May 1, 1775, and died in Ohio, Aug. 14, 1851. The mother of John was born Feb. 24, 1783, and died in Kirkville, Iowa, Aug. 16, 1872.

The subject of this sketch was reared on a farm in his native State, and in 1830 was united in marriage with Mary A. Kygar, who was born Feb. 5, 1812, and is a daughter of Daniel and Ann (Henthorn) Kygar, the former of whom died April 27, 1849, and the latter June 9, 1859. To our subject and wife were born the following children: Mary A., deceased; Hannah J.; Eliza, deceased; Henry married Agnes Lamme, and lives in Richland Township; Daniel was killed in the United States service at Mark's Mills, Ark.; Thomas married Martha Hirst; J. M. married Lizzie Zeitz.

In 1833 Mr. Kirkpatrick moved from Ohio to Illinois, and lived there until 1844, when he moved to Wapello County, Iowa. He made the trip from Ohio to Illinois on a keelboat, which he poled up the Wabash River. When he came to Iowa he made the trip with three yoke of oxen. On coming to this county, he located on the site of the present village of Kirkville, which he had surveyed and platted in 1848. On the 28th day of April, 1850, he started across the plains with an ox-team for California, in company with Daniel Kygar and David Bates, the latter dying of cholera while en route. Mr. Kirkpatrick landed in California Aug. 28, 1850. For five months of the time spent in California, he was too sick for work, and the remainder of the time he spent in prospecting. In 1851 he returned home by way of the Isthmus of Panama, New Orleans and the Mississippi River, landing at home March 17 of that year. In 1863 he drove 200 head of cows to Pike's Peak, his cattle swimming the Missouri River at Plattsmouth, and all other streams on the route. He arrived at home from this journey on the the 25th day of December, 1863. Previous to the time he went to California, he spent some five years in trading upon the lower Mississippi and upon the coast near New Orleans.

The life of Mr. Kirkpatrick has been an active one. Coming to this county in 1844, he has been a witness of all the improvements that have been made, and few men have been more actively engaged and are better known than John Kirkpatrick. No man in Wapello County enjoys the respect and esteem of his fellow-citizens more than he. Financially he has been quite successful, and in his old age can enjoy life without any of its worry. He is a Master Mason, a member of the Methodist Episcopal Church, and politically is a Republican.

FREDERICK HARNESS, a retired farmer living in the city of Ottumwa, was born in Fayette County, Ohio, Dec. 25, 1813, and is a son of John and Helen (Trotwine) Harness, both natives of Virginia and early settlers of Fayette County. Our subject was reared upon a farm, receiving but limited advantages in the way of securing an education, and when about twelve years of age, left Fayette and went into Greene County, where he worked on a farm for a Mr. Gideon Spohr till he was sixteen years of age, when he went to La Fayette, Ind., where he remained until he was twenty-one. He then, in the following year, was engaged for himself in farming, having had a farm left to him by his grandfather. This, however, he soon sold, and returned to Greene County, Ohio, where he rented land for four or five years, when we find him making another move. This time he went into Darke County, Ind., where he resided for eight years. Here he bought a farm of eighty acres, which he sold at the expiration of the time mentioned, and moved on a farm in Randolph County, the same State, which he had also become the owner of. Two years was the allotted time, seemingly, for his sojourn here, as at the end of that time we find him on his journey westward. He arrived in Wapello County May 10, 1850, since which time, however, he has abandoned the roving spirit so characteristic of him in his early life, for this has been his permanent home since. For a year after his arrival he rented a farm in Center Township, when he went into Green, where he bought 200 acres of land, most of which was raw prairie. This he improved and brought to a high state of cultivation, and lived upon it until 1881, when he retired from the active labors of life and moved into the city of Ottumwa, where he could better enjoy the accumulations of his earliest efforts.

Our subject was united in marriage, July 26, 1835, with Miss Rosanna McDill, a native of Pennsylvania, and a daughter of John and Mary (Halladay) McDill, also natives of the Keystone State. To them six children were born, namely: Elmira, who died at the age of one year; Mary Ann was the wife of George L. Moyer, of Missouri, and died in 1874 at the age of twenty-eight years; John Henry was born July 16, 1839, and became a member of the 7th Iowa Infantry, enlisting in 1862, and gave his life in the defense of his country, having been killed at Corinth, Miss., after a service of two years. He was a valiant soldier and served in all the battles of his regiment till his death. He was wounded at Belmont and again at Donelson, and killed at Corinth, Oct. 20, 1862. Elizabeth Ellen is the wife of James Heckart, of Green Township, this county; Gideon died in 1862, aged seventeen years and six months. The mother of this family died April 27, 1880, aged seventy-one years, and our subject was united in marriage with Mrs. McLain, widow of John McLain, of Memphis, Mo., and formerly a Miss Kirkpatrick. Mr. H. has also reared a grandchild named Elmira Moyer.

Mr. H. is a member of the Christian Church, while his wife is connected with the Presbyterian. Politically he is a Republican, and has ever taken an active interest in public affairs. He began life a poor boy, his father having died when he was two years old, leaving him to the care of his mother, who died in 1862. He has accumulated a handsome property by his own efforts, and is regarded as an excellent and representative citizen of the county.

S P. CRIPS, of Ottumwa, the son of W. H. Crips, of Center Township, this county, is a native of the State of Pennsylvania. His early life was spent on the farm of his father, and he attended school in the winter season and in summer assisted in the duties around the homestead as soon as he became of suitable age. He remained under the parental roof until he was twenty-one years old, and after a year spent in Kansas, in the spring of 1879, came to Ottumwa and engaged on the Transfer Line, then owned by Michael Crips, with whom he remained until September, 1884.

Mr. Crips then went to Chariton, Iowa, and purchased a restaurant, which he operated until the 20th of March, 1886. The 1st of April he returned to Ottumwa, and purchased an interest in the livery and transfer line with which he is at present engaged, the name and style of the firm being W. S. Crips & Bro. They are carrying on business in a straightforward and systematic manner, and the firm is one of the useful factors in the business element of the city.

The subject of our sketch was united in marriage with Miss Anna V. Jeffries, who was born in Wapello County, on the 4th of August, 1867. Mrs. Crips is the daughter of B. W. and Mary (Allcock) Jeffries, the former a native of Kentucky. She is prominently connected with the Main Street Methodist Episcopal Church. Mr. Crips is Republican in politics, and socially is connected with the A. O. U. W.

REV. WILLIAM ANSELM NYE, one of the popular local preachers of Wapello County, while dispensing the Gospel of peace to numbers of his fellow-beings, has sought his recreation in the tilling of the soil, and is the owner of one of the most valuable farms in Cass Township, located on section 36. Here he has a beautiful residence, good barns and out-buildings, and all the appurtenances of a modern country seat. He has pursued his agricultural operations with more than ordinary intelligence and skill, and has reached the just reward of his labors in being the owner of one of the finest homesteads in this section of the State. In addition to his evident talents as a business man and a farmer, he is also a valuable member of society, has been zealous in his religious work, devoted to the cause of temperance, and socially is one of the most genial spirits of his age. His course as a minister has been popular, his warm sympathies and cheerful services gaining him a passport to the confidence and affection of a host of friends.

William Anselm Nye is the son of Ludwig and Mary (Habig) Nye. He was born in Bavaria, May 25, 1824. In the spring of 1830 he commenced attendance in the school of his native town, where he continued the following four years, and then his father sold his property at a great sacrifice in order (as he said) to emigrate with his children to a free country. They embarked in July, 1834, and after a voyage of thirty-seven days landed in New York City where, after a few days, they resumed their journey westward, and located in Waverly, Pike Co., Ohio. After a few days the father was seized with fatal illness, and died on the 8th of October, 1834. After this misfortune the family removed to a farm near Waverly, where our subject attended the country school and began to learn the English language. This school was conducted only three months in the year, and of these meager opportunities he availed himself until he was eighteen years of age, in the meantime assisting his mother's family in the duties of the farm.

On the 3d of October, 1844, Mr. Nye was united in marriage with Miss Rebecca Wicker, and five days later, he left Ohio with his bride to seek his fortune in the farther West. They stopped for a few months near Abingdon, in Knox County, Ill., and thence came to Wapello County, Iowa, arriving here on the 1st day of March, 1845. In due time Mr. Nye selected the tract of land which, under his cultivation and supervision, has now become the beautiful farm estate of which he is the proud possessor and still occupies. The township was not then organized, but when this was effected Mr. Nye was elected the first Justice of the Peace, by the unanimous vote of the people, and was retained in the office several terms. In 1879 he was elected County Treasurer, which position he held four years with credit to himself and satisfaction to all concerned.

Upon his first arrival here Mr. Nye at once became interested in the establishment of schools and everything tending to advance the cause of education. He has served as School Director for nearly twenty years, and has been the stanch friend of every measure calculated to advance the community in intelligence, morality and religion. In early life he was identified with the Whig party, and upon the abandonment of the old party cordially indorsed the principles of the Republicans, and has uniformly cast his vote with them since that time. He was active in the organization of the latter party, being one of the delegates to the State Convention at Iowa City at the time it assumed the dignity of a party.

Mr. Nye became a member of the Methodist Episcopal Church in April, 1842. In March, 1845, the first religious services in the township were held at his house, and in April following he secured the Rev. Cyrus Spurlock, who preached the first sermon ever delivered in the township. In June following a Sabbath-school was organized at his house, probably the first in the county, of which he was appointed Superintendent, and the good work which he began at that early day he has continued faithfully since. On the 19th of March, 1853, Mr. Nye was duly licensed as a Christian minister, and at the Methodist Episcopal Conference held in September, 1860, he was ordained Deacon by Bishop Scott, and in 1864 was ordained Elder by Bishop Jaynes. For six years he was a circuit supply, and at an early day gave his gratuitous services wherever called for to people who had no regular minister. He has probably attended more funerals and solemnized more marriages than any minister in the county.

The first wife of our subject, Mrs. Rebecca W. Nye, became the mother of five children, and departed this life at the homestead in Cass Township Aug. 18, 1855. He married for his second wife Mrs. Mary A. (Hoyt) Persons, and they became the parents of five children, one of whom is deceased.

JOSEPH W. WORKMAN, Sheriff of Wapello County, and a resident of Ottumwa, is a native of Coshocton County, Ohio. He was born on the 26th of May, 1840, and is the son of James and Hannah (Walker) Workman, natives of the same State as their son and among the earliest settlers of Coshocton County, to which they removed from Guernsey County. James Workman, after his removal from his native county, entered a claim in Coshocton, and after laborious toil, opened up a farm in the wilderness and established a comfortable home. The parental household included eight children, of whom six are living, as follows: Lavina became the wife of Richard Hunter, of Knox County, Ohio; Hiram B. is also a resident of that county; J. W. came West and located in Wapello County, Iowa; Rebecca married Adam Sapp, of Knox County, Ohio; Hattie became the wife of Frank Stringfellow, of Greene County, Ind., and George B. lives in Coshocton County, Ohio.

The father of our subject was a man of high moral principles and decided views; and was an enthusiastic Democrat. He departed this life in March, 1880, at his residence in Coshocton County. The companion of his early manhood and the mother of his children preceded him to the better land twenty-two years before, dying in 1858. They were both prominently connected with the Baptist Church, of which James Workman was a Deacon for many years. He was a man of more than ordinary intelligence, and well posted upon all matters of general interest.

Joseph W. Workman was reared in the county of his birth and received his early education in the pioneer log cabin, with puncheon floor and slabs for seats and desks. Into these light was admitted through a square place sawed out of the logs and covered with greased paper. He received careful parental training, being reared to habits of industry and economy, and remained under the parental roof until the breaking out of the late Civil War. He was drafted twice, first in 1862, and also the following year, procuring a substitute on both occasions.

The subject of our sketch was married in Ohio, in 1863, to Miss Lydia Draper, who died of consumption the following year. He was the second time married, in 1865, to Miss Phœbe Barnes, of Holmes County, Ohio. She was born on the 19th of December, 1843, and is the daughter of Permenus and Margaret Barnes. In 1868 they removed across the Mississippi into Wapello County, Iowa, and located in Green Township upon a farm, where Mr. W. engaged in agricultural pursuits, and by his upright and straightforward manner of doing business at once secured the esteem and confidence of his neighbors. He was intrusted with the various township offices and became prominent in the affairs of this locality. In 1883 he was nominated by the Democratic party to the office of Sheriff, and elected, taking his office the following year. He was re-elected in 1885, and continues to hold the office, the duties of which he has fulfilled with credit to himself and satisfaction to all concerned. He is the friend and encourager of education, and every enterprise which has for its object the progress and welfare of his county and community. He and his excellent lady are highly esteemed in this community, and their home is the resort of the cultured people of the city of Ottumwa. Mr. Workman belongs to the I. O. O. F., being a member of Ottumwa Lodge No. 9 and Patriarch Circle. He is also a member in good standing of the A. O. U. W.

ANDREW J. BRYANT, a rising attorney of the city of Ottumwa, is a native of Wapello County, and was born in Adams Township on the 30th of March, 1853. His parents were Benjamin and Rachel (Chilton) Bryant, the father a native of Kentucky, born in 1827, and the mother of Missouri, born on the 4th of July, 1829. They were married in Missouri, and removed to Henry County, Iowa, in 1846. They soon afterward came into Wapello County, and settled in Adams Township, being among the pioneers of this section. In 1868 they left Wapello County to locate in Davis County, Iowa, and at present are residents of Bloomfield, that county. The parental household included eleven children, of whom eight sons and one daughter are living. The parents are prominently connected with the Methodist Episcopal Church. In early life Benjamin Bryant affiliated with the Democratic party, but at the breaking out of the Rebellion he considered that he had reason to change his status and, joining the Republican party, has uniformly supported its principles since that time.

Andrew J. Bryant received his primary education in the common schools, afterward attending Troy

Academy, and later, the State Normal School at Kirkville, Mo., where he completed the scientific course. He then entered upon the study of law in the office of Temple & Phelps, at Atlantic, Iowa, and was admitted to practice in the courts of Iowa in 1879. Previous to this he had been employed as a teacher, and for a year was Principal of Milford High School.

Mr. Bryant came to Ottumwa in April, 1880, opened an office, and has since confined himself to the duties of his profession. He took an active interest in the campaign of 1884, and the year following was elected Chairman of the Republican Central Committee. In 1886, much against his wishes, he was re-elected. He is an enthusiastic Republican, and has fulfilled the duties of his position as Chairman of the Central Committee with credit to himself and the party. Although still a young man he has made a record to be proud of, and has attained his position in the community by his own efforts. He is held in high esteem by his fellow-citizens, who are always ready to encourage worthy efforts and will rejoice at his future successes.

Mr. Bryant was married on the 27th of October, 1881, to Miss Lizzie Bills. Mrs. B. is a native of Missouri, and the daughter of John C. and Mary A. Bills, of Wapello County. By her union with our subject she has become the mother of two children—Stella M. and Leila C. The parents are regular attendants of the Methodist Episcopal Church. Socially Mr. Bryant belongs to the Masonic fraternity, having attained to the degree of a Master Mason. He is is also a member of the I. O. O. F., the A. O. U. W. and the Sons of Veterans

J. B. HELMAN, a farmer and stock-raiser on section 36, Pleasant Township, was born in Ashland County, Ohio, Nov. 15, 1835, and is the son of David and Elizabeth (Smith) Helman, both of whom were natives of Pennsylvania. The mother died in Ohio in 1874, and the father Oct. 26, 1886, in Wayne County, that State. In 1866 the subject of this sketch moved from Ohio to Wapello County. He was married in 1858 to Lydia Smalley, who was born in Ashland County, Ohio, in 1837, and was the daughter of Benjamin and Mary (Smith) Smalley. Her mother died in Ashland County, Ohio, in 1874; her father still survives, and is living in that county.

Mr. and Mrs. Helman became the parents of six children: Frank O. lives in Ashland, Ohio; Charles E. resides near Cleveland, Ashtabula Co., Ohio; Walter W. is in Wellington, Lorain Co., Ohio; David C. lives in Ashtabula County, the same State; Benjamin F. also lives in Ashtabula County; Tibbie makes her home with her father. Mrs. Helman died in January, 1873, and is buried in the Batavia Cemetery.

During the war of the Rebellion Mr. Helman enlisted in Co. F, 176th Ohio Vol. Inf., and served as a non-commissioned officer from June, 1862, to June, 1865, when he was discharged at Columbus, Ohio. He was in the battles of Nashville and Franklin, Tenn. Mr. Helman is the owner of 144 acres of good farm land, all of which is under a high state of cultivation, the farm being one of the best watered in Pleasant Township. On the place is a fine orchard, a fine natural grove, and a maple grove. Our subject is a member of the G. A. R., and politically he is a Republican.

ROBERT SCOTT GILCREST, M. D., of the firm of Thrall & Gilcrest, Ottumwa, was born in Mt. Vernon, Knox Co., Ohio, Aug. 5, 1823. His father was an officer in the War of 1812, a man of good business capacity, and was often chosen by the people of his section in Ohio to fill places of honor and public trust. The subject of this sketch in his youth attended the district schools until sufficiently advanced to enter the Martinsburg Academy, which he did in 1839, and after attending for some years took a partial course at Kenyon's College.

May 7, 1847, Mr. Gilcrest commenced the study of medicine, under the instruction of Dr. H. L. Thrall, of Gambier, Ohio, attending his first course of medical lectures at the Western Reserve College, Cleveland, Ohio, in the winter of 1850–51. On the close of the lecture term, by request, he went to New Albary and took charge of Dr. Brooks' practice during his temporary absence. Returning to Cleveland he attended another course of lectures, and received his medical degree in the spring of 1853. April 1 of the same year he began the practice of his profession at De Graff, and there resided until 1886, when he came to Ottumwa. Notwithstanding the fatigue of a laborious general practice he managed to read and inform himself of the latest discoveries and improvements in medical science. His confidence in the power of judiciously chosen remedies is as great now as on his entering his profession. He made a visit to California as a delegate to the American Medical Association that met in San Francisco, May 2, 1871. While on the Pacific coast Dr. Gilcrest visited the Yosemite Valley, the Guysers, and most places of interest to travelers, and en route spent a day at Salt Lake City.

In 1852 Dr. Gilcrest was united in marriage with Filena Brooks, of Columbus, Ohio, who died in 1854. In 1856 the Doctor married Annie B. Brooks, of De Graff, Ohio, and of this latter union one child was born, named Fay, who is now deceased.

The Doctor is a member of Logan County Medical Society, the Ohio State Medical Society, the American Medical Association, and an honorary member of the California State Medical Society.

GEORGE BANE, a resident of Ottumwa, and Treasurer of Wapello County, Iowa, is a native of Ohio County, Va., where he was born on the 6th of January, 1833. He is the son of Absalom and Sarah (Dowley) Bane, who removed from Virginia to Ohio in 1835, locating in Champaign County at an early period in the history of that region. There they established a permanent home, and remained there until the close of their lives. Absalom Bane was a farmer by occupation, and cleared a farm in the midst of a heavy timber tract. The household circle consisted of ten children, of whom six are still living, as follows: Nancy is the widow of George Leavitt, and lives near Paris, Edgar Co., Ill.; Lovina married Henry Holton, of Ohio; Sarah A. married Chauncey Jones, of Dana, Ill.; Mary Jane became the wife of Samuel McCaughey, of Mutual, Ohio; Susan, Mrs. Granville Smith, is a resident of the same place; the next was George, our subject. Absalom Bane departed this life in 1864. His wife survived him sixteen years, dying in 1880. She was an estimable Christian lady, and a devoted member of the Methodist Episcopal Church.

George Bane was reared in Champaign County, Ohio, and received his early education in the district schools of his native county. The schoolhouse was at a long distance from his home, and he was eleven years old before he commenced attendance there, his first text-book being an elementary speller. He attended school three months each summer and winter until he was fourteen years old, and thereafter was engaged in the various duties around the homestead, being his father's right-hand man, following the plow and assisting in the other work. After he left school, however, he still pursued the study of instructive books, and taught school during the winter seasons, with the exception of two years, up to 1871-72, his duties in this line embracing twenty years. He was possessed of a good amount of native talent, and kept himself well posted upon matters of general interest, and is now what might be called a self-made man, for the position which he holds in the community is the result of his own worthy effort and his determination to become a man among men.

In 1872 the subject of our sketch crossed the Mississippi, and coming into Wapello County, located in Richland Township, where he was alternately engaged in farming and teaching for several years. Upon coming here his abilities were at once recognized, and after holding other important positions in the county, in the fall of 1883 he was nominated for County Treasurer on the Democratic ticket, being elected after a hard-fought battle, and in 1885 was re-elected. He has fulfilled the duties of his office in a creditable and satisfactory manner, and is highly respected in the community. He belongs to the I. O. O. F., the principles of which order he thoroughly believes in and cheerfully supports.

Mr. Bane was married in Urbana, Ohio, in 1861,

John C. Fisher
Sarah E Fisher

to Miss Rebecca J. McCaughey, a native of Washington County, Pa. They have become the parents of three children—William, Charles and George A. Mr. B. is the owner of a farm in Highland Township, which is finely located on sections 21, 22 and 27, where are living his sons who carry on the business connected therewith.

JOHN C. FISHER, one of the most highly respected of the earliest pioneer settlers of the Hawkeye State, came into Wapello County in 1844, and has been a resident of the city of Ottumwa since 1855. He is a native of Wayne County, Ind., where he was born in 1817, and is the son of Richard and Elizabeth (Helphinstine) Fisher, natives respectively of Delaware and Virginia. His father was a farmer by occupation, and our subject remained with his parents during his early years, and received a fair education in the common schools, common to the frontier settlements. When he was a child of one year old, his parents removed from his native State to Darke County, Ohio, remaining there until the fall of 1829, and then moved into Hamilton County, Ind., near "Strawtown," being early settlers of that locality. Here Richard Fisher opened up a farm from a tract of unimproved land, and remained there with his family until the fall of 1831. He then removed to Tippecanoe County, same State, and repeated his former experiment of developing a new farm out of the wilderness. They only remained there, however, until the following year, removing thence to Parke County, and from there went over into Illinois and settled in Fulton County, making it their home until the spring of 1841. The father of the family then determined to cross the Mississippi, and made his first settlement in Jefferson County, Iowa, upon a tract of rented land, upon which they remained until purchasing the present homestead in Wapello County, coming into possession of it on the 1st of January, 1844. This was located on section 12, in Center Township. The land was uncultivated, and it required incessant labor for a number of years to bring it to a profitable condition.

Richard Fisher departed this life Aug. 29, 1864, at the ripe old age of seventy-seven years. He was a farmer by occupation, public-spirited and liberal, and was always willing to contribute of his time and means to promote any worthy enterprise. He was one of the first Justices of the Peace in this county and possessed a wise discretion in matters connected with his office. When a young man he was a great traveler, and frequently went over the Alleghanies in the early times, on horseback. The faithful wife and mother survived her husband for a period of fifteen years, and died Aug. 16, 1879, aged nearly eighty-four years, and, like him, was connected with the Catholic Church.

The maternal grandfather of our subject, Peter Helphinstine, kept the White House tavern in Virginia, near Winchester, and often entertained Gens. Washington and Jackson while they were on their way to and from Washington, D. C. He was a soldier in the War of 1812, and received a land grant from the Government through Harrison before he was elected President. At that time land was almost worthless in Ohio.

The subject of our sketch remained with his parents until 1848, when he opened up a farm of his own, and on the 29th of June, 1854, he was united in marriage with Miss Sarah Elizabeth Lewis, a native of Champaign County, Ohio, and the daughter of William and Ruey (Pierce) Lewis, natives respectively of Benton County, Ky., and Ohio. He was already the possessor of an improved farm, located on section 1 of Center Township, and immediately after his marriage removed to it, where the young couple commenced the joint business of housekeeping and farming. They resided upon this place for a period of about one year, when Mr. Fisher decided to abandon agricultural pursuits and remove to town. They became residents of Ottumwa on the 25th of August, 1855. Mr. Fisher erected a frame residence at the intersection of West Fifth and Washington streets, and since then has built a two-story brick which he now occupies. In the spring of 1856 he was elected Justice of the Peace, which position he resigned in a short time, and was then appointed Deputy Sheriff, serving over two years. He was appointed Postmaster by President Buchanan, but was also compelled to resign this office after a short time on account of ill-health.

Mr. Fisher and his wife are connected with the Catholic Church, and are well and widely known throughout this community as being genial and pleasant people. They enjoy an extended acquaintance among the people of this vicinity, and number among their warmest friends the most highly cultured people of Ottumwa.

It is with pleasure that we present in this connection the portraits of Mr. and Mrs. Fisher.

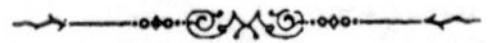

CAPT. CHARLES C. CLOUTMAN, deceased, who lost his life while defending his country at the battle of Ft. Donelson, was a native of Conway, N. H., born June 10, 1824. There he spent his early life, and received his primary education in the common schools, afterward attending a select school, and altogether received a liberal education. At the age of twenty-two he came west to Burlington, Iowa. While in his native town he had learned the trade of a blacksmith in his father's shop, but was not particularly fond of this employment, his natural tastes leading him into the sphere of the finer arts. He possessed great musical talent, and after coming to Burlington became identified with the first band of the city as its instructor, and during the winter seasons taught singing-school. In the meantime, however, he established a blacksmith-shop, and for a time was employed at his trade, but subsequently sold out the business and engaged in the grocery trade.

The subject of our sketch was married in Burlington, this State, April 11, 1850, to Miss Rachel Scott, cousin of Gen. Winfield Scott, and a native of Switzerland County, Ind., born July 30, 1830. She was a daughter of William and Lydia (Iler) Scott, natives respectively of North Carolina and Ohio. They then became residents of Ottumwa, where Mr. Cloutman was interested in a plow factory, which he assisted in operating until the Rebellion began to assume alarming proportions, and then, laying aside personal and private interests, at once engaged himself in raising a company of infantry, which was named Company K, and numbered as the 2d Iowa. Of this he was commissioned Captain by Gov. Kirkwood, and they were at once sent to the front, and soon afterward participated in the siege of Ft. Donelson, where Capt. Cloutman was killed by a ball which passed through his heart.

Mr. W. S. Moore, a soldier in the same regiment, wrote of this sad event as follows: "Many surviving members of the 2d Iowa Infantry will remember the tall and manly figure of Capt. Charles C. Cloutman, of Company K. It was my pleasure to be well acquainted with him personally, and to enjoy and value his friendship. As early as 1854 I became acquainted with him as a citizen of Burlington, subsequently renewed my acquaintance with him at Ottumwa, and cultivated with him a warm intimacy after the fortunes of war associated us together as members of the same regiment. Though I was but a private soldier and my friend a commander of the company, we frequently met and conversed upon various matters, on terms of entire equality. Capt. Cloutman was a man of highly cultivated intellect, and conscientious in his views upon all subjects of vital concern. He was a patriot, true and steadfast. When Sumter was fired upon he was Captain of a company of militia in Ottumwa, and promptly telegraphed Gov. Kirkwood a formal tender of his company for the service. Other men did the same, but it is plain that the telegram of Capt. Cloutman was the first received by the Governor of Iowa. Sitting upon the guard of the boat on the evening before embarkation, the Captain drew his chair close to mine and engaged in conversation as to the prospects at Ft. Donelson. 'What' said he, 'do you think of the prospect?' I replied briefly that I thought we would have the fight at Donelson, for which the boys had been spoiling for months. 'Yes,' rejoined the Captain, 'I realize the awful truth of that fact, and feel that many of us will not pass through the battle alive. I have a continual presentiment that I will be killed in the first battle I am in, and it has been to me a subject of serious thought for months. Indeed I have at times seriously meditated upon the question as to whether I had better resign and disgrace myself for the benefit of my family, or go into the battle and be killed. I have considered the matter in all its bearings, and have chosen the latter alternative. I feel sure I will be killed in the first battle and at the first fire from the enemy's guns, and cannot resist the conviction.'

"Not being much of a believer in presentiments, I was disposed to make light of the Captain's apprehensions, and assured him that it was a hallucination, that he was no more liable to be killed than I was, and that I had never allowed such thoughts to enter my head. He finally admitted that there was a remote possibility that his life would be spared and his honor saved. 'If,' said he, 'I have the good fortune to pass through the Ft. Donelson battle alive, I will immediately thereafter resign my commission and return home. I cling tenaciously to life and am devotedly fond of my family; I am in poor circumstances financially, and if I survive this battle I will resign at once.'

"After parting with my friend I gave the subject of our conversation no special thought. We continued upon our voyage and the next day joined the investing force at Ft. Donelson. The following day it fell to our lot to lead the great charge which brought about the surrender of the fort. When the firing had ceased, I was approached by Lieut. John E. Mobley, of Company K, an acquaintance of many years, who asked me if I had seen Lieut. Mastic. Being answered in the negative, Mobley said, 'Capt. Cloutman is killed, and I cannot find Mastic.' Capt. Cloutman killed! The announcement filled me with horror as the convictions of the Captain, expressed to me on the boat, echoed through my brain. Killed in the first battle, and at the first fire from the enemy's guns as he had predicted! The reader is left to estimate the patriotism of the heroism, or the heroism of the patriotism, which impels a man, while laboring under the conviction of certain death, to march into the jaws of the grim monster."

Capt. Cloutman was a man greatly beloved by the soldiers under his command, as well as by the community of which he had been a resident in Ottumwa. He left a widow and four children, one of whom, a son Frank, was killed while an employe of the C., B. & Q. R. R. Those surviving are, Ella, a music teacher; Life, who is a ticket agent at Ottumwa, and Charles C., employed in a freight office in Kansas City. Mrs. Cloutman is still living in Ottumwa, and is a lady fully deserving of the universal sympathy which is extended her by many of the citizens of Ottumwa, in consideration of her great afflictions.

Capt. Cloutman was the first officer from this vicinity who fell in battle. He was Democratic in politics and his name is prominently connected with the G. A. R. Post of Ottumwa. Cloutman Post is named in honor of the Captain.

E L. LATHROP, M. D., a prominent and successful physician of Ottumwa, claims as his birthplace Madison County, N. Y., where he first opened his eyes to the light on the 19th of September, 1844. He is descended from an old and excellent family, his father being Rev. Samuel G. Lathrop, a man of more than ordinary ability, and his mother, Cynthia (Clary) Lathrop, descended from relatives of Henry Clary, who were prominently and favorably known in that section.

When a lad of thirteen years old Dr. Lathrop went with his parents to Chicago, Ill., where they located and where his primary education was supplemented by attendance at the High Schools of that city. He afterward spent two years at Rock River Seminary, and at the age of sixteen commenced reading medicine in the office of Dr. W. W. Winn, at Dixon, Ill., where he gained great proficiency, but was refused a diploma on account of his minority. He then, in 1862, went to Chicago, in the office of N. S. Davis, and attended two courses of lectures, but there also was refused a diploma on account of his age. In the meantime, however, the Civil War was in progress, and on the 8th of October, 1864, he enlisted as a soldier in the 12th Illinois Cavalry. He received an honorable discharge from this regiment the following month, in order to accept a commission as Assistant Surgeon of the 10th Illinois Cavalry, with which regiment he remained until the close of the war, and was but two months past twenty years old when he assumed the post of Assistant Surgeon. He was mustered out at San Antonio, Tex., and discharged in January of the following year.

After returning from the army Dr. Lathrop entered upon the practice of his profession for a short time at Joliet, thence went to Chicago to attend a course of study at the Rush Medical College, from which he received his diploma with honors, in 1868. Three years thereafter he came to Ottumwa, and since 1871 has practiced his profession continuously and with success. His genial disposition and warm, generous temperament have proved an irresistible attraction to a large circle of friends and patrons, and he now occupies an enviable position among his brethren of the profession in this locality.

The marriage of Dr. Lathrop with Miss Emma Hedrick was celebrated in Ottumwa, in 1872. Mrs. L. is a daughter of John W. Hedrick, a highly esteemed citizen of this county, and is an educated and accomplished lady. Of her union with our subject there has been one child, Edward H., born Oct. 7, 1876.

Dr. Lathrop is prominently connected with the Des Moines Valley Medical Association of Iowa, and is a member of the G. A. R., being at present Surgeon of C. C. Cloutman Post. In 1877 he was commissioned Surgeon of the Fifth National Guards of Iowa.

D. McKECHNIE, M. D., of Ottumwa, is a licentiate of the Royal College of Physicians of Edinburgh, and a licentiate of the Faculty of Physicians and Surgeons of Glasgow, Scotland. He is also a graduate in medicine of Toronto and Victoria Universities, Canada, and a member of the College of Physicians and Surgeons of Ontario. Dr. McKechnie was born in Lanarkshire, Scotland, July 31, 1857, and is the son of Neil and Isabella (Henderson) McKechnie, natives of Argyleshire, Scotland. His father was engaged in the large iron manufactories of his native country for upward of thirty years. In 1871 he emigrated to Canada with his family and engaged in farming. The Doctor, however, soon returned to Scotland to finish his professional studies, and remained there until the close of 1880, when he came back to Canada and settled near London, engaging in the active practice of his profession. In June, 1886, he came to this State and decided to locate in Ottumwa, where he at once entered upon active practice. The Doctor's medical education and his credentials from the best medical schools and colleges of Great Britain alike entitle him to the respect of his medical confreres and the confidence of the general public.

Dr. McKechnie was married near London, Canada, to Miss Sarah Shoff, who was born in Canada, March 14, 1856. Of this union one child has been born, Menie, June 3, 1884.

E. W. MOORE. Among the representative farmers and stock-raisers of Wapello County, the gentleman of whom we write the following brief personal sketch is prominently identified. He resides on his excellent farm on section 18, of Competine Township, where he is surrounded by all the necessaries and comforts of life. He is the son of James and Eliza (Wayman) Moore, the former a native of Tennessee, where he was born about the year 1802, and the latter of Indiana, where her birth took place in 1803. She was the daughter of Emanuel Wayman, a native of England, who came to this country when he was about twenty years of age.

When James Moore was a lad of fourteen he moved with his family into Indiana, where he met and married Miss Wayman. They had a family of nine children, four of whom were sons. The children bore the following names: Mary, who died in infancy; E. W., our subject, was born Aug. 31, 1826, in Clark County, Ind.; Mary A., born in 1828, is the wife of W. H. Ring, a farmer of Sullivan County, Ind.; W. H. was born in 1830, in Clark County, Ind., and is now a farmer of Clark County, Ill.; Nancy M. was born in 1832, and is the wife of Jesse Willis, a resident of Effingham County, Ill.; Ann M., the wife of Gideon Lashbrook, was born in 1835, and they are farmers in Ralls County, Mo.; Reason was born in 1837, and is now living in Jackson County, Ind.; Margaret

E., who was born in 1839, is the wife of S. Schoonover and resides in Louisville, Ky.; John W. was born in 1841, and is a resident of Effingham County, Ill., where he is engaged in farming.

The early years of Mr. Moore's life were spent with his parents on a farm. In 1846 he enlisted in the 2d Indiana Infantry, under Col. William A. Bowls, to serve in the Mexican War. He was in the battle of Buena Vista, and after a service of one year was discharged at New Orleans. He then returned to his home in Indiana, and March 27, 1851, was married to Miss Clorinda R. Wells. This lady is a daughter of James and Susan M. (Thompson) Wells, both of whom were natives of Indiana. The father was born March 15, 1806, and died in 1874, in Labette County, Kan.; the mother was born May 20, 1814, and died in 1879, her remains being interred in Dickins Cemetery, this county. Mrs. Moore is the third of a family of eleven children, six of whom, two daughters and four sons, are now living—Sarah, born May 12, 1831; Clarissa W., June 7, 1832; Clorinda, Feb. 26, 1835; Reason R., May 30, 1837; William T., Nov. 8, 1839; Laura A., July 3, 1842; Emma R., Jan. 4, 1845; Joshua T., Aug. 9, 1847; James H., April 17, 1850; Francis M., March 14, 1853; Harriet M., June 22, 1856.

Our subject came to this county in 1873, buying 200 acres of raw land, and immediately began its improvement, and has been so prospered that to-day he is surrounded by all the comforts of life. To himself and wife have been born a family of ten children, equally divided between sons and daughters. Eliza M., the eldest, born May 7, 1852, is the widow of Peter H. Bottorff, who died Oct. 17, 1885, and is buried in Silver Creek Cemetery, Clark County, Ind.; Sarah J., born Nov. 9, 1853, died Aug. 1, 1854; James W., born March 14, 1855, is a farmer on section 18, Competine Township; Rella Z., who is the wife of William E. Mowrey, was born Aug. 8, 1857; Mr. M. is now attending medical lectures in Cincinnati; Mary A., born Aug. 3, 1859, died April 15, 1869; George E., born May 13, 1864, is a farmer living on section 19, Competine Township; John H., born Dec. 21, 1867, is now attending school at Ottumwa; Laura M. was born June 23, 1872, and died May 27, 1876; Calvin T., born Dec. 8, 1874, died Dec. 26 of the same year; Charles H., born Jan. 25, 1878.

Both Mr. and Mrs. Moore are members of the Baptist Church, and politically he is a Republican. He has been prominently identified in all worthy enterprises of his community, and has held several offices of the township. He is a member of the I. O. O. F. and is regarded as one of the solid men of his community. A lithographic view of his residence is shown on another page of this work.

J M. ELDER, a prosperous farmer of Wapello County, owns and occupies a fine homestead in Highland Township, pleasantly located on section 13. He is a native of Decatur County, Ind., and was born in 1845. His parents were William M. and Sarah (Sellers) Elder, natives of Kentucky.

Mr. Elder came to Wapello County in 1870, and for three years rented land and carried on agriculture in Highland Township. He then purchased a tract of eighty acres, on section 4, which he occupied for eight years and then sold. In 1881 he purchased 115 acres on section 13, where he permanently established himself, and since that time has been industriously engaged in the improvement and cultivation of his property. He has been prominently connected with the affairs of this county since coming here, has served as Assessor for five terms, and held the office of Justice of the Peace.

Mr. Elder was married, in 1867, to Miss Lydia Pratt, a native of his own county, and the daughter of Vactor and Valeria (Baldwin) Pratt. They have become the parents of two children—Louis and Valeria L.

During the progress of the late war, Mr. Elder enlisted as a Union soldier in Co. H, 5th Ind. Vol. Cav., and served nearly two years. He went all through the Atlanta campaign, and was with Stoneman's raid, in July, 1864, where he was captured and taken to Andersonville prison, being a prisoner four months and ten days. After his release he rejoined his regiment, and put in most of his time afterward hunting the Bushwhackers. He is Republican in politics.

William M. Elder, the father of our subject, was of Irish descent, and a farmer by occupation. He departed this life in the spring of 1875, at the ripe old age of seventy-four years. His wife, Mrs. Sarah S. Elder, died in 1855, when the subject of our sketch was a small boy. The father of Mrs. Elder is still living, upon a farm in Highland Township.

AMMI D. WHIPPLE, who departed this life in Ottumwa, Oct. 16, 1864, was one of the early pioneers of the Hawkeye State. He was a native of Warren County, N. Y., and was born July 16, 1805. He grew to manhood in his native county, receiving a common-school education, and was there married, in 1831, to Miss Sylvina Marsh, a native of Pennsylvania, born about the year 1810. They remained in New York until 1845, when Mr. W. started West with his family, crossing the Mississippi and coming into Wapello County, their first stopping-place being at what is now known as the Old Garrison. Here Mr. Whipple purchased a small tract of land where the pork house now stands, and at once engaged in its cultivation and improvement. He only remained here, however, until 1858, when he removed to Keokuk Township and engaged in the lumber business, felling the trees, sawing them, and disposing of the lumber thus manufactured to builders. The same year he purchased a small farm, which he operated in connection with his lumber trade, and from the two received a comfortable income.

In the meantime Mr. Whipple had experienced his joys and sorrows. Six children had been born to the household, who were left motherless in 1849, his wife departing from the scenes of earth in that year. Of these, three are now living: Catharine, who became the wife of W. E. Jones; Mary, the wife of John M. Jones, deceased, and Joseph, of Guthrie County, Iowa.

During the existence of the Whig party Mr. Whipple was numbered among its adherents, but upon the abandonment of the old by the organization of the new Republican party, he cordially indorsed the principles of the latter, and uniformly cast his vote to uphold its principles. Although his early education was limited, he was a man keenly observant of what was going on around him and took an active interest in public matters generally, being especially interested in the welfare of his own county and community. He was well posted in local and general history, and an interesting man to converse with. Although not connected with any religious denomination he contributed liberally to objects of charity, was strictly honest and honorable in his business transactions, and by his upright life secured the highest respect and esteem of his associates and the community at large. His name is kindly remembered by a large circle of friends and acquaintances, who name him as an example worthy of imitation by the rising generation.

P. T. OVERMAN, an esteemed citizen of Ottumwa, is a native of Wayne County, Ind., his birth taking place in 1834. He is the son of Reuben and Jane (Spencer) Overman, natives respectively of North Carolina and Virginia. They removed to Indiana at an early period in its history and engaged in farming pursuits. The subject of our sketch remained with his parents during his childhood, and in 1846 with them crossed the Father of Waters and came into Iowa the same year in which it was admitted as a State into the Union. They located in Wapello County, settling in Center Township on section 23, and purchased a claim of unimproved land, which they brought to a good state of cultivation, and there established a comfortable home.

Mr. Overman was married in 1856, to Miss Mary M. Young, a native of Ohio, and the daughter of Benjamin Young, of the same State. They became the parents of four children, as follows: Alfred B. died in 1859, at the age of two years; Harriet E. became the wife of F. Michael, and lives in Emporia, Kan.; Eva died in 1881, at the age of twenty-two years; Rubin B. died in 1864, when a child.

Mr. Overman has been prominent in the affairs of his community, having been one year on the police force of Ottumwa, and was elected Constable in the fall of 1886. After coming to this city he learned the trade of plastering, at which he worked for ten years. In 1864 he took an overland trip to California, and for three years was engaged in the mining regions of the Golden State, meeting with fair success. He returned home in 1871, and since that time, in addition to other pursuits, has been cultivating a little farm of thirty acres near the city of Ottumwa, and quite agrees with Horace Greeley in regard to having a small tract and giving it thorough attention. The wife of our subject is prominently connected with the Methodist Episcopal Church, and politically Mr. O. uniformly casts his vote with the Democratic party.

The father of our subject was a soldier in the War of 1812, and departed this life in 1845; the mother survived for twelve years, dying in 1857. They were both connected with the Society of Friends, and were most excellent and worthy people, enjoying the respect and esteem of the community in which they lived.

ALONSON BULL COMSTOCK, now residing in the southwest part of Richland Township, was born in Franklin County, Ohio, near Columbus, on the 1st day of March, 1818. When about six years old his father moved to Hamilton County, the same State, to the village of New Haven, which was the precinct or voting place for Crosby Township, where our subject lived until his thirteenth year, when his father sent him and his younger brother, Hiram, to Augusta College, Kentucky, where he remained for about four years, or until the spring of 1834, when he returned and began reading medicine in his father's office, and so continued until the spring of 1837, when he came to Iowa, at that time a Territory. He came to what is now Van Buren County, in April, 1837, and in the fall of that year located at Benton's Post and began the practice of his profession.

On the 17th day of June, 1838, our subject married Sarah Ann Sullivan, and continued to reside in the same county, at several different places, until the spring of 1843, when he came to his present location, where he continued to reside, engaged in practice in connection with his farm, until 1865, when his hearing became so much impaired that he quit the practice, and has since devoted his time to farming, stock-raising, etc. He now owns about 520 acres of land, most of which he has under cultivation.

Mr. Comstock never took much interest in political affairs, never seeking office, but was, on a non-partisan vote, elected to represent Wapello County, in 1846, in the first Legislature of the State of Iowa, he being a Whig. The election in 1848, party lines being drawn, showed the county to be Democratic by a large majority.

Dr. James and Chloe (Bull) Comstock, parents of our subject, were both natives of Vermont, being born near Bennington. His ancestors on his father's side were originally from Scotland, and on his mother's side from England. His wife, Sarah Ann Sullivan, was born July 2, 1821, on the north side of the Des Moines River, about half way between Sweet Home and St. Francisville (which are on the opposite side of the river in Missouri, which is now in Lee County, Iowa), and it is claimed was the first white child born in what is now the State of Iowa. Her father, Giles O. Sullivan, was born in Kentucky, of Irish descent. Her mother, whose maiden name was Letisha Tane Tolbert, was of Scotch descent. Giles O. Sullivan was a nephew of John Sullivan, who located the northern boundary of the State of Missouri, which was the cause of a very hot dispute, and in 1839 came near ending in war between the State of Missouri and Territory of Iowa. Mrs. Comstock remembers a great many incidents that occurred during the Black Hawk War, the place of her nativity being near the scene of conflict. The settlers had a block house at Sweet Home, and her father was an independent scout under Gen. Dodge, father of one of Iowa's old and much beloved ex-Senators, A. C. Dodge. Mrs. C. is the only surviving member of her father's family.

Dr. and Mrs. C. have had twelve children born to them, five only now living: F. J. Comstock, born Nov. 21, 1839; J. H., Dec. 1, 1841; Chloe J., now Mrs. Shields, Oct. 25, 1843; Frances M., now

Mrs. Williams, March 24, 1850, and Sally Ann, now Mrs. Abernathy, July 27, 1859. The two sons served the full term in the late Civil War. Dr. Comstock is independent both in politics and religion.

J. N. BARKER, a highly respected citizen of Wapello County, resides on the old homestead of his mother, two miles east of Kirkville, where he is carrying on agricultural pursuits in an intelligent and successful manner, and, besides the ordinary pursuits of farming, is giving much attention to raising stock for the markets. He has been a resident of this county since his boyhood, and has fully established himself in the esteem and confidence of his community. Mr. Barker was born Dec. 20, 1839, and is the son of James and Anna D. Barker, the former born March 27, 1801, and the latter on the 21st day of April, 1806. She was the oldest daughter of George Lues, who emigrated from Germany in 1787. The Lues family possessed in a remarkable degree the excellent traits of the substantial German character, of which Mrs. Barker inherited her full share. She received a careful parental training and a fair education in her native State, and remained there, making her home with her parents, until her marriage to James Barker, which occurred in 1824. Fourteen years later they removed northwest to Indiana, and in 1848, the husband, after a long and weary illness, died of consumption, and left the mother of our subject with nine children, and in very limited circumstances, having barely enough to enable her to keep her family together; but she fortunately, by her excellent personal traits, had gathered around her a circle of friends and acquaintances who proved of great assistance and comfort in her time of need. These mostly belonged to the Society of Friends, or Quakers.

Mrs. Barker had reared her boys to habits of industry, so that labor was no hardship for them; and the mother had always practiced close economy, notwithstanding that she was generous almost to a fault. With the assistance of the boys, who worked industriously at whatever they could find to do, and saved their earnings, Mrs. Barker, in the course of time, was enabled to purchase a home in Iowa. While in Indiana they had cultivated rented land, and in 1852 they crossed the Mississippi and settled in this county. In the meantime her eldest son had been removed by death, which was a sore affliction to the widowed mother, and interfered greatly with her plans for the future. But with that courage and resolution which was one of her chief characteristics, she bravely recovered from the blow, and prepared herself for the duties of the future. They started overland from Indiana to Iowa, and, after a journey of twenty days with ox-teams, arrived in this county on the 10th of October, 1852, and were welcomed at the house of an old friend, Joshua Marshall.

As soon as convenient Mrs. B. rented a house in Kirkville, which belonged to John H. Carver, into which she removed with her family for the winter. In the meantime she and her sons set about the erection of a frame house on the farm which she had purchased, and which was completed by April of the following year. This consisted of four rooms, and stood out in the middle of the prairie, and here Mrs. Barker and her boys commenced the improvement and cultivation of the farm. The first work done was to build fences, and put up a barn and pig-pen, and for this the boys were obliged to haul the rails and timber five miles. They also did hauling for the neighbors, and the nearest point of timber was two miles away. This was accomplished with ox-teams, as was also the breaking of the prairie. They put up what were called "stake and rider" fences, and these were required to be made seven rails high, with double riders. This involved a vast amount of labor, but it made sturdy men of Mrs. Barker's boys, and fitted them for the later duties of life. The mother and children were prospered in their labors, and it was not long before they were established in a comfortable home, where they enjoyed all the necessaries and many of the luxuries of life. As one by one the boys attained their majority they passed out from under the parental roof, and when the war broke out, in 1861, Mrs. Barker was left with only one son at home. Daniel L. was married and living in Ringgold County, this State, and he

now enlisted in the 29th Iowa Infantry, as also did William I. and Joshua H. William lost his life on the field of Mark's Mills, as did many others as brave men as ever marched to the front. J. N., our subject, had the management of the homestead, and Mrs. Barker lived with him until her death, which occurred on the 21st of April, 1876, when she had arrived at the age of seventy years. She was a devout Christian, and left behind her a record of womanly virtues and kindly deeds. From early childhood she had been a member of the Baptist Church, with which she was connected until her removal to Iowa.

J. N. Barker was united in marriage with Miss Rachel J. Stout, Nov. 29, 1860. Mrs. Barker was born in Parke County, Ind., in 1842, and is the daughter of Charles Stout. Of the union of our subject and his wife there have been born eight children: The eldest, a boy, died in infancy; Josie became the wife of Gus G. Griffith, an attorney at law, who is engaged in the practice of his profession in Little Rock, Ark.; Ida was married to Stephen Buckner, of this county; the remaining five children—Stella, Cora, Fred A., and Nelson and Nellie (twins)—are at home.

The homestead of Mr. Barker consists of 200 acres of finely improved land, and the estate is supplied with all the appliances for carrying on agricultural pursuits after the most modern and improved methods. In 1881 our subject concluded to abandon farming, and accordingly leased the place for five years and moved to town. After five months' residence in the city he paid his tenant $650 to let him have his farm back, and returned to it, satisfied that the country, for him at least, was the best place in which to live.

The early education of Mr. Barker was necessarily quite limited, but he kept his eyes open to what was going on in the world, and pursued a course of instructive reading as opportunity afforded, and consequently has been enabled to keep himself well posted in regard to matters of general interest. During the first years of his residence in this vicinity he worked in the coal mines of Kirkville during the winter season and on the farm in summer, and consequently had but little time to spend in school. He has been remarkably successful in his stock operations, and feeds from forty to fifty cattle and from sixty to seventy-five hogs each winter. He buys his cattle when about two years old, feeds them one year, and when ready for market they yield him a handsome profit.

Mr. Barker has contributed his full quota toward the building up of his community, in that he has been the staunch friend of education, morality and religion. The whole family are regular attendants of the Methodist Episcopal Church, and have contributed liberally to its establishment and maintenance. Mr. Barker, politically, affiliates with the Democratic party, and uniformly casts his vote in support of its principles. He has fulfilled all his obligations as an honest man and a good citizen, and is held in the highest esteem by the community of which he has been a resident for over thirty years. A view of his place is shown on another page.

HENRY WILSON, a prominent and respected resident of Ottumwa, was a pioneer of Wapello County, coming to this section at an early period in the history of the Hawkeye State, in the spring of 1849. Although the advance of civilization within the two or three years preceding had been quite rapid, still it bore no comparison with its present aspect, and Mr. Wilson, in common with his brother settlers of that day, has witnessed with pleasure and gratification the march of civilization which has so changed the face of the country in a period of over thirty-five years.

The subject of this history is a native of Harrison County, Ky., the date of his birth being Jan. 9, 1822. He is the son of William and Charity (DeVour) Wilson, and when he was a lad nine years of age, his parents removed from Kentucky to Monroe County, Ind. There the father purchased a tract of timber land, from which he opened up a farm. After years of incessant industry and perseverance, the heavy timber gave place to cultivated fields, and in due time a comfortable homestead was established. Here young Wilson was reared and received his education in the subscription schools, which were carried on in log cabins with puncheons for flooring, slabs for benches and desks, and greased paper for window-panes. He was also carefully trained to habits of industry, and in early years was instilled with those principles of courage and resolution which served him so well in the after battle of life.

Mr. Wilson was married in Monroe County, Ind., in 1841, to Miss Jane Farmer, a native of his own State, who had removed with her parents to the latter. Of their union there were born two sons, Pryor S. and William, who are both residents of this county. Eight years after his marriage, Mr. Wilson not being quite satisfied with his condition or his prospects in Indiana, resolved to cross the Father of Waters, and seek his fortune in the Hawkeye State. They located first in Bonaparte, Van Buren County, where they resided about eighteen months, and then, coming into this county, purchased a tract of land in Center Township, upon which stood a small cabin, and thirty acres of the land had been broken. Here they settled down and determined to lay the foundation of a future home. Mr. Wilson and his wife "pulled together" in the labors around the house and farm, and in due time were rewarded for their toil. As their means accumulated, Mr. Wilson added to his first purchase, and finally became the possessor of 400 acres, most of which was improved by himself, with such assistance as he could secure. The log cabin finally gave place to a handsome farm residence, and the rude pig-sty to a barn of goodly proportions, with all necessary out-buildings, farm implements, and the appliances of a first-class agriculturist.

Upon the homestead thus established our subject and wife remained until 1870, when he retired from active labor and removed into the city of Ottumwa, where he is enjoying a competency, the result of his own industry and perseverance. The companion of his early manhood, Mrs. Jane Wilson, rested from her earthly labors in 1866. She was an amiable and highly respected lady, a sincere Christian, and a devoted member of the Baptist Church. It may be fairly said of her that, "None named her but to praise," and she has left behind her a record of womanly virtues and kindly deeds. Mr. Wilson was the second time married, to Mrs. Elizabeth Cox, the widow of William Cox, by whom she became the mother of one child, James, who is familiarly known as James Wilson.

Politically Mr. Wilson is a stanch Democrat, and cast his first presidential vote for Franklin Pierce. Although always having been a prominent man in his community, he has steadily declined to become an office-holder, being more content with the peaceful pursuits of his farm and the quiet life of a private citizen. At the time of his coming here Ottumwa was an humble hamlet, and he often compares the present city with its 12,000 inhabitants, to the little village which greeted his eyes upon his first arrival west of the Mississippi.

The parental family of our subject and the offspring of William and Charity Wilson included eleven children, all of whom lived to mature years, but of these, three only are now surviving, viz., Christopher and William, of Chariton, Iowa, and Henry, our subject. The parents were connected with the Baptist Church for many years, were straightforward and upright in their daily lives, and instilled into the minds of their children those principles which they had made the rule of their own lives, and which constituted them highly respected and valued citizens.

LEWIS MULFORD, deceased, was an honored pioneer of Wapello County, crossing the Mississippi from far New England, at an early period in the history of the Hawkeye State. He was a native of Trenton, N. J., his birth taking place Nov. 26, 1812. He was reared in his native State, receiving a liberal education, and after having attained his majority went to Ohio and located in Delaware County. He there became acquainted with Miss Amy Miller, who subsequently became his wife. Mrs. M. was the daughter of Christian Miller, who was born on the Delaware River in 1777, and when a young man removed to the Wyoming Valley. He was united in marriage with Miss Sarah Partridge, a native of Massachusetts, who was born Oct. 19, 1782. Their wedding occurred in Northampton County, Pa., in 1800, and they became the parents of ten children, of whom the record is as follows: Andrew, born June 24, 1802, died Jan. 2, 1880; Eunice, born Sept. 3, 1804, died about 1878; Sarah, born Dec. 22, 1806, is a resident of Kendall County, Ill.; Mary, born June 15, 1809, died in 1863; Elizabeth, born Oct. 3, 1811, resides near Ithaca, N. Y.; Susan, born Feb. 18, 1813, died March 9, 1815; John, born May 17, 1816, died April 14, 1817; Amy, born Feb. 5, 1818; Frances, born March 13, 1821, is now deceased; Caroline, born Sept. 15, 1826, died in Washington, D. C. Mr. and Mrs. Miller died in the Wyoming Valley in 1840 and 1877 respectively.

Mr. and Mrs. Mulford were married in Delaware County, Ohio, April 30, 1840. They afterward removed to Morrow County, the same State, and in 1855 resolved to seek the country beyond the Mississippi. They accordingly started out with teams and journeyed across the States of Indiana and Illinois, fording creeks, and making their way laboriously over rough and uncertain roads. After crossing the Father of Waters they came into Wapello County, and located in Green Township, on section 3, southwest of the present site of Ottumwa. Mr. M. purchased 160 acres of land, to which he subsequently added and laid the foundations for the fine farm estate which became one of the attractive spots in the landscape of this section. His purchase consisted mainly of timber, and the clearing of this involved months and years of incessant industry. Ottumwa, now a city of 12,000 inhabitants, was then but a small village, and in the exchange which they received for their produce, there was but a small amount of hard cash. They were made of that stuff, however, which was not easily dismayed, and, in common with their brother settlers, had no thought of turning back or abandoning their first purpose of establishing a home beyond the Mississippi. In due time they received the reward of their labors in the picture of smiling fields and growing grain around them.

Of the union of Mr. and Mrs. M. there were born seven children, four of whom are living, as follows: Harvey Webb, born in Delaware County, Ohio, April 2, 1845, during the late Civil War enlisted in Co. D, 17th Iowa Vol. Inf., on the 21st of March, 1862. He proceeded with his regiment to the scene of conflict, and at the battle of Champion Hills, which occurred on the 16th of May, 1863, was mortally wounded, conveyed to the hospital, and died six days later; Frances, born March 25, 1843, died in Ohio, April 17, 1848; Sarah H., born Dec. 10, 1845, is the wife of Samuel Holloway, of Plattsmouth, Neb.; Florence, born Sept. 26, 1848, died October 11 of the same year; Exira born Dec. 24, 1849, is the wife of John Prosser, of Wapello County; William DeBoise, born May 9, 1853, is a resident of Seward, Neb.; Charles E., born Feb. 28, 1856, in Wapello County, is still a resident here.

Lewis Mulford departed this life Feb. 7, 1873, at the age of sixty-one years. He was a sincere Christian and a devoted member of the Methodist Episcopal Church, honorable and upright in his dealings with his fellow-men, and possessed of admirable traits of character. He contributed liberally and cheerfully to the support of his church, of which he was Steward, both in Ohio and after he came to this county. He was Republican in politics, and a staunch supporter of the Union cause, and although the loss of his son was a most terrible affliction to both himself and wife, Mr. M. felt that he had accomplished his whole duty by this sacrifice of his affection. This son, Harvey W., had been married and left one son, who was reared by his grandmother, Mrs. M., and bears the name of Walter Cook Mulford. The maiden name of his mother was Sarah Michaels.

VACTOR PRATT, a successful agriculturist of Highland Township, was born in Boone County, Ky., in 1817, and is the son of Artemus and Nancy (Parker) Pratt, natives respectively of New York and Virginia, the former being of Scotch-Irish descent and the latter descended from the English.

The subject of our history removed with his parents from his native State to Indiana, where he lived until 1871. He then crossed the Mississippi and coming into Wapello County, settled in Highland Township, which has been his home since that time. He was married in 1843, to Miss Valeria Baldwin, a native of Indiana and the daughter of

David Baldwin, who, by her union with our subject, became the mother of seven children, briefly recorded as follows: Oliver C. served in the Union army a few months and died in 1871, at the age of twenty-four years; Lydia A. is the wife of J. M. Elder, of Highland Township; George R., of Creston, Iowa, is engaged in railroading; Albert is a cattle-breeder of Montana; Alice, a twin, died in 1882, at the age of twenty-seven years; Rebecca J. is the wife of Newton Baker, of Competine Township; Henry H. is at home.

The father of our subject died when the latter was an infant of thirteen months old; his mother survived her husband nearly sixteen years. After the death of his mother, Mr. Pratt learned the trade of a stone-cutter at Greensburg, Ind., and was thus occupied for a number of years, and until the time of coming to Iowa. He is an energetic and enterprising citizen, the friend of morality and sobriety, and takes an intelligent interest in everything pertaining to the welfare of his county and community. Politically he is a Republican and uniformly votes in support of the principles of his party.

DAVID H. EMERY. Among the professional men of Ottumwa who have attained prominence in the practice of their profession is David H. Emery, now residing in this city. Mr. Emery was born in Fulton County, Ill., Dec. 4, 1837, and is the son of F. W. and Hannah (Gaffney) Emery, natives of Pennsylvania, who emigrated to Illinois in 1833. In the spring of 1838 F. W. Emery removed to Stark County, Ill., and there engaged in farming. He was a gentleman of considerable prominence and popularity, and held several offices within the gift of the people. He was well read and possessed of more than ordinary ability, and won the respect of those with whom he came in contact by his integrity and straightforward and manly dealings with his fellowmen.

The parental family included four sons and one daughter: Amanda J. became the wife of Samuel Pritchard, a resident of Woodland, Ill.; Oliver P. is living at Galva, that State, where he is engaged in the insurance business, and has held the office of Justice of the Peace for many years, having been admitted to the bar in Charles City, Iowa, in 1862; David H. is the subject of this notice; John G. is a well-to-do farmer of Knox County, Ill.; William E. was a soldier in the 42d Illinois Infantry and participated in all the battles in which his regiment engaged up to the battle of Stone River, where he fell mortally wounded. The father of our subject departed this life in 1846, and his widow married her brother-in-law, Henry Emery, in 1859. He died in 1878, and Mrs. Emery departed this life in 1884, aged seventy years; she was a member of the Christian Church.

The subject of this notice was brought up to the calling of a farmer, and received his education in the common schools, supplementing the same by an attendance of two terms at Abingdon College, after which he performed the duties of a pedagogue for some time. Mr. Emery commenced the study of law at Toulon, Stark Co., Ill., in the spring of 1859, in the office of Hon. Martin Shellenbarger, and remained under his instruction for eighteen months. He then went to Montezuma, Iowa, where he entered the office of the late Hon. M. E. Cutts of that place, who has held the office of Attorney-General, Member of Congress, and other prominent positions, and received instruction from him.

In February, 1861, our subject was admitted to the bar at Montezuma, Iowa, with the privilege of practicing in all the courts of the State. He did not, nevertheless, immediately enter upon the practice of his profession, for the following August he enlisted in Co. F, 10th Iowa Vol. Inf., which he and Capt. Head had been instrumental in raising. Mr. Emery was commissioned First Lieutenant by Gov. Kirkwood, and Albert Head, Captain. In the winter of 1861 his company was sent to Cape Girardeau and from there to Bird's Point. They participated in the campaign against Island No. 10, and were then in the bloody battle of Ft. Pillow, after which they were ordered back, and arriving at Shiloh soon after that battle, they engaged in the advance on Corinth. While near Corinth, and prior to his being permitted to participate in the battle, our subject was sent home on a recruit-

ing expedition. He remained there until the spring of 1863, when he returned to his regiment, arriving in time to fight under the gallant old silent soldier at the battle of Jackson and Champion Hills. After this he participated in the siege and capture of Vicksburg. He then went to Chattanooga, Tenn., by way of Memphis, where he participated in the battle of Mission Ridge, and was there shot through the thigh by a minie ball from the gun of the enemy. After confinement in the hospital for twenty days he was sent to Keokuk, and after treatment for a while returned to the army and received an honorable discharge Sept. 28, 1864.

On returning from the war, our subject located at Montezuma, Iowa, and entered upon the practice of his profession. In 1865 he was elected on the Republican ticket to the House of Representatives. In 1870 he moved to Ottumwa, where he at once began the practice of law, and where he has continued to reside until the present, meeting with success in his practice.

Mr. Emery was married in Oskaloosa, Iowa, May 23, 1867, to Miss Sarah C., daughter of Rev. B. Holland, a minister of the Methodist Episcopal Church. She was born in Lee County, Iowa, Sept. 15, 1846, and their union has been productive of the birth of seven children—Roscoe, Wilbur, Edwin H., Herbert, Alice A., Irving and Clara. Both our subject and wife are members of the First Methodist Episcopal Church of Ottumwa.

MAJ. S. K. CRAMER, a well-to-do farmer and stock-grower, and a gentleman whose life has been passed in agricultural pursuits, is pleasantly located on his exceedingly fine place on section 24, Agency Township. Mr. Cramer was born in Somerset County, Pa., Aug. 31, 1818, and is a son of Samuel and Rebecca (King) Cramer. Samuel Cramer, Sr., was born in York County, Pa., Nov. 12, 1777, and was of German ancestry. He was a Captain in the War of 1812, and a brave and noble officer. He was also a gentleman of more than ordinary popularity in any and all communities in which he lived, and held the offices of County Treasurer and Collector of this county. He was married in 1798, to Rebecca King, of Somerset County, Pa. She was the daughter of Michael King, a Methodist minister of considerable prominence, and of English ancestry. The Cramers were of German lineage. The union of Samuel Cramer, Sr., with Miss King, was blest by the birth of eleven children, our subject being the tenth. The remaining children are Eliza, John S., Mary A., Joseph, Hester A., James, Martha, David P., Henry and Michael, all of whom are deceased except John S. and David P.

Our subject was married to Miss Hulda Frantz, March 22, 1843. She was born in Alleghany County, Md., March 23, 1823, and was the daughter of John and Catherine Frantz. Of this union nine children were born: Leonidas B., Jan. 22, 1847; Licurgus L., Dec. 10, 1850; Kate L., April 18, 1854; Brutus F., April 30, 1856; Augustus C., Feb. 10, 1858; Americus V., April 10, 1860; Cincinnatus C., March 12, 1862; Minnie D., Oct. 12, 1865; Dora F., Oct. 11, 1868. Americus V. met his death by being thrown from a spirited horse, while returning from a Sunday-shool picnic. He lay unconscious for three days, and expired Sept. 10, 1877, aged seventeen years and five months. Mrs. Huldah Cramer remained the faithful and loving wife of our subject until called to that better home, July 31, 1878. April 29, 1880, Mr. Cramer was again married, Mrs. N. E. Macky, widow of J. D. Macky, being the other contracting party. She is the daughter of Solomon Frantz, and was born in Alleghany County, Md., March 5, 1840. Her father was of German and her mother of Irish ancestry. Mrs. Cramer had three children by her former husband: Lucy M., William H., who died in infancy, and Jennie D.

The subject of this notice was a volunteer in the 7th Regiment of the Canal Guards, which was uniformed and armed by the Government for the purpose of going into actual service against Great Britain, on the disputed boundary of the State of Maine. Mr. Cramer was chosen and elected Major of the 7th Pennsylvania Regiment; prior to this he was Orderly Sergeant of Company C for four years. He was commissioned Major by Gov. Porter, of Pennsylvania, and served nearly four years, resigning his position on account of removal from the State of Pennsylvania to Iowa. This latter event took place in 1844, and since that time our subject has continued to remain a resident of Wapello County. He is a gentleman of great popularity, and has been elected to the State Legislature from this county, serving two terms. He was also nominated for a third term, but declined to serve. He has also held the office as President of the Wapello Agricultural Society.

Mr. Cramer is the owner of 600 acres of good land, on which he has a fine brick dwelling, second to none in the county. He also has four barns on his place, and other necessary improvements, and has met with success in the prosecution of his vocation. He and his wife are members of the Methodist Episcopal Church, and in politics Mr. Cramer is a Republican.

D W. GRAVES, of Ottumwa, is one of the honored pioneers of Wapello County, having crossed the Mississippi and come into Iowa in 1851. He is a native of Franklin County, Mass., and was born in 1807. He received careful parental training, pursued his primary studies in the public schools of his native State, and remained with his parents until he attained the age of manhood. He was united in marriage with Miss Roxana D. Fuller, a native of the same State, and his junior by nine years, her birth occurring in 1816. They afterward removed to Connecticut, where they remained until coming West. After reaching Wapello County they located in Ottumwa, where Mr. Graves, having previously learned the trade of a woolen manufacturer, took charge of the woolen-mills of Hammond & Bowen, with whom he remained for several years. In the meantime he met with a serious accident, which resulted in the loss of his arm, it having been caught in the machinery and torn off. After he abandoned his position with this firm he purchased a tract of land in Wapello County, and engaged in farming.

The family of Mr. and Mrs. Graves consisted of five children, one of whom died in infancy. The eldest son, H. H., is the senior partner of Graves Bros., of Ottumwa, who are engaged in the manufacture of cigars. He was born in Berkshire County, Mass., Aug. 5, 1840, and was eleven years old when his parents came to Iowa. At the first three-years' call for troops to defend the Union he enlisted in Co. K, 2d Iowa Vol. Inf., and after participating in the battle of Ft. Donelson was discharged from the service on account of disability. The firm of which he is at present a member was established in 1886. The other children are Sarah E., the wife of H. W. Briggs, who resides at Findlay, Ohio; F. J., connected with the firm of Graves Bros., and Emma J., the wife of D. F. Morey, of Ottumwa.

Our esteemed subject and his wife have lived together in peace and harmony for a period of fifty years, and present in their lives a striking example of the noble results of high morality and integrity. Mrs. G. is a member in good standing of the Congregational Church, and our subject is a strong temperance advocate, being an active worker in the cause in this locality. In politics he is a staunch Republican, and has kept himself well posted on matters of general interest. He occupies a high position in his adopted county as embodying all that constitutes an honest man and a good citizen.

MISS ALICE M. STARK, M. D., a practicing physician of Ottumwa, is a lady of fine abilities, well read in her profession, and has built up for herself in this vicinity a large and increasing patronage. She is a native of Ypsilanti, Mich., where she was reared and received her early education. She afterward entered the State Normal School near her home, where she graduated, and afterward was engaged as a teacher for several years, her father being opposed to her studying medicine. She finally, however, yielded to her own inclinations and entered upon a course of study in the office of Miss Ruth Gerry. In 1876 she entered the Medical Department of the State University, at Ann Arbor, and pursued her studies there until 1878. She then went to Boston, Mass., and spent six months in the hospital for women and children, afterward returning to Ann Arbor, and graduating in the class of 1879. During that year she came to Iowa, and entered upon the practice of her profession in Ottumwa, with remarkable success from the start. She now has more business than she can conveniently attend to, frequently being obliged to send patients elsewhere for the lack of time to give them proper attention.

Dr. Stark is a close student, a lady of more than ordinary ability, and deserves great credit for the position which she now occupies, being the result of a love of learning and persevering industry. She stands high in her profession in this locality, and has been admitted to membership in the county and Des Moines Valley Medical and State Societies. She is also a member of the American Medical Association, and has been intrusted with important offices in most of these.

Miss Stark came to Ottumwa a perfect stranger, and secured the confidence of the people of this locality simply upon her own merits. Her parents were John B. and Harriet (Aber) Stark, both natives of New York. They were greatly respected in the community where they resided, and her father during the greater part of his life, was engaged in farming pursuits. Mrs. Harriet Stark, the mother of our subject, departed this life at her home in Michigan, in 1883. Her father is still living.

JOSEPH LEIGHTON, deceased. Among the pioneers of 1843 was the subject of this sketch, a man who made his impress upon the time in which he lived, and who was well known to every citizen of Wapello County. He was a native of Maine, born in Harmony, Jan. 10, 1810. His early life was spent among the hills of his native State, and doubtless their rugged nature was impressed upon his life. At least this is common among the people of every nation and clime, their surroundings having much to do with their character in life. The educational advantages enjoyed were those of the common schools of that early day, but an active and observing life tended to give him a practical knowledge, which is even better than that taught in books. Before reaching his majority, he learned the trade of a carpenter, which occupation he followed for some years. In 1837 he turned his face toward the setting sun, with the hope that has actuated many young men before him, and which will doubtless control many more—that of bettering himself in life. Arriving in Manchester, Ill., he at once engaged at his trade, contracting and building a number of residences in that place and vicinity.

March 1, 1838, Mr. Leighton was united in marriage with Mary L. Coe, of Manchester, a native of Greene County, Ill., born June 25, 1821. Of this union there were six children: Alvin C., born June 2, 1839, is now engaged in the real-estate business in Ottumwa; Ann, born in 1842, died in 1846; James, born in November, 1844, died Dec. 15, 1882; Joseph, born Feb. 1, 1848, is now engaged in the banking business at Miles City, M. T.; Mary, born Oct. 9, 1851; Abbie, Aug. 25, 1854.

The Territory of Iowa having been thrown open to emigration, Mr. Leighton decided to make that his home, and in 1841 he moved to Des Moines County and located in Dodgeville. But the location was only temporary. There was territory still farther West yet in possession of the Indians, but which it was hoped would soon be secured for settlement by the whites. With many others he had his eye fixed on the beautiful land, and when the treaty was made in October, 1842, by the Indians, by which they ceded much territory to the General Government, agreeing to give possession May 1, 1843, he was ready to enter in and take possession. On that day he staked a claim in what is now Competine Township, and at once erected a log cabin fourteen feet square, in which he moved his family and commenced the improvement of his farm.

The selection of a farm being made, its improvement was not such an easy matter. Like thousands of others it took his all to get the promised land, and when here, there was no market for produce, and yet it was necessary that a living should be made for himself and family. During the winter following he assisted in building Mulk's Mill, at Bonaparte, Van Buren County. While engaged in this work he walked to and from his home each week, with his pack upon his back, as he had no means of conveyance. But the work was a blessing to him, as what he secured for his services enabled him to provide for his family. During the winter he set traps for prairie chickens, and was successful in capturing all they desired for their use. In this manner he managed to care for those he loved during the first few years of life in Wapello County.

Being of a jovial disposition, it was easy for him to make friends, and in 1846 he was nominated and elected to the office of Treasurer and Recorder of the county, being the first in this county. On his election he moved to Ottumwa, and lived for about two years in a little log cabin where the First Methodist Episcopal Church now stands. He then moved into a more pretentious house on Main street, a small brick building which yet stands, being used as a laundry. On the expiration of his term of office, he was re-elected and served a second term. Shortly after retiring from office he formed a partnership with Dr. C. C. Warden in the dry-goods and grocery trade at Ottumwa. The firm operated a branch store at Blakesburg, this county. The partnership continued about one year, being then dissolved, Dr. Warden taking the Ottumwa store, and Mr. Leighton that in Blakesburg. This business he continued only till the fall of 1853, when he sold out, and entered upon the discharge of the duties of Justice of the Peace at Ottumwa, to which office he was then elected.

Soon after coming to Ottumwa, Mr. Leighton purchased a number of town lots, which proved a valuable investment, the rise in value after the building of the B. & M., now the C., B. & Q. R. R., being so great as to make him a comfortable fortune. But this he was not permitted long to enjoy, death claiming him for his own, June 26, 1858. His widow yet survives him, and is living at Ottumwa, where she enjoys the love and respect of all who know her.

In the death of Joseph Leighton, Ottumwa lost a valuable citizen, a man who was ever ready to do his utmost to further its interests; the wife and children, a loving husband and kind father. His many excellent traits of character endeared him to a host of friends, who, with the family, join in mourning his untimely death, while yet in the prime of life.

WILLIAM H. CRIPS has been an honored resident of Wapello County since 1849, and during a period of nearly forty years has witnessed with interest and satisfaction the remarkable changes which have been going on in the Hawkeye State. He also, in common with his brother pioneers of that period who came to Iowa while it was still new, contributed his quota to the general advancement of civilization by opening up his farm, encouraging industry and economy, and by setting a good example of sobriety and morality to the rising generation around him.

The subject of this history is a native of Ross County, Ohio, and born May 12, 1818. He is the son of Henry and Mary (Clouser) Crips, natives of Pennsylvania, who removed from their native State in 1816, soon after their marriage, and joined the pioneer settlers of Ross County, Ohio. There their son William was reared to manhood, received a fair education in the subscription schools, and was trained to farming pursuits. April 27, 1843, he was married to Miss Martha A., daughter of Enos Jones, a native of Virginia. Mrs. C. was born in the same county as her husband, and after their marriage they emigrated to Iowa and settled in Green Township, Wapello County, upon a tract of land on section 1, which constitutes the present homestead. The section where they located has since been attached to Center Township. It consists of ninety-eight acres, and from its original condition Mr. Crips has brought it to that of a finely cultivated estate, producing all the cereals and vegetables known to this section of country.

Prior to his marriage Mr. Crips had given much attention to music, having great love for the art and no small degree of talent. He perfected himself as a performer on the violincello under the instruction of Prof. T. B. Mason, of Cincinnati, Ohio, and for two months thereafter was engaged as a teacher of both vocal and instrumental music. His

a honored
nce 1849,
orty years
on the re-
on in the
with his

ota to the
opening up
nomy, and

Crips, ma-
a their ma-
rriage, and

manhood,
ubscription
; pursuits.
Martha A.,
f Virginia.
e her hus-
nigrated to
, Wapello

given much

der the in-

music. His

S. E. O'Neill. M. D.

residence in Cincinnati was during the period of the Harrison campaign, and he remembers seeing that popular General riding through the streets of the city.

Mr. and Mrs. Crips became the parents of ten children, as follows: James Henry, who died when two years old; Mary Hannah became the wife of L. P. Michael, of Ottumwa; William S. is engaged in the livery business in Ottumwa; Harlin P. is also in the same city; Enos J. is a locomotive engineer, having his residence at Creston, Iowa; Joseph Edward died in the city of Ottumwa at the age of twenty-nine years; Alice became the wife of George Z. Cowan, a farmer of Center Township; Simon P. is engaged in the livery business, at Ottumwa, with his brother; John O. is operating a lunch counter at Chariton, Iowa; Edgar W. is living in Ottumwa.

Mr. and Mrs. C. are connected with the Congregational Church, and in the Sunday-school our subject has been an active worker in this township for a number of years. He is recognized as an able, efficient laborer in this important part of the Lord's work. He is a strong temperance man, Republican in politics, and an energetic supporter of every measure calculated to promote sobriety, morality and religion.

Henry Crips, the father of our subject, after a useful and busy life, in 1868 ended his earthly labors, in Ross County, Ohio, at the advanced age of eighty-one years; the mother survived her husband and died in the same place when eighty-seven years of age. They were both devout Christians and prominently connected with the Presbyterian Church. It affords the publishers of this ALBUM pleasure to present the portrait of so upright and honorable a citizen as one of the representative men of Wapello County.

SALISBURY EUGENE O'NEILL, M. D., one of the leading medical practitioners of Ottumwa, was born near Chambersburg, Franklin Co., Pa., Sept. 29, 1836, and is a son of Charles O'Neill, who was born on the Emerald Isle. Charles O'Neill emigrated to the United States when twenty-four years of age, and located in the Cumberland Valley, Pa. There he married Miss Elizabeth Shormann, who was born in Adams County, that State. Their union was blest by the birth of seven children, five of whom are living at the present writing: Mary C. is the widow of Jacob Yost, and is living in the beautiful city of Dayton, Ohio; Elizabeth was united in marriage with John Albright, of Kokomo, Ind.; S. E. is the subject of this notice; William S. resides at Dayton, Ohio, where he is engaged in the mercantile business; Jennie became the wife of Dr. Samuel Souders. The father of our subject was well posted in the affairs of county, State and nation, and became somewhat prominent for his forensic effort in debate. He died in 1846, and his wife survived him until 1873, when she passed to meet him on the other shore. They were both members of the Catholic Church.

The subject of this notice was reared to manhood in his native county. He was orphaned by the death of his father when ten years of age, and his mother being left with a large family on her hands, young O'Neill was obliged to work out to aid in the maintenance of the family. This he did for seven months, at a remuneration of $13.50, being less than $2 per month. Returning home, during the winter, he worked for his board and attended the district schools, and later supplemented his education by a course of study at Fayette Academy. Thus growing up into manhood and passing on in the rugged school of experience, he was prepared to meet every emergency with a steady and ready hand. We soon find him employed as a teacher in the district schools. He performed the duties of a pedagogue for three years. It is obvious that the Doctor himself must have fully availed himself of all privileges of instruction to which he found access, and a distinguishing characteristic of his is the possession of quickness of mind and talent. While teaching he had access to the library of Dr. George W. Smith, of Green Village, and afterward read medicine under the instruction of Dr. J. C. Richards, who was his firm friend, and did much to advance him in his professional studies. In 1863–64 our subject attended lectures at Jefferson Medical College, Philadelphia, after which he engaged in practicing, and continued in the same until 1871. In 1872 he went to Bellevue Hospital Medical College, where he received his degree.

In 1872 Dr. O'Neill went to Clinton County, Mo., and locating at Lathrop entered upon the practice of his profession. Continuing at Lathrop until 1876, during which time he had met with success, he moved to Carrollton, Carroll Co., Mo., and in the spring of 1879 came to this State and located at Ottumwa, where he has since been actively engaged in the practice of his profession. The Doctor is a member of the Des Moines Valley Medical Society, the Wapello County Medical Society and the American Medical Association. He stands high in the scale of professional integrity, and has had many honors conferred upon him by his professional brethren, of which he is justly proud. He is a favorite among the members of the Democratic party, and is Chairman of the Democratic County Central Committee.

Dr. O'Neill was married in Franklin County, Pa., in 1860, to Miss Maria Baney, a native of that county. Their union was blest by the birth of two children—Harry E. and Myrtie L. Mrs. O'Neill died in 1875, and in 1877 the Doctor formed a second marriage, Miss Mary Quirk, a native of Illinois, becoming his wife. Of this latter union two children, Ralph and Marguerita, have been born.

It is with pleasure that we give, accompanying this sketch, a portrait of Dr. O'Neill.

SAMUEL S. NORRIS, deceased, was one of the early pioneers of Wapello County, to which he came in 1845, and by his goodly life and high moral character, replete with benevolence, kindness and charity, won for himself a high place in the estimation of his fellow-citizens. Mr. Norris was a native of the Old Granite State, having been born in the town of Sandwich, N. H., about 1777. His father, Samuel Norris, was a soldier of the Revolutionary War, in which he served for a period of eight years, or during the struggle of the colonies for independence. The family were descendants of stanch Scotch and Irish ancestry, and represented in this country by three brothers who came over and made settlement, one in Sandwich, N. H., one in New York State, and one in Norristown, Pa., the latter being the progenitor of those who originated the large locomotive foundry.

The subject of our sketch was reared in his native State, and when he arrived at the age of manhood was united in marriage with Miss Anna M. Bean, a native of his own State, their wedding taking place about 1800. They subsequently removed to Canada at the time of the rebellion of 1836, where he lost his property, returning to his native State in the fall of the same year. He then resolved to seek another locality, and turned his steps southwestward toward the prairies of Illinois. From there, in 1845, he crossed the Father of Waters and, coming into Wapello County, Iowa, located in Ottumwa. The trip was made with teams, and they crossed the Mississippi at Burlington, whence they proceeded to Fairfield and Agency City before coming to this vicinity. Here our subject followed his trade of shoe-making, and established the first shop of the kind in Ottumwa, also making the first pair of boots manufactured in this city.

From the time of his coming here Mr. Norris gained the good-will of his associates, which in the course of time ripened into the profoundest esteem and respect. He was an uncompromising Abolitionist, and his house was one of the stations of the "Underground Railroad," and in the course of time suffered mob violence, but he was firm in his convictions of right and courageous in carrying out what he solemnly believed to be his duty, and, notwithstanding the machinations of hate and opposition, many a poor slave was rescued from bondage and his temporary wants provided for by Mr. Norris and his family. Had he lived until the present day he would feel amply repaid for all he had suffered in the cause of human freedom. But he passed from earthly scenes while the question was still under deep agitation, having folded his hands for his final rest in 1859.

Mr. Norris, after coming to this vicinity, thoroughly identified himself with the interests of his adopted State and county. He was the friend and encourager of morality, education and religion, and actively assisted in the organization of the first Congregational Church in the county, the six members of which it was then composed holding their meetings at his house. They were S. S. and Maria Norris, Julia Noris, Bela White, Sarah Burgess and Ann N. Norris. Mr. Norris was elected the first Deacon, and ever afterward contributed liberally of his time and means for its maintenance and support.

Mr. and Mrs. Norris became the parents of nine children, five of whom died before arriving at mature years. The four who lived to be adults were as follows: James W., whose sketch appears on another page of this volume; Ann N., the wife of Rev. Benjamin F. Spaulding, deceased, who was first Pastor of the Congregational Church of Ottumwa, and a graduate of Andover College, Mass.; Julia M., the wife of Col. Samuel S. Summers, of Ottumwa, who died in this city, and George P., a brief history of whose life will be found elsewhere in this volume. Mrs. Norris survived the death of her husband five years, dying in 1864, after having made a good record as a true-hearted and amiable Christian lady, and one well fitted to be the companion of such a man as Samuel S. Norris.

JOHN F. HARLAN, of Polk Township, owns and occupies a comfortable farm homestead on section 36, and is successfully engaged in agriculture and stock-raising. He has been a resident of the Hawkeye State for thirty-nine years, and has generously identified himself with the interests of his county and community, contributing as opportunity affords to its general welfare and prosperity. He presents the example of an industrious, enterprising and energetic farmer and business man, and is highly respected by his neighbors and fellow-citizens.

Mr. Harlan was born in Fayette County, Ind., Feb. 11, 1819, and is the son of Aaron and Julia (Jackson) Harlan, natives of South Carolina, who were born the same year, 1793, and after their marriage removed to Fayette County, Ind., whence, in 1821, they removed to Parke County. There our subject lived with his parents until he had attained his majority. He assisted his father to clear and improve their farm of 100 acres in the latter county, the family having been among the early settlers, and locating there when the country was practically a wilderness, and when its population consisted of but six families within the boundaries of Parke County, so far as they knew. The younger brother of our subject was the first white child born in this latter county. The household circle included seven children, three of whom died in infancy, one in later years, and three sons lived to manhood and reared families of their own.

John F. Harlan is now the only living member of his father's family. Aaron Harlan died in 1853, at the age of sixty years and seventeen days; his wife, the mother of our subject, departed this life seven years later, Feb. 17, 1860, at the age of sixty-six years. They were deeply religious people, and the father officiated as a Baptist minister, preaching for a period of thirty years, without money and without price. Both parents are buried in the family cemetery of Green Township, Parke Co., Ind.

On the 5th of March, 1840, the subject of our sketch was united in marriage with Miss Ann Edgman, in Parke County, Ind. Mrs. H. was born in Tennessee, June 25, 1820, and is the daughter of Braxton and Sarah (Deathridge) Edgman, the father a native of Tennessee and the mother of North Carolina. In 1849 Mr. and Mrs. Harlan removed westward and came to Iowa, purchasing 114 acres of land in Polk and Adams Townships, this county, and set about the establishment of a permanent home. Our subject was prospered in his farming and business operations and added to his original purchase as time passed on until he became the possessor, at one time, of 660 acres, 520 of which he divided among his children, who were ten in number, four sons and six daughters. The record is as follows: Sarah, born Dec. 21, 1840, is the wife of William Draper, a farmer of Adams Township; Ulysses, born April 24, 1842, is carrying on farming in Polk Township; Sareptha was born July 6, 1845; Julia, born Jan. 15, 1847, became the wife of W. L. Colvin, a farmer of Gage County, Neb.; Mary, born Dec. 11, 1848, died at the age of eighteen years, and George, born April 11, 1851, at seven years; Jane, born Sept. 13, 1853, married Mr. O. P. Ralston, a farmer of Gage County, Neb.; Martha, born July 7, 1856, is deceased; Aaron, born Nov. 9, 1858, is farming in Polk Township, and Joseph, March 30, 1860, in Adams Township.

Mrs. Harlan is connected with the Baptist Church, of which her honored parents were members during a greater part of their lifetime. Her father died in Shelby County, Ky., where his remains were interred. Subsequently the mother came to Iowa and made her home with our subject and his wife, where she departed this life Nov. 3, 1873, at the advanced age of eighty-five years, and her remains were laid to rest in Polk Township.

Since coming to this locality Mr. Harlan has been prominently connected with its welfare and prosperity, and has fully established himself in the confidence and esteem of his fellow-citizens. He started out in life with no capital but his own strong hands and energy of purpose, and has climbed up the ladder step by step until he now occupies an enviable position among the worthy men of the Hawkeye State. He has been upright and honorable in his business transactions, industrious and economical, wise in his expenditures, and is now enjoying the fruits of his early toil and self-denial in a handsome competency. In his earliest efforts to attain a worthy position in life he has been seconded by his excellent and amiable partner, the wife of his youth and the mother of his children, who stood by him through all his difficulties and rejoiced with him in his prosperity. During the years that are gone Mrs. Harlan was fully as industrious and self-sacrificing as her husband. In addition to the ordinary duties of a large household she spun and wove all the clothing which they wore until her children were grown to mature years, and in all other respects performed fully the duties of a faithful wife and affectionate mother. The surviving children of this excellent and worthy couple are now all established in homes of their own, and by their creditable lives are living out the principles which were instilled in them during their childhood years and which have constituted them worthy citizens and honored members of the community.

Mr. Harlan has held the various offices of his township, and in 1867 was elected a member of the Board of Supervisors, which office he filled in a creditable and satisfactory manner for four years, and he has often been called upon as a counselor in matters of importance connected with the welfare of his township and community. Politically Mr. H. is a stanch Democrat of the Jackson type, and uniformly casts his vote in support of the principles which he believes to be the true foundation stone of law and good order. He has been the encourager and supporter of education, morality and sobriety, and all the worthy enterprises of his locality have found in him a stanch and substantial friend.

WILLIAM H. LEWIS, a highly esteemed citizen of Ottumwa, is a gentleman of fine abilities, well read and intelligent, and occupies a prominent position among the better class of citizens of this locality. He has been a resident of Ottumwa since 1857, first occupying himself at his trade of plastering, and subsequently became a successful contractor, which business he followed until the spring of 1876. He then moved upon a farm in Center Township, and followed agricultural pursuits until 1882, when he returned to Ottumwa and was elected to the office of Justice of the Peace. The duties of this position he fulfilled with great credit to himself and satisfaction to his constituents; he is now retired.

The subject of this history was born in the little city of Urbana, Champaign Co., Ohio, Aug. 30, 1832. He is the son of William and Ruth (Pearce) Lewis, and his father was a native of Kentucky, in which State he was born on the 15th of May, 1810; the mother was a native of Ohio. The parental household included six children, who are recorded as follows: William H., our subject, was the eldest born; Sarah Elizabeth, now Mrs. John Fisher; Louisa is deceased; Theophilus enlisted as a soldier in the late war and was killed in battle near Oldtown, Miss., in 1862; George died in infancy; Clara died in California about 1877. When our subject was about thirteen years of age his father removed into Illinois, and there the mother's decease occurred in 1845.

When he had arrived at the age of fifteen years young Lewis was apprenticed to the trade of a plasterer in Peoria, Ill., where he remained four years. He then went to the rapidly growing town of Pekin, where he was at once busily engaged at his trade, and the father received the contract in his department for some of the largest buildings then in process of construction. On the 10th of September, 1857, in Kappa, Ill., he was united in wedlock with Miss Mary A. Jones, and soon afterward removed to Ottumwa, Iowa. Mrs. L. is the daughter of Charles, Jr., and Mary (Vining) Jones, natives of Massachusetts. She was born in November, 1840, and by her union with our subject became the mother of five children, as follows: Josephine L. was born Nov. 14, 1858; Jennie A., Oct. 13, 1862; Walter A., Oct. 19, 1864; Clara A., Feb. 11, 1867, and Arthur, Aug. 12, 1875.

Mr. Lewis has given his children the advantages of a liberal education, and his daughter, Miss Clara, is an artist of considerable merit, and has painted a portrait of her father which does great credit to her skill and genius. The family residence is pleasantly located, and in all respects is indicative of the cultivated tastes and the education of its inmates. Mr. Lewis is an extensive reader, and is the encourager and supporter of education, temperance and morality. In politics he is a Republican, and socially belongs to the I. O. O. F. of Ottumwa.

SENECA BROWN THRALL, M. D. Among the medical practitioners of Ottumwa, who have attained to no small degree of prominence in the practice of their profession by their constant attention to their business, Dr. Thrall certainly deserves mention. What success he has attained has been due to close application as a student and also continual practice. He was born in Utica, Licking Co., Ohio, Aug. 9, 1832. The father of our subject, the late Prof. H. L. Thrall, of Kenyon College, Ohio, was well known throughout the West for his general scientific attainments as well as for his skill as a physician, having filled the chair of Chemistry and Geology in that institution from 1840 to 1852; the chair of Materia Medica and general Pathology in the Starling Medical College, Columbus, during the years 1855–56. The honorary degree of M. D. was conferred on him by the Medical Department of the University of New York, in 1844.

The subject of this notice passed through all the departments of Kenyon College, graduating A. B. in 1851, and A. M. in 1855. He commenced the study of medicine in 1849; attended a course of lectures at Starling Medical College, in 1851–52, and then at the University of New York, where he graduated M. D. in 1853. He had begun practice a year prior to his graduation, in company with his father, at Columbus, Ohio. In April, 1854, he removed to Belle Center, Logan County, that State, where he continued in active practice until November, 1855, when he returned to Columbus, and in May, 1856, came to this State and located at Ottumwa, where he is at present residing and enjoying a large and responsible practice. At the time of locating in Ottumwa it had a population of about 900 and there were fifteen nominal physicians candidates for practice. Now the population is 12,000, and there are thirty physicians, including all schools.

The Doctor is a member of the Wapello County Medical Society and was President of the same in 1871. He is also a member of the Iowa State Medical Society, and has been ever since 1856, being its Secretary in 1864, its President in 1869, and President *pro tem* in 1870. He was re-elected Secretary in 1873, and continued his own successor until 1877. The Doctor was a delegate to the American Medical Association held in San Francisco in 1871, and is an honorary member of the California State Medical Society. On a visit to the Pacific Coast he made short excursions to places of note and stopped at Salt Lake City on his return home. Our subject is likewise a member and ex-President of the Des Moines Valley Medical Association. For a period of fifteen years he was a member of the City School Board of Ottumwa. He has contributed some papers to medical literature and likewise some admirable addresses to the State and county medical societies, some of which are contained in their transactions. He also wrote a report of the epidemic of peritonitis which prevailed in Wapello County in 1876. In February, 1862, Dr. Thrall was appointed Surgeon in the Military Hospital at Keokuk. In November of that year he was commissioned Assistant Surgeon of the 13th Iowa Volunteers, and served with it, in the 17th Corps, until May, 1864. Returning from the war Dr. Thrall resumed his practice at Ottumwa, and has continued the same until the present time. He was married, in 1856, to Miss Mary Brooks, of Columbus, Ohio, and they have three children—Frank B., Nellie and Homer N.

LEWIS W. THORNBURG, residing on section 11, Center Township, is a grower of small fruit and vegetables, which he has pursued intelligently and industriously for many years. He is a native of Highland County, Ohio, born Oct. 26, 1820, and is a son of Joseph and Matilda (Higgins) Thornburg, the father a native of North Carolina and mother of Maryland. When Lewis W. was but seven years of age his parents moved from Ohio to Randolph County, Ind., where they remained until 1862, thence removing to Keosauqua, Van Buren Co., Iowa, where the mother died shortly after their arrival, and the father in about 1864.

The subject of this sketch was reared upon his father's farm, and remained at home until twenty years of age, when he came to what was then Iowa Territory, locating in Salem, Henry County, and worked at the cabinet-maker's trade. In 1840, just before coming to Iowa, he was united in marriage with Miss Matilda Jacobs, the daughter of Gabriel Jacobs, a native of Pennsylvania. To this union there were born two children—Cecelia and Joseph, both of whom are now deceased. The mother of these children died Sept. 22, 1842. In 1845 Mr. Thornburg contracted a second marriage, choosing as his bride Miss Martha Miller, a native of Ohio, and a daughter of Thomas Miller, of Clarke County, that State. Seven children blest this union: William and Millard, deceased; Thomas, now living at Ottumwa; Sarah, the wife of Joseph Bower, of Albia, Iowa; Alice, who married N. D. Hinsey, and is now deceased; Charles, living in Omaha, Neb.; Angie, living with her brother in Plattsmouth, Neb. Mrs. Martha Thornburg died Jan. 9, 1879.

Mr. Thornburg, on March 30, 1882, married Mrs. Ellen McPherson, the widow of Isaac McPherson, and a daughter of Dr. Galland, of Nashville, Iowa. She was born Jan. 3, 1830, and is believed to be the first white child born in the State of Iowa. She is remarkably well preserved, and it is a real pleasure to meet her; it is wonderful, considering the progress and development in the State that the first citizen could yet be found in her borders, looking so hale and hearty. Mr. Thornburg owns eleven acres of land, on which is one of the finest orchards in Wapello County. He is a member of the Methodist Episcopal Church and also of the I. O. O. F. Politically he is a Republican.

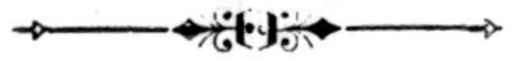

LEONIDAS M. GODLEY, a resident of Ottumwa, and one of the early settlers of Wapello County, is a native of Mason County, W. Va., and was born June 13, 1836. When he was a lad fourteen years old, in 1850, his parents emigrated to Jefferson County, Iowa, and since that time he has been a resident of this section. He is the son of Mahlon and Nancy (Newman) Godley, natives respectively of Virginia and Pennsylvania. After living in Jefferson County for a period of four years they came to Wapello County, settling in Ashland, where Mahlon Godley followed the trade of a carpenter. He had formerly been a cabinet-maker, but after coming into Iowa there was but little demand for anything in that line and consequently he worked at carpentering.

The parental household consisted of eight children, all of whom lived to mature years, as follows: Edward died in 1849; Walter N. served during the late war as a soldier in the 1st Kansas Cavalry, under Gen. Lyons. He was wounded at the battle of Wilson Creek by a ball which cut its way through the outer surface of the skull. Although the shock was severe he recovered in due time, and remained in the ranks until the close of the war.

After returning from the army he located in Sedgwick County, Kan., where he departed this life in January, 1879; Elizabeth C. is a resident of this county; Martha A. became the wife of James Marshall, and died in 1857; Milton L. enlisted in Co. E., 17th Iowa Vol. Inf., returned home safely from the war, and is now a resident of this county; Mary E. married John D. Boswell, and died in 1853; Virginia H. became the wife of C. F. Graves and died in 1860.

Mahlon Godley, the father of our subject, was a man of more than ordinary ability, of decided views and principles, and a stanch Jeffersonian Democrat. He was an extensive reader and kept himself well posted on State affairs. He was no office-seeker, but was always ready to aid in every enterprise pertaining to the welfare of his community and in supporting the principles of his party. He was the friend of education, and gave his children the best advantages which could be obtained in this locality. Both he and his wife were earnest and active members of the Methodist Episcopal Church, to the support of which they contributed of their means liberally and cheerfully, and at the same time spared no labor to promote its prosperity and growth. They were honorable and upright in their lives and transmitted to their children those principles which had always been the rule by which they lived. The father departed this life in 1879, and the mother in 1866.

L. M. Godley, our subject, received judicious training at the hands of his parents, and a fair education in the common schools. He was trained to habits of industry, and in 1858, removing from Iowa to Kansas, learned in the latter place the trade of a carpenter, being located at Paris, the county seat of Linn County. In the fall of that year a term of the United States Court was held there, when John Brown, Montgomery and other Free-State men were there at the time. Indictments were found against those parties in the United States Court for aiding in the liberation and escape of slaves, and Mr. G. was called upon to serve in a posse of 135 men, under command of the Sheriff of the county, to assist in the arrest of the offenders. There was a small fort on Little Sugar Creek to which they were marched and disbanded, it having been ascertained that John Brown and his party were in the fort. The barricade was unusually strong, and the Sheriff retired to the town without the desired prisoners. The rabble who were with Montgomery and Brown were unprincipled ruffians, who were ready to shoot everybody but their friends, and Mr. Godley was solicited to carry a dispatch to the Governor at Le Compton. He was a stranger in the country and the distance was seventy-five miles, but he undertook it, and after a cold, dreary ride on horseback, succeeded in fulfilling his mission. After returning he was met by some of the adherents of John Brown, who had ascertained the object of his journey, and was notified that he must leave that section of the country within ten days. Believing discretion to be the better part of valor he went down in Missouri, located in Syracuse, and engaged at his trade as a carpenter. He here became acquainted with the lady destined to share his joys and sorrows, Miss Julia A. Walker, to whom he was married in August, 1859. She was a native of Kentucky, and the daughter of William M. Walker, of the same State.

From Syracuse, Mo., Mr. Godley moved to Sedalia at about the time of the breaking out of the late Civil War. He enlisted in the 27th Missouri Infantry, and was sick at Sedalia during the siege of Lexington. After his term of service expired he returned to Wapello County, and upon his recovery enlisted again, in Co. E, 22d Iowa Vol. Inf. The regiment rendezvoused at Iowa City whence, after a short time, it was ordered to Port Gibson, and participated in the battle at that place, which was soon followed by the battles of Champion Hills, Black River Bridge, and the seige and capture of Vicksburg. At the last mentioned place, during the first assault upon the works Mr. G. was wounded between the knee and ankle by a ball which carried away a portion of the bone. His wound was very painful, and he lay down between the fire of the contending armies, but finding that his limb was bleeding profusely he raised up, and while trying to get his handkerchief to tie around his leg, he was shot in the right breast, the ball coming out at the shoulder-blade, and subsequently was shot through the same knee which had before been wounded. While sitting up the general charge had ceased, but many shots were fired at him before he resumed his recumbent position. He lay upon the field for three hours between the two lines. There was a small stream between him and the rebel lines, and while lying there he saw two of his comrades skulking down the stream. He called to them, but being in an exposed position, within hearing of the rebels, they did not dare to approach him, but procured a long pole and, reaching it out to him, pulled him into the river, from which he was enabled to get under the shade of a tree. There he lay until midnight, in company with twenty others who had also been disabled. He then made up his mind that he must get away from there that night or remain through the following day. A rebel picket was within call, and he asked him to remove him inside of their lines on a stretcher, which was done by a couple of "darkies." He was taken into what was called the Texas Legion, and a surgeon was called, who, after examining his wounds, informed him that he could do nothing for him before morning; otherwise he was very kindly treated by the Confederates.

The next morning our subject was carried out and laid into a hole beside the railroad bridge upon some leaves, and this arrangement served for a dissecting table. Two stout men were on hand for the purpose of holding him, and the surgeon gave him to understand that he had no chloroform and the limb would have to be removed without the use of an anæsthetic. The two stout men stood by to hold him, but he finally prevailed upon the surgeon to dispense with their services, and braced himself up for the amputation. His determination was equal to the emergency, and, after the limb was removed, the patient was placed on a lumber wagon in company with a sick rebel, and they started for town to be placed in a residence which had been converted into a hospital. It was a beautiful structure and afforded a striking illustration of the exigencies of war.

While on their journey thither they encountered a company of Union Sharpshooters, who gave them a warm reception and compelled the driver to put his team to the utmost speed. They rattled over the road at a lively rate and reached their destination in safety. After being comfortably located inside the hospital, the blue coats continued shelling the building, and the rebels with their disabled captive were forced to vacate. When it was discovered that they had a Union soldier in their charge Mr. G. was paroled and sent through the lines. After reaching the Union lines he was sent to St. Louis, and placed in Lawson Hospital, where he remained until his final discharge in September, 1863, after which he returned to his home in this county. After returning home the bone of his amputated leg began to decay, and he was obliged to have three inches more removed. It was a long time healing, and he justly deserves the pension which he receives from his Government.

After the close of his military career, the loss of his limb debarring him from further occupation at his trade, Mr. Godley turned his attention to business and political matters, and in 1864 was elected to the office of County Clerk, which he held by re-election for seven successive terms. He was appointed Revenue Agent in 1883, and the following year was appointed Deputy of the same office. He is a member of Cloutman Post No. 69, G. A. R., and belongs to the I. O. O. F. He passed all the chairs and has represented his Lodge in the Grand Lodge.

Mr. and Mrs. Godley are members of the Methodist Episcopal Church. They have become the parents of five children, viz.: Terasita, William G., Mattie A., Charles L. and Harry L. They occupy a handsome residence in Ottumwa, and are highly esteemed residents of this community. In politics Mr. Godley has been a Republican since 1860, and has always taken a prominent part in the councils of his party in this portion of the State.

S. A. FLAGLER, Superintendent of the Union Coal Mining Company of Ottumwa, is a native of Hudson, N. Y., and was born June 28, 1837. He is the son of William B. and Cornelia C. (Edmonds) Flagler, the latter being a sister of Judge Edmonds. In early life William B. Flagler was Sheriff of Columbia County, N. Y. He was a gentleman well posted in county, State and national affairs, and was very popular in

his community. For many years he was bookkeeper of the Leather Manufacturers' Bank of New York City. Subsequently he was clerk at Blackwell's Island for many years, and died there in 1855. His wife died at Ottumwa in September, 1885. She was a sincere Christian, holding fellowship with the Episcopal Church, and her entire life may be said to have been passed in the cause of the Master.

The parental family consisted of three sons and two daughters: Cornelia E., the wife of D. S. Davie, of Illinois, crossed the river of death Nov. 29, 1868, at Anna, Ill.; William Edmonds died Aug. 25, 1858, at Pulaski, Ill.; John Edmonds, who succeeded his father to his position on Blackwell's Island, spent thirty years of his life there, handling millions of money, and died of paralysis June 18, 1885; S. A., our subject, is the only surviving member of the family, Frances M. having died in childhood.

The subject of this notice was reared to manhood in the busy metropolis of New York. There he received his education and continued to reside until 1853, when he was apprenticed to learn the saddler's trade, which he followed for nine years. He then came West and located at Carbondale, Ill., and was a resident there for about ten years. In 1861 Mr. Flagler was appointed Deputy United States Marshall for the State of Illinois, with headquarters at Springfield, and continued to serve in that capacity until the close of the war. After the war Mr. Flagler went to Moberly, Mo., where he became Superintendent of the mines at that city, and was sent by that company to Ottumwa to take control of the Union Coal & Mining Company, which position he still holds.

Mr. Flagler was married at Anna, Ill., Oct. 24, 1858, to Miss Melvina D. Browne, a daughter of A. B. Browne, who was County Clerk of Massac County, Ill., for a period of twenty-five years. By this union they had two daughters and one son—Frances E., Carrie C. and William B. Socially Mr. Flagler is a member of the I. O. O. F., and has held all the offices of that order. He is also a member of the Patriarchal Circle, and is at present Supreme Oracle. During the years 1869–70 our subject was a member of the City Council of Carbondale, and during the year 1871 acted as Mayor of that city. In politics Mr. Flagler has been a Republican ever since the rebels first fired on Ft. Sumter.

JAMES NEYLON, of Ottumwa, Roadmaster of the C., B. & Q. R. R. at this point, is a native of County Clare, Ireland, and was born Dec. 6, 1842. He was reared in his native country and educated in the common schools, remaining with his parents until twenty-two years of age. He then left Ireland, and emigrating to America located in the city of Pittsburgh, Pa., where he was first employed as laborer on the Pittsburgh, Fort Wayne & Chicago Railroad, and was subsequently promoted to foreman of a gang of men. In May, 1868, he left the vicinity of the Smoky City and journeying west to Chicago, became employed on the Western Transportation Line, receiving for his services a salary of $50 per month. On the 8th of September of that same year he went to Afton, where he became foreman of a grading gang on the C., B. & Q. R. R., receiving now $65 per month. He was also, for a short time, employed by the Superintendent of the track between Afton and Cromwell. He then became foreman of the track and was connected therewith for a period of twelve years and until he was promoted to foreman of a construction train, and was employed laying steel rails. He was then solicited to take a section on the road west of Afton, which he run from April 2, 1869, until April 1, 1881. In 1882 he was appointed Roadmaster of the division between Ottumwa and Des Moines. He has filled since that time many responsible positions and made many improvements connected with the details of the system of procedure, thus becoming a practical railroad man, and has abundant reason to feel proud of his continued success and advancement. During these years Mr. Neylon has lived sensibly and economically and has become the owner of valuable property. He has a farm of eighty acres in Union County, Iowa, all under improvement, and several lots in the village of Afton.

The subject of our sketch was married in Union County, Iowa, in February, 1871, to Miss Mary

Brannan, a native of La Salle County, Ill. Mrs. N. was born in 1852, and by her union with our subject became the mother of five children, all of whom are living—Katie, Margaret, Thomas, Mary and Terrance.

Mr. Neylon is a man of energy and enterprise, and highly respected among his associates. Socially he belongs to the Ancient Order of Hibernians. He and his family occupy a pleasant and comfortable home and enjoy a large share of the good things of life.

WILLIAM E. JONES, one of the prominent business men of the city of Ottumwa, is senior member of the firm of Jones & Buchanan, who are successfully operating as flour and feed merchants. Mr. Jones was born in Ross County, Ohio, Jan. 28, 1843, and is the son of Enos and Hannah (Jones) Jones, natives of Augusta County, Va. The date of his father's birth was May 18, 1793, and that of his mother Dec. 25, 1803. Before their marriage they crossed the Ohio River into the Buckeye State, and were among the early pioneers of that section. They located in Ross County, where they were married in 1821, and located upon a new tract of land. Here Enos Jones improved and cultivated a farm, after laborious and persevering industry. It had originally been a heavy timber tract, and he experienced, to the full degree, the toil and hardships of pioneer life. In 1849 they decided to leave their old home and cross the Mississippi, and accordingly came into Wapello County, Iowa, and located upon a farm in Center Township, where they purchased a claim, a small portion of which was broken, and upon which had been erected an humble cabin. This they took possession of, established a comfortable homestead, and lived upon it the remainder of their lives, Enos Jones dying on the 6th of December, 1864, and the mother, Aug. 6, 1885.

The father of our subject was a man of more than ordinary intelligence, and well posted upon the affairs of the country. Politically he was a stanch Democrat, possessed of decided views and fearless in the expression of his sentiments. He was straightforward and upright in his business transactions and, with his estimable wife, was held in the highest respect in the community where they made their home for so many years. The parental household included nine children, four sons and five daughters, who lived to become men and women, and of whom the record is as follows: Martha A. became the wife of William H. Crips, and resides in Center Township; Mary is the wife of James H. Goldsberry, of Ottumwa, Iowa; Jemima married John Coiner, of Newton, Jasper Co., Iowa; Matilda, the wife of Judge Marion Williamson, died in Oquawka, and her husband, Judge W., died in Peoria, Ill.; Peter C. is a resident of Jackson County, Mo.; Thomas M., of Taylor County, Iowa; Ann married Austin Allcott, of Taylor County, Iowa; John M. served as a soldier in Co. B, 36th Iowa Vol. Inf., contracted an incurable disease while on the Yazoo expedition, and died in Ottumwa in 1863; the youngest was William E., of our sketch.

William E. Jones of this history came with his parents to Wapello County in 1849, and here grew to manhood. He received a good education in the district schools, and remained upon his father's farm until he was twenty-six years of age. He had been trained by his excellent parents to habits of industry, and when not in attendance in school during his earlier years, assisted in the labors around the homestead, and shared with his brothers and sisters the hardships of pioneer life. In December, 1869, he decided to go into business for himself and accordingly came to Ottumwa and associated himself with the firm of Lively, Lewis & Co., with whom he remained two years, and afterward became proprietor of the public scales, and was engaged to a considerable extent in grain operations. In 1880 he associated himself with Mr. Buchanan in the flour and feed business, in which they have operated successfully since that time.

Mr. Jones was united in marriage with Miss Catharine Whipple in 1865, in Wapello County. Mrs. J. is a daughter of A. D. Whipple, one of the early settlers of this region, and a sketch of whom will be found in another part of this work. Of this marriage there have been born two children—Etta M. and Carrie M. Mr. and Mrs. J. are prominently connected with the Congregational Church and are held in high esteem in this community. Mr. J. has long been identified with the business and industrial interests of Wapello County, and has viewed its progress and advancement with unabated interest. He is Democratic in polities, and in 1882 was elected a member of the Board of Supervisors. At this time the prohibition movement was the occasion of great excitement, and Mr. J. made a firm stand in favor of temperance, and as a law-abiding citizen cast his influence upon the side of sobriety and good order. Like all prominent men with decided views and force of character, he has his enemies, but takes satisfaction in the conviction that he has endeavored to follow the principles of truth and justice in all respects.

W. A. WORK, of the firm of Sloan, Work & Brown, of Ottumwa and Keosauqua, Iowa, attorneys at law, is successfully engaged with his partners in the transaction of legal business in this county, the firm commanding a large and lucrative business.

Mr. Work is a native of Jefferson County, Iowa, and was born on the 25th of December, 1844. He is the son of Joseph Work, a native of Clark County, Ind., who, in 1843, was united in marriage with Miss Eleanor Huckleberry, and soon afterward, coming to Iowa, located in Jefferson County. The following year they removed to Van Buren County and engaged in farming pursuits. Joseph Work, in early life, affiliated with the Whig party and upon the abandonment of this and the organization of the Republican party, he cheerfully indorsed the principles of the latter and uniformly voted in support of them. He was a man of reliable and substantial character, possessed of good, sound common sense, and a keen observer of what was going on around him. He kept himself thoroughly posted upon the events of the day and became a leader in his community. His views and opinions were of the most decided character and he was largely in sympathy with the Grangers of that time, being in 1872 elected to the Iowa Legislature on the Granger ticket. He is still living in Van Buren County, and his wife also, the mother of our subject. They are connected with the Methodist Episcopal Church, to the support of which they have contributed liberally for many years, and are greatly esteemed in the community where they have lived so long for their excellent personal traits of character.

The subject of our sketch was reared in Van Buren County and received careful home training at the hands of his excellent parents. His primary studies were pursued in the common schools and later he entered the Iowa Wesleyan University at Mt. Pleasant, Iowa, graduating from there in 1867. During the progress of the late war he enlisted in the navy and was one of the crew of the gunboat "Benton" of the Mississippi fleet, being in the service until the early part of 1864. In the fall of 1867 he entered the office of Judge Sloan at Keosauqua, with whom he pursued a course of law study for one year, and was admitted to the bar in January, 1869, succeeding to the practice of the Judge at the time the latter was elected to the bench. Eight years later he associated himself with Judge Alexander Brown at Keosauqua, under the firm name of Work & Brown, and in 1882, Judge Sloan, after leaving the bench, became a member of the firm. In 1883 Mr. Work came to Ottumwa, where he opened an office which he still retains and, with his partners, as occasion requires, attends the courts of Wapello and Van Buren Counties.

The subject of our sketch possesses the staunch and substantial qualities of his father and, like him, has developed remarkable business capacity and an excellent store of knowledge, both in regard to his practice and to matters of general interest. In politics he is a conscientious Republican, although he has declined political offices and prefers to confine his attention to the duties of his profession. The firm is a strong one, each member of which brings to it those qualities which are of a high order and essential to success.

W. A. Work and Miss Hinda H. Marlow were united in marriage at Keosauqua in 1869. Mrs. Work is a daughter of Benjamin P. Marlow, a native of Van Buren County, and by her union with our subject became the mother of five children, as follows: Craig M., Benjamin M., Emmett A., Esther B. and Ruth E. Mr. and Mrs. W. are members in good standing of the First Methodist Episcopal Church of Ottumwa, and occupy a pleasant home on Maple avenue, where they are surrounded by the comforts of life and a circle of warm friends.

ISAAC BRAY WHITAKER, M. D., residing at Ottumwa, occupies an enviable position as a highly respected member of the profession in the Hawkeye State, and has been a resident of Iowa since 1880. He is a gentleman of enterprise and energy, and has made the most of his opportunities, and after a long and busy career is enjoying the fruits of his early industry in the reward of a handsome competency.

The subject of this sketch is a native of Surry Co., N. C., and the date of his birth July 15, 1838. His parents were William and Jane (Bray) Whitaker, his father a native of Rowan County, N. C., and his mother, who was born in France, came to America with her parents when a child five years old. They located in North Carolina and were both reared and educated in that State, and in 1831 were united in marriage. Eleven years later they started northwest, to Indiana, with teams, and located in Monroe County. There, William Bray first purchased a farm, only a portion of which was improved; this he afterward disposed of and entered a large tract of land, which, in the course of time, he converted into a valuable homestead. In 1865 he also disposed of this, and after a residence of over twenty years in Indiana, he removed from that State across the Mississippi to Decatur County, Iowa, where he remained for the following ten years, and then, in 1875, removed from there to Schuyler County, Mo., and settled upon the farm where he still resides. The parental household included five children, as follows: Julia became the wife of Col. O. P. Gray, of the 50th Indiana Regiment; Isaac B., our subject, was the second child; Martha married Dr. P. Mullinix, who is now deceased, having been assassinated by unknown parties in Missouri; Mrs. M. was married again, to George W. Dixon, of Lyonville, Iowa; Americus served as Second Lieutenant of the 82d Indiana Regiment, and was wounded at Perryville, Ky., whence he returned to his home in Monroe County, Ind., and died soon afterward; Richard is a farmer of Grundy County, Mo. The wife and mother departed this life in 1874, while a resident of Decatur County. She was an earnest Christian lady, highly esteemed by all who knew her and prominently connected with the Baptist Church. Mr. Whitaker is still living, having arrived at the advanced age of seventy-five years, is Democratic in politics, and religiously is connected with the Baptist Church.

Isaac Bray Whitaker remained under the parental roof until he was a youth of sixteen years, receiving careful home training, and his primary education in the common schools. He then entered Jacksonville Institute, where he spent three years of a scientific course, and graduated in 1856. He then commenced the study of medicine under the instruction of Dr. Dunlap of Jacksonville, and in the winter of 1859–60 took a course in Miami Medical College, Cincinnati, receiving his degree in the spring of 1861.

In the summer of 1861 Dr. Whitaker went to Henderson, Ky., and commenced the practice of his profession. At this time there began to be heard in the land the mutterings of Civil War, and at the call for 300,000 troops for the preservation of the Union, he enlisted as a soldier in Co. B, 6th Ind. Vol. Cav. Soon after the organization of the regiment he was sent to Louisville, Ky., on detached duty, and was promoted First Lieutenant. He was soon afterward sent to Santa Fe, N. M., where he was Surgeon of the Post at that point, and stationed there until the close of the war, when he received his honorable discharge, and returning to Terre Haute, Ind., resumed the practice of his profession.

In 1880 Dr. Whitaker removed West, across the Mississippi, and located in Wapello County, Iowa, and has successfully followed his profession in this locality since that time. He has identified himself with the business and industrial interests of this section, and is the encourager of education, morality and religion. He has been connected with the Baptist Church for a period of sixteen years, and contributes, as his means justify, to the spread of the Gospel and the building up of educational and reformatory institutions.

While a resident of Louisville, Ky., Dr. Whitaker was united in marriage with Miss Mary E. Cupps, in 1866. Of this union there has been one child, a daughter, Alice. Mrs. Mary Whitaker departed this life at the home of her husband in Ottumwa, in 1881.

The second marriage of Dr. Whitaker was with Miss Fannie Anderson, in 1882, and they have also become the parents of one child, John H. Their home surroundings are pleasant and desirable, and their friends and associates comprise the most cultured people of the city.

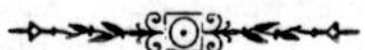

W. HARKINS owns and occupies a comfortable homestead in Highland Township, on section 18, and has been a resident of this county since February, 1872. He was born in Crawford County, Pa., in 1832, and is the son of Daniel and Lydia (Williams) Harkins, both natives of Pennsylvania. Mr. H. left his native State in the spring of 1853, first going to Warren County, Ill., where he lived twenty-one years, and then, coming into Wapello County, settled on the farm which is his present homestead.

Our subject was married, in 1864, to Mrs. Malinda (Chapman) Johnson, the daughter of Samuel and Polly (Jones) Chapman, natives of Kentucky and Ohio respectively. Of this union there were born six children, only one of whom is living, George W., a young man of nineteen years, who has the principal charge of his father's farm. Loretta died at the age of twenty-two months; William, at the age of four years; Gracie, eighteen months, and the others died in infancy. Mr. and Mrs. H. are members in good standing of the Methodist Episcopal Church. Our subject has been greatly interested in the prohibition movement, is a strong friend of temperance, and a Republican in politics. Mrs. H. has been an invalid for thirteen years.

The grandfather of our subject, John Harkins, was a native of Ireland, born in 1773, and died in 1829. The maiden name of his wife was Susanna Miller, who was of German descent, born in this country, and died in 1850. His grandfather Williams was a Captain in the War of 1812, a prominent man in his time, and at the close of his military career engaged in farming pursuits. The father of our subject died in 1861 in Illinois, at the age of fifty-nine years; the mother survived until 1874, and departed this life in Wapello County at the advanced age of seventy. She was a most estimable lady, and a worthy member of the Methodist Episcopal Church. The parental family consisted of fifteen children, eight of whom are now living.

The grandparents of Mrs. Harkins were natives of Kentucky, and her parents of Ohio. Her father, Samuel Chapman, was a Union soldier in the late war for a period of six months, and received his discharge on account of disability. He is still living; both parents were connected with the Methodist Episcopal Church. The mother died in 1873, at the age of fifty-one years. Mrs. H. received careful home training, and remained with her parents until her first marriage, to Richard Johnson, who served in the late war in Co. H, 83d Ill. Vol. Inf., and participated in the battle of Ft. Donelson and the other engagements of his regiment. He died at Donaldson June 19, 1864. Of this marriage there were born two children—Lewis E., who is with his mother at home, and Clara, who became the wife of Preston Hough, of Keokuk County.

J B. HILL, a Methodist minister, is pleasantly located on a small fruit farm in Agency Township, and is meeting with success in the prosecution of his labors. Rev. Hill was born in Pocahontas County, W. Va., July 25, 1822, and is the son of Abraham and Sarah (Burr) Hill. Abraham Hill and wife were natives of Virginia, and he followed the calling of a farmer in that State until his demise, which occurred about 1865. His wife died in the same State about three years previous to the demise of her husband. The parental union was blest by the birth of nine children, John B. being the second in order of birth.

The other children are Richard, Rebecca, Aaron, Thomas, Peter, Joel, Doctor C. and William.

John B. Hill left the parental homestead when he had reached the age of maturity, and having attended the common schools prior to this time and received therein a good common-school education, he supplemented the same by a course of study at the academy at Hillsboro, Va. When twenty-five years of age he was licensed to preach, and at once engaged in the ministry, and, in connection with other vocations, has continued to follow the same until the present time.

Our subject was married to Eliza J. McCoy in 1843. She was born in Greenbrier County, Va., and was the daughter of William and Elizabeth (McMillen) McCoy. The union of our subject with Miss McCoy was productive of the birth of one child, Nathan, who is deceased. The mother departed this life in 1845, and three years later, in 1848, our subject was again married, Miss Mary J. Cottle being the other contracting party. She was born in Nicholas County, W. Va., June 6, 1829, and is the daughter of William D. and Elizabeth (Groves) Cottle. Of this latter union eight children have been born—John W., Sarah E., Sophronia A., Mary E., Frank S., Stella R., Cora M. and Edda C. Mr. Hill is the proprietor of forty acres of good land under an advanced state of improvement, and has thereon a good residence, together with substantial out-buildings and other improvements, and is surrounded by a happy family and all that gives comfort to his declining years.

W. J. ANSON, an attorney at law, now following the practice of his profession in the city of Ottumwa, is an honored member of the legal fraternity in this section. He is a native of the Hawkeye State, and was born in Van Buren County on the 10th of December, 1849. His parents were Flarius and Amanda (Goodrich) Anson, natives respectively of Kentucky and Ohio. They were among the early pioneers of Iowa, crossing the Mississippi while it was yet a Territory, in 1837, each with their parents, who located in Van Buren County. The elder Anson was an energetic and enterprising man, and erected the first saw and grist mill on Lick Creek, in that county. To this the people came for miles around, not only the residents of Van Buren County, but many from Wapello County adjoining. Flarius Anson was occupied in the business of the mill for a period of several years, and then abandoned it to engage in agricultural pursuits.

The parental family consisted of five children, four of whom are living, as follows: Henry F. is a farmer of Van Buren County; W. J., our subject, was the next in order of birth; Mary E. became the wife of William M. Orr, of Van Buren County; Martha married E. P. Rogers, of Gilroy, Cal. To the latter place the elder Anson moved in 1869, where he and his wife at present reside. She is a devoted member of the Methodist Episcopal Church, and a sincere Christian lady, greatly esteemed by all who knew her.

The subject of this history was reared by his parents in Van Buren County, and received his early education in the pioneer schools. His studies were pursued in a log cabin with puncheon floor and slabs for seats and desks. These latter were supported by poles driven into the logs, and, as may well be imagined, the system of study pursued within those primitive structures was widely different from that of the present day. After completing his primary studies, Mr. Anson attended the High Schools of Fairfield, which he entered in 1866, and continued there for about two years. He then became a teacher in Van Buren County, being thus occupied, however, only one year. He then went to California, where he resided until the fall of 1871, and then entered the Iowa Wesleyan College, at Mt. Pleasant, for the purpose of further perfecting himself for the profession of law, which he had had in view for some time. After a course in this institution he went to Iowa City and entered the law department of the State University there, from which he graduated in 1875, and received his license to practice in all the courts of the State of Iowa.

Mr. Anson came to Ottumwa in 1875, arriving here for his final location on the 29th of July. He at once entered upon the practice of his profession, and soon afterward associated himself in partnership with P. H. Riordan, the firm doing business under the style of Anson & Riordan. They operated together until the fall of 1877, and then Mr. Anson continued business alone until the 20th of October, 1882. He then became associated in partnership with D. T. Miller, the firm name being Miller & Anson. This partnership was dissolved two years later, and since June, 1884, Mr. Anson has carried on his business alone.

The marriage of Mr. Anson and Miss Jennie E. Scott, of Ohio, was celebrated on the 14th of October, 1875. Of this union there have been born three children—David F., Floyd and Eugene. Mr. Anson closely confines himself to the practice of his profession and the details of his additional business. He is Republican in politics. He and his family occupy a handsome residence at the corner of Benton and Second streets, and are surrounded by all the comforts and refinements of life.

W. T. THOMPSON, a prosperous farmer and stock-grower of Richland Township, may be found on section 36, following his peaceful pursuits successfully, and enjoying the confidence and esteem of his neighbors. He was born in Ohio County, Ky., Dec. 29, 1820, and is a son of John and Sarah (Iglehart) Thompson, the former a native of Kentucky and the latter of Maryland. At quite an early day the family removed from Kentucky to Indiana, and lived there till 1844, when they came to Wapello County, Iowa, and were thus numbered among the pioneers of this county. Here they lived until 1857, when they moved to Adams County, Iowa, where the father died soon after, the mother surviving him until February, 1877.

The subject of this sketch was reared on a farm, and on the 30th day of October, 1842, in Warrick County, Ind., was united in marriage with Miss Polly Ann Evans. Mrs. Thompson was born July 25, 1821, and is the daughter of James and Sarah (Garret) Evans. Her father was a farmer and moved with his family from Indiana to this State, where he remained a short time and then returned to Indiana, where himself and wife subsequently died. In 1847 Mr. Thompson came from Indiana to Wapello County, making the journey with team. On his arrival he bought 120 acres of land of the Government, which comprises his present farm. Of this eighty acres are under cultivation, and he owns thirty-eight acres of wood and pasture land on section 17, Dahlonega Township. The home farm is well improved; on it is a tasteful and substantial dwelling, good barn and a fine orchard.

Mr. and Mrs. Thompson are the parents of nine children: Sarah J., who married N. W. Bliles, is now a widow, living in Kansas; John E. married Miss Mary Dunn, and lives in Adams County, Iowa; he was a member of the 29th Iowa Infantry, and served until the close of the war; William F. married Miss Louisa Falkner, and is living in Wapello County; Martha is the wife of C. C. Ingersoll, and lives in Republic County, Kan.; Julia is deceased; Ellen is the wife of J. F. Gowdy, living in Cass County, Iowa; Polly Ann, Mrs. Albert D. Rickett, is living in Keokuk County, Iowa; Belle is the wife of Lewis N. Gowdy, of this county; Anserna is living at home with her parents. Politically Mr. Thompson is a Republican.

JOHN FULLEN, of Agency, is a dealer in lumber, agricultural implements and live stock. He also has a branch store in Ottumwa, and in both places does a large and profitable business. He has the exclusive control of some of the best farm machinery made. John Fullen was born in New York City, Sept. 28, 1832, and is a son of Benjamin and Mary (Barnes) Fullen. His parents were both of Scotch-Irish descent, his father being a farmer by occupation. His mother died in Essex County, N. Y., in 1858, aged fifty-five, and his father in the same county in 1882, at the advanced age of ninety-three years. The subject of this sketch, while in his teens, learned the trade of carpenter, joiner and bridge-builder, which he followed for a number of years. For some years he was also engaged in cutting and rafting timber and lumber on the Upper Hudson River.

In 1858 Mr. Fullen married Maggie Sage, a native of Clark County, Ind., born Feb. 23, 1841, the daughter of James and Rebecca (Powell) Sage. Six children have been given to this union—Charles Douglas, Lora Ella, Nellie Blanche, Bertha Belle, Maggie May and John Clifford.

John Fuller is one of the leading business men of Agency City. He was a member of the City Council, and served in the same for a number of years. He was also a member of the School Board for many years, and for years was Treasurer of the school funds of the city. He owns a farm of sixty acres of well-improved land on section 6, Agency Township, on which is a fine orchard, with large and small fruit of all kinds. He also owns four dwelling-houses in Agency City. Mr. Fuller was the principal founder of, and is a stock-holder in, the Agency District Fair, and also holds stock in the Wapello County Fair, being a Director of the latter. Socially he is a member of the A. A. S. Politically he is a Democrat, and is quite an active politician.

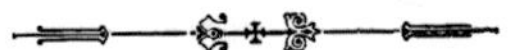

OHIO L. MILLER, a prominent resident of Ottumwa, occupies the position of Superintendent and proprietor of the Ottumwa Business College. He is finely educated, is an excellent business man, and fills the duties of his position in a successful and creditable manner. Prof. Miller is a native of Keokuk County, Iowa, having been born in Sigourney Jan. 15, 1859, and is the son of John W. and Matilda (Ford) Miller, his father a native of Fayette County, Pa., and born on the 28th of March, 1798, and his mother of Washington County, Ohio, born May 2, 1814. They both removed to Ohio with their parents and were married on the 1st of September, 1835, in Licking County, that State, where they settled, and where young Miller became engaged in iron work, to the trade of which he had been apprenticed in his earlier years. He was thus occupied in that locality until the fall of 1855, and then, coming to Iowa, located in Sigourney, and erected the first foundry in Keokuk County. Thence he removed into Marion County, locating near Knoxville at the time of its early settlement. He was an ambitious and enterprising man, and was actively engaged in business for a period of forty-five years after coming West.

John Miller, in early life, identified himself with the Whig party and was a great admirer of Henry Clay. After the abandonment of the old party, he cordially indorsed the principles of the new Republican party, with which he uniformly cast his vote. The parental household consisted of eight children, seven sons and one daughter, as follows: Chancey J. died in 1855; Charles S. served as a soldier in the late war, in Co. F, 5th Iowa Vol. Inf.; he entered as Sergeant and was promoted to Lieutenant; he participated in all the engagements of his regiment, was at the battle of Shiloh, the siege of Corinth, the capture of Vicksburg and Iuka, and at Lookout Mountain, being mortally wounded on the 24th of November, 1863, his death taking place eleven days afterward; David T., also a soldier, served in the 15th Iowa Infantry; Benjamin F., a member of the same regiment, died in the army at Marietta, Ga., on the 23d of September, 1864; he also had participated in the principal engagements of the war, and became a victim of hardship, exposure and the wearisome marches through the malarial districts of the South; Winfield S. is a resident of Keokuk County, Iowa; Hannah A., a teacher, is the wife of A. F. Harris of Marquette, Hamilton County, Neb.; Leroy D. is a farmer of Wapello County, and Ohio L., of our sketch, completes the number. The parents of our subject have lived together as husband and wife for fifty-one years.

The subject of our sketch received his primary education in the public schools of Sigourney, and in 1885 graduated at the Business College of Ottumwa, and was soon afterward appointed to his present position. He is a printer by trade, and has traveled over most of the States and Territories of the Northwest. In common with most members of the craft, he is exceedingly well informed, and possesses a valuable store of knowledge concerning general matters connected with the history of the country. After coming to Ottumwa in 1886, he was united in marriage with Miss Rofeno Graves. Mrs. M. is a native of Ottumwa, her birth occurring on the 10th of October, 1859. Her father, A. L.

J. C. Hensley M.D

Graves, was one of the early settlers of Wapello County, and has been a resident of the Hawkeye State for a period of forty-six years, crossing the Mississsippi and locating within its boundaries while it was yet a Territory.

JOSEPH C. HINSEY, M. D., one of the oldest practicing physicians of Wapello County, and a resident of Ottumwa, is a native of the proud and wealthy State of Ohio, and was born in Butler County on the 9th of June, 1829. When a mere child, his parents, William and Mary (Haines) Hinsey, emigrated to Illinois, and locating in Tazewell County, settled near where the city of Pekin now stands. At that time an old fort was the only dwelling in that vicinity, and within its walls a few adventurous pioneers had gathered with the expectation that in time their numbers would so increase that they would be enabled to venture out in safety, the country in that section being then full of Indians. The first winter of their sojourn here the mother of our subject was taken ill, and her little son, Joseph C., of our sketch, was taken care of by an Indian squaw. The father opened up a farm of 160 acres, but only lived a short time, being stricken down in the prime of manhood in 1837, leaving his widow with a family of three children, one son and two daughters: Joseph C., our subject; Elizabeth, now Mrs. Robertson, of Dayton, Ore., and Nellie, Mrs. I. S. Milam, of El Dorado, Butler Co., Kan.

William Hinsey was a man of decided views and character, and a devoted member of the Baptist Church. Mrs. Hinsey was married again in due time to William Ayers, and by this union became the mother of six children, five sons and one daughter, one of whom is deceased. They are, William, James, George, Jonathan and Benjamin. Mrs. Ayers departed this life in 1847, in Whiteside County, Ill., to which place the family had moved in 1845. She was a lady highly respected in the community wherever she made her home, and was also connected with the Baptist Church.

The subject of our sketch remained with his mother until 1843, removing before her from Tazewell to Whiteside County, Ill. In the latter place he went into the employ of his uncle, Jonathan Haines, who was the patentee of the famous Haines' Harvester and Header, and our subject assisted in the construction of the first machine and operated it through the neighborhood. He had entered into a contract with his uncle to learn the trade of carpenter and joiner, with the agreement that he should be sent to school such portion of the time as he could be spared, but the latter not living up to the terms, our subject left his employ and engaged at whatever he could find to do. For some months afterward he was variously occupied, and then became an employe of Dr. A. Brown, a follower of the Thompsonian or Botanic system, and young Hinsey had access to his library and assisted him in manufacturing pills. He contracted to stay with Dr. Brown three years, with the understanding that he should be allowed money to attend a botanic medical college. He completed one term of study, and took a course at the Cincinnati Medical, the Eclectic, and also the Ohio Medical Colleges, dividing up his time about equally between the three institutions. After he had completed his studies he returned to Whiteside County, and in the winter of 1849 went to Pekin, Ill., and entered the office of Drs. Fitch and Quigley, where he remained for one year, and then, entering Rush Medical College, of Chicago, Ill., graduated in the class of 1851, before he had attained his majority. He then returned to Pekin and commenced the practice of his profession.

Soon after receiving his diploma Dr. Hinsey was united in marriage, in March, 1851, with Miss Olive R. Upson, a step-daughter of Dr. Brown, and a native of New Haven, Conn. She was born in 1830, and of this union there were two children—Norton D., a printer of Des Moines, and Olive, who died in infancy. Mrs. Olive Hinsey departed this life in August, 1853. She was a devoted member of the Methodist Episcopal Church and highly respected by all who knew her.

In the winter of 1853 Dr. Hinsey went to Philadelphia, and attended a course of lectures in the medical department of Pennsylvania College, where he received the *ad eundem* degree, and in the fall of 1854 he came across the Mississippi into Iowa, and located at Dahlonega, in Wapello County. This was then the leading town, and our subject opened an office and in due time built up an extensive and successful practice. At the time of his arrival here he had \$2.50 in money and \$40 in worthless script. But he was rich in determination and enterprise, and he had no other intention than to push ahead and battle with the difficulties which might beset him, and the result is an apt illustration of what perseverance and resolution may accomplish.

During the late Civil War Dr. Hinsey was appointed Assistant Surgeon of the volunteer army, and assigned as Surgeon of the Board of Enrollment for the 4th Congressional District of Iowa, in which capacity he examined all the men enlisted in the district, and had charge of the returned sick and wounded soldiers.

In the spring of 1863 Dr. Hinsey moved to Ottumwa, since which time he has been a resident of this city, and has been engaged continuously in the practice of his profession. He occupies a high position among his medical brethren in this vicinity. He is a member of the State Medical Society of Iowa, the Des Moines Valley District Society, the American Medical Association, of which latter he has been a member for a period of thirty-three years, and the Wapello County Medical Society. He has been President of the District Society and of the Wapello Society, and first Vice President of the State Society.

The marriage of Dr. Hinsey and Miss Louisa F. Leitner, of Ohio, was celebrated in 1856. Mrs. Hinsey was born near Athens, Ohio, in 1838, and by her marriage with our subject became the mother of eleven children, of whom all except one are living, the record being as follows: Ida B. is the wife of W. C. Kinsely, and resides near New Philadelphia, Ohio; Mary Alice was united in marriage with Henry Phillips, Secretary of the Phillips Coal Company; Ellen, the third daughter, is book-keeper for the Phillips Coal Company; William is book-keeper for W. A. Jordan & Son; Mattie C. is a teacher in the city schools; the remaining children are Laura, Gertrude, Joseph, Louisa and Edith. The Doctor and his family occupy a handsome residence, and enjoy the confidence and esteem of a large circle of friends. Since coming to this county he has identified himself with its interests, and has done what he could toward the promotion of every worthy enterprise.

Socially Dr. Hinsey belongs to the A. F. & A. M., his first connection with the fraternity being before he came to Wapello County, becoming then a member of Pekin Lodge No. 29. He subsequently joined Ottumwa Lodge No. 16, and withdrew from it afterward in order to organize Empire Lodge No. 269, of which he was made Master, serving two years, and in the meantime represented this in the Grand Lodge of the State. He is also a member of Clinton Chapter No. 9, and Malta Commandery No. 31. In these orders he has always taken an active interest, and until of late years has devoted much time in seeking to advance their prosperity and increase their membership. As a representative citizen of the county and a prominent resident of Ottumwa, the publishers are pleased to present the portrait of Dr. Hinsey in this ALBUM.

PROF. JOHN H. RHEEM, prominent in the musical circles of the city of Ottumwa, and an instructor of rare merit, has been finely educated in this profession, and during a residence of thirteen years in this city has built up a reputation as an adept, and is well qualified for the successful prosecution of his present business as a dealer in music and musical instruments, of which he carries one of the finest stocks in this section of the State.

Mr. Rheem is a native of Carlisle, Pa., and was born on the 12th of April, 1835, his parents being George W. and Lydia (Updegraff) Rheem, also natives of the Keystone State. He grew to manhood and received his early education in the schools of Carlisle. At a very early age he displayed unusual talent as a musician, and when eight years old sang in the church choir of his native town. At the age of twenty-one years he went to Boston, Mass., where he was placed under the very best teachers and pursued his musical studies for two years, attaining great proficiency. He then returned to Carlisle, and was a teacher in the public schools for four years. Thence he removed to Reading and engaged as a teacher of music. Not being satisfied with the prospects in that vicinity he resolved to cross the Mississippi, and in 1871 went to Chariton, Iowa, and continued as a teacher there also. Two years later he came to Ottumwa, and for a period of ten years thereafter was employed as an instructor of music in the public schools of this city. At the expiration of that time he abandoned teaching and established his present business, since which time he has given his whole attention to the sale of musical instruments, of which he carries a full line and stands at the head of the business in this locality.

In September, 1886, Prof. Rheem secured a patent on the Rheem Accompanist, one of the best devices that has ever been produced, and designed to assist beginners to play. Following this he organized a company for the purpose of its manufacture, which has for its officers the following prominent citizens: J. H. Rheem, President; W. H. Lehman, of Des Moines, Secretary, and R. S. Field, Treasurer. The company gives employment to five men, and is turning out a goodly number of machines. The work is carried on under the oversight of Mr. Rheem and the device may be attached to any musical instrument. He has been employed ten years in perfecting and completing it, and has succeeded in producing an attachment which will be universally adopted in every household wherever there is an organ or similar instrument. He deserves great credit for his perseverance and integrity.

Mr. Rheem was married in his native town in Pennsylvania on the 5th of April, 1860, the maiden of his choice being Miss Fannie A. Ritter, a native of the same place. Of this union there were born three children: Lillie, the wife of R. S. Field, of Ottumwa; Mary, at home, and Jessie, the wife of W. G. Field, of this city. They occupy a handsome residence which is finely fitted up, and on every hand gives evidence of taste and refinement. Their friends and acquaintances embrace the cultivated and educated people of the city.

Socially Mr. Rheem belongs to the K. T., and I. O. O. F., and was a representative in the Grand Lodge two years. He is Past Grand Chancellor of the K. of P., and assisted to organize the Supreme Lodge of the World. Mr. and Mrs. R. are prominently connected with the Methodist Episcopal Church of Ottumwa, and are the generous supporters of morality, education, and everything which tends to elevate the standard of religion, education and morality.

JOHN JOHNSON, a successful farmer of Green Township, is pleasantly located on section 4, where he owns 340 acres of good farming land and is industriously engaged in its improvement and cultivation. He is a native of Holland, born in 1820, and the son of John and Johanna (Degrut) Johnson, natives of the same country. He remained with his parents until he had attained to manhood, and in 1848 made his preparations to sail for the New World. After a voyage of seventy-three days he landed in New Orleans, the trip having been made in a sailing-vessel, the "Albright." It was a very tempestuous voyage, and upon several occasions the passengers and crew anticipated a watery grave, but they finally arrived in safety and were none the worse for their experience, except, perhaps, the loss of valuable time.

After a short time spent in the Crescent City, Mr. Johnson came up the Mississippi to St. Louis, from there to Keokuk, remaining a few days in each city, and then coming into Wapello County, soon afterward located in Green Township, on section 2, where he rented a tract of land and became occupied in its cultivation. He then removed to Richmond and carried on a farm for Mr. J. Overman for two years, and then rented a farm on section 3 of Center Township, which he occupied for two years and then purchased his present homestead. He was prospered in his farming pursuits and business transactions, and added to his landed possessions as time passed and his means accumulated. He is now the owner of 340 acres, all improved and under a good state of cultivation. This he has acquired solely by the exercise of his own energy and perseverance, having commenced at the foot of the ladder, without money or friends to whom he could apply for financial aid.

Mr. Johnson was married in his native country in 1840, to Mrs. Cornelia Venderlow, also a native of Holland, who by her former marriage had become the mother of two children: Cornelius, who lives in Green Township, and Dora, deceased. By her union with our subject there were born three children; Henry, who is conducting a meat market in Ottumwa; Mary M., the wife of Henry Turnson, of Green Township, and Peter, who died in infancy. Mr. and Mrs. J. are connected with the Catholic Church of Ottumwa. He is Democratic in politics and takes that interest which all good citizens manifest in the welfare of their township and county.

The parents of our subject spent their early lives in their native country, and after emigrating to the United States came to Iowa and located in Eddyville, Wapello County, where the father died in 1851, and the mother ten years later. Both were members of the Catholic Church.

WILLIAM GIFT, a highly respected farmer and resident of Green Township, is the possessor of a comfortable homestead finely located on section 11, where he is carrying on farming pursuits after the most improved methods and with success. Our subject is a native of Tennessee, and was born in Washington County, in 1828. His parents were Adam and Sarah (Smith) Gift, natives respectively of Pennsylvania and Maryland, who removed from Washington to Bedford County, Pa., when our subject was a child of two years old. They remained there only a short time, however, and thence went to Alleghany County, Md., where they remained residents until 1852. Adam Gift departed this life in Fairfield, Iowa, Jan. 19, 1868, at the age of seventy-three years, and the following month the faithful wife and mother joined her husband on the other shore. They were most excellent and worthy people, upright and honorable in their lives, and are held in kindly remembrance by a large circle of friends and acquaintances.

In the year mentioned William Gift started for the West, and having crossed the Mississippi came into Iowa, first locating near Fairfield, where he engaged in farming pursuits, having been reared to that occupation. He was thus engaged for the following thirteen years, and then, in 1865, came into Wapello County and purchased the tract of land which is included in his present homestead, and is located on section 11. In the meantime he was married, July 27, 1856, to Miss Catherine Walmer, a native of Wayne County, Ohio, and the daughter of Jacob and Sarah (Shuey) Walmer, of Lebanon County, Pa. Mr. and Mrs. G. have become the parents of the following-named children: Sarah Jane is the wife of James A. Neil, a farmer of St. John County, Kan.; Joseph Walter married Ella Dickerson, and is a locomotive engineer, having his home in St. Paul, Minn.; Charles Wesley is in the employ of the N. P. R. R., and resides in Kansas City, Mo.; Pluma B., Elizabeth, Ada and William Ray are at home with their parents.

Mr. and Mrs. Gift are highly respected in their community and are devoted members of the Methodist Episcopal Church. During the late Civil War Mr. Gift served as a soldier in the 30th Iowa Infantry, two years and ten months, and participated with his regiment in the battles of Haines Bluff, Arkansas Post, the two battles of Jackson, Miss.; Lookout Mountain, the siege of Vicksburg, Mission Ridge, Buzzard's Roost, Kenesaw Mountain, Resaca, and went through the Atlanta campaign. At Resaca he received a flesh wound in the neck, and at the battle of Atlanta was slightly wounded in the head. After his honorable discharge from the service he returned home and resumed his former occupation as an agriculturist.

The homestead of Mr. Gift comprises 238 acres of land, mostly improved and under a good state of cultivation. When he first took possession it was mostly in its original condition, and the beautiful and fertile fields which now greet the eye were mainly brought to their present condition by the hand of the proprietor, and that which he has not performed by his own hand, he has closely directed and superintended. He has been wise and judicious in the disbursement of funds, and his business transactions have been conducted in a straightforward manner, while his farming operations have been carried on with that system and good order which are indispensable in the arrangement of a comfortable homestead. Since becoming a resident of this township he has enjoyed the hearty and cordial esteem of his neighbors and fellow-citizens, and has been prominent in all their councils concerning the general welfare of the community. He has been Township Trustee, Road Supervisor, and a member of the School Board, and in all respects is fulfilling the obligations of a good citizen.

In politics Mr. Gift is a stanch Republican. A view of his residence, farm buildings and stock is shown on another page.

HON. WILLIAM McCORMICK, a highly respected citizen of Highland Township, has been a resident of Wapello County since the spring of 1848, when he purchased a farm of eighty acres, which he has occupied since that time. He has been prospered in his business and farming operations, and doubled his first possessions so that he now has 160 acres, all of which is improved and under a good state of cultivation. He has held the various offices of his township, been Clerk for a number of years, and in 1858 was a member of the State Legislature. He has been a peaceable and law-abiding citizen, never engaged in a law suit, and never upon a jury.

The subject of this history was born in Gallatin County, Ky., in 1814, and is the son of John and Nancy (Cox) McCormick, natives respectively of Maryland and Kentucky. In the spring of 1835, they removed from the latter State to McDonough County, Ill., where our subject remained for the following thirteen years, and then became a resident of this county.

Mr. McCormick was married to Miss Elizabeth Stevens in 1838. This lady was the daughter of Jacob and Rhoda Stevens of Kentucky, and was born in 1820. After being the faithful and affectionate companion of her husband for a period of forty-eight years, she departed this life on the 18th of August, 1885, at the age of sixty-five years. The home circle was completed by the birth of fourteen children, who are recorded as follows: Lavina was born Aug. 8, 1839, became the wife of James Reeves, and died June 17, 1866. Albert and Melissa were twins; the latter died in infancy; they were born March 24, 1841, and Albert married Miss Martha Gray, March 28, 1866; he afterward went to the Black Hills, and when last heard of was at Boulder, Col. Hezekiah was born Jan. 25, 1843, and married Miss Phebe N. Turner, June 28, 1866; they live in Jasper County, Iowa; John, born March 18, 1845, was married to Miss Sarah Ann Reeves, of Mahaska County, Aug. 19, 1868; Jacob, born Oct. 9, 1847, married Miss Sarah E. Dennis, in this county, and they are residents of Highland Township; Mary Jane, Mrs. Knight, of Highland, was born Oct. 14, 1848; Sarah Maria married John A. Dennis, but is now a widow; Rhoda, born Feb. 10, 1854, is at home with her father; William B., born Dec. 29, 1857, is a resident of Nebraska; Theodore S., born Jan. 4, 1859, died in infancy; Elizabeth, born Dec. 15, 1860, was married March 12, 1885, to George Bender, of Highland Township; Matilda Catherine was born Jan. 15, 1863, and lives at home; Chloe, born May 2, 1865, died in infancy. Mr. McCormick has been a faithful member of the Baptist Church for a period of twenty-seven years, and politically is a Greenbacker.

ELIAS KITHERMAN, an honored pioneer of Wapello County, has been a resident of the Hawkeye State since the spring of 1843, and in a period of forty-three years spent in this locality has earned the high esteem of his fellow-citizens. He has been a man of high moral character, upright and honorable in his transactions, industrious and enterprising, and possesses all the qualities which constitute an honest man and a good citizen. The subject of our sketch is a native of Virginia, and was born in Franklin County, near Richmond, on the 1st day of September, 1809. He is the son of Henry and Anna (Damer) Kitherman, of Pennsylvania, and his father died in Virginia, leaving his widow with a family of eleven children. Soon after the death of her husband, Mrs. K. removed to Indiana and settled in Perry

County, where she entered a tract of wild land, and, with the assistance of her children, opened up a farm in the midst of the heavy timber. She was a lady of great energy and business talent, and determined to keep her little family together, which she accomplished. She trained them carefully to honest and worthy lives and to habits of industry and economy, and presented to them an example of a sincere and worthy Christian life. She was prominently connected with the United Brethren Church, and died upon the homestead which she had established in Perry County. Of her large family of children only two survive, the subject of our sketch and his brother Peter.

Elias Kitherman was reared among the wilds of Indiana, and received his early education in the pioneer schools, which were conducted in rude log cabins. The first structure wherein he began his rudimentary studies was built of round back-logs, with puncheon floor and slabs for seats, and one end of the floor was occupied by the huge fireplace, the chimney being composed of mud and sticks. Daylight was admitted through a square place sawed in the logs, with greased paper for window-panes, and the school books of those primitive days passed from the eldest to the youngest of the family and were perused as long as they would hold together, which system was widely different from that of the present day with its frequent changes of text books. As soon as able Elias Kitherman assisted in the labors around the homestead, and remained with his mother's family until his marriage, which occurred in 1828. The maiden of his choice was Miss Sarah Archibald, who bore him two children—William, who is now deceased, and Mary Ann, who became the wife of Martin Koontz, of California. Mrs. Sarah Kitherman only remained the companion of her husband for three years, dying in 1831. Mr. K. for his second wife married Miss Lydia Redman, and of this union there were born four children: Sarah, the wife of Alfred Bowland, of Highland Township, Wapello County; Nancy, married to Jefferson Thompson, also of this county; John, a resident of Mitchell County, Kan., and George W., of Ottumwa.

In 1842 Mr. Kitherman removed from Indiana to Bureau County, Ill., where he spent the winter, and the following spring came to Wapello County, and located in Dahlonega Township, where he entered a claim and commenced the opening up of a farm. He had previously learned the trade of a blacksmith, and he now worked alternately upon the farm and in the blacksmith-shop, and was the first man to build a shop of the kind in the township of Dahlonega. In early manhood he exhibited those traits of character which afterward earned for him so thoroughly the respect and confidence of his associates. He was well informed and intelligent and kept himself posted upon general matters of interest. He was elected the first Justice of the Peace in Dahlonega Township, serving four years, and was intrusted with other local offices.

Mrs. Lydia Kitherman departed this life in Ottumwa in 1875. She was a most estimable Christian lady, and highly respected by all who knew her. Her kindness of heart was proverbial, and it was remarked of her that she was always seeking to do a kind action. Her name is held in kindly remembrance by a wide circle of friends and acquaintances, and also by numbers of those to whom her inherent charity and benevolence had been of great assistance. The third marriage of Mr. Kitherman took place on the 19th of November, 1876, the lady of his choice being Miss Kate Cooper, of Illinois. They occupy a handsome residence in Ottumwa, and are surrounded by all the comforts and many of the luxuries of life in a home which possesses all the appliances of cultivated tastes and ample means.

When Mr. Kitherman first came to Wapello County he was obliged to have his milling done at Bonaparte, in Van Buren County, the trip frequently consuming a week's time. He commenced life at the foot of the ladder and has climbed up to his present position solely through his own efforts and the inheritance of enterprise and industry transmitted to him by his excellent and worthy parents. In the old pioneer days he was sometimes compelled to work for twenty-five cents per week, but was always disposed to make the best of circumstances and do the very best he could, whatever might be the difficulties by which he was surrounded.

Mr. Kitherman cast his first vote for Andrew Jackson and subsequently affiliated with the Whig party, and when the latter was abandoned by the substitution of the new Republican party, he cordially supported the principles of the latter and has uniformly cast his vote in their support since that time. He is now living in the enjoyment of the fruits of his earlier toil, and looks back with satisfaction over a well-spent and honorable life.

R H. TINDELL, a prosperous and skillful farmer and stock-grower, of Richland Township, owns and occupies a valuable homestead on section 27. He was born in Knox County, Tenn., Jan. 30, 1821, and is the son of Nathan and Margaret (Ross) Tindell. In 1829 his parents removed from Tennessee to Indiana, where they lived until 1848, when they came to Wapello County and settled upon the place which now constitutes the home of our subject. In 1856 they removed from the farm into the city of Ottumwa and retired from active labor. The father died there in 1862, and the mother in 1880, and they are both buried in Ottumwa Cemetery.

The subject of this sketch came to Wapello County with his parents and has lived upon the present or an adjoining farm since that time. In 1852 he was married to Miss Angeline Sloan, who was born in McMinn County, Tenn., March 17, 1819, and is the daughter of James and Nancy (McCartney) Sloan. Her father died in Tennessee in 1819. Her mother removed to Illinois in 1840, and spent the remainder of her days in McDonough County.

Mr. and Mrs. Tindell are the parents of four children, as follows: Margaret, who was born Nov. 20, 1852, is the wife of Franklin Wright; and Ellen, born Aug. 2, 1854, married Harvey Millard; both live in Clarke County, Iowa; Nina F., born Feb. 25, 1858, was married July 20, 1879, to Janna Dalrymple. The latter was born in Hunterdon County, N. J., Jan. 27, 1856. He moved to McDonough County, Ill., in February, 1878, and came to this county in September following. The parents of Mr. Dalrymple are natives of New Jersey; his father was born Jan 4, 1822, and died May 3, 1885, in New Jersey. The mother was born Jan. 6, 1834, and is still living in her native State. Mr. Dalrymple, Sr., was a blacksmith by trade but the last years of his life were spent upon a farm. Both parents were members of the Methodist Episcopal Church. The eldest child of Mr. and Mrs. Dalrymple was Iva E., born July 1, 1880, and died March 20, 1882; Lola A. was born Feb. 12, 1883; Ruie E. was born June 12, 1886. Mrs. D. is a member of the Methodist Episcopal Church; Mr. D., in politics, uniformly votes the Republican ticket. Amelia A. Tindell, the fourth child of our subject, born April 3, 1860, is the wife of Edward Jenks and lives in Clarke County, Iowa.

Mr. Tindell is the owner of 198 acres of valuable farming land with a good house and barn and all necessary out-buildings, which are kept in good repair and correspond with the general neat aspect of the homestead. Our subject has been prominent in the local affairs of his township for many years, having held the offices of Road Supervisor, Township Trustee and School Director. He and his wife are members of the Methodist Episcopal Church, and in politics Mr. T. uniformly casts his vote with the Republican party. A fine lithographic view of the Tindell homestead is given in connection with this biography.

REV. ANTHONY ROBINSON, a pioneer preacher of Wapello County, first opened his eyes to the light in Orange County, N. C., on the 15th of April, 1810. His parents were William and Sarah (Scott) Robinson; the former was born in "Old Virginia" in 1790, and died in May, 1855, in Indiana; the mother was a native of Maryland, born in 1777, and only survived her husband until the next year, departing this life in 1856. While yet young they both became residents of North Carolina and were there married, becoming the parents of one child only, the subject of our sketch. The mother, before her marriage to William Robinson, had become the wife of Joshua Underwood and the mother of a son and daughter, both of whom are now deceased.

In 1816 William Robinson emigrated with his

family from North Carolina to the Territory of Indiana, locating in Davis County, near Washington, which was then the county seat. They remained there for four years and then moved to Greene County, where they located upon a tract of uncultivated land and commenced the improvement and cultivation of a farm. After a season of laborious toil, and just as Mr. Robinson had accumulated sufficient means to enter the land for purchase, another party slipped in before him and secured it. In the meantime, Mr. R. had also made a claim in another part of the county, upon which he removed with his family and established a permanent home. At that time the country was a vast wilderness, peopled only by a few scattering Indians who were encamped upon what was known as the New Purchase, and they did not see the face of a white man, frequently for weeks at a time.

The first purchase of Mr. Robinson included 160 acres, to which he added from time to time until he became an extensive landed proprietor and the owner of nearly 400 acres. He was also a carpenter and joiner by trade, very industrious and enterprising, and allowed no time to run to waste. His mechanical skill saved him every year the outlay of hundreds of dollars, and in time he accumulated a fine property. He was strictly upright in his business dealings and prompt in meeting his obligations, and no man could say that William Robinson was indebted to him or refused to pay. Politically he affiliated with the Whig party, and was a great admirer of Henry Clay. He and his excellent lady were active members of the Methodist Church for many years, and contributed of their means for the promotion of education and morality. Mr. R. regularly attended the religious meetings of his church, whether formal or informal, and was one of the pillars upon whom the brethren leaned for aid and counsel.

The subject of our sketch was a child a little more than six years old when his parents removed from North Carolina to the Territory of Indiana. For three months in the year he attended the pioneer school in the log cabin, and during the summer seasons assisted his parents in the lighter labors of the homestead. He yet distinctly remembers the school building of his childhood days. It was built of round logs, 12x16 feet in dimensions, and during the first winter the only floor within it was the trodden ground. The huge fireplace extending across one end was built of what was called "cattle clay." The writing-desks and seats were made of slabs supported by poles placed in holes in the wall, and the square place sawed out of the logs, which served as a window, was supplied with panes of greased paper. This cabin was afterward closed against school purposes, and the children of the pioneers were provided with a large log house in Bloomfield, the county seat, where a gentleman by the name of Cushman erected a more comfortable structure and conducted the school. He was well educated, possessed more than ordinary ability as an instructor, and was a man of fine Christian character.

Young Robinson was fond of his books, pursued his studies faithfully, improved his opportunities, and succeeded in acquiring a liberal education. He had already selected his profession in life, and when eighteen years of age was baptized by Rev. John Strang, then Presiding Elder of the Vincennes District. He then began to study for the ministry, and was often employed as a local exhorter, and gave indications in early life of the talents which have since distinguished him. At the age of twenty-six he entered the Indiana Conference and continued in that conference and work for twenty-one years, with remarkable success. In the meantine he had charge of the Mt. Vernon Circuit, which included all the territory between the Ohio and Wabash Rivers for a distance of about twenty miles. Within the space of two years, under the ministrations of himself and Rev. Stephen Ravenscroft, there were 1,400 persons taken into the Methodist Episcopal Church, and many others who had been converted under their preaching joined other churches. They wound up the last year with a camp-meeting which, opening on Friday, closed the following Tuesday, and it was said there were only two persons at this last meeting who were not professed followers of Christ, there having been 100 converts since it opened.

After leaving Mt. Vernon Rev. Robinson was located at Vincennes, Ind., for two years, and was very successful, being sent thence to Point Commerce, in Greene County. In 1845 he was stationed at Bloomington, Ind., and appointed Presiding Elder, which office he held for the four succeeding years. He held eight camp-meetings in one year and also filled vacancies in Vincennes, Evansville and other towns. In 1857, his parents being both deceased, and the parents of his wife being residents of Iowa, he also concluded to locate in the Hawkeye State, and by his request was transferred from the Indiana Conference, being stationed at Ottumwa, and held his first meeting in this city. He was stationed here for two years, and then had charge of Blakesburg Circuit, thereafter the Agency City Circuit, and in 1860 went to Mt. Pleasant, having been appointed Presiding Elder of the Burlington District. At the close of four years spent in Iowa, he was appointed to Mt. Pleasant Circuit, and then traveled a year and a half, being thereafter appointed by Bishop Janes to Mt. Pleasant District to fill a vacancy caused by the decease of Rev. David Worthington. Afterward he was sent to the Middletown Circuit two years, Winfield Circuit two years, Canaan three years, Dahlonega two years, and Batavia one year. His health then began to fail, and at the conference of 1883 he was kindly placed on the superannuated list, being broken down, but holding a membership in the conference.

After forty-seven years of continued labor in the ministry, Rev. Anthony Robinson, now at the age of seventy-six years, is taking a well-earned rest from active labor. He was possessed of more than ordinary ability, and cheerfully gave his time and his talents for the Master's cause. He has fought a good fight, and feels that he has done his work well in proportion to the light that was given him. He is an Abolitionist in principle, and has been an earnest temperance worker, having exerted his influence wherever possible against the evil of spirituous liquors.

Rev. Anthony Robinson was united in marriage with Miss Mary Ann Hammond, in Warrick County, Ind., on the 7th of October, 1838. Mrs. Robinson is a native of Bowling Green, Ky., her birth occurring on the 26th of July, 1821. Their union was blest by the birth of six children, all living except one: Mary R. became the wife of Rev. J. W. McDonald, a minister of the Methodist Episcopal Church, now stationed at Mt. Pleasant, Iowa; Sarah W. married T. J. Zollers, of Denver, Col.; Martha became the wife of Rev. Edward E. Schreiner, of Centerville, Iowa, also a Methodist minister; William T. is located at Concepcion, Chili, S. A., engaged as a missionary and teacher, and went out under Bishop Taylor; Edward A. is an attorney at law of Ottumwa.

T. P. SPILMAN, ex-Sheriff of Wapello County, is a native of Decatur County, Ind., and was born Jan. 11, 1845. He is a son of J. D. and Amelia (Perceval) Spilman, natives of Kentucky. Mr. Spilman of this notice was reared and educated in his native county, where he attended the common schools, worked on his father's farm, and continued to reside until the breaking out of the Civil War. On attaining his sixteenth year and almost at the very beginning of the war our subject enlisted in Co. B, 52d Ind. Vol. Inf., as private, and went forth to battle for the perpetuity of his country's flag. He participated in the fight at Donelson, also in that of Shiloh, and the bloody battle of Nashville. In October, 1863, he was discharged on account of disability. Returning home he soon afterward assisted in raising a company, which became known as Co. A, 146th Ind. Vol. Inf., of which our subject was elected Captain and subsequently was promoted Major. He was in the army of the Shenandoah Valley and continued with his regiment until the close of the war, receiving an honorable discharge.

In the spring of 1866 Maj. Spilman came to Ottumwa, and in the neighborhood of this city engaged in farming. He was elected Sheriff of Wapello County in 1873, and re-elected in 1875, serving four years. He is Republican in politics and held the office of Sheriff by the votes of that party. In the spring of 1880 Maj. Spilman was employed as agent for the large packing-house of John Morrill & Co.

Maj. Spilman was married at Ottumwa, Sept. 10, 1866, to Miss Almira Randel, a daughter of Benjamin R. Randel, of Indiana. She was born in

1848, and has borne our subject three children—Thomas H., John M. and Maggie. During the years 1876–77 Maj. Spilman was Chairman of the Republican County Central Committee. He is a self-made man in every respect the word implies, and has gained many friends in Ottumwa and throughout the State by his straightforward and manly dealings with his fellow-man, as well as strict integrity. Socially he is a member of the G. A. R., belonging to Cloutman Post at Ottumwa, and is also a member of the I. O. O. F.

FREDERICK LAWRENCE BACHMAN, a prosperous and enterprising German of Green Township, is comfortably located on section 30, and successfully engaged in the peaceful pursuits of agriculture. His birthplace was in the Electorate of Hesse-Cassel in the northern part of Germany, and he first opened his eyes to the light on the 26th of April, 1815. His parents were Charles and Elizabeth (Reinhard) Bachman, and they spent their early lives in their native country, emigrating to the United States in the latter part of 1837, on a sailing-vessel, the "Copernicus," which carried a cargo of wheat, and sixty-five passengers. After a tedious voyage of ten weeks they landed in Baltimore Jan. 16, 1838, with a family of six children, and during that same winter made the trip across the Alleghany Mountains in wagons to Muskingum County, Ohio, where they bought a farm near Taylorsville, and there the mother died in 1847, at the age of thirty-nine years. The father subsequently married and moved to Wapello County, Iowa, in 1865, where he lived until his death, which took place about 1872, in his seventy-first year. The parents were both connected with the Lutheran Church, and carried out in their daily lives those principles of honor and integrity which they carefully sought to instill within the hearts of their children.

Our subject was twenty-two years of age when he came to America, and with his parents and family proceeded to Wheeling, W. Va., where they staid eight days, and then hired a team to take them to Muskingum County, Ohio. He remained with his parents two years and at the expiration of this time removed to Zanesville, where he lived for a period of nine years, engaged in operating an oilmill. From there he moved across the Mississippi into Wapello County, Iowa, and purchased a farm of 200 acres, where he established a permanent home, and upon which he has remained since that time. He was the first settler in this immediate vicinity, and there were no farms or roads yet laid out. He first put up a log cabin 18x20 feet, in which he settled and lived until 1862, when he built a more pretentious dwelling, which he still occupies. At that time the present city of Ottumwa was composed of only a few log cabins, and upon his first trip to the town he carried his ax along and cut a road for his team through the woods and underbush. In contrasting the past with the present he reviews the interval with pleasure and satisfaction. The Indian trail of the wilderness has given place to the magnificent system of railroads, and the primitive ox-team to the snorting iron horse, while the rude implements of agriculture have been replaced by more expeditious farm machinery, a large part of this great change being due to the brave old pioneers who first courageously ventured into the Western wilds to make way for the later civilization.

Three years after he became a citizen of the United States, on the 21st of June, 1840, Mr. Bachman was united in marriage with Miss Susanna Spangler, of Westmoreland County, Pa. She was born Feb. 20, 1820, and is the daughter of George and Barbara (Rose) Spangler, both natives of Westmoreland County, and whose parents emigrated from Wurtemberg, Germany, at an early day and settled in Pennsylvania. Her parents emigrated from Westmoreland County to Ohio, where they became farmers and spent the remainder of their lives. Of the union of our subject and wife eleven children were born, the record being as follows: Maria is the wife of Alexander Martin, of this county; Charles W., who married Sarah J. Kent, and after her death married her sister, Rebecca, also deceased, is a resident of Adams Township; Susanna is the wife of William P. Powell, of Anderson County, Kan.; Augusta Louisa married Isaac N. Brown, of Holt County, Neb.; John F.

married Mary Reinhard, and is a resident of Green Township; Loretta is the wife of Harrison Wellman, of Douglas County, Kan.; Henry L. married Sarah E. Baker, and is a resident of Adams Township; Samuel is a Nevada ranchman; George was a machinist by trade, and died in Nevada in June, 1882, aged twenty-five years; Rosa is the wife of Michael Heckert, of Green Township; Frederick married Armilda Overturff, and is a resident of Davis County, Iowa.

Mr. and Mrs. Bachman are prominent members of the Lutheran Church, to which they contribute liberally and cheerfully. Mr. Bachman has been prominently connected with the affairs of his township for a third of a century. He is a Democrat in politics, and has held the office of Justice of the Peace for twenty-four years. He has enjoyed in a marked degree the confidence of his fellow-townsmen, and has been honored with many offices by them. A view of Mr. Bachman's home is shown on another page of this work.

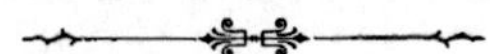

CHARLES F. HARROW, an early pioneer of Wapello County, was born in Bracken County, Ky., in September, 1800, and is consequently nearly rounding up the last half of a century of life. He grew to manhood in his native State, and was married within its boundaries, in Fleming County, to Miss Gracie Frane, in 1821. They located in Montgomery County, remaining there for the following twelve years, and then removed north into Indiana, where they remained for ten years. In 1842 Mr. Harrow concluded to go into the country beyond the Mississppi and, coming into Wapello County, Iowa, purchased a large tract of land in the immediate vicinity of where the city of Ottumwa now stands. He was one of the first County Commissioners, and prominently identified with the interests of this section from the start. The family of Mr. and Mrs. Harrow included ten children, of whom only three are living: John G., of California; Lovina, the wife of Quincy A. Wood, of Creston, Iowa, and Mary A., who married John Hardin, of Agency City.

Francis M. Harrow, a son of the subject of our sketch, was born in Kentucky in 1826, and was a youth of eighteen years old when his parents came to Iowa. He was married in Ottumwa, Feb. 18, 1852, to Miss Harriet F. Humphrey, and they became the parents of three children, two of whom are living: Albert G., of Ottumwa, and Frances M., married to F. M. Hunger, of Little Rock, Ark. Francis M. Harrow died on the 1st of October, 1855, and his wife on the 2d of February, 1864. The latter was a devoted member of the Methodist Episcopal Church. Mr. Harrow politically affiliated with the Whig party.

L. T. BAKER, a successful farmer and stock-grower, will be found industriously engaged in his chosen occupation on his fine farm on section 35, Richland Township. Our subject was born in Warrick County, Ind., March 10, 1824, and is the son of John and Mary (Johnston) Baker. His father, who was a farmer by occupation, came to Wapello County in the spring of 1844, and died here in 1863; his widow survived him six years, her death taking place in this county in 1869.

L. T. Baker, when a youth, learned the trade of a wool-carder and was an expert in running carding-machines. In the fall of 1844 he came to this county and followed his occupation for eight years, since which time he has been engaged in farming.

Oct. 14, 1847, Mr. Baker was united in marriage with Jane Hill. Mrs. B. is a native of England, born June 15, 1826, and a daughter of John and Ann Hill. Her parents came to this country from England in 1846, proceeding to Chicago, where they remained two years, and from there came to Wapello County, where they spent the remainder of their lives, the father dying Nov. 24, 1882, and the mother July 30, 1883. Six children were born of the union of our subject and wife: William J., born July 4, 1848, married Emma J. Harris, and is now living in Ottumwa; Sarah A., born Aug. 9, 1850, is the wife of D. W. Terrell, and lives in West Virginia; John H., born Feb. 22, 1852, married Sarah I. Akins, and is living in Richland

Township; Minerva J., born June 5, 1855, is the widow of D. S. Akins, and lives in this township; Frank D., born Oct. 24, 1860; Eunice M., March 26, 1870.

Mr. Baker is the owner of 200 acres of well-improved land. Himself and wife are members in good standing of the Methodist Episcopal Church. Politically he is a Democrat. A view of the residence and surroundings of Mr. Baker is shown on another page of this work.

G. F. MYERS, residing on section 35, Cass Township, where he is successfully engaged in the occupation of a farmer and stock-raiser, was born in Harrison County, W. Va., March 27, 1813. The parents of our subject, John P. and Susanna (Tiller) Myers, were natives of Virginia, and of German descent. They had eleven children, of whom the record is as follows: Elizabeth is the widow of James Duffy, a former resident and farmer of Polk Township; G. F., our subject, was the next in order of birth; Mary became the wife of Peter Ell, and they have both crossed the river to the home beyond; David is a farmer in Wayne County, Iowa; Canzady is deceased; Henry is farming in Hocking County, Ohio; Jesse is deceased; Lucinda is the widow of Harrison Hornback, a farmer of Tama City, Iowa; Emanuel is deceased; John is likewise deceased, and Hester is living with our subject.

In the fall of 1820 the father of these children moved with his family to Fairfield County, Ohio. There he rented a farm, and with his children was industriously occupied in agricultural pursuits until 1830. During that year he moved to Hocking County, Ohio, and purchased 160 acres of land, the same being well improved, and on which he continued to reside until his death, in about 1843. He was connected with the Presbyterian Church. The mother died the year after their removal there, in 1831. She was a member of the Methodist Episcopal Church, and a kind, loving, consistent Christian lady.

The early years of the life of our subject were passed on his father's farm in Hocking County, Ohio, and it was there that he received what education he possesses, in the common schools. He was united in marriage with Miss Hannah R. Butin, March 15, 1838. She was born Feb. 23, 1818, in New York, and is the daughter of Abraham and Olive (Coleman) Butin, the former a native of Holland and the latter of New York. The union of Mr. and Mrs. Myers has been productive of seven children, as follows: Alvira R., born June 12, 1839, became the wife of John Swope, and is now deceased; Abraham, born Nov. 3, 1842, died December 19 following; Sarah J., born June 4, 1844, died Sept. 26, 1845; Emma J., born Oct. 16, 1848, died Sept. 22, 1850; Emily V., born Aug. 28, 1851, died Sept. 18, 1852; Ella M., born Sept. 2, 1854, died March 23, 1856; George D. was born Nov. 3, 1859.

In 1844 the subject of this notice emigrated from Ohio to Iowa, making the trip overland with teams, occupying thirty-one days' time. Arriving in this county he purchased eighty acres of uncultivated land, on which he erected the log cabin common to the pioneers of that day. Into this he moved with his family, and at once began the improvement of his land, with the determination of making it the future abiding-place of himself and family. He had great faith in the future development of the country, and his judgment proved correct. He has lived to see the broad, uncultivated waste transformed to smiling meadows and fields of growing grain, and the log cabin of the pioneer replaced by the handsome and convenient farm residences. Mr. Myers added to his original purchase until he now has a fine farm of 187 acres, all fenced, and the major portion under an advanced state of cultivation. He has one of the finest rock quarries on his farm to be found anywhere within the boundaries of this great commonwealth, and everything on the premises is indicative of his energy and good judgment.

On the 23d day of February, 1885, our subject was called to the death-bed of his loved companion. She passed away with peace and contentment on her countenance, believing she was entering the home where sorrow and pain would trouble her no more. Mrs. Myers was a consistent Christian lady, holding fellowship with the Methodist Episcopal Church.

In 1862 our subject was elected County Supervisor, and has held various other township offices, in all of which he acquitted himself to the satisfaction of all concerned. He is at present Township Trustee, having been the incumbent of that office for upward of five years. Politically he is a Democrat, and seldom fails to cast his vote with that party when opportunity occurs.

Mr. Myers was enrolled in the State militia when eighteen years old, and the following year was elected Lieutenant, which commission, issued by Gov. Robert Lucas, he holds to-day. He was afterward elected Captain, but his term of service was so near at a close that he never asked for his commission.

WILLIAM E. CHAMBERS, senior partner of the law firm of Chambers & McElroy, of Ottumwa, Iowa, was born in Darrtown, Butler Co., Ohio, on the 7th of June, 1846. He completed his school studies at Earlham College, Richmond, Ind., and commenced the study of law with Hon. Jesse Liddell, of that city, in 1866. The following year, his parents having removed to Eaton, Ohio, he returned there and entered the office of Judge A. L. Harris, where he completed his law course, and was admitted to the bar in May, 1869. In June following he came to Ottumwa, and commenced the practice of his profession. In 1870 he became associated in partnership with Hon. A. H. Hamilton, and they operated together until the retirement of Mr. H. from practice, in 1875, and Mr. Chambers then became associated with E. E. McElroy, the firm being now Chambers & McElroy. Mr. Chambers has been a close student and an extensive reader, and has given his entire attention to the duties of his profession. As an advocate he is able and eloquent, and in counsel the firm ranks with the strongest of the profession in this locality.

The wife of our subject was formerly Miss Nannie A. Munson, a lady of fine education and accomplishments, and who was Principal of one of the city schools of Ottumwa. Both Mr. and Mrs. C. are greatly respected in this community, and enjoy the friendship and association of its most cultured people.

M E. S. RUBEL is a farmer and stock-grower on section 3, Richland Township. He was born in Washington County, Tenn., Nov. 16, 1843, and is a son of Henry W. and Margaret (Walter) Rubel, both of whom were natives of Tennessee. Mr. Rubel is of German descent. His great-grandfather, Peter Rubel, came from Bavaria, Germany, in 1760, and settled in Frederick County, Md., where he married Catharine Wirt, March 19, 1770; these were the parents of Henry Rubel, who was born Sept. 23, 1776. In 1798 Peter Rubel and family moved to Washington County, Tenn, where, in 1800, Henry married Miss Barbara Hunter. The youngest child but one born to these parents was Henry Wirt, whose birth occurred May 9, 1821, and who was married to Miss Margaret Walter, Jan. 26, 1843.

All of the brothers and sisters having left Tennessee the care of the aged parents devolved upon Henry W., who with his family moved upon and occupied the old homestead, in 1853. In 1858 the family came to Wapello County, Iowa. The grandparents dying soon afterward, were buried at Mt. Pleasant, Iowa, where also was buried their son, John Rubel, a pioneer Methodist preacher, who died there in 1836. Henry Rubel was widely known in Washington and adjoining counties in Tennessee as a local preacher and exhorter of the Methodist Church.

At the time the family moved to Wapello County the subject of this sketch was but fifteen years of age. He continued with his parents until the death of the mother, which occurred in 1863; the father surviving some years, and dying in Bates County, Mo., in 1878. On Dec. 25, 1865, E. S. Rubel was united in marriage with Miss Jane Bennett, who was born in Hocking County, Ohio, in 1847, and was the daughter of DeWitt and Sarah Bennett. Three children were born to this union—Albert S., Wilbur D. and Lucy B. Mrs. Jane Rubel died March 6, 1874, and Sept. 2, 1877, Mr. Rubel again married, choosing as a companion Miss Susan A. Neer, born in Clarke County, Ohio, Sept. 21, 1849, and daughter of Isaiah and Ann (Lafferty) Neer. To this union four children have been born: Ross N., who died in infancy; Maggie D., Chester W. and Walter G. Mr. Rubel has been successful in his stock-raising, and is also engaged in dairying to a limited extent. He is also breeding graded Holstein cattle. He owns 148 acres of land, all of which is in a high state of cultivation. On the farm is a comfortable dwelling, a good barn, and all the accessories of a well-regulated stock and grain farm.

Mr. Rubel is Clerk of the School Board, having been elected in 1876, serving continuously ever since, and is at present serving his second term as Township Clerk. During the late war he enlisted in Co. B, 36th Iowa Vol. Inf., Aug. 4, 1862. After eight months' service he was discharged on account of sickness and returned home. Regaining his health he again enlisted in the same company and regiment, and served till the close of the war. He was in Gen. Steele's expedition from Little Rock, Ark., to the Red River, and was taken prisoner at Mark's Mills, Ark., and held some months at Camp Ford, Tyler, Tex. With three others he at one time succeeded in escaping from the prison, but after traveling forty miles was recaptured with blood-hounds. He was exchanged at the mouth of Red River, Feb. 25, 1865, and mustered out and discharged at Davenport, Iowa, in September, 1865. Mr. and Mrs. Rubel are members of the Methodist Episcopal Church, and politically our subject is a Republican.

HON. JAMES R. BURGESS, Representative of the Sixth District in the Lower House of the Iowa Legislature, is one of its youngest members and a gentleman of marked ability, both in business transactions and a general knowledge of current events. Mr. Burgess is a native of Bullitt County, Ky., the date of his birth being April 5, 1857. He is the son of John Burgess, a native of Wheeling, W. Va., born Aug. 27, 1829, who removed from his native State to Ohio when a young man, and was there married, Oct. 22, 1852, to Miss Mary Carlisle. She was a native of Brooke County, W. Va., born Aug. 25, 1834, and a daughter of James Carlisle, of Portsmouth, Ohio. From there he removed to Kentucky, and located in Bullitt County, where he engaged in agricultural pursuits; thence removed to Iowa in the spring of 1860, becoming a resident of Keokuk County, and continuing his former vocation. Not long thereafter the trouble between the North and South necessitated a call for troops to defend the Union, and Mr. B. enlisted, becoming a member of Co. K, 33d Iowa Vol. Inf. He marched with his regiment to the scene of conflict, and participated with his comrades in the various engagements and skirmishes which they encountered until the close of the war. He was in the battles at Jenkins' Ferry, Prairie d'Anne, being wounded at the latter place, and was at the siege and capture of Spanish Fort, in Texas. He was subsequently transferred to Company I, in the same regiment, and with his comrades, received an honorable discharge on the 15th of August, 1865.

After his discharge from the service of the Union, John Burgess returned to his home in Keokuk County, where he remained until 1873, and then removed with his family to Ottumwa. In politics he was a Jackson Democrat, and after removing to Ohio was elected Deputy Sheriff of Pike County, serving in 1853–54. He was a man of great force of character and decided views, and wherever he located was recognized as a man eminently fitted to be a leader among his fellows.

The parental household of our subject included six children, four of whom are living, as follows: Lida is the wife of B. Goldsberry, of Bedford, Iowa; Nannie graduated in the High School of Ottumwa, and is a teacher in this city; Willie W. is engaged as a clerk in a dry-goods house, and the fourth is our subject. Mrs. Mary Burgess is still living in Ottumwa, and has been a devoted member of the Methodist Episcopal Church for many years.

James R. Burgess was educated in the city schools of Keokuk County, and came to Ottumwa with his parents. He is a self-made man in every respect, when young being without means or influence, and having nothing to depend upon but his own exertions. He gladly accepted employment at whatever he could secure, using his leisure hours in studying instructive books, and in this way has acquired a fund of knowledge superior to many who have taken a full college course. In addition to this he assisted in educating his sister and brother, and in the course of time, by incessant industry and rigid economy, found himself the possessor of sufficient means to enable him to take a course at the Ottumwa Business College, from which he graduated in 1875, with high recommendations from his instructors.

After leaving college, finding nothing better at hand in which to engage, our subject went on the road as traveling salesman for a firm which dealt in the manufacture and sale of pumps, and two years later purchased the interest of the proprietor, H. M. Fair, and continued the business himself for the following three years. In 1881 he associated himself in partnership with Mr. M. H. Giltner, and they are now operating under the firm name of Giltner & Burgess, and have added to their stock, farm machinery, wagons, buggies, etc.

Notwithstanding the demands of business, Mr. Burgess keeps himself well informed in regard to political and general matters, and has received ready recognition at the hands of his fellow-townsmen as a man well qualified to become a leader in their midst. He became a member of the City Council in the spring of 1885, being elected on the Republican ticket with a majority of between fifty and seventy-five votes, being the first Democratic official elected to this position in sixteen years. In the fall of 1885 he was elected by a union of the Democratic and Greenback parties to the General Assembly of the State, being the youngest member but one in the House. While there he made a vigorous fight on the Cassett Mining Bill, extracts of which were published in the leading papers of this State and Illinois.

In politics Mr. B. has vigorously upheld the principles of the Greenback party, and has uniformly cast his vote in support of its principles. He has always taken a lively interest in the leading questions of the day, and since he became of age has been an out-and-out anti-monopolist. He has represented his district in all the conventions since 1879, and was a delegate to the Indianapolis convention of 1884, and cast his vote for Ben Butler for President. Socially he belongs to the K. of P., the Modern Woodmen, etc.

CHRISTOPHER MEYERS, a saddler and harness-maker doing business at Ottumwa, where he resides, and in which he is meeting with that success which constant attention to his trade has brought him, was born in Elkhart County, Ind., July 6, 1835. He is a son of Joseph Meyers, one of the early settlers of this county, and whose biography is given elsewhere in this work.

Christopher Meyers was but seven years of age when he accompanied his parents to this State, in 1843, and located with them at Agency, this county. It was in that place, attending the log school-house, which was 16x16 feet in dimensions, and had its puncheon floors and slabs for seats as well as writing-desks, that our subject obtained his education. When fourteen years of age young Meyers was apprenticed to the shoemaker's trade, and after working at the same for three years thoroughly mastered it, but during that time only received his board and clothes as remuneration for his services. At the expiration of his apprenticeship he received a suit of clothes and $5 in cash, and started out in the world to do for himself. He continued to work at his trade until 1865, when he added thereto that of harness-making. In 1871, while a resident of Agency, he embarked in the grocery business and was thus occupied for some years. Closing out the latter business he engaged in the sale of confectionery, and in 1884 went to Pierre, Dak. There he was engaged in business for a time, but not liking the country, and still less the poor success he was meeting with at that place, he returned and settled at Ottumwa, where he has been engaged in the saddle and harness business until the present time.

Mr. Meyers was married at Agency City, in 1854, to Miss Martha E. Brantner. She was born in Pennsylvania, and has borne our subject four children, three daughters and one son: Florence E.;

Josephine, wife of C. H. Sage, station agent for the B. & M. R. R. at Endicott, Neb.; Claude M., and Rena May, who died in infancy. In politics Mr. Meyers is a stanch Democrat. He is always to be found at county conventions and has been a delegate to State conventions for a number of times. He always takes an active part in all the campaigns, and has held several local offices within the gift of the people. Having passed almost an entire lifetime within the boundaries of the county, he has seen it develop from a wild, uncultivated district to the prominent position it occupies in comparison with other agricultural counties in the State. From a little village he has watched the growth of Ottumwa until it has attained to the population of 12,000 inhabitants, and in place of the log cabins which were to be seen in every direction throughout the county when he first came here, one can now see beautiful farms with fine and magnificent residences upon them, and surrounded by such modern improvements as go to make up happy homes. Socially Mr. Meyers is a member of Magnolia Lodge No. 24, I. O. O. F., and has represented his lodge in the Grand Lodge. He is also a member of the Camp, and has held all the offices of that division of the order.

EVAN JONES is a highly respected resident of Ottumwa, and a master mechanic of the C. B. & Q. R. R. He is a native of the British Empire, being born in England on the 21st of June, 1845. When he was six years of age he came with his parents to the United States. He is the son of Evan and Margaret (Ashton) Jones, and soon after reaching American shores, they located at Utica, N. Y. Evan Jones was a tanner by trade and established himself in business there in company with Richard Moses, the firm title being Moses & Jones. In 1853 the elder Jones severed his connection with the business at Utica, and coming west as far as Illinois, located near Jonesboro, where he engaged in mercantile pursuits for a short time, and thence removed to Burlington, Iowa. In 1855, at the commencement of the grading of the B. & M. R. R., he expected to obtain employment in connection with the building of this road, but being disappointed went to Griswold City, Mo., and entered the employ of the Missouri Pacific, with which he remained for the two years following. He then crossed back over the Mississippi to Nauvoo, Ill., where he was engaged in the county produce trade for the following nine months. This venture proving unsuccessful he returned to Iowa and located in Henry County, where he engaged in keeping boarders, which latter business proved successful. He was finally burned out, losing all his worldly effects. He died in Henry County, Iowa, in the fall of 1858. His wife, the mother of our subject, is still living and is a resident of Ottumwa. Both parents were connected with the Episcopal Church, and in politics, Evans Jones, Sr., was a pronounced Democrat.

The subject of this sketch was reared under the parental roof and received his primary education in the public schools. He afterward took a course in the High School, but is principally a self-educated man, being fond of books and making the most of his opportunities. He commenced his railroad work in the employ of the B. & M. in August, 1864, and remained with that company until the fall of 1868. He then abandoned this position to take a more desirable one with the Toledo, Peoria & Warsaw, with headquarters at Peoria. He was thus occupied for one year, and then returned to Burlington and to the B. & M.. In December following he came into Ottumwa, where he entered the shops under the superintendence of J. D. Carder. In September, 1880, he was promoted as general foreman of the locomotive department, which position he has since occupied and takes pride in the excellence of his work.

Mr. Jones since coming here has been prominent in the affairs of his community and is one of the Aldermen of the Second Ward. In politics he is a stanch Republican and socially belongs to the Masonic fraternity, Des Moines Lodge No. 1

Evan Jones was united in marriage with Miss Emily Eads, at Burlington, Iowa, in January, 1868. Mrs. Jones was born and reared in Burlington and received her education in the schools of that city. Of her union with our subject there have been

born eight children, viz., Anna, George, Charles, Maude, Paul and Clarence; Ella and Cora are deceased. Their home is pleasantly located on East Second street, and they number among their friends and acquaintances the most cultured citizens of Ottumwa.

R. W. HUSTON, M. D., a skillful and prominent physician of Eldon, is a native of Ohio, born in Ashland County near Hayesville, June 15, 1848. He is the son of Samuel and Jane (Ginn) Huston, both natives of Scotland. The father emigrated to the United States in 1811, and the mother two years later. They first settled in Washington County, N. Y., and were married there in 1843, whence they removed to Cuyahoga County, Ohio, and from there went to Ashland County two years later and engaged in farming pursuits.

Our subject remained with his parents and assisted in the lighter duties around the homestead until he was sixteen years of age, and then went to Vermillion Institute at Hayesville, where he took a literary course of three years; then went to Nebraska and entered the Literary Department of Otoe University, in 1867, where he was occupied alternately as teacher and student. From there he went to Wooster, Ohio, and after taking a three years' course in the university graduated from that institution Feb. 25, 1871. He had in the meantime also pursued his medical studies, and now took a course in the College of Physicians and Surgeons at Keokuk, Iowa, graduating Feb. 25, 1879. He began the practice of his profession at Champaign City, and became a resident of Eldon in 1873, and from that time to the present has been continuously engaged in practice, and has thoroughly established himself in the confidence and esteem of the citizens of this locality.

Dr. Houston was married, Nov. 26, 1874, to Miss Hortense J. Scott, of Warsaw, Ind., the daughter of George Washington and Elizabeth (Horn) Scott, of Ohio. Of this union there have been born five children, as follows: Willis, who died at the age of nine months; Milton C., George Garfield, Robert Monroe and Myrtle F. The Doctor has been prominently identified with public affairs since coming to this section. He was Mayor of the city for six terms and Trustee in 1879. In politics he is a reliable Republican and during the war served in the Home Guard for three months. Socially he is connected with the I. O. O. F. and the K. of P.

Samuel Huston, the father of our subject, departed this life in 1867, at the advanced age of eighty-seven years. He was a Captain in the War of 1812, and at the close of his military career returned to his homestead in Washington County, N. Y., and superintended the operations of his farm until his hands were folded for his final rest. He was a good man in every respect, honest and upright in his transactions with his fellow-men, and was prominently connected with the Presbyterian Church. His wife passed from the scenes of earth Nov. 11, 1866, one year previous to the decease of her husband; she was seventy-nine years of age. She also was a member of the Presbyterian Church, and left behind her a record of kindly deeds and womanly virtues. The parental family consisted of ten children, of whom six are now living: Samuel, Lucinda, and Jane, the latter the widow of Charles Jarvis, all live in Ohio; John; Jasper is a resident of Jefferson County, Iowa; Mary Ann is the wife of F. E. Crocker, and lives in Gage County, Neb. A lithographic portrait of Dr. Huston is shown on another page of this work.

PETER FRANCIS, wagon and carriage manufacturer residing at Eddyville, and Mayor of that city, was born March 30, 1828, near Wheeling, W. Va. He is the son of Emanuel and Sabra (Crow) Francis, both natives of West Virginia. The former was born in the year 1800 and is yet living, residing in Marshall County, W. Va. Our subject's mother died in 1863, at the age of sixty-five. Peter Francis was reared on his father's farm and there continued to reside until September, 1844, in the meantime attending the common schools and assisting in the labors on the farm. He then engaged to learn the wagon-maker's trade in Moundsville, the county seat of Marshall County, W. Va., where he continued to work at his trade for eleven years. In the spring of 1855 he came to Eddyville, this county, the journey being made by river and requiring two weeks of irksome travel. He was thus one of the early residents of that place and has since made it his home, becoming one of the leading and most enterprising men there. On his first locating there he engaged in running a sawmill and was thus occupied until 1870. He then took a contract in company with Jacob Bausher for the furnishing of rock for the building of bridges for the Iowa Central Railroad Company. He established his present business Jan. 1, 1872, and has since conducted it in his customary business-like way, and as a consequence, has met with signal success.

Mr. Francis was married, Aug. 17, 1848, to Mary Raymond, a native of Delaware, and a daughter of Joseph H. Raymond. Their union has been blest by the birth of the following children: Florence, wife of John F. Skelton, a jeweler by trade and a resident of California; William P., living at home; Edward M., a butcher of Albion, Iowa; Clara Belle, who became the wife of a Mr. Cline, of California, is deceased.

Mr. Francis has considerable town property, and at this writing is Mayor of the thriving little city of Eddyville, having been elected to that office in March, 1886. Mr. Francis is a member of the Masonic fraternity, having joined that order at Moundsville, W. Va., in 1854.

As a representative not only of the pioneer element of Wapello County, but of her excellent business men, we are pleased to present the portrait of Mr. Francis in this connection.

JOHN HARNESS. The subject of this history has been a resident of the Hawkeye State for a period of over thirty years, and during his long residence in this section has undeniably built up for himself a reputation as an honest man and a good citizen. He owns and occupies a comfortable homestead in Green Township, on section 20, which consists of 100 acres of finely cultivated land, a handsome farm dwelling, good barns and outhouses, and everything pertaining to a first-class farm estate.

Mr. Harness is a native of Darke County, Ohio, the date of his birth having been July 8, 1840. He is the son of Gideon and Sarah (Shook) Harness, both natives of Ohio. After their marriage and after the birth of our subject, they started for the farther West, and, crossing the Father of Waters, came into Wapello County, Iowa, and settled upon the tract of land which is the present homestead of our subject. At the time of their coming here John H. was a small boy, just old enough to assist in the lightest duties around the farm. He was reared under the parental roof and obtained a fair education in the common schools. He remained with his parents until he had attained to years of manhood, and during the progress of the late Civil War became a soldier of the Union, enlisting Aug. 14, 1862, in Co. E, 36th Iowa Vol. Inf., serving until Sept. 25, 1864. In the meantime he participated in the following battles: Ft. Pemberton; Coffeeville, Miss.; Helena, Ark.; and many others until April, 1864, when, at the battle of Mark's Mills, he received a gunshot wound through the left knee, left hip and right side, the three wounds disabling him so much that he was unfitted for further service, and accordingly received an honorable discharge. After his enlistment he was promoted Sergeant, and at the time of being wounded was among the troops detailed to open a passage for the waters of the Mississippi to flow into the bayous of Moon Lake in order that steamboats might effect the passage up the Yazoo River. To add to his distress at the time he was wounded he was also captured by the rebels and confined as a prisoner from the 25th of April to the 3d of July. At the date last mentioned he was removed to St. John's Hospital at Little Rock, Ark., where he remained until he was discharged from service the following September.

Mr. Harness then returned home and resumed his studies at the district schools for two years following, for the purpose of fitting himself for a teacher. He entered upon the duties of his profession soon afterward, and was thus occupied for the following five years. He then purchased a stock of general merchandise and opened a store at

Ormanville, which he operated until 1877, when he engaged in farming for three years following, and in 1880 was elected to the office of Recorder of Wapello County. At the expiration of his first term he was re-elected, serving two years more, and then retired to the old homestead, where he has since been engaged in general farming.

John Harness and Miss Linnia Ann Heckart were united in marriage Oct. 13, 1867. Mrs. H. is a native of this county, and the daughter of Joseph and Polly (Brashear) Heckart, and by her union with our subject has become the mother of eight children, as follows: John Irvin, Sarepta Ellen, William Frederick, George Elder, Gideon Ralph, Joseph LeRoy, Alice May and Walter Henry. Mr. Harness, politically, is a stanch Republican. He is a member of the G. A. R.; and was first Post Commander of Cloutman Post No. 69, and is one of the prominent officials of his order.

Gideon Harness, the father of our subject, departed this life at his home in Green Township in 1856, at the age of forty-one years, eight months and sixteen days. The mother survived him twenty-nine years, dying Sept. 14, 1885, at the age of sixty-six years. She was a highly respected Christian lady and a devoted member of the Methodist Episcopal Church.

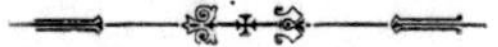

S. S. COCKERILL, an honored resident of Green Township, and pleasantly located on section 14, has been a resident of Wapello County since 1855, and during a period of more than thirty years has fully established himself in the confidence and esteem of his fellow-citizens. He is occupied in the peaceful pursuits of a farmer, and in all respects is filling the place of a valued citizen and worthy member of the community. Mr. Cockerill is a native of Hampshire County, Va., and was born in 1818. He is the son of William S. and Anna (Leadman) Cockerill, natives of the same State, who, after their marriage and birth of their son, our subject, removed to Fayette County, Ohio, where the latter was reared to farming pursuits. The affectionate wife and mother died when our subject was a little lad six years old, and he was taken from his home and cared for elsewhere. At sixteen years of age he returned to his father and lived with him for the following five years. He then went to Greene County, Ohio, and engaged in teaming from Beaver Creek Mill to Dayton, being thus occupied for a period of four years. He then returned to Fayette County and remained until the fall of 1855, when he crossed the Hoosier State to Illinois and located in Peoria County, remaining there until the following spring. Then, setting his face for the further West, he crossed the Mississippi and coming to Wapello County, Iowa, purchased eighty acres of land in Green Township, on section 14, which constitutes a part of his present homestead. He immediately set about the improvement and cultivation of his purchase, and added to it as time and means permitted until now the estate consists of 200 acres, all improved and under a good state of cultivation.

In 1843 Mr. Cockerill was united in marriage with Miss Eveline Mason, of Ohio, and they became the parents of three children, as follows: William S. died in 1868; Mary Ellen became the wife of James Fishback, of Highland County, Ohio; Henry Milton is engaged in the wholesale tea and spice business at Ottumwa, Iowa; Mrs. Eveline Cockerill departed this life in 1848, at the home of her husband in Fayette County, Ohio.

Mr. C. was married, the second time, in 1853, to Miss Elizabeth Smith, of Ohio, who became the mother of one child, a daughter, Laura, who married William Branch, of Ohio, and died in 1881. Mrs. Elizabeth Cockerill died the year of her marriage, in 1853.

The third marriage of Mr. C. occurred in July, 1857, when he was united with Mrs. Catharine (Jackson) Wilson. Of this union there were born two children—Charles Clarence and Flora D. Mrs. C. is a highly respected lady and a devoted member of the Methodist Episcopal Church.

Mr. C. has visited Ohio four times since becoming a resident of the Hawkeye State. The greater part of his life has been devoted to farming pursuits, although he followed the trade of a painter for seven years, in Ohio. Before the organization of the Republican party he was a thorough Whig in sentiment, but since the abandonment of the old party has cordially indorsed the principles of the new. He has always taken an active interest in the general welfare of the community, and has filled the office of Constable for two years in Green Township.

William S. Cockerill, the father of our subject, was a soldier in the War of 1812, and Captain of Militia in Ohio. He was a Justice of the Peace for a number of years, and was a prominent member of the Methodist Episcopal Church. He was a man of decided views and great force of character, a good judge of human nature, and keenly observant of what was going on around him in the world. He departed this life in 1879, at the ripe old age of nearly ninety years, at peace with his neighbors and with a conscience "void of offense."

JOHN W. WELLMAN, one of the honored pioneers of Wapello County, and at present Postmaster of Amador, is a native of Lawrence County, Ky.. where he was born in 1822. His parents were Michael and Anna (Adams) Wellman, of Virginia, who, when young people, removed to Kentucky. Their family consisted of nine children, five living: J. W., of our sketch; Mary, the wife of Benjamin Jones, deceased, is now living in this county; Nancy, Mrs. Spaulding; Harrison, of Jefferson County, Kan., and Lucius H., of this county. Michael Wellman came to this county in 1844, while Iowa was yet a Territory, and settled in Adams Township, on section 14. He was a Whig in politics, and, with his estimable wife, was a member of the Christian Church. Both died in this county.

Mr. Wellman was educated in Kentucky and visited Iowa in 1842. He at that time met Gov. Chambers, with whom he spent many pleasant hours. Our subject was married, in Maysville, Aug. 22, 1847, to Miss Mary Hendrickson, also a native of Kentucky and born April 15, 1825. They became the parents of eight children, seven now living: William H., and Angeline, who became the wife of Anderson Hunter, live in this county; Winfield S. is in Davis County; Kittie, Mrs. John Hendricks, is in this county; Belle is the wife of Albert Green, of Jefferson County, Kan.; Georgiana, Mrs. Alfred Marts, lives in Center Township; Frank is at home.

Our subject came to this county in 1848, and purchased a section of land in Adams Township. Two years later he sold out and moved to Ottumwa, where he embarked in mercantile pursuits, and in 1851 returned to Adams Township, where he has since resided. He is Democratic in politics and has held the various local offices. In 1883 he was appointed Postmaster by President Arthur, which position he has since held. In connection with his office he has a grocery stand which he runs to advantage. Mr. Wellman still retains possession of his farm of 140 acres, and since the time of coming here has been closely identified with the industrial and agricultural interests of this section. He came to the county poor in purse, but by industry and enterprise has accumulated a competency. Mrs. W. is a member of the Christian Church, and our subject in religious views adheres to the doctrines of the Methodist Episcopal Church.

JAMES RUSH, a prosperous farmer and stock raiser of Adams Township, is pleasantly located on section 12, and in his operations is meeting with success. He is a native of Brown County, Ill., and was born on the 3d of August, 1834, his parents being John and Martha (Lanning) Rush, natives of Somerset County, Pa., who, when children, went with their parents to Ohio and settled in Athens County. They were married in the latter county in 1830, and the following year went to Brown County, Ill. The mother of our subject died in about 1851, at Ottumwa. She was a lady highly respected wherever known for her kindness of heart and noble principles, and was prominently connected with the Christian Church.

The second marriage of Mr. Rush was with Miss Luanna McCallister, of Lucas County, Iowa, and of their union there was one child, Sarah, now the wife of Thomas Summers, and residing in Arkansas. The father of our subject died in the latter State in 1878. He was Democratic in politics, and wherever he made his home ranked among the most useful and worthy citizens.

The subject of our sketch was the second child of his parents' family, and was eleven years old when they removed to Wapello County. Iowa was then a Territory and the face of a white man seldom seen, but Indians were plenty and roamed over the country in bands. After arriving at years of manhood our subject went into Schuyler County in 1856, where he had already secured a farm and had begun to improve it. He was married, May 16, 1856, to Miss Eliza Jane McAlister, who was born in Washington County, Jan. 18, 1840. Her parents were John and Luanna (Stone) McAlister, natives respectively of Indiana and Connecticut. Of the union of our subject and wife there were born three children: William J., a teacher in Adams Township; Alice, at home, and Bertha who is attending school.

Mr. and Mrs. R. are valued members of the community, and have watched with genuine interest and satisfaction the growth and development of their adopted county. Their homestead now includes 220 acres of fine farming land, embellished with a tasteful residence, good barns and outbuildings, and all the accessories of a first-class country home.

JAMES KISINGER, an honored pioneer of the Hawkeye State, came to Iowa with his parents in 1841, while it was yet a Territory, settling first in Van Buren County, and has been a resident of Wapello County since 1852. He has witnessed with interest and pleasure the remarkable changes which have taken place in the condition of the country, and as a good citizen has contributed of his time and means as he was able, to every worthy enterprise, and now, in his later days, established upon a comfortable homestead, is reaping the reward of industry and economy.

The subject of this biography is a native of Berkeley County, Va., and was born May 3, 1817. His parents were George and Nancy (McCormick) Kisinger, the former a native of Maryland and the latter of Virginia. He removed from his native State with his parents in 1836, going first to Ohio and settling in Champaign County, where they carried on farming pursuits upon rented land for the following five years. They then determined to go farther westward and, crossing the Mississippi, came to Iowa, first settling in Van Buren County. They remained there for a period of nine years and then removed to Wapello County, and purchased 167 acres of land in Green Township, on sections 18 and 19. The land was in its original condition and they immediately began its improvement and cultivation, establishing a comfortable home which is still in possession of our subject, although he has parted with a portion of the land.

The marriage of James Kisinger and Miss Ann Young was celebrated in Ohio, July 31, 1838. Mrs. K. is a native of Franklin County, Ohio, and the daughter of James and Eleanor Young, the former of Irish birth and parentage and the latter a native of Pennsylvania. Of this union there were born the following: Mary E. became the wife of William Simpson and is living in Clarke County, Iowa; George is a farmer of Young County, Tex.; John is a resident of the same locality; Margaret N., the wife of Madison Parker, and Rebecca are in Texas; Isabell is at home; Rosa, the wife of David Green, of Texas, died Sept. 29, 1886, aged twenty-seven years and six months; Henry, born in 1845, died in Des Moines County, Iowa, May 9, 1848; Nancy died when a child, in May, 1848; James died in 1862, aged eight months.

In 1850 Mr. K. took an overland trip to California, being on the road from April 17 to August 28. After reaching the Golden State he entered the mines and was very successful in his search for the yellow ore. He remained there two years, reaching home on the 17th of June, 1852. He made the journey homeward by way of the Isthmus and New Orleans, and upon his return continued his farming operations until the present time. During his sojourn in California Mr. Kisinger met with quite a serious accident occasioned by the caving in of a sand bank, which crushed him so that he was disabled for three months.

George Kisinger, the father of our subject, was Postmaster at Pittsburgh for a number of years. He died in August, 1872; the mother passed to her rest in November, 1852. George Kisinger, Sr., the grandfather of our subject, was reared near Mt. Vernon, the home of Washington, and was well acquainted with the Father of his Country. He also frequently saw Gen. Lafayette when he was in the United States, in 1827.

JOB P. JAY, an early settler of Wapello County, has been a resident of the Hawkeye State since 1854, when he located in Adams Township, where he has since resided. He at one time was the owner of 1,400 acres of land, and twelve miles of rail fence. Mr. Jay was born in Miami County, Ohio, Oct. 28, 1816, and is the son of Samuel and Bathsheba B. (Pugh) Jay, both natives of North Carolina, and reared in the faith of the Society of Friends. His father was born in 1784, and the mother in 1788. In early life they emigrated to Miami County, Ohio, when the latter was but a wilderness, and there Samuel Jay opened up three farms amidst the heavy timber, which, as may be supposed, involved a vast amount of labor.

The parental family consisted of ten children, only two of whom are now living: Verlinda, the wife of Robert Jenkins, with her husband, is deceased; David died in Grant County, Ind.; Rachel became Mrs. Samuel Jenkins, and she and her husband both died in Miami County, Ohio; Elizabeth, Mrs. Russell, is living in Wayne County, Ind.; Job P. was the next in order of birth; Samuel died in Grant County, Ind.; William, in Miami County, Ohio, and Thomas, in Indiana; Lydia, the youngest daughter, died in early childhood. Mr. Jay was a hard worker, and kept himself well informed upon matters of general interest. Both he and his wife remained connected with the Friends during their lifetime, Samuel Jay being an Elder for many years. He departed this life Dec. 14, 1859, aged seventy-five years; the mother died Jan. 1, 1850, when sixty-two years of age. They were greatly respected, and had trained their children to principles of honor and morality.

The subject of our sketch was educated in the by-gone log school-house, and remained under the parental roof until he attained to years of manhood. He was married, Sept. 24, 1840, to Miss Rachel Commons, a native of Wayne County, Ind., who was born Aug. 14, 1817. Her parents were John and Elizabeth (Mouch) Commons, the former of Virginia and the latter of Georgia. Mr. and Mrs. Jay became the parents of ten children, four deceased. Those living are as follows: Mary E. became the wife of William Asbury, and lives in Ottumwa; David lives in Adams Township; Martha and Rhoda are twins; the former is married and lives in Shelby County, Iowa; Rhoda married Dr. Arnolds, of Wayne County, Iowa; Austin lives in Franklin Township; Charles M. is in Los Angeles, Cal.

WILLIAM WADDINGTON, a prosperous dry-goods merchant of Ottumwa, Iowa, is a native of the Buckeye State, where he was born in 1845. His parents were James and Ellen (Kerr) Waddington, natives of England, who emigrated to this country in 1843, and located in Seneca, Ohio, where, however, they remained but a short time, soon afterward removing to Steubenville, where the father pursued his calling as a shoe manufacturer. In 1849 he came west with the intention of taking up a tract of land, but was stricken down with cholera, and died at St. Louis, Mo. The family included five children, three only now living: John, of this county; James, a merchant of Chillicothe, and our subject. After the death of her first husband Mrs. Waddington was married to Abram Jewett, and of this union there were born five children, three now living—Ellen, Mary J. and Joseph. Mr. and Mrs. Jewett came to this county in 1861.

The subject of our sketch attended school eight years in his native county, and in after years pursued his studies at night after the labors of the day were ended. By this means he obtained a fund of useful information and ranks among the intelligent men of the day. In 1869 Mr. Waddington commenced business in Chillicothe, and by close attention to business has accumulated a fine property. He came to Ottumwa in 1880, and erected the building which he now occupies. He carries a stock of $4,000, and enjoys an extensive and profitable trade.

The marriage of our subject with Miss Mary Morgan was celebrated at Oskaloosa in 1871. Mrs. Waddington is the daughter of Fielding and Keziah J. (Harding) Morgan, who were pioneers of Van Buren County, settling there in 1835, and there Mrs. Waddington was born on the 12th of June, 1849. Mr. and Mrs. Waddington are the parents of three children—Albert H., Gracie and Bessie. Their pleasant home is the resort of the cultured people of the city. Mr. Waddington has attained to a high standing in the business and social world, and is considered one of the most valued members of the community. He belongs to the Masonic fraternity, being a member of Ottumwa Lodge No. 16.

L. Z. RUPE, prominently located on section 27, in Keokuk Township, is successfully engaged in farming and stock-raising, and by his upright life and straightforward business methods has fully established himself in the confidence and esteem of his fellow-citizens.

Mr. Rupe is a native of the Buckeye State, having been born in Gallia, Feb. 4, 1824. He is the son of John and Rebecca (Lewis) Rupe, the father a native of Virginia and the mother of New Jersey. The parental household consisted of the children whose record is as follows: John enlisted in the 7th Iowa Cavalry during the war, and was frozen to death while in service near Ft. Kearney; Israel, a farmer by occupation, is a resident of Kingman County, Kan.; he also served in the late war as a member of the 7th Iowa Cavalry; Samuel is farming in Washington County, Ark.; Enoch is carrying on agricultural pursuits in this county; Prudence, the widow of Parker Gee, lives in Oregon; Hannah became the wife of John Hubler, and is now deceased; Mary A. and Rosetta are also deceased; William is a farmer of Davis County, Iowa; Jerome Tillotson married Miss Ellen Rupe, and is engaged in farming pursuits in this county.

Mr. Rupe of our sketch spent the early part of his life on the farm and in attendance at the subscription schools of his native county in Ohio. He was reared by his excellent parents to habits of industry and economy, and at an early age began to "paddle his own canoe." Soon after becoming of age he took unto himself a wife and helpmeet in the person of Miss Mary M. Smith, the daughter of Solomon and Catharine (Hartsook) Smith, who were early pioneers of Ohio and are now deceased. They were most excellent and worthy people, useful members of society and devoted to the Baptist Church, of which they were prominent and valued members.

Mr. and Mrs. Rupe became the parents of seven children who are recorded as follows: John M. was born Sept. 9, 1845, and is now a farmer of Keokuk Township; Rosena married M. A. Thomas, who is also pursuing agriculture in this township; Christina became the wife of William R. Coen, a farmer of Shasta County, Cal.; Emma married John H. Loy, a farmer of Wapello County; Mary was united in marriage with W. T. Turner, who is carrying on farming in Keokuk Township; Daniel accidentally shot himself, and died on the 21st of March, 1879; Addison operates a farm in Keokuk Township.

Mr. Rupe came to this county with his parents in 1845, and is well acquainted with the hardships of pioneer life. He and his parents were early settlers of this region before there had been erected any mills and before there was any market for their farm produce. They were obliged to haul their grain twenty-five or thirty miles to mill, the nearest institution of this kind being at Bentonsport, in Van Buren County. The father of our subject entered forty acres of land to which he subsequently added, and as time passed on became possessed of eighty acres.

L. Z. Rupe was an industrious and energetic man and during his younger years learned the art of basket-making, which, in his later days, proves a source of amusement and employment and assists in whiling away the time which might otherwise hang heavy on his hands, as he is never happy when idle. In stormy weather especially, he may be still found working at his trade, and is ever ready to relate interesting incidents of the time when he first crossed the Mississippi and located in the Hawkeye State. In his younger years he was prominent in the affairs of his township, holding the office of Justice of the Peace for about thirty-five years, and has been Secretary of the Board of School Directors for the past twenty years. Politically he is a Republican in a Democratic township, and is esteemed a useful man, a good neighbor and a valued citizen. Mr. R. is a member of the Universalist Church.

ANDREW JACKSON HICKS, a prominent farmer and successful stock-raiser of Green Township, is pleasantly located on section 29, and in his joint operations is meeting with that success which perseverance and industry almost invariably accomplish. The subject of this history was born in Indiana, Aug. 11, 1832, and is the son of Joseph and Elizabeth (Bower) Hicks, natives respectively of West Virginia and Ohio. The mother died in 1834, and was buried in Owen County, Ind. The father survived his partner until 1872, dying in the same State and county at the age of sixty-seven years, and was buried by the side of his wife. They were most excellent and worthy people of true Christian character, and carried out in their daily lives the religious principles which they had professed. Joseph Hicks, in his younger days, was a member of the Indiana State Militia, and took great pride and pleasure in the military drill.

The first marriage of our subject occurred in 1850, with Miss Mary A. Luther, the daughter of Michael and Polly (Nicholson) Luther, natives of North Carolina. They became the parents of four children, of whom Joseph M. is deceased; Marila was the second child; Margaret is deceased, and Andrew Jackson Hicks, Jr. Mrs. Mary A. Hicks died in Green Township, Dec. 12, 1864.

After the death of the mother of these children, who was deeply mourned on account of her devotion to duty and her tender and affectionate care over her family, Mr. Hicks made his first trip across the Mississippi, and coming into Wapello County, Iowa, purchased 160 acres of land. The following spring he returned to Indiana for his children, and after coming back settled upon his purchase and began its improvement and cultivation. After remaining here one season and being not quite satisfied with the result of his operations, he returned to Indiana, in the meantime, however, retaining possession of his Iowa property. The trips between the States were made overland and occupied about fifteen days. In 1864, again taking his team, Mr. Hicks once more proceeded westward and crossed the Father of Waters to the land he had located in Wapello County, resolving now to remain upon it and establish a permanent home. He has been prospered in his undertaking and has added to his landed property as time passed on. He is now the owner of 260 acres, which embraces a part of sections 19, 20, 29 and 30, all improved and under a good state of cultivation. In 1885 he erected a substantial farm residence on section 29, and his barns and out-buildings are indicative of the thrifty and thorough-going agriculturist.

A. J. Hicks for his second wife married Mrs. Mahulda J. (Ashcroft) Harness, widow of Hiram Harness, in Wapello County, April 9, 1871. Mrs. Hicks is a daughter of Elijah and Eliza (Dalton) Ashcroft, natives respectively of Kentucky and Indiana. Of this union there were born five children, viz., Sylvia, Samuel L., Myrta, Harvey H. and Lee.

The family residence of our subject is a model of convenience and comfort. The barns and out-buildings are substantial structures, fitted up with conveniences for the storing of grain and the shelter of stock. To the breeding of the latter Mr. Hicks has given much attention. His herd of cattle includes some of the finest animals in this section. In 1880 he purchased a full blood Durham, expecting to make a specialty of this breed of cattle, and so far has been successful in all his operations in this direction.

Since coming into this county Mr. Hicks has been prominent in its public affairs, and has held nearly all the township offices. Politically he has identified himself with the Democratic party, and has always been willing to assist in maintaining the principles of temperance and good order. He came to this vicinity a poor man, and his present possessions are the result of his own energy and industry.

He is fulfilling all the obligations of a good citizen, and is enjoying in a marked degree the friendship and respect of his fellow-citizens.

GEORGE W. MANRO, an early pioneer of Wapello County, crossed the Mississippi from the State of Ohio with his parents while in infancy, in 1846, and therefore really "grew up with the country." He has known no other home since that time and is as much a native of the Hawkeye State as though he had been born here. The real place of his birth, however, was Tuscarawas County, Ohio, and the date thereof June 1, 1846. His parents were James and Sarah (Fisher) Manro, and soon after the birth of their son, our subject, they started for the western country and coming into Wapello County, Iowa, made their first location in Keokuk Township. Here, James Manro entered a tract of wild land and commenced the improvement of a farm. He continued at this calling for the following six years, meeting with fair success, and then ceased his earthly labors, being stricken down in the prime of life and dying in 1852. The parental household included thirteen children, who are recorded as follows: Sarah Ann is the widow of John Alleshouse, and resides in Ohio; Elizabeth is deceased; Catharine, the widow of David Dibbles, resides in Ottumwa; Eveline, deceased, was the wife of William Pedrick; John T. is deceased; Nathan F. is a citizen of Ottumwa; James A. is deceased; George W., our subject, and five who died in infancy.

George Manro was left an orphan at the age of six years. He remained at the home of his uncle, Mr. McNamee, for a time, and then went to live with a gentleman by the name of Luther Hite, within whose household he remained until he was seventeen years of age. At this time, the Civil War being in progress, he enlisted as a soldier in the 8th Iowa Cavalry for three years under Col. Dorr. He was mustered in at Davenport and soon afterward sent with his regiment to Western Tennessee, where he first experienced the hardships and privations of army life. They were there engaged in fighting Bushwhackers and guarding railroads until the following spring, when they were ordered to Nashville and thence to Atlanta. Here the division of the army to which the regiment of young Manro belonged was engaged in fighting the rebel General Hood, who was finally driven across the Tennessee River. The regiment continued in active service for the year following, and in the winter of 1864–65 went into winter quarters. In the spring following they joined the command of Gen. Wilson and were sent to Tuscaloosa, where they fought Forrest with bad results. Here young Manro was captured by Forrest's men and held for twenty-four hours, after which he was paroled and remained with the regiment until he was exchanged. Subsequently at Macon, Ga., he was taken ill and was there at the time Jefferson Davis was captured and brought in. Here also his regiment was mustered out and then sent to Clinton, Iowa, where they received their final discharge in August, 1865. Although young and strong when entering the army, the exposures and privations which Mr. Manro endured undermined his health, and to-day he is a broken-down man. His two brothers, James and Nathan, were also in the army. The former was wounded between Iuka and Corinth at the time of the battles in that vicinity and died on the field; Nathan served three years and escaped serious injury.

In 1873 the subject of our sketch was married to Miss Augusta L, the daughter of L. A. and Elizabeth (McNatt) Myers. The parents of Mrs. M., formerly of Ohio and Tennessee respectively, now reside near Eldon in this county. Our subject and his wife became the parents of four children, as follows: Fred M. was born July 9, 1874; Lizzie D., Feb. 20, 1878; Iva G., July 17, 1881; Lewis L., Nov. 10, 1882.

After his return from the army Mr. Manro purchased a tract of land in Keokuk Township, and is now successfully engaged in farming and stock raising. Although not able to do hard labor, he is fully equal to the task of superintending the affairs of his homestead and is considered one of the representative farmers and business men of this section. The family occupy a comfortable dwelling, and the barn and outhouses of the estate are all in first-class condition and amply suited for the storing of grain and the shelter of stock. All the surroundings indicate substantial comfort and the pleasures of a peaceful farm life. Mr. and Mrs. Manro enjoy in a marked degree the confidence and esteem of their neighbors and are members in good standing of the Methodist Episcopal Church. In politics Mr. M. is a stanch Republican and conscientiously casts his vote in support of the principles of that party.

A lithographic view of Mr. Mauro's place is shown in this work.

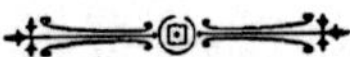

T. J. LAYNE, a prominent and respected citizen of Chillicothe, where he is passing the sunset of life retired from active labor, was born in Goochland County, Va., Feb. 27, 1812. The parents of our subject were Elisha and Elizabeth (Layne) Layne, natives of the Old Dominion. The father died Nov. 27, 1860. He was a member of the Baptist Church, took great interest in promoting the cause of the Master and also in all public enterprises that were calculated for the good of the community in which he resided. The mother of our subject died Nov. 31, 1860. She was also a member of the Baptist Church, and bore her husband ten children, four daughters and six sons: Matilda, Mrs. Doyle, is deceased; Eliza A. is the widow of John Galey, and is living with her children; T. J., our subject, was next in order of birth; Elisha B. died in 1849, being at the time of his demise a candidate for the Legislature of his State; Elizabeth, now deceased, was the wife of W. A. Long; Jacob V. was killed in 1880 by the running away of a team; Samuel M. is a farmer of Montgomery County, Ind.; Preston M. is a prosperous physician of Crawfordsville, Ind.; Letitia died in 1846. In 1815 the parental family of our subject moved from Virginia to Kentucky, where the father at once entered upon the task of clearing and improving a farm. He lived in that State until 1830, when he moved to Montgomery County, Ind., and there purchased 160 acres of land, on which the old folk lived until their death.

In 1835 the subject of this notice was united in marriage with Miss Sallie, daughter of Daniel and Nancy (Edgman) Easley. She was born in 1818, and their union has been blest by the birth of three children: James T., a farmer of Adams Township, this county; Franklin M., residing near Swan Lake, Dak., and Walter H., Sheriff of Cherokee County, Kan. On the 4th of March, 1842, Mrs. Layne, mother of the above children, departed this life in Montgomery County, Ind., where she is buried. In 1847 our subject formed a second matrimonial alliance, with Miss Sarah G., the daughter of Baxter and Polly Edgman. Of this latter union four children have been born, two sons and two daughters: Joseph S. is a farmer of Cass Township; H. D., and Nancy A., the wife of William Galey, reside in Chillicothe, this county; Sarah E. died in infancy.

Mr. Layne came to Wapello County in 1843, and soon thereafter entered 320 acres of Government land in what is now Polk Township. On this he located and at once began its improvement, and lived there until 1875, meeting with success in his labors. During the latter year he sold his farm, it being at the time one of the best improved in Polk Township, and moved to Macon County, Mo. There he purchased 120 acres of land, on which he made his home for about five years, and until the death of Mrs. Layne, which occurred March 1, 1879, when he sold out, and returning to Chillicothe, has since made that his home, residing with his daughter, Mrs. Galey. He is well preserved in mind and body and has been no inactive factor in the upbuilding and growth of Wapello County, having held numerous offices of trust and taken an active part in politics, always upon the side of the Democratic party.

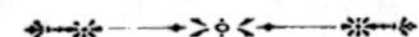

JEROME D. FERREE, Secretary of the Iowa Mutual Aid Association and of the Ottumwa Loan and Building Association, is a native of Illinois, and was born near Hillsboro, Montgomery County, June 10, 1838. The father of our subject, Thomas M. Ferree, was a native of Bracken County, Ky., but in early life moved to Clermont County, Ohio, and was there married to Miss Esther Ann Nelson, a native of that county.

After marriage Thomas M. Ferree engaged in mercantile pursuits in Clermont County, and was thus occupied until 1835. During that year he emigrated to Illinois, purchased a farm in Montgomery County, and remained on it until 1845. He then moved to St. Louis, Mo., and took a contract for sprinkling the streets of that city, which he continued until his death, from cholera, in 1849. His wife, the mother of our subject, after the demise of her husband, returned to their farm in Montgomery County, Ill., where she lived several years, and then removed to Litchfield, Ill., where she died, at the advanced age of seventy-one years, in October, 1882.

The parental family of our subject comprised six children, of whom one died at the age of four years; Marshal O. enlisted in the United States service in 1861, was taken prisoner after the siege of Vicksburg, and died in that foulest of Southern prisons, Andersonville. The four living children are Snoden R., a resident of Wellington, Kan.; Thomas M., living in Morton County, Kan.; Sarah A., wife of Joseph A. Coatney, a resident of Litchfield, Ill., and our subject.

Jerome D. Ferree is the second in order of birth of his parents' children. After the death of his father at St. Louis, he returned to Hillsboro, Ill., and there worked out by the month during the summer seasons on a farm, and attended school winters, and thus his life was spent until about eighteen years of age. He then attended school at Litchfield for nearly three years, receiving a good education, which he afterward supplemented by teaching for about three years. In 1860 our subject was united in marriage with Miss Susan F. Nelson, of Keokuk, Iowa. In 1864 Mr. Ferree engaged as an employe in the fire-insurance business, at Keokuk, and in 1868 commenced in the same business for himself, and added thereto transactions in real estate. In 1871 he took the general agency of Iowa for the St. Louis Mutual Life Insurance Company, and held that position until 1873, after which he was Special Agent for the Connecticut Mutual Life Insurance Company for Iowa, and in 1875 became General Agent for Iowa of the Penn Mutual Life of Philadelphia, which he held until 1878. Mr. Ferree then came to Ottumwa, Iowa, and organized the Ottumwa Loan and Building Association, and in 1881 he organized the Iowa Mutual Aid Association of Ottumwa, and has served as Secretary of the two latter companies since they were organized.

Mr. and Mrs. Ferree have had nine children, two of whom are deceased—one dying at the age of two years, and the other when nine years old. The seven living are: Mary E., wife of Henry E. Redenbaugh, a resident of Newton, Kan.; Bernie L., George N., Fannie F., Grace B., Daisy L. and Violet M. Politically Mr. F. has always been a staunch Republican, but is not an active politician. He has been a member of the Methodist Episcopal Church since 1869, and his good wife belongs to the Episcopal Church.

WILLIAM M. KING, a prominent resident of Columbia Township, and successfully engaged in the prosecution of agriculture on section 27, comes of good old Scottish ancestry, having been born in the land of the thistle, near the city of Glasgow, on the 4th of March, 1833. He is the son of John and Rose (Morton) King, and was the third of a family of six children. His father was a Captain of the Scottish Fusileers, and participated in the battle of Waterloo, under the Duke of Wellington. He was a man of strong character, energetic and ambitious, and after the country had resumed the garb of peace, returned and passed the remainder of his life among the hills of his native land.

William M. King, when a youth of fifteen years, set sail from his native shores for the United States. He had heard much of the opportunities afforded the young and enterprising emigrant in this country, and he now affirms with pride and pleasure that his hopes have been more than realized. He landed in Boston during the winter season, and from there proceeded to Oregon, where he enlisted in the army, becoming a member of the 1st Oregon Mounted Infantry, each man of which furnished his own horse. Our young hero became a member of Kit Carson's company, and served about thirteen months, in which time he gained great proficiency with the rifle. He became a friend of Kit Carson, and one of his warmest admirers, viewing the brave acts of his leader with that enthusiasm which is natural to the young. In 1855 Gov. Stevens sent Carson through the Indian Nation, accompanied by a half-breed boy. During the journey they were pursued by a band of thirty Indians; their horses were worn out, and he dismounted and distracted the attention of the red men while the boy lassoed two ponies belonging to them. These the boy and Carson then mounted and made good their escape.

After his term of service had expired young King went down into California, and was engaged there in the mines for about six years. He was fairly successful in his search for the shining ore, and secured enough to start him in business. He accordingly proceeded to San Francisco, and until 863 engaged in buying and selling horses, which yielded him a good income. He then came East as far as Iowa, and purchased eighty acres of land in Wapello County, with the intention of establishing a permanent home. He began the improvement and cultivation of his purchase, to which he added from time to time, and in the meanwhile erected a comfortable farm-house, with a good barn and other necessary out-buildings. He is now the possessor of 254 acres in this county and 160 acres in Dent County, Mo. He has given much attention to the breeding of fine stock, for which purpose he has unusually fine accommodations. His yards are supplied with water from a never-failing spring, which is conducted to the adjoining fields through convenient pipes. His sheds and stables are of first-class description, and everything in and about the estate denotes the supervision of a wise judgment and an intelligent mind.

The marriage of William King and Miss Jessica Knox was celebrated on the 10th of December, 1863, at the home of the bride's parents in Columbia Township. Mrs. King was born on the 28th of April, 1841, in Logan County, Ohio, and is the daughter of Peter and Mary (Peach) Knox, natives respectively of Virginia and Ohio. By her union with our subject she has become the mother of six children: Leonard died in infancy; Mary, William, Lillian M., Myrtle L. and Cora are all at home. Mr. King has afforded his children the advantages of a good education, which has included musical and art studies, all of them being fine pianists and having decided musical talent.

Mr. King made the passage to this country on the ship "John Gilpin," and came by the way of Calcutta and the East Indies, serving as cabin-boy to pay his passage. During the trip he saw many strange things and strange people, and can relate a host of interesting incidents which transpired on the long voyage hither, and which, to the ears of the young who have never seen the sea, appear like a fairy tale in a story book.

In politics our subject is an uncompromising Democrat, and takes pride in the fact that he has made a record in his community as an honest man and a good citizen, and as one who has taken a genuine interest in the welfare of his county and township.

A lithographic view of the residence of Mr. King is shown on another page of this volume.

JOSHUA MARSHALL, a retired farmer, living in the village of Kirkville, Wapello County, is a native of Surry County, N. C., his birth taking place Oct. 24, 1807. His father, William Marshall, was born in Chatham County, N. C., in 1766, and died in Hendricks County, Ind., March 7, 1840; his occupation was that of a farmer. His mother, Elizabeth (Bills) Marshall, was born in New Jersey about 1772, and died in Kirkville in March, 1861.

Joshua Marshall was reared upon a farm and received but a very limited education. In company with his parents he moved from North Carolina to Indiana in 1826, where he remained till the fall of 1847, when he removed to Wapello County, Iowa. Before leaving Indiana he was united in marriage with Mary Cook, who was born in Stokes County, N. C., in 1803, and the daughter of John and Lydia (Hussey) Cook. Her parents both died in Indiana. Seven children were born of this union: Lucinda, widow of Nelson McCracken, lives in Leavenworth, Kan.; Melinda is deceased; J. W. married Mrs. Burkey, and is now living in Omaha, Neb., engaged in the real-estate business; William B. and Mary A. are deceased; Nancy J. is the wife of J. W. Woods, of Plattsmouth, Neb.; Joshua B. is deceased. Mrs. Marshall died Jan. 9, 1853, and Mr. Marshall was again married in 1854, to Rebecca Morrow, born in Highland County, Ohio, April 18, 1818, and the daughter of John and Abigail (Patterson) Morrow. They have three daughters: Angeline Parker is married to Daniel McLane, and lives in Kirkville; Sarah E. is the wife of Edward A. Oliver, and lives in Plattsmouth, Neb.; Fannie S. Morrow is the wife of B. F. McGothlen, and lives in Kirkville.

Mr. Marshall is the owner of a good home, and also four other dwelling-houses, which he rents, in the village of Kirkville. He has held the office of Justice of the Peace for fifteen years in Kirkville. He is an ordained Elder of the Methodist Episcopal Church, having been set apart in that office in 1849. His wife is also a member of the same church. Politically Mr. Marshall is a Republican. His son, John W., was a Captain in Co. H, 2d Neb. Vol. Cav., and served as Postmaster of Plattsmouth, Neb., for twenty-two years.

SAMUEL LILBURN & CO., of Ottumwa one of the most prominent and successful business firms of this city, are conducting a thriving trade as shippers of butter and eggs, the business being established by Samuel Lilburn in 1871. Mr. Johnson is head book-keeper and general manager of the business. A. J Chambers, assistant book-keeper and manager, having been with Mr. Lilburn for many years, is held in high esteem for his business qualifications.

Mr. Lilburn comes from an excellent old family of Scotch-Irish ancestry, and was born near Belfast, Ireland, in 1830. He is a son of Hugh and Jane (Strong) Lilburn, also natives of the Emerald Isle. His father spent his entire life in his native country, and died there at the age of seventy-nine years. He was a farmer by occupation, a straightforward honest man, and transmitted to his son those excellent qualities which have constituted him a good business manager and upright in his transactions with his fellow-men. The mother of our subject died in Ireland in 1845.

Samuel Lilburn emigrated from his native country in 1864, and made his first location in St. Louis, Mo., where he engaged in the produce business for seven years. He came to Ottumwa in 1871 and established his present business, which has been successful from the start.

The subject of our sketch was married in 1853 in Ireland, to Miss Isabella J. Lilburn, a native of the same. They became the parents of four children, one of whom, Emma, died at the age of two years, and was buried in St. Louis. Sarah is the wife of A. W. Johnson, and Annie is at home.

Mr. and Mrs. L. are members in good standing of the Presbyterian Church. They occupy a handsome residence and are surrounded by all the comforts and many of the luxuries of life. Mr. L. began at the foot of the ladder, and has climbed up without other aid than his own perseverance and industry. He is the possessor of valuable real estate in Ottumwa, including several business buildings on Main street and seven dwelling-houses. He is Republican in politics, and the suppporter and encourager of every enterprise calculated to promote the welfare of his community.

Mr. A. N. Johnson, the son-in-law of our subject, has been a resident of Ottumwa for the past eight years, and during that length of time has established himself in the confidence of the community as a straightforward business man and a citizen worthy of honor. He is a native of Seneca County, Ohio, born in 1854, and the son of L. S. and S. R. Johnson, natives respectively of England and Ohio. His father was a minister of the Methodist Episcopal Church. He received a good education and taught school in Ohio two years after he had completed his studies. He then took up the study of law, and was admitted to the bar in August, 1878, after which he came to the city of Ottumwa, practicing his profession here until 1881, and then practically abandoning it to engage in his present business.

Mr. Johnson was married, in June, 1884, to Miss Sadie Lilburn, the daughter of Samuel Lilburn. He is the owner of valuable real estate in this city, and occupies a pleasant home on East Fourth street. He and his wife are connected with the Methodist Church. Mr. J. is a member of the I. O. O. F. and the A. F. & A. M. His parents are still living and reside in Huron County, Ohio.

LAFAYETTE CAMPBELL, physician and druggist of Chillicothe, has been a resident of this State since 1851, and in that time has established himself in the confidence of the people of this section as a skillful practitioner, a straightforward business man, and a useful member of society.

Dr. Campbell was born in Union County, Ohio, on the 11th of June, 1845. He is the son of John B. and Elizabeth (Kerner) Campbell, his father a native of Pennsylvania and the mother of Ohio. The former died when our subject was about eighteen months old, and at the tender age of five years he was bound out to Samuel Hoover who, in the fall of 1850, emigrated to Missouri, and the following spring came to Iowa. In the fall of 1852 he came to Ottumwa and from there went to a farm in Richland Township, which he only occupied until the following spring. In this latter year our subject was placed in a woolen factory, where he served three years, and then Mr. Hoover died, in the spring of 1858. After the death of Mr. H., young Campbell, for the following four years, worked on the farm of Peter Knox, with whom he remained until the 4th of August, 1862. The late war being then in progress, he enlisted in Co. D, 36th Iowa Vol. Inf., and joined his regiment at Keokuk, Iowa, whence they proceeded to St. Louis, and were soon afterward sent to Memphis, Tenn., and not long afterward engaged in the battle of Shell Mound, Ark. Returning to Helena young Campbell, with others of his company, was placed on picket guard under a heavy fire from the enemy, which lasted about ten hours. During this engagement he was captured, made his escape three times and was three times recaptured. At every opportunity he tried to escape, but was taken by the enemy to Little Rock, where he was detained a prisoner until the 28th of September. He was then paroled and taken to the Federal lines near the north of the Arkansas River, and thence again to Benton Barracks. He soon afterward joined his regiment at Little Rock, remaining at that point until the 25th of March, 1864, and then started on the Camden campaign, during which the entire brigade was captured, with 240 wagons. On the 25th of April, about sunset, the rebels started away with their prisoners, and marched that night and the next day a distance of sixty miles, without rest or food. After crossing the Washute River they drew their first rations, a pint of corn meal, which was wet with water and cooked. They then returned to Camden, where the prisoners were robbed of everything they had, their money and the main part of their clothing, and after lying at this place a few days were started for Shreveport. When within about thirty miles of the place our subject with one of his comrades, Thomas West, attempted to escape, and were out four days and nights. They were overtaken, however, near Mendon, Ark., and started once more for Shreveport, young Campbell at every opportunity still trying to escape, but each time failing. After spending about four days at this place they were started on a march of 120 miles for the rebel stronghold situated in Tyler, Tex., which they reached in about twenty days, where young Campbell, true to his former instincts, a number of times attempted to get away. He was here run down by blood-hounds and put into the Tyler prison, where he remained in close confinement for about a month, when he again attempted his escape and was successful. This was effected in the following manner: He had a friend who acted as nurse in the hospital, just outside, and sent out his haversack for this friend to fill with grapes. The friend, upon returning the haversack, slipped into it a pass for two, and with this our hero and one of his comrades, B. F. Gordon, marched boldly out. They had secured for their provisions five pounds of cooked flour. After journeying twenty-one days Gordon was recaptured near Camden. Our subject made his way to Little Rock, a distance of 300 miles, without a guide and unarmed. The first night the fugitives were out rain fell continuously, and the darkness was such they were obliged to grope their way by slow degrees, and when daylight came secreted themselves in the swamps. The bread soured the fifth day out, and they soon used all the matches with which they had provided themselves in order to build a fire. On the tenth night out the fugitives succeeded in capturing two horses, with which they made a distance of thirty miles that night. They finally concluded this was altogether too stylish a mode of conveyance and would attract the attention of their enemies, so they turned the horses loose and pursued their way on foot as before. The second night they crossed the Sabine River three times, each time by swimming, and for two nights thereafter were in the rain and without any fire. On the thirteenth night out they crossed the Sulphur River, near its confluence with the Red River; our subject now was nearly destitute of clothing, and on the fourteenth night was obliged to swim this river also. The following day it began to rain, and they lay in the Red River bottom without even a fire. To add to their distress Mr. Campbell had twenty-seven boils, and on the morning of the twenty-first day they came in contact with three rebel officers, near Camden, Ark., whom they attempted to convince of their identity as rebels. In this, however, they failed, as the officers coolly informed them that they were escaped "Yanks," and if they did not go with them willingly they should go by force. Neither party were armed, and the rebels started off for re-enforcements; in the meantime Campbell and his friend started for a swamp in the opposite direction, in which they traveled for several hours, and after striking dry land made as good time as they could in their half-starved condition, and at three o'clock that day ate their last bread. For eight days afterward they had nothing but raw corn, and Mr. Gordon, almost mad with suffering and privation, resolved to face death in the attempt to procure something to eat. Starting for a shanty at some distance away he remarked to our subject, "If I am not back within an hour or where I can signal you, I will be captured or killed." He was again taken prisoner and sent back to Tyler, Tex. Young Campbell waited until about sundown and resumed his journey to Little Rock, which was ninety miles away. That night he got two biscuits of an old lady, and with a part of one pacified the blood-hound which was ready to follow him. After four nights of travel he finally reached Little Rock, having had nothing but the biscuit and a half during the last four days of forty miles' travel. This terrible journey had consumed twenty-five days and nights. When Mr. Campbell started out from Tyler he weighed 140 pounds, and when he reached Little Rock he pulled down the scales at just 100. After this bitter experience he was allowed a thirty days' furlough, and returned home to recruit. He then rejoined his regiment, finding however, only a remnant of the brave old 36th, some of his comrades having been captured and fallen the victims of rebel cruelty, privation and exposure, and some being shot down in battle. The troubles of our subject, however, were not ended. On the 4th of July, 1865, while on guard at the headquarters of Gen. Shaylor he received a sunstroke, from the effects of which he is now partially paralyzed. No one can say that he did not suffer for the cause of the Union, and on the 24th of August of that same year he received his honorable discharge at Devall's Bluff, and reached his home on the 8th of September following.

In October of that same year Mr. Campbell went to Union County, Ohio, and in March following entered the State University at Athens, where he pursued a thorough course of study for one year. He then returned to Union and entered the office of Dr. J. Q. Suthard, of Newton, Ohio, and with him pursued the study of medicine until the fall of 1868, and spring of 1869. He then attended two courses of lectures in the Cleveland Medical College, and commenced the practice of his profession in Chillicothe, this State. He was in partnership with Dr. S. P. Johnson until the spring of 1870.

Dr. Campbell and Miss Mary Olney were united in marriage in Chillicothe on the 23d of March, 1870. They removed to Newton, Putnam Co., Mo., remaining there one year, from there to Unionville, Mo., and then, returning to Chillicothe, our subject resumed his old practice with good results. In the meantime he had become the father of three children—Elsie E., Marcus D. and Emma M. Jan. 7, 1877, the young wife and mother was called to her long home, leaving her husband and three little children to mourn an irreparable loss.

On the 30th of September, 1877, Dr. Campbell was married to Miss Isabel Stodghill, and of this union there were born two children—James B. and Orpha D. On the 29th of September, 1886, our subject was bereft of his second wife.

Dr. Campbell was stricken down with partial paralysis, in June, 1884, which principally affected his left side. He partially gave up practice, and bought out the drug stock, where he is now found ready to give advice and put up prescriptions for the sick and afflicted. During the active years of his practice he was remarkably successful and built up a large patronage, and is now in the enjoyment of a competency. Our subject is a stanch Republican in politics, and a member of the G. A. R., Cloutman Post No. 69, Ottumwa. He also belongs to the County Medical Association, and is an honored member of the profession in this portion of the State.

MOSES O'BRIEN, a successful farmer and stock-raiser of Keokuk Township, occupies a fine homestead on section 29, and in the various branches of his business is meeting with success. Mr. O'Brien is a native of Ireland, having been born on Vinegar Hill, County Wexford, Aug. 15, 1826. He is the son of Michael and Catharine (Doyle) O'Brien, who passed their entire lives in their native land, and are now deceased.

The maternal grandfather of our subject was a Captain in the Rebellion of 1798, in Ireland, and took an active part in that Revolution. He was finally captured by the English, shot and gibbeted. In those days the manner of executing the latter ignominy was by taking a large gunny sack covered with tar and pitch, into which was placed the body of the victim and was then hung upon a triangle, remaining there until it fell to pieces, and even after this the bones were not allowed Christian burial, but were to remain upon the ground in sight as an example to rising generations.

Moses O'Brien arrived in the United States in 1854, landing in New York City. He remained there until the following year, and then removed to Pennsylvania, going thence to Galena, Ill., and from there to New Boston, Mercer County, where he engaged on a ferry-boat. His fortunes then led him into Mt. Pleasant, Iowa, where he accepted a situation in the asylum, and was employed there for the following ten years. In 1866 he came to Wapello County and purchased forty acres of land, upon which he began to establish a home and to which he has added in acreage and value until he is now the possessor of 120 acres, finely improved and cultivated, and supplied with a valuable set of farm buildings. He has all the necessary farm machinery and implements for the successful prosecution of agriculture, and in addition to mixed husbandry, is giving much attention to the breeding of fine cattle. The homestead is a model one and one of the attractive spots of this section of country.

The marriage of Mr. O'Brien with Miss Bridget Brennen was celebrated on the 29th of August, 1857, after he had become a citizen of the West. The parents of Mrs. O'Brien were natives of Ireland, where they spent their entire lives, and where their remains are buried. They were devoted members of the Catholic faith, to which religion their daughter also adhered during her entire life. Mrs. O'Brien remained the faithful and affectionate companion of her husband until 1874, when she departed this life at their home in Keokuk Township. Of their union there were born five children—Michael, Edward, Richard, Thomas and Mary C.

On the 20th of October, 1874, Mr. O'Brien was the second time married, to Miss Mary, the daughter of James and Mary (Ryan) Finn. The parents were natives of Ireland, but are now residents of Northumberland, Upper Canada. Of the second marriage of Mr. O'Brien there have been born seven children, as follows: Patrick J. was born July 24, 1875; Moses John, Oct. 19, 1876; Julia A., Feb. 25, 1878; Joseph L., Sept. 6, 1880; Margaret E., Oct. 14, 1882; William D., Sept. 13, 1884; Elizabeth J., Dec. 13, 1885.

Mr. O'Brien in all respects is fulfilling the obligations of a good citizen. He possesses a great amount of energy and industry, and has been prominent in the affairs of his township, holding its various local offices, and being the encourager and supporter of everything calculated to promote its welfare, morally, educationally and religiously. He and his wife are faithful adherents of the Catholic Church, and Mr. O'Brien in politics is an uncompromising Democrat.

THOMAS M. DICKENS, of Wapello County, is a native of North Carolina, and was born March 12, 1802. His parents were James and Mary (Haskins) Dickens, both natives of West Virginia. The parents removed to Ohio, where the father died near Gallipolis in 1812, when our subject was but ten years old. The latter was then taken into the home of Mr. Langford, where he remained five years and then started out to seek his fortune. He had no particular point in view, but after walking thirty-five miles found employment in Jackson County, in the salt works. After two years he started on foot for the Kanawha salt works in Virginia, a distance of 100 miles. He worked there five years, then returned to Jackson County, Ohio, and from there went to Sandusky.

In December, 1824, Mr. Dickens was united in marriage with Miss Elizabeth Staley, of Crawford County, Ohio. He then bought up a lot of cattle, but being taken ill was unable to care for them and they got away and were scattered over the county. He was disabled for two years. In 1827 he purchased a farm of eighty acres, adding to it until it aggregated 400 acres. He then decided to come West, and landing in Wapello County in 1845, waited one year before the establishment of a land-office so that he could purchase. When this was effected he secured 320 acres and put in his crops. He then went back to Ohio after his family, and returned to Iowa in October. He then proceeded uninterruptedly with the improvement of his farm, and made other purchases from time to time until he became one of the largest land-owners in that part of the State.

The household of our subject was completed by the birth of ten children, seven sons and three daughters: Mary, the wife of John Hooker, died in Wyandotte County, Ohio, in 1847; James A. and Thomas M. died May 21, 1847; Catharine A. and Anthony died in Ohio; Malachi and Harvey are both living in this county; Elizabeth is the wife of A. B. Phelps; George W. lives in this county; Hiram H. died Nov. 21, 1864, and is buried in Dickens Cemetery. Mrs. Elizabeth Dickens departed this life May 21, 1863. The second wife of our subject was Miss Margaret Williams, who became the mother of two children, a son and daughter: Emma is living at home; E. D. died Nov. 18, 1875.

Politically Mr. Dickens is a staunch Republican. He is in all respects a representative citizen, and has filled many of the local offices with credit.

CAPT. DAVID L. HARDY, a prominent and prosperous farmer of Adams Township, owns and occupies a fine homestead on section 7, and is one of the representative agriculturists and business men of Wapello County.

Our subject first opened his eyes to the light among the rugged New England hills, having been born in Franklin County, Vt., on the 22d day of February, 1828. His parents were David and Martha (Taft) Hardy, natives respectively of New Hampshire and Massachusetts. The mother was reared in the Society of Friends. Her parents removed to Franklin County when she was quite young, and her father was a Lieutenant in the War of 1812, in which he distinguished himself for bravery, and for which he was promoted. The grandfather of Mrs. H. served in the Revolutionary War and in the War of 1812, although not having regularly enlisted, constituting himself one of the guard to protect the women and children at the time of the battle of Plattsburg, in which he did good service with his musket. When found near the battle-ground he was asked by some what he was doing there, and he replied, "You well know I couldn't stay at home when I heard of the enemy coming from Montreal." This sturdy old gentleman was of Scottish extraction and a fine representative of the honest and sturdy character of his race, and took a great interest in the affairs and prosperity of the colonies.

The parental household of our subject included seven children, two sons and five daughters, who are recorded as follows: Benson is a resident of

Cleveland, Ohio; Mary became the wife of Harrison Morgan, now deceased, and lives in Kansas City; Frances married J. D. Tyler, of Chicago; Rebecca, Mrs. R. Rumble, lives at Wheaton, Ill.; David, our subject, was the youngest of the family. In 1838 the father removed to Chicago. He died in 1852, and the mother a year later, in Chicago; both were members of the Presbyterian Church.

Capt. Hardy of our sketch went with his parents to Chicago, Ill., when a lad of ten years old. Two years later he left home and went to sea, his first cruise being from New Orleans to Rio Janeiro, Brazil, thence to France. At the time of the Mexican War he enlisted in the navy, and was on the frigate "Cumberland," under Perry. After leaving Mexico he was detailed as one of the party under Lieut. Lynch to visit the Holy Land, and assist in the coast survey from Jerusalem to Joppa. Here Lieut Dale died, and Capt. Hardy assumed the position of master's mate, spending about nine months in the East. He returned to America in the winter of 1848, and the following spring went to California, and engaged in mining until 1853. Then, on account of failing health, he resolved upon another sea voyage and was placed in command as Captain of the brig "Etna," making a trip to Honolulu, the Sandwich Islands, thence to Sitka, Alaska, and then returned to the mines of California. In 1858 he went east as far as Chicago, and was there married to Miss Elizabeth M. Gunsall, of Schenectady, N. Y. After their marriage Capt. Hardy and his wife came to Wapello County, Iowa, which has remained the home of our subject since that time, with the exception of a few years spent in Colorado.

At the breaking out of the late war in 1861, Capt. Hardy raised a company of volunteers with the intention of forming an Iowa regiment. But the company was afterward transferred to the First Cavalry, and Capt. Hardy was promoted to the command of Company M, thus becoming a military Captain. After brave and faithful service of three and one-half years he was mustered out at Ft. Leavenworth, Kan., on the 10th of December, 1864. He then returned to Wapello County, of which he has been a resident since that time. He is now engaged in farming pursuits and is the owner of a snug homestead in Adams Township, which embraces eighty acres of land, with a comfortable dwelling, barns and outhouses, and is enjoying the good things of life.

Capt. Hardy is Republican in politics, and has been identified with the interests of the township as one of its most valued citizens. He has held the office of County Commissioner, and in other respects has contributed his share toward its prosperity and advancement. The household of our subject and his wife includes three children: Frank, now of Blakesburg; Fred, who is in Colorado, and John, at home with his parents.

WILLIAM CLOYD, a pioneer settler of this county, was born in North Carolina on the 11th of April, 1824. His father was born in 1796, and his mother in 1802, both being natives of that State. In 1826 they emigrated to Ohio, whence, four years later, they removed to Rush County, Ind. Here the father opened up a farm and established a comfortable home, which they occupied until 1847. They then came to Wapello County, and he entered a tract of land in Adams township.

The subject of our sketch was the eldest of his parents' family, and was but two years old when they removed to Ohio, and six when they went to Indiana. His early education was obtained in the subscription schools of Rush County, and was exceedingly limited; but he was trained to habits of industry and honesty, and enjoyed the respect and confidence of all who knew him. In 1845 he crossed the Mississippi and spent two years in Linn County, Iowa, where he taught school. He was married in November, 1845, to Miss Elvira Christie, who was born in Arkansas Oct. 8, 1824. They afterward settled in Adams Township, this county, on section 9, before the soil had been disturbed by the plowshare. Here our subject opened up his farm and still holds the patent, which was signed by President Taylor.

Mr. and Mrs. Cloyd became the parents of three children: Cynthia, Mrs. Harlan, of this county; Ella, Mrs. John T. Parker, of Leavenworth, Kan., and Perry E., living in this county. Our subject is Democratic in politics, and has held various local offices. He has been County Supervisor, and at one time saved to his county the sum of $3,000 by the substitution of gold for greenbacks. He has always been actively interested in the welfare and prosperity of his community, and presents a striking illustration of a man who commenced life poor in purse but with an abundance of courage and determination. The possessions which he enjoys to-day have been accumulated by hard work, and his excellent personal traits of character have won for him hosts of friends. Mrs. Cloyd is connected with the Baptist Church and is greatly esteemed for her many virtues, having been a faithful and affectionate wife and mother, a generous friend, and the liberal helper and encourager of the poor and needy.

CHARLES SCHICK, engaged in the manufacture of staves and barrels, also a dealer in hardwood lumber, at Ottumwa, has his office on the corner of Samantha and Benton streets, and is doing a thriving business. He was born in Hesse Darmstadt, Germany, July 24, 1847, being the son of Jacob and Charlotte (Dinsdorf) Schick, who emigrated to the United States in 1849, accompanied by our subject. They located in Buffalo, N. Y., where they remained about a year. During that year the mother and one daughter died with cholera, leaving the father with two small children, and in destitute circumstances. In 1850 he removed to Racine, Wis., and after a residence there of about seven years went to Lawrence, Kan., where they were engaged in the bakery business during the border ruffian war. At this time the older son, Valentine, left home without giving any warning, and was not heard from until 1872. Then Charles S. accidentally heard of him through a comrade who was in the same company with him during the Rebellion; he was running a hack line in Montana. After receiving a letter from his brother he immediately sold out and came home, where he was made welcome by the father and brother who had anxiously sought his whereabouts for these long years. Soon after Valentine left home Mr. Schick was compelled to take his son Charles and leave Kansas for a more peaceable section, abandoning his bakery and other business to the ruffians of that Territory. They then located in Le Claire, Iowa, and were there residents for about two years. In 1859 the father and son sailed for New Orleans, and thence to California on board of the steamship Daniel Webster, landing in San Francisco, where they lived for about one year, during which time the father followed his trade, that of a baker. He then sold out and went to Carson City, where he was prospecting for a time, and thence moved to Santa Clara, Cal., where the father engaged in the bakery business, and the son attended the University of the Pacific, for two years. From the latter place they went to San Jose, where the father engaged in the manufacture of brick, and made the brick for the first depot built in that place. Living there until 1866, they returned, by the way of New York, to Davenport, this State, which latter city they reached after a tedious voyage of twenty-six days. They remained in Davenport during the winter, and in the spring of the following year moved to Lee County, Iowa, where the father purchased a farm on which they located, and where he engaged in its cultivation and improvement. They lived on this farm for three years, when the father with his son moved to Ottumwa, where he has made his home until the present time.

Jacob Schick was born in Darmstadt, Germany, April 10, 1821, and is a son of Valentine and Margaret (Lawrence) Schick, both of whom died in Germany. He was the second time married, to Mrs. Lucinda Carpenter, widow of J. W. Carpenter, one of the worthy pioneer settlers of this county, their wedding taking place Dec. 27, 1885. Mrs. Schick was a daughter of Nathaniel and Anna (Leech) Robison. Her parents were natives of Pennsylvania and Maryland respectively, and were both members of the Baptist Church. Mrs. Schick was born and reared in Indiana, and is a member of the Methodist Episcopal Church. The one daughter of herself and her former husband, who was the wife of L. E. Gray, of this county, died in 1881.

Charles Schick, the subject of this sketch, was maried to Elizabeth Lawson Oct. 24, 1869. She was born in Danville, Ill., Oct. 4, 1852, and is a daughter of D. S. Lawson. Her father and mother are living at Rose Hill, Iowa. Of the union of our subject with Miss Lawson four children have been born—Iowa, Maggie, Charles J. and William D. Mr. Schick and son of this notice are the proprietors of 367 acres of fine farming land, eighty of which are in pasture. He only has thirty acres under cultivation, and thirty acres of his land are where the brick-works are located. He has a good dwelling on his place, and is also the proprietor of several tenement houses in the city. Socially he is a member of the Masonic fraternity, belonging to Lodge No. 269, of Ottumwa. In politics he is a Republican.

HENRY REINHARD, a highly respected resident of Green Township, is located on section 30 and successfully engaged in general farming. He is a native of the German Empire and was born in Prussia in 1822. His parents were Frederick Lawrence and Elizabeth (Miller) Reinhard, both natives of Germany, where the father followed the peaceful occupation of a farmer. Young Reinhard remained under the parental roof until he was eighteen years of age and then resolved to emigrate to the United States. He embarked on the American sailing-vessel "Ottoliam," commanded by Capt. Sampson, of Boston, and sailed from the harbor of Bremen on the 16th day of May, 1840. After a voyage of sixty-three days, during which they encountered several severe storms, our subject landed in Baltimore, Md. After two months spent there he went to Ohio and located in Muskingum County and engaged in farming through the summer season, and during the winter shipped wood down the river to New Orleans. He was thus occupied until the beginning of the Mexican War, when he enlisted as a United States soldier, and after being in camp two months was discharged on account of an overplus of numbers. He then came to Wapello County, Iowa, and purchased 213 acres of unimproved land. In the course of a few weeks he leased this to a man named John L. Wissan for two years, and then returned to Ohio where he engaged in coopering. He was thus occupied until 1851, when he again started overland for the West. After leaving Muskingum County he was twenty-one days on the road, which was then considered a very quick trip. He arrived on the 7th of October and has been a resident of this township since that time.

Mr. Reinhard was married, May 16, 1849, to Miss Elizabeth Cline, a native of his own country, born in 1831, and the daughter of John F. and Mary C. (Young) Cline, also of German ancestry and parentage. Our subject and his wife became the parents of ten children, who are recorded as follows: Mary, a teacher, married John Bachman, of Wapello County; Catharine, Mrs. John W. Proctor, is a resident of Davis County, Iowa; Elizabeth is at home; F. L., a teacher, resides in this county; Martha is at home; Charles H. lives in Center Township; John W., a teacher, makes his home with his parents; George E., a teacher, lives in Green Township; Emma, a teacher, and Sophia are at home.

Mr. Reinhard commenced life a poor boy, his present possessions being the result solely of his own persevering industry and good management. He is now the owner of 480 acres of land, 300 of which are finely improved and under a good state of cultivation. The home dwelling is a model of convenience and comfort, and the barns and outbuildings correspond with the residence. The farm and its appointments constitute one of the finest estates in this locality.

Mr. Reinhard has been prominent in the public affairs of this section, and has held various offices within the gift of his townsmen. He has served fifteen years on the Board of Supervisors, has been School Treasurer and in all respects the encourager and supporter of every work and purpose. He is Democratic in politics, and with his wife is connected with the Protestant Methodist Church.

The father of our subject died in his native land in 1828, being cut down in the prime of life at the age of thirty-five years. The mother survived her husband for seventeen years, dying also in the old country in 1845, when fifty years of age. They were most excellent and worthy people and members in good standing in the Lutheran Church.

Henry Reinhard received his early education in

the High Schools of his native Germany. He is one of the oldest members of the I. O. O. F. in this county and has taken great interest in the success of the order. He has given his children a liberal education, thus fitting them to become worthy citizens of the great Republic whose development and growth has been largely assisted by the efforts of his countrymen, who brought with them to this land the staunch and substantial character of the representative German citizen. A view of his homestead appears on another page.

A. R. BURNS, occupying a comfortable homestead in Dahlonega Township, was born in Allegheny County, Pa., Nov. 4, 1835. His parents were Robert and Jane (Marshall) Burns, both natives of the same State and county. His paternal grandfather, Alexander Burns, was a native of Scotland, born in the town of Ayr, and after coming to this country was married to Miss Nancy Barnes, a native of Maryland. Robert Burns was the youngest of ten brothers and two sisters, all of whom lived to be over seventy years old, but none reaching fourscore. He died in Allegheny, Pa., in 1874, at the age of seventy-five years. The mother survived until 1878, and departed this life when seventy-four years old. The parents were both reared in the Presbyterian faith, and lived consistent Christians. Their remains rest in the Valley Church Cemetery in Allegheny County, Pa.

The subject of our sketch removed from his native State in the spring of 1871, and crossing the Mississippi came into Iowa, and purchased 120 acres of land, which constitutes his present homestead. It is located on section 14, and he took possession of it in September following his arrival here.

Mr. Burns was married, in Jefferson County, Iowa, to Mrs. Kirkpatrick nee Ball, who was born in what is now Hancock County, W. Va. She is the daughter of Joseph and Margaret (Langfitt) Ball, the father a native of Loudoun County, Va., born Dec. 23, 1803, and the mother of Beaver County, Pa.

The little household of our subject included two children only, Margaret M., born July 14, 1872, and Robert B., July 31, 1879; they are both at home with their parents. The homestead of Mr. Burns includes 250 acres of land which is in a good state of cultivation, and ninety acres of which is prairie. He is principally engaged in stock-raising, and keeps upon an average eighty head of cattle and ten head of horses. He also owns fifty acres of the old homestead in Allegheny County, Pa.

Since coming to this vicinity Mr. Burns has been prominent in the local affairs of his community, having served as Township Trustee, and has been Justice of the Peace for a period of eleven years. In 1877 he was nominated by the Republicans for Representative, but was defeated by seventy votes by the fusion of the Democrats and Greenbackers. During the late Civil War he was a strong Union man, and although he did not go to the field, he did good work at home in aid of the cause, being persuaded by his friends and others interested that he could labor more effectually at home than by shouldering his musket and repairing to the scene of conflict. Before coming to Iowa Mr. Burns was the tax collector of his native county in Pennsylvania. The family residence is pleasantly located, and its inmates enjoy the friendship and association of a large circle of friends. Mrs. Burns is a lady highly esteemed for her excellent qualities of character, and is prominently connected with the Christian Church.

Joseph Ball, the father of Mrs. Burns, was a descendant of the same family of Balls from which Mary, the mother of George Washington, descended. His parents belonged to the Society of Friends, and in politics he was a Republican with strong abolition principles, and represented his district in the Lower House of the Legislature in 1869–70. His eldest son, John F., was a soldier in the late war, and met his death at the battle of Prairie Grove, Ark., Dec. 7, 1862, when only nineteen years of age. Joseph Ball departed this life Dec. 29, 1875, when seventy-two years old. He was an Elder in the Christian Church, and a good man in every sense of the word.

Margaret Ball, the mother of Mrs. Burns, came from a family of strong military propensities. The grandfather was a soldier in the Revolutionary

War, and her father in the War of 1812. Two brothers engaged in the Mexican War, and her two sons, John and William, served in the late Civil War. Mrs. Ball was a lady of more than ordinary intellect, with a remarkable memory, and was standard authority on ancient history and the Bible. Her sympathies were always with the poor and distressed. Besides a large family of her own, she raised three orphan children, and toward them performed the part of a kind and faithful mother. She was beloved by all who knew her, and a consistent member of the Christian Church, having been baptized at the same time and place as her husband. She departed this life April 14, 1875, aged sixty-seven years, and lies by the side of her husband in the cemetery at Fairfield, Iowa.

The former husband of Mrs. Ball, Gilbert B. Kirkpatrick, was an attorney at law, and served as a Union soldier in Co. B, 4th Iowa Vol. Inf.; he enlisted July 4, 1861, as a private, and was promoted, first to Commissary Sergeant and afterward to First Lieutenant. He participated in all the engagements of his regiment up to and during the siege of Atlanta, after which his health failed, and, returning home, he died Nov. 16, 1864, at the age of twenty-seven years. His remains also rest in Fairfield Cemetery.

W. L. McCLELAND, of Ottumwa, is a native of the Hawkeye State, having been born in Des Moines County Dec. 27, 1846. His parents were John and Eliza (Patterson) McCleland, natives of Pennsylvania, who emigrated to Iowa while it was yet a Territory, in 1844, and located in Des Moines County. In 1851 they removed to Washington County, where our subject received his education in the public schools. In 1863 he entered the office of the Washington *Press*, but the following year became a soldier of the Union army, having enlisted in Co. B, 45th Iowa Vol. Inf. They awaited orders at Keokuk, and from there were sent to Tennessee, where our subject was detailed for bridge duty, and after his term of four months had expired he was mustered out, and returned to his former employers. Two years afterward he purchased the office of the Washington *Gazette*, and operated with a partner until 1874, when he came to Ottumwa. Here he became foreman of the job department of the Ottumwa *Courier*, which position he held until 1880.

Mr. McCleland was married in Ottumwa, in May, 1877, to Miss Frances McPherson, of Missouri. He is a member of Malta Commandery No. 31, of Ottumwa, of Clinton Chapter No. 9, and of Blue Lodge No. 26, in Washington.

MINOR KIRKPATRICK, an honored pioneer of Wapello County, has been a resident of the Hawkeye State since 1849. He first located in Highland Township upon a tract of Government land, which he improved and cultivated, and where he established a comfortable home which he occupied until 1885. He then practically retired from active labor and purchased a pleasant homestead two miles north of Ottumwa, where he now resides.

Mr. Kirkpatrick is a native of Loudoun County Va., and was born on the 15th of September, 1817. He left his native State when a young man and went over the river into Madison County, Ohio, where he became acquainted with Miss Hannah Godfrey, from which there sprang a mutual attachment which resulted in marriage. Mrs. K. was born in Hocking County, Ohio, April 16, 1819, and still remains the companion of her husband.

After their marriage Mr. and Mrs. Kirkpatrick located in Ohio, where they remained until 1849, and where Mr. K. was engaged as a stock-drover, buying and shipping extensively. They then came into what is now Highland Township, this county, which was then a wilderness. They took up their quarters in an humble log cabin, and prepared to endure their share of the difficulties that beset the life of a pioneer. There were no neighbors in sight, and Mrs. K. did not often see the face of a white woman. Their milling was done at Bonaparte, in Van Buren County, and the surplus grain which was produced from the new farm was hauled to the Mississippi River for shipment. The many turns which had to be made in order to sustain life and derive from it a moderate degree of comfort would form an interesting volume. But they had come to stay, and hand to hand prepared to meet every emergency that might arise. In due time they received the reward of their labors; the rough tract of land in the wilderness gave place to smiling fields and growing grain, the log cabin to a modern farm dwelling, the rude shelter for stock was supplanted by good barns and outhouses, and Mr. Kirkpatrick, after the lapse of years, found himself the possessor of a valuable homestead.

From the time of coming here Mr. K. took a genuine interest in the progress and development of the county, and contributed his full quota toward bringing it to its present position. His energy and enterprise proved an inspiration to his neighbors, and they were ambitious to emulate the example of thrift and industry which he set before them. He had little but his own hands to depend upon when first coming here, and his present possessions are mostly due to his own industry, energy and economy. He was a man of great force of character, was at once acknowledged as a leader in the community, and from the organization of the township has been prominent in its enterprises, and contributed liberally to whatever was calculated to promote its welfare.

Mr. K. is a member of the Cumberland Presbyterian, and Mrs. K. of the Methodist Episcopal Church. The household circle included seven children, five of whom are still living, and whom they trained to those principles of honor and integrity which have secured to themselves in such a marked degree the respect of a wide circle of friends and acquaintances in this vicinity.

THOMAS EYRE, a farmer of Green Township, and a gentleman well and favorably known in his community for his many good qualities, was born in Ohio, May 9, 1823. He is a son of Robert and Elizabeth (Cockerill) Eyre, natives of Virginia. Mr. Eyre of this notice was reared to manhood in his native State, and there lived until 1856, engaged the while in farming. During the year last named he came to this State and located in Wapello County, where he purchased 200 acres of wild land, on which he located and at once entered with energy and perseverance upon its improvement, determining to make it a future abiding-place for himself and family.

Mr. Eyre was married, Nov. 13, 1845, to Miss Sarah E. McClure. She was born in Ohio, of which State her mother was also a native; her father was born in Virginia. Of the union of our subject with Miss McClure four children have been born: James W., deceased; Mary E. is the wife of A. B. Saum, and a resident of Page County, this State; Sarah E. is the wife of G. L. Shaul, and they are also residing in Page County; and Eldridge L. is deceased.

Mr. Eyre is a gentleman who has never sought office at the hands of his neighbors or friends, but has held the position of Steward of the Poor Farm and also the office of Road Overseer. Socially he belongs to the I. O. O. F., holding fellowship with Lodge No. 9, of Ottumwa. In politics he is Republican, and he and his wife are members of the Methodist Episcopal Church.

A. C. STECK, attorney at law, of Ottumwa, occupies a high position in the legal profession of this locality. He is a native of Westmoreland County, Pa., and was born on the 12th of September, 1851. His parents were Daniel F. and Sarah (George) Steck, also natives of Pennsylvania. His father was a railroad contractor and held the office of Sheriff of Westmoreland County, Pa. He was a man of much force of character, more than ordinary ability, and Democratic in politics. The parental household consisted of three sons and two daughters: Frank G. is a commission merchant at the stockyards in Chicago, Ill.; A. C., our subject, was the second in order of birth; Kate became the the wife of R. G. Ford, Superintendent of Bells Gap Railroad, in Pennsylvania; Ed. M. is the General Passenger Agent of the same road and located at Bellwood, Pa.; Dot, the youngest daughter, is at home.

The subject of our sketch was reared in his native county and received his primary education in the common schools, which was supplemented later by an attendance at the High School. He was fond of his books, attended closely to his studies, and at the age of fifteen years taught school two terms in the district near his home. In 1866 he was Deputy Sheriff under his father, occupying the position for one year. Then, desiring to further perfect himself in his studies he took a preparatory course at Ligonier Academy, but instead of going to college as he had intended he accepted a position in the office of the County Clerk, which he occupied for two years. He availed himself of this opportunity of reading law, having for his instructor, Hon. Jacob Turney, of Greensburg, Pa., and in 1869 he attended the law department of Michigan University at Ann Arbor, from which he graduated in the class of 1873.

After returning to Greensburg, Pa., his father persuaded him to cross the Mississippi and seek for honors in the western country. He accordingly proceeded to Leavenworth, Kan., and entering the office of Maj. Housley, confined himself to a still more thorough course of study and in due time was admitted to practice in the courts of Kansas. He remained there only a year, however, and returning home entered the office of Hon. Edgar Cunan, ex-United States Senator, and was soon afterward appointed Deputy Recorder.

In 1875 Mr Steck came to Ottumwa, Iowa, where he associated himself in partnership with L. F. Portsen, and they operated under the style of Portsen & Steck. Two years later the partnership was dissolved and Mr. Steck associated himself then with E. Robinson, the latter being junior partner. After two years this firm also dissolved, and Mr. Steck operated for the following three years by himself. On the 1st of January, 1833, he became the partner of Judge I. S. Moore, and they remained in business together also two years, when, on account of the failing health of Mr. M., the latter withdrew from active business.

Mr. Steck was married in Ottumwa, Iowa, on the 4th of February, 1878, to Miss Ada Washburn, a native of this county and born in 1858. Mrs. S. is the youngest daughter of E. Washburn, Esq., Auditor of Wapello County, and by her union with our subject has become the mother of two children—Alice and Daniel F., Jr. Mr. Steck was invested with the office of County Attorney by appointment in 1884 and elected in October, 1886. He is Democratic in politics and socially belongs to the Masonic fraternity and K. of P. He is successful in his practice, is a close student and well read, and transacts his business in a straightforward and upright manner. He is held in high esteem by his associates in the profession and is accounted an able attorney as well as a valued citizen.

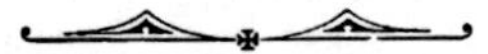

LEANDER T. STUART, Postmaster of Blakesburg, was born in Charlestown, Clark Co., Ind., on the 30th of November, 1823, and is the son of Alexander and Elizabeth (Humphreys) Stuart, natives respectively of Pennsylvania and Virginia. His mother was the daughter of John Humphreys, a soldier of the Revolutionary War, who served from the beginning until its close. While they were still young, the parents of our subject became residents of Kentucky, and after arriving at suitable years were married near Louisville. They soon afterward removed to Indiana and settled in Clark County. Thence they removed to the county seat, where Alexander Stuart opened a boot-and-shoe trade. Only two of their children are living. The brother of our subject is State editor of the Galveston (Tex.) *News*. He was Mayor and Collector of Customs of that city for several years preceding the war. The mother died in Charlestown, Ind., in 1829, and the father in Galveston, in 1858.

The subject of this history received his education in the country school-house, and spent two terms in Clark County Seminary. When seventeen years old he went to Putnam County, Ind., where he was apprenticed to the potter's trade with John S. Perry, serving about two years. He was married, Sept. 25, 1844, to Miss Hannah Turbeoille, who was of French descent and born in Knoxville, Tenn., in 1826. Of this union there are two children: Eudora A., the wife of George Haff, of Nebraska, and Lizzie F., now Mrs. Frank Loomis.

After his marriage our subject located in New

Albany, Ind., and with a partner engaged in the pottery business one year, under the firm name of Keller & Stuart. Then, in 1847 he came to Wapello County, and established the first pottery shops in the county, locating in Dahlonega Township. Besides being the only industry of the kind in this county, there was none further west of it. He hauled his wares to Des Moines, and they were the first of the kind sold in that city.

After a few years thus occupied Mr. Stuart removed to a tract of Government land three-fourths of a mile west of Dahlonega, and in connection with farming resumed his former business. In 1852 he returned to Dahlonega, resumed his former occupation there for eight years following, and then selling out, purchased a farm in Highland Township. He afterward made other removals, and in 1868 came to Blakesburg, where he has been employed at his old occupation and has also found time to interest himself in the welfare of his township. He has been Assessor several times and Justice of the Peace. In 1854 he was a candidate for the Legislature, being defeated by only fifteen votes. In 1882 he was again nominated by the Republicans, and ran 100 votes ahead of his ticket. In politics he is Democratic.

WILLIAM R. JONES, who occupies a prominent position in the community of Adams Township, and is pleasantly located on section 4, was born in Shelby County, Ky., on the 16th of March, 1831, and in October of that same year accompanied his parents to Montgomery County, Ind. There were then no schools or school-houses, the country at that time being wild and new, but our subject learned to read and spell at home, and after nine years of age, when a school was finally established near his father's homestead, attended for a few months in the year until he was twelve. He remained at home two years afterward, during which time his mother died, and then went out into the world to earn his own living. He served an apprenticeship of three years at wagon and carriage making and two years at general blacksmithing, all in Putnam County, Ind.

At twenty years of age Mr. Jones set up a shop for himself in Russellville, that county, and on the 24th of June, 1852, was married to Miss Sophia Jane Ham, the daughter of James and Elizabeth Ham, and born in 1832. After his marriage he continued at his trade until the spring of 1855. In the meantime he had invested in some choice live-stock, three stallions and one fine Kentucky jack, and in the following fall removed to Hendricks County, Ind., where he engaged in general farming and keeping improved stock. In the fall of 1857 he took the first premium on hogs and the second on sheep at the Indiana State Fair, beside other premiums on horses and sheep at county and district fairs, and became quite noted as a breeder in that section of country.

Mr. Jones came into Wapello County in 1868, locating in Adams Township on section 4, where he engaged in general farming and stock-raising. In 1873 he made some fine purchases, and his stables contained choice specimens of draft animals, Cleveland Bays and Hambletonians. His stock almost invariably took first premiums at the various county fairs. Mr. Jones, however, had labored too industriously, both mentally and physically, and he was forced to retire from active labor, and is now passing his days in the enjoyment of the fruits of his early industry and enterprise.

To our subject and wife were born four children, all of whom are living: Horace G. and Rebecca E. were born in Putnam County, Ind., their births taking place April 13, 1853, and Aug. 30, 1854, respectively; Isaac N. was born in Hendricks County, Ind., July 6, 1857, and Selmon F., June 6, 1875, in Wapello County.

The father of our subject, Joshua B. Jones, was born near Richmond, Va., Dec. 3, 1804. His parents removed to Shelby County, Ky., four years later, where he worked on a farm until he attained his majority. On the 17th of June, 1830, he was married to Miss Rebecca Carman. They removed to Montgomery County, Ind., at an early period in the history of that State, and settled in a timber tract, opening up a farm in the wilderness, and there the mother died on the the 28th of March, 1844. They had become the parents of five children: William R.; Isaac S.; J. W.; Mary E., who died in March, 1871, and a son who died in infancy. The year following the death of his first wife, Mr. Jones married Mrs. Rachel Dickerson, and of this marriage there were born four children—Henry, Robert K., Jesse H. and Sarah. In 1856 they removed to Wapello County, Iowa, and located on the farm where he still lives, having arrived at the advanced age of eighty-three years.

The paternal grandfather of our subject was also named Joshua Jones, and was born near Richmond, Va., in 1770. He moved to Shelby County, Ky., with his family in 1808, having been married in 1792, in Virginia, to Miss Mary Richardson. They had four children, three of whom died before they were of age. Joshua Jones served under Gen. Harrison in the War of 1812, and when the colonists had once more subdued Great Britain, Mr. J., in 1831, moved to Indiana and opened up a farm in the wilderness, where he spent the balance of his days, dying at the age of seventy-six years. He was the fourth son of Benjamin Jones, who was also born near Richmond, Va., in 1740. In early years he was crippled for life by a log falling upon him at a house-raising. He was therefore not able to bear arms in defence of the colonies, but was so outspoken in regard to the rights of the people that the Tories appropriated about forty head of his cattle to the use of King George's army. His family had been living on James River since the first settlement there by the English.

The paternal grandmother of our subject was born near Richmond, Va., in 1765, and after her marriage with Joshua Jones removed with her husband to Kentucky and afterward to Indiana, dying in the latter State at the age of eighty-four years. She was the only child of Capt. Richardson, a Welshman, and a sailor who made regular trips from England to the mouth of the James River in Virginia. He was shipwrecked on the Atlantic in about 1869. His wife having died, he left his daughter with an uncle to be reared and educated, for which he provided ample means, and she became a highly accomplished and intelligent lady. At her knee the subject of our sketch obtained the first rudiments of his education.

The mother of our subject, whose maiden name was Rebecca Carman, was born Dec. 12, 1811, and was the eldest daughter of Isaac Carman, a Baptist minister of Shelby County, Ky. He was born in 1772, in Virginia, and in 1798 was married to Miss Mary Huges, who died of cholera in Kentucky, in 1833. They became the parents of ten children, —Joseph, Benjamin, Thomas H., Rebecca, Mary, George W., Elizabeth, Isaac H., Barbara and William N. They removed to Indiana in 1835, where he died at the age of eighty-four years. He was the second son of Joseph Carman, who was born at Bordentown, N. J., in 1745, and went to Virginia, where he married a French lady, Miss Mary LaRue, in 1768, and they became the parents of seven children—Caleb, Isaac, James, Joshua, Mary, Phœbe and Elizabeth. In 1779 he boarded a flatboat with his family, came down the Ohio River with Col. Clark, and was sent out by the commonwealth of Virginia to protect the frontier. They landed where Louisville, Ky., now stands, and Joseph and his family went to the fort at Lynch's Station, now in Shelby County, Ky. A few years afterward he was killed by the Indians on Carman's Creek, in what is now Henry County in Kentucky. He was the youngest child of Caleb Carman, who settled at Bordentown, N. J., in 1827. He had six children—John, Joshua, Benjamin, Mary, Elizabeth and Joseph. He was the son of James Carman, born at Cape May, N. J., in 1677. He was for many years Pastor of the Baptist Church at Hightstown, N. J. He died Oct. 29, 1756, aged eighty-nine years. James was the son of Caleb Carman, who came from Long Island, N. Y., and settled at Cape May, N. J., in 1665. Caleb was the son of John and Florence Carman, natives of Hampstead, England. They emigrated to America, landing at Roxbury, Mass., Nov. 4, 1631, whence they removed to Long Island and founded the town of Hempstead, L. I., in 1643.

Mrs. William R. Jones was born in Putnam County, Ind., Oct. 29, 1832, and was the fourth daughter of James and Elizabeth (Hicks) Ham, the former of whom was born in Kentucky, Oct. 19, 1800. His marriage took place in 1825, and in the fall of that year they removed to Montgomery County, Ind., where he died Sept. 13, 1867. His wife was born in Kentucky, July 14, 1806, and died in Indiana in September, 1877. She was the eldest daughter of John and Elizabeth (Sandusky) Hicks, of Kentucky.

Mr. and Mrs. Jones have belonged to the Christian Church since 1851. In politics Mr. J. is a liberal Republican Greenbacker. He has been doing business for over forty years, dealing with all classes and large numbers of men, and was never involved in a law suit with any one, and as far back as he has any record his ancestors pursued the same peaceable course with their fellow-men. The family is an old one and widely known, and have made a good record, filling up the measure of their days with honesty and usefulness.

SANFORD KIRKPATRICK, one of the early settlers of Wapello County, is a native of the Buckeye State, having first opened his eyes to the light in Madison County, on the 11th day of February, 1842. When a child of seven years his parents started for the West, and crossing the Mississippi came into Wapello County, Iowa. He enjoyed but a limited education, which was principally carried on by his own efforts, as in his duties around the homestead, he kept with him his book, paper and pencil, and studied at every leisure moment, in the fields of his father's farm. He remained under the parental roof until he was nineteen years of age, and until there came the first three years' call for volunteers to aid in the preservation of the Union. He then enlisted in Co. K, 2d Iowa Vol. Inf., which was first sent to Keokuk and then to St. Joseph, Mo. He remained with his regiment after it arrived at Ft. Donelson, and at the battle of Shiloh was in the same regiment with Capt. Cloutman, who was subsequently killed at Ft. Donelson, and whose death was so deeply lamented. Young Kirkpatrick was also engaged in what was known as the Hornet's Nest, from its dangerous proximity to the fire of the rebels. He also participated in the siege of Corinth, the siege and capture of Atlanta, and with his regiment accompanied Gen. Sherman in his march to the sea, he in the meantime being promoted First Lieutenant. They closed up with a grand review at Washington, were mustered out at Louisville, Ky., and discharged at Davenport, Iowa.

Upon his return home Mr. Kirkpatrick occupied himself in farming pursuits up to 1877. He then engaged in trade, associating with himself a partner, and they operated in Ottumwa, Iowa, under the firm name of S. Kirkpatrick & Co. In February, 1886, Mr. Kirkpatrick sold his interest in the business, and was commissioned United States Revenue Agent at Omaha, Neb., having under his supervision Iowa, Kansas, Nebraska, Colorado, Dakota, Wyoming, Montana and Indian Territory.

In 1865 Mr. Kirkpatrick was united in marriage with Miss Hester M. Lentner, of Ohio, and they have become the parents of three children—Maude E., Stella M. and Miron, Jr. They occupy a pleasant home in Ottumwa, and enjoy the confidence and respect of their neighbors and acquaintances. Our subject has been identified with the business interests of Wapello County nearly all his life, and has watched the growth and development of the Hawkeye State with interest and satisfaction. He is a man of good abilities and well posted in matters of general interest.

Politically Mr. Kirkpatrick affiliates with the Greenback party, and has been prominent in the affairs of the city, being at present a member of the City Council. Socially he belongs to the A. O. U. W., the Modern Woodmen, K. of H. and K. of L., holding a prominent position in each, and is also a member of Cloutman Post No. 69. He is the friend of temperance and good order, and in all respects is fulfilling the duties of a worthy and honored citizen.

JACOB PETERSON, a highly respected farmer and stock-raiser of Adams Township, is of Scandinavian origin, and born in Sweden on the 8th of April, 1844. His parents were James and Mary (Dram) Peterson, who came to America in 1855, in a sailing-vessel, landing in New York City after a voyage of six weeks. They proceeded directly westward to Van Buren County, Iowa, where Jacob Peterson was engaged at whatever his hands could find to do until the spring of 1860. They then came to Wapello County, where the father cultivated rented land for a few years and then purchased a farm. The parental household included three children: Axel, now living in Clark County, Mo.; Anna, the wife of John Anderson, supposed to be in Idaho, and Jacob, our subject. Mr. Peterson died in 1875, his wife having preceded him to the silent land ten years. In religious faith they adhered to the doctrines of the Methodist Church.

The parents of our subject were in limited circumstances and consequently his early education was but slight. He was early trained to habits of industry, and long before he had reached manhood had learned to depend upon himself. After the death of his father he purchased the old homestead, where he followed farming until the spring of 1886. He then sold out and purchased his present property in Adams Township, on section 7. This consists of eighty acres of choice land, under a good state of cultivation. He has a good set of farm buildings and all the accessories of a skillful and intelligent agriculturist.

Mr. Peterson was married on the 20th of May, 1874, and is the father of four children: John H. was born March 12, 1875; James Otto, May 11, 1877; Jacob O. H. and Nelse O. E. (twins), June 13, 1882; the latter died when nine months old.

In politics our subject is Democratic, and has officiated as Road Supervisor and School Director. He is connected with the Lutheran Church. Mr. and Mrs. Peterson are well known and highly respected throughout this locality and have finely illustrated the results of industry, economy and upright lives.

DAVID C. BEAMAN, a highly respected gentleman and attorney at law of Ottumwa, crossed the Mississippi in 1846, and came into Iowa the same year of its admission into the Union as a State. He first located with his parents in Montrose, Lee County, opposite Nauvoo, Ill., and was educated in the common schools. After he had completed his primary studies he entered the preparatory department of Oberlin College, in Ohio, where he remained nearly two years. His studies were then interrupted, and, returning to Lee County, he was appointed railroad agent at Croton, occupying this position for the next two years, and afterward going to Selma (then Independent), Van Buren County, occupied a similar position for six or seven years.

In 1864 Mr. Beaman engaged in mercantile pursuits, in company with Jacob T. Overturff. Our subject was then engaged in railroading until 1867, when he took up the study of law, to which he closely attended for the two years following, under the instruction of Judge Robert Sloan, being admitted to the bar in the year 1869 at Keosauqua, Van Buren County, when he at once opened an office and entered upon the practice of his profession. During the administration of President Lincoln he was appointed Postmaster of Independent, which office he held for several years. In 1874 he associated himself in partnership with Rutledge Lea as junior partner, and they practiced law together for the following five years, at Keosauqua, where Mr. Beaman had removed. The firm was then dissolved, and Mr. B. became associated with Judge Joseph C. Knapp, the firm name being Knapp & Beaman, which continued until the death of Judge Knapp, in 1882. Mr. Beaman then removed to Ottumwa, and formed a partnership with Hon. E. H. Stiles, the latter being senior member of the firm. They operated in company until January, 1886, and the partnership was then dissolved, on account of Mr. Stiles going to Kansas City, Mr. Beaman continuing in the practice alone.

Mr. Beaman is an extensive reader and a close student, and it has been his constant aim to excel in his profession. He has been intrusted with important matters since the beginning, and since 1878 has been employed as the attorney for the C., R. I. & P. R. R., and also the C., B. & Q. He makes a specialty of land cases, and has become familiar with the intricacies of the vexed questions of boundaries, titles and deeds.

The subject of our sketch is a native of Ohio, and was born in Lawrence County in 1838. He is the son of Rev. G. C. and Emelia C. Beaman, natives of Massachusetts and Scotland respectively. He remained with his parents during his earlier years, and in 1860, at Athens, Mo., was united in marriage with Miss Luella A. Smith, a native of St. Louis, Mo., her birth having taken place in February, 1838. They became the parents of four children: James L., who occupies the position of foreman in the *Courier* job office at Ottumwa; George C., Alice M. and Arthur D. Their home in Ottumwa is pleasantly located, and they enjoy the respect and esteem of a large circle of friends and acquaintances.

JAMES W. LAFORCE, M. D., a prominent and successful physician of Eldon, has been a resident of Wapello County since 1843, and during the long period which has elapsed since that time has built up for himself an enviable reputation, both as a physician and a citizen.

Dr. LaForce is a native of Woodford County, Ky., born in 1826. His parents were Daniel G. and Nancy (Stodgehill) LaForce, both natives of Kentucky. The family removed from their native State to Iowa in 1841, first settling in Van Buren County, where they remained until April of the following year and then removed to Washington Township, this county, where Daniel LaForce took a claim and afterward purchased 160 acres of land which he proceeded to improve and cultivate, with the view of establishing a permanent home. Upon this farm the subject of our sketch was reared and received a good education in the common schools, remaining under the parental roof until 1848. He had been a studious boy, fond of his books and ambitious to excel, and after he had arrived at a suitable age, engaged in teaching school. In the meantime he had already planned his future course in life and selected his profession, that of a physician. Soon after leaving school and while engaged in teaching, he occupied his leisure time in the study of medical works. In 1850 he went overland to California, where he engaged in mining for one year. He then returned to this county and made preparations to pursue the course of study which had been interrupted, and in due time entered the medical department of the Iowa State University, where he remained until he graduated and received his diploma, in 1856. He returned at once to Washington Township and entered upon the practice of his profession, which he pursued continuously until the fall of 1862. Then, during the progress of the late Civil War, he enlisted as a private in Co. C, 7th Iowa Vol. Cav. Soon afterward he was commissioned Second Lieutenant, and the following year was appointed Assistant Surgeon of his regiment, in which capacity he served until the time of his honorable discharge, in December, 1864, having been obliged to abandon the army on account of failing eyesight.

While in the service Dr. LaForce had charge of the camp hospital at Ottumwa for some time and from here was sent to Davenport to Camp Hendershott Hospital. Thence he was appointed to the charge of the Cottonwood Springs Hospital at Ft. McPherson, where he remained until the fall of 1864. He was then detailed for station duty, and the consequent exposure incident to this position brought on a severe cold which settled in his eyes and incapacitated him for further duty. He then returned home, and as soon as able entered upon the practice of his profession, and employed his spare time in agricultural pursuits.

Dr. LaForce was united in marriage with Miss Margaret Ann Morgan, in 1849. Mrs. LaF. was a native of Davis County, Iowa, and by her marriage with our subject became the mother of two children, both of whom died in infancy. The wife and mother departed this life in the spring of 1853.

The second marriage of Dr. LaForce was with Miss Mary Jane Black, of Lee County, Iowa, which was celebrated Aug. 2, 1865. Of this union there were born four children, recorded as follows: Carrie died in childhood; Mary Frances is the wife of W. H. Baker, of Plattsburg, Neb.; Mattie M. grew to womanhood and became the wife of J. R. Swinney, of Davis County, Iowa; Jesse is at home. The family residence is pleasantly located, and its inmates are surrounded by all of the comforts and many of the luxuries of life.

Dr. and Mrs. LaForce are prominently connected with the Congregational Church, and the Doctor belongs to the A. F. & A. M. He has been prospered in his profession and in his agricultural operations, and is the owner of 1,700 acres of land, the most of which is improved and under a good state of cultivation. He carries on general farming, and is devoting much attention to the breeding of fine stock, particularly horses and cattle.

ANDREW J. HOUDYSHELL was numbered among the pioneers of Wapello County. He was born in Clarke County, Ohio, May 26, 1821. When a young man he went to Indiana and located in Wells County, where he became acquainted, and was united in marriage with Miss Eizara Mace, on the 23d day of February, 1841. His wife was a native of Meigs County, Ohio, and the daughter of Henry, Sr., and Rachel (Townsen) Mace. In 1848 Mr. Houdyshell came to Iowa and located in Wapello County, near the present village of Agency, where he purchased a claim and opened up a farm.

At the breaking out of the Rebellion, Mr. Houdyshell enlisted in Co. H, 7th Iowa Vol. Cav., and served until the close of the war. In 1881 he removed to Kansas, and is now residing in Salem, Jewell County, that State. His wife died in Kansas, Oct. 27, 1884. She was a sincere member of the Christian Church, with which she was connected for many years.

Mr. and Mrs. Houdyshell were the parents of ten children, six of whom lived to maturity: William A., now living in Ringgold County, Iowa, enlisted in Co. E, 22d Iowa Vol. Inf., and served till the close of the war; Henry S., now living in Ottawa, Kan., was a member of Co. C, 7th Iowa Vol. Cav.; Rachel A. married Berry Roberts, and died in Ft. Madison, Iowa, in 1864; Mary, the wife of Lewis Ludwig, now resides in Mahoning County, Ohio; David went west in 1881, and has not been heard from since; Martha, the wife of C. B. Streeby, now resides in Smith County, Kan.; James is now residing at Ottumwa, Iowa, serving as County Recorder.

As stated, Mr. Houdyshell was among the pioneers of 1848. At that time the country was but a wilderness, no improvements of any kind having been made, but he lived to witness a complete transformation. Instead of the Indian trails, followed by the slow-going ox-team, he has seen the iron rails stretched across the country, over which the iron horse traverses day by day, carrying its thousands of passengers and many thousand tons of the produce of the country.

James Houdyshell, County Recorder of Wapello County, is a native "Hawkeye," born in Wapello County, Nov. 18, 1858. He was reared in this county and educated in the district schools, which was supplemented by an attendance at the Normal School of Mrs. M. A. Peck, at Ottumwa, for several terms. He also attended the Ottumwa Business College. After finishing his studies in the Normal School, he commenced teaching, and followed that profession for some years, in all teaching some twenty-three terms. In the fall of 1884 he was nominated by the Democratic party, and elected Recorder of Wapello County, by a majority of sixty-four votes. In 1886 he again received the nomination, and was elected by a majority of 567. The increased majority shows the confidence placed in him by the citizens of the county, and that many, not of his own party, gave him their support.

On the 21st day of February, 1881, Mr. Houdyshell was united in marriage with Miss Lettie Fleming, daughter of Henry and Priscilla (Whitmore) Fleming. She is also a native of Wapello County, born Oct. 3, 1862. She was engaged as a teacher, having taught some ten terms of school. They have one child, Lura G., born July 31, 1885. In politics Mr. and Mrs. Houdyshell are Democrats.

ALFRED LOTSPEICH, an honored pioneer of the Hawkeye State, is a citizen of Ottumwa, and after a long life of energy and industry is passing his later days in the enjoyment of a competency. He occupies a handsome home, and, possessing the esteem of a large circle of acquaintances, is going down the hill of life with the consciousness of duty performed and obligations fulfilled as becomes a good man and a worthy citizen.

Mr. L. is a native of Greenville, Tenn., born June 17, 1817, near the home of Andrew Johnson, and many a time in his younger days saw that gentleman working at his tailor's bench before the idea of future greatness had dawned upon him. The parents of our subject were William and Hannah (Doan) Lotspeich, his father a native of Tennesee and his mother of North Carolina. The mother was of Quaker faith, to which religion the son has loyally adhered since leaving the parental roof. The father was a member of the Methodist Episcopal Church. They were married in Tennesee in 1810, and became the parents of two children, Ira and Alfred, the former of whom died in Athens, Tenn., in 1837. The mother departed this life the same year. She was an earnest and devoted Christian.

The second marriage of William Lotspeich was with Miss Rebecca Wells, of Tennesee, who by her union with the father of our subject became the mother of three children, one of whom died in infancy. Those surviving are George H., a farmer near Creston, Iowa, and Hannah E., the wife of Emory Crist, of Los Angeles, Cal. For his third wife William Lotspeich married Mrs. Norris, a widow lady and a resident of Iowa. Mr. L. departed this life Feb. 16, 1863, in Dahalonega Township, this county. He was a useful and prominent citizen, a Whig in politics, and a great admirer of Henry Clay.

The subject of our sketch grew to manhood in his native State, receiving his primary education in the private schools, completing his studies at Holston Seminary, in New Market, Tenn., thus receiving a liberal education. At the death of his brother he was forced to abandon the plans which he had marked out for himself, and resumed farming. He afterward engaged as clerk in a store, and while there he saw in the *Intelligencer* that a new Territory had been organized west of the Mississippi, composed of a beautiful tract of country which offered great inducements to the young and enterprising emigrant. This set him to thinking and he determined to go and see for himself if the report were true. He left his home on the 17th of September, 1840, on horseback, going by the way of Nashville, which was about 200 miles from home. He crossed the Father of Waters at Ft. Madison, and made his way to Mt. Pleasant, the county seat of Henry County. He was favorably impressed with the appearance of the country, and returning to Tennessee disposed of his interests in that section, and coming back to Iowa, purchased a tract of land in Henry County. Here he resumed his law studies and in due time was admitted to practice in the courts of the Territory. In 1847 he was elected Prosecuting Attorney, and during his creditable occupation of this office paved the way for his future success.

Mr. Lotspeich was united in marriage with Miss Rebecca A. Moore on the 26th of May, 1846. Of this union was born a son, Ira M., June 30, 1848. Mrs. L. was a native of Sangamon County, Ill., and was born Sept. 20, 1826. She came with her parents to Iowa when a child ten years of age and remained with them until her marriage with our subject. She was carefully trained by wise and judicious parents and received a fair education in the pioneer schools.

In the spring of 1849, on account of the failing health of his wife, Mr. L. resigned his office and started with her across the plains to California. They were the first to enter upon this long journey toward the Pacific, and after traveling five months arrived at their destination in safety. Her father accompanied her. After remaining one year, Mrs. L., receiving no benefit from the change of climate, decided to return with her father, Mr. L. wishing to remain longer on the Pacific coast. The father and daughter, together with her infant son two years old, determining to make the return trip by water, embarked on the brig Meteor, Aug. 22, 1850. The vessel was never afterward heard of and is supposed to have gone down with all on board. The loss of his wife was a sore bereavement to Mr. L. She was a lady of most excellent traits of character, greatly beloved by all who knew her, and a devoted member of the Methodist Episcopal Church. Mr. L. for two years made every endeavor to gain information of the lost vessel, but in vain.

In 1852 our subject returned to Mt. Pleasant, Iowa. Two years later he removed into Wapello County, and not long afterward, in 1854, was united in marriage with Mrs. Susannah Lotspeich, his cousin by marriage. She was a native of North Carolina, from which her parents removed in her childhood to Alabama. Of this union there was born one child, William G., the date of his birth being April 5, 1855. He died when a young man, Sept. 16, 1876. He was a bright and promising youth and a graduate of the Commercial College, of Ottumwa. Mrs. Lotspeich departed this life Nov. 20, 1873, of consumption; she was a lady highly esteemed and prominently connected with the Methodist Episcopal Church.

Mr. L. was again married, at Des Moines, Oct. 23, 1878, to Mrs. Mary P. (Armstrong) Jones; she is connected with the Baptist Church and possesses those excellent qualities of character which command the respect of all who enjoy her acquaintance. Mr. L. was County Treasurer from 1870 to 1874 and has held the office of Justice of the Peace for seven years, besides having held many other important offices in the county. He has been a member of the A. F. & A. M., Ottumwa Lodge No. 16, since 1854; and Clinton Chapter No. 9; also Malta Commandery No. 31, of Ottumwa. In politics Mr. L. was originally a Whig but is now a Republican. He is connected by membership with the Methodist Episcopal Church.

A. J. JENKINS, a prosperous farmer of Cass Township, residing on section 26, is a son of Solomon and Sarah (Jackson) Jenkins, natives of Virginia, who became the parents of a family of ten children, four yet living, and the record of the family is as follows: Levi is deceased; Elizabeth is the wife of Jacob Strayer, a farmer in Carroll County, Ohio; Sampson is a farmer, and lives in Jefferson, Ohio; Mahala was the wife of Joseph Shadduck, and is now deceased; Nancy is the widow of Caleb Wagner, who was a merchant at Richland Center, Wis.; Amanda became the wife of John Holmes, and is now deceased; Sarah became the wife of George Adams, and they have both passed to the land of the hereafter; Solomon, Jr., is also deceased; Elvira, deceased, was the wife of Philip Jolley, and A. J. is our subject.

A. J. Jenkins is the youngest of his parents' children. His father died on the old home farm at the age of seventy years. He was not a member of any church, but charitable to a fault, and endowed with an unlimited amount of energy and perseverance, to which his success in life is attributable. The age of our subject's mother at the date of her demise was also about seventy years. She was a devoted member of the Methodist Episcopal Church, and her death occurred about 1860, that of her husband having taken place three years previously, in 1857, and they are both buried in Jefferson County, Ohio.

The early years of our subject were spent on the farm, assisting his father in the maintenance of the family, and attending the subscription schools of that day and locality. Oct. 10, 1850, he was married to Miss Martha Stephenson, born May 1, 1832. She was a daughter of Richard and Elizabeth (Cloakey) Stephenson, natives of Pennsylvania, and both members of the Presbyterian Church; they are now deceased. Mr. and Mrs. Jenkins became the parents of two children: Kiturah A., born Nov. 30, 1852, is the wife of James Gardner a farmer of Columbia Township, this county; Alonzo, born June 2, 1856, died Sept. 7, 1857.

During the year 1855 our subject and family moved to the farm on section 26 where they now reside. At that time he purchased 200 acres of unimproved land, having since then been continuously occupied in its improvement, and has added thereto until his landed interests now amount to 235 acres of as good farm land as is to be found in Wapello County. In 1857 our subject sustained a great loss in the demise of his faithful and loving companion. She was a consistent member of the Presbyterian Church, and is buried in the Kirkville graveyard. April 29, 1858, Mr. Jenkins was again married, Miss Mary Butin being the other contracting party. She was born Dec. 17, 1832, in Hocking County, Ohio, and is the daughter of Abraham and Olive (Coleman) Butin, the former a native of Holland and the latter of New York. Both are deceased. The father died May 3, 1853, over sixty-three years of age, and the mother Jan. 5, 1855, sixty-two years old. They were members of the Methodist Episcopal Church, and are buried side by side in the Chillicothe Cemetery. Of the latter union of our subject four children have been born, the record of whom is as follows: Mary E., born Oct. 29, 1861, is a graduate of the Mt. Pleasant school, and at present is teaching in the public schools at Agency; Sarah R., born March 18, 1864, is a graduate of the Chillicothe schools; George E., born Jan. 1, 1867, is living at home, and Myrtie B. was born Oct. 21, 1871.

Mr. Jenkins has held the office of Assessor two terms, and likewise various other township offices. Socially he is a member of the Masonic fraternity, holding fellowship with Lodge No. 16, of Ottumwa, and is likewise a member of the I. O. O. F. Mrs. Jenkins belongs to the Methodist Episcopal Church, and is an active worker in the cause of the Master. Mr. Jenkins has always been identified with every movement calculated to benefit the community in which he lives. In politics he votes with the Republican party. A view of his residence and surroundings is presented on another page of this work.

J S. McCLELAND, a highly respected resident of Ottumwa, was born in Pennsylvania on the 10th of June, 1843, his parents soon afterward removing to the Territory of Iowa, their first location being in Washington County, where our subject lived until a young man, and entered the office of the Washington *Press* to learn the printer's trade. The Civil War then coming on he enlisted in Co. H, 2d Iowa Vol. Inf., and was in the division under Gen. McPherson until the latter was killed, afterward under Gen. Logan. He participated with his comrades in the various battles and minor engagements which they encountered, marched from Atlanta to the sea with Gen. Sherman, and found himself unharmed at the close of the war, being mustered out in July, 1865. He then returned to his former occupation. In 1866 he went to Galesburg, and purchased an interest in one of the leading journals there, remaining one year, and in 1867 was connected with the Dixon *Advertiser*.

Mr. McCleland was married in Galesburg to Miss Florence Maguire, a native of Hartford, Conn., who was born in 1852. He soon afterward removed to Carthage, and thence to Washington, where he worked upon the *Gazette* for five years. He afterward went to Sigourney, Iowa, and in 1881 became a resident of Ottumwa, where he has since remained.

Mr. McCleland is a member of Washington Lodge No. 26, A. F. & A. M., Cyrus Chapter No. 13, and Clinton Chapter No. 9, also of Malta Commandery No. 31. The family circle includes two children—Mazie E. and Willie S.

MORIARTY, EGAN & CO., wholesale grocers of Ottumwa, established their present business in the spring of 1882. Their sale room is 44x98 feet in dimensions, and they occupy the larger portion of a brick building, two stories in height, keeping three men constantly employed in traveling through Southern Iowa and Northern Missouri. They have a trade of $300,000 annually, which they have secured by strict attention to business and straightforward dealing. Their transactions extend throughout this and adjacent States, and they may justly be proud of the patronage with which they have been favored by their honorable, systematic business methods. The firm bears a prominent part in the business interests of this section, and is widely and favorably known along the Mississippi Valley.

JOHN B. MAXON, Assistant Superintendent of the Middle Iowa Division of the C., B. & Q. R. R., is a self-made man. He was born in Clarke County, on Mad River, near Fairfield, Ohio, Sept. 29, 1833, and is the son of James and Eliza (Hardman) Maxon, pioneers of that State, going there when children with their parents. They were married in Greene County. They settled upon a farm where five children were born to them. Three died in infancy, the others living to the age of majority. The daughter became the wife of A. W. Hempleman, of Richmond, Ind., and died in 1877, leaving three children. James Maxon was a man of more than ordinary ability, a great reader, and strictly honest in his dealings with his fellow-man. He was a sincere member of the Methodist Episcopal Church, was an active Mason during his life, and filled all the chairs in his lodge. He departed this life in 1836, and was buried with Masonic honors. His wife formed a second matrimonial alliance, Finneas Davis being the other contracting party, and by this union there were four children, three of whom are yet living. Mrs. Davis departed this life in 1859, mourned and respected by all who knew her; she left a family of five children.

The subject of this notice was reared and educated in Greene County, Ohio, receiving only a common-school education. He was left an orphan with four others when fifteen years old, and being the eldest of the children, the responsibility of rearing and educating his younger brothers and sisters naturally fell upon him. Young Maxon was equal to the emergency, and throwing off his coat went to work upon the farm, and succeeded with the assistance of friends, in procuring a comfortable home, and with what he could earn contributed to their support until they were old enough to lend a helping hand, and the family was unbroken until they had attained the age of maturity, and had all of them procured homes of their own. After seeing all his brothers and sisters provided for, our subject, hoping to better his financial condition, came West with a family who were moving to Illinois. He first located at Hennepin, Putnam County, on the Illinois River. There, by accident, he met some relatives, with whom he remained a short time and, in the fall of 1851, went to Aurora, where he attended High School, doing chores nights and mornings for his board. The following spring he was employed as a clerk in a dry-goods store, and was thus occupied until the spring of 1855.

During the year last named our subject went into Henry County, where he became connected in a mercantile and coal enterprise, and in which he continued until 1869. On account of failing health, he was compelled to abandon the position, although it was bringing him $1,000 a year. He then took a position on the C., B. & Q. R. R. as brakeman, receiving for his services only $45 per month. In January, 1870, he was promoted foreman upon the track, and subsequently was promoted conductor of a construction train. In 1872 he was again promoted, becoming Roadmaster between Mendota and Galesburg, and subsequently being transferred to Aurora. Here he was given charge as Roadmaster of the Chicago Division, including the Mendota and Fox River branches. Mr. Maxon for several years managed the work entrusted to two Roadmasters, and rendered excellent service to the company.

In August, 1882, our subject was sent to Ottumwa as Superintendent of the Middle Division of the C., B. & Q. At that time, there was, beside the main line, only the Albia & Des Moines and the Albia & Moravia, a small portion of the south branch and Indianola embraced in the mileage. Now the total mileage is 475 miles, and embraces five divisions, namely: Ottumwa to Creston, Albia to Des Moines, Albia to Moravia, Des Moines to St. Joseph, Mo., and Bethany Junction to Grand City, Mo. During Mr. Maxon's administration about sixty miles of double track were completed, making the Middle Division practically the best built road in the State. Early in 1885 the additional responsibilities of the track and bridge building departments were turned over to him, placing the following army of men under his control: Station service, 201; train service, 202; track service, 1,114; new bridge building and water service, 164 switchmen, 40; engineers and firemen, 130. With this army of employes and all their various pursuits to manage, there is hardly to be found anywhere within the State a harder worked man than Superintendent Maxon. A year ago, Mr. Maxon seeing the necessity for more yard room in the city, conferred with the officials at Chicago and secured the enlargement of the yards, costing $100,000, which work is just now being completed. Superintendent Maxon is justly credited with having the finest railroad division and most perfect system of any in Iowa, and he, together with Superintendent Duggan of Creston, and Assistant Superintendent Stewart of Burlington, are considered the most successful men in their line within the boundaries of the State. Mr. Maxon's popularity with the public and his employes is marked, and though he requires strict obedience to his orders, he is courteous and kind, and in consequence, is held in very esteem. He is assisted in his work by four roadmasters, two trainmasters, a foreman of the building department, and a train dispatcher.

Mr. Maxon was married at Aurora, Ill., in March, 1857, to Miss Maria Hackney, daughter of Adam Hackney, a native of New York. Their union has been blest by four children, two sons and two daughters: Edward C., who was private secretary for his father until his health failed, went to Mexico, where he died in the twenty-seventh year of his age; the others are Kate N., William F. and Helen E. Mr. Maxon and family are living in the city of Ottumwa, surrounded by a large circle of friends and acquaintances. He is a member of the Masonic fraternity.

HON. PAUL C. JEFFRIES, deceased, was born May 4, 1790, in Mecklinburg County, Va. He was the son of Richard Jeffries, a wealthy planter of the Old Dominion, and like most sons of wealthy men of the South, he had no special calling, in other words, was a youth of leisure. The parents of the subject of this sketch, not intending him for any of the learned professions, did not afford him an opportunity for a classical education, yet he was given a very thorough English course.

Young Jeffries remained at home most of the time until his marriage, which took place Dec. 4, 1817, the lady of his choice being Miss Mary B. Evans, born and raised in the same county, and four years his junior. After his marriage he followed the business of a planter, in the county of his birth, until the fall of 1826, when he moved to Nicholas County, Ky., where for some years he devoted himself to teaching, and until he purchased a large plantation in Mercer County, the same State. In connection with the business of farming in Mercer County, he bought and drove hogs and horses to the South Mississippi and Alabama, more or less every year, until 1837, when through the failure of banks in the South and in Kentucky he became financially crippled, and had to dispose of his large plantation and such personal property as he had on it. With the exception of one year when he lived in Harrodsburg, he continued in the business of farming on a limited scale until the spring of 1842, when he removed to Iowa, settling in Van Buren County.

When he moved to Iowa Judge Jeffries had very little left of what had been an ample fortune. Our subject's family consisted of himself, Mrs. Jeffries, a daughter and two sons. His daughter, now the wife of Judge Hendershott, of Ottumwa, and one of his sons, Mr. B. W. Jeffries, residing in South Ottumwa, alone are living. Paul C. Jeffries settled in Ottumwa with his family on the 16th day of May, 1844. He was one of the original proprietors who located and laid out the town of Ottumwa. At the election held in the county of Wapello, in April, 1844, being the first election held in the county, Mr. Jeffries was elected to the office of Judge of Probate; the importance of said office is pointed out elsewhere in this volume.

That Judge Jeffries filled his station with marked ability and unquestioned integrity is cheerfully conceded by all who knew him while in office, and there are many such now living in the county. In the language of another we quote: "It is natural to associate crude men with new counties, and to expect to find imperfect records of early events; but in the case of this county (Wapello) one is agreeably surprised to find evidence of clear minds, well drilled business habits, and methodical ways. This good impression is due in no small degree to the care and experience of Judge Paul C. Jeffries."

Judge Jeffries at one time, and for some years after settling in Ottumwa, held the office of United States Pension Agent for this district, located at the place of his residence. He was a popular officer, and left the office with honor and credit, and without the slightest intimation from any source that his record was not pure and clean. He also, while the sessions of the Iowa Supreme Court were held at Ottumwa, acted as Clerk of that court, and as in the other official station filled by him, rendered entire satisfaction to the Court, the bar and the people. In sectionizing portions of the Government lands in Wapello County, a man by the name of Barrow had been appointed to do the work, and under his appointment had sectionized, or pretended to do so, five or six townships. It was ascertained, however, that Barrow's survey was so defective and inaccurate that a re-survey would have to be made. This service was assigned to Judge Jeffries, who did the work to the entire satisfaction of the Government.

Judge Jeffries was at an early day Postmaster at Ottumwa. He held many other official trusts, and in each it may be truthfully said he was an honest, honorable, capable and faithful officer. In politics he was a Democrat of the old school, not from policy, but from conviction of the right. And while it may be said of him that he was a strict partisan, he had the most considerate regard for the feelings and judgments of his opponents, and most scrupulously avoided giving offense in urging the right of his party. He had no enemies. In religion Judge Jeffries was a Presbyterian, and at the time of his death, Dec 17, 1876, and for many years before, was a member of that church in Ottumwa. He lived an honest, upright life and died a Christian.

Of Mrs. Jeffries, who died June 19, 1882, it is appropriate here to say, that she was a noble woman, and in every way worthy of such a long life companion. Their home was the abode of love and affection. Their friends were all who knew them. It may not be inappropriate to give here an account taken from the press at his home, of the celebration of the golden wedding of Judge and Mrs. Jeffries, Dec. 4, 1867:

"The fiftieth anniversary of the marriage of Mr. Paul C. Jeffries and Mrs. Mary B. Jeffries was celebrated at the residence of Judge Hendershott, in this place, on the evening of the 4th inst. There were in attendance on the occasion about 200 persons. About 10:30 o'clock, the formal part of the occasion transpired. The bride and groom made their appearance, attended by two bridesmaids, Miss Laura Jones and Mrs. S. Coffin, and a corresponding number of groomsmen, Col. Thompson, of Fairfield, and Maj. Mahon, of this place.

"The parties passed in from the west rooms of Judge Hendershott's large building to the parlor, Col. Thompson and Miss Jones leading the way, they followed by the bride and groom, and they in turn by Maj. Mahon and Mrs. Coffin. After they had been placed in position, Judge Hendershott introduced the happy pair to their friends in a few well-timed and feeling remarks, giving an account of their marriage, and a short, brief history of Judge Jeffries and wife from childhood to the present. After this introductory, the Rev. Mr. McElroy, Pastor of the Presbyterian Church, of which Judge Jeffries and wife are members, pronounced one of the most happily conceived marriage ceremonies we ever listened to.

"After the ceremony a general good time of joyous congratulations followed, when the many golden tokens, which were prepared by the friends of Judge Jeffries and wife for the occasion, were presented in an address full of feeling and eloquence, by Hon. E. H. Stiles. Then was most sweetly sung a piece of music entitled 'The Golden Wedding' by Mr. Howerton, Mr. Hastings, Master C. D. Hendershott and Mr. Green. Then followed the presentation of a massive and very valuable Bible, by Gen. Weaver, in eloquent and appropriate remarks. After these ceremonies were gone through with, the joyous company did ample justice to the delicacies which had been prepared for the occasion. The whole affair wound up with a brilliant dance which closed at 3:30 A. M. Take the occasion all in all it was the grandest affair that ever took place in our city"

REV. I. P. TETER, Presiding Elder of the Methodist Episcopal Church in the Ottumwa District, is a native of Lewis County, Va., and was born May 11, 1829. He is a son of James and Barbara (Reger) Teter, both natives of the Old Dominion and both now deceased. Of their five children the record is as follows: Alvah lives in Virginia; John is a large cattle-dealer in Kansas; Jacob is in Virginia; Isaac, our subject, was the fourth son; Granville is deceased.

The subject of this history grew to manhood in his native county, received careful training at the hands of most excellent parents, and obtained his early education in the common schools of that section. Early in life he determined to become a minister of the Gospel, and with that end in view closely pursued a course of Scriptural study. He was married in Buchanan, Va., Oct. 25, 1849, to Miss Rebecca Jackson, who was born July 25, 1831. Her parents, Edward H. and Rebecca (Love) Jackson, were also natives of Virginia, and both descended from excellent families. Their household included four sons and seven daughters, as follows: Margaret married Job Hinkle, of Virginia, who is now deceased; Sarah became the wife of William Sexton, and lives in Virginia; Mary was united in marriage with Val Strader, of Virginia; Elizabeth is deceased; John G. married Miss Salina Norman, of Virginia; William L. is a bachelor; Minter J. married Miss Mary Cummins; Winford E. became the wife of Will S. Peterson, of Iowa; and they are now residents of Washington, D. C.; Prudence A. is deceased; the wife of our subject was the next in order of birth; E. N. B. married a Miss Wilkinson, of Iowa, and they reside in California. Our subject and wife are the parents of two children: Joseph C., a resident of Burlington, and Frank Elbert, of Ottumwa.

After becoming fitted for ministerial labors Mr. Teter resolved to come West for a permanent location, and accordingly, crossing the Mississippi in 1853, became identified with the Iowa Conference. In the fall of 1861, having fully established himself in the confidence and esteem of the people of this section, and deeply interested in its welfare, he was elected to the Ninth General Assembly of the State of Iowa, as Senator from the Sixteenth District. He fulfilled the duties of this position with great credit, and then, the Civil War being in progress, became Chaplain of the 7th Iowa Infantry and also of the United States Hospital at Keokuk. In this capacity he sympathized with the unfortunate, cheered and encouraged the sick and wounded, and became the object of affectionate attachment by many who never lived to tell the tale.

At the close of the war Mr. Teter became Presiding Elder of the Burlington District, and since then has spent the greater part of his time in building up the cause of religion and morality. He is an earnest advocate of prohibition, and by his influence and public speeches has contributed in no small degree to bringing the State to its present high position on the temperance question. He has taken an active interest in all matters pertaining to the general welfare of his adopted State, and has labored with but little recompense for the good of his fellow-men. He possesses a keen insight into human nature, and has made the most of his opportunities of reading and study. He is a fluent speaker, possesses a valuable fund of information, and without apparent effort secures the close attention of his audiences. His words are well selected and his line of argument at once takes hold of the reason and sympathy of his hearers. He has built up a good record and made for himself hosts of friends in this county.

JOHN C. PROSSER, an esteemed citizen of Center Township, has been a resident of Wapello County since 1856, and after living here for a period of nearly thirty years has established for himself a record as an honest man and an industrious and enterprising citizen.

The subject of this history was born in Pennsylvania in 1844, and is the son of John and Margaret (Gittins) Prosser, who were natives respectively of Wales and Pennsylvania. While still a young boy the parents of our subject started via the Erie Canal on a journey to the farther West, crossing the intervening States to the Mississippi River, which they were ferried across, and, coming into Wapello County, Iowa, made their first location in Ottumwa, where the father worked as a carpenter, and when his son became of suitable age taught him the same trade.

In the meantime young Prosser took a trip to St. Louis, both to get a farther sight of the country, and to engage at his trade. He remained there until 1874, and then returned to his parents in Wapello County, soon afterward purchasing the tract of land which he now owns and occupies. In the meantime, in 1862, he had taken to himself a wife, in the person of Miss Eliza Mulford, a native of Marion County, Ohio, and the daughter of Lewis and Annie (Miller) Mulford, natives respectively of New Jersey and Pennsylvania. Of this union there were six children, as follows: Charles Lewis was born July 10, 1870; Rosa May, born May 14, 1872, died October 27 of the same year; Edna Pearl, born Aug. 15, 1874, is at home; Harry Otto, born Aug. 10, 1878, died April 8, 1881; Walter C., born April 4, 1882, died May 27 of the same year; Harvey John was born March 10, 1885. Mr. and Mrs. P. are members in good standing of the Methodist Episcopal Church, and politically Mr. P. affiliates with the Republican party. He has been President of the School Board for three years, and is interested in everything pertaining to the general welfare of his county and community.

The father of Mrs. Prosser departed this life in February, 1873, at the age of sixty years. Her mother still lives at Ottumwa, Iowa. John Prosser, the father of our subject, was a soldier of the late war, and died June 9, 1884, at the age of sixty-three years. His wife, Margaret G. Prosser, and the mother of our subject, died when the latter was a child, in Birmingham, Pa., of cholera, in 1849.

REV. S. L. BURNHAM, at present a resident of the city of Ottumwa, is a native of St. Albans, Vt., and was born on the 23d of May, 1835. He is the son of Philander and Electa (Beals) Burnham, who were the parents of nine children—six sons and three daughters—recorded as follows: Sheppard, the eldest, is a resident of Stoughton, Mass.; Miranda is the wife of Timothy Soule, of Canada; Ebenezer lives in Dakota; Philander is deceased; Charles enlisted as a soldier of the Union during the late Rebellion, was captured by the rebels, and it is supposed that he died in some Southern prison; George is deceased; Electa married W. H. Clark, of St. Albans, Vt.; S. L., our subject; Sarah became the wife of J. Ballard, also of St. Albans.

When Mr. Burnham of this sketch was a youth of fourteen years he was deprived of his father by death. He had received his primary education in the public schools of his native town, and after the decease of his father he was sent to Georgia Academy in his native State, and subsequently to New Hampton College and Theological Institute, where he completed his studies, being fully qualified to enter upon his chosen profession, that of a minister of the Gospel. He commenced his labors in 1861, taking charge of the Baptist Church at Nicholville, N. Y. He remained there one year, and in 1862, having a desire to visit the western country, crossed the Father of Waters and came to Muscatine, Iowa, where he was placed in charge of the Baptist Church, and continued three years. During this comparatively short time he collected funds and erected a church at a cost of $12,000, and baptized and added about sixty members to the society. He then came to Ottumwa, and took charge of the Baptist Church in this city for two years. During his pastorate here, in company with Rev. Morgan Edwards, known as the "sailor preacher," Mr. Burnham held a very successful revival, adding to the church some sixty souls. About this time he gave up the pastorate of the church, which thus lost an earnest worker and an able advocate. Since leaving the ministry Mr. Burnham has held the office of Superintendent of Schools of this county, and in other respects has materially aided in the advancement of education and morality.

The life of our subject has been an energetic and industrious one. He has been moderate and temperate in his manner of living, and is now the owner of a fine property, consisting of 800 acres of land, all improved and well fitted for his present business, breeding fine stock, to which he has given the greater part of his time and attention for a number of years. His herd now consists of about 100 head of high-grade Short-horn cattle, and his stud of sixty Clydesdale and Percheron horses are models of beauty and symmetry, very valuable, and possess as draft animals that strength and endurance for which those breeds are so noted. Mr. Burnham has established an enviable reputation in this section of the Hawkeye State as a breeder of fine stock, and is not afraid to exhibit his animals with any others in the Mississippi Valley. Our subject, finding that he had still a little spare time, has also been quite extensively engaged in real-estate transactions, which are yielding him a handsome income. He recently purchased 768 acres of land and a herd of cattle in Kansas, and intends soon to establish a ranch there, where he proposes to breed high-grade stock.

The subject of this history, on Sept. 6, 1864, was

united in marriage with Miss Josephine E., the daughter of Orin and Sally (Remington) Andrews, natives of St. Lawrence County, N. Y. Of this union there are two children: Sandford A. was born Oct. 5, 1868, graduated at the Ottumwa High School, and is now the book-keeper of White Breast Coal Company; Fred H., born Dec. 20, 1872, is still a student. Mrs. Burnham is a lady of fine accomplishments, and interested in many good works. She is State Secretary of the National Primary Sabbath-school Union, and has been connected officially with the local and county W. C. T. U. since its organization. She is an earnest worker in the temperance cause, having for years given to it much of her time and attention. She now holds the office of President of the county W. C. T. U., and is Secretary of the Ottumwa Society for the Relief of the Poor. She is also Secretary of the Woman's Foreign Mission, and the Occaboso Baptist Association. She is a strong advocate of equal suffrage. Mrs. B. is a lady of broad culture and refinement, and always prominent in every worthy movement for the good of society at large.

Mr. and Mrs. B. occupy a handsome and comfortable residence, and enjoy the esteem and friendship of a large circle of acquaintances. Mr. B. is a Republican in politics, and as a business man and citizen ranks among the representative men of Wapello County.

J. H. CARVER, a farmer and stock-grower, of Richland Township, was born in Harrison County, Ohio, Dec. 2, 1818. His parents were John and Abigail (Wilson) Carver. His father died in Ohio in about 1820, and the mother came West with our subject in 1849. He was married, in about 1841, to Miss Mary, the daughter of Stephen Thackery, and they became the parents of three children: The eldest son is a conductor on the Rock Island Division of the C., B. & Q. R. R., from Keokuk to Des Moines; James M. died in 1853; I. M. and his wife live in Kansas; their children are as follows: H. B. lives in Benton County, Iowa; Clara M., near Kirkville; C. O., at Albia; S. A. W., at Ottumwa; F. M. is teaching in Chillicothe; C. E., H. L. and Jesse are at home.

Mr. Carver is the owner of 583 acres of land, supplied with five dwelling-houses, two barns, and other substantial and necessary farm buildings. He has been a man of influence in this vicinity, and represented the county in the State Legislature in 1875. In politics he is a staunch Republican, and he and his estimable wife are members in good standing of the Methodist Episcopal Church.

G. W. DICKINS. There are through this section of Iowa many extensive and prosperous farmers, those who came here at an early day, when the fertile prairie land was covered with a verdant growth of waving grass, and the wolf and deer were frequently seen around the little settlement. Among this number, and one who is highly respected and greatly esteemed by a multitude of friends, is our subject. He was born in Wyandotte County, Ohio, Sept. 18, 1843, and is the son of T. M. Dickins, a prominent early settler of this county, and with whom G. W. came to the county as early as 1846. The mother's maiden name was Elizabeth Stayle.

Our subject was reared here, nothing of special importance occurring in his life until his enlistment, in 1862, to defend his country's banner, which had found an enemy in those whom it had for nearly 100 years sheltered. He enlisted in Co. I, 1st Iowa Vol. Cav., Aug. 12, 1862, at Davenport. From there he went to St. Louis, where he was taken sick, and for two months lay in the hospital. Regaining his strength he joined his regiment, which had marched to Forsythe, Mo., when the army was ordered back to Rolla. In 1863 the regiment was at Pilot Knob, under Gen. Steele, 7th Army Corps. They were then ordered to Little Rock, and on the 1st day of January, 1864, the regiment veteranized, expecting to come home on a veteran furlough, but Gen. Steele took all the available forces to join Gen. Banks on the Red River expedition. The men of the regiment to which our subject belonged, having sold their horses, marched on foot, traveling some 600 miles on what is known as the Camden expedition. After the Red River expedition the regiment was sent to Jefferson City, Mo., thence to Little Rock, and thence to Memphis. While at the latter city the joyful news of the surrender of Lee came to them, and the sad, sad news of the assassination of Abraham Lincoln was also made known to them while there. They thought that they would soon be mustered out and return home, but they were disappointed, for the regiment was ordered to Alexandria, La., marching first to Hempstead, Tex., then to Austin, Tex., thence to Waco, where they received orders to return to Austin to be mustered out, which they did, and were there discharged, and paid off at Davenport, Iowa. Mr. Dickins has a grand war record, having served three years and ten months, and participated in forty-six engagements, and may justly feel proud of the record which he leaves to his posterity.

Returning from his many fields of conflict to his home in this county he engaged in farming, and has since followed that vocation. He was married, June 2, 1864, to Miss Elizabeth M. Hawthorne, and four children have been born to them, three sons and one daughter: Wilbur T. died in June, 1871; Anthony departed this life in infancy; Mary D. was born July 10, 1869; Hiram H., Oct. 7, 1871. Mrs. Dickins died June 20, 1874, and March 30, 1875, our subject was again married, Miss Martha C. Eller, a daughter of Harvey and Mary C. Eller, being the other contracting party. She was born Sept. 19, 1855, and their union has been blest by the birth of three children: Scott M., born Aug. 1, 1876; Rella M., Feb. 5, 1879, and Katie, May 30, 1881.

In politics Mr. Dickins is a Republican. He has held many of the local offices of the township and County, has been a member of the Board of Supervisors, and in 1881 was elected to represent his district in the State Legislature. He is a self-made man, and has accumulated handsomely of this world's goods, being the proprietor of 760 acres of fine farming land in Wapello County. He makes a specialty of Short-horn cattle, Clydesdale horses and Poland-China hogs, and has a barn on his place with a capacity for 200 head of stock. Mr. and Mrs. Dickins are both members of the Baptist Church. He is one of the foremost citizens of Wapello County, and in all business transactions his word is as good as his bond. Mr. Dickins is Commander of the G. A. R. Post of which he is a member.

As one of the representative farm homesteads of Wapello County, we present in this ALBUM a view of the fine farm property of Mr. Dickins

JOSHUA B. JONES has been a resident of the State of Iowa since 1856. He came from Indiana by team to this State, the trip occupying twenty-one days. After arriving here he purchased 2,000 acres of land and began the opening up of a farm, which he intended should become a permanent homestead for himself and family. He now owns and occupies a valuable estate in Adams Township, which is located on section 5, and forms one of the most attractive spots on the landscape of Wapello County, and during a long residence of over thirty years has fully established himself in the respect and confidence of his neighbors and acquaintances.

The subject of our sketch is a native of Virginia, and was born Dec. 3, 1804, in Henrico County. His parents were Joshua and Mary (Richardson) Jones, natives of Virginia. The mother, in early life, was deprived of the protecting care of both parents. After her marriage with the father of our subject and the birth of their son, they removed from Virginia to Kentucky, locating in the latter State in 1807. They staid there until the fall of 1831, and then removed to Indiana, where the father died in about 1845, at the age of seventy-five years. The mother survived her husband four years, and at her death was eighty-four years old. Both parents were members of the Baptist Church, and their remains are buried in Montgomery County, Ind.

The subject of our sketch was married to Miss Rebecca Carman, on the 17th of June, 1830. Mrs. J. was the daughter of Isaac and Mary (Hughes) Carman. She was stricken down with the cholera and died in 1844. She was forty-two years old, and her remains were laid to rest in Shelby County,

Ky. Of this marriage there were five children: William R. is a farmer in Adams Township; Isaac S. resides at Albia; Joshua W. is also a farmer: Mary E. died at the age of thirty-two years, and a son died in infancy.

Mr. Jones removed from Indiana to Iowa in the fall of 1856, with his family, as above stated. He had been married again, about a year after his first wife's death, to Mrs. Rachel Dickerson, the widow of Solomon Dickerson. She was born in Ross County, Ky., Aug. 10, 1810, and on her father's side was descended from the German. Her mother died when she was too young to remember her. Our subject and his wife became the parents of four children, namely: Henry, who is engaged as a farmer and gardener in Union, this State; Robert K. was born April 11, 1848, and Jesse H., Jan. 15, 1850; Sarah C., born March 16, 1852, is the wife of James Kinney, and they are now living on the old homestead. Mr. Jones and his wife are members in good standing of the Baptist Church, and politically our subject affiliates with the Democratic party. (For parental history of our subject see sketch of William R. Jones.)

EDWARD ULREY. The subject of this sketch is pleasantly located on section 13, Competine Township, and is successfully following the joint occupation of farmer and stock-raiser, and has been a resident of the Hawkeye State since 1868. During this period he has established a reputation as a good citizen, and his example of industry has been an incentive to many others to follow in his footsteps, as being an illustration of what a spirit of determination can accomplish.

The subject of this history is the son of David and Margaret (Richardson) Ulrey, natives respectively of Pennsylvania and Maryland. The birth of the father occurred Aug. 23, 1791, in Washington County, and he departed this life Oct. 12, 1859, in Knox County, Ohio, whither he had emigrated several years before. By a previous marriage with Miss Mary Clark there were born eight children, as follows: Valentine, born April 29, 1814, died in Knox County, Ohio, in 1884; William, born July 28, 1816, died March 15, 1849; John, born Sept. 1, 1819, died Sept. 30, 1844, in Knoxville, Ohio; Stephen, born May 20, 1821, died Sept. 24, 1846, in Allen County, Ohio; Elizabeth, born April 17, 1823, became the wife of John Brackney, and resides in Auglaize County, Ohio; Emma, born July 26, 1825, died in about 1861, in Allen County, Ohio; Jane, born Sept. 2, 1827, is the wife of J. H. Lusk, a farmer and stock-raiser of Auglaize County, Ohio; Thamar, born Feb. 14, 1830, died Nov. 28, 1849, in Allen County, Ohio. The mother of these children departed this life Feb. 19, 1833, in Knox County, Ohio.

By the second marriage of Mr. Ulrey there were the following children: David, born Aug. 28, 1834, is a resident of this county; Mary, born July 29, 1836, died Sept. 3, 1860, in Knox County, Ohio; Edward, of our sketch, was born Feb. 13, 1838; Hugh, born March 5, 1840, is a resident of Monterey County, Cal., being engaged as a farmer and stock-raiser; Hannah, born June 13, 1842, is the wife of G. W. Spencer, a farmer of Nebraska.

In 1862, while a young man, Mr. Ulrey started on a trip overland to California, where he was engaged in mining and in various other pursuits. After a residence of four years in the Golden State he returned to his father's home in Ohio, and the year following again crossed the Mississippi, coming into Wapello County in the fall of 1867. He purchased 320 acres of partly improved land and made arrangements for a temporary location. In the winter of 1868 he went back to Ohio for the purpose of securing a partner to share his contemplated new home in the West. The lady of his choice was Miss Nancy Dudgeon, a daughter of William and Anna M. (Breitlinger) Dudgeon, the father of Irish and the mother of German descent, but both American born. William Dudgeon was born Feb. 23, 1823, and at the time of the marriage of our subject was a resident of Auglaize County, Ohio. The mother was born April 15, 1825, and died July 11, 1860; her remains are buried in the latter-named county.

Mr. and Mrs. William Dudgeon became the parents of eight children, three sons and five daughters, all living but Mary Jane, who died Jan. 28, 1886;

she was born June 6, 1847, and was the wife of William Gullett, a farmer in Keokuk County, Iowa. Nancy, born Feb. 18, 1849, is the wife of our subject; Andrew, born June 3, 1850, resides on the old homestead in Auglaize County, Ohio; Lucinda, born Nov. 27, 1851, is a resident of Cowley County, Kan.; Elizabeth, born Nov. 12, 1853, is in Auglaize County, Ohio; Rachel, born Jan. 6, 1855, resides in Cowley County, Kan.; John, born Nov. 8, 1857, is also a resident of that county; Samuel, born Dec. 9, 1859, is in Auglaize County, Ohio.

The marriage of Mr. and Mrs. Ulrey has been blest by the birth of the following children: Rose Ann, born June 16, 1870; Sarah M., June 7, 1872; William F., Aug. 26, 1873; Edward L., Jan. 15, 1875; Priscilla J., March 22, 1876. Mr. and Mrs. U. are highly respected in their community and are members in good standing of the Regular Baptist Church. They have a comfortable home surrounded by all the necessaries and many of the luxuries of life.

In his stock-raising operations Mr. Ulrey is giving considerable attention to the breeding of Shorthorn cattle, and exhibits some very fine animals. He has been straightforward in his business transactions and is considered one of the leading farmers of Competine Township.

The second wife of David Ulrey, father of the subject of our sketch, was the widow of Mr. Durbin, by whom she became the mother of one child, a son, Ambrose, born Nov. 29, 1826, and now a resident of Wapello County. Margaret Ulrey was born June 25, 1799.

W. H. GILTNER, a well-to-do farmer and stock-raiser, residing on section 4, Competine Township, is the son of A. Giltner, a native of New York, and who removed from that State to Indiana in 1810. The mother of our subject was Sarah (Hendrickson) Giltner, born in New Jersey. She married Mr. Giltner in 1830, near Brookville, Ind, and their union was blest by the birth of ten children, six sons and four daughters. The father of our subject moved to this county in 1856, and here engaged in agricultural pursuits. W. H. accompanied his parents when they came to this county and has made this his home until the present time.

The early years of the life of our subject were spent on his father's farm and in acquiring a common-school education. In 1858 he was married to Harriet, daughter of John H. and Frances (Rosser) Turner. Her father was born in Maryland and her mother in Virginia, and both are now deceased. The mother was born in 1802, and died in 1866, and is buried in Agency City. The father was born in 1801, departed this life in 1854, and is buried in the churchyard near Burlington, Iowa.

Mr. and Mrs. Giltner are the parents of four children, three daughters and one son, namely Emma, born Nov. 21, 1859, is the wife of M. L. McLinn, and they are living in Pleasant Township, this county, where he is engaged in farming and stock-raising; Sarah T., born Jan. 18, 1862, is at present engaged in the occupation of a teacher; Laura A., born Oct. 9, 1864, is living at home; Zarah A., born March 22, 1874, is also living with the old folk. Mrs. Giltner is a member of the Methodist Episcopal Church. Mr. Giltner is a self-made man and is indebted for his success in life to his own energy and perseverance.

REV. M. P. ODEN, of Ottumwa, is the present pastor of the Swedish Lutheran Church, and is fulfilling the responsible duties of his office with great credit and faithfulness. He was born in Ousala, Sweden, Nov. 13, 1852, and is the son of John and Anna Magnuson, natives of the same Province as their son. They emigrated to the United States in June, 1876, and settled in Ludington, Mich., where they still live. The father of our subject followed the sea for twenty-three years, during which period he sailed around the world several times. Their son, our subject, pursued his clerical studies for seven years in his native country, beginning when a boy of seventeen years old, taking his primary course in the parish school, and the academy in his native town. He was also in the "Gymnasium" (college) in the city of Gothenburg, for a period of five years. After coming to this country he attended Augustana College and Theological Seminary, at Rock Island, Ill., for three years, and in 1879 was ordained at Chicago, from which he went directly to Big Rapids, Mecosta Co., Mich., and spent his time alternately in that city and Muskegon as pastor of the Swedish Lutheran Churches. He was thus occupied until 1881, and was then appointed to take charge of a church at Ottumwa, where he has since remained.

The subject of our sketch was united in marriage, June 29, 1879, with Miss Emma Carlberg, a native of his own country, and the daughter of C. J. Carlberg and Jaquette Gyllenhammar, and they have become the parents of three children, viz.: Elis Martin Josua, Rudolph Justus Emanuel and Anna Naemi Jaquette.

Mr. Oden has been remarkably successful in connection with his charge in this city. The congregation was organized Feb. 16, 1871, with forty members, and there are now about 200 adult members, making a total of 300.

Mr. Oden is the second pastor of this church. The present building was erected in the fall of 1884, and is 36x70 feet, located at 130 Jefferson St., north. Services are held twice on Sunday, and every Thursday evening. The cost of the edifice was about $6,000, and the whole property in connection with it is valued at $10,000. The society is in a flourishing condition, and the Sunday-school embraces ten classes, with about seventy children. The congregation has also a parochial school three months every year, with about fifty children.

A view of the neat and tasteful church building and parochial residence will be found on another page.

THOMAS W. McDILL, a farmer and gardener, residing on section 20, Center Township, was born in Preble County, Ohio, April 28, 1828. He is a son of Robert and Mary (Porter) McDill, who came to this State in 1844, and made settlement in Henderson County, where the father followed the calling of a farmer. His good wife died there in the latter part of September, 1886, and he is at present engaged in the sale of dry-goods at Griggsville, Pike County, and meeting with signal success.

Mr. McDill was married to Martha Troy in 1867 She was born in Benton County, Ill., and by her union with our subject six children have been born Martha E., John A., James T., Josephine, Louisa and Robert. Mr. McDill was a soldier in the late Civil War, having enlisted in the 91st Illinois Infantry. He was Hospital Steward, and after a service of nine months was discharged at Benton Barracks, Mo., on account of disability contracted in the army. Mr. McDill has been engaged in agricultural pursuits all his life and in the prosecution of that calling, together with the occupation of gardening, has met with far more than ordinary success. In politics he is a stanch Republican.

J. M. WINN, successfully engaged as a photographer of Ottumwa, is a native of Yorkshire, England, and was born on the 29th of January, 1838. He is the son of John and Ann (Smith) Winn, natives of the same country as their son, and who emigrated to America in the summer of 1848. They proceeded directly to Pennsylvania and located at Brownsville, Fayette County. John Winn was a carpenter and wagonmaker, and a skilled mechanic. The parental household consisted of nine children, five of whom are still living: Isaac and William are residents of Brownsville, Pa.; Frank lives in Libertyville, Jefferson Co., Iowa; the next was J. M., our subject; Annie W. married Joseph A. Phillips, of Des Moines, Iowa. The father died in Brownsville in 1879, the mother having preceded him to the home beyond in 1870. They were both connected with the Episcopal Church for many years, Mr. W. being one of the Wardens at the time of his death. They were held in high esteem for their excellent personal traits of character and the high moral principles which they not only followed themselves but transmitted to their children in a marked degree.

The subject of this history was ten years old when his parents came to the United States. He remained with them and obtained a fair education in the district schools. At the age of fifteen he was apprenticed to learn the trade of a machinist, at which he served for two years, and one year afterward started out from the parental roof, and, turning his face toward the setting sun, crossed the Father of Waters and came into Iowa. He set himself to work at whatever his hands could find to do, traveling over various portions of the Hawkeye State. In 1858 he crossed the plains to Utah and California, and was, as before, engaged in various pursuits. The struggle between the North and South now began to assume serious proportions, and on the first call for troops, while in San Francisco, he enlisted in September, 1861, in Co. B, 2d Cal. Vol. Cav., under Captain John C. Cremorny. With his company he spent the greater part of his time in Arizona and New Mexico for the protection of the frontier, and at the close of his term of enlistment was mustered out at San Francisco on the 12th of October, 1864, having been in service three years. During his army life he was often employed as scout and despatch bearer, and made many narrow and thrilling escapes.

Five days after receiving his discharge Mr. Winn boarded a vessel at San Francisco and proceeded to New York City, thence to Brownsville, Pa., to visit his parents, with whom he remained until the February following, when he enlisted in Co. A, 3d Regiment, U. S. Vet. Vol., at Washington City. The regiment remained about the capitol until about the 10th of July, and was then sent to Springfield, Ill. A few days later the company to which Mr. Winn belonged was sent to Ft. Snelling, Minn., where it remained on duty through the following winter, and in February, 1866, those whose term of enlistment had expired were discharged, our subject being among the number. Mr. Winn then returned to Brownsville, Pa., and spent the year following as an apprentice to his present business, photography.

In 1867 Mr. Winn once more turned toward the West, locating first in Libertyville, Iowa, from which he removed to Ottumwa in 1871, where he has since remained. Three years after coming here, having inherited much of his father's mechanical skill, he took up the duties of a civil engineer, being first employed at Ladd's pork-house until 1864, and then became engineer of the steam fire-engine of Ottumwa, which position he occupied for four years, and then established his present business. In this latter he has kept pace with all the improvements of the day, and has built up a prosperous and lucrative business. He is a gentleman of fine tastes, and has proved himself worthy to administer in an artistic manner to the taste of the cultured people of this city

Mr. Winn was united in marriage with Miss Aurora R. Russell on the 1st of June, 1881. Mrs. Winn is a daughter of Peter Russell, a pioneer settler of Lee County, Iowa, and was born in that county in 1853. By her union with our subject she became the mother of twin daughters, Bonnie and Birdie, both deceased. Politically Mr. Winn is a Greenbacker, and socially both he and his wife are held in high esteem by the leading citizens of Ottumwa.

CHARLES MICK is a prosperous and successful farmer and stock-raiser, living on section 3, Competine Township. He was born Dec. 13, 1840, in this State, and is the son of John and Mary (White) Mick, the former a native of West Virginia and the latter of Ohio. John Mick was the father of five children: James, a farmer of Highland Township; Sarah, married and living in Mahaska County; Charles, our subject; Peter, deceased; Mary is married and also living in Mahaska County. These children were by his first wife, who was buried in Virginia. The second wife of John Mick was Elizabeth (Thompson) Mick. They came to this county in 1856, and took up their residence in Highland Township, where he engaged in agricultural pursuits.

Charles Mick accompanied his parents to the county in 1856, and remained on the old homestead until 1862, engaged the while in farm labor. He then enlisted in Co. D, 19th Iowa Vol. Inf., and was mustered into the service at Keokuk. He enlisted for three years, or during the war, and on the 4th of September, that year, his regiment left Keokuk for St. Louis. They then went to Benton Barracks, thence to Rolla, Mo., then participating in the battle of Prairie Grove, Ark., and going to Van Buren, that State, drove the rebels out of the town and buried five steamboats, loaded with provisions. The regiment then returned to Vicksburg and from there was ordered to New Orleans, where our subject was taken sick, and in November, 1863, he received a furlough and went home. He remained at home until the following May, when he returned to his regiment and participated in all the battles in which it was engaged. Our subject received his discharge at Davenport, Iowa, and returning home again engaged in the peaceful pursuits of life.

Mr. Mick was united in marriage with Julia A. Mowery, daughter of Joseph Mowery. This union has been blest by the birth of seven children, two sons and five daughters. The record is as follows: Minnie, born Nov. 12, 1867; Annie, Sept. 17, 1869; Joseph B., Sept. 20, 1872, deceased; Mary A., Oct. 5, 1873; Nellie M., July 13, 1875; Charles F., Sept. 1, 1877; Ida, Dec. 28, 1880. Mrs. Mick departed this life June 2, 1881. She was a true and consistent Christian lady and held fellowship with the Christian Church. Socially Mr. Mick is a member of the G. A. R. and belongs to Post No. 402.

RUEL NIMOCKS is a farmer and stock-grower, residing on section 10, Washington Township. He was born in Lewis County, N. Y., Aug. 19, 1817, and is a son of Roland and Zermah (Bosworth) Nimocks. His parents moved from New York to Michigan, where his father died in 1864, and his mother the year following. In 1835, when but eighteen years of age, Ruel moved from New York to Kane County, Ill., where he lived three years, and in 1838 went to Adams County, in the same State, and in 1840 there married Amy Thomas, born in Switzerland County, Ind., Dec. 15, 1821, the daughter of George and Elizabeth (Jackson) Thomas. Her mother died in Morgan County, Ill., and her father again married, and in 1850 moved to Wayne County, Iowa, where he died in 1861.

Mr. and Mrs. Nimocks are the parents of nine children: Lucretia married Milton Crail, and is now deceased; Flint is now in Kansas; George W. married Elvira Newell, and is now living in Great Bend, Barton Co., Kan.; Clara married A. W. Roberts, and is now living in Marysville, Mo.; Mary is the wife of Henry Haydock, and is living in Ness City, Kan.; Sophia married D. T. Foster, and is now living in this township; William A. married Martha Robinson, and is now living in Nickerson, Kan.; Ruel L. married Maria Acton, and is now living in Kansas; Lucy is the wife of Harrison Creamer, and lives in Washington Township; Frank A. is living at home with his parents.

Mr. Nimocks has a fine farm of 300 acres, with good dwelling-house, barn, and all other necessary improvements. He and his wife have been members of the Methodist Episcopal Church since 1838, and in politics he is a Republican.

J. J. PADDEN, of Ottumwa, occupies the responsible position of assistant foreman of bridge building along the route of the C., B. & Q. R. R., and is accredited with being a skillful mechanic and having a thorough knowledge of the duties devolving upon him. Mr. Padden is a native of Ogden, N. Y., the date of his birth being Aug. 15, 1846. He is the son of Patrick and Bridget (Millet) Padden, of Irish birth and parentage, and possessing the warm and generous character of the Celtic race. While the subject of our sketch was a mere boy his parents removed to Chicago, Ill., where he was educated in the city schools. Patrick Padden was a carpenter by trade, and his son became his apprentice. At an early age he exhibited natural talent as a mechanic, and under the excellent instruction of his father soon developed into a first-class workman. While in Chicago he was employed by the American Bridge Company for seven years. He afterward went South and engaged in the construction of bridges on the railroads of that section, having charge of a gang of men. He subsequently returned to the Garden City, and in 1882 crossed the Father of Waters and proceeded northwest to Dakota, with the idea of changing his occupation. He located 160 acres of land in Barnes County, where he remained for the space of two years, and in 1884 returned southeast and came into Ottumwa. Being inclined to his old occupation, he afterward entered the employ of the C., B. & Q. R. R., and soon afterward was promoted to his present position.

Mr. Padden was married on the 3d of July, 1876, to Miss Josephine Hill, of Chicago, Ill., and they have become the parents of two sons—Edwin A. and Harry I. They have a pleasant home at 1,006 Plum street, and are surrounded by all the comforts of life. Mr. P. is highly respected in this community and a member in good standing of the Select Knights of A. O. U. W.

ALEXANDER MARTIN, of Adams Township, is a native of the Hawkeye State, and was born in Van Buren County, March 9, 1839. His parents were James and Rebecca Martin, who were born in Pickaway County, Ohio, and there reared and married. They afterward came to Van Buren County, Iowa, and settled near Keosauqua, where James Martin made a claim which he occupied with his family until 1843. They then removed to Davis County, where he took up another tract of Government land, opened up a farm, established a permanent home, and spent the remainder of his days, dying of cholera in 1852. He was a man of considerable force of character, and was an old-line Whig up to the time of his death. The parental household consisted of eight children, who lived to maturity: Harriet became the wife of Madison McIntyre, of Monroe County, Iowa; Rachel married Jacob Zegler, of Davis County; James is a resident of Monroe County; Mary, Mrs. Enoch Demeris, lives in Oregon; Rebecca married James Gordon, of Oregon, and they are both deceased; John is a resident of Washington Territory; Alexander is at home, and Samuel is in Oregon. Mrs. Martin, the mother of these children, died in 1884, at the advanced age of seventy-nine years. She and her husband were members of the Methodist Episcopal Church.

The subject of our sketch removed with his parents from Van Buren to Davis County, and from there to Wapello County. He received a common-school education, and after arriving at years of manhood was married in this county on the 21st of March, 1861, to Miss Maria Bachman, the daughter of Fred L. and Susan (Spangler) Bachman, who were among the early settlers of Wapello County. Mrs. Martin, the wife of our subject, was born in Muskingum County, Ohio, March 12, 1841. Of this union there were born nine children, as follows: Mary, born July 2, 1863, was married Dec. 18, 1883, to Thomas A. Green, M. D., a graduate of Des Moines Medical College, who is now traveling for a drug-house at Kansas City; Charles W., born April 11, 1866, lives in this county; Frederick L., born Jan. 18, 1868, and Alex W., April 10, 1877, are at home; Alexander, born April 13, 1865, died in infancy; Elnora A., born Jan. 20, 1870, died Aug. 7, 1871; Rebecca F., born July 24, 1873 died June 8, 1876; Henry C., born March 11 1875, died June 15, 1876; John R., born Dec. 8, 1879, died July 28, 1881.

In 1864 Mr. and Mrs. Martin crossed the plains to Idaho and Oregon and located in Pioneer City, where he engaged in the dairy business, but only remained one year. In 1865 he came to this township, opened up a farm, erected a log cabin, and commenced the establishment of a permanent home. In 1886 he built his present fine residence, at a cost of $1,000, and has one of the most attractive homes in this part of the county. His possessions have been accumulated by the industry of his own hands, and he presents the happy spectacle of a representative citizen and a straightforward business man, who is fulfilling all his obligations in a creditable and praiseworthy manner.

Mr. M. is Township Trustee, and is connected with the business and general welfare of the township and county. His father, James Martin, was often requested to allow his name to be used as a candidate, but always refused, having no ambition in that direction, but made himself useful by doing the writing for the early settlers.

THOMAS J. HALL has been a resident of Ottumwa since the spring of 1866, is successfully engaged as a builder and contractor, and also interested in the Ottumwa Screen Factory. He first opened his eyes to the light on the rugged coast of New England, being a native of Maine and born in Machias, on the 3d of October, 1839. He is the son of Thomas and Mary (Kinney) Hall, and his father was a native of Suffolkshire, England, descended from excellent English ancestry. The latter was a soldier in the army of his native country at the time of the battle of Waterloo, but being under age his father bought him off, and he subsequently became a member of the Queen's Guard. He afterward enlisted in the regular services of the English army, serving eleven years and nine months in Ireland and Scotland. In 1822, becoming heartily tired of military life he deserted the ranks, and boarding a vessel bound for the United States, arrived here after a narrow escape from being captured, taken back and shot. He located in Maine, where he was subsequently married to the mother of our subject, and they became the parents of four children—Rebecca, Thomas J., James and Lydia. In 1847 the family removed to Hempstead, L. I., where another child was born, a son, William. The following year they removed to Sing Sing, where they remained until 1857, and where, in the meantime, another son, Charlie, was added to the little household. Thence they removed to Toledo, Ohio, which remained their home until the death of the father in 1872.

Thomas Hall was a man of decided views and opinions, warm-hearted and generous in his disposition, and was an active sympathizer in the cause of right and justice. At the breaking out of the trouble between the North and South he proffered his services as a soldier of the Union, but was rejected on account of his age. His son, our subject, however, was accepted and enlisted on the 22d of August, 1862, in Co. H, 111th Ohio Vol. Inf., at the call for 600,000 troops. His regiment proceeded to Bowling Green, Ky., and with twenty-three others Thomas J. Hall was detailed in a pioneer corps. He afterward participated in the battle of Stone River, upon which occasion his closest friend and comrade, Horace Cooper, fell at his post. In the winter of 1863 they camped at Loudon, Tenn. Our subject was present at the siege of Knoxville, and at a large number of subsequent battles and skirmishes. At the battle of Rocky Face he laid down his knapsack with the expectation of never taking it up again. He, however, escaped serious disaster, and was enabled to remain in the service with his comrades until the close of the war, and was mustered out at Cleveland, Ohio, July 14, 1865. During his term of enlistment he was in the following battles: Stone River, Huff's Ferry, Campbell Station, siege of Knoxville, Ft. Sanders, Strawberry Plains, Rocky Face, Resaca, Pumpkin-Vine Creek, Burnt Hickory, Lost Mountain. Nickel Jack Creek, Kenesaw Mountain, Decatur, Peachtree Creek, Atlanta, Jonesboro, Stone Mountain, Franklin, Nashville, Ft. Anderson and Town Creek.

Thomas J. Hall was married in Toledo, Ohio, in 1859, to Miss Mary A. Blair, of Michigan. She then became a resident of Toledo while her husband was in the army, and after his return they crossed the Mississippi and located in Ottumwa, which has remained their home since that time, highly respected by a large circle of friends and acquaintances. Of their union there was born one child, which died in infancy.

Mr. Hall is a Greenbacker in politics, and socially belongs to Cloutman Post No. 69, G. A. R., of Ottumwa, and represented his lodge (I. O. O. F.) in the sessions of the Grand Lodge at Ottumwa and Council Bluffs, in 1864–65.

REV. J. T. SIMMONS, of Center Township, was born in New Castle County Del., Jan. 11, 1829. His father died six months before he was born, and his widowed mother afterward resided with his grandfather. At the age of seven years he moved with his grandfather, Hiram Talley, to Morgan County, Ohio. They located on a farm near McConnelsville, and in this home young Simmons spent his early years, attending such schools as the country afforded, and by close application to study acquired a good education. When eighteen years of age he engaged in the manufacture and sale of agricultural implements. He was married, in his twenty-second year, to Miss Martha Arganbright, of Jackson County, Ohio, and four years later moved to Iowa, in 1855. Of this marriage there were born four sons and two daughters: Lydia J. married E. G. Chapman; Frank W. and George B. are engaged in the hardware business; Kittie L., John W. and Ed. S. are at home.

In 1854 Mr. Simmons was licensed as a local preacher of the Methodist Episcopal Church, and the year following joined the Iowa Annual Conference, and entered upon what has been thirty years of active ministerial life. What was lacking in scholarly attainments he tried to make up in close study and hard work. He has filled some of the leading appointments in the Iowa Conference, representing the Conference as a delegate to the General Conference, which convened at Brooklyn, N. Y., in 1872, and has served two terms of four years each as Presiding Elder. He was one of the original committees who organized Clear Lake and Bluff Park Assembly grounds. He has been for years a Trustee of the Iowa Wesleyan University and for two years its Financial Agent. In August, 1862, he was commissioned Chaplain of the 28th Iowa Infantry, in which he served faithfully until the close of the war. This was one of the Iowa regiments which saw the hardest field service, and was with Grant in the long Mississippi campaign until the fall of Vicksburg; then with Gen. Banks in the Red River expedition; again with Grant and Sheridan in the Shenandoah campaign, and finally transferred to Sherman in Georgia, where it closed its eventful service.

Mr. Simmons was with his regiment in every battle it fought, being in some of the hardest battles of the war. His activity in the army gave him more than an ordinary record. He was detailed on the staff of Gen. Prentiss in the winter of 1863, and put in charge of the contraband camps at Helena, Ark, which he superintended under great difficulties with the scanty means. He relieved the suffering of thousands of refugees, who, escaping from bondage, sought refuge in the Union lines, sending hundreds of them North to find employment out of the reach of slavery. When the Government armed the negro, he had the pleasure of recruiting the first company at Helena, Ark., mustering them under a huge tree on which the slave power hung a Methodist preacher in 1858.

Mr. Simmons interested himself in the law concerning the Chaplains as officers, since they received no pensions. He wrote to Mr. Grinnell and Mr. Harlan and other members of Congress, and kept up a persistent effort until the cross legislation of Congress was secured and the rank of Chaplain created, by which the Chaplains were paid and received pensions as other officers, and while he has never received a dollar as personal benefit he rejoices that many worthy men have. He was detailed by the General commanding the 2d Division of the 13th Army Corps at Champion Hills battlefield, to register the wounded and form descriptive rolls; and when the Colonel of a Confederate Kentucky regiment captured the camp and demanded the rolls, Mr. Simmons buried them under a brush heap and saved 1,800 soldiers from being parolled. The Colonel swore and threatened, but the Chaplain was firm and he did not obtain them.

Arduous duties and hard work during the siege of Vicksburg brought our subject down with typhoid fever, which necessitated a leave of absence of six weeks, after which time he rejoined his regiment and accompanied it in all its marches and battles. Active in caring for the wants of his regiment, he was often brought in contact with the officers of the army, by whom he was always treated with much courtesy. On the 3d of July, during the siege of Vicksburg, he was in Gen. Grant's tent soliciting assistance for one of his regiment, when the first message from Gen. Pemberton was received proposing to surrender the city and 20,000 prisoners of war. Gen. Grant's face was firm; not a muscle twitched, and in characteristic simplicity he said to Gen. Rawlins, "If he wishes to surrender, he knows our terms." It was a good time to secure a favor, and the Chaplain succeeded in getting the man a leave of absence. But Gen. Grant was always kind. Once on personal application for leave the General directed that it be given, and walked out, but soon returned and said, "Give the Chaplain transportation."

The Red River campaign was the most severe service in which the regiment of Mr. Simmons was engaged. In the spring of 1864 the regiment left New Orleans, nearly 800 strong, and in fine condition; but hard service and two severe battles in that campaign left its strength less than 400 on its return to Alexandria. Being transferred to the army of the Potomac, it was put in the 19th Army Corps under Sheridan, and in the Shenandoah campaign helped to destroy Lee's army under Early; fought the battles of Winchester and Cedar Creek, and witnessed the famous ride of Sheridan.

With the consciousness of a life well spent Mr. Simmons is cheerfully living and hoping to meet the future in the same confidence in God by which he has met each day of the past. One year ago he settled on a small farm two miles west of Ottumwa, and is yet active and at present engaged in ministerial labor.

GAMALIEL C. BEAMAN, deceased, formerly a resident of Massachusetts, was a native of Winchendon, Mass., and was born on the 20th of March, 1799. His rudimentary education was carefully conducted, and after the completion of his primary studies he entered Union College at Schenectady, N. Y., from which he graduated, and after taking a course in Andover Theological Seminary, in Massachusetts, entered the Presbyterian ministry. After a service of several years in New England, Mr. Beaman journeyed southwestward to Ohio, settling in Piketon, Pike County, in 1831, where he organized the pioneer church of that region.

Mr. Beaman was a man of kindly and generous impulses, with a rigid belief in the rights of human freedom. He was bitterly opposed to slavery and was one of the leaders of the anti-slavery movement in Ohio. In April, 1835, he assisted in organizing the Ohio State Anti-Slavery Society at Putnam which helped many a fugitive to freedom.

Rev. Gamaliel C. Beaman was united in marriage with Miss Emelia Crichton, in 1836. This lady was a native of Scotland and a descendant of the same family as Admiral Crichton. Mr. and Mrs. B. two years later removed to Burlington, Lawrence County, where he preached the Gospel and taught in the High School. In 1842 he opened an academy at Burlington, and continued in charge until 1846, when he removed to Iowa and settled in Montrose, Lee County, where he organized a church, holding services in the Government Barracks, there being no church building. He also preached half the time in Nauvoo, just across the Mississippi River, which was then the seat of Mormonism. The Mormon War occurred that year, resulting in the capitulation of the Latter-Day Saints on the 17th of September, 1846, after which many of them removed to Salt Lake City.

Montrose being at the head of the great rapids on the Mississippi, had become the resort of thieves, gamblers and roughs of every description, and was justly reputed to be the most wicked place on the river. Here Mr. Beaman opened a school, which was attended by many of the characters referred to, partly from a desire to learn and partly to break up the project. Personal conflicts between them and the teacher were not infrequent, but by strategy and firmness, combined with muscle, the result was invariably favorable to good order and discipline. The mob element finally became divided, a part abandoning the school and others submitting to its government, so that it was carried on quite successfully for several years, and finally surrendered to other hands. In 1848 the majority of the Mormons had left the country, and on the 9th of September of that year their magnificent Temple at Nauvoo was destroyed by fire, presumably by themselves to prevent its use by the Gentiles, who had been reaping a rich harvest by exhibiting to visitors its inner splendors. After five years of discipline the morals of the town of Montrose became quite respectable.

In 1852 Mr. Beaman removed to Croton, on the Des Moines River, where he had previously organized a church. A few miles above, at Salubria, was the house of Abner Kneeland, who had a few years before been imprisoned in Boston for blasphemy, and the leader of a sect known as Pantheists. His followers were infidels of the most pronounced character, and their doctrines had infected a wide region. For the next twenty-one years Mr. Beaman preached in that region and the conflict of doctrine was constant and fierce; but in the end the Pantheistic leaders died, and the last vestige of their doctrines have disappeared, until but few people in the community now remember what they were.

In 1873 Mr. B., in response to an urgent call

from his old church, removed back to Montrose, leaving the churches on the Des Moines River in charge of other ministers, who had then become quite numerous. Three years later his physical frame gave way, and he removed to the residence of his son at Keosauqua in Van Buren County, where he remained until the final summons came, on the 26th of October, 1876. He was in his seventy-seventh year, having spent forty-four years in the ministry. Since the commencement of his ministerial labors Mr. Beaman had delivered 3,542 sermons, 474 lectures on slavery and temperance, and had organized seven churches, twenty-seven Sabbath-schools, four anti-slavery societies, twenty-eight temperance societies, and obtained 2,700 names to anti-slavery and temperance pledges. He also received into the church 317 persons, baptized 298, married 227 couples, preached 299 funeral sermons, examined and licensed seventy-five school-teachers, distributed 337 Bibles, and 7,000 tracts.

The funeral sermon of this lamented citizen and Christian minister was preached at Keosauqua by his friend, Rev. Dr. W. G. Craig, of Chicago, Ill. In the course of his remarks Dr. Craig, in reviewing the life of the deceased, said that he was indeed one of the soldiers of the Cross, and had stood during his entire ministerial life on the "high places of the field" and in the forefront of the battle.

The good which one such life has accomplished can scarcely be estimated within the limits of a comparatively brief biography. The influence of his Christian character was one that has spread far beyond his own day and time, and its effects will extend far beyond the present generation in the lives of those who, as children of those who came under the sphere of his influence, are made better, happier and more useful, even unto the third generation.

HON. DANIEL A. LAFORCE, M. D., a physician and surgeon of considerable prominence, residing at Ottumwa, was born in Jefferson County, Ind., May 17, 1837. The father of our subject, Daniel G. LaForce, was a native of Woodford County, Ky., where he grew to manhood. He was married to Miss Margaret Monroe in Jefferson County, Ind. He was a farmer by occupation and at different times in life was engaged in mercantile pursuits. He removed from Kentucky to Jefferson County, Ind., where he continued to reside until 1842, and during that year came to this State and first made settlement in Van Buren County. Subsequently he removed to this county, and locating in Washington Township there followed his chosen vocation, farming, until his demise, which took place Aug. 2, 1863. His good wife survives him and is at present residing at Agency.

Daniel LaForce came to Iowa with his parents in 1842, when about five years of age. Here he attended the common schools and supplemented the education received therein by an attendance of several terms at the Mt. Pleasant (Iowa) Western University. It was during the year 1858 that our subject came to the conclusion that he would study medicine, and made a beginning in the office of a local physician. Subsequently he entered the College of Physicians and Surgeons at Keokuk, and graduated therefrom in 1862. Immediately after receiving his diploma he was commissioned Surgeon of the 56th U. S. Colored Troops, and after nine months' service was placed in charge of a U. S. general hospital at Helena, Ark.; he was also appointed Medical Director for the district of Eastern Arkansas. During this time he also served on the staff of Gen. E. A. Carr about twelve months. Dr. LaForce continued in the service until Sept. 15, 1866, when his regiment was mustered out.

Returning from the field of conflict Dr. LaForce located at Mt. Pleasant, Iowa, and there entered upon the practice of his profession and continued the same with success until 1869. He then removed to Burlington, and after a residence there of two years, engaged in practice, he took up his abode in Agency City, where he enjoyed an extensive practice for fourteen years. He then removed to Ottumwa, which he has continued to make his home, and has devoted himself closely to his profession. He is a member of the Wapello County Medical Society, the Iowa State Medical Society, and the American Medical Association.

Politically Dr. LaForce is Republican, and represented his county in the Twenty-first General As-

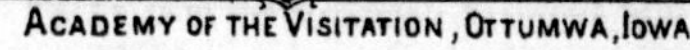

ACADEMY OF THE VISITATION, OTTUMWA, IOWA.

ST. PATRICKS CHURCH,-SOUTH OTTUMWA. REV. FRANCIS T. WARD, PASTOR.

sembly of Iowa. In 1884, when first coming to Ottumwa, he purchased the Castor House, and changing the name to the LaForce House, has continued its proprietor until the present time. It is a four-story brick structure and contains 100 rooms.

Dr. LaForce was married, Oct. 18, 1866, at Mt. Pleasant, Iowa, to Miss Mahala J. Dudley, the daughter of Rev. Edward and Eliza (Dudley) Dudley, natives of Athens, Ohio. Rev. Edward Dudley was a man of prominence and a leading divine in the Free-Will Baptist Church. He moved with his family to Agency City, Iowa, and was among the pioneers of the Hawkeye State. His good wife departed this life Sept. 20, 1884; he is yet living and resides in Agency City. Mrs. LaForce was born in Ohio, and by her marriage with our subject has become the mother of four children, namely: William B., Burdett D., Edward F. and Charles R. Socially Dr. LaForce is a member of the Masonic fraternity, the I. O. O. F. and the Knights of Pythias. Religiously he is connected with the Methodist Episcopal Church.

REV. FRANCIS T. WARD. The history of St. Patrick's Church at Ottumwa, and the personal history of Father Ward are so interwoven that we give both a brief mention in this sketch. St. Mary's Parish, of Ottumwa, with a small beginning and few members, increased like the Scriptural mustard seed, under the fostering care and zealous attention of Rev. John Kreckel, who may truly be called its first Pastor, and not only Wapello County and its principal town, but the six or seven adjoining counties, with a thinly scattered Catholic element, were dependent on his spiritual ministrations, and received their share of his watchful care.

In 1880, Rt. Rev. John Hennessey, Bishop of Dubuque, and then the whole State of Iowa, judged it expedient from the growth of the parish to establish a new parish from the settlements south of the Des Moines River. Rev. Francis T. Ward was appointed as its first Pastor. He was born in County Langford, Ireland, and pursued his preparatory and classical studies in St. Bernard's School, and in the German and French colleges at Black Rock, Dublin. In 1873 he entered St. Patrick's Eccelesiastical College, of Carlow, Ireland, where he spent six years, one year in the rhetoric class, with two years of philosophy and three of theology. June 9, 1879, he was ordained Priest for the diocese of Dubuque, Iowa. After spending a few months with friends, he sailed on the 25th of October following on the Cunard steamer, "Bothnia," from Queensstown, landing in the city of New York on the 4th of November.

In 1881 Father Ward secured lots from W. B. Smith, M. D., of Ann Arbor, Mich., and in the following year a brick church was erected, in South Ottumwa, 40x80 feet in dimensions, with a stone basement and trimmings, slate roof and stained glass windows, at a cost of between $9,000 and $10,000. In 1884, the congregation having no parochial house, and encouraged by the people of Ottumwa, who lent not only moral but substantial aid in the erection of their church, came a second time and contributed to the erection of a parochial residence that would do no discredit to any parish in Iowa. It is trimmed with white Milwaukee stone, is built of brick, with a slate roof, and cost $3,500. The mission proper has, on a rough calculation, 100 families attached to it, and the station thirty or forty more families, in all perhaps 140. A view of both church and residence is given in this connection.

CHECKART, who is a highly esteemed resident of Green Township, was born in Dauphin County, Pa., Nov. 17, 1832, being the son of Jost and Mary (Schneider) Heckart. He left Pennsylvania with his parents when a boy of eight years old, and went to Ralls County, Mo., where he lived until the fall of 1862, and thence went to Hancock County, Ill. This was during the progress of the late war, and he enlisted as a Union soldier in Co. K, 119th Ill. Vol. Inf., and served two years and ten months. He participated in numerous skirmishes and one general engagement in Mississippi. He was subjected, however, to much hardship and exposure, which greatly impaired his health, and in March, 1865, he received his honorable discharge on account of disability.

He was confined in the hospital at St. Louis during the latter part of his army life, but able to officiate as nurse. His observations convinced him that the inmates of the hospital did not receive proper attention, and he addressed a letter to Gov. Yates to that effect, requesting the Governor to come and see for himself. This he did, being disguised, and our subject was removed to better quarters in a few days.

After the war Mr. Heckart returned to Illinois, and thence to Ralls County, Mo., where he engaged three years in farming, and then, in the fall of 1868, came into this county and settled in Green Township, where he has since lived.

Mr. Heckart was first married in 1851 to Miss Lydia M. Brown, a native of Virginia, and of this union there were born four children: Elias V., who is a plasterer by trade and now living in St. Louis; William Henry, a farmer of Montgomery County, Mo.; Perry Eugene and James C., the latter a resident of New London, Mo., and engaged in railroading. The second wife of our subject, to whom he was married in 1878, was a widow lady and formerly Miss Rosa E. DeValt, a native of Kentucky. Mrs. H. by her first marriage became the mother of six children, of whom one is deceased, and five are living with our subject and his wife.

Mr. Heckart is the owner of eighty acres of good land with a comfortable dwelling and all necessary out-buildings. He is Republican in politics and keeps himself well posted upon all matters of general interest. He is a member of the Presbyterian Church, and Mrs. H. is connected with the Methodist Episcopal Church.

E. D. SOMERS lives in the city of Ottumwa, and is book-keeper and manager of the agricultural warehouse of John Fuller. He was born in Hancock County, Ill., March 25, 1855, and is a son of Albertus and Caroline Somers, the former a native of Germany and the latter of Vermont. In 1859 the family moved from Hancock County, Ill., to Davis County, Iowa, where they remained two years, and then moved back to Hancock County. In 1867 they again returned to Davis County, Iowa, remaining there one year, and then moved to Jones County, Iowa, where they remained ten years. The father and mother reside in Ottumwa, Iowa.

The subject of this sketch is one of a family of six children, and is second in order of birth. The others are Ella E., who was married to J. N. Ellis, but is now deceased; Charles G., now living in Anamosa, this State; Susan B. is the wife of Charles E. Fliesbach, and has one child; they live in Sigourney, Iowa; America A. is the wife of W. R. Kizer, and lives in Ottumwa; James A. is married, and also resides in Ottumwa.

E. D. Somers was married, April 26, 1877, to Hester A. Jenkins. The father of Mrs. Somers is deceased; her mother, Hannah Jenkins, survives, and makes her home in Hancock County, Ill. Mr. Somers is a man of good executive and business abilities.

J. F. LEWIS, an honored pioneer of Wapello County, came to Iowa in March, 1839, seven years before it was admitted into the Union as a State. This section of country was then a wilderness where the feet of white men had seldom trod. Wild animals were abundant and wild Indians were the only human beings scattered over the country, with an occasional white man. The remarkable changes which Mr. Lewis has witnessed since first crossing the Father of Waters would form an interesting volume. He has observed the developement of this State and the march of civilization with pleasure and satisfaction, and has materially aided in bringing about its present condition of prosperity, for he was one of those enterprising and industrious characters, without which very little could have been accomplished. The present wealth and population of the Hawkeye State is due to such men as the subject of this sketch.

Mr. Lewis is a native of Champaign County, Ohio, and was born on the 27th day of August, 1830. His father, George Lewis, was born in

Greenbriar County, (now West) Virginia, Dec. 2, 1801, and his mother, Sophia (Woolly) Lewis, was born near Elizabethtown, N. J., Jan. 11, 1806. They both went to Ohio with their parents while young, and were there married in 1827. They became the parents of seven children, five born in Ohio and two in Iowa. Of these four only are now living: William died in Ottumwa in 1875. He was a man of more than ordinary ability and was the Sheriff of Wapello County in 1858-59; J. F., our subject, was the second in order of birth; Dr. C. G. is a resident of Ottumwa; Martha became the wife of David Warner of Van Buren County, Iowa; George is also a resident of Van Buren County; Jane became the wife of Henry Warner, and departed this life in 1880 near Winchester; Nelson died in 1871 in Van Buren County.

George Lewis removed from the State of Ohio in 1838 to Warren County, Ill. He remained a resident of that locality until the following year, and on the 10th of March came into Van Buren County, Iowa. He purchased a claim of 160 acres of wild land, ten acres of which was partly improved, and upon it stood a rude cabin sixteen feet square. Into this he removed with his own and two other families, the total number of inmates being thirteen. They existed in this manner for the space of three weeks. Provisions were scarce and difficult to obtain, and Mr. Lewis was compelled to go down into Missouri and buy corn at $1 a bushel, which he carried to a small mill on Chequest Creek to be ground into meal. Even this was not always reliable, and when the water was low the pioneers had to pound their corn in a rude mortar in order to make bread. Mr. Lewis remained on this farm until 1871, and during that time had converted the wilderness into broad and smiling fields, and the rude cabin was succeeded by a handsome and comfortable farm dwelling. At the expiration of this time he retired from active labor and removed from the farm into the city of Ottumwa, where he resided until his death, which took place on the 1st of May, 1877. Mrs. Lewis survived her husband three years, dying in October, 1880. She was a highly respected Christian lady, and left behind her a record of womanly virtues and kindly deeds.

Although George Lewis was not connected with any church organization he was a man of strict morality, straightforward in his business transactions, and enjoyed the entire confidence of his neighbors and acquaintances. He was a man of great force of character and more than ordinarily intelligent, keeping himself well posted in regard to local and general matters. Politically he was an uncompromising Democrat, and fearlessly upheld the principles of the party of his choice.

The subject of our sketch came with his parents to Iowa when a little boy of seven years old. They located first in Van Buren County, and he was reared and educated in the log cabin with its puncheon floor and slabs for seats and desks. This rude structure was provided with a small square opening for a window, and light was admitted through panes of greased paper, and the chimney was made of mud. In order to reach the "schoolhouse" he traveled a mile through all kinds of weather in the winter, and worked upon the farm during the summer seasons.

Mr. Lewis remained under the parental roof until after he had attained to years of manhood, and on St. Valentine's Day, 1856, was united in marriage with Miss Sarah L. Neal, a native also of Champaign County, Ohio, her birth having occurred on the 11th of June, 1836. The following October Mr. L. with his young wife removed from Van Buren to Wapello County, and located in the township of Dahlonega. Two years later he was appointed Deputy Sheriff and then removed to Ottumwa, of which city he has since been a resident. He has been prominent in local affairs here, and was elected City Marshal, serving in 1860-61. His time not being fully occupied with his official duties he became employed as a clerk in the dry-goods establishment of W. C. Moss, Jr., & Co., with whom he remained until 1865. In that year he went into business for himself as member of the firm of Lively & Co., operating thus until 1871. He then disposed of his interest in the business, and since that time has been engaged as an insurance, real estate and loan agent.

Mr. and Mrs L. have become the parents of seven children, all living, and the record is as follows: Josephine is the wife of William Hunt, of

Ottumwa; Leon D. is also a resident of this city; Minnie, Charles L., Louisa, John and Anna are at home with their parents. The family residence is pleasantly located and its inmates are surrounded by all the comforts of life.

Mr. Lewis has been identified with the Masonic fraternity of Ottumwa for many years. He was originally a member of Ottumwa Lodge No. 16, but subsequently, with sixteen others, withdrew and founded Empire Lodge No. 269, and is a member of Clinton Chapter No. 9, and Malta Commandery No. 31. He has taken great interest in the prosperity and advancement of the order, and is esteemed one of its most valued members. In his political affiliations Mr. Lewis is an ardent supporter of the Democratic party.

HISTORICAL

TIME is ever moving on. The deeds and actions of to-day form the subject of history to-morrow. From the record of these deeds men form ideas of duty, which govern them in all their actions, present and future. In the foregoing pages has been traced the life history of many of the best citizens of Wapello County. In those that follow will be presented in a brief manner facts in common to all, which go to make up the history of this county. The plan of this work, as doubtless well understood by our patrons, will not admit of more than this. In the biographical department we have given all an opportunity to have their sketches satisfactory and complete, and as history is no more nor less than a record of the lives of the people, much of the history of this county is therein given.

The question is often asked why men leave the comforts and pleasures of civilized lands, and strike out into a new and almost unknown country, bearing the toils and privations which are unavoidable. Not more from choice than necessity did the old pioneers bid farewell to the play-grounds of their childhood and the graves of their fathers. One generation after another had worn themselves out in the service of avaricious landlords, or to eke out a miserable existence upon barren or worn-out land, which they called their own. From the first flashes of the morning light until the last glimmer of the setting sun, they toiled unceasingly on from father to son, carrying home each day upon their aching shoulders the precious proceeds of their daily labor. Money, pride and power were handed down in the line of succession from the rich father to his son, while unceasing work, continuous poverty and everlasting obscurity were the heritage of the working man and his children. For the sons and daughters of the poor man to remain there, was to follow and never to lead—to be poor forever.

Without money, prestige or friends, the old pioneer drifted along, seeking the garden spot, the place where he might establish a home, where he might educate his sons and daughters, giving them privileges he never enjoyed himself. The broad prairies and beautiful groves of Wapello County in that early day, were indeed inviting to those seeking a home in a more favored land, and here planted their stakes, many of whom the present generation have reason to rise up and call blessed. To secure and adorn the homes desired by the pioneers, more than ordinary ambition was required. greater than ordinary endurance demanded. How well they succeeded, let the broad, cultivated fields and fruit-bearing orchards, the flocks and the herds, the palatial residences, the places of business, the spacious halls, the clattering car-wheels and ponderous engines all testify.

Generation after generation come and go like the leaves of autumn. Nations have been born, have had their rise and fall, and then passed away, leaving scarcely a ripple on the great ocean of time to show that they ever existed, so imperfect and mutable have been their means to perpetuate their achievements. It was left to modern ages to establish an intelligent, undecaying, immutable method of perpetuating this history; immutable in that it is almost unlimited in extent, and perpetual in its action; and this is through the art of printing. Nations may become disintegrated and pass away, monuments and statues may crumble into dust, but books will live. This art has been rapidly advancing from its first inception, until now it would seem that there were no longer any further ground for improvement. This is pre-eminently an age of printing, an age of books.

To the present generation, however, are we indebted for the introduction of the admirable system of local history and local biography. By this system every man, though he has not achieved what the world calls greatness, has the means to perpetuate his life, his history through the coming ages; so alike has every community.

We come now to the work before us: To our patrons we say, that the scythe of Time cuts down all; nothing of the physical man is left; the monument which his children or friends may erect to his memory in the cemetery, will crumble into dust and pass away; but his life, his achievements, the work he has accomplished, which otherwise would be forgotten, is perpetuated by this book through coming ages. Shakespeare has said:

> The evil that men do lives after them:
> The good is oft interred with their bones.

Our aim in this work has been only to preserve the good, to record such acts as will tend to make men better, to show how the early settlers labored, and how the present development of the county has been brought about. Many of the pioneers came into this beautiful country without a dollar in their pockets, but with the unflinching determination to carve out their fortunes and build up a community. With undaunted hearts and a courage equal to that of the great heroes of our country, they began life.

Early Settlement.

WAPELLO, though comparatively a new county, is to-day classed among the best counties of the State of Iowa, the "beautiful land." It is bounded on the east by Jefferson, on the west by Monroe, on the south by Davis, and on the north by Mahaska and Keokuk Counties. It comprises twelve congressional townships, and is well watered by the Des Moines River and its tributaries. The Des Moines River enters the county on section 6, township 73, range 15, and flowing in a southeasterly course, leaves the county from section 35, township 71, range 12, thus dividing the county into nearly equal parts. The surface of the county is much broken, especially along the streams, though there are some as fine prairies as are to be seen in any part of the State. The whole country is probably underlaid with coal, many valuable mines being worked, Wapello ranking next to Mahaska in the amount of its coal productions.

Like various other parts of the State Wapello has a history previous to the advent of the white men. Evidences exist of the great unknown race to which has been given the name of Mound-Builders, well developed mounds being in plain view, some of which have been examined and human remains found interred therein, together with flint implements, and other productions of a race lost to view. Following the Mound-Builder came the wily red men, of which so much has been written, and so little true knowledge given to the world. When the Sacs and Foxes were driven from Illinois, some of the tribe settled in what is now Wapello County, establishing villages at several points. In the limits of this volume, an account of the Indian settlement cannot be given, however fascinating it might be, especially to the young; suffice it to say that here for some years was the home of Wapello, a chief friendly to the whites, a great friend of Gen. Street, the first Indian Agent whose headquarters were on the site of the present village of Agency. Wapello died March 15, 1842, at the forks of Skunk River, and his remains were brought to the Indian Agency, in an ox-wagon, and buried toward evening of the same day, with the customary Indian ceremonies. At his own request he was buried by the side of Gen Street, in the garden of the Agency.

The history proper of the county of Wapello begins with the establishment of the Indian Agency. Early in 1838, and soon after the ratification by the United States Senate of the treaty of 1837, with the Sacs and Foxes, Gen. Street took steps for the establishment of an agency within the boundaries. and as convenient as possible to the villages of the Indians. The first building complete was the old council house, which was ready for occupancy early in the summer of 1838. The agency house was soon afterward completed, and in April, 1839, Gen. Street moved his family down from Prairie du Chien and took possession. But he was not permitted long to exercise the duties of an Indian Agent, his health soon afterward failing, and in May, 1840, he passed away. It is said the Indians were so greatly attached to the General that on the news of his death reaching their village, opposite the present city of Ottumwa, many of them immediately went to the agency, and their expressions of grief were so demonstrative as to augment the distress of Mrs. Street.

On the death of Gen. Street, Maj. John Beach was appointed to the agency and took possession June 1, 1840. At the time of his arrival, according to a statement given by himself some years ago, the settlement here was as follows: "In the agency house was Mrs. Street, and the nine youngest of her children, of whom William B. Street, of Oskaloosa, (now of Council Bluffs) was the senior. Just over the branch, in the rear of the agency, was Josiah Smart, the interpreter, one of God's noblemen, who combined in his character every brave, honest and generous sentiment that can adorn man, and within a few steps of his residence was the blacksmith, Charles H. Withington. There was also Harvey Sturdevant, the gunsmith, but, being unmarried, he boarded with Withington, until, a year or so later, he put up a cabin, where the writer now lives [August, 1874], and dug that famous old well. As distance (from the rest of us) did not lend enchantment to the view of his bachelorhood, he soon switched onto the matrimonial track. Then there was the household of the Pattern Farm, some half dozen in number, except in extra times, such as harvesting. This was the actual agency settlement. On the Des Moines, a mile or so below the county farm, where the bluff approaches nearest to the bank, was the trading-post of P. Chouteau, Sr., & Co., but later more familiarly known as the 'old garrison.' This was usually superintended by Capt. William Phelps. And just above the mouth of Sugar Creek, at the old road crossing, lived the miller, Jeremiah Smith, Jr., with his family. This embraced all the whites lawfully living in the county at the time."

In the summer of 1840, J. P. Eddy was licensed by Maj. Beach, the Indian Agent, as a trader, and established his trading-post at the Indian village of Hardfish, where the village of Eddyville is now located. He continued to trade there until the final cession of the Indian lands in 1842, and was very fortunate in his business. About the time Eddy located here, P. Chouteau, Jr., & Co. also obtained permission and located near the same point. In the winter of 1840-41, W. G. & G. W. Ewing, of Indiana, obtained a license, and were assigned as a point for this trading post just at the mouth of Sugar Creek, below the present city of Ottumwa. Mr. Hunt was their representative and managed the post for one or two years. The Indian Agent and traders were all who were lawfully permitted to remain upon the soil of Wapello County till the spring of 1843.

In 1842 the Indians made a final cession of all their lands in the Territory of Iowa and agreed to leave, allowing its settlement by the whites. The treaty was to go into effect May 1, 1843. Before night of that day it is claimed there were not less than 2,000 persons actually inhabiting the county. For some time previous these pioneers had been making arrangements to take possession of the land as soon as thrown open for settlement, and had encamped upon the imaginary boundary line, ready when the hour of midnight was struck to enter in. The greater number of these persons were engaged the last half of the night of April 30, and morning of May 1, 1843, in marking out their claims, which embraced from 80 to 320 acres. The marking was done by setting stakes in the prairie and by blazing trees in the timber.

As remarked by Judge Hendershott, in an address delivered before the Old Settlers' Society of Wapello County some years ago, the work was very inartistically done, being made by lanterns or blazing torchlights. "Many of the boundary lines," said the Judge, "were crooked, disjointed, and encroached the one upon the other. This inevitably led to many disturbances, called 'claim difficulties.' It must be quite apparent that these difficulties must find some peaceable means of adjustment. To meet this necessity the earlier inhabitants organized what was called 'claim committees.' A claim, when *bona fide* made and held, was as sacredly protected as are houses and lands of the present inhabitants. The judgment of these crudely organized though necessary tribunals was enforced by summary process. This process was generally a plain, written statement of the claim committee, setting forth the right of the injured party and the wrong complained of, and an order to the wrongdoer to abide by and submit to the judgment of the court, in default of which the power of the court was invoked to carry out and enforce on the spot the judgment. From the judgment of these claim committees there was no appeal or stay of execution. It was well understood that when the committee reported it meant business, and generally, like Crockett's coon, the erring brother came down. Occasionally, however, these judgments were met by insubordination, and when it did occur there was war on the spot, without any formal declaration."

Some amusing instances are related of these claim wars, and some that were a little serious in results. Judge Hendershott, in his address already quoted from, gives some instances. The address may be found in the local papers of 1874, and also in the History of Wapello County, prepared by the Western Historical Company in 1878.

When Christ asked the demoniac his name, he responded: "My name is legion, for we are many." So it can be said of the first settler of Wapello County, his name is legion, for, as already stated, the morning of the 1st day of May, 1843, found many here who became permanent residents of the county, some of whom have been prominently identified with its history from that time to the present, but the majority of whom have either moved to other parts or have passed on to the other shore.

ORGANIZATION.

ON the 13th of February, 1844, the Territorial Legislature passed an act for the organization of the county, previous to which time it had been attached to Jefferson County for judicial purposes. The first section of the act declared "that the county of Wapello be and the same is hereby organized from and after the 1st day of March next," March 1, 1844. The act declared the Clerk of the District Court of said county, aided by the Sheriff of the county, should be the organizing officers. The duty of the Clerk was to appoint the Clerks and Judges of Election, fix the place of voting, receive, open and canvass the returns, declare the result, and issue certificates of election. H. B. Hendershott, who for so many years has been a leading attorney in Ottumwa, was Clerk of the Court, and J. M. Peck, Sr., yet living, two miles north of Ottumwa, a pioneer among pioneers, was the Sheriff, whose duty it was to post notices of the time and places of holding the election, and deliver to the Judges and Clerks the poll books.

The first election was held April 1, 1844, resulting in the choice of the following named: James M. Montgomery, Lewis F. Temple and Charles F. Harrow, County Commissioners; Charles Overman, Commissioner's Clerk; Paul C. Jeffries, Judge of Probate; Joseph Hayne, Sheriff; James Caldwell,

Assessor; Thomas Foster, Treasurer; Milton J. Spurlock, Recorder; Hugh George, Surveyor.

With the election of the foregoing officers, and their qualification, the county of Wapello was duly organized. At this time, or when the census was taken in the summer of that year, the county had a population of 2,814, all of whom had become citizens within one year. As may easily be inferred, all, or nearly all were in limited circumstances, but they had brave hearts, invincible will, and a strong determination to carve out for themselves homes in this fertile country. How well they have succeeded, let the cities and villages, the school-houses and churches, the finely cultivated farms, testify.

The act for the organization of the county provided for the appointment of Joseph B. Davis, of Washington County; John H. Randolph, of Henry County, and Solomon Jackson, of Lee County, as Commissioners for the location of the county seat. They were to meet at the house of George Wilson, near the old Indian Agency, on the first Monday in May, 1844, or at such time in that month as might be agreed upon by themselves. The Commissioners met according to appointment, and selected the present site of Ottumwa, to which they gave the name of Louisville. This name, however, did not suit the people here, and it was soon afterward changed to Ottumwa by the Commissioners.

The first meeting of the Board of County Commissioners was held on the 20th day of May, 1844, at "Louisville, the county seat of Wapello County." Charles Overman was appointed Clerk of the Commissioner's Court, and duly qualified.

The first business transacted was the granting of a license to David Glass to keep a grocery at Ottumwa, the Commissioners even then being favorable to a change of name, and doubtless with the intention of changing it.

Washington Township was organized at this meeting, while at the June session Pleasant, Competine, Columbia, Center, Dahlonega, Richland and Adams Townships were created. Keokuk and Polk Townships were created in April, 1846, and Agency Township not until April, 1851.

At the July, 1844, session J. P. Eddy was granted a license authorizing him to establish a ferry at Eddyville. The prices permitted to be charged were: Footman 6¼ cents; man and horse, 18¾ cents; two horses and wagon, 37½ cents; four horses and wagon, 50 cents; cattle, 4 cents; hogs, 2 cents.

A jail was ordered built on the east end of lot 136, block 11, in Louisville, but definite action was postponed, but in 1845 a contract was awarded to David Armstrong for its building on lot 140, block 11, at a cost of $2,000.

In November of this year the Board first officially recognized Ottumwa as the name of the town, previous to which time it had been using the names of Louisville and Ottumwa interchangeably.

COUNTY officers having been elected and the machinery of its government put in operation by the Board of County Commissioners, the county entered upon its career. While there has been nothing of a very startling nature in its history, it will show a gradual increase, year by year, in its growth and development. The first session of the District Court for the county of Wapello, was ordered held on Monday, Sept. 16, 1844. H. B. Hendershott was Clerk of the courts. The first records were kept on common foolscap paper stitched together, somewhat in contrast to the large, well-bound record books of the present time. Hon. Charles Mason was the Judge who presided upon this occasion. On account of his absence the term did not begin until Wednesday, September 18. The court was held in a log house, situated on the lot where the First National Bank of Ottumwa now stands. The first case that came up for trial was that of "Josiah Smart, who sues for the use of S. S. Phelps, *vs.* Elias Orton, assumpsit." The damages claimed were $500. By the consent of the parties interested the case was ordered dismissed at the cost of the defendant, which amounted to $7.52½.

A Grand Jury was empaneled at this term, consisting of the following named: James Weir, George W. Knight, Seth Ogg, Robert H. Ivers. Thomas Pendleton, Henry Smith, William Brinn, Lewis F. Temple, John Humphreys, Martin Fisher, Paul C. Jeffries, John Fuller, Finley Lindsey, William Pritchell, William C. McIntire, John Clark, James R. Boggs, John Kirkpatrick, John Murray, Ison Garrett, Shannon Hackney, Philaster Lee and Thomas Wright. Upon the panel being called the following named answered not: Robert H. Ivers, Martin Fisher, John Fuller, John Clark and John Kirkpatrick. The Court ordered the Sheriff to complete the panel, whereupon William A. Winsell, Peter Barnett, Richard Fisher and Jacob Hackney were added to the list. James Weir was appointed foreman, while George B. Warden was appointed bailiff and the jury placed under his charge. Only one indictment was found, that against Joseph S. Hendricks, for larceny. The case was taken up at once by the Court. Hendricks plead "not guilty," and the case was postponed till the next term of court, in April, 1844. It was continued at that term till the September term, 1845, when the Prosecuting Attorney refused to prosecute, and the case was stricken from the docket. There were forty cases on the first docket and the term lasted five days.

The first probate business transacted was in September, 1844, in the settlement of the estate of Thomas Crawford, deceased. Hon. Paul C. Jeffries was Judge of the Probate. William Crawford was appointed administrator, and gave bond with John Stout as surety. The administrator appointed Isaac McKeon, Paris Caldwell and Sylvester Warner to appraise the estate, which was done and a copy of the appraisement filed in court. Among the bills filed against the estate was one by the administrator, amounting to $9.59½, principally for whisky. Whether the whisky was necessary to drown his sorrow on account of the death of Mr. Crawford, or essential to a proper discharge of the duties of the administrator, is not stated.

And there "was marrying and giving in marriage" in that day as well as at the present time. Even before the county was fully officered an application was made, on the 15th day of March, 1844, for a license to the Clerk of the Court, Hon. H. B. Hendershott. The license was for Andrew Crawford and Mary Ann Montgomery. The couple being under age the consent of the father of Andrew and the guardian of Miss Montgomery was first obtained. They were married at the residence of Peter Walker, by R. R. Jones, a Justice of the Peace. The groom was nineteen and the bride sixteen years of age. On the same day a license was granted Dr. C. W. Phelps and Miss Lizzie Weaver. But before even this date, and when Wapello was yet Indian territory, there is said to have been a marriage solemnized at the agency. Harvey Sturdevant, the gunsmith of the post, and a widow, a relative of C. H. Withington, the blacksmith of the post, were married in 1841. The work of organization of the various townships, laying out of roads, building bridges, and the erection of public buildings, occupied much of the attention of the Board of County Commissioners for some years, or until they were legislated out of office. The jail, as already stated, was erected in 1845. In 1846 the court-house was built. One of the provisions in the articles of agreement by the Appanoose Rapids Company, which laid out the town of Ottumwa, provided for the donation to the county of one-half of the lots in the town, should the seat of justice of the county be located here, and also for the erection of the court-house. John Fuller, Paul C. Jeffries and J. R. McBeth were appointed a building committee. The building was erected on the corner of Market and Third street, and was a frame structure, twenty-four feet square, two stories high. The lower story was used for court purposes, and when not thus occupied was used for school and religious purposes, all denominations having an equal right. The second story was divided into three rooms, and occupied by the Clerk of the Courts, the County Treasurer and Recorder. "It was a very necessary and useful building, when first erected," says a local chronicler, "and, indeed, continued to be so for many years. Beside its legal uses, it served a multitude of purposes, for all sorts of public gatherings were held there—political, agricultural, plankroad, railroad and river improvement meetings. The first meeting in behalf of the Burlington & Missouri Railroad enterprise was held there." After being used by the county for twelve years, it was sold to the Christian Church, and used by them for a place of worship for several years. It was purchased from the county for $600. The lot alone on which the house stood is now estimated to be worth $10,000.

In 1848 was established the first paper in Wapello County, the Des Moines *Courier*, now the Ottumwa *Courier*, which has had a continuous existence for a period of thirty-eight years, and has always been recognized as one of the leading papers of the State. With a newspaper to advocate its interests, progress must be made in the county. At this time the Des Moines River improvement scheme was being extensively agitated, and the *Courier* as a matter of course advocated it with all its power. To those living at the present day it seems absurd to think of making the Des Moines River navigable, and that thousands of dollars should ever have been squandered for that purpose. But it did not look absurd to those living here during the first decade, and who were long distances from a general market with no regular means of communication. When the Indians were removed from this section, they moved up the river and located near the Raccoon Fork, and the Government thought proper to locate a body of troops at that point. For the conveyance of soldiers and their equipage to that place, the little steamer Ione was employed, and, laden with stores and a detachment of troops, landed on the site of the present city of Des Moines on the 9th day of May, 1843. This was the first steamer that had ever ventured so far up the stream, and having made a successful trip, added greatly to the expectation of the estimated importance and value of this thoroughfare. The attention of Congress being called to the fact, on the 8th day of August, 1846, a law was enacted giving to the State of Iowa, for the purpose of aiding to improve the navigation of the river from its mouth to the Raccoon Fork, an equal moiety in alternate sections of the public land remaining unsold, in a strip five miles wide on each side of the river, to be selected by an agent or agents, who should be appointed by the Governor of the Territory, subject to the approval of the General Government.

In 1847 the Legislature passed an act creating a Board of Public Works, and providing for the improvement of the river. During this year $150,000 was expended near Keokuk in digging a canal from the mouth of Nassau Slough to St. Francisville, the first place on the river where it was thought practicable to build a dam. The effort was, however, abandoned, but early in the spring of 1848 the canal and three dams were put under contract and about 500 hands were put to work. On the 21st of August, the building of ten more dams was contracted for, and there seemed to be a fair prospect for the speedy completion of the entire improvement. But little was known of the resources of the valley of the Des Moines River at that time, so provisions were made by the General Government for a geological surveyin Iowa, and a party was sent up the river, which explored it to its source. A flattering report was made. They reported that "coal was found for 200 miles on the Des Moines, and, from indications heavy deposits of iron ore were believed to exist; that gypsum in abundance, forming cliffs for miles, was encountered; and that limestone that makes a superior lime existed in abundance; limestone suitable for lime, clay suitable for brick, rock suitable for polishing, for grindstones, whetstones, and for building purposes, some of superior quality, were found in abundance along the Des Moines." Col. Samuel Curtis, the chief engineer of the improvement, in his report to the Legislature, led the people to anticipate great results from the improvement. He said: "No country can afford like accommodations to manufacturers; no country can produce more agricultural wealth than that within sixty miles on either side of this river. Taking all things into consideration, the matter is mathematically certain (except in times of high water in the Missouri) the trade of Council Bluffs will incline to follow down the improvement. But it is not this point alone that is reached. We enter the great valley of Nebraska, and the upper branches of the Missouri, and offer the commerce of these valleys the cheapest and most expeditious routes for their products. A country of a thousand miles in extent, capable of furnishing vast and unknown agricultural and mineral products, may, by wise and discreet energy in the prosecution of this work, become tributary to the improvement now in progress on the Des Moines."

It is no wonder that when such glowing reports were made of the advantages to be gained by the improvement of the river, that the citizens of Wapello County, alike with those of the rest of the State, were enthusiastically in favor of the work. But much time and money was spent with no real or apparent result. Charles Negus, in the "Annals of Iowa," published some years ago, gave a very full history of this improvement scheme, and after speaking of the grant by Congress of lands, and of their disposition, concluded as follows: "This was a most magnificent grant, embracing some of the best lands in the State; and if the proceeds had been judiciously and properly expended, would have made a great thoroughfare for steamboats, besides affording an immense water-power for driving machinery. But through the incompetency of managing the means, and the intrigues of designing men, the whole of the lands below the Raccoon Fork, and a large quantity above, were disposed of, and very little practical good accomplished toward the navigation of the river."

In the spring of 1849 the water in the river was unusually high, and early in April, the steamer Revenue Cutter came up the river, arriving at Ottumwa about daylight. This being the first steamer seen on the river in several years, was quite a novelty to the inhabitants. A number of citizens joined those on board from other points down the river, and proceeded on an excursion up the river. The farmers and their families, living near the river, lined the shore and cheered those upon board as the vessel proceeded on its voyage. Several boats passed up the river and made the return trip this season, but this it is believed, ended navigation on the Des Moines.

In 1856 the present court-house was erected at a cost of $13,000, and in 1858 the old building was sold to the Christian Church, and used by that body for some years as a house of worship. It was subsequently converted into a wagon-shop and afterward burned. The present structure, which is of brick, was quite a respectable edifice in its day, but the busy city of Ottumwa and rich county of Wapello, have outgrown the old court-house. The second jail building was erected in 1857 at a cost of $9,000.

The next great event to the people of Wapello County was the war for the Union. Its record in that war was a glorious one. While some may not have shown that enthusiasm in its prosecution that was naturally expected of them, the great body of people were truly patriotic and were willing to make any sacrifice necessary to a restoration of the union of States. As this subject is more fully treated elsewhere in this volume under the title of "War for the Union," it is not necessary to repeat in this connection.

Railroad enterprises had in the meantime been inaugurated, an account of which is given in articles on railroads.

In the growth and development of the county, the extensive coal mines that have been opened form no inconsiderable part. For many years the people of the county did not dream of the vast mines of wealth beneath the surface of the earth. True, they saw cropping out here and there along the streams or on the hillsides considerable coal, and thus congratulated themselves on a sufficient supply of fuel to last for a few years at least. The attention of the pioneer was given to agriculture, each desiring to secure land, the fertility of the soil being unquestioned. But at last they began to realize that they had overlooked that which, being developed, would bring to them a competence which could not be realized by agriculture in long years. Lands which had been regarded as of little or no value took an upward rise, and the fortunes of many were made even without a stroke.

According to the report of the State Mine Inspector for 1885, there were twenty-two mines in operation in the county, a large majority of which were in the vicinity of Ottumwa. The largest mines in the county are those of the Wapello Coal Company, which was organized and incorporated Oct. 22, 1881. T. J. Potter is the President; H. L. Waterman, Vice-President and General Manager; A. C. Hatfield, Treasurer; H. E. Jarvis, Secretary. There are in the employ of the company 450 men, the average wages being $2.50 per day. Five engines are used, and the capacity of the mines is 900 tons per day.

The Eldon Coal Company's mines are located in Washington Township, Wapello County, and in Salt Creek Township, Davis County. The company was organized March 8, 1882, with a capital stock of $50,000, and a shaft seventy feet deep sunk. They employ from 80 to 100 men regularly, and ship much of their coal to Kansas and Nebraska. The present officers are O. M. Ladd, President and Business Manager; C. H. Merrick, Secretary and Treasurer.

The output of the various mines in the county, as reported to the State Mine Inspector for five years is as follows: 1881, 131,815 tons; 1882, 207,721 tons; 1883, 237,821 tons; 1884, 240,720 tons; 1885, 187,911 tons. The amount given is only approximate, as many mines failed to report. Enough is given to show that the coal industries are extremely valuable to the county.

In agriculture, Wapello County will compare favorably with other counties in the State. For a number of years the farmers of the county have been turning their attention to stock-raising, and to-day show as fine horses, cattle, sheep and hogs, as can be found elsewhere. Much of the fine stock is imported; especially is this true of horses, there being several men in the county engaged in the importation of Norman, Percheron, and other fine breeds. The dairy business is constantly on the increase. The many streams in the county make it peculiarly well adapted for that purpose.

Wapello County has had a steady and sure growth since its first settlement. Every year in which the census has been taken, save two, has shown an increase over the preceding one in number of inhabitants and material wealth. The following is a statement of each enumeration, showing the population: 1844, 2,814; 1846, 4,422; 1847, 5,660; 1849, 7,255; 1850, 8,479; 1851, 8,500; 1852, 8,888; 1854, 10,521; 1856, 13,246; 1859, 15,060; 1860, 14,578; 1863, 16,729; 1865, 18,794; 1867, 18,930; 1869, 20,672; 1870, 22,346; 1873, 22,261; 1875, 23,855; 1880, 25,285; 1885, 25,803.

FOR many long years the question of slavery was the bone of contention between the North and South, the latter ever being fearful that its rights were being encroached upon. Various compromise measures were resorted to for the purpose of allaying the fears of the Southern people, or to prevent open rebellion. When the compromise measure of 1820, known as the Missouri Compromise, was passed, it was thought there would be an end of future trouble. But the slave power was ever aggressive and determined to have an equal voice in all governmental matters, whether their population and territory warranted it or not. New Territory being thrown open for settlement, north of the line fixed beyond which it was not to go, slave-holders were determined to enter with their slaves, and, if possible, make of it slave-holding States. The Missouri Compromise was repealed by the passage of what is known as the Kansas-Nebraska Act, permitting the question as to the admission of slaves to be left to the people of any given Territory. The doctrine of popular sovereignty was a pet measure of Stephen A. Douglas, and it was thought by him that this would settle all difficulty in the future, as none could object to the right of the majority to govern. But the measure was neither satisfactory to the slave-holders of the South, nor the liberty-loving people of the North. The former objected to it on what they termed constitutional grounds, slavery being recognized by the Constitution, and therefore the Southern man had the same right to take into the Territories of the General Government, his property, be it slaves or cattle, as the Northern man his horses and sheep. The latter objected on the ground that while slavery may have been recognized where it already was in existence, it was never designed by the fathers to perpetuate, much less to spread it, and that the

Territories must ever be reserved for free men.

The passage of the Kansas-Nebraska Act served to solidify the free-soil sentiment in the North, that resulted in the organization of the Republican party, while at the same time it divided the great Democratic party. In the Presidential campaign of 1860 there were four candidates for the Presidency. Abraham Lincoln, of Illinois, was the nominee of the Republicans, Stephen A. Douglas, of Illinois, of that wing of the Democratic party favorable to the Kansas-Nebraska Act, while John C. Breckenridge, of Kentucky, of that wing of the Democratic party opposed to the bill, and John Bell, of Tennessee, of the Union party. The divided state of the Democracy made possible the election of Lincoln, and when the ballots were counted, it was found that he had a majority of electoral votes.

The South had given notice that in the event of the election of Lincoln, some, if not all, of the Southern States would secede from the Union. This assertion was regarded as an idle threat by the people of the North, who could not conceive it possible that any body of people would be so foolish as to plunge the country into a civil war. When the result of the election was made known, led by South Carolina, several of the Southern States soon after passed acts of secession. By the people of that section United States forts and arsenals were seized, and everything at once done to rob the General Government of its power. Abraham Lincoln was inaugurated March 4, 1861. He delivered an address, on the occasion of his inauguration, full of kindly terms and entreaties to the people of the South to stay their mad hand. But his words were unheeded. On the 12th of April, 1861, fire was opened upon Ft. Sumter, and on the third day the brave and gallant Maj. Anderson was compelled to lower the American flag and surrender to the rebel forces. The first shot that was fired echoed and re-echoed throughout the North, and was as much a call to arms as the proclamation of President Lincoln, which quickly followed, calling for 75,000 men.

There was no lack of response to this call among the Northern States, and no State more enthusiastically or patriotically responded than the State of Iowa. Men and money were offered without reserve. Volunteers came from all vocations in life, and offered up their lives on the altar of their country. Patriotism was dominant in every heart. Party lines were ignored, and political conflicts were forgotten, and all formed themselves together for the preservation of the Union. The news of the conflict reached the citizens of Wapello County as soon as received by any other section, and aroused the same state of feeling as elsewhere existed. The *Courier*, of Ottumwa, voiced the sentiment of almost the entire people of the county when it said in its issue of April 17: "The North, cool, unimpassioned and deliberate, is slow to move, but it will now be seen when she does move, as she is now moving, that it will be as the ocean in its sublime upheavings, with a current of such irresistible power that secession and treason will be swept from the land. There are but two sides now. One is the side of the Union as our fathers gave it to us; the other is the side of the enemies of the Union, who are waging war for its dismemberment."

A large and enthusiastic meeting was held at the court-house Tuesday, April 23, at 1 o'clock. C. W. Kittredge was made Chairman, and J. M. Hedrick was elected Secretary. The Chairman stated the object of the meeting was to express an opinion in favor of sustaining the Government, after which S. W. Summers arose and moved the adoption of the following resolution:

"*Resolved*, That we are in favor of sustaining the Government."

The resolution was adopted amid deafening applause. Col. Gillaspy then addressed the meeting, concluding by offering a resolution requesting the business men to hoist the American flag at their places of business, which was also adopted amid great cheering. Other resolutions were then offered expressing the sense of the meeting in relation to the war, its causes, and the duty of all patriotic men and women with reference to the support of the General Government. A committee was appointed, consisting of Thomas Devin, Sr., J. Loomis, E. Washburn, C. C. Warden and James Hawley, to receive and hold in trust such contributions as might be made for the support of the families of the members of the City Guards, during their absence in defense of the country, while E. F. Cody, J. C. Hinsey and Charles Dudley were appointed to solicit subscriptions for that purpose.

Union meetings were also held at Ashland, Chillicothe, and in country school-houses, in which strong resolutions were passed in support of the General Government. A company of infantry and one of cavalry was also organized at Ottumwa for home defense.

On Friday, May 10, the Ottumwa City Guards, commanded by Capt. C. C. Cloutman, were sworn into the service, the first company from Wapello County. It left for Keokuk, where it was to rendezvous, on Friday, May 24, almost the entire city and surrounding country following the brave boys to the depot from which they were to depart. There were wives with their little ones, striving in vain to keep back their tears as they bid their loved husbands good-bye. There were also gray-haired fathers and mothers to bid farewell to dutiful and patriotic sons, while they prayed the blessings of Almighty God might rest upon them. The scene was a tearful though thrilling one, and will never be forgotten by those participating, though before the war was ended it was often repeated, with the sad consciousness, as with the first company so with the others, some would leave never to return.

The first call of President Lincoln was quickly followed by another, and then by another, and another, until it seemed as if there were not enough loyal men in the North to respond to the calls. For what were they fighting, and why was the war permitted to go on? These were questions asked over and over again. As if in answer to these questions, Capt. C. C. Cloutman, one of the bravest and best men that went from Wapello County, and one of the first that fell in defense of his country, just before the battle of Ft. Donelson, wrote the following letter to the Ottumwa *Courier*. It was found in his trunk after his death and published in that paper. No better presentation of the question was ever made:

"The war in which we are now engaged, to a superficial observer, might seem to be a mere strife of personal or sectional ambition; or a controversy about the negro; or an insurrection of local prejudices, because Mr. Lincoln was elected President rather than Mr. Douglas, or Mr. Breckenridge, or Mr. Bell; or as some will have it, because of the persistent intermeddling of the North with the 'peculiar institution' of the South. All this may show itself on the surface, but in fact, the war is, at the bottom, no such thing, and whoever takes this view only, altogether fails to comprehend the contest and the real questions and interests at stake. The contest is not of persons or sections as such, but of principles. The election of Mr. Lincoln has served as the occasion, but not the cause of the disturbance. It is no strife between the North merely; it is a conflict between two hostile and irreconcilable theories of government and human rights. It is two distinct types of civilization; or rather it is civilization and barbarism grappling in a hand-to-hand conflict for the possession of this Government. The negro is but the representative of the essential equality and absolute rights of man. The South stands to-day upon the same platform on which absolutism has always stood. It enunciates the same philosophy and puts forth the same arrogant claims. It sets up a banner and ascribes on it that old lie of tyrants that 'might makes right.' It scoffs at the idea of human equality. It renounces the sentiment of absolute justice. It despises the masses as fit only to be ruled. It affirms that capital sustains its true relation to labor only when it owns the laborers. It builds its sham confederacy on the doctrine that one class of men is born to be trampled upon and chattelized by another. In a word, it sneers at the fathers of the Republic as dreamy and fanciful enthusiasts; it denounces the Declaration of Independence; rejects every principle of the Revolution; despises the doctrines of a genuine Democracy; substantially plants itself upon the assumption of the Divine rights of kings, and represents ideas as thoroughly and cruelly despotic as ever sat upon a throne or ground the people into the dust. We shall not stop to produce the evidence to sustain the above assertions. Let those who question the fairness of the representations consult De Bow's Review for 1860 and 1861, and we think there will be no mistaking the premises upon which the South has planted herself. There is no mistaking the principles or logical results of the political philosophy which are there furnished. If these are granted then must the Republican constitution and government which our fathers framed be thrown away. All that the friends of freedom have through the ages been contending for must be given up. Austria and Naples must be accepted as the only just interpreters of political science. Every popular movement which has made a despot tremble, or a tyrant shake in his seat, is proved wrong, and our vaunted bill of rights is only so much lying paper that should as soon as possible be committed to the flames.

"Seventy years ago William Pinckney, of Maryland, himself a slaveholder, foretold that unless Democracy destroyed slavery, slavery would destroy Democracy; and this is what it is now trying to do. This conflict, we repeat, is one of principles, and not of persons or sections. We have no quarrel with the men of the South, as such. They are our brethren, our friends. We have eaten with them at their tables, and they have eaten with us at ours. We are linked together, not only by the memories of common history, but by ties of business, and by the sanctities of domestic and social affections, and should be thus linked together as one people. It is a fratricidal strife, and we would fain be relieved from the necessity of drawing the sword against them. We love not Cæsar less, but Rome more. The war is none of our making. We have done nothing to invite or justify it. We have claimed no authority to meddle with slavery in the States where it exists. We have simply exercised our American right of free discussion in carrying our principles to the ballot box. Believing slavery to be wrong, morally, politically, economically and socially, we have said so. This is all. Defeated at the election, the South has rebelled. They have protested against the doctrine that majorities have the right to rule, and unable longer to control the Government, they have resolved to disorganize and destroy it. They have defied the Government and commenced the war. The doctrine of liberty, the principles of justice, the Government reared by our fathers' toil and cemented by their blood, standing amid the thrones and despotisms of the world, the grand assertions alike of the people's right and the people's ability to govern; these, and the flag which has symbolized them, we are called upon to surrender. Being forced by the South between war and a surrender of these, we say let the war come, and may God defend the right."

Right did prevail, but it was after more than four years of hard service, in which blood and treasure were poured out like water. In the struggle Wapello County did its duty as proudly and as well as any county in this fair State, or in the Union. Some who went out were brought back in coffins, others were buried upon the battle-field, others returned minus an arm or a leg, while still others came back without a wound upon their body, yet suffering from disease contracted while in service.

More than a score of years have passed since the war terminated, but it is not forgotten, though the weeds of mourning may have disappeared. In too many homes there still stands the vacant chair; too many hearts mourn the loss of father, husband and brother, for the memories of that unhappy conflict to fade away. Our cemeteries are too full of the dead who lost their lives upon the battle-field, or died from the effects of wounds or imprisonment, for the heart to forget its sorrow, or the memory to become oblivious. No! the war is not forgotten, neither are the brave men who sleep in soldiers' graves. Once each year the survivors, with their friends and the children, meet and strew upon their graves beautiful flowers, while lessons of patriotism are repeated o'er and o'er. Never will these brave men be forgotten. Their noble deeds, their sacrifices, will be remembered in years to come, and then, as now, will come the thought "How beautiful it is to die for one's country."

"All hail to our gallant defenders, all hail!
Our noblest, our bravest, our best;
Proud peers of the world's worshiped heroes ye stand,
By freedom's dear attributes blest.

"Ah, the voice of the past to your heart and ours,
It brings in its eloquent breath
The wild tones of victory, softened and blest,
With the low, mystic cadence of death.

"But the angel of faith with her magical wand,
Lifts the veil from our grief, and behold!
The invisible arm of a pitying God
Hath gathered them into the fold."

THE doctor is said to be the first person thought of when one is taken ill, and the last one thought of in health. There is probably too much truth in the statement, but surely no class in any community is more desirable than the well-read, common-sense physician. Whatever may be said of the physicians of the present day, it cannot but be acknowledged that those residing here in the early day had a hard life to live. To minister to the wants of the afflicted they were often compelled to ride many miles over tractless prairies, facing danger from exposure to the cold rains of spring and autumn, or the chilling blasts of winter, while the remuneration would be small, indeed, if anything at all.

The first physician to permanently locate in the county was Dr. C. C. Warden, yet residing in Ottumwa and numbered among its honored citizens. The Doctor long since retired from active practice.

The first physician in the county and who resided here a few months was Dr. J. C. Ware, who came from Fairfeld, and removed back and there died many years ago.

Dr. Hackleman, a brother of the Brigadier General, came to the county in 1843, and remained for a time.

Dr. Phelps resided at the Indian Agency for a time previous to the advent of the white men. He was a rough character, and adapted more to the frontier than to more refined society.

Dr. Cunningham came in 1843 and located about three miles north of Ottumwa, in Dahlonega Township. He was then a young man, of some ability, and now resides in Knoxville, Marion County, where he removed many years ago,

J. C. Comstock, now a retired physician, came about the same time as Dr. Cunningham.

Dr. William Ross was also one of the physicians who came in 1843. He settled at Eddyville, where he remained several years. He was one of the first physicians to locate in the Territory of Iowa, and resided for some years at Burlington.

Dr. McClintock came either in 1843 or 1844, and located in Dahlonega Township, where he remained some years, and then went West. He was a man of limited education.

Dr. V. C. Coffin, a relative of Mrs. Maj. Hamilton, came in about 1846.

Dr. George Wright came about 1848 and settled in Ottumwa. He was a man of fine personal appearance, a strong frame, but was exceedingly high-tempered. As a physician and surgeon, he ranked among the best in the State. While living at Burlington he got into an altercation with an old and highly respected physician, and knocked him downstairs. He came to Ottumwa soon afterward and tried to form a partnership with Dr. C. C. Warden, but without success. In a quarrel with a man by the name of Ross, in regard to a land claim, he was shot in the stomach, the wound causing his death. He first shot Ross in the chest.

In 1848 Dr. A. D. Wood came to Ottumwa. (See sketch.)

Dr. S. Smythe was also numbered among those who came at an early day. He was a man of good ability, and now resides at Denver, Col., where he has a large and lucrative practice.

Dr. D. L. Hubbard purchased the practice of Dr. Smythe. When he came to Ottumwa he was quite wealthy, but lost it all through intemperance, so it is reported.

Dr. L. D. Morse, who came to Ottumwa in the fall of 1856 or 1857, was from New Jersey. He was a graduate of a New York medical school. After remaining here about two years he went to some town near St. Louis, afterward moving to that city, but is now in California.

Dr. D. W. Stewart came to Ottumwa in 1866. He was a man of more than ordinary ability, a graduate of a Chicago medical college, but lacked the ability to adapt himself to his surroundings. He is now in Des Moines.

Dr. G. F. Foster, a graduate of the Cincinnati Medical College, came to Ottumwa in 1868 from Davenport. After remaining here five or six years, he quit the general practice and made a specialty of diseases of the eye. He is now located in St. Louis.

Dr. William Fuller came to Ottumwa in 1871. He was a college graduate, and a physician of undoubted ability. He is at present residing in Indianola, Iowa.

Dr. James Carter was a graduate of a Chicago medical college and began practice here in 1880. Dr. Carter was reared in this county, his parents being among the pioneers. He is at present filling a chair in a medical college at Omaha, and is regarded as a growing man.

The medical profession in Wapello County to-day is represented by some of the ablest men that adorn that high calling.

At Ottumwa reside the following named: Drs. J. C. Hinsey, E. L. Lathrop, C. G. Lewis, J. W. Nichols, S. E. O'Neill, E. C. Pyle, S. A. Spilman, S. B. Thrall, R. S. Gilcrest, I. B. Whitaker, J. Williamson, J. Jackson Crider, William Blauw, T. J. Douglas, B. F. Hyatt, C. D. Powell, H. W. Roberts, A. O. Williams, J. E. Wilkinson, B. W. Searle.

At Eddyville: Drs. F. M. McCrea, A. C. Olney, George Sheffield, M. H. Sprague.

At Eldon: Drs. E. M. Arenchild, John Box, William Brownfield, R. W. Huston, J. W. LaForce, B. S. Shaug, H. Strickling.

At Agency: Drs. M. L. Davis, William Hilton, Eli Sage. At Chillicothe: Dr. A. K. Berry.

At Kirkville: Drs. William Abegg, J. H. McCune.

At Competine: Dr. G. M. Cowger.

At Ormanville: Dr. L. P. Torrence.

At Blakesburg: Dr. C. N. Udell.

The Press.

NOTHING is a greater instrumentality toward building up a country than the newspaper. This is being realized and acted upon by the pioneers of our Western States and Territories much more than by the early pioneers. In the creation of a new town at the present time, almost the first building erected is for a printing-office, and the advantages of the proposed city and surrounding country are at once heralded throughout the length and breadth of the land. Capital is invited in, and all who will come are assured a hearty welcome. Forty years ago the power of the press had not been fully realized—the people were not then as now a reading people, and in many homes such a thing as a newspaper was seldom found. A printing-press was a great curiosity and a printer was regarded as a superior being and looked upon with awe. The advent of a printing-press, and the appearance of a bright, clean paper, marked an era in the history of a town and county never to be forgotten.

Four years after the organization of Wapello County, when it had a population of more than 6,000 inhabitants, two young men—J. H. D. Street and R. H. Warden—had the courage to establish in Ottumwa its first newspaper. At that time in all the vast country west of it, now inhabited by more than 8,000,000 people, there was not a single newspaper printed. This is, indeed, hard to realize, but such was the fact. To-day the weekly newspapers in that region are numbered by the hundreds, the dailies by the score, together with several excellent monthly magazines. The press of this region will compare favorably with Eastern publications, and is wielding a great power for good.

The Ottumwa Courier.

THE pioneer newspaper of Wapello County first made its appearance Aug. 8, 1848, under the name of the *Des Moines Courier*, with J. H. D. Street and R. H. Warden as editors and proprietors. It was a six-column folio, neatly printed, and edited with considerable ability. Politically it was the advocate of Whig principles, advocating the election of Zachary Taylor and Millard Fillmore for the Presidency and Vice Presidency. In its first issue appear the advertisements of a number of merchants and professional men of Ottumwa. Lane & Devin have a card as attorneys. Dr. Charles C. Warden and Dr. A. T. Alt have professional cards offering their services to the afflicted. L. C. Nichols advertises a livery, "with horses and buggies to carry persons to any part of the State. He also keeps a four-horse omnibus that will carry fourteen persons, which he will run whenever occasion requires." S. Richards, by H. P. Graves, advertises dry-goods, groceries, hardware, etc. F. W. Taylor advertises drugs, paints, oils, etc. A. Mudge & Co., dry-goods and groceries. W. S. Carter & Co., the "Farmers' Cheap Store." Hunter & Baldwin, general store. Of the foregoing, Dr. Warden and H. P. Graves yet reside in the city, highly respected citizens.

At the beginning of the second volume, the paper was enlarged to a seven-column folio. Street & Warden continued the publication of the paper till Jan 20, 1851, when Mr. Warden became sole proprietor, and continued as such till Dec. 20, 1855, when J. W. Norris purchased the office, and in connection with his brother, G. W. Norris, published the paper until 1866, when N. D. Mussleman, W. H. Caldwell and W. C. Holden became the proprietors. J. W. Norris at one time was associated in the publication of the Chicago *Journal*. In his editorial utterances, he was quite conservative, though a warm supporter of Republican principles. In August, 1869, Gen. John M. Hedrick and Maj. Augustus H. Hamilton became editors and proprietors and continued in partnership until January, 1878, when A. H. Hamilton became sole owner. Since that time no change has been made in ownership, though R. H. Warden, the greater part of the time has occupied the position of general editor, city editor or business manager.

The *Daily Courier* was established in 1865, and is now in its twenty-second year. Both the weekly and daily have large circulations. The *Courier* has always been recognized as one of the leading papers of the State of Iowa, and has contributed its share in the upbuilding of every public enterprise. Politically it was an advocate of Whig principles as long as that party had an existence, but when it ceased to be, it was one of the first papers to espouse Republican principles. In its advocacy of the principles of the latter party it has never wavered, though decidedly independent in tone. The name of the paper was changed in 1857 from the *Des Moines Courier* to the Ottumwa *Courier*. In connection with the paper is a well-equipped job office.

The Ottumwa Democrat.

IN March, 1868, a Democratic paper called the *Copperhead*, was removed from Pella, Marion County, to Ottumwa, and its publication continued by M. V. B. Bennett, H. M. McCully and S. B. Evans until December of that year, when Mr. Bennett withdrew. In December, 1870, Mr. McCully also withdrew. On thus succeeding to the sole ownership of the paper, Mr. Evans changed its name to the Ottumwa *Democrat*, and continued its publication alone for some time, and then associated with himself J. W. Norris.

On the 4th day of April, 1874, the Ottumwa Printing Company, composed of N. M. Ives, O. G. Graves, Dr. G. F. Foster and others, began the publication of the *Spirit of the Times*. Dr. Foster soon withdrew from the firm, and in 1875, H. M. Ives, son of N. M. Ives, purchased Mr. Graves' interest, and the publication of the paper was continued by N. M. Ives & Son, until July, 1876, when I. T. Flint purchased a one-third interest, and the name of the paper was changed to the Ottumwa *Times*. Mr. Flint's connection with the paper was of short duration, he retiring from the firm in February, 1877. It was then continued by Ives & Son until Nov. 14, 1878, when it was consolidated with the Ottumwa *Democrat* under the name of *Democrat and Times*, with Ives & Evans as publishers, and N. M. Ives and S. B. Evans, editors. In 1881 J. W. Norris became sole proprietor, running it for some months and then selling out to Edwin Green, who disposed of it to the Ottumwa Printing Company, who continued its publication with A. Melick as editor. In September, 1884, S. B. Evans again assumed control, and has since had exclusive management.

Notwithstanding the many changes in ownership, the *Democrat* has always been ably edited, and has exercised great influence in molding political opinion in Wapello County. Throughout the State it has also been recognized as a leading paper of the Democratic faith. At no time has it ever exercised greater power than at present, its editor, Mr. Evans, wielding a strong pen, striking stalwart blows in defense of those principles which he believes to be right. The name of the paper was changed to the Ottumwa *Democrat* while controlled by Mr. Green. Daily and weekly editions are now issued. The former was commenced in 1875, but existed but a few months when it was compelled to suspend from a lack of support. In 1880 it was revived, and has since been continued, with gratifying success. Its merits as an advertising medium seem to be appreciated by the business men of Ottumwa, as a glance at its columns will testify.

The Ottumwa Saturday Press.

ON the 28th day of August, 1880, the first number of the *Independent Press* made its appearance, with J. W. Dixon as editor and proprietor. It was an eight-column folio, and seemed to have for its object the defeat of J. C. Cook for Congress, it opposing his election with considerable vim. The paper was continued by Mr. Dixon until Jan. 1, 1881, when the office was purchased by George Riley, Jr., and Edwin A. Jones, who changed the name of the paper to the Ottumwa *Saturday Press.*

The paper remained an eight-column folio until the summer of 1882, when it was changed to a nine-column folio. In June, 1884, it was again changed, taking the form of a six-column quarto, which form it yet retains. When Riley & Jones purchased the paper it had a circulation of between 300 and 400. It now has a circulation of 4,000 copies, and is still on the increase. This remarkable increase has been brought about by careful attention to business and hard work. At the time of their purchase the junior member of the firm had no knowledge of the printing business, and had not reached his majority by several years. Mr. Riley was a thorough practical printer, although a young man of but twenty-five years of age. He had been schooled in some of the best offices in Central New York, and had served about two years in New York City, the greater part of the time as a reporter. The junior member pulled off his coat, went to work, and is now numbered among the best practical printers in Ottumwa.

In the general management of the office Mr. Riley attends to the outside work, Mr. Jones having the management of the office work. The *Press* has a large corps of correspondents in the neighboring towns, who furnish all the local news of importance up to the hour of going to press, on Saturday morning. No item of interest is allowed to escape. By this means the *Press* has attained a large circulation outside of Wapello County, and has therefore become an excellent advertising medium, which is appreciated by business men generally. In the discussion of all matters of public interest the *Press* gives no uncertain sound. Every enterprise calculated to build up finds in this paper an earnest champion. Politically it is independent in the strictest sense of the term. While bowing the knee to no party, as such, it feels free to advocate the election of any person it may desire. It is not an offensive partisan, but independent in all things, neutral in nothing. Such papers as the Ottumwa *Saturday Press* are a blessing to any community, and deserve a large patronage.

The Journal and Frie Press.

THIS is the only German paper printed in Wapello County. In 1871 A. Danquard commenced the publication of the Ottumwa *Journal*, a six-column folio German-Democratic paper, continuing its publication alone until 1879, with varying success. In 1878 the Ottumwa *Frie Press* was commenced by Theodore Danquard. This latter was an eight-column folio, and was likewise in politics Democratic. The German population in and tributary to Ottumwa was hardly sufficient to support two German papers, even if of opposite political faith, much less two of the same faith, so a consolidation became a necessity. This was effected in 1879, and the publication was continued under its present name, the *Journal and Frie Press*, with A. & T. Danquard as editors and prietors. This firm continued until 1881, when J. A. Wagner purchased T. Danquard's interest, the paper being continued by Danquard & Wagner. In April, 1885, J. A. Wagner purchased the interest of A. Danquard, and yet remains as sole proprietor.

The *Frie Press* is now a nine-column folio, the enlargement taking place in February, 1886. In politics it yet adheres to the Democratic faith, and is exerting a great influence among those speaking the German language in Wapello and adjoining counties. The circulation of the paper is now 800, among an intelligent class of citizens, and being among many who are conversant with no other language than the German, makes it a good advertising medium. The editor of the *Journal and Frie Press* is a young man, a native of Wapello County, though of German parentage.

The Des Moines Valley Journal.

THIS is a seven-column folio, published at Eldon, by Conger & Connell, at $1.50 per annum. The first number made its appearance Oct. 2, 1886. The material of the office was that on which the Agency *Tribune* had been published, which suspended a week or two before the *Journal* made its appearance. The *Journal* is a well-edited paper, Democratic in politics, and says "it has come to stay."

The Industrial Appeal.

FOR years the labor question has forced itself upon the people, and until the issue between capital and labor is settled, and that, too, in favor of the working class, it will always be an element in the politics of the nation.

The *Industrial Appeal* was started with a view of agitating this question and advocating the rights of the laboring man. Its first number made its appearance, Aug. 1, 1882, with N. M. Ives as editor and proprietor. It was an eight-column folio, which form it still maintains, and Mr. Ives is still editor and publisher. As announced by the editor, it is "anti-monopoly in its teachings, independent in politics, and severely neutral in religion, 'forninst' political bosses and machine politics." The *Appeal* has had fair success. Mr. Ives is an editor of ability, and publishes a readable paper.

The Eldon Review.

THE *Review* is a neat, seven-column folio, published at Eldon, the first number of which appeared in November, 1881, under the management of E. H. Thomas, now of the West Point *Appeal*. In April, 1885, C. E. & L. R. McKinney took possession of the office, and have since edited and published the paper. Under their management the *Review* has proved a success, and is in a most flourishing condition, with bright prospects for the future. The senior member of the firm is a practical printer, while the junior member is a writer of much ability, having for some years been a contributor to various metropolitan publications.

The *Review* deserves good treatment at the hands of the business men of Eldon, who should patronize it liberally. In thus doing they will help themselves as well.

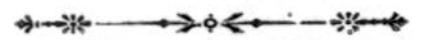

Various Papers.

LIKE every other organized county, Wapello has had published within its boundaries quite a number of papers that had a longer or shorter period of existence.

Among the best-known papers that were published that have ceased to exist was the Ottumwa *Democratic Statesman*, the publication of which was commenced in 1858, by G. D. R. Boyd, who ran it a short time and then sold to J. D. H. Street. In 1861 H. B. Hendershott and E. L. Burton became editors and proprietors, and changed its name to Ottumwa *Democratic Union*. In 1862 Mr. Heindershott retired, and S. B. Evans became associated with Mr. Burton in its publication, and its name was again changed. The *Democratic Mercury* was the name chosen by Burton & Evans. In the winter of 1863-64 S. H. Burton purchased Mr. Evans' interest, and the firm of E. L. & S. H. Burton continued until October, 1865, when Russell Higgins purchased the interest of E. L. Burton, but in one month sold to S. B. Evans. In March, 1868, Mr. Evans retired, leaving S. H. Burton sole editor and proprietor. A few months later the publication of the paper was permanently discontinued.

In 1870 H. S. Bailey and Dr. G. F. Foster commenced the publication of the *Reveille*, a lively local paper, but which survived only about six months.

The *Table Talk* was another lively local sheet which had an existence for a few months, in 1885, in Ottumwa.

The Eddyville *Free Press* was started in 1853, by J. W. Norris, and continued by him for a time, and then by J. N. Yunker, who in turn gave place to B. H. Palmer, who, in 1856, changed its name to the *Commercial*. The paper was discontinued in 1859.

The Eddyville *Observer* was the next newspaper venture in Eddyville, its publication being some time after the suspension of the *Commercial*. It was short lived.

In 1862 Melick & McConnell started the Eddyville *Star*, which they published about three years, and then sold to Charles Sherman, who soon after discontinued its publication.

Melick & Bitner commenced the next paper at Eddyville, called the *Independent*. It was also short lived.

The material of the *Independent* office was sold to Mr. Straight, who, in 1868, started the *Des Moines Valley Gazette*, but soon associated with himself in its publication John Wilcox, subsequently disposing of his remaining interest to Maj. Wilcox. The paper survived about five years.

In February, 1869, W. L. Palmer commenced the Eddyville *Advertiser*, a weekly Republican paper, which was continued for a number of years.

The Eddyville *Record* was the last newspaper enterprise in Eddyville. It ceased to exist in the spring of 1886.

The first newspaper published at Agency City was the Agency City *Newsboy*, commenced in 1869 by William Axline. It was continued until the spring of 1871, when the office was moved to Chariton, Lucas County. In the spring of 1874 the Agency *Independent* was commenced, the office being removed here from Eldon. The Agency *Tribune* closes the newspaper enterprises of Agency. The *Tribune* had a fairly prosperous career for a time, but from a lack of proper support was compelled to suspend in the fall of 1886.

At Eldon several newspapers have been commenced, among which were the Eldon *Herald*, in 1873; the Eldon *Messenger*, in 1875; the Eldon *Times*, in 1875. The latter paper had a longer period of existence than its predecessors, but in June, 1876, its name was changed to the *Western News*. Its publication was suspended in 1878.

Railroads.

SOME interest was manifested by the people of Wapello County, during the years 1850 and 1851, in plank roads. At this time it was hardly considered in the range of possibility that a railroad would soon be built, and the difficulty experienced in going to and coming from a general market was so great it was felt by all that something should be done. In February, 1850, a meeting was held at Ottumwa to discuss the construction of a plank road from that place which would intersect the Burlington & Mt. Pleasant Plank Road at Mt. Pleasant. All present at that meeting expressed themselves heartily in favor of the project, and a committee of prominent citizens was appointed to attend a plank road convention at Mt. Pleasant on the 27th of February. In this county subscription books were opened, and Ottumwa responded with $8,700; Agency City with $5,000, and Ashland with $4,500. Notwithstanding the effort made the road was never built, for the reason that a more important project was started.

The scheme which was far greater than that of building a plank road was the construction of a railroad over substantially the same route as that of the plank road. The railroad fever struck this county in 1851, and many of the leading citizens took hold of the work, advocated its interests, made liberal donations of money, and spent much time in securing the road. Their efforts were successful, and, though the additional subscription of the county to the capital stock of the road, to the amount of $100,000, the Burlington & Missouri River Railroad, now the C., B. & Q., was obtained, although it was not completed here till 1859, the first train of cars arriving at Ottumwa Saturday, August 13, though for some months previous Agency had been the terminus.

The Keokuk, Ft. Des Moines & Minnesota Railroad was the next one completed through the county, the cars on that road arriving at Ottumwa but a few months subsequent to the completion of the B. & M.

The county had now two lines of railroad, one east and west, the other north and south, thus giving it the advantages of an eastern and southern market. The citizens were therefore happy. Other railroads have been completed into and through the county, and, as this history is being prepared, it boasts of four of the great lines of railroad—the Chicago, Burlington & Quincy, the Rock Island, the Chicago, Milwaukee & St. Paul, and the Wabash—with an almost certainty of the Chicago & Northwestern.

The war was ended in 1865, and with the return

of the Union soldiers, enterprises that for more than four years had lain dormant, were again revived. Manufactories were established, railroads built, churches, school-houses and other public buildings were erected, and a perfect boom was inaugurated. Money was plenty and there was no disposition to hoard. It was kept ever on the move.

As a result of the good times, several railroads were projected into and through the county. Among the number was the St. Louis, Ottumwa & Cedar Rapids Railroad. A company was organized, which in time gave way to the St. Louis, Kansas City & Northern Railway, which built and operated the road to Ottumwa, where it remained for some years. The road finally passed into the hands of the Wabash Company and was made a part of that great system. It now has Des Moines for its terminus. There was no corporation subscription to this road in the county, but private citizens subscribed stock to the amount of $125,000, thus securing the road.

In 1873 commenced a financial panic and but little was done for several years either in railroad building or in other public enterprises. Finally the Cedar Rapids, Sigourney & Ottumwa Railroad Company was organized, which secured the right of way, and, backed by the Chicago, Milwaukee & St. Paul Railroad Company, built the road from Cedar Rapids to Ottumwa, the first train of cars reaching the city from the north Dec. 31, 1883. This road soon passed into the hands of the C., M. & St. P. Co., and is now a part of its great system. As this work is being printed, having been extended southward, it is nearing Kansas City.

Wabash, St. Louis & Pacific Railway.

THE Wabash, St. Louis & Pacific Railway, widely and commonly known as the Wabash, is one of the most important roads centering at Ottumwa, Iowa, and has done much to promote the growth and development of the city and Wapello County. The policy of this road has always been to foster and encourage local enterprise. Through a system of consolidation unparalleled in American railway history, it has become a giant. This consolidation, it is estimated, has added more than $50,000 to the value of bonds and shares of the various companies now incorporated in the Wabash system. The road takes its title from the river of that name, a tributary of the Ohio, which in part separates the States of Indiana and Illinois.

Thirty-four years ago, in April, 1853, the initial steps were taken in behalf of a line of road to extend from Toledo, Ohio, to the Mississippi River, such road to be subject to the direction and control of one official management. Upon examination of the laws of the States through which it was to pass, it was found impracticable to prosecute the enterprise under one corporate organization, and consequently distinct corporations were organized in each State.

In April, 1853, the Toledo & Illinois Railroad Company was incorporated, under the general railroad laws of Ohio, with power to build a railroad from Toledo to the western boundary of the State. The capital stock was originally fixed at $500,000, but in 1855 was increased to $2,500,000.

In August, 1853, the Lake Erie, Wabash & St. Louis Railroad Company was incorporated in the State of Indiana, with the power to construct a railroad from the east line of the State to a point on the western line in the direction of Danville, Ill. The road was constructed in 1856, and the companies consolidated under the name Toledo, Wabash & Western. Financial embarrassments confronted the company during the panic of 1857, and various changes in management and name followed. St. Louis as an objective point, as indicated in the name of one of the corporations, was lost sight of; the road was built across Illinois, terminating at Meredosia, with a branch from Bluffs to Naples. From Meredosia to Camp Point a road was owned by the Quincy & Toledo Company. In conformity to the laws of Ohio, Indiana and Illinois, then but recently adopted, authorizing consolidation where the roads of various companies formed a continuous line, these roads were placed under one management, the Toledo, Wabash & Western Railway Company.

In August, 1870, arrangements were made with

the Decatur & East St. Louis Railroad Company for the construction and equipment of a railroad between Decatur and East St. Louis, the understanding being that on completion thereof the bonded debt of the Decatur & St. Louis Railroad Company, to the extent of $25,000 per mile, should be assumed by the Toledo, Wabash & Western, and that the capital stock of the Decatur and East St. Louis Railway Company, to the amount of $15,000 per mile, should be exchanged at par for the stock of the Toledo, Wabash & Western. The road to St. Louis was completed and opened for business in 1871. During the two years following, the Wabash acquired by lease the Hannibal & Missouri Central, the Pekin, Lincoln & Decatur, and the La-Fayette & Bloomington. In the early part of 1873 the Toledo, Wabash & Western controlled and operated 905 miles of road, with average gross earnings for the whole system of more than $6,000 per mile per annum, and it promised, although capitalized at a high figure, to realize the most sanguine expectations of its owners. The financial panic of 1873 seriously affected the road, so that it failed to meet its obligations, and in 1874 the property was placed in the hands of a Receiver.

This road remained in the Receiver's hands and under the control of the court until 1877, when, arrangements having been effected by the company, transfer of the property was made to the Wabash Railroad Company. Soon after it underwent a re-organization under the name of Wabash, St. Louis & Pacific Railway Company, following which several branches were added to the Wabash, St. Louis & Pacific system, either by purchase or lease, viz: July 15, 1881, the Peoria, Pekin & Jacksonville, eighty-three miles in length, was acquired by purchase; July 15, 1881, the Springfield & Northern Railroad, forty-seven and one-half miles in length, was also acquired by purchase; Aug. 15, 1881, the Detroit & Butler Road, 112.6 miles in length, completing the line to Detroit, was acquired by purchase; Sept. 1, 1881, the Indianapolis, Peru & Chicago Road, running from Indianapolis to Michigan City, 161 miles, was acquired by purchase; Oct. 1, 1881, the Cairo & Vincennes, the Danville & Southwestern, and the St. Francisville & Lawrenceville Railroads, 267.3 miles in length, forming the Cairo Division, were acquired by the purchase and since returned to original owners.

The Quincy, Missouri & Pacific Road was extended from Milan to Trenton, a distance of thirty-one miles, and opened for business Aug. 5, 1881. The Attica & Covington branch, extending from Attica to Covington, fourteen and one-half miles, was built by this company, and opened for business Sept. 1, 1881. A branch road leading from the Chicago division to the Braidwood coal fields, a distance of twelve miles, was built by this company. The Des Moines & Northwestern Railway (narrow gauge) leading from Des Moines, Iowa, to Jefferson, Iowa, a distance of sixty-six and nine-tenth miles, was acquired by lease. There is also a branch line extending from Champaign to Sydney, a distance of ten and one-half miles, connecting their Champaign, Havana & Western Road with the main line. The St. Louis, Jerseyville & Springfield Railroad was also built under the auspices of this company, from Bates to Grafton, Ill., a distance of seventy-five miles. The Des Moines & St. Louis Railroad, from Albia to Des Moines, and Northwestern Road was extended to Eads Station, a distance of twenty-one miles north of Jefferson.

This company, in connection with the Chicago, Burlington & Quincy Railroad, built the Humeston & Shenandoah Road, from Humeston to Shenandoah, for the purpose of forming a connection between their Missouri, Iowa & Nebraska Road and their Council Bluffs branch, which reduced the distance on this line between Omaha and Chicago nearly 100 miles, and gave the Wabash a short and direct line between Omaha and all points east. In connection with the Missouri Pacific Road, this company perfected a lease of the St. Louis bridge, taking effect Oct. 1, 1881.

The various branches of the Wabash system are in excellent condition; the road-bed and bridges are substantial, well tied, and laid with steel rails, and the rolling stock is first-class in every respect. The passenger department is unexcelled for the elegant and substantial comfort afforded travelers. On several of the more important branches of the system dining cars are run. The number of miles operated west of the Mississippi River is 1,226.7, and east 2,296.8, giving a total of 3,513.5 miles.

The Wabash does an immense passenger and freight business between Kansas City, Omaha, St. Joseph, St. Louis, and Chicago, and the principal commercial points East. From Chicago to Kansas City via St. Louis this road has a large and increasing patronage in the passenger department, and is recognized as the most popular route.

RIGHTLY regarded, the city of Ottumwa is one of the most enterprising cities in the State of Iowa. Its very name implies perseverance or self-will, according to the best authorities, and was given because of the dogged determination of Appanoose and his band making it their dwelling-place against the wishes of Wapello and other members of his tribe. Those afterward founding the place as a home for white men had something of the same spirit which has descended to those of the present generation. Even before the land was formally ceded to the whites by the Indians, it had been determined to make all counties west of Jefferson of a uniform size, consisting of twelve congressional townships, or twenty-four miles from east to west and eighteen miles from north to south. Wherever possible to be done, taking into consideration the surrounding country, the county seat would most naturally be attracted to the geographical center of the county. While no regular survey had been made, yet sufficient was known of the country to approximately fix upon the center of the county of Wapello. For the purpose of securing the town site and building up a town, a company was formed in the spring of 1843 under the name of the Appanoose Rapids Company. The following named were members of the company: J. R. McBeth, Uriah Biggs, John Lewis, Thomas D. Evans, Paul C. Jeffries, Hugh George, David Glass, Sewell Kenny, William Dewey and Milton Jamieson.

As soon as the county was thrown open for settlement these men at once selected the site for the proposed town, and on the 20th of May, 1844, met at the place and entered into formal articles of association "for the better organization of the Appanoose Rapids Company." By these articles it is shown that the company claimed that they were "proprietors of the following property or claims near and adjoining the Appanoose Rapids of Des Moines River, known by the Indian name of Ottumwa, in Wapello County, Iowa Territory, viz: What is supposed to be the northeast quarter and the southeast quarter and the east half of the northwest quarter, and the east half of the southwest quarter of section 24; and so much of the north half of section 25 as lies on the left bank of said river, including the island therein, in town 72 north, range 14 west; and also the west half of section 30, town 72 north, range 13 west, and the southwest quarter of section 19, town 72 north, range 13 west." The town, at that time, had been partially platted by John Arrowsmith, a local surveyor, who had, it appears, made partial survey of quite a large section of country in that vicinity. The company, in its articles of agreement, in consideration of the location here of the county seat, agreed to donate to the county every alternate lot in the town, provided the donation should not exceed one quarter section of land. It was also agreed to donate the mill site at the rapids, together with sufficient ground for milling purposes, to any company who would build a dam and erect either a flouring or saw mill. It will thus be seen that the proprietors of the town had an eye to business, and were determined to hold out every inducement possible to settlers.

The name chosen by the company was Ottumwa, the Indian name. When the commissioners appointed to locate the seat of justice of the county selected the site for that purpose, they gave it the name of Louisville, in honor of Louisville, Ky. The early records of the County Commissioners show that that name was accepted, as probably they were compelled to do, but it was but a few months before the Indian name was restored.

For two years after the platting of the village it grew but slowly. According to J. W. Norris at that time "there were three stores, a tinshop, a blacksmith-shop, a tailor-shop, two hotels, a whisky shop and about fifteen log houses, more or less, scattered about. There were no churches, no school-houses, and no public buildings, except a little temporary jail, though there was a civil corporation, a county organization, with the various offices and officers, and the courts and terms of court." But in 1845 new settlers began to come in and the town began to take on some life. A mill was begun and completed some time during the following year, at which time a court-house was built on the corner of Third and Market streets. This was a most useful building, being used for all public meetings.

In 1848 the first newspaper in Ottumwa was established by R. H. Warden, yet an honored citizen of that city, and at present the city editor of the paper of which he was the father. The Ottumwa *Courier* did much in making known the merits of the place, and the year following its advent a veritable boom set in. Business was very brisk, and many buildings were erected, the latter being hindered, however, by the scarcity of lumber, owing to a lack of sawmills. Several steamboats came up the river during the spring and summer, the water being unusually high.

The town continued steadily to increase until 1851 when there was found to be a number sufficient to incorporate, and accordingly in the spring of that year a town organization was effected, with George Gillaspy President of the Board of Trustees.

Two years later the town, according to a local writer, was very flourishing. Says the writer: "In November, 1853, Ottumwa was a thriving village with busy streets and an active, wide-awake population. One sign of prosperity was constantly intruded upon the citizens, and that was the eager inquiry for houses and places of business to rent, which conveniences could not be had, as the town was completely full. There were then eight dry-goods stores, two drug-stores, one clothing store, one grocery store, one stove store with tin-shop connected, one saddle and harness shop, two hotels, two churches—Congregational and Catholic—and a Methodist church in process of erection, an excellent tannery, two steam saw and grist mills, a carding-machine, one wagon-maker's shop, three blacksmith-shops, four shoe-shops, three tailor-shops, one bakery and confectionery, one printing-office (the *Courier*), a land-office for the sale of river lands, and one daguerrean gallery. The various charitable orders were well represented, as there was a Masonic lodge, an Odd Fellows' lodge, a division of the Sons of Temperance, and a section of the Cadets of Temperance. There were seven lawyers and six physicians. An excellent chain ferry was kept constantly running immediately opposite the town. There was a railroad actually surveyed from here to the Mississippi River at Burlington, and about $600,000 had been subscribed to build it. Another railroad had been surveyed to the mouth of the Platte on the Missouri River."

There has never been anything of the spasmodic in the growth of Ottumwa. While, of course, some years will show a larger increase in population than in others, there has always been a steady increase each year over the one preceding. At the present writing (in December, 1886) there is a population of 14,000 inhabitants, and in commercial importance the city ranks among the first in the interior of the State. It is the business and industrial center of a large area of thickly populated territory, and is the center of four important railroads, giving excellent facilities for transportation. The volume of its business is indicated by the condition of its banks, the deposits of which are about $1,000,000, with loans and discounts nearly as much.

Ottumwa is beautifully situated upon the Des Moines River, the main part of the city being upon the north side. From the banks of the river there is a gradual ascent for about one-half mile, then broken by a hollow, from which another ascent is made for another half mile. From the elevation a beautiful scene presents itself. Lying below is a busy city, teeming with life, while the river Des Moines can be seen winding in and out and passing on toward the Father of Waters, with which it mingles and then flows on to the sea. Along the banks of the river is seen a perfect network of iron rails, on which the iron horse is steaming, carrying tons upon tons of merchandise, tons upon tons of live stock, and hundreds of human beings going North, South, East and West. There is no intermission. As fast as one train pulls out another comes in.

From this elevation you see the handsome dwellings of the rich and the humble cottages of the poor. You see school-houses and churches, mills and factories, and you wonder how came they here. You remember it has been but a few short years since upon this very site the rude wigwam of the Indian was erected, while nature and the red men had sway all over this country. Change, change, is written upon every hand. The Ottumwa of 1845 or 1853, of which special mention has been made, cannot be compared with the Ottumwa of to-day. With its increase in population, its trade has increased in a corresponding ratio. The wholesale trade will compare favorably with many larger and more pretentious cities. Its manufactories afford employment to hundreds of persons, while its railroad interests keep busy a small army of men.

Educational.

THE public schools of Ottumwa are the pride of the city, and rank among the best in the State. There are at present five school buildings in the city, as follows: Douglas, on West Second street, erected in 1870, with an addition built in 1877. The building seats about 300 pupils, and with grounds is estimated worth $17,000. The Lincoln school building was erected in 1879, at a cost of $20,000. while the grounds are worth $8,000. It is located on Court street, at the head of Washington, and has a seating capacity for 530 pupils. The Garfield building was erected in 1882, on Ash street, and seats 400 pupils. The value of the ground is about $1,000, and the building $15,000. The Adams school building is located on College street, between Second and Fourth. It is the handsomest and costliest structure for school purposes in the city, being erected in 1884, at a cost of $30,000. The grounds are valued at $12,000. The building will seat 700 pupils. A new building was erected in South Ottumwa, in the fall of 1886, at a cost of $15,000, on grounds valued at $1,000. At present forty-one teachers are employed in addition to a music teacher and a teacher of penmanship. The number of pupils enrolled is 2,200. The cost of the schools for the past year was $35,-000.

THE ACADEMY OF VISITATION.

This institution, a view of which is given in this work, was established in 1864, and is conducted by the Sisters of Visitation. It is situated on Fourth street, adjoining the Catholic Church so long ministered to by Rev. John Kreckel. The school is first class in all its appointments, and its well-known advantages for securing a thorough education in science, literature and art, will be sufficient guarantee to parents desiring to place their daughters at school. For twenty-two years it has been making a record of which it is not ashamed, the graduates of the institution being such as to reflect credit upon themselves and the school alike.

The location of Ottumwa on the beautiful Des Moines River is pleasant and healthy, and the several lines of railroad make it easy of access from all parts of the country. The school building, of which a handsome lithographic view is given on another page, is well adapted to the purposes for which it is used, and is heated by steam and supplied with pure water on every floor, by the Ottumwa Water Works Company. Fire escapes, readily accessible and perfectly safe, have been placed in various parts of the building, so that but little danger is experienced in case of fire.

Every encouragement is held out to the pupils to make them attentive and create within them a desire for an education. A system of rewards has been adopted for this purpose, which has proven of great advantage to pupils. In addition to the literary work the young scholars of the institution receive instructions in mending during an hour on Saturday.

The academic year is divided into two sessions of five months each, commencing on the first Monday in September and February, though pupils are received at any time during the year, and charged only for such portion of the session as may remain.

While the Sisters of Visitation profess the Catholic faith, they will at all times respect the religious belief of their pupils, no discussions upon religion being permitted. Any information desired in relation to the school will be cheerfully furnished by simply addressing a letter to the "Directress of Visitation Academy," Ottumwa, Iowa.

THE OTTUMWA BUSINESS COLLEGE.

In June, 1871, W. C. Caldwell and J. W. Oldham commenced this school with one student, but with a determination to establish here a practical educational institution. For a number of years its success was problematical, and it passed under the control of different persons, who labored hard to place it upon solid footing. In 1885, Prof. W. L. Howe, of Oskaloosa, purchased the fixtures and good-will of the institution, and in May, 1886, sold a half interest to Prof. O. L. Miller, who had been in charge during the entire period of Mr. Howe's ownership. In the fall of 1886 Prof. Miller purchased the remaining interest of Prof. Howe, and has now full control. The school is now in a flourishing condition, with prospects of great usefulness. Prof. Miller is a thorough teacher, and every department of a first-class business college is represented here.

Religious.

OTTUMWA is well supplied with church edifices, some of which are very creditable structures indeed. The first minister of the Gospel to locate here was Rev. B. A. Spaulding, of the Congregational Church, in the spring of 1844. Other ministers, representatives of other denominations, soon afterward came in, and the moral interests of the place were carefully attended to. At present the denominations are represented by the Catholics, with one church on each side of the river; Congregationalists, with a church on each side of the river; Christian, Colored Methodist, Colored Baptist, Episcopal, First Methodist Episcopal, Main Street Methodist Episcopal, First Baptist, Free Methodists, German Methodists, Presbyterian and Swedish Lutheran. There is also a chapel in the east end of the city, and an Independent Congregation meets in Liberal Hall.

The Methodist Episcopal denomination was first represented in this place by Rev. Thomas Kirkpatrick in 1844, but an organization was not effected until the following year, when the First Methodist Episcopal Church was organized with fourteen members. The church has had a very prosperous existence, and is now occupying one of the handsomest church edifices in this section of the county.

The Main Street Methodist Episcopal Church was organized in 1869, with seventy members. Like the parent church it has been very successful, its membership being composed of some of the best citizens of the city and country.

The First Congregational Church was organized Feb. 15, 1846, with eight members. Rev. B. A. Spaulding was its first pastor, and served for twenty-two years. The church edifice is on Fourth, between Market and Green streets, and is a handsome structure, with a seating capacity of 600. Rev. A. W. Archibald is the pastor.

The Presbyterian Church of Ottumwa was organized Dec. 24, 1853, with twenty members. Rev. J. M. McElroy, who is yet living in the city, was its first pastor. The present church edifice is situated on the corner of Fourth and Green streets, and is a neat building. Rev. Ben E. S. Ely is the present pastor, and is well liked by church and society. The church is prosperous.

The Catholics are well represented in this city, with a handsome and substantial church building on the corner of Fourth and Court streets. Rev. John Kreckel has been the priest in charge of the congregation since 1853, and is well liked by the entire community, Protestants as well as Catholics. The school in connection with the church is also flourishing.

The St. Mary's Episcopal Church is located on the corner of Market and Fourth streets. Rev. A. C. Stilson is the present rector, and the church is doing well. The parish was organized in 1857.

The First Baptist Church was organized March 14, 1855, with eighteen constituent members. Its house of worship is on Third street, between Washington and Court. The church is in a prosperous condition, and well organized for work.

The Christian Church of Ottumwa was organized in 1845 about three miles north of Ottumwa, with nine members. In 1858 the congregation bought the old court-house and for some years held service therein. Their present church edifice, on West Second Street, between Cass and McLean, was erected in 1873.

The Swedish Lutheran Church in Ottumwa was organized in 1871. Rev. M. P. Oden is the present pastor, and the society is in a prosperous condition. The church building is on North Jefferson street, between Second and Fourth.

The Second Congregational Church is in South Ottumwa. Rev. LeRoy S. Hand is the present pastor, and the church is prospering.

The Free Methodists have a house of worship on the corner of Main and McLean streets.

The Colored Methodists and Colored Baptists have each organizations.

The Woman's Christian Temperance Union is an organization which is exerting great power, and is composed of some of the best Christian women in the city.

The Ottumwa Loan and Building Association.

THIS association was organized in March, 1848, by the present Secretary. Its incorporators were: J. Williamson, George Haw, J. M. Hedrick, J. B. Field, R. Douglass, J. D. Ferree, J. T. Hackworth, William Daggett, Daniel Eaton, W. E. Chambers, O. M. Ladd, A. G. Harrow. This association is organized on what is known as the permanent serial plan. The association has now issued and has in successful operation nine series. Several hundred persons have procured through this association beautiful and comfortable homes for their families. Over $200,000 has been invested by this association in this way. Probably no one institution ever organized in Ottumwa has done so much toward building up the city. The Ottumwa association is without doubt one of the best managed institutions in Iowa. As a proof of this assertion we need but state that in nine years' business, covering nearly $300,000, not $1 has been lost in its investments, nor has it ever had idle money on hand. Such an association cannot be too highly appreciated by the community in which it exists, and no management could do better for its members.

The Ottumwa Turnverein.

AS there are a number of prominent and well-to-do Germans residing at Ottumwa, it was thought an excellent idea to organize a society among them. In 1867 this idea was materalized by the organization and incorporation of the Ottumwa Turnverein, which is a branch of the National Turner Union. Their hall was burned in 1871, and three years later was rebuilt. It is a liberal society and includes in its membership the more prominent German citizens of the county. John Wagner is the President, and A. Danquard, Secretary. The hall is at the corner of Market and Fourth streets.

The Iowa Mutual Aid Association of Ottumwa.

THE above named association was organized April 4, 1881, by Mr. J. D. Ferree, its present Secretary. This association is purely mutual and does business on the assessment plan. It issues but one certificate of $2,000 on any one life, and does strictly a life business. Its officers and directors are men of high character and standing, and they look well after the business of the association. The record of the business of the association bears evidence of the above fact. The association has had in six years, twenty-seven deaths, all paid. The association has complied with the laws of the State, and doubtless is the safest and best assessment association in Iowa. Officers: Dr. J. Williamson, President; Hon. J. G. Hutchison, Vice President; J. D. Ferree, Secretary; C. F. Blake, President Iowa National Bank, Treasurer; Dr. J. Williamson, Medical Director; D. C. Beaman, Counselor. Directors: Hon. J. G. Hutchison, A. C. Stilson, John L. Moore, George F. Hall, W. W. Douglas, D. C. Beaman, B. J. Boulton, Dr. J. Williamson, Dr. H. W. Roberts.

Manufacturing.

OTTUMWA is fast taking rank as a manufacturing center. With the advantages possessed as to water, fuel and railroad facilities, there is nothing to hinder the city being one of the best manufacturing points in the State. Like its growth in population, the manufactories have steadily increased from the start, while all have been built upon a solid basis. Those here have come to stay, and will form a nucleus for others.

Among the most noted of the manufactories are the Ottumwa Iron Works and Johnson Ruffler Company. While two separate institutions, they are yet controlled by the same persons, the capital stock of each being $24,000.

Among other manufacturing institutions worthy of notice are the following: Robert Bigham, Julius Fecht, Graves Bros., Win S. Leas, cigars; C. F. W. Bachman and Daniel Eaton, furniture; W. H. Boston & Co., harness; W. T. Harper & Co., linseed oil; J. E. Langford, artificial stone; C. E. McDaniel & Co., boilers; H. W. Moses & Co., butter tubs; C. Myers, harness; Peter O'Connell, boilers; Porter Bros. & Hackworth, harness; Pollard & Belmont, carriages; Sanchez & Son, soap; T. K. Shepherd, pumps; Schick & Son, cooperage; S. H. Worcester & Son, show cases and office furniture; Western Machine Works, Cutlery Works, Starch Works, Woolen Factory.

THE WHITE BREAST COAL COMPANY.

This company is represented in this city by J. A. Kebler, General Superintendent. It was organized in January, 1876, at Burlington, Iowa, with a capital stock of $60,000. William Haven was its first President and Superintendent, and J. C. Osgood, Secretary and Treasurer. Some of the gentleman of this company had been prospecting along White Breast Creek, in Lucas County, with very gratifying results. On the organization of the company it immediately commenced operations, purchasing the necessary machinery and sinking a shaft. From the start the company has been very successful in its operations, and from time to time has increased its capital stock until it now amounts to $1,000,000. The offices of the company have been removed from Burlington to Ottumwa, and on completion of the First National Bank Building in this city a handsome suite of rooms was arranged in the second story, which apartments are used by the company.

The coal mined by this company at Cleveland and Swan is said to be superior to any other the State of Iowa has produced. The perfect care displayed in cleaning, assorting and separating the various grades, has made the coal popular with consumers. The company have succeeded in finding a market for their product in Iowa, Illinois, Missouri, Kansas and Nebraska. In addition to their own mines they have contracted for the output of several other mines. Their shipments are reaching over 1,000,000 tons per year.

The present officers of the company are: J. C. Osgood, President, Chicago; C. M. Schenck, Vice President and Treasurer, Chicago; T. C. Mauro, Secretary, Ottumwa; J. A. Kebler, General Superintendent, Ottumwa; S. A. Forbush, General Agent, Ottumwa.

Miscellaneous.

THE FIRE DEPARTMENT.

ONE of the most useful institutions in Ottumwa is its fire department, which was first organized in 1868. At present the company is composed of eight men, with T. J. Ward as Chief; Mark Bush, Foreman; Joseph Crawford, Assistant; C. A. Calhoun, Secretary. In the past year there has been an average of three calls per month. The department has in its main building, on Market street, one engine and 1,500 feet of hose, with hose-cart, truck, etc. In different parts of the city there are four hose-carts, with 500 feet of hose attached. The engine is never used, there being sufficient force to throw a stream over 100 feet high in almost any part of the city where water-mains have been laid. At a test on Court street, near the court-house, a stream was thrown from the hydrant, through 1½-inch hose, 146 feet high. Three men sleep in the engine house each night, while there is an electric bell in the residence of each of the others, connecting with the engine room. A salary of $100 per year is paid each of the men for their services.

THE POLICE DEPARTMENT.

For the further protection of the city a Police Department has been organized, consisting of a Marshal, Deputy Marshal and seven policemen. Henry C. Williams is the present Marshal, and O. C. Truitt, Assistant Marshal. The Marshal and four policemen serve in the day, and the Deputy and three policemen at night. In addition to the regular police the merchants employ one.

LIGHTING THE CITY.

For illuminating purposes there is gas, the Brush electric light and the incandescent electric light. The gas company was organized in 1870, the Brush in 1885, and the incandescent in the fall of 1886.

THE WATER SUPPLY.

A company was organized in 1877 for the purpose of introducing water-works in the city, and secured a charter from the city for the same. Water is obtained from the Des Moines River, and is distributed by mains throughout almost the entire city. Hydrants are put in at various points for protection against fire. The force of the water is so great as to send a stream through 1½-inch hose over any building in the city.

THE POST-OFFICE.

The post-office was established in 1844, with Paul C. Jeffries as Postmaster. The office of Postmaster has been held by but eight persons in that time, in order as follows: Paul C. Jeffries, Richard H. Warden, Stephen Osborn, Thomas J. Holmes, J. W. Norris, J. M. Hedrick, A. H. Hamilton and S. B. Evans. It will be seen the majority of them have been newspaper men, publishers of the party papers represented by the administrations. The affairs of the office have generally, if not always, been well managed, and to the satisfaction of its patrons. Maj. Hamilton, of the *Courier*, held the office a greater period of time than any other person, receiving his first appointment in 1870, and serving till July, 1885, when he was succeeded by Capt. S. B. Evans, the incumbent.

The office is now located on the corner of Market and Second streets, probably the most convenient point in the city for all classes of its people. Thirteen men are required to transact the business of the office—the Postmaster, Capt. Evans; his Deputy, J. M. Murray; one mailing clerk, one money-order clerk, one general delivery clerk, one night clerk, one special messenger, and six carriers. From December, 1885, to December, 1886, there were delivered by carriers 2,465 registered letters; 524,687 unregistered letters; 116,866 postal cards received by mail; 55,613 local letters; 24,577 local postal cards; 379,596 newspapers, magazines and pamphlets. There were returned to the office by carriers 181 letters. Of mail matter collected by carriers there were 368,879 letters; 98,051 postal cards; 33,571 newspapers, etc. Amount of postage collected by carriers, $1,779.69. For the year there were sold of stamps and postal cards $15,-295.96; envelopes and newspaper wrappers, $5,-352.08. The money-order business amounted to about $100,000.

Academy of the Visitation.

THE Order of the Visitation is not a recent organization, but has existed for nearly 280 years, having been founded in 1610 by St. St. Francis de Sales, Bishop and Prince of Geneva, and St. Jane Frances, Baroness de Chantal. During this long period the integrity of this Order as a religious and educational factor in the training of young girls has never been impaired. Constantly increasing in strength and vigor, by the establishment of new houses, it has gradually spread over nearly the entire world, even being represented in the Holy Land. It had already numbered over seventy foundations before the death of its saintly founders.

The first house established in this country was at Georgetown, D. C., and is regarded, on that account, as the Mother House in the United States. Although each is entirely independent of all the others, as far as the management of temporal affairs is concerned, yet by a wide and beautiful arrangement of St. Francis de Sales, the entire Visitation Order is considered as one family. Intercourse between the different houses is constantly maintained by circular letters, giving full particulars of whatever may have occurred touching the welfare of each and all.

In case of a death in the community notice of the same is at once sent to the other houses, that special prayers may be offered for the dear departed. A sketch of the entire life of the deceased is also prepared and becomes the common property of the Order. A few of these "Lives" have already been given to the public. Many of those never yet published—except for private circulation—would furnish a unique form of literature, fully equal, in the charm and interest of detail, to any biography ever published.

As the Visitation is essentially a teaching Order, the time and talents of its members are mainly devoted to that noble work, and, let us add, not in a time-serving, money-making spirit, but conscientiously, from the purest of motives and the noblest of aims, viz.: the culture of the minds and hearts of their pupils, desiring that their progress in science may keep pace, not supercede, their advancement in whatever may lead them to become ornaments to society, the pride and comfort of the home circle, in a word, truly virtuous. For, although the Sisters of the Visitation do not restrain or constrain the religious tendencies of those under their care, yet they cannot in conscience follow the too prevalent spirit of the age, and ignore even tacitly the existence of God, the most solemn obligations of the creature to the Creator, as well as the highest truths of morality. Considering these to be the fundamental principles of true education they never fail to inculcate the same in their general instructions.

The Academy of the Visitation in Ottumwa was established on the 25th of October, 1864, at the request of Rev. John Kreckel, now entering upon his thirty-fourth year as Pastor of St. Mary's Catholic Church. Although the accommodations were at first very limited yet the list of boarders and day-scholars was soon more than filled, representing the best Catholic and Protestant families of Iowa, as well as the neighboring and far-distant States, both East and West. Temporary buildings were added to meet the present urgent needs of the community and pupils. More substantial quarters were needed, and although finances were at a low ebb, yet, after mature deliberation, trusting in assistance from on high, steps were taken to erect an academy.

Ground was broken on Friday, July 2, 1869, and in one year from that date possession was taken of the new and commodious building still occupied by the Sisters of the Visitation and their pupils, being used both as a Monastery and an Academy. For some time past it has seemed inevitable that additions must be made to the present quarters, or, what would be more desirable, a more retired locality, with additional grounds and larger buildings, for the accommodations are wholly inadequate to the needs of the Sisters and pupils.

The first Superior was Mother Mary Stanislaus Scott, of Washington, D. C. She still holds the same honorable position, two intervals alone, of three years each, interrupting her firm and gentle guidance of those placed under her charge. To her wise and skillful direction of affairs, and to the zealous labors of Rev. Father John Kreckel, may be attributed the success which has thus far made the Visitation Academy a model educational institution. Pupils of all ages are received here, special care being taken to have them well grounded in the fundamentals, then advanced to higher grades according to proficiency, rather than on account of time spent upon a study. Those who are not so far advanced as others of their own age, on account of illness, want of opportunity, or from other causes, will find at the Visitation Academy that kind and considerate attention and assistance which will supply all natural deficiencies, and prevent any embarrassment they might otherwise feel. The terms are as follows, per session of five months: Entrance fee, paid but once, $5; board and tuition in the English branches, washing, bed, bedding, fuel and lights, per session, $100; the same, per quarter, or half session, $50; primary department for children under ten years of age, $80; the same, per quarter, $40.

For day scholars: Graduating class, per quarter, $12; 1st and 2d classes, per quarter, $8; division of the 2d, 3d and division of the 3d, per quarter, $6; 4th and 5th classes, per quarter, $4; primary department, per quarter, $3.

Extra charges: Short-hand terms, according to number of lessons; book-keeping, per quarter, $4; Latin, French and German, each, per quarter, $3; lessons on piano, with use of instrument, per quarter, $10; lessons on harp, with use of instrument, per quarter, $15; lessons on guitar, with use of instrument, per quarter, $10; extra practice on either of the above, per month, $1; class lessons in vocal music, per quarter, $3; private lessons in vocal music, per quarter, $10; lessons in drawing, per quarter, $4; lessons in painting (water colors), per quarter, $5; lessons in oil painting, per quarter, $10; lessons in embroidery and tapestry, per quarter, $3; ten lessons in lace or wax work, two hours each, $5; twenty lessons in hair flowers, two hours each, $4; lessons in hair jewelry, according to style of work. Books furnished at current rates. A view of the Academy is given in this work.

St. Joseph Convent and Hospital.

THE Sisters of the Humility of Mary came to Ottumwa in August, 1877, at the request of Rev. J. Kreckel. They devote their time to teaching, caring for the sick and providing for the homeless orphans. They purchased their beautiful home on Court street the year of their arrival in Ottumwa. In this they were liberally assisted by Mrs. Mary Tally, a benevolent lady, who afterward made her home with them until her death. This home is at present the Mother House of the Sisters in Iowa.

In 1880 they built a hospital at a cost of about $4,000, and for a short time cared for the insane of the county, until the County Poor-house was completed. Last year the hospital was temporarily closed. Within the last six years they have cared for more than forty orphans, until they could secure for them respectable homes, and at present are supporting quite a number without any cost to the public. They hope in the near future to have a regularly established Orphan's Home.

The Sisters act as teachers in St. Joseph's School, for boys, and also have schools in Marshalltown and Ft. Madison. A view of St. Joseph's Convent is given in this volume.

Agency City.

AGENCY CITY is situated upon section 36, township 72, range 13 west, of the 5th principal meridian. As stated in the article on the early settlement of the county, an Indian Agency was established at this point in 1838. Out of this agency grew the present village, the first settlers being those employed at the agency. As soon as the country was thrown open for settlement, it was determined to locate a town at this point. A post-office was established here in 1843 with Shapheth Dwire as Postmaster. Mr. Dwire was the first merchant in the place. It was incorporated as a village in 1859.

The town is beautifully located on a high, level

tract of land, and while it has never attained a remarkable size, it is, nevertheless, a pleasant place in which to live, and numbers among its citizens some of the best people in Wapello County. The growth of the place was somewhat slow until the completion here of the railroad in 1859, and it being the terminus for quite awhile, made business quite lively. Its population has fluctuated somewhat, it numbering at the last census, in 1885, but 514 persons, a falling off of 144 since 1875, when it had 658 inhabitants.

The village is well represented by the various lines of trade, and its business men seem to be doing a fair business, The public schools rank among the best in the county, and are a matter of pride among its citizens. Religiously the village is represented by the Baptists and Methodist Episcopals, the latter being one of the first organized in the county. Rev. Thomas Kirkpatrick organized the society. The Congregationalists for some years maintained an organization here, which was set in motion by Rev. B. A. Spaulding. It has long since ceased to exist. The Presbyterians had an organization here some years ago, but which has ceased to exist. The benevolent orders are represented by the Odd Fellows, Masons and Knights of Pythias, each of which maintains a good lodge, and are working for humanity in the way which seems to them best.

Eldon.

THE village of Eldon was originally laid out in 1870, though quite a settlement was made previous to that time. A flag station was established here in 1859 on the completion of the Keokuk & Des Moines Railroad, known as Ashland Crossing, and afterward Williamsburg. When the Southwestern division of the Chicago, Rock Island & Pacific Railroad was completed to this point there was no doubt but a thriving town could here be located, accordingly O. Baldwin, of Keokuk, was employed by the proprietors, Judge J. M. Love, Col. George Gillaspy, Hon. Edward Johnston, Col. William Leighton and George Williams, to survey and plat the town. It is located on section 27, township 71, range 12, in the civil township of Washington.

Shortly after the town was surveyed a post-office was established here, with E. I. Cummings as Postmaster. The present Postmaster is William Huston. The town is very pleasantly located, and is surrounded by a rich agricultural country, which is underlaid with rich coal deposits. For a time after it was laid out it grew quite rapidly, having a population in 1872 sufficient to entitle it to incorporation. D. K. Taylor was elected its first Mayor.

When the C., R. I. & P. Railway Company obtained control of the K. & D. M. Railroad, they decided to locate here a round-house and repair shops. This brought in a large number of men and greatly added to the population of the place, making it emphatically a railroad town.

As regards its schools. Eldon has no cause to be ashamed of what has been done, its school privileges being excelled by few towns of its size in the State. In religion it is represented by several of the denominations who guard the moral tone of the town. The benevolent societies are also well represented, the Odd Fellows taking the lead of the purely benevolent. The railroad men are well organized and guard closely their interest as laboring men.

Two newspapers are published here, the Eldon *Review* and the *Des Moines Valley Journal*, which do much toward advancing the interests of the place. These papers have proper mention elsewhere in this volume under the head of "The Press." Other newspaper ventures have been started here, these two being the "survival of the fittest."

The village of Eldon had a population in 1885 of 1,288, which has been increased somewhat, being now estimated at 1,500. The business of the place is good, and its merchants an enterprising set of men. The Eldon Mineral Springs bring the town into notice quite extensively throughout the Union. With a good country tributary to it, and with the patronage of the railroad company, Eldon should be a prosperous town.

Eddyville.

THIS is one of the oldest towns in the county, and is situated on the left bank of the Des Moines River, on section 6, in Columbia Township. The first settlement made here was by

J. P. Eddy, an Indian trader, from whom the place derives its name. Mr. Eddy came here in 1841, some two years before the Indian title became extinct, and on obtaining possession of the country, the Government permitted him to enter an entire section of land. Selecting section 6, township 73, range 15, he laid off 160 acres of it for the town. A post-office was soon afterward established here with Mr. Eddy as Postmaster. He opened a stock of goods here, more suited to the wants of the whites than he had been keeping, and was the first engaged in the regular trade. He also built the first school-house in the place, which was used for all purposes, religious as well as educational. Mr. Eddy only remained in the place until sometime in 1844, when he sold out and moved to St. Louis, where he has since died.

E. D. Fish purchased the stock of Mr. Eddy and continued business for some years. Richard Butcher, who is yet an honored citizen of the place, in 1846, in company with William Cox, commenced business in the place. He is still in the general merchandise trade.

The town gradually increased in numbers and wealth for some years. Every branch of trade was soon represented. Martin Tucker was the pioneer hotel man. Dr. Ross the pioneer physician, locating here in 1843, and followed in a year or two by Dr. Fish and Dr. Nosler. J. W. Caldwell and J. T. Wiley were the first blacksmiths. Joseph Perry the first wagon-maker. John M. Fish kept the first regular lumber-yard. J. M. McNamee ran a pottery from 1847 till 1857. James Brady erected a woolen-mill in 1851. A plow manufactory was established in 1856 by Thurbaugh & Phillips. The first child born was George, son of Mr. and Mrs. J. W. Caldwell. Their daughter, Clara, was the first to die in the new settlement.

As the population of the place increased and business became active a newspaper was considered a necessity. Accordingly in 1853, J. W. Norris commenced the publication of the Eddyville *Free Press*. Other papers succeeded this, and the village has seldom been without its local paper; though at present, in the winter of 1886–87, it has none.

It was incorporated as a village in 1857. The completion here of the C. & D. M. Railroad added an impetus to the trade of the place, and increased its population considerably. About 1860 the population was estimated at 2,500 inhabitants, and the town presented quite a metropolitan appearance. For some time the merchants of Oskaloosa, Mahaska County, were compelled to haul their goods from this point. Its proximity to other larger towns having greater advantages, has operated against Eddyville, so that it now numbers but about 1,000 inhabitants, though considerable trade is yet carried on, quite a large scope of country being tributary to it.

The moral influence of the place is good, there being representatives of various religious denominations, including Baptists, Christians, Congregationalists, Catholics, Lutherans, Presbyterians and Methodists. The houses of worship will compare favorably with other places of its size.

The educational interests are carefully guarded, and the public schools are numbered among the best. At present they are under the charge of Prof. J. J. Thompson, who has had control for two years. The Professor is a good disciplinarian, a fine scholar, and takes pride in his work. He is assisted by six teachers. The enrollment is 330.

The secret and benevolent societies are represented by the Masons, Odd Fellows, United Workmen, and the G. A. R., each of which is flourishing, and in its special field is working for good.

The manufacturing interests of the place have been suffered to decline, which accounts somewhat for the decline in population and wealth of the place.

One of the most noted objects of interest in the place is the monument erected in 1866, to the memory of its fallen soldiers, thus inculcating patriotism in the rising generation.

Chillicothe.

THIS village is situated on the right bank of the Des Moines River, on section 36, township 73, range 15, the civil township of Cass. The C., B. & Q. R. R. passes through the place. It was laid out in 1849, by A. J. Wicker, and the first house erected on the village plat was for the residence of Rev. A. J. Pierce, a Methodist Episcopal minister. A Methodist Episcopal class had been organized here the previous year, and Mr. Wicker being of that denomination, determined that the cause should be firmly planted here. A house of worship was soon afterward erected.

The post-office was established in 1849, with A. J. Wicker as Postmaster. He was succeeded by W. A. Nye, and he in turn by N. Poston, J. J. Ellison, J. G. Henshaw, S. P. Heacock and F. M. Bush.

Its proximity to Ottumwa, the county seat, has operated against the growth of the village, so that it numbers to-day but about 250 inhabitants, though the various branches of trade are pretty well represented. The village is a great convenience to citizens of Cass Township, and that section of country upon the south and west side of the river tributary to it. Peter Young opened the first store.

Kirkville.

WHEN John Kirk settled in Richland Township, he determined to locate here a village, and accordingly had surveyed a portion of his claim, on sections 7 and 8, township 73, range 14. Until the development of the coal mines in the neighborhood the town grew but slowly, although considerable trade was carried on. Since these mines were developed and the completion here of the Ottumwa & Kirkville Railroad, a thriving village has sprung up, presenting the best appearance of any mining town in the country, and with a population of 1,000 inhabitants. The principal business of the place is done by the Kirkville Supply Company and I. E. Page.

The educational interests of the place are well maintained, the schools ranking with those of any town of its size. The religious interests are guarded by the Methodist Episcopal and Presbyterian denominations. The former society was organized by Rev. Thomas Kirkpatrick, about 1844, and erected its first house of worship in 1852–53. Its present church edifice was erected in 1870, and dedicated in September of that year. The Presbyterian congregation was organized at Eddyville in 1850, and transferred to Kirkville in 1854. Their present church edifice was erected and dedicated in February, 1876. Its cost was $4,700.

Kirkville is a growing town, and is surrounded by a rich agricultural region, with an inexhaustible supply of coal. Here are located the mines of the Wapello Coal Company, in which are employed 450 men, and who mine an average of 900 tons of coal per day. The wages paid men are from $2 to $4 per day, an average of $2.50 per day.

Blakesburg.

IN 1852 T. Blake had laid out upon section 7, township 71, range 15, in the civil township of Adams, to which he gave the name of Blakesburg. Four years after the town was laid out it contained a population of about 500 inhabitants, but on account of the building of railroads upon every side, but never to the place, many persons removed to more favored localities, so that its population was reduced to about 200, at which figure it remained for many years. In the fall of 1886 the C., M. & St. P. R. R. was built through the place, and the prospects are now that it will once more take on its old-timed activity. The village is situated upon a high, rolling prairie, adjoining a heavy body of woodland, and in the vicinity there is an abundance of coal. The land in the vicinity is very fertile, and the beauty of the scenery is unsurpassed. In December, 1886, there were 4 general stores, 1 drug-store, 2 hotels, 2 blacksmith-shops, 1 pottery, 1 wagon-shop, 2 meat-markets, 1 graded school, 2 churches, Methodist Episcopal and Baptist. The citizens of the village and vicinity donated $2,500 for depot purposes to the C. M. & St. P. R. R.

BIOGRAPHICAL.

S

T

U

V

W

Y

Z

Views.

HISTORICAL

CPSIA information can be obtained
at www.ICGtesting.com
Printed in the USA
LVOW07s1025130517
534409LV00007B/307/P